Latino Image Makers in Hollywood

Performers, Filmmakers and Films Since the 1960s

FRANK JAVIER GARCIA BERUMEN

WITHDRAWN

McFarland & Company, Inc., Publishers

Jefferson, North Carolina

D0555312

LIBRARY OF CONGRESS CATALOGUING-IN-PUBLICATION DATA

Berumen, Frank Javier Garcia.
Latino image makers in Hollywood : performers, filmmakers
and films since the 1960s / Frank Javier Garcia Berumen.
p.   cm.
Includes bibliographical references and index.

ISBN 978-0-7864-7432-5 (softcover : acid free paper) ∞
ISBN 978-1-4766-1411-3 (ebook)

1. Hispanic Americans in the motion picture industry.
2. Hispanic Americans in motion pictures.   I. Title.
PN1995.9.H47B475 2014   791.43'652968073—dc23   2014023489

BRITISH LIBRARY CATALOGUING DATA ARE AVAILABLE

© 2014 Frank Javier Garcia Berumen. All rights reserved

*No part of this book may be reproduced or transmitted in any form
or by any means, electronic or mechanical, including photocopying
or recording, or by any information storage and retrieval system,
without permission in writing from the publisher.*

On the cover: top row: Cheech Marin, Raquel Welch, Antonio Banderas,
Salma Hayek (all from the author's collection); bottom row: Danny De La Paz
and Alma Martinez in Jesus Trevino's *Seguin*, 1982, PBS (photograph
by George Rodriguez); Lupe Ontiveros (courtesy Lupe Ontiveros,
photograph by Bill Gamble); Efrain Figueroa (courtesy Efrain Figueroa);
Silvana Gallardo (courtesy Silvana Gallardo, photograph by Elsa Braunstein)

Printed in the United States of America

*McFarland & Company, Inc., Publishers
Box 611, Jefferson, North Carolina 28640
www.mcfarlandpub.com*

CT

OCT 1 8 2016

Latino
Image Makers
in Hollywood

To my late sister,
Martha Berumen Adams, with love.

To the late Lupe Ontiveros,
a brilliant actress and an untiring activist for
the improvement of the cinematic images and
employment of Latino performers.

To the late actress Silvana Gallardo,
a versatile and outstanding actress of theater,
film, and television; and as well a dear friend.

Table of Contents

Acknowledgments

I wish to thank and acknowledge the following people:

Lupita Tovar Kohner, a Latina film pioneer, for her invaluable recollections of the Hollywood film industry, her family, and contemporaries.

The late Ricardo Montalbán for his gracious and illuminating interview.

The late Rosaura Revueltas for her invaluable interview and insights into the making of *Salt of the Earth* and the Hollywood blacklist.

The late Silvana Gallardo for her most informative interview and constant support for this book.

The late Lupe Ontiveros for her gracious interview and support for this book.

The following contemporary performers, directors, and filmmakers whose stories helped me immensely to contextualize the film history of Latinos in the Hollywood film industry: María Conchita Alonso, Miguel Arteta, Lumi Cavazos, Danny De La Paz, Efrain Figueroa, Silvana Gallardo, Rubén González, Efrain Gutiérrez, Sal Lopez, Alma Martínez, Bob Morones, Annette Murphy, Edward James Olmos, Pilar Pellicer, Julieta Rosen, Jesús Salvador Treviño, Luis Valdez, and Richard Yniguez, among many others.

The staff of the Academy of Motion Pictures Arts and Sciences for years of assistance and support while researching this book.

The following publications and publishers for their kind permission: *Variety; The Hollywood Reporter;* the *Los Angeles Times*; the *New York Times*; New York University Press for quotations from *The Latino/a Condition: A Critical Reader;* the University Press of New England for quotations from *Tropicalization Transcultural Representations of Latinidad*: Harper & Row for quotations from *Occupied America*; Viking for quotations from *Harvest of Empire: A History of Latinos in America*; the State University of New York Press for quotations from *Ethnic Identity and Power: Cultural Contexts of Political Action in School and Society;* the British Film Institute for excerpts from *Mediating Two Worlds: Cinematic Encounters in the Americas*; the University of Minnesota Press for excerpts from *Chicanos and Film: Representation and Resistance*; Harper Perennial for excerpts from *The Film Encyclopedia*; Crescent Books for excerpts from *The Movie Star Story*; and the University of California, Los Angeles, for excerpts from *The Latin Image in Latin American Film*.

Finally, I wish to thank my brother Enrique Berumen and friend Angel Parga Guzmán for their important assistance on Spanish-language grammar.

Introduction

The purpose of this book is to document the history of Latino film images and icons in the Hollywood film industry from the 1960s to the present. The presence of Latinos in the Hollywood film industry spans more than one hundred years. As we enter into the second decade of the 2000s, the Latino experience is transforming the demographic, political, and cultural landscape of the United States. This is already evidenced in popular culture, especially music, radio, print media, and literature. Ironically, the two most powerful media, those of cinema and television, remain to a large degree preserves of exclusion. However, this was not always so and this is one more reason why the history of Latinos is both overdue and timely.

These historic changes have also compelled the Latino community to reexamine its own identity and self-naming in the context of globalization and the post-nation states world. This discourse has centered on what to call ourselves as a community-at-large, "Latino" or "Hispanic?" I have used the term "Latino" because it is a term designated by the community itself. In its narrower definition it includes the heterogeneous peoples who were formerly under the colonial dominion of Spain and Portugal. In addition, as Ángel R. Oquendo writes, "it calls to mind the Latino/a struggle for empowerment in the United States.... The adoption of the term 'Latino' could be regarded as part of a broader process of self-definition and self-assertion.... It accentuates the bond between the Latino/a community and the Spanish language."[1] The term "Hispanic" was coined by the U.S. Census in 1980. It connotes a link to the Spanish empire in Latin America. But, as Suzanne Oboler wrote, "like other ethnic labels currently used to identify minority groups in this country, the term Hispanic raises the question of how people are defined and classified in this society and in turn how they define themselves in the United States. It points to the gap between the self-identification of people of Latin American descent and their definition through the label created and used by others."[2]

Much of this debate centers on the manipulation and positioning of such terms as "Latino" and "Hispanic," as well as the conceptions of cultural identity. For example, Juan Flores has noted, "The demographic conceptions of Latinos or of a 'Latino community' refers to an aggregate of people whose existence is established on the basis of numerical presence.... The definition of the Hispanic community by official measurements is of course instrumental, since the immediate goal is really to identify, not so much social groups or lines of cultural diversity, but voting blocs and consumer markets."[3] For Francis R. Aparicio, "the growing visual, linguistic, and cultural presence of Latinos/a in the United States is concomitant to the historical and cultural crisis ... ultimately epistemological—by which the United States has to recognize the failure of the dominant paradigm (American exceptionalism, individualism, democratic capitalism) that has 'glued' this country together since its constitutional inception. The fact that certain Anglo sectors have begun to dismantle the homogeneous concept of American culture and now include 'subordinate' cultural practices as part of their daily lives and social interaction is a positive, progressive step forward a more democratic and inclusive society."[4] In a similar vein, Beatriz Urraca has indicated, "National identity in the United States was—and continues to be—a function of existing between two worlds: Europe and the other America."[5]

The modern construct of the term "Latino" is at times not without difficulty and controversy. Latinos come in different hues of skin color, brown, black, white, and everything in between. The modern Latino mosaic includes Native Americans, mestizos, mulattos, and others. Some Latinos in the United States and in Latin America speak Native American languages and dialects; others Spanish and Spanglish; while others speak French and Portuguese; and some even English. They are products of their diverse history.

Mexico, for example, had 80 percent of the Native American population of the American continent at the time of European contact. Immigration to Mexico was almost nonexistent until the 1930s with the arrival of Spanish refugees (fleeing Franco's fascist dictatorship) and others after World War II. Some Mexicans would rather be called "detribalized native peoples" rather than Latino. This applies as well to many of the more than twenty million Mexican-Americans who live in the United States. In addition to Mexico, other countries in Latin America have Native American majority populations: Guatemala, Honduras, Peru, Bolivia, and Nicaragua. Many of these Native Americans still live in traditional native cultures. For these peoples especially, the term "Latino" is irrelevant or even offensive.

The Caribbean nations (Cuba, Puerto Rico, Haiti, and the Dominican Republic, among others) and those nations on the rim of this part of the continent (Venezuela, Panama, Colombia, and Brazil) have predominantly or significantly Spanish and African cultural roots. Many of the native peoples in those regions became extinct in the aftermath of European diseases and the genocidal tendencies of most conquistadores. In turn, three nations in South America—Brazil, Argentina, and Chile—are the product of the immigration of millions of Italians and Germans to those particular regions.

In summary, history, conquest, geography, and the push and pull of economics has created the current Latino mosaic. It is a cultural experiment in progress. The term "Latino" is a convenient and practical one for the sake of cultural unity, political expediency, and economic cohesiveness.

All this notwithstanding, both terms, Latino and Hispanic, used interchangeably, include people from Spain and Portugal as well. For example, actor Antonio Banderas, who was born in Spain, calls himself a "Latino." At times, both the self-naming and imposed naming is contradictory and perplexing. For example, Carlos Gardel, the legendary singer, is revered as Argentinean but was actually born in France; and Carmen Miranda, who was christened by Hollywood as the "Brazilian bombshell," was actually born in Portugal. Another example of this cross-ethnicity is Xavier Cugat, the famous orchestra leader and film performer. Many believe he was born in Cuba or somewhere in the Caribbean, but in fact Cugat was born in Spain.

In this book I have used the particular ethnic designation of the particular Latino community, such as Puerto Rican, Nuyorican (Puerto Ricans born in New York), Dominican,

Cuban, Cuban-American, and so on. In the case of performers and film characters of Mexican ancestry, I have used the term that evolved in historical sequence: Mexican or Mexicano, which refers to individuals born in Mexico or in the Southwest before the annexation into the United States in 1848; Mexican-Americans, the most common term in use until the 1960s to designate people of Mexican ancestry born or raised in the United States; and the most recent designation of "Chicano," a term coined during the Chicano movement of the 1960s.

Included in this book are the contributions of a number of Spanish-born or Spanish-origin film stars, although they do not compose part of the contemporary construct of "Latino." The reason for their inclusion is that Hollywood films more often than not lumped all Spanish-speaking people together into one group. Historically, Spanish-origin performers played mostly Mexican or Latin American roles. Antonio Moreno, Rita Hayworth (Cansino), Sarita Montiel, Antonio Banderas, and Penélope Cruz are but some of the most prominent examples of this long pattern.

Latinos in film and television today are not as visible, despite becoming this nation's largest minority. But once upon a time this was not the case in the Hollywood film industry. In the "golden age of Hollywood," Latinos were not incidental and bit players, they were major stars: they were handsome and romantic heroes, beautiful and sophisticated women, and versatile actors who earned critical acclaim by playing every type of role. In the golden age, Latino film stars stirred the hearts of women, the aspirations of men and the dreams of children. The first Latino Hollywood film star was the Mexican-born Ramon Novarro, who came to prominence and fame in 1922. He was followed at the end of the decade by the first Latina film star, the Mexican-born Dolores del Río (who was Navarro's second cousin). At their prime they were able to demonstrate the wide range of roles that talented Latino film actors could play when not impeded by the confines of prejudice and racism. In subsequent years the staple of the Latino male brought back the bandit image, as well as new ones like the docile peon, the crooked government official, the murderous *narcotraficante*, the violence-prone revolutionary, the gang-banger and the illegal alien. For the Latina, the later stereotype consigned them to the roles of temperamental *cantineras*, boisterous prostitutes, oversexed *campesinas*, docile domestics, welfare mothers, and violent gang members.

Novarro's enormous popularity facilitated the arrival and stardom of other Latino film stars of the 1920s: Dolores del Río, Lupe Vélez, Gilbert Roland, Don Alvarado, Raquel Torres, and Lupita Tovar. In the following decades some of the best and brightest stars were Latino: Anthony Quinn, Rita Hayworth (Cansino), Maria Montez, Ricardo Montalbán, Cesar Romero, Pedro Armendáriz, José Ferrer, Cantinflas, Rita Moreno, Raquel Welch (Tejada), Raúl Juliá, Edward James Olmos, María Conchita Alonso, Jimmy Smits, Jennifer Lopez, and Salma Hayek. Some were less durable and flickered only briefly, but not less memorably: Rosaura Revueltas, Lalo Ríos, Pina Pellicer, and Jaime Sánchez, among others.

Each in their own way was affected by the prevalent prejudice and discrimination in society and the film industry. Some were compelled to endure stereotypes and others type-casting. Many attempted to alter the negative images individually or collectively. For some the price was blacklisting, deportation, self-destruction, and/or unfulfilled promise. But regardless of the trials and tribulations experienced by Latino film stars and filmmakers, they contributed and left an indelible mark on United States cinema. Some earned legendary fame, great wealth and international awards and adulation. Others toiled at their craft, devoid of fame, fortune or honors.

The golden age of Latino film stars in Hollywood was between 1922 and the 1950s. Thereafter, Latinos were for the most part relegated to supporting roles and incidental roles in both films and television. Bona fide Latino film stars and even Latino character actors became increasingly rare. But aside from the presence of major actors must also be added the contributions of Latino directors, writers, cinematographers, technicians, bit players, and extras that enriched Hollywood and international cinema. The presence of a significant number of Latinos behind the camera began in the early 1930s when Hollywood began producing Spanish-language films (in the aftermath of talking films). After the vogue of these films had passed, Latinos continued as a creative presence, although in diminishing numbers into the present day.

I would like to explain a little about my methodology. First, the book is divided by decade, beginning with the 1960s and finishing with the present decade. I have provided an overview of each decade, with particular emphasis on the Hollywood film industry, trends, major political and economic events, and the prevailing Latino images. Finally, I have listed representative films depicting the key Latino images and finished with the biographies of major Latino film stars and filmmakers. The purpose of this approach is that in a very real sense the particular socioeconomic factors within each decade determined the appeal and popularity of each film star and roles. They are the product of their time. For example, the "Latin lover" vogue and such film stars as Don Alvarado and Antonio Moreno are very much a phenomenon of the 1920s; similarly the Technicolor escapist "easterners" of Maria Montez reflect the World War II years. Film studios responded to filmgoers' demand at the box office by creating and packaging a certain type of film and film star. In addition, the advent of certain technological developments (like sound) and the rise and fall of the studio system had an incalculable impact on how films were made and distributed. Thus, every film star, film, and film image is very much reflects its time.

Second, I also focus on the major Latino film stars (and their film images) and filmmakers (directors, screenwriters, etc.). (Though I have also included some of the better-known Latino supporting and character actors, as some earned comparable fame to the big stars.) As a consequence, the longer biographies are of the most significant individuals. I have purposely avoided an encyclopedic approach or a mere recitation of credits and vital statistics. Rather, I have focused on the actors' unique film personae and/or typecasting. Most of the biographies include direct quotes in reference to their film image or experience as Latinos in the Hollywood film industry in particular, as well as some key aspects of their lives. Many of them contain capsule reviews of their key films. I hope that this will make both their life and career come alive for the reader. I have made a point of avoiding tabloid and sensationalized accounts of their private lives, which are irrelevant to their film achievements. The major film stars were prized possessions of the studios as they brought moviegoers to the box office; developed a particular style and film image; affected fashion; and were the object of desire by millions of fans around the world. They still spark nostalgia and interest today. Each biography has been placed in the decade in which that film star or filmmaker reached stardom or gained fame. Some proved to be durable and resilient, while others had short-lived careers.

Third, I provide an overview of Latino film images and stereotypes prevalent in each decade. I have included a list of representative films from each decade that depicted the Latino image or stereotype. Not ironically, the major Latino film stars avoided playing the worst of the stereotypes and negative roles, although there were exceptions. Latino film stars were well aware of the prejudice and obstacles facing them in the Hollywood film industry. During the golden age of Hollywood, film stars like Ramon Novarro, Dolores del Río, and Anthony Quinn were able to play a wide assortment of roles and ethnicities, while others were not and were often typecast in a certain type of role, such as exotics or romantic lovers. Most often, the worst of the Latino stereotypes were played by non–Latino performers. Thus, the representative films presented are in the latter category, with some recent exceptions. Oftentimes, I have included reviews of the particular film. They bring a unique, time-based perspective as to how society at large viewed Latinos, as well as their history and culture.

I have viewed most of the films that are mentioned in this book, on video, DVD, television, cable or in theaters. Some films have been lost due to the negligence of the studios or distributors. In some cases, I have relied on the reviews that appeared about them, the comments of others or persons that I have interviewed. I have attempted to assess these films through a critical eye, especially those films allegedly based on historical events, and where possible have refuted inaccuracies, revisionism, or outright prejudice. I have viewed these films from a Latino point of view.

I have tried to keep Hollywood film jargon to a minimum, but some terms are unavoidable and merit definition. A "sleeper" is a film, often with a modest budget, that becomes an unexpected critical and commercial success. An "A" film is a big-budget film with big stars and an important director, while a "B" film is a low-budget film with new or past-their-prime talent. In Hollywood's golden age, most major studios released both types of films. An "oater" is a western; a "weepie" or "sudser," a sentimental melodrama; a "film noir," a dark crime drama in vogue during the 1940s and 1950s, but at times undergoing revival; and a "screwball comedy" is a comedy popular in the 1930s with eccentric or offbeat characters and stories.

My research for this book really began when I was a child and began viewing films, both U.S. and Mexican. From the beginning, the contrast in reference to how the characters were portrayed and how the films dealt with Mexican and Latino culture and history was drastically different and illuminating. I began amassing clippings, books, photos, and later videos and DVDs of English- and Spanish-language films. I did acting in high school and was part of a Chicano acting ensemble called Teatro a la Brava in college. Through these experiences I began to meet many people in the U.S. and Mexican film industry, actors, directors, and others who furthered my understanding about the history of Latino performers and their contributions. Unfortunately, there was nothing about this history until 1977 with the publication of Allen L. Woll's *The Latin Image in American Film*. In 1985, Gary D. Keller edited *Chicano Cinema Research: Research, Reviews, and Resources*, an anthology of essays on different aspects of Chicano cinema and images, which filled a large void in this area of study. Since then, other books have been published, most notably the works of Chon Noriega on film theory. Other works have provided only a cursory perspective of Latino film images bolstered by a sumptuous display of photographs encompassing the one hundred years of

Latino film images; and still others have been biographies and autobiographies of the most famous Latino film stars. However, while I have found these works of great interest and merit, I wanted to go in a different direction, that is, to provide a historical analysis and political analysis of the powerful social forces that have shaped the film art form, especially Latino film images. This is the conception of this book.

In the process of my research I have relied on a multitude of different sources and resources: general works on film and film history, biographies, newspaper and magazine articles, reference books, interviews, and, last but not least, repeated viewing and analysis of the films themselves and long discussions about them with friends, relatives, acquaintances and strangers. I have conducted many interviews with Latino performers and filmmakers over the years. The interviews are a cross-section of the different voices from different eras of the Latino film experience. The experience of Latinos in short films, documentaries, and television is beyond the scope of this book, and as such I have kept that history to a minimum.

I had intended to use the term "Latino/a" to be inclusive of gender representation. However, this term has proved too obtrusive, especially in a book of this size. Thus I have followed the widespread practice of using the term "Latino" in both masculine and feminine contexts.

The struggles and triumphs of Latino film actors and filmmakers within the Hollywood film industry is an important legacy for both Latinos and non–Latinos. The images of and opportunities for Latinos have mirrored the history and sociopolitical conditions in the United States. Nevertheless, this writer remains optimistic and hopeful that the both the images and opportunities will improve and reflect the considerable contributions of this community.

I

The Origins of Latino Stereotypes
A Historical Perspective

Although inaccuracies and derogatory images of Latinos have become the norm in U.S. motion pictures, I propose that the roots have their origins in history.

They began in the clash of two civilizations (and empires): one, Protestant-oriented and derived from England and northern Europe; and the other Catholic and based in Spain. Both the British and Spanish empires (as well as others) appropriated the entire American continent through force of arms and genocide against the indigenous peoples, while at the same time expounding the virtues of their "civilization" and "culture." They transplanted to their American-based empires and, later, to the nation-states that evolved, their particular prejudices about one another, their religions and their way of life. However, they reserved the worst of these prejudices, hatreds, hostilities, and stereotypes for the indigenous peoples that they conquered, enslaved, and exterminated. Later, added to the catalogue of "otherness" were more people with dark skins, the mestizo, the African, and the mulatto.

By the mid–18th century, the United States began to establish hegemony over Latin America through the Monroe Doctrine and "gunboat diplomacy." A justification of these policies was the belief that indigenous peoples and other people of color were inferior. For example, President Thomas Jefferson described Native Americans as "blood thirsty barbarians," among other things. Not surprisingly, it was during his administration that indigenous peoples were forcefully removed from the East Coast to reserves east of the Mississippi River.[1] Even the race-pure Senator John Calhoun would rather pass up the conquest of the Mexican Southwest if it meant undermining racial purity: "To incorporate Mexico, would be the first instance of the kind of incorporation of an Indian race ... I protest against a union of that! Ours, sir, is the Government of a white race."[2] Mexico had some 80 percent of the Native American population on the continent when Europeans arrived. This long-standing antipathy against Mexicans has been documented by historians. David Weber noted, for example, "American visitors to the Mexican frontier were nearly unanimous in commenting on the dark skin of Mexican *mestizos* who, it was generally agreed, had inherited the worst qualities of Spaniards and Indians to produce a 'race' still more despicable than of either parent."[3]

In 1848, Rufus B. Sage, a journalist and former trapper, wrote, "There are no people on the continent of America, whether civilized, with one or two exceptions, more miserable in the condition or despicable morals than the mongrel race inhabiting New Mexico."[4] Another United States historian, Walter Prescott Webb, in 1935 expressed in no uncertain terms his lack of objectivity and disdain for Mexicans: "The Mexican nation arises from the heterogeneous mixture of races that compose it.... The result is a conglomerate with all gradations with grandees at the top and peons at the bottom. The language is Spanish, or Mexican, the religion is Catholic, the temperament volatile and mercurial."[5]

The denigration of Mexicans and other peoples in Latin America led to the belief that the United States had the right to determine their destiny, as they were incapable of doing so. For example, President Theodore Roosevelt, in an annual message to Congress, added his own corollary to the Monroe Doctrine: "Chronic wrongdoing, or an impotence which results in general loosening of the ties of civilized society, may in America, as elsewhere, ultimately require intervention by some civilized nation, and in the Western Hemisphere, the adherence of the United States to the Monroe Doctrine may force the United States, however reluctantly, in flagrant cases of such wrongdoing or impotence, to the exercise of an international police power."[6] Inevitably, this gospel of hegemony contributed to a long and tumultuous relationship between the United States and Latin America: war, intervention, hostility, suspicion, and animosity.

The first military conflict between the United States and a Latin American country occurred over the growing expansion of slavery into then Mexican Texas in 1836. The newborn Mexican republic had abolished slavery upon its independence from Spain in 1821, while in the United States a precarious balance existed between slave and "free states," one that would continue until the Civil War. The Texas Rebellion of 1836, which was mostly made up of and led by recent U.S. arrivals, in turn led to the Mexican-American War (1846–1848). The war resulted in the loss of more than half of the national territory of Mexico. Once again, as in previous historical periods, inherent economic and cultural differences had contributed to misunderstanding, rivalry, and ultimately war.

These conflicts, more than any others, between two neighbors laid the foundation of distrust, animosity, and stereotyping between the peoples of the United States and Latin America, especially Mexico. Dwight Conquerwood, for example, has written, "Borders bleed, as much as they contain."[7] The Mexico–United States border has remained an open wound for more than one hundred years. Gloria Anzaldúa has noted, "The U.S.–Mexican border *es una herida abierta* where the Third World grates against the first and bleeds. And before a scab forms it hemorrhages again, the lifeblood of the two worlds merging to form a third country—a border culture. Borders are set up to define the places that are safe and unsafe, to distinguish us from them.... The prohibited and forbidden are its inhabitants."[8]

Moreover, these fractured images would remain frozen in collective memory. For example, historian Rodolfo Acuña wrote, "Most Anglo-Americans believed that, based on their right of conquest, they were entitled to special privileges and special citizenship status: this was reinforced by the belief in their cultural and racial superiority. The Chicano, in contrast, was a conquered person, an alien, and a half-breed. When a small number of Chicanos turned to highway banditry, Anglo-Americans did not bother to investigate why they committed anti-social acts or why the Chicano masses supported them. They merely stereotyped the entire group as criminal, justifying further violence against the Mexican-American community."[9]

The ethos of United States foreign policy was reflected in race relations within the nation. The United States Supreme Court itself had ruled in *Plessy v. Ferguson*, in 1896, that the doctrine of "separate but equal" was constitutional. The court's ruling at the national level gave legal justification of the seeming superiority of Euro-Americans over peoples of darker skins. Although de jure segregation was primarily directed at African Americans, numerous de facto practices and local ordinances had segregated Mexicans, Native Americans, and Asians for decades.[10] Mexicans were confined to "Mexican schools" and the "Mexican" part of town. Native Americans were for the most part contained in reservations and their children forced into boarding schools to be "civilized"; while Asians (primarily Chinese at that time) were confined to "Chinatowns."[11] The legal legitimacy of segregation was undermined by *Mendez v. Westminster* (1947) and later in *Brown v. Board of Education* in 1954, but it would take a national civil rights movement and continued federal legislation to ensure the demise of de jure segregation. However, de facto segregation, as well as racism, would continue to gnaw at the nation's conscience.

In the meantime, the Latino population of the country continued to grow, directly related to U.S. foreign policy in Latin America and patterns of capital investment. Both had the result of stimulating mass migration from Latin America to the United States. People would come either as political refugees seeking a haven or as cheap labor responding to supply and demand. In Puerto Rico, people abandoned the countryside for the cities, where they found they outnumbered the jobs created by the economy. According to Juan González, "To prevent renewed unrest, Muñoz and officials in Washington started to encourage emigration to the north. By the early 1950s, their policy was sparking the largest flight of Latin America to the United States."[12] In turn, the Cuban Revolution in 1959 resulted in the migration of hundreds of thousands during the 1960s and 1970s. The first wave was largely the affluent and middle class, while the second wave, in the 1980s, was poorer and darker-skinned. A failed popular uprising in the Dominican Republic in 1965 was crushed militarily by the United States under the rationale of preventing "another Cuba." It had the effect of igniting a Dominican migration for several decades.

The liberal administrations of Kennedy's "New Frontier" and Johnson's "Great Society" responded to the exigencies of the civil rights movement with social programs and inclusionary policies like affirmative action. However, a conservative retrenchment began with Nixon and flourished during the administrations of Reagan and George H.W. Bush. The demise of the Soviet Union and the "evil empire" deprived ideologues and the New Right of their sense of mission, purpose and identifiable enemy. The globalization of world economies (the North American Free Trade Agreement, the European Union, etc.) signaled the decline of the traditional nation-states and accentuated the transnational nature of cheap Third World labor to the industrialized world. For example, anthropologist Marcelo Suárez-Orozco noted, "The global impetus undermined the old boundaries that served to contain not only political and economic projects but also to structure local identities and cultural psychologies. The upheavals brought about by these unprecedented global changes have affected the political and economic realm as well as the symbolic and psychological order. A particularly subversive aspect of the global upheaval has been the tearing down of a feeling of 'home'—the sense of rootedness, the feeling of continuity and familiarity with one's social space."[13]

This post–Cold War era has coincided with the demise or flight to Third World countries and cheaper labor of many of the old mainstay industries like steel and manufacturing, and the metamorphoses to a knowledge- and service-oriented economy. Global economic forces have fueled an unprecedented immigration of labor from Latin America (primarily from Mexico), but also significantly from countries further impoverished by U.S.–sponsored counterinsurgency efforts: El Salvador, Guatemala, and Nicaragua. Latinos are no longer confined to the agricultural fields and segregated barrios. They have a marked presence in many school districts. Many are employed as laborers in restaurants and hotels, as gardeners, and as domestics. The increased Latino visibility has resulted in a political backlash laced with paranoid rage. Immigrants, especially Latino immigrants (as well as U.S.–born Latinos) have become the object of unbearable inner tension and catharsis. The media has served to manifest much of this. For example, Bob Herbert wrote, "Immigrants from countries and cultures that are incompatible with and indigestible to the Euro-American cultural core of the United States should be prohibited."[14] The xenophobia and intolerance has resulted in a proliferation of state laws and measures directed at denying social services, education, and health care access to "foreign-looking people." Marcelo Suárez-Orozco observed, "At a time when nothing else can be kept steady, there is a desperate drive to maintain and defend the basic markers that give meaning and structure identity. Fascist anti-immigrant sentiment, whether in France, Belgium, or California, captures the tools of anthropology to construct landscapes of Otherness around the incommensurability of cultural forms and the tantalization of human differences."[15]

Latinos (whether undocumented or documented) have joined the media pantheon of stereotypes such as the "black welfare queen," "the Arab terrorist," and the "lazy homeless." For Latinos, it appeared that art imitated life and vice versa. According to the *Los Angeles Times*, a study undertaken by the National Association of Hispanic Journalists found that "only 1 percent of network news coverage focuses on Latinos or issues related to Latinos.... And based on a study of the 1995 evening newscasts of ABC, CBS, and NBC, 85 percent of stories that do cover Latinos fall in four negative categories—crime, immigration, affirmative action and welfare. Latinos are symbolically annihilated in terms of their representation in network news stories ... they are seen only occasionally and then in roles of illegal aliens, welfare recipients, criminals."[16]

In conclusion, history, conquest, foreign policy, and economics have constructed and shaped: the images and stereotypes of Latinos in the United States. These events created perceptions, attitudes, and images, which made their way into literature and then into film.

II

The Evolution of Latino
Film Images (1894–1919)

The first image of Latino culture in the United States cinema was in an obscure 1894 short entitled *Pedro Esquirel and Dionecio González: Mexican Duel*. It was the first character reference as well. It froze in time forever the violence-prone, crime-oriented Mexican with a pronounced inability to control his primitive passions. It is a distorted image that has remained static for more than a century.

This stereotyped image was transplanted into the infant art form of film from the prevailing prejudices and attitudes of the time that had been constructed and nurtured by the historic experience of the Texas Rebellion, the Mexican-American War, Manifest Destiny, the Monroe Doctrine, and segregation. But even before the advent of film, these images had already been encapsulated into the popular imagination in literature and in the less reputable dime novels of the Old West.[1] For example, Arthur G. Pettit noted, "The basic fictional stereotypes of Anglo and Mexican appeared at the time and place where the characters and incidents first appear: that is, in works written in the heat of emotion generated by the Texas Revolution, the war with Mexico, and the invasion of the Southwest. Yet, for more than a century, few authors have attempted to refute these images."[2]

The writers of these dime novels, short stories, and Mexican southwest conquest literature were of two types. Half of them were Texas-born or migrants from Texas.[3] As such, they tended to be directed or influenced by the folklore about the Texas Revolution or the prevailing prejudice against Mexicans. Another group of writers were easterners without a direct knowledge of the Southwest or of Mexicans.[4] The epitome of the dime novelists was Ned Buntine (Edward Zane Carroll Judson, 1821–1856), a well-known bigamist and confidence man. During the 1840s and 1850s, he produced a prolific output of dime novels that established the basic Mexican stereotypes. Later, Buntine would mastermind Buffalo Bill's transformation into a show business superstar. Much later, Buffalo Bill himself would recreate the fictional Wild West invented by Buntine in early films.

Other writers who contributed to perpetuating Mexican stereotypes and a revisionist history included the well-respected Bret Harte (Francis Brett II, 1839–1901) and O. Henry (William Sydney Porter, 1862–1910). Still other purveyors of such images included Sam Hall, Roy Lander Lightfoot, Paul Wellman, Eugene P. Lyle, Arthur Carhart, Birdsall Biscoe, Willis Vernon Cole, Gertrude Crownsfield, and Clara Driscoll, among many others. The most enduring and popular images invented by these writers were the Mexican *bandido* and his counterpart, the half-breed harlot. Pettit wrote of the former, "Bandidos are characterized by complexions shading from pitch black through dark brown to orange, yellow, olive, and gray. Such polychromatic blemishing earns a long list of descriptive adjectives: dusky, dingy, sooty, swarthy, inky, pitchy, and greasy. These mixed-blood unfortunately are variously called greasers, Mexes, Mexikins, yellers, breeds, mongrels, and niggers—seldom Mexicans."[5] Other Mexican male types included the overbearing and blue-blooded caballero, the conniving and indolent peon, and the corrupt and fastidious priest.

The gender representation of Mexican women in this literature was no more flattering. According to Pettit, "The harlot fulfills the libidinous needs of the man who will eventually reject her, and she guarantees the chastity of the women he will eventually marry. Always, however, she is a secondary character. The primary sexual emphasis is on the purity of the white heroine and the corresponding ultimate redemption of the white hero, who is rarely condemned for his transgression unless he sows oats with white virgins."[6] The cast of Mexican female characters included the dark and oversexed peasant maiden, the embittered *cantinera*, and the long-suffering mother and/or grandmother. But these were overshadowed by the Castilian-blooded *señorita*, which in films always ended with the white hero in both love and war against the brown rabble; and the "half-breed" harlot who could never control her sexuality and temperament. Mexican women were not only the object of ethnic stereotypes but also outright sexist misrepresentation, and of class bias.

Some feminist writers propose that the genesis of Latina stereotypes is based on how the Spanish conquest is interpreted. For example, Christine List noted, "*La Malinche* is regarded as the first person to betray the indigenous collectivity. She is the Eve of Mexican culture, a woman who contaminated the purity of the native with European blood. She is regarded as the person responsible for the fall of the continent, and is referred to as *la vendida* (the sellout). She is known as la *chingada,* the one who was violated by Cortez, and it is a common belief (like Adam and Eve tale of European culture) that her action generated evil in all those of the female sex. The notion that *La Malinche* as the '*chingada*' is also used to justify the view of women as naturally passive and, following the same logic, a view of men as active agents and penetrators."[7] This enduring image survived through history and was transplanted intact into the infant art form of cinema that began at the end of the 1890s and flourished in the next century.

Similarly, an equally popular and distorted image of the "phony West" was disseminated by Buffalo Bill's Wild West Show, which featured Mexican bandits and bloodthirsty Indians. These distorted images were further disseminated through paintings, illustrated magazines, and photographs.

By the time the first Mexican image arrived in 1894, in the form of *Pedro Esquirel and Dionecio González: Mexican Duel,* the Mexican image in the popular imagination was already firmly established. Motion pictures simply followed the patterns and formulas of Mexican stereotypes already established by their literary predecessors. For example, during the early teens of the 20th century, a popular staple was the grotesque Mexican bandit. A series of films with epithetic titles were produced, especially in the western genre, such as *The Greaser's Gauntlet* (1908); *Tony, the Greaser* (1911); *Bronco Billy and the Greaser* (1914); *The Greaser's Revenge* (1914); *The Greaser, Majestic* (1915); and *Guns and Greasers* (1919), among many others. During this period, that epitome of yellow journalism, William Randolph Hearst, helped to partially finance a melodramatic fifteen-part serial entitled *Patria* (1916), which chronicled the Mexican-Japanese invasion of the United States. This film proposed a justified U.S. intervention into the then raging Mexican Revolution.

These early films and numerous others established the fundamental stereotypes of Mexicans, and later Latinos. Mexican males were either docile or violent. Neither type could think for themselves. The docile characters could only be saved by a stalwart Yankee hero, as in *The Aztec Hero* (1914). The unrepentant, violent Mexican always would meet with a Darwinist ending at the hands of a white hero, such as in *Why Worry?* (1923). A third characteristic of these scenarios was that the Yankee, whether a recent transplant from the East or a stoic hombre of the West, would always prove himself superior to his Mexican counterpart in both love and war. Inevitably, the virtuous señorita always discarded her Mexican lover for the white tenderfoot hero, and similarly, the Mexican miscreant would always dump his Mexican *cantinera* to pursue the Euro-American women, as in *In Old Arizona* (1929, 20th Century–Fox). Margarita De Orellano noted, "Unlike the men, the women of Mexico are ascribed very different qualities, among them docility and sensuality. The representation of Mexican women is the 'beautiful *señorita*,' a figure as picturesque as the greaser, but not as depreciated. The model of the beautiful señorita is not the *mestiza* or the Indian, but the while *criolla* Spanish woman."[8]

Another characteristic of these early film representations was that Latino roles were invariably played by Euro-American performers. This was the norm at the beginning of motion pictures. Native Americans, African Americans, and Asians were also played by exclusively by Euro-American actors. The earliest Mexican-American performers (this was well before Hollywood's star system was created) were Myrtle González (1891–1917) and Beatriz

Left: Ramon Novarro (1899–1968) was born in Durango, Mexico, and began in Hollywood films as an extra and singer in 1917. He became the first Latino Hollywood star by playing the villain in *The Prisoner of Zenda* (1922). He also became a matinee idol, but played an unusually diverse array of roles. He had a fine tenor voice, which he capitalized on when sound arrived. Key films include *Scaramouche* (1923); *The Student Prince* (1927); *The Pagan* (1929); and *Mata Hari* (1931).
   Right: Ramon Novarro in *Ben-Hur* (1925, Metro-Goldwyn-Mayer). He starred in two important films in France and Mexico: *Le Comedie du Bonheur* (1940) and *La Virgen Que Forjo una Patria* (1941). Tragically, he was murdered on Halloween in 1968.

Michelena (1890–1942). Both were California girls and played numerous roles during the teens of the 20th century. Other Mexican performers and craftsmen worked in front of and behind the camera, especially after filmmaking relocated from New York and New Jersey to California. California was blessed with every type of landscape and films could be shot outdoors almost every day of the year. It was close to the Latin American market, and across the Pacific Ocean laid the vast Asian market as well. The first bona fide Latino film stars would appear in the 1920s: Ramon Novarro, Dolores del Río, Lupe Vélez, Gilbert Roland, Lupita Tovar, and others. Other Latino film stars would come later. (I have documented the era from the 1920s to the 1950s in a previous book.)

The fact that the motion picture industry was brought to California provided entry to many Mexicans. The film industry became centered in Hollywood (a former orange grove area), a nearby suburb of Los Angeles. Mexicans were native to the city and preceded its founding (when they were called Native Americans). The Southwest had been part of Mexico and its culture has always been clearly stamped into this geographic area. Mexicans and the history of the Southwest became part of the movies that were made, especially westerns. Latinos from Puerto Rico, Cuba, and Central and South America were on the other side of the continent and were decades away into the future in terms of migration and public consciousness. Hollywood was a little over one hundred miles from Mexico, an important market for Hollywood films. All these coincidences and realities contributed to the Mexican presence in the film industry and to the content of many films. As a consequence, of the thousands of Latino roles and characters in Hollywood films, the vast majority have been Mexican in ethnicity.

During the teens of the

Dolores del Río (1905–1983) was born in Durango, Mexico, and was the second cousin of Ramon Novarro. She arrived in Hollywood and became the first Latina Hollywood film star in *What Price Glory?* (1926). She was originally typecast as an "exotic" but later went on to play diverse roles in dramas, comedies, and musicals.

Dolores del Río (center) in *Bird of Paradise* (1930, RKO Pictures). After 1942, she left Hollywood for Mexico where she starred in important films directed by Emilio "Indio" Fernández. Her other films included *Flor Silvestre* (1943); *Maria Candelaria* (1943); and *Bugambilia* (1944). Later, she made sporadic appearances in U.S. films and television. In Mexico, she did theater and television.

20th century, performers who became more recognizable became "stars." They had box-office appeal and brought in the moviegoers. These stars were able to negotiate lucrative contracts with the studios. Typically the contracts were for seven years. Tailor-made directors, screenplays, make-up personnel, costumes, camera angles, and other considerations were provided for the great stars. The studios protected their prized possessions by morality clauses in their contracts, legal counsel, and a culture of silence about the stars' private lives (i.e., addictions, sexual orientations, pregnancies, abortions, and any other "misdeeds"). Movie magazines created a cottage industry around the gossip and scandal, career rise and fall, romances and divorces, and films of the great stars.

Movie studios became powerful and influential in politics and economics. Everybody was caught up in the glamour, idolatry, and culture of these beautiful people. Studios became owners of the thousands of theaters for which they provided new films every week. Thousands of young men and women traveled to the West Coast to break into the movies and become part of the dream factory. The golden age of Hollywood films was from the 1920s to the 1950s. During this era the Hollywood film industry was the most creative, powerful, and influential in the world.

The beginning of the decline of the Hollywood film industry would begin in the late

1940s, when it was decreed by the U.S. Supreme Court that the studios' ownership of theaters was in a violation of antitrust legislation. Later, television and professional sports took a heavy toll on film audiences in the 1950s. The studios began to falter with expensive and super-colossal spectacles made to bring movie audiences back to theaters. However, they could no longer afford their expensive roster of long-term contract film stars. The 1960s witnessed the final death throes of the studio system and the beginning of the modern era of motion pictures.

This new era of the Hollywood film industry deeply affected the images of Latino performers, as well as the opportunities and lack of opportunities. It is this modern era of cinema that is the subject of this book.

III
The 1960s

The turbulent decade began with the idealistic inauguration of President Kennedy, who stated, "Those who possess wealth and power in poor nations must accept their own responsibility. They must lead the fight for those basic reforms which alone can preserve the fabric of their society. Those who make peaceful revolution impossible make revolution inevitable."[1] However, the ideological rigidity of the Cold War and the self-interest of both sides made self-determination impossible and conflict inevitable.

Throughout the Third World, nationalist liberation movements proliferated, challenging the moribund empires of Britain, France and Portugal in Africa and Asia, and newer hegemonies such as the United States in Latin America. In the Americas, the United States attempted to undermine the Cuban Revolution, through invasion in 1961 and an economic blockade thereafter. The U.S. military intervention in the Dominican Republic in 1965 was euphemistically justified as "preventing another Cuba." In 1962, the Cuban Missile Crisis brought the world to the brink of annihilation. Gradually, the idealism embodied in Kennedy's Alliance for Progress gave way to Green Berets and military advisors as the Cold War was replicated throughout the Americas between the status quo military regimes and insurgent guerrilla movements.

At home, the assassination of President Kennedy in 1963 foreshadowed the emergence to plain view of social tensions and divisions of long standing. The impetus of President Johnson's "War on Poverty" lost ground as U.S. involvement in the Vietnam War depleted funds for the social agenda. Racial integration met with increasing violent resistance, the anti–Vietnam War movement became a mass movement, hundreds of ghettos broke into riots, and in 1968, two more political assassinations (Martin Luther King, Jr., and Robert Kennedy) ripped the national social fabric. The FBI escalated a number of illegal activities, from harassment of dissidents and wiretaps to shootouts with the Black Panthers. By the end of a decade a "law and order" presidential candidate, Richard M. Nixon, made a spectacular political comeback. He had been written off after his defeat in the 1960 presidential election and in the 1964 California gubernatorial election. In 1968, he was elected president.

During the 1960s, Latinos were making their own history, political and otherwise. The end of the Bracero Program in 1965 gave momentum to the rise of the United Farm Workers union led by Cesar Chavez. In 1967, Reies López Tijerina of New Mexico led the Alianza de los Pueblos Libres (Alliance for Free City-States) in a movement to reclaim land based on colonial land grants. In the cities, the Chicano movement flourished as a new generation struggled for political empowerment, equitable education, and an end to segregation. Chicanos accounted for 10 percent of the population of the Southwest, but 19.4 percent of the

17

Southwest casualties of the Vietnam War.[2] As Chicanos died in large numbers, their Mexican relatives were accused of "stealing jobs" and deported. In December 1969, the National Chicano Moratorium Committee held its first anti–Vietnam War mass demonstration.

Latinos during the decade made up some 6 percent of the U.S. population and the second-largest minority group in the nation. As the large Cuban influx declined in mid–decade, a significant migration of Puerto Ricans took place. Marginalized by both poverty and racism, they struggled to build a social movement to redress their plight. By the end of the decade, the Latino was no longer the "invisible minority."

Film Images and Film Stars

The 1960s saw the continued decline of the Hollywood film industry in both quantity and quality. The old Hollywood was being challenged both from within and without.

Several factors contributed to the trend. First, the previously World War II-ravaged film industries in Europe and Asia (especially in India and Japan) reemerged and became more competitive. Second, the rise of professional sports (such as basketball and baseball) provided an alternative and live form of entertainment. Third, television rose to become the main entertainment of entire families in the comfort of their own homes. Fourth, the personal manner of running film studios by autocratic moguls came to a complete end and they were replaced by talent agency personnel and more often by multinational corporations, which were oriented more towards short-term profits than long-term quality. Fifth, the Hollywood film industry continued to remain irresponsive to the youthful audience (until the breakthrough of *Easy Rider* in 1969) who now became the predominant moviegoer.

Finally, the decade witnessed the remarkable turnover of film stars and filmmakers in a scale only comparable to the silent-to-sound period. A great number of the stars of Hollywood's golden age passed from the scene during the late 1950s and 1960s: Ramon Novarro, Antonio Moreno, Errol Flynn, Humphrey Bogart, Tyrone Power, Clark Gable, Gary Cooper, Alan Ladd, Ronald Coleman, Richard Barthelmess, Marilyn Monroe, Margaret Sullavan, Leo Carrillo, Gail Russell, Don Alvarado, Wayne Morris, Paul Muni, Claude Rains, Ann Sheridan, Spencer Tracy, and Robert Taylor, among others. Many others retired from the cinema: Duncan Renaldo, Susan Kohner, James Cagney, William Powell, Gloria Swanson, Vivien Leigh, Dorothy Gish, Kay Francis, and Franchot Tone. The great directors of that era made their last films during the late 1950s or during the 1960s: John Ford, Raoul Walsh, William Wyler, George Stevens, Henry Hathaway, William Wellman, Alfred Hitchcock, Orson Welles, Anthony Mann, and Michael Curtiz, among others.

Although the Latino population continued to grow and was the second-largest minority community, Latinos lacked both political and economic power. This lack of empowerment, coupled with the U.S. policy of containment in Latin America, shaped the images of Latinos in U.S. cinema. The predominant images of Latinos during the 1960s, with minor exceptions, were of two kinds: one, that of the subservient, ideological or cultural disciple, who was unable to think for himself or herself; and two, the amoral bandit/desperado and *cantinera* woman. The majority of these roles were in westerns, in which lawlessness was the central theme. Two other discernible genres were films with the Mexican Revolution as a back-

Ann Blyth and Fernando Lamas in *Rose Marie* (1952, Metro-Goldwyn-Mayer).

ground and other historical films. The inevitable fate of Latinos in these films was to be benignly docile or subservient, in accordance with the Monroe Doctrine or Manifest Destiny; or to be violent bandits and consequently doomed to be annihilated like the revolutionaries in Latin America.

The image as ideological or cultural disciples had been glimpsed in the 1930s in films like *Juarez* (1939, Warner Brothers), which proposed that the concept of "democracy" emanated only from Euro-American mentors like Abraham Lincoln, and that the Monroe Doctrine was a benevolent gesture for the benefit of Latinos who needed to be guided. These images flourished with the advent of the Cold War. Invariably, these films depicted Latinos, especially Mexicans, as pathetic, childlike figures, humble but cowardly, incapable of defending or fighting for their lives or rights without the condescending and fearless European-American hero. The most representative and reprehensible of these films during the decade were *The Magnificent Seven* (1960, United Artists), *Guns of the Magnificent Seven* (1969, United Artists), and *The Magnificent Seven Ride* (1972, United Artists). The first film was based on Akira Kurosawa's *Seven Samurai* (1954). In the original classic film, a Japanese village was pillaged and plundered frequently by a band of marauding bandits. The villagers decide to pool their meager resources and hire seven Japanese samurai warriors to protect them. In the Americanization of the story, the warriors became seven European-American gunfighters; the bandits became Mexican, as did the villagers. The metaphors of Manifest Destiny and the Monroe Doctrine, within the context of the Cold War, were evident.

The Mexican bandit and desperado image had a spectacular resurgence with the phenomenon of the "spaghetti western," which developed in Italy in the mid–1960s and was popularized later in the decade by the work of Sergio Leone: *A Fistful of Dollars* (1966, United Artists), and its two sequels, *For a Few Dollars More* (1967, United Artists), and *The Good, the Bad and the Ugly* (1970, United Artists). The trio of films catapulted the former television star Clint Eastwood, cast as the "man with no name," into major stardom. The films were based on another classic Akira Kurosawa film, *Yojimbo* (1961), in which Toshiro Mifune had played the sardonic and amoral samurai. The international popularity of the spaghetti western lasted into the 1970s. They were mostly produced in Italy, later in Spain, and even Germany, where a series of the genre were headlined by two expatriate Hollywood stars, Stewart Granger and Lex Barker. The genre was a godsend for many former Hollywood stars, as well as for some character actors. For some it brought a second career of fame and fortune and for others the first taste of success. Among the stars that experienced the former were the veterans Gilbert Roland and Stewart Granger and former heartthrobs Guy Madison and Lex Barker. Two former stars of the "sand and sandals" epics, Steve Reeves and Gordon Scott, prolonged their careers in the new genre. Former television stars like Ty Hardin (*Bronco*) and Edd "Kookie" Byrnes (*77 Sunset Strip*) found their careers resurrected. Even such unlikely western heroes as Rod Steiger and Eli Wallach found new careers; while long-time character actors like Charles Bronson and Lee Van Cleef were catapulted to world fame.

Gilbert Roland (1905–1994) was born in Mexico and fell in love with Hollywood films at an early age. He began acting as an extra in the 1920s and by 1926 had achieved stardom in such films as *Camille* as a romantic leading man. He went on to play every type of role in many types of film. He is shown here in *The Passionate Plumber* (1932, Metro-Goldwyn-Mayer) with Irene Purcell.

These new Mexican bandits in the spaghetti westerns were a different breed: "good-bad bandidos." The "good" was in reference to their technical skills, ingenuity, duplicity, and ability to do a fast draw. In these amoral films, the European-American protagonist descended to the level of the stereotypical and caricatured Mexican bandit. But the Mexican characters, unlike their European-American counterparts, were more violent, treacherous, and intellectually and technically inferior. As a consequence, these Mexican bandits were always the villains in the spaghetti westerns. Their female counterparts were always *cantineras*, oversexed, seedy and duplicitous. The other Mexican image on display in the genre was the docile kind, usually a peon, predictably backward, illiterate, foolish, and cowardly. As for the Mexican nation, Christopher Frayling noted, "Mexico tended to be presented in American cinema as a place of escape, a refuge; a noisy, exotic alternative; a place for seeking lost ideals; and (its most characteristic role in silent films) as a breeding ground for particularly vicious bad guys. The Mexican Revolution of 1911–1920 routinely provided a colourful backdrop for footloose American heroes to discover for themselves that 'a man's gotta do what a man's gotta do.'"[3]

Some films in the spaghetti western genre are *Adios, Gringo* (1968, Translux); *Flaming Frontier* (1968, Warner Bros.) with Stewart Granger; *A Stranger in Town* (1968, Metro-Goldwyn-Mayer) and *Any Gun Can Play* (1968, Raft) with Gilbert Roland and Edd Byrnes; *The Ugly Ones* (1968, United Artists); *Seven Guns for the MacGregors* (1968, Columbia); *Payment in Blood* (1968) with Guy Madison and Edd Byrnes; *A Minute to Pay, a Second to Die* (1968, Metro-Goldwyn-Mayer) with Tony Anthony; *The Big Gundown* (1968, Paramount) with Lee Van Cleef; *A Bullet for the General* (1968, Avco) with Gian Maria Volante; *Aces High* (1969, United Artists); *Death Rides a Horse* (1969, United Artists) with Lee Van Cleef; *God Forgives, I Don't* (1969, American International) with Terence Hill; and *Day of Anger* (1969, National General) with Lee Van Cleef, among many others. The amoral spaghetti western reached a climax with Sergio Leone's masterpiece *Once upon a Time in the West* (1969, Paramount), shot on location in the U.S. Southwest, in which the unlikely hero turned out to be a Mexican gunfighter called the "man with harmonica" (Charles Bronson).

In the meantime, the traditional Mexican bandit continued during the 1960s with such films as *The Magnificent Seven* and *The Outrage* (1964, Metro-Goldwyn-Mayer). The latter film was based on yet another Akira Kurosawa film classic, *Rashomon* (1951), which chronicled a bandit's rape of a woman of the landed gentry. In the U.S. adaptation, the bandit became Mexican, Juan Carrasco (played by the miscast Paul Newman), while the rancher (Laurence Harvey) and his wife (Claire Bloom) were inevitably European-American. In the British-made *The Singer Not the Song* (1961, Warner Bros.), Dirk Bogarde played Anncleto, an atheistic Mexican bandit in control of a small town. He becomes so enraged with the arrival of a Roman Catholic priest (John Mills) that he begins killing peasants alphabetically. In *Rio Conchos* (1965, 20th Century–Fox), Anthony Franciosa played a stereotypical Mexican bandit who pays with his worthless life for his treachery. In *The Appaloosa* (1966, Columbia), the horse of a buffalo hunter (Marlon Brando) is stolen by a sadistic Mexican bandit, Chuy Medina (John Saxon), who is also dumped by his *mujer* (Anjanette Comer). In *Blue* (1969, Paramount), Ricardo Montalbán played a Mexican bandit, Ortega, whose adopted European-American son (Terence Stamp) turns against him. In *MacKenna's Gold* (1969, 20th Century–Fox), a sheriff (Gregory Peck) battles to defend his newfound treasure against an unsavory *bandido*, Colorado (Omar Sharif). Mexican *bandidos* menaced and prevented peace-loving Confederates (John Wayne, Rock Hudson) from supporting the Juaristas in *The Undefeated* (1969, 20th Century–Fox). And in *Butch Cassidy and the Sundance Kid* (1969, 20th Century–Fox), the two outlaws literally decimate the Bolivian army single-handedly.

The third type of film in evidence during the decade was the film with the Mexican Revolution as a backdrop. Increasingly, U.S. westerns were influenced by the amoral spaghetti westerns. As a consequence, films portrayed both the reactionary government federales and the liberal revolutionary forces as decadent. The former were portrayed as pompous, class-conscious and corrupt, while the revolutionaries were equally violent, but also promiscuous, alcoholic, and seedy. This body of films proverbially had European-American soldiers of fortune (mercenaries) as ideological mentors providing technical and political expertise. In *The Professionals* (1966, Paramount), several ex–soldiers of fortune who fought on the side of the revolution (Burt Lancaster, Lee Marvin, Robert Ryan) are paid to abduct the wife (Claudia Cardinale) of a revolutionary leader (Jack Palance), only to realize that she left willingly the arms of her reactionary rancher. In *100 Rifles* (1969, 20th Century–Fox), one superstud black sheriff (Jim Brown), on the trail of a Yaqui Indian (Burt Reynolds), easily seduces the latter's promiscuous girlfriend (Raquel Welch). In *Viva Rides!* (1968, Paramount), the image of Pancho Villa was an improvement over the caricature of *Viva Villa!* (1934, Metro-Goldwyn-Mayer), although the trigger-happiness of his right-hand man (Charles Bronson) bordered on caricature.

The most famous of the films with the Mexican Revolution as a background was Sam Peckinpah's *The Wild Bunch* (1969, Warner Bros.), which chronicled the demise of an aging and anachronistic gang of the Old West, who seek a redemption in the Mexican conflict.

A fourth type of film prominent during the decade was the revisionist historical film. The key film of this type was the John Wayne–directed *The Alamo* (1961, United Artists), which reprised the assorted romanticized myths within a Cold War allegory. Later in the decade, *Viva Max!* (1969, Commonwealth United) was set in a contemporary setting and had a buffoonish Mexican general (Peter Ustinov), recapturing the Alamo and recycling stereotypes dormant since the 1930s. In the low-budget *Frontier Uprising* (1961, United Artists), a stalwart European-American scout (Jim Davis) battled hordes of Mexicans and Indians in accordance with Manifest Destiny. In turn, the epic and star-studded *How the West Was Won* (1963, Metro-Goldwyn-Mayer) gave only one fleeting second to the dispossession of the Mexican Southwest and had one incidental Mexican character, a bandit (Rodolfo Acosta) who participates in the train robbery at the grand finale.

Joaquin Murietta was portrayed in a trio of low-budget films. Carlos Thompson depicted him as a vengeful man who becomes demented in *The Last Rebel* (1961, Hispano); and Jeffrey Hunter portrayed him in the Spanish-filmed *Murietta* (1965, Warner Bros.). The third film, *The Firebrand* (1962, American Pictures–Fox), Murietta (Valentin de Vargas) successfully eluded pursuing rangers and returned to Sonora, Mexico. A more contemporary history was depicted in *Hell to Eternity* (1960, Allied Artists), which focused on the exploits of Guy Gabaldon (Jeffrey Hunter), the Mexican-American marine hero of World War II. It was only the second Hollywood film to deal with the contributions of Mexicans and/or Latinos in the armed forces. Finally, derision, ridicule and caricature were the trademarks in *Che!* (1969, 20th Century–Fox), the purported biography of the Latin American revolutionary Ernesto "Che" Guevara.

The fifth type of film attempted a more honest and genuine depiction of Mexican and Latino characters. During this decade, the body of work constituted only three films. The western *One-Eyed Jacks* (1961, Paramount), which was directed by Marlon Brando, provided two long-overdue characters of Mexican women with a measure of dignity, portrayed by newcomer Pina Pellicer and the veteran Katy Jurado, respectively. In *Dime with a Halo* (1963, Metro-Goldwyn-Mayer), Barbara Luna played a working-class and independent-minded young woman, who responsibly looks after her younger brother in the Tijuana shantytown. *The Royal Hunt of the Sun* (1969, Rank) finally chronicled the infamous Spanish conquest in South America and provided a sympathetic perspective of Atalhualpa (Christopher Plummer), the captive Inca king tormented by the avaricious Pizzaro (Robert Shaw).

Latina characters during the 1960s, with the exceptions of characters in *One-Eyed Jacks* and *Dime with a Halo,* were generally depicted as *cantineras* to their male *bandido* counterparts. Promiscuity, easy virtue, and an inability to control their primitive sexual passions were the characteristics of these reel Latinas. In *The Appaloosa* (1966, Universal), for example, Trini (Anjanette Comer) develops a sudden and overwhelming hatred for her Mexican bandit lover, Chuy Medina (John Saxon) and a primitive desire for the great white scout, Matt Fletcher (Marlon Brando). In *The Professionals* (1966, Paramount), the *soldadera* Chiquita (Maria Gomez) spends most of her time provocatively dressed and satisfying the sexual needs of an entire regiment. In *100 Rifles* (1969, 20th Century–Fox), Sarita (Raquel Welch), already romantically involved with Yaqui Joe (Burt Reynolds), is seduced at will and whim of a black superstud sheriff (Jim Brown). In the spaghetti western genre, swarms of seedy, promiscuous and insatiable *cantineras* filled the screen. Seemingly, loyalty, honor, and self-respect were not virtues attributable to Latinas.

Finally, the tail end of the decade saw the first Chicano film, a fifteen-minute documentary chronicling the four hundred years of Latino and Mexican history since the intrusion of the European. Entitled *I Am Joaquin* (1967), it was based on the epic poem by Rodolfo "Corky" González. It was produced by Luis Valdez (who also narrated) and his brother Daniel (who provided the music score). *I Am Joaquin* complemented and was part of the growing Chicano and Latino efforts to find a voice and space in all different media. On television it was reflected in *Canción de la Raza* (KCET), a dramatic series; and *¡Ahora!* (KCET), a weekly public affairs program. It also included documentaries such as Jesús Salvador Treviño's *La Raza Nueva* (1969) and *¡Ya Basta!* (1969). Chon Noriega has noted, "The first generation of Chicano/a filmmakers emerged from the context of the farm workers' struggle and the student movement, where political activism and poetic discourse developed together as part of a social movement that drew and addressed the lived experience of Chicanos/as in the Southwest."[4] By extension, Rosa Linda Fregoso wrote, "If we recognized that Chicano cinema developed within the context of the Chicano Power Movement's struggle of antiracism (equality, self-determination, human rights, and social justice), then its cinema must somehow remain bound by these ideals."[5] The evolution of Chicano cinema and other Latino cinemas would be to a lesser or greater degree inspired and conceived by the passion for social justice and inclusion.

The decade saw a marked decline of Latino film stars from previous decades. Although the films of the 1960s had a lesser number of Latino roles, they were more often than not portrayed by non–Latinos.

Several factors contributed to this trend. First, Latinos, specifically Mexican characters, had always been more visible in westerns than any other genre. The overexposure of the genre during the late 1950s and early 1960s on television (i.e., *Bonanza, Wagon Train,*

Cheyenne, among others) led to an almost virtual demise of western films early in the decade and with them the Mexican roles. Second, the reemergence of the genre later in the decade in the guise of the spaghetti western was fortuitous for Mexican characters, but not Mexican or Latino players, as they were shot in Italy, Spain, and Germany and used local performers in those roles. Third, the studio system, which had nurtured and developed the previous Latino film stars, was history by the 1960s. The studios that survived into the decade did not have the star-making long-term contracts or personnel of before. Under these conditions, new Latino film stars were unable to grow and develop a loyal following. Fourth, many of the existing and aging Latino film stars were beginning to pass from the scene or retire (Ramon Novarro, Dolores del Río, Antonio Moreno, Don Alvarado, etc.). Gilbert Roland, Ricardo Montalbán, and Katy Jurado worked infrequently in film during the decade and mostly on

José Ferrer (1912–1992) was of Puerto Rican heritage. He was the first Latino to win an Academy Award for Best Actor, for his role in *Cyrano de Bergerac* (1950). He won accolades in theater before entering films. Later, he went on to direct several films and continued performing as an actor in film, television, and theater.

television. Even the Latino film stars of the previous decade were no longer on the scene. Rosaura Revueltas was blacklisted; María Elena Marqués, Rita Macedo, and Sarita Montiel did not continue their careers in U.S. films; Lalo Ríos, Rafael Campos, Valentin de Vargas, among the younger players, disappeared into bit parts. Rita Hayworth, José Ferrer, and Rita Moreno worked sporadically in Hollywood films. The most visible and bona fide Latino star during the 1960s was Anthony Quinn.

Lastly, while the familiar cliché in Hollywood was

Katy Jurado (1924–2002) was already an established Mexican film star before Hollywood films beckoned. She had memorable roles in *The Bullfighter and the Lady* (1951); *High Noon* (1952); and *One-Eyed Jacks* (1961). She became the first Latina to be nominated for an Academy Award for Best Supporting Actress, for *Broken Lance* in 1954.

(Left to right) Lloyd Bridges, Katy Jurado, Gary Cooper, and Grace Kelly in *High Noon* (1952).

Lalo Ríos (1927–1973) with E. G. Marshall (left) and Gerald Mohr (right) in *The Ring* (1952, United Artists). The film depicted the struggles of a young Chicano boxer from East Los Angeles. Ríos was a gifted and sensitive actor who died too soon to display his complete talents.

Rosaura Revueltas and the author in Cuernavaca, Mexico, in 1992.

Left: Rosaura Revueltas (1910–1996) in *Salt of the Earth* (1954, IPC). Revueltas was already well established as a film star in Mexico when she made this film, which focused on the issues of labor, women, Mexican culture, and racism. There was a storm of controversy in the context of the McCarthy era which resulted in the film receiving limited screenings. Revueltas, screenwriter Michael Wilson, producer Paul Jarrico, and director Herbert J. Biberman were blacklisted.

Right: Maria Montez (1912–1951) was born in the Dominican Republic and became a huge star during the 1940s. She was typecast mostly in adventure and romantic films in Technicolor that showcased her beauty.

Maria Montez and two of her frequent costars, Jon Hall (center) and Sabu, in the Technicolor hit *Arabian Nights* (1942, Universal). She left Hollywood for Europe in the late 1940s, hoping to break the typecasting. She made several films in Europe and was recalled to Hollywood by her studio, but died prematurely of a heart attack at the age of 39.

that there were "no qualified Latino actors and actresses," the studios badly squandered the Latino talent that they did use. For example, the internationally acclaimed and Luis Buñuel favorite Silvia Pinal was reduced to small roles such as in *The Guns of San Sebastian* (1968, Metro-Goldwyn-Mayer). Other notable talent like Pilar Pellicer, David Reynoso, Aurora Clavel, Alfonso Arau, and Emilio Fernández suffered similar fates.

All this notwithstanding, some Latino film stars did shine. The one who enjoyed the most spectacular rise to fame was Raquel Welch, alias Raquel Tejada. She began as a beauty contest winner, then had bit parts, and then there was an expensive build-up orchestrated by her husband and 20th Century–Fox. By the end of the decade, she had been transformed into the reigning international sex symbol. A Latina star of this magnitude had not evolved since the time of Dolores del Río, Lupe Vélez, Rita Hayworth, and Maria Montez. Welch would be typecast for the most part as the sultry Latina, but by the late 1970s she begin to win accolades as a serious actress and light comedienne.

A bright promise early in the decade was Pina Pellicer, who debuted in Marlon Brando's *One-Eyed Jacks* (1961, United Artists), as the tender but independent-minded leading lady. Sadly, after four more films in Mexico she committed suicide in 1964. Another young Mexican actress, Ana Martín, was brought in to costar opposite Robert Taylor in *The Return of the Gunfighter* (1968, Metro-Goldwyn-Mayer). Although she made an impact, she thereafter concentrated on Mexican films.

New male Latino film stars were similarly rare and had a short life span. Among the most impressive and promising was the Puerto Rican Jaime Sánchez, who first scored in Sidney Lumet's *The Pawnbroker* (1965, Warner Bros.) as a troubled youth. Subsequently, he made even more impact as Angel in Sam Peckinpah's *The Wild Bunch*. However, after these roles his career languished and he was subsequently consigned to small roles. Among the others who had some success was the Mexican-born Alfonso Arau, who would enjoy more lasting success as a director in future years. Another Mexican leading man, David Reynoso, turned in an impressive performance in one U.S. film, *Rage* (1966, Columbia Pictures) but nothing else came his way to sustain a career. The legendary and veteran Mexican director Emilio Fernández made his U.S. acting debut in *The Wild Bunch* and thereafter played other supporting roles in less distinguished films. Latino leading men had more success on television, Henry Darrow being the most prominent example, in the *High Chaparral* television series.

Rita Hayworth (1918–1987), alias Rita Cansino, in *Gilda* (1946, Columbia). She was the daughter of a famous Spanish dancing couple and she began as a singer and dancer in the early 1930s. By 1939, she was a top film star, sex symbol, and the epitome of Hollywood glamor.

Representative Films

The Alamo (1960, United Artists/Batjac)

The key historical Latino-themed film of the decade was John Wayne's *The Alamo*. The film was released at the height of the Cold War, and as such was an allegory between East and West ideologies. It also recycled myths and legends about the Alamo, many of which had already been depicted in previous films about the event.

The film was produced (for $15 million) and directed by John Wayne, who was also the star. In the film's press kit, Wayne reiterated the film's point of view: "However, this is not a story that belongs only to Texas; it was filmed to convey to Americans and people everywhere a sense of the debt they owe to all men who have died fighting for freedom." Ironically, the concept of "freedom" is arguable, as the founders of an independent Texas established the institution of slavery as indicated in the 1836 Texas Constitution (General Provisions, Section 10): "All persons of color who were slaves for life previous to their emigration to Texas, and who are now held in bondage, shall remain in the like state of servitude." Indeed, one of the most pathetic characters is Jethro (Jester Hairston), the aged black slave of Jim Bowie (Richard Widmark). In one of the film's most preposterous scenes, Jethro is finally given his freedom by his master in the midst of the siege of the Alamo, when he could hardly be expected to leave. Then, once he is given his "freedom," he decides to stay and fight for a cause that will institutionalize slavery in Texas. At the end, Jethro sacrifices his own life for his master, when the latter battles against the Mexican soldiers.

The Mexican characters are equally pathetically depicted. A case in point is the scene where Davy Crockett (John Wayne) and his men arrive in San Antonio. They find droves of the proverbial happy-go-lucky Mexican *cantineras*, who at the drop of a hat fraternize with the very people who will dispossess them of their land. Similarly, the Mexican male characters are all emotionless mannequins with thick serapes on their shoulders, presumably worn so they can sleep at moment's notice. One of the few Mexican characters with dialogue is Juan Seguín. The real Seguín (1806–1890) was one of the key leaders of the Texas revolt and would later fight on the Mexican side during the Mexican-American War. He is depicted condescendingly as an octogenarian in one fleeting scene where he is treated with contempt by William Travis (Laurence Harvey). Thereafter, he disappears completely from the film.

The film propagates a decidedly European-American perspective. It nevertheless has some bizarre glimpses of love-hate for Mexicans. For example, after one Mexican attack has been repulsed by the besiegers, one of them comments on how pretty the Mexican army looks, and states, "You know, I was proud of them even as I was killing them." As for the character of General Santa Anna, he is portrayed as a silent and expressionless observer. The only Mexican character with any sense of dignity is one named Lieutenant Reyes (played by the Spanish bullfighter Carlos Arrúza). The film's press kit describes him as "the courier sent by Santa Ana to the Alamo, first, to demand surrender, then to offer safe evacuation for the non-combatants. He represents the gallantry, dignity and bravery of Mexican soldiery." Dignity is in short supply with regard to Mexican characters in this

(Foreground, left to right) John Wayne, Richard Widmark, and Laurence Harvey in *The Alamo* **(1960, United Artists/Batjack). The film perpetuated all of the Alamo myths within the context of the Cold War.**

film. The film ends with Mrs. Dickinson (Joan O'Brien), her infant daughter, and a black boy (presumably Jethro's son) departing the battle-strewn area in a striking silhouette, not unlike Jesus, Mary and Joseph, with an imposing crescendo provided by Dimitri Tiomkin's music score.

A growing film scholarship has emerged around the film since its release, but none has tackled the underlying issues at the heart of this historical conflict which set the stage for the Mexican-American War, namely Manifest Destiny and slavery. They are issues which this film and other films dealing with this historical event refuse to confront even in passing. Rodney Farnsworth in his critique nevertheless makes a thrust in this direction: "*The Alamo* is an often beautifully, often powerfully crafted film about a myth and by a myth: aesthetically, at least, one of the finest epics ever made; ideologically, both a tragedy and a divine comedy. Wayne's film is a tragedy because of its uncanny foreboding of the thinking that got the USA into Vietnam.... Most significantly, it offers an often penetrating analysis of how rhetoric functions—for the bad as well as for the good."[6]

The Alamo was nominated for several Academy Awards, including Best Picture, but it was not the commercial success envisioned. Wayne, a political conservative and hawk most of his life, most notoriously during the McCarthy era, would go on to make a diametrical shift in his ideological position in 1979. He would travel with Panama's General Omar Torrijos to support and campaign for the passage of a referendum in support of returning the Panama canal to that nation. It was an act ironically contrary to his character of Davy Crockett in *The Alamo.*

Che! (1969, 20th Century–Fox)

The film *Che!* was the only Hollywood feature to focus on the revolutionary upheavals in Latin America after the advent of the Cuban Revolution in 1959. Not surprisingly, this studio film was hobbled by a rigid ethnocentrism, an ethos of Manifest Destiny, and the Cold War. The result was a superficial depiction of profound and timely events unfolding in Latin America.

Unlike the past, when filmmakers made no attempt to account for derogatory Latino images, the makers of *Che!* felt compelled to justify their film. For example, producer Sy Barlett commented to the *Hollywood Reporter*, "This story was done with the greatest attempt at objectivity, and we have been criticized for not taking a point of view which is precisely what we set out to do."[7] The film's director, Richard Fleischer, stated to *Newsweek*, "We're dealing with one of the phenomena of our time. As of this moment [Che is] a tremendous

Woody Strode (second from left), Omar Sharif (center, as revolutionary Ernesto "Che" Guevara), and Linda Marsh in *Che!* (1969, 20th Century–Fox).

symbol for young people all over the world. But I'm not so sure that five years from now anyone will remember him, because there's no residue, no substance to the man. When you analyze it, Che is a big loser."[8] History would prove Fleischer sadly mistaken.

The focus of the film was Ernesto "Che" Guevara (1928–1967), doctor, revolutionary, and writer. He was born to a middle-class Argentine family. He was asthmatic since childhood. He acquired the nickname "Che" from the Argentine expression for "Hey, you!" He traveled widely throughout Latin America, where he witnessed the poverty and injustice. After graduating from medical school he worked in Guatemala during 1954, when the C.I.A.–sponsored invasion overthrew the democratically elected President Jacobo Árbenz. Guevara subsequently obtained political asylum in Mexico, where he met several Cuban revolutionaries who were planing an insurrection against Cuban dictator Fulgencio Batista. Guevara went on to emerge as a military theoretician, economic minister, diplomat, and writer. He disappeared from public view in 1965. Later, he was executed after capture by U.S.–trained counterinsurgency forces while leading a guerrilla movement in Bolivia on October 9, 1967.[9]

The film proved incapable of understanding or conceptualizing the complex historical, political, and economic forces that shaped the life of Guevara, the Cuban Revolution or Latin America. The film's screenplay underwent numerous changes. At one point, the formerly blacklisted screenwriter Michael Wilson, who had scripted *Salt of the Earth* and had been one of the Hollywood Ten, was employed to do one draft. Later, screenplay credit was given to Sy Barlett and Michael Wilson and story credit to Sy Barlett and David Karp. The film also contained a disclaimer that stated, "None of the various texts written on Che Guevara, nor his published diary penned by the revolutionary during the Bolivian episode, was utilized in the final treatment from which this screenplay was adapted." Removed from the final film was anything before the Cuban Revolution, the repressive and corruptive nature of the Batista and Barrientos (in Bolivia) regimes, the Bay of Pigs, the Cuban Missile Crisis, the Congo campaign, and several important historical characters in the Bolivian campaign (Régis Debray, Inti Peredo, Tania). Removed from a historical context, the film was reduced to a melodrama characterized by simplistic myopia and ambiguous motives. The cardboard rendition of Guevara reduces his idealism and activities to delusion and buffoonery, thus justifying the filmmaker's derision. Egyptian actor Omar Sharif was cast as Guevara and Jack Palance in the role of Fidel Castro. Palance's excessive mannerisms reduced the role to the level of a stand-up comedian's caricature.

Given the dubious quality and truthfulness of the film, various Latin American countries banned it, including Mexico. Angered by this, producer Sy Barlett stated to anyone who would listen, "I'd be glad to take him on, a young man who audaciously questions some of the world's most professional observers and people who were on the scene. I'd like to know who this expert is who challenges the authenticity and the objectivity of 'Che!'"[10] Not surprisingly, Barlett never revealed the bogus "professional observers." Omar Sharif, in contrast, stated, "To say the film is 100 per cent honest is absurd.... It's being made by a bunch of capitalists."[11]

Reviewers of the film were surprisingly cognizant of the film's appalling shortcomings. *Variety* noted, "Che talks in vague terms about his theories of revolution, but his comments on the U.S. are confined to few references to 'Yankee imperialism,' always quickly stated in the middle of a sentence about something else. The specific reasons for bitterness of many

Latin American intellectuals and guerrillas toward the U.S. are hardly mentioned.... It had been thought that at least 'Che!' would attempt to explain just what was the charisma inherent in this leader which has caused such a cult and mystique as saint by many youth elements.... But the effort in 'Che!' appears to be entirely one of demystification, a denial of Guevara's appeal."[12] *Time* wrote, "The men who made 'Che!' chose folly. As scenarists Michael Wilson and Sy Barlett saw it, the Cuban Revolution was just a Caribbean comic strip drawn in that country's green and pleasant land.... Striving to placate all factions, the film actually represents none. One moment Che is a cultural hero; the next he is a messianic psychopath."[13]

Sergio Leone's Trilogy: *A Fistful of Dollars* (1966, United Artists), *For a Few Dollars More* (1967, United Artists), and *The Good, the Bad, and the Ugly* (1968, United Artists)

Italian director and screenwriter Sergio Leone (1921–1989) was the most important creative force behind the "spaghetti western" genre which emerged during the mid–1960s in Italy and revitalized the moribund western genre. The genesis and epitome of the spaghetti western are Leone's trilogy of *A Fistful of Dollars, For a Few Dollars More,* and *The Good, the Bad, and the Ugly.* Unfortunately, these films and others of the genre brought back some of the most racist stereotypes from the 20th century's teen years when the Mexican "greaser" image was predominant.

Leone had served a long apprenticeship with several notable U.S. directors (including Robert Wise, William Wyler, Raoul Walsh, and Fred Zinnemann), who had all shot on location in Italy during the latter part of the 1950s. He was heavily influenced by them, as well as by the U.S. western genre. Leone's first spaghetti western, *A Fistful of Dollars,* was based on Akira Kurosawa's *Yojimbo* (1962), which had starred Toshiro Mifune. Like previous films (*The Magnificent Seven, The Outrage*) based on Kurosawa's work, in the latter film adaptations the villains or bandits became exclusively Mexican, whereas in the original versions all the characters were Japanese. According to Christopher Frayling, "Sergio Leone said at the time that he, too, rejected 'the romance of the sombrero' in Hollywood films, but because of his disillusionment with recent political and artistic developments in Italy, he found the cinematic rebuttals of this romance equally resistible."[14]

A Fistful of Dollars told the tale of a violent and amoral European-American gunfighter, "the man with no name" (Clint Eastwood), who is employed by two bands who want to control a town. He proceeds to play each band against the other, taking their money and facilitating the destruction of each. At the end, the inhabitants of the town include only a now-wealthy coffin maker, a pathetic bell ringer, and a bankrupt bartender.

A Fistful of Dollars contains some reprehensible stereotypes, as well as technical deficiencies. The majority of the Mexican characters are bandits, violent, treacherous, and greasy-looking. Seemingly, they are unable to control these innate characteristics and thereby meet the proverbial Darwinistic extinction at the hands of the "man with no name." Other Mexican characters are *cantineras* and/or docile peons. All the Mexican characters are played by Italian performers very unconvincingly. Both the landscape and architecture lack authenticity; they are clearly not the U.S. Southwest. Finally, like the Italian-made "sandal and spear" genre whose heyday had just ended, this film has some significant dubbing shortcomings.

Nevertheless, *A Fistful of Dollars* despite its flaws was able to revitalize the moribund western film genre. This was both due to the film itself and to its timing. Leone infused his film with a non–Hollywood operatic and visual style. He complemented this with impressive spatial compositions of extreme close-ups and background, and then interjected Ennio Morricone's eerie music score, which consisted of grunts, groans, and stereolike gunfire. Leone had incorporated all the nuances of the Hollywood western, and had then proceeded to reinterpret it through the context of Italian cinema. The final product was unlike anything the genre had experienced and the impact was electrifying.

Although the film was made in 1964, it was not released in the United States until 1967, by which time the western genre had undergone an overexposure on television. In addition, most of the great directors and film stars associated with the genre were passing from the scene. The western genre was for all practical purposes dead in the United States. *A Fistful of Dollars* catapulted Clint Eastwood, the costar of television's *Rawhide* (1959–1965) into international stardom. His fee climbed from $15,000 for *A Fistful of Dollars* to $50,000 in *For a Few Dollars More,* and then to $250,000 plus a percentage of the profits for *The Good, the Bad, and the Ugly.*

Surprisingly, only a few of the critics noted the impact of *A Fistful of Dollars* upon its release. The *Los Angeles Herald-Examiner* commented, "If *A Fistful of Dollars* doesn't blaze a new trail in Western, shoot-'em style motion pictures, it'll be a miracle of this preposterous age, and you will be wise not to bet against it."[15] Although the spaghetti westerns predated Leone's work, it was his work which brought the genre international recognition and sparked its widespread popularity for another decade. According to Christopher Frayling, "Well over 300 spaghetti westerns were released in Italy between 1963 and 1969 alone; the peak year for production was 1966–1967 (when 66 were made). Fewer than 20 percent of these spaghettis have been distributed internationally."[16] Later, spaghetti westerns were made in both Spain and Germany. They would have a definite and permanent impact on U.S. western films.

Leone's second spaghetti western, *For a Few Dollars More,* was made in 1965 but not released in the United States until 1967. It brought back "the man with no name" (Clint Eastwood). He establishes an opportunistic association with an aging gunfighter, Colonel Douglas Mortimer (Lee Van Cleef), in order to capture or kill a psychopathic Mexican bandit, Indio (Gian Maria Volonté). Indio has a large reward on his head and has plans to rob a supposedly impregnable bank in El Paso, Texas. Mortimer's incentive is not the bounty but revenge for Indio's rape and murder of his sister.

Gian Maria Volonté (who had played another Mexican bandit in *A Fistful of Dollars*) played Indio as violent, treacherous and brutal. He is willing to kill his entire gang for the bank's loot. However, he is not astute enough to discover that "the man with no name" has infiltrated his gang and acquired the trust and support of his own men. Indio spends most of his waking time under the influence of marijuana, laughing sadistically and beating his adversaries to a pulp. The European-American hero is equally sadistic and brutal, but more efficient. His inherent cruelty is cause for glorification, which is not the case with Indio. In one scene, for example, "the man with no name" grabs a Mexican boy by the throat and threatens him: "Listen to me, you sawed-off little runt, how many were there?" In a later scene, after "the man" has killed half a dozen Mexican bandits, one of his victims stumbles around, apparently not yet mortally wounded. For a few seconds, "the man" observes him with cool calculation, and then suddenly shoots him dead.

Reviewers of the film were decidedly less enthusiastic about *For a Few Dollars More* than its predecessor. For example, the *New York Daily News* commented, "More than two dozen people get killed in one way or another, so the cost is large."[17] The *New York Times* noted, "That this film is constructed to endorse and generate glee in frantic manifestations of death is, to my mind, a sharp indictment of its so-called entertainment in this day."[18] Despite the growing outcry against the spaghetti western's gratuitous violence, no reviewer pointed out the racist stereotypes of Mexicans.

Leone's third spaghetti western, *The Good, the Bad, and the Ugly* (1968), was both the most expensive (with a budget of more than $1 million) and the longest (161 minutes). The film traces the efforts of "the man with no name" (Clint Eastwood) and his uneasy partnership with a violent and crude Mexican bandit, Tuco (Eli Wallach). They come upon a dying Bill Carson, who informs them of gold loot buried in a cemetery. However, each is able to hear only part of the details, and as such must depend on the other to find the gold. The pair are subsequently captured by an avaricious Union sergeant, Sotenza (Lee Van Cleef), who is also on the trail of the loot. He is unable to extract the information from his two prisoners, so they make an alliance of convenience, which ends in a climactic gunfight.

The Good, the Bad, and the Ugly is the most visually impressive and dramatically effective of Leone's three westerns. The scenes in the Civil War battlefield are especially evocative and painstakingly realistic. However, the film is marred by the ludicrous, caricatured Mexican bandit, who is grotesquely overplayed by Eli Wallach (he had played a similarly reprehensible Mexican bandit in 1960's *The Magnificent Seven*). While Tuco is the only major Mexican character, there is an underlying stereotype about all Mexicans. In one particular scene, Tuco's brother, who is a friar, reminds him, "Where we were born, one is only a bandit or a priest." For once, this was noted by reviewers. For example, the *New York Times* wrote, "Wallach makes his eyes dance, he emits horrible gastrointestinal noises to communicate emotion and laughs incessantly."[19] *Time* commented, "Bad is the word for the wooden acting, and Leone's addition to the cramped values and stretched probabilities of the comic strip. And ugly is his insatiable appetite for beatings, disemboweling and mutilations, complete closeups of mashed-in faces and death-rattle sound effects."[20]

In Leone's subsequent masterpiece, *Once Upon a Time in the West* (1969), the film's hero was an exception to the rule of Mexicans being bandits and villains in spaghetti westerns in that the hero turns out to be a Mexican gunfighter. In his last spaghetti western, *Duck, You Sucker* (1972), Leone featured yet another grotesque Mexican bandit as one of the two protagonists, this time played by Rod Steiger. Although he was an undeniably gifted director, Sergio Leone's body of work in this writer's estimation is marred by his fixation with Mexican stereotypes.

The Magnificent Seven (1960, United Artists)

The Magnificent Seven remains as one of the key films that represent Mexicans as helpless and cowardly ideological disciples.

The Magnificent Seven was a remake of Akira Kurosawa's classic *Seven Samurai* (1954), which had earned an Academy Award as Best Foreign Film and starred Toshiro Mifune. The film is about seven down-and-out samurai warriors who come to the aid of village farmers pillaged by a warlord and his band of marauders. All of the characters in the film are Japanese. However, in the U.S. version the samurai became European-American gunfighters, the farmers became docile and cowardly Mexican peasants, and the marauders became violent and slimy Mexican bandits. This version was set somewhere in northern Mexico. After the first attack of the bandits, the peasants quiver in fear. One peasant cries out, "We must do something!" A second asks, "But what?" Yet another shouts, "I don't know!" Rather than seek government aid, they travel to the United States with the meager resources they have pooled in search of seven misfit gunfighters to protect them. The film was made at the height of the Cold War and the metaphor is apparent, Latinos, especially Mexicans, cannot think or fight for themselves without the benign guidance of their neighbor to the north. The ethos of the Monroe Doctrine is prevalent throughout the film.

One of the most ludicrous characters is the Mexican bandit Calvero, played by Eli Wallach, in a throwback to the Mexican greaser roles of the teen years. Calvero is depicted as part barbarian and part buffoon, both violent and treacherous, and physically greasy and dirty. Adding insult to injury, Wallach would give a similarly grotesque performance as yet another Mexican bandit in *The Good, the Bad, and the Ugly* (1968). The role of Chico, a

Left: Anthony Quinn (1915–2001) was born in Chihuahua, Mexico, to Tarahumara natives. The Quinn surname came from an Irish grandfather. He began as an extra in the mid–1930s and played virtually every type of ethnic role in scores of films before reaching stardom in the early 1950s. He won two Best Supporting Actor Academy Awards: for *Viva Zapata* (1952) and *Lust for Life* (1956).

Right: Anthony Quinn in *Lust for Life* (1956, Metro-Goldwyn-Mayer). In his legendary career he had many memorable roles, including the title role in *Zorba the Greek* (1964), which he later reprised on stage. He became a highly respected painter, sculptor, and writer.

sort of disciple to the gunfighters, was played badly by the miscast Horst Buchholz, who at that time was a German heartthrob. Russian character actor Vladimir Sokoloff played the village elder, and other small roles were played by Mexican actors Jorge Martínez de Hoyos, Valentin de Vargas, and Enrique Lucero. The role of Petra was played by newcomer Rosenda Monteros, who would enjoy modest fame as a leading lady in U.S. "B" films. Mexican director Emilio Fernández was hired as casting director and choreographer of Mexican dances.

The film had a checkered history before it was completed. The film's star, Yul Brynner, had made the initial arrangements for a remake of Kurosawa's film and had arrived at an agreement with Anthony Quinn to costar. The film was to be produced by Brynner's Alciona Productions, but when Brynner sold the rights to Mirisch Productions, Quinn sued him for breach of contract. They subsequently settled out of court. Enlisted to direct was veteran director John Sturges (1911–1992), whose films included such socially conscious works as *Right Cross* (1950, Metro-Goldwyn-Mayer) and *Bad Day at Black Rock* (1955, Metro-Goldwyn-Mayer), as well as the hugely successful western *Gunfight at the O.K. Coral* (1957, Paramount). Sturges later commented about *The Magnificent Seven*, "My thought was that the original film held the basis for a story and characters that would make a very good western. We developed that story to the best of our ability without regard to whether or how it differed."[21]

While on location in Mexico to make the film, Sturges submitted the script to the Mexican government as required. Subsequently, he was informed by Jorge Ferretis, the official censor, that they had found the screenplay to be anti–Mexican, and requested changes. Sturges, who certainly knew better, resisted the request: "The idea of Americans coming into Mexico to do a job involving physical prowess and courage for the Mexican government presented an instant censorship problem. We had difficulty selling the idea that the villagers were farmers, men of peace—not an aspect limited to Mexicans!"[22] He added, "The censor was just picking on anything that might be objected to by some member of the lunatic fringe. I think his only concern was that there must be nothing that someone in Mexico might conceivably consider anti–Mexican."[23] He concluded, "If it weren't for the censor, Mexico would be a wonderful country for making movies. But as it is now, it is okay so long as you are making an American movie with a boy and his dog."[24]

The film went on to become a huge commercial success, one that owed more to the box-office magnetism of star Yul Brynner and the chemistry of his fast-rising costars (Steve McQueen, James Coburn, Charles Bronson, and Robert Vaughn) than to the reprehensible stereotypes. *The Magnificent Seven* went on to spawn three sequels, which became more and more mediocre and low-budget: *Return of the Seven* (1966), *Guns of the Magnificent Seven* (1969), and *The Magnificent Seven Ride* (1972). As for the recalcitrant John Sturges, he would go on to direct more commercially successful films, including *The Great Escape* (1963). In one of his later films, *Valdez Is Coming* (1973), the leading character, ironically, is a Mexican peasant who successfully outwits and defeats a group of marauding European-Americans.

One-Eyed Jacks (1961, United Artists)

One-Eyed Jacks, an offbeat and evocative western, is the only film directed by Marlon Brando. It is also a film that has three of the best-developed and dignified Chicano roles in contemporary times.

The film endured a long and conflicted history before being made. Stanley Kubrick was originally slated to direct, but with his sudden departure after the start of the film, the film's star took the directorial helm. Due to this and other delays, the budget rose from the original $1.8 to some $6 million; the shooting schedule became longer (December 1958 to October 1959), and the film's length doubled. In his quest to realize his vision, Brando shot more than one million feet of film, which added up to four hours and forty-two minutes of footage. In the subsequent effort to wrest creative control from Brando, producer Frank P. Rosenberg and his editors then spent several months winnowing down the film to two hours and twenty-two minutes. The finished film, which was produced by Brando's own Pennebaker Productions, was then released during March 1961.

The film told the tale of two European-American outlaws, Rio (Brando) and Dad Longsworth (Karl Malden), who rob a bank in Mexico in 1880, and then become trapped on a lone hill when one of their horses is shot. Longsworth wins a toss of the coin to leave on their only remaining horse. He promises to return for his companion when he gets another horse. However, upon reaching safety and finding another horse, he decides to ride off across the border with the loot.

In the meantime, Rio is captured and imprisoned for five years. Sometime later, he breaks out with a friend, Modesto (Larry Duran). Embittered and sworn to revenge, he and

Modesto strike up with another pair of bank robbers, Amory (Ben Johnson) and Johnson (Sam Gilman), who have masterminded a plan to rob the bank in Monterey, California. There Longsworth has become sheriff and settled down with Maria (Katy Jurado) and his teenage daughter Louisa (Pina Pellicer). When he meets Longsworth again, Rio does not reveal to him what happened to him as a consequence of Longsworth's duplicity. However, in a show of contempt for Longsworth's hypocrisy, he purposely seduces and abandons Louisa.

Rio is subsequently arrested by Longsworth for killing a man in self-defense, and the latter breaks his gun hand to further handicap his desire for revenge. Rio seeks refuge in a hamlet along the seashore. Increasingly impatient, Amory and Johnson decide to rob the bank on their own, and when Modesto refuses to betray Rio, they kill him. Louisa visits Rio

Pina Pellicer (1934–1964) and Marlon Brando in *One-Eyed Jacks* (1960, Columbia). It was the only film directed by Marlon Brando. Pellicer played a memorable role as a lovelorn Mexican girl.

to inform him that she is pregnant, and to her surprise he confesses both his guilt and his love for her. Rio is blamed for Amory and Johnson's robbery; he is arrested and sentenced to be hanged. As he is making a daring escape, a gunfight ensues with Longworth in which the latter is killed. Rio flees, but promises Louisa that he will return for her.

In a refreshing exception to the Hollywood rule, the three Mexicano/Chicano roles are three-dimensional, with both depth and dignity. The mother, Maria, and the daughter, Louisa, are depicted as strong-willed and independent-minded, although they understand that both their gender and ethnicity limit their aspirations. Maria has married the very unattractive Longsworth, partly as a means to remove herself from the marginalized ranks of being both poor and Mexican. She has resigned herself to be a good wife, and puts up with her husband's self-righteous sense of superiority: "I took you out of the beanfields and gave you respectability!" Maria is also either a widow or an abandoned mother with a teenage daughter, and this is another reason for to her marriage to Longsworth. Consequently, when Louisa becomes pregnant with Rio's child, both are acutely aware of the stigma of being an unwed mother, Mexican and poor. Both realize the weakness and power of love.

In a film where most of the male characters are duplicitous, the character of Modesto is the only one who remains true to his code of loyalty. Although he is an outlaw, he is unable to succumb to the opportunism of both Amory and Johnson, even for gold. At the end, his loyalty to his friend Rio results in his death.

The film affectionately acknowledges the Mexicanness of California. It captures the ambiance of the Mexican culture in Monterey, as well as the prevalent racism against it. It also depicts the early presence of the Chinese community. Among the Latinos in the cast are Rodolfo Acosta as a leader of the *rurales* and Puerto Rican actress Miriam Colón as a señorita who is the object of Rio's interest.

The film's critical reaction was mixed. Many critics blamed Brando for the bloated budget and delays. However, over the years *One-Eyed Jacks* has deservedly acquired a cult status. Some reviewers noted the film's worth. The *New York Times* commented, "At his acting peak, Marlon Brando also elected to direct himself. The result is an extraordinary sort of Western drama, proceeding in two contrasting styles, one hard and realistic, the other lush and romantic.... The realism is curiously surrounded by elements of creamed-cliché romance—Brando's tender idyll with a charmingly delicate girl, played by Pina Pellicer— and a kind of pictorial extravagance."[25]

Mexican actress Pina Pellicer made an impressive film debut and appeared to have bright promise. She won the Best Actress award at the San Sebastian Film Festival. Regrettably, her short life came to end by suicide in 1964.

The Professionals (1966, Columbia)

Richard Brooks' *The Professionals* epitomizes U.S. films set during the Mexican Revolution in which the main characters are opportunistic and coolly efficient European-Americans who single-handedly alter Mexican history. This scenario had been continuing since the 1920s when Victor McLaglen and Edmund Lowe played similar macho and amoral adventurers in a series of films beginning with *What Price Glory?* in 1926. Thereafter, the 1954 film *Vera Cruz* resuscitated two similar characters (Gary Cooper, Burt Lancaster) carrying out daring exploits for the patriot Juaristas as they battled the French Intervention in Mexico during the 1860s. These characters would become the genesis for the amoral and technically efficient spaghetti western European-American heroes in the next decade.

The Professionals centered around the efforts of a powerful rancher, J.W. Grant (Ralph Bellamy), who hires a group of professional gunmen, Dolworth (Burt Lancaster), Fardin (Lee Marvin), Ehrengard (Robert Ryan), and Sharp (Woody Strode) to rescue his wife Maria (Claudia Cardinale), who has been kidnapped by a Mexican revolutionary, Jesus Reza (Jack Palance). The group had previously fought alongside Pancho Villa, and had entered victoriously into Mexico City. At present, however, the U.S.–supported Carranzista forces have the Villistas on the defensive. Subsequently, the group fights their way into Reza's camp, rescues Maria and returns her to her husband, who they finally realized was really Grant's hostage. The group decides to return her to Reza. An angered Grant confronts Farden and shouts at him, "Bastard!" "Yes, sir!" responds Farden. "In my case, an accident of nature. But you're a self-made man!"

The Professionals perpetuates the myths that four European-American soldiers of fortune could decimate hundreds of Villista revolutionaries, something that General Pershing's entire army and the Carranzistas were unable to do. The film is laced with amorality and sardonic cynicism, elements common to the spaghetti western genre.

Aside from the old staple of depicting European-American superiority of arms and efficiency, the film's other stereotype is that of Mexican women as promiscuous sexual objects. For example, the leading woman character, Maria, has prostituted herself to Grant in order to raise money for the revolution. She justifies her conduct to Dolworth on one occasion as follows: "My husband stole millions from this land, our land. If we can keep the revolution alive for even one more day then I'll steal and cheat and whore!" She then attempts to entice Dolworth by baring her breasts, so that he can release her. Another important Mexican character and Dolworth's former girlfriend, Chiquita, is another insatiable sexual predator. Dolworth asks her about her sexual promiscuity, "Don't you ever say no?" "Never!" she responds. "Anybody?" inquires Dolworth. "Everybody!" she responds.

The film received mixed reviews but went on to become one of the top-grossing films of 1966. Few of the critics questioned the protagonist's far-fetched exploits and noone noted the appalling stereotypes of Mexican women.

Villa Rides! (1968, Paramount)

Hollywood's love-hate fascination with Pancho Villa continued with *Villa Rides!,* after a ten-year absence since *Villa!* (1958). Doroteo Arango (1878–1923), who later became known in history as Francisco "Pancho" Villa, was a peasant leader from northern Mexico during the Mexican Revolution (1910–1920).

The film was based on a screenplay written by Sam Peckinpah in 1959, when he was directing television. It was a film project he hoped to direct. However, by the time of *Major Dundee* in 1965, which had been cut and altered without his consent or participation, he had acquired a reputation as an independent-minded, maverick director, as well as a difficult director. After he was fired from *The Cincinnati Kid* in 1965, he was compelled to sell his screenplay about Villa, much to his regret. Subsequently, when the film project got the green light, Yul Brynner (1915–1985) was cast as Villa. Brynner demanded that the script be rewritten and questioned Peckinpah's historical accuracy. An angered Peckinpah shot back, "I've spent a great many years in Mexico, I married a Mexican girl, and I know Mexican history."[26]

Nevertheless, Brynner had his way and Robert Towne was brought in to do a rewrite. Towne was still several years away from fame as the writer of *Chinatown* (1974) and *Shampoo* (1975). However, Towne himself would later denounce *Villa Rides!*, and Peckinpah would go public about his original screenplay being butchered. Rightly expecting that the Mexican censor would object to the Hollywood distortions of Mexico and Mexicans, Paramount had the film shot in Spain. Later, as expected, Mexico banned the film.

Villa Rides! indeed was filled with historical distortions and stereotypes, but it nevertheless depicted one aspect never before presented, namely Villa's innovations of air power in war. *The Motion Picture Herald* wisely noted, "Villa invented or rediscovered military tactics that left his enemies in awe. He was a political-sociological thinker who organized his army as a weapon for peace and his peaceful countrymen as an army in reserve. One of his tradition-breaking departures was his use of aircraft in guerrilla-type warfare."[27]

The film revolved around this military contribution and Villa's friendship with a European-American flyer, Lee Arnold (Robert Mitchum), during the lean years of 1912 and

Robert Viharo as Urbina, Yul Brynner as Pancho Villa, Charles Bronson as General Fierro, and Robert Mitchum as a U.S. pilot in *Villa Rides!* (1969, United Artists). The film continued Hollywood's love-hate relationship with Mexican revolutionary Pancho Villa.

1913. Unfortunately, the film turned out to be a trivial and superficial account of this part of Mexican history. What added to the incongruity of the narrative was the non–Mexican/Latino cast, all of whom brought their own different accents: the Russian-born Yul Brynner as Villa; the Lithuanian-American Charles Bronson as General Fierro; the Italian Maria Grazia Buccello as Fina; the Czech Herbert Lom as General Huerta; and the British Alexander Knox as President Francisco I. Madero. The only believable and effective actor in the film was the underestimated Robert Mitchum as the flyer.

The definitive portrayal of Villa remained that of Pedro Armendáriz, who played him in a trilogy of Mexican films directed by Ismael Rodríguez: *Así Era Pancho Villa* (1957); *Pancho Villa y la Valentina* (1958); and *Cuando Viva Villa es La Muerte* (1958).

Film reviewers were surprisingly critical of *Villa Rides!* The *Los Angeles Times* noted, "Perhaps if Sam Peckinpah had had the chance to direct the script he wrote for *'Villa Rides'* it might have been worthy of the legendary Pancho Villa. The result is that deadliest kind of picture, the one that's neither good nor bad but merely routine.... Mitchum, easily the more talented of the two, seems to walk his way through a role that wasn't much to begin with and as such had the unintentional offensive effect of making it seem that Villa couldn't have gotten by without the help of this resourceful American.... Brynner, on the other hand, hasn't much to give.... His Pancho Villa cannot stand comparisons with Brando's subtle Zapata...."[28]

West Side Story (1961, United Artists)

The film musical *West Side Story,* based on a play by the same name, remains as the key U.S. film about Puerto Ricans. Nevertheless, the Puerto Rican images depicted are grossly distorted and stereotypical.

To some, *West Side Story* exudes a nostalgia for the ill-fated lovers and has appealingly kinetic choreography. The play was written by Arthur Laurents and based on a concept by Jerome Robbins. The play nevertheless borrowed heavily from William Shakespeare's *Romeo and Juliet.* The play opened in September 1957 and went on for 734 performances at the Winter Garden Theatre in New York City. Thereafter it was revived several times, and it has remained a popular vehicle ever since.

Both the play and the film perpetuated the otherness of Puerto Ricans, whose great migration to the United States, especially New York City, had begun and grown in the 1940s. The push and pull of their migration was due to the insatiable demand for cheap labor thanks to the booming economy of the United States, and the impoverishment of Puerto Rico, which had been under the control of the United States since 1898 and the Spanish-American War. Sonia Nieto noted, "The nature of the migration has also profoundly influenced such issues as language use, identity, and cultural fusion and retention."[29] Neither a state nor an independent nation, Puerto Rico maintained a status defined as a "commonwealth."

Several films in the 1950s and 1960s established the stereotype of the Puerto Rican: a picturesque people who were unable to control their violence, sexuality, and temperament. Inevitably, they were depicted as violence-prone and remorseless street gang hoodlums or as irresponsible people living on public assistance. *Blackboard Jungle* (1956, Metro-Goldwyn-

Mayer) and *Cry Tough* (1959, United Artists) established the image of Puerto Rican youths' inclination to criminality. Thereafter, both *The Young Savages* (1961, United Artists) and *The Pawnbroker* (1965, Allied Artists) perpetuated that image. In *Popi* (1969, United Artists), a Puerto Rican widower with two sons masquerades as a Cuban refugee in order to be a recipient of federal assistance. *West Side Story* followed this pattern in its portrayal of Puerto Ricans.

The film revolves around the rivalry between two New York City youth gangs: the Jets, made up of a variety of European-origin nationalities and headed by Riff (Russ Tamblyn); and the Sharks, a Puerto Rican gang led by Bernardo (George Chakiris). Against this backdrop is the emerging love story between Maria (Natalie Wood), the sister of Bernardo, and Tony (Richard Beymer), an ex-leader of the Jets. On the night of a rumble between the gangs, Maria begs Tony to be a peacemaker. However, after his manhood is challenged, Tony ends up stabbing Bernardo to death after the latter has killed Riff. Subsequently, Tony flees and holes up at the store cellar of Doc (Ned Glass). When Anita (Rita Moreno) is sent with a message for Tony, she is received with racial epithets by members of the Jets. After this treatment, and in a fit of anger, Anita tells the Jets the lie that Maria is dead, that she was killed by Chino (Jose De Vega), a vengeful Shark. A grief-stricken Tony leaves his hiding place despite knowing that Chino is out looking for him. Maria goes out to find Tony. When they find each other, Chino shoots Tony dead. Tony dies in Maria's arms.

Natalie Wood (1938–1981), the popular Russian-American actress, was cast in the role of Maria. A former child star, she had gone on to earn a cult status in a trio of films exploring the ethos of adolescent yearning: *Rebel Without a Cause* (1955) with James Dean; *Splendor in the Grass* (1961) with Warren Beatty; and *West Side Story*. Richard Beymer, who was a former child actor himself and grew up to enjoy a short vogue as a leading man, played Tony, and Russ Tamblyn, another former child actor, played Riff. The role of Bernardo was played by the Greek-American George Chakiris (who won an Academy Award for Best Supporting Actor). The only Puerto Rican performer in an important role was Rita Moreno, who played Anita and won an Academy Award for Best Supporting Actress. She became the first Latina to win an Academy Award. *West Side Story* won ten Academy Awards, including Best Picture, and was both a commercial and critical hit.

However, the film is filled with stereotypical shortcomings. The Jets are a metaphor for the glue of the "melting pot" and the Puerto Ricans are represented as the intruders whose very being challenges white harmony. No socioeconomic context is provided as to the marginalization of these characters or the factors that determined their departure from Puerto Rico. All the Puerto Rican males are portrayed as gang members and their female counterparts as temperamental sexual objects of gratification. Their hopes and aspirations are nonexistent. Maria is only able to see beyond her world of Spanish Harlem and greater expectations at Tony's urging. Compounding the behavior of the Puerto Rican characters is the stereotypical "Hollywood standard Spanish accent" circa the 1930s, vocal gymnastics which are thick and border on the caricature. Another aspect of Hollywood artificiality is the absence of black or mulatto Puerto Ricans.

The thing that resonates about *West Side Story* through the years is the choreography (by Jerome Robbins, who also codirected with Robert Wise), the dancing, and the music (by Leonard Bernstein).

The Wild Bunch (1969, Warner Bros.)

Sam Peckinpah's *The Wild Bunch* remains as one of the decade's most important films. The film's stature continues to grow with the passage of time.

The film was painstakingly shot on location in Parras, Coahuila, Mexico, and featured a large number of Mexican performers, among them the famed director Emilio "Indio" Fernández; the long-absent Elsa Cárdenas, who had been so impressive in *Giant*; and newcomer actor-director Alfonso Arau. Unfortunately, producer Phil Feldman and the studio took the film from director Sam Peckinpah and trimmed it down to 143 minutes. A 190-minute restored version was released in 1986. It is the latter version's that provides a richer context of both characters and narrative.

The film is set in Texas in 1913, a time when the Old West is fading fast into the sunset of history and World War I is soon to usher in a new era of a different kind of violence. An aging wild bunch (William Holden, Ernest Borgnine, Jaime Sánchez, Ben Johnson, Warren Oates, Bo Hopkins) rob a bank. However, it is a trap organized by a vengeful railroad owner (Albert Dekker) and carried out by an ex-member of the bunch, Deke (Robert Ryan), and some bounty hunters (Strother Martin, L.Q. Jones). The remnants of the group flee into Mexico, only to realize that the expected loot is only metal washers.

Their failure contributes to a fracturing of the bunch. The bigoted Gorch brothers

Ernest Borgnine (left) and William Holden in Sam Peckinpah's *The Wild Bunch* (1969, Warner Bros.). The film told the story of the two Mexicos at odds during the Mexican Revolution.

(Johnson, Oates) bait and threaten the Mexican member of the group, Ángel (Sánchez). However, an old member, Sykes (Edmond O'Brien), Pike Bishop (Holden) and Dutch (Borgnine) side with Ángel. Pike warns them and attempts to instill in them a code of honor: "You're not getting rid of anybody. We're gonna stick together just like it used to be. When you side with a man you stay with him and if you can't do that you're like some animal. You're finished. We're finished! All of us!" As they ponder their future, Pike adds, "We got to start thinking beyond our guns. Those days are closing fast."

They find some respite in Ángel's village, where Ángel discovers that the renegade General Mapache (Emilio Fernández), a follower of the usurper Victoriano Huerta, has killed all the young men and that his girlfriend Teresa (Sonia Amelio) has gone willingly with him. The bunch considers hiring themselves out to Mapache. Ángel dissents: "I'm not going to seek guns for that devil to rob and kill my people ... I care about my people, my village, my Mexico ... this is their land and no one is going to drive them away.... If I can take guns I will go with them." Pike makes him an offer: "One case, you give up your half of the gold." Ángel agrees. However, at Mapache's camp, Ángel in a moment of sudden anger kills Teresa, who has become a prostitute. Only when Mapache is convinced that they did not come to assassinate him does he hire them to rob several cases of U.S. rifles.

The bunch carries out the task and gives the promised case of arms to the Villista villagers as Pike had promised. However, Mapache learns of the deception after Teresa's father tells him. Dutch himself abandons Ángel, who had saved his life, while taking the rifles. He tells Mapache, "He's a thief, you take care of him."

When Pike lashes out to him for his treachery—"He gave his word!"—Dutch responds, "That's not what counts! It's who you give it to!" Once more pursued by Deke and the bounty hunters, the bunch seeks solace with prostitutes in Mapache's camp. Pike, who is totally disillusioned with the empty life he has lived, even with his tarnished code of loyalty, decides to seek retribution with one noble act, to rescue Ángel. The bunch is obliterated in gun battle with Mapache and his men. Later, the bounty hunters arrive to recover the bodies and seek the bounties. Shortly after leaving with the bodies, they are killed by the Villista villagers. Sykes arrives with some of the villagers. He tells Deke, "Me and the boys here got a job to do. Wanna come along? It ain't like it used to be, but it'll do."

Peckinpah presented the two Mexicos of the Mexican Revolution through the allegorical characters of Ángel, the flawed, lost youth who finds himself again as a Villista, who makes his people his cause; and Mapache, the corrupt and opportunistic counterrevolutionary, whose cause is his own self-aggrandizement. It is Ángel who becomes the redeeming messenger of fate for the lost and fractured bunch. Arthur Pettit, in his in-depth work of Peckinpah and his films, wrote, "His commitment to my people, my village, Mexico, separates him from the bunch, who are committed only to each other until Ángel's execution takes them to their own deaths—if not for Ángel's values, a least for his spirit. It is Ángel who wins our sympathy early in the action by flinging the Bunch's racism in their faces, and it is Ángel who shows the bunch an alternative to Mapachismo by taking them to his native village.... It is Ángel who is the catalyst for both the physical destruction and the moral resurrection of the Wild Bunch. By awakening his fellow outlaws to the moral dimensions of the revolution, Ángel serves as the spiritual center, the conscience, the moral burden, and, ultimately, the redeemer of the bunch."[30]

Peckinpah's characters are three-dimensional. Mapache, for example, exhibits touching concern for his men when they are outgunned by the Villistas and suppresses his desire to retreat when he notices the hero-worship of a little boy. Mapache is cruel and tenacious, but only when it threatens his people. Peckinpah pays homage to the Villista villagers, who lack technical skills but who possess courage and resourcefulness, as when they outwit the bunch and come to retrieve their guns. General Pershing's troops, who defend the arms shipment, are less than indomitable men of war. They prove be bumbling and incompetent.

The bunch from the beginning are depicted as thieves and killers, filled with tarnished remnants of morality and ethics. Unlike in *Butch Cassidy and the Sundance Kid* (1969, 20th Century–Fox), another well-known western released the same year, the bunch are not pristine, romanticized and sugar-coated good-bad men. Given this context, the controversial battle at the end of the film is a metaphor for the death throes of one era and the birth of another.

Latino Film Stars and Filmmakers

ANTONIO AGUILAR

Mexican actor-singer Antonio Aguilar established a lengthy and successful career playing Mexican revolutionary heroes and typical *rancheros*.

He was born in Villanueva, Zacatecas, Mexico, on May 17, 1919. He began as a professional singer of *rancheras* in the 1940s and broke into films with the help of film idol Pedro Infante at the end of the decade. In the 1950s, he played leads in "B" films and supporting roles in important films usually top-billed by Pedro Infante, Pedro Armendáriz or Luis Aguilar. His role in Ismael Rodríguez's epic of the Mexican Revolution, *La Cucaracha* (1958), with Dolores del Río, Pedro Armendáriz, and María Félix, finally propelled him into the higher brackets.

He produced some of his films beginning in the 1960s and specialized in populist *ranchera* comedies and tales of Mexican Revolution heroes usually costarring his singer/actress wife Flor Silvestre and a stock company of players. His popular film fare in the 1960s included *Rumbo a Brasilia* (1960), about a Mexican engineer building a national highway, and *Los Hermanos Hierro* (1961) with Columba Domínguez. His Mexican Revolution films began with Miguel Zacarías' *Los Cuatro Juanes* (1964) and *El Hijo de Gabino Barrera* (1964). Others include Zacarías' *Juan Colorado* (1965) with Elsa Cárdenas, and *Los Alegres Aguilares* (1965); René Cardona's *Caballo Prieto Azabache* (1965), with Flor Silvestre; *El Caballo Bayo* (1965) with Maricruz Olivier; *Lauro Puñales* (1966) with Flor Silvestre and Elsa Cárdenas; and *Lucio Vásquez* (1966).

Among his *ranchera* films are *Escuela Para Solteros* (1964), with Luis Aguilar; *El Padre Diablo* (1964) with Kitty De Hoyos; René Cardona's *El Alazán y el Rosillo* (1966) with Flor Silvestre; *Alma Llanera* (1964); and Zacarías' *Los Dos Rivales* (1965) with Lucha Villa.

In 1969, he made his U.S. film debut in the costarring role of General Rojas, a supporter of Benito Juárez battling French occupation forces, in Andrew V. McLaglen's *The Undefeated* (1969, 20th Century–Fox) with John Wayne and Rock Hudson.

In the next two decades his film output diminished but he exhibited impressive reserves as an actor of depth and substance, especially as Pancho Villa in *La Muerte de Pancho Villa* (1974), with Ana Luisa Peluffo, and as Emiliano Zapata in two evocative films directed by Felipe Cazals: *Emiliano Zapata* (1985) and *La Traición de Zapata* (1986).

Antonio Aguilar toured extensively as a singer and rodeo performer throughout the world, including the United States. He died on June 19, 2007, of pneumonia.

ALFONSO ARAU

Mexican actor/writer/director Alfonso Arau was part of a new infusion of talent in Mexican cinema during the innovative and liberal 1960s. He has made several forays into U.S. films as an actor and more recently as a director.

He was born on January 11, 1932, in Mexico City. He worked as a dancer, singer, mime and satirist. In 1953, he began working as part of a comic dance team and continued on his own when the team broke up. He spent a year in Paris while studying pantomime with Marcel Marceau's teacher Etienne Dacroux. He wrote a dumb-show for himself entitled "Happy Madness," which met with much success in Paris' Théâtre Comedie des Champs-Élysées. When he was offered a lucrative contract to tour, he turned it down. Later, he would comment, "My life's dream was to become a film maker. The prospect of spending twenty or thirty years touring the world as a stage performer dismayed me."[31]

He returned to Mexico during the liberalization period in its cinema. He had previously made his film debut in *Caras Nuevas* in 1955. Upon his return, he won a supporting role in Alberto Isaac's evocative film adaptation of Gabriel García Márquez's *En Este Pueblo No Hay Ladrones* (1964) and then followed it up with the role of Saltaperico in Carlos Velos' adaptation of Juan Rulfo's famous novel *Pedro Páramo* (1966), with Pilar Pellicer, Ignacio López Tarso and a miscast John Gavin.

Arau made his U.S. film debut in Sam Peckinpah's powerful tale of the Mexican Revolution, *The Wild Bunch* (1969, Warner Bros.), with the stellar cast of William Holden, Robert Ryan, Ernest Borgnine, Ben Johnson, Emilio Fernández, and Jaime Sánchez. Arau played the role of Herrera, General Mapache's right-hand man. He was then cast in *Scandalous John* (1971, Disney), a somewhat contemporary retelling of the tale of Don Quixote of La Mancha.

Meanwhile, his Mexican film career went into high gear when he directed and starred in *Calzonzín Inspector* (1973), a strong political satire that won wide acclaim. He costarred in Albert Isaac's surrealistic *El Rincón de Las Vírgenes* (1972) with Emilio Fernández. Isaac retained Arau's services for the role of a burlesque comic caught in a futile effort to save an old theater in *Tivoli* (1974). During those years of openness in Mexican cinema, Arau directed a documentary about Cuba entitled *Caribe, Estrella y Aguila* (1976). In 1979, Arau wrote, directed, produced, and starred in *Mojado Power*. The film (in which this author was cast in a bit part) chronicled the misfortunes of a Mexican undocumented worker and his attempt to organize a union.

As the Mexican film industry went into doldrums, Arau found it increasingly difficult to find financing for his offbeat, independent-minded films. He returned to roles in U.S. films of decreasing merit: Manuel in the obscure comedy *Used Cars* (1980) with Kurt Russell;

a Colombian smuggler in the popular *Romancing the Stone* (1984) with Michael Douglas; the caricatured Mexican bandit El Guapo in John Landis' abysmally stereotypical *Three Amigos* (1988); and the filibuster in the misfire *Walker* (1987).

In 1991, he was given the opportunity to direct the film adaptation of Laura Esquivel's novel *Like Water for Chocolate* with newcomer Lumi Cavazos and Italian star Marco Leonardi, of *Cinema Paradiso* fame. *Like Water for Chocolate* went on to become an international and critical hit. In the United States, it became the highest-grossing foreign film of all time. Arau later stated, "*Like Water for Chocolate* opened the doors, not only for Mexican filmmakers, but also for Latin-American filmmakers.... Definitely, every filmmaker from Mexico coming to Hollywood now—I mean, at least they will answer their phone calls."[32]

Of his previous films he commented, "My previous films have been political satires— very wild comedies, very, very political. But it's humor with a lot of poetry, they are very romantic in a way. Always very romantic heroes trying to fix the world. So romanticism is a common denominator in my films."[33]

His next directorial assignment was *A Walk in the Clouds* (1995, 20th Century–Fox), with Anthony Quinn, Giancarlo Giannini, Spanish actress Aitana Sánchez-Gijón, and Keanu Reeves. Of the film, Arau stated, "'A Walk in the Clouds' is about love and life—it's a chant to all family and human values and the love of human beings for the earth."[34] *Like Water for Chocolate* had been made on a budget of two million dollars but Arau was given twenty million dollars to make *A Walk in the Clouds* by Twentieth-Century–Fox. Arau noted, "This film is the first time in my life that I am shooting a film without having to go on Saturday and Sunday to get the money next week.... It's a blessing to me and I'm grateful."[35] The film was set in the Napa Valley in 1945 and centered on a Mexican-American wine-owning family. Of the time frame, Arau commented, "If you put contemporary things in the past, you can analyze it with more distance, with more perspective. And 1945, the period in which the film is set, is the beginning of this era of extreme materialism. All the look is definitely, intentionally, old."[36] He talked of one of the reasons for directing a Hollywood film: "Part of this dream to make a film in Hollywood was like writing a letter to Santa Claus. I wanted to work with these giants, Anthony Quinn and Giancarlo Giannini. I was a little intimidated because they were so big, but I realized that they were good actors and good actors are always modest and disciplined and humble. It was a pleasure to work with those two guys—and all the cast."[37]

However, *A Walk in the Clouds* compared to *Like Water for Chocolate* was a modest critical and commercial success. *Entertainment Today* expressed the typical critical response to the film: "If the lead performance doesn't cut it, can you still enjoy the movie? I mean, really enjoy it, recommend it to your friends, cry in your popcorn? This is the sad dilemma posed by *Walk in the Clouds,* the film which represents director Alfonso Arau's post–*Like Water for Chocolate* love song to Hollywood. As breathlessly romantic as *Legends of the Fall* but not nearly as silly, *A Walk in the Clouds* brings Arau's Magic Realist sensibility to the vineyards of the Napa Valley and the aftermath of the second world war."[38] The anemic performance by the badly miscast Keanu Reeves virtually wrecked the film. However, Anthony Quinn in a character role effortlessly redeemed the film, giving it its only worth.

In recent years Arau has appeared mostly on Mexican and U.S. television. He directed the U.S. film *Picking Up the Pieces* (2000) and the Mexican film *Zapata: El Sueño de un Héroe* (2000). However, both films met with critical and commercial failure.

Arau's marriage to author Laura Esquivel ended in 1996. Arau has one son from a previous marriage.

Pedro Armendáriz, Jr.

Pedro Armendáriz, Jr., was the son of the legendary Mexican film star Pedro Armendáriz. Pedro, Jr., met with moderate success in Mexican films as a leading man and as a supporting and featured actor in U.S. films.

He was born on March 9, 1947, in Mexico City, the oldest of three offspring, which included two sisters. He was educated as an architect. His Mexican film debut in came in a western, *Los Gavilanes* (1965), with Luis Aguilar and Irma Serrano.

He then played leads in a trio of low-budget westerns: *Fuera de la Ley* (1965) with Sonia Furio and David Reynosa; *El Cachorro* (1965) with the veteran David Silva; and *Temerario* (1965). He then played a costarring part in three big-budget films: *Los Tres Mosqueteros de Dios* (1966) with Javier Solis; Jose Bolaños' impressive Mexican Revolution–based *La Soldadera* (1966) with Silvia Pinal and Aurora Clavel; and the melodrama *Matar No Es Fácil* (1966) with Arturo de Córdova. He was top-billed in an ordinary western, *Bandidos* (1966), with Pilar Pellicer and Robert Conrad.

He made his U.S. feature debut in a featured role as Father Lucas in *Guns for San Sebastian* (1968) with Anthony Quinn and Silvia Pinal. John Wayne, one of his father's close friends, cast him in two of his westerns: *The Undefeated* (1969) and *Chisum* (1970). He moved up to supporting roles in the western *Macho Callahan* (1970) with Jean Seberg and David Janssen; *The Magnificent Seven Ride* (1971) with Lee Van Cleef; *The Soul of Nigger Charley* (1972) with Fred Williamson; and *The Deadly Trackers* (1973) with Isela Vega and Richard Harris. He next appeared in the science fiction film *Chosen Survivors* (1974) with Jackie Cooper and Alex Cord.

He has had supporting and featured roles in several television films: *River of Gold* (1971, ABC); *Hardcase* (1972, ABC); *Killer by Night* (1972, CBS); *Don't Be Afraid of the Dark* (1973, ABC); *A Home of Our Own* (1975, CBS); *The Log of Black Pearl* (1975, NBC); *Evita Perón* (1981, NBC); *Agatha Christie's Murder in Three Acts* (1986, CBS); and two miniseries, *The Rhinemann Exchange* (1977, NBC) and *On Wings of Eagles* (1986, NBC).

During this time, he was relegated to small roles in U.S. films: *Earthquake* (1974) with Ava Gardner and Charlton Heston; *Survival Run* (1980) with Ray Milland; the actioner *The Dogs of War* (1981) with JoBeth Williams; the French comedy *Le Chevre* (1985) with Gerard Depardieu; the Mexican Revolution–based misfire *Old Gringo* (1989), in which he portrayed Pancho Villa (whom his father had played memorably in four films); and *Licence to Kill* (1989) with Timothy Dalton as the new James Bond.

His Mexican film career has been mixed. Among his better films have been *El Cuarto Cuatro* (1979) with Ana Martín; and *Cadena Perpetua* (1979) with Pilar Pellicer and Ana Martín. He has worked extensively in Mexican *telenovelas* and U.S. television commercials. During 2000, he got a prized role in the *La Ley de Heródes*, a controversial Mexican film which depicted the rise of the PRI (Partido Revolucionario Institucional), the political party which has dominated Mexico for more than seventy years.

His more recent U.S. films include George P. Cosmatos' tale of Wyatt Earp entitled *Tombstone* (1993), in which Armendáriz played a helpless Mexican priest, and *The Mask of Zorro* (1999), in which he played a *hacendado*.

He died of eye cancer on December 26, 2011, in New York City, soon after being diagnosed with the disease while working on a Mexican *telenovela*.

AURORA CLAVEL

The talented, dark-haired and attractive Mexican actress Aurora Clavel has played an assortment of supporting roles as Native Americans and alluring camp followers in both Mexican and U.S. films in the 1960s and 1970s.

She was born in Santiago, Pinotepa, Oaxaco, Mexico, in 1936. She gravitated to acting at an early age. She made her film debut in the film *Rosa Blanca* in 1961. She was in her late twenties when she appeared in Gerardo Wenzine's experimental short *Huástica* (1964). As a consequence of her strong impression in that film, she was cast in the female lead in Luis Alcoriza's memorable *Tarahumara* (1965). The film chronicled the efforts of an anthropologist (Ignacio López Tarzo) to study the customs of the remote Tarahumara Indians in the Mexican state of Chihuahua. He is befriended by a couple (Aurora Clavel, Jaime Fernández) whose way of life is altered fatefully. The film was a winner at the Cannes Film Festival and gained international acclaim. Aurora (herself of indigenous roots) won wide praise for her best role of her career. The Mexican magazine *Siempre* commented, "La Clavel and the others give authenticity in their roles of Tarahumara. Greater acclaim cannot be accorded to them."[39] However, Aurora's was a talent that would never be fully realized.

She made her U.S. film debut when she was selected by director Sam Peckinpah for the role of the Indian maiden Melinche in the dark and offbeat western *Major Dundee* (1964) with Charlton Heston and Richard Harris. She made two routine Mexican films: *¡Viva Benito Canales!* (1965) with Elvira Quintana and *Rancho Solo* (1965) with Lilia Prado. She then had a strong role as a *soldadera* in Jose Bolanos' impressive *La Soldadera* (1966) with Silvia Pinal and Jaime Fernández. Aurora played Magdalena in Henri Vernevil's mixed-quality U.S. adventure tale *Guns for San Sebastian* (1968) with Anthony Quinn. She worked for a second time with Sam Peckinpah in the role of a *soldadera* of the counterrevolutionary Mapache in the classic *The Wild Bunch* (1969, Warner Bros.) with William Holden and Robert Ryan. She was cast as a Juarista in Don Siegel's *Two Mules for Sister Sara* (1969), lensed by Gabriel Figueroa, shot on location in Mexico and top-billed by Shirley MacLaine and Clint Eastwood.

She essayed the role of an Indian woman massacred by the U.S. Cavalry in Ralph Nelson's allegorical *Soldier Blue* (1970) with Candice Bergen. She had a role in the misfire adaptation of a B. Traven story, *The Bridge in the Jungle* (1971) with Katy Jurado and John Huston, and she had a small role in Sam Peckinpah's *Pat Garrett and Billy the Kid* (1973) with Bob Dylan, James Coburn and Kris Kristofferson.

She continues to work infrequently in Mexican films.

Miriam Colón

One of the most outstanding and durable Latina actresses of the contemporary times has been the Puerto Rican–born Miriam Colón, who has performed on stage and in television and films.

She was born in Ponce, Puerto Rico, on August 20, 1936, one of three children. She began acting in high school and then continued in the University of Puerto Rico's Department of Drama. Later she was accepted at New York's famous Actors Studio on the basis of her first audition. There, she studied under the tutelage of Lee Strasberg and Elia Kazan. On Broadway, she went on to perform in *In the Summer House* with Dame Judith Anderson, *The Innkeepers* with Geraldine Page and *The Wrong Way Lighbulb* with James Patterson. Among her numerous Off-Broadway plays are *La Carreta*, which is the most performed play in Puerto Rico; *Matty and the Moron and Madonna*, directed by the renowned José Quintero; *Winterset;* and *The Passion of Antigona Perez.*

Moving to the West Coast, she made her television debut in *Tragedy in a Temporary Town* on *Playhouse 90.* Her numerous television appearances include *The DuPont of the Week, The Defenders, The Dick Van Dyke Show, Gunsmoke, Jesse James*, and *Dr. Kildare.*

She made her film debut in the low-budget *Crowded Paradise* in 1956. She won praise for her second film appearance, in which she played the Mexican girlfriend of Marlon Brando in *One-Eyed Jacks* (1961, Paramount), which the latter directed and starred in. It costarred Pina Pellicer and Katy Jurado. Colón said of the film, "I think it is a beautiful motion picture. Even the villain is not an ordinary villain. He has dimensions that make you wonder about him. You know, somehow, he is not merely a ruthless character. He is a human being."[40]

She played a Filipina guerrilla in the World War II film *The Battle at Bloody Beach* (1961, 20th Century–Fox) with Audie Murphy; an Indian maiden in Delbert Mann's impressive *The Outsider* (1962, Universal) with Tony Curtis; and thereafter was wasted in two routine low-budget films, *Harbor Lights* (1963) and *Thunder Island* (1963). She was reunited with Marlon Brando in Sidney J. Furie's offbeat western *The Appaloosa* (1966, Universal), in which she played a Mexican wife. She followed this with the role of Rosita in *Joaquin Murietta* (1969) and the *curandera* in *The Possession of Joel Delaney* (1972, Paramount) opposite Shirley MacLaine.

In 1967, she founded the Puerto Rican Traveling Theatre in New York, a showcase for all ethnic groups which performs in the barrios and ghettos. For this and other dedicated community involvement, she was honored with a special Golden Eagle Award by Nosotros for "her outstanding contributions to theatre."

She played Mama Montana in Brian De Palma's gangster epic *Scarface* (1983, Universal), with Al Pacino as the violent mobster, and she played a ruthless madam in Martin Ritt's evocative *Back Roads* (1981, Warner Bros.) with Sally Field.

She has had featured roles in several television films: *The Desperate Mission* (1971, NBC); *They Call It Murder* (1971, NBC); *Dr. Max* (1974, CBS); and *Best Kept Secrets* (1984, ABC).

She has been a tireless advocate for better opportunities for the Latino community in film and television and the eradication of stereotypes. In one interview she stated, "The Mexican girl is never a school teacher. She's always the widow of the man who was killed, or the harlot in the bar. If she's Mexican can't she ever be a nurse or a wife? Let's face it, there are scientists who are Latin Americans."[41]

Her most recent play, *Floating Islands*, had a successful run in Los Angeles during 1994. She earned accolades for her long-overdue lead role of a Mexican matriarch businesswoman in John Sayles' evocative tale of south Texas, *Lone Star* (1996), opposite Elizabeth Peña and Kris Kristofferson. In 2013, she played the prized role of Ultima, the *curandera* in the film adaptation of Rudolfo Anaya's classic novel *Bless Me, Ultima*.

HENRY DARROW

One of the busiest Latino actors in the late 1960s and early 1970s was the versatile and amiable Henry Darrow.

He was born Enrique Delgado in New York City on September 15, 1933. Of Puerto Rican ancestry, he grew up in New York City and Puerto Rico. He attended the University of Puerto Rico, where he majored in political science and psychiatry. Later, he earned a bachelor of theater arts degree from the Pasadena Playhouse, which he attended on a scholarship.

After graduation he headed for Hollywood in 1960, where he played bit parts in films, bigger ones on television and an assortment of roles in theater. He found significant resistance from casting directors due to his Spanish surname. His first professional appearance as Henry

Henry Darrow has worked for decades in film, television, and theater.

Darrow occurred in the television series *Iron Horse* episode "Cougar Man" in 1966. He would later recall, "In films, a man named Delgado was hopelessly typed.... He played a Mexican or an Indian, nothing else. On the stage I did Hungarians and Irishmen and American southerners and even a Cockney. It made no difference. For Delgado, there was no such parts in movies and television."[42]

He spent a year with a professional classical repertory company that was based at the Pasadena Playhouse, playing a diverse number of roles in plays by Shakespeare, Ibsen and Shaw.

Darrow met with his greatest success when he was cast as the Mexican *vaquero* Manolito Montoya (a cast regular) in the popular NBC western *The High Chaparral* opposite Linda Cristal, Leif Erickson and Cameron Mitchell. He obtained the part after the series producer saw him in the Ray Bradbury play *The Wonderful Ice Cream Suit*. Darrow later stated, "I only had one year to go on my own five-year limit. My wife has had to help me support our kids for so long I had decided that if I didn't make it in five years—zap—I was going to toss the whole bit and find another way to make my living."[43]

About his role of Manolito he said, "In the Mexican community ... *The Chaparral* [sic] was known as a program that portrayed a Mexican with dignity as a man of substance and worth. In Mano's father's home hangs a Goya! It was also a program that employed many Chicanos."[44] Darrow's tenure as a costar of *The High Chaparral* ran from 1967 to 1971.

The series was praised by *TV Guide*, which wrote, "David Dortort, executive producer and creator of *Bonanza*, has thrown mostly old secrets into his newest western, *The High Chaparral*. The exception is a heretofore totally obscure young actor named Henry Darrow. Darrow plays Manolito, dashing Mexican brother-in-law to a trio of white group-heroes, something like the folks on the Ponderosa but not exactly."[45]

Darrow went on to costar in five other television series: *The New Dick Van Dyke Show* (1973–74); *Harry-O* (1974–76) with David Janssen; *Zorro and Son* (1983); *Me and Mom* (1985); and *Zorro* (1990). He also guest-starred in numerous top-rated television shows: *Police Woman, The Waltons, Kojak, Vega$, Hart to Hart, The Bionic Woman, Baretta, Wonder Woman,* and *Quincy,* among others.

He costarred in several television films: *Brock's Last Case* (1973) with Richard Widmark; *Hitchhike* (1974) with Cloris Leachman; *Aloha Means Goodbye* (1974) with Sally Struthers; and *Attica* (1980). His theatrical-film credits include *Cancel My Reservation* (1972) with Bob Hope and Eva Marie Saint; *Badge 373* (1973) with Robert Duvall; *Walk Proud* (1979) with Robby Benson; *Losin' It* (1982) with Shelley Long; *Maverick* (1994); with James Garner; *Primo* (2008); and *Soda Springs* (2012). His most memorable film performance remains the role of the patriarch in Jesús Salvador Treviño's *Seguin* (1982) with Edward James Olmos and A. Martinez.

Along with Ricardo Montalbán, Anthony Quinn, and others, he was the cofounder of Nosotros, an organization dedicated to creating better opportunities and images for Latinos in the media. Darrow served on the Ethnic Minorities Committee of the Screen Actors Guild, a watchdog body monitoring the use of minorities in films and television.

ANA MARTÍN

Popular Mexican leading lady Ana Martín made her U.S. film debut upon reaching stardom in her native country.

Ana Martín was born on May 14, 1947, in Mexico City, Mexico, the daughter of popular Mexican television comedian Jesús "Palillo" Martínez. She made her film debut in a bit part in *El Gangster* (1964) with Arturo De Córdova and the same year blossomed to stardom in Gilberto Martinez Solares' *Marcela y María*. She was then cast in some programmers: *La Muerte Punctual* (1965) with Maricruz Oliver; *El Ángel y Yo* (1966) with Tin-Tan; *Acapulco a Go Go* (1966); and *Blue Demon contra Cerebros Infernales* (1966) with David Reynosa. She was recognized as a talented young dramatic actress and was given Mexico's Diosa de Plata Award of 1967 as Newcomer of the Year.

In 1968, she was cast as the female lead in Metro-Goldwyn-Mayer's impressive but underappreciated *Return of the Gunfighter* opposite Robert Taylor and Chad Everett. She played a Mexican girl who has witnessed a murder and who is protected by the victim's friend (Taylor), who seeks revenge.

The vivacious and attractive Martín returned to Mexico where she continued to develop into a highly respected actress and comedienne in film, television and theater, as well as a top box-office draw. Among her popular films are: *Los Corrompidos* (1971) with Rita Macedo; *El Profesor Mimi* (1973) with Ignacio López Tarso; *Los Indolentes* (1979) with Rita Macedo; *El Verano Salvaje* (1980) with Jorge Rivero; and *Vivir Para Amar* (1980) with Kitty de Hoyos.

During 2000, she was cast in an important role in the film adaptation of Julia Alvarez's *In the Time of the Butterflies.*

TOMÁS MILIÁN

Tomás Milián won fame in European films in the late 1950s and 1960s under the helm of several important directors and prolonged his fame with several spaghetti westerns during their vogue.

He was born Tomás Rodríguez on March 3, 1937, in Havana, Cuba. He was raised in the United States and studied acting at the Actors Studio. Soon thereafter, he appeared in several plays in New York City. He moved to Italy in the late 1950s after appearing in the Spoleto Festival, where he met Italian director Mauro Bolognini, who convinced him about the opportunities in Europe.

He made an impressive film debut in *La Notte Brava/On Any Street* in 1959. He specialized in playing amoral heroes. Among his well-known films were: *Il Bell'Antonio* (1960); *L'Imprevisto* (1961); one segment directed by Luchino Visconti in *Boccaccio '70* (1962) with Romy Schneider; *Il Disordine/Disorder* (1962); and *Time of Indifference/Gli Indifferenti* (1964), directed by Francisco Maselli, with Paulette Goddard and Shelley Winters.

In 1965, he was cast in the role of Raphael in the film adaptation of Irving Stone's novel about Michelangelo, *The Agony and the Ecstasy* (1965, 20th Century–Fox), directed by Carol Reed and starring Charlton Heston and Rex Harrison. At this point, he reinvigorated his career as a popular star of a series of spaghetti westerns: *The Bounty Hunter/El Precio de un Hombre* (1966); *Django Kid* (1967); *The Big Gundown/La Resa dei Conti* (1968) with Lee Van Cleef; and *The Violent Four/Bandit of Milano* (1968).

He made infrequent appearances in U.S. films in supporting roles like *A Fine Pair* (1969) with Claudia Cardinale and Rock Hudson; and in Dennis Hopper's *The Last Movie* (1971).

Beginning in 1975 with his appearance in *Winter Kills,* he began to make frequent forays into U.S. films in supporting roles. Among his films were: *Monsginor* (1982) with Christopher Reeve; *King David* (1985) with Richard Gere; *Salome* (1985); *Revenge* (1990) with Anthony Quinn; *Havana* (1990) with Robert Redford; Oliver Stone's *JFK* (1992); and *Death and the Maiden* (1995) with Sigourney Weaver.

Other films include *I Cannibali/The Cannibals* (1970); *Cronaca criminale del Far West* (1972); *I Consigliori* (1973); *Folle a' tuer* (1975—France/Italy); *Il Quatro dell' Apocaisse* (1975); *La Luna* (1979); *Roma a Mano armata* (1979); *Milano Odia* (1980); *La Polizia no puo sparare/Almost Human* (1980); *Identificazione di una Donna/Identification of a Woman* (1983); *Money* (1991—France/Italy/Canada).

In recent years, he made an impressive comeback as a character actor in such films such as *Traffic* (2000) and *The Lost City* (2005).

PILAR PELLICER

Distinguished Mexican actress Pilar Pellicer, the older sister of Pina Pellicer, has appeared in two U.S. films. She continues to be one of Mexico's noted actresses.

She was born on February 2, 1938, in Mexico City, and while still in her teens she was trained as a dancer in the Modern Dance Ballet of Bellas Artes. She was given sympathetic support by her well-known and respected uncle Carlos Pellicer, a writer. As dancer, she toured Mexico and the United States for two years before turning to theater and eventually films.

She made her Mexican film debut in a bit role in the comedy-drama *El Gangster* (1964) with Arturo De Cordova. She acquired film stardom and rave reviews in her second film, Juan José Gurrola's *Tajimara* (1965), part of a new and innovative current in Mexican films during the decade. She then played the female lead, Susana, in the film adaptation of Juan Rulfo's *Pedro Páramo* (1966) with Ignacio López Tarso. She starred in the inconsequential western *Los Bandidos* (1966) with Robert Conrad and then had a small role in Luis Buñuel's *Nazarín* (1959).

She has appeared on Mexican and French television and in numerous plays in Mexico, such as *The Little Foxes* in 1983. In 1968, she was contracted by Metro-Goldwyn-Mayer (MGM) to play the distraught widow Lydia opposite Glenn Ford and Arthur Kennedy in Jerry Thorpe's sardonic western *Day of the Evil Gun,* which was lensed on location in Durango, Mexico. Her second U.S. film was the comedy spoof *Zorro, the Gay Blade* (1981) with George Hamilton.

Among her commercial and critical successes are *La Trinchera*, a drama about the Mexican Revolution; *Golfas de Talón* and *Las Porquianchis* (1976), a pair of somber films about the lower depths of the red light district; *Cadena Perpetua* (1978), a crime drama with Ana Martín and Pedro Armendáriz, Jr.; the controversial *Tres Mujeres de la Hoguera* (1979) with Maricruz Oliver; and *Amor a la Vuelta de la Esquina* (1985).

She gave a memorable performance in Emilio Fernández's *La Choca* (1974), in which she played an embittered and poverty-stricken illiterate peasant wife. For her performance she won the Ariel Award as Best Actress of the Year. Another notable role was as the solitary sculptress in *El Festín de la Loba* (1972) opposite Isela Vega.

She keeps busy in Mexican *telenovelas* and theater.

She married a U.S. sculptor and has two daughters.

PINA PELLICER

Pina Pellicer had a meteoric career not unlike James Dean's, brief but significant, as she died young and tragically. She became a star in her very first film, opposite Marlon Brando, and would later star in four other films, including the Mexican classic *Macario.*

Pina was born Josefina Pellicer López de Elergo on April 3, 1935, in Mexico City. Her older sister Pilar Pellicer would also go on to become a distinguished actress of stage and screen. Pina's childhood was sad and solitary, and since a young age she has been exceptionally sensitive. She was an excellent student and it was with dismay that her parents assented to her wish to pursue an acting career.

She joined a university theater group and through the influence of her uncle Carlos Pellicer (a noted writer) joined the group Poesía en Voz Alta, forming part of a chorus. A few months later she was chosen for the lead in the play *The Diary of Anne Frank*. The immediate box-office success and critical raves confirmed the emergence of a new and great actress.

A U.S. producer was in Mexico searching for a Mexican actress to play the female lead of Luisa opposite Marlon Brando in *One-Eyed Jacks* (1961, Columbia Pictures), and when he saw Pina he knew his search was over. Brando (the star and director of the film) agreed. Overnight, she had gone from obscurity to fame.

However, the experience caused her both fear and insecurity. Later, she would recall, "When they invited me to test for the film, I took it as a joke. Nevertheless, I took it out of curiosity: I wanted to know what Hollywood film tests consisted of. As other aspiring actresses tested, I became more confident of myself. When my turn came, for the first time in many years I felt completely at ease.... However, on arriving in Hollywood I became nervous. I was advised that I needed to go to California and take the final tests. A couple of minutes before the test, Marlon called me and told me 'Miss, I want you with me in the picture, do exactly what is indicated in the screenplay and nothing more. I order you not to be nervous.' I guess I believed in him, because I acted very much at ease: but on completing the test I thought I was going to get a heart attack. I was a bundle of nerves and at the point of becoming hysterical."[46]

Stanley Kubrick, whose early pictures *The Killing and Paths of Glory* Brando admired, was hired to direct, but the men could not agree on the concept of the characters and Brando took over as director. Shooting began in December 1958 and finished during June 1959. The film was finally released during March of 1961. Due to the budget ($6,000,000) and the fact that the studio cut the film contrary to Brando's wishes, the film was not a big commercial success as expected. In critical terms, Pina garnered the bulk of the acclaim, winning the Best Actress Award at the San Sebastian Film Festival in Spain. *One-Eyed Jacks* (the title which refers to the duplicity of humankind) is a flawed film, but one that is permanent in historical memory because of its stunning visual beauty and sensitivity of the scenes between Pina and Brando.

Upon returning to Mexico, she starred with Ignacio López Tarso in Roberto Gavaldón's classic *Macario* (1961). The film is a parable about man's obsession with death. She played the wife of the peasant who attempts to cheat death. The film won numerous awards, including the Mexican film industry's Cuauhtémoc Award, which went to Pellicer as the year's most promising star. During 1960, she starred on the U.S. television show *Hitchcock Presents* in the segment "Juan Diego."

She next went to Spain to film *Rogelia* (1961), directed by Rafael Gil, which was neither routine nor distinguished. She then replaced Silvia Pinal in Roberto Galvaldón's *Días de Otoño* (1961), in which she played Luisa, a young woman frustrated by a deceptive love affair. Because she had just experienced a failed and brief marriage with Ramón Naves, Jr., she could empathize with the role only too well. She turned in an outstanding performance, winning the Mexican film industry's Diosa de Plata de Pecime for Best Actress, the Onix of the Iberoamerica University and another Cuauhtémoc Award which she received in person.

In her final film, *El Gran Pecador* (1961), she starred with several luminaries of the Mexican screen, Arturo De Córdova, Marga López, and Javier Solis.

She was a very reserved person and once spoke of her attitude: "I don't like to talk about sentiments because if others discover how I am, they will use it as arms against me to do me harm."[47]

Her turbulent life, solitude, and her rebellious spirit may have influenced her to take her own life. One of her favorite poems by John Donne read, "Send not to know for whom the bell tolls, / it tolls for thee." She left a handful of outstanding performances laced with her gentle spirit.

Pina Pellicer was only twenty-four years of age at the time of her suicide on December 10, 1964.

SILVIA PINAL

In the history of Mexican cinema there has perhaps never been such a versatile entertainer as Silvia Pinal. She has appeared in two U.S. films.

She was born on September 12, 1931, in Guaymas, Sonora, Mexico. She began acting on radio while still a student and went on to experimental theater. It was her first husband, Rafael Banquella, who started her in the theatre. Among the plays she acted in was Alejandro Casona's *Nuestra Natacha*.

She attracted the attention of film director Miguel Contreras, who contracted her for her first film, *Bamba,* in 1948. Her versatility and vivacious beauty and personality quickly won the hearts of moviegoers and earned her film stardom. Among her early notable films were *Puerta Joven* (1949) with Cantinflas; *El Rey del Barrio* (1949) with Tin Tan; and a pair of films with Pedro Infante, *La Mujer Que Yo Perdí* (1949) and *Un Rincón Cerca del Cielo* (1952).

She branched out as a singer, a dancer and an actress in both dramatic and comic roles. During the 1950s, her successes included Emilio Fernández's *Reportaje* (1953) and *El Inocente* (1955), both with Infante; Fernández's *Una Cita de Amor* (1956); *Cabo de Hornos* (1955) with Spain's heartthrob Jorge Mistral; Tito Davison's *La Dulce Enemiga* (1956); and Tulio Demicheli's *Mi Desconocida Esposa* (1955).

By the 1960s, she had established herself as the preeminent Mexican film actress and one of its foremost box-office attractions. Her decade began auspiciously with leads in three of Luis Buñuel's best films: *Viridiana* (1961), co-winner of the Grand Prize at Cannes; *The Exterminating Angel* (1962); and *Simon of the Desert* (1965), winner of five prizes at the Venice Film Festival. She won the 1966 Pecime Award as Best Actress for the last-named film. Later, Buñuel would state that she was his favorite actress. Among her other notable films of the decade were: *Buenas Noches, Año Nuevo* (1964) with Ricardo Montalbán and Fanny Cano; *Los Cuervos Están de Luto* (1965) with Lilia Prado and Kitty De Hoyos; Jose Bolaños' *La Soldadera* (1966); Alberto Gout's *Estratega Matrimonio* (1966); the episode directed by Luis Alcoriza in *Juego Peligroso* (1966); Rogelio A. González's *La Guerra Xochitl* (1966); and Federico Curiel's *María Isabel* (1969).

She made her U.S. film debut as an aristocratic adulteress in Henri Verneuilis' weak adventure tale *Guns for San Sebastian* (1968, Metro-Goldwyn-Mayer), set in 18th-century Mexico, in which she costarred with Anthony Quinn and Charles Bronson. In her second U.S. film, she played Anna, a ruthless femme fatale, in Samuel Fuller's dark but uneven *Shark* (1970) with Burt Reynolds and Arthur Kennedy.

After her two unworthy U.S. film features she concentrated more on theater, television, and singing, and worked in films with less frequency. She spent three seasons playing in *Mame, Annie Get Your Gun*, and *Same Time, Next Year* on the Mexican stage. Her second marriage began on July 8, 1967, to Mexican pop singer Enrique Gúzman but ended in divorce. It produced one daughter, Alejandra, who later pursued a modest career as a singer.

She was lured back to films after a long absence by Conacine, one of the more innovative and independent Mexican film enterprises, for the title role of Marigaile in *Divinas Palabras* (1976), based on Valle Inclán's dark and somber novel. The film was directed by Juan Ibañez and lensed by the noted cinematographer Gabriel Figueroa. It costarred Rita Macedo. A raw and controversial film due to its depraved characters, profanity and nudity (especially for the then forty-five-year-old Pinal), it nevertheless contributed immeasurably to the maturity of Mexican cinema. She was impressive again the next year as the love-starved, manipulative spinster in Sergio Verjar's *El Llanto de la Mariposa*.

Thereafter, she concentrated on television and the publication of a women's magazine. She served a term as a deputy in the Mexican congress and has continued to appear on the stage, more recently in *Hello Dolly!*

Her films include *El Pecado de Laura* (1948); *Escuela Para Casados, Mujer de Medianoche* (1949); *La Marca de Zorillo, El Amor No es Ciego, Recién Casados, No Molestar, Una Gallega Baila el Mambo, Azahaes Para tu Boda* (1950); *La Estatua de Carne* (1951); *Por Ellas, Aunque Mal Paguen, Me Traes de una Ala, Dona Mariquita, El Casto Susano, Cuando los Hijos Pecan, Si, Mi Vida* (1952); *Reventa de Esclavas, Yo Soy Muy Macho, Las Tres Viudas Alegres, Las Carinosas, Si Volvieras a Mi* (1953); *Hijas Casaderas, Un Extraño en la Escalera, Pecado Mortal, La Vida Tiene Tres Días, Historia de Un Abrigo de Mink, El Vengador de Muñecas, Amor en Cuatro Tiempos, La Sospechosa* (1954); *Locura Pasional* (1955); *La Adultera, Dios No Lo Quiera, El Teatro del Crimen, Viva el Amor* (1956); *Préstame tu Cuerpo, Desnúdate Lucrecia, Una Golfa* (1957); *El Hombre Que Me Gusta, Las Locuras de Barbara* (1958); *Charleston, Uomini y Nobiluomini* (Italy) (1959); *Adiós, Mimi Pompón, Maribel y la Horas de Extraña Familia* (1960); *Divertimento* (1966); *El Cuerpo del Delito, Lobo, Veinticuatro El Despertar del Placer* (1968); *La Mujer de Oro, Los Novios, La Hermana Trinquete* (1969); *Bang, Bang y al Hoyo, Secreto de Confesión* (1970); *Como Hay Gente Sinvergüenza, Los Cacos* (1971); *Pubis Angelical* (1982—Argentina); *Modelo Antiguo* (1991).

In the 1990s and 2000s, she served as a federal deputy and senator and as a member of the assembly of the Partido Revolucionario Institucional (PRI). She continues to be very active in social causes.

DAVID REYNOSO

Brawny and rugged Mexican leading man David Reynoso personified the working-class man and antihero in scores of Mexican films (including two U.S. features) beginning in the early 1960s.

He was born on January 29, 1926, in Aguascalientes, Mexico. He worked as a taxi driver, factory worker and publicity agent, among other professions. At the age of seventeen, he was briefly a bullfighter. Upon becoming a radio broadcaster, he caught the attention of director Roberto Gavaldón, who cast him in his debut film, *Aquí Está Heraclio Bernal* (1957), opposite Antonio Aguilar, who became a helpful friend in the film industry.

Throughout the late fifties and early sixties he worked continuously as a journeyman all-purpose supporting actor, including in Emilio Fernández's epic of the Mexican Revolution *La Cucaracha* (1958) with Dolores del Río, Pedro Armendáriz, and María Félix, in which he portrayed a cowardly general. In 1964, he won the Mexican film industry's Pecime Diosa de Plata for Best Supporting Actor in *Canción del Alma*. However, the award and film (one of ten in 1964 in which he costarred) did not appear to have immediate impact upon the fortunes of his career as he continued to be cast in scores of mostly mediocre "B" films, usually as a villain. The exceptions to this trend were a few noteworthy films: the excellent comedy *El Gangster* (1964) with Arturo De Córdova; a pair of films directed by Rafael Baledón, *Los Hermanos Muerte* (1964) with Luis Aguilar, and *El Amor No Es Pecado* (1964) with Arturo De Córdova and Marga López.

Other films of this period included routine fare: *La Juventud Se Impone* (1964); with teen idol Enrique Guzmán; the comedy *El Tragabalas* (1964) with Flor Silvestre and Julio Aldama; the summer teen film *Guadalajara en Verano* (1964) with Elizabeth Campbell; the Jules Verne science fiction adventure *Aventura al Centro de la Tierra* (1964) with Kitty de Hoyos and Javier Solís; and the melodrama *Diablos en el Cielo* (1964) with Marga López. During this period he made his Mexican television debut and worked extensively.

At this juncture, he was unexpectedly given perhaps the best role of his career by first-time director Servando González, who cast him as the embittered widower and railroad engineer in the dark and arresting *Viento Negro* (1964). The film and Reynoso won wide international acclaim. He would recollect later, "*Viento Negro* gave me the opportunity to make a film of an international standard like *Rage*.... From there have come many films with me as the lead. As of this date I have more than 90 films, good, bad and indifferent."[48]

Despite the triumph of *Viento Negro*, four more routine films followed: *Joselito* (1965), the Spanish child star Joselito's third and last film; two westerns, *Alma Grande* (1965) and *Sangre en el Río Bravo* (1965) with Julio Alemán and Joaquín Cordero; and the melodrama *Tirando a Gol* (1965) with Lola Beltrán and Julissa. He then had one of his better roles in the excellent U.S.–Mexican co-production *Rage* (1966), filmed in Mexico and costarring Glenn Ford and Stella Stevens. Reynoso played a miner whose wife needs a cesarean childbirth while the down-and-out U.S. doctor (Ford) is infected with rabies. *Variety* noted, "It stars Glenn Ford and David Reynoso, to have equal attraction in the Latin American market ... the performances are excellent, the direction firm and the production first class."[49]

Reynoso's costars praised him. Ford stated, "In Hollywood, I have heard that Mexican cinema was undergoing a time of crisis. I cannot comprehend why: with such talents it would very well become the best cinema in the world."[50] Stevens commented, "Working with David Reynoso and Jose Elías Moreno has made me comprehend that there are actors of international stature that merit the opportunity to become acclaimed internationally. David is one of the most sensitive actors that I have ever known."[51]

Unfortunately, Reynoso followed this excellent film with a slew of films of mixed quality: the western *Fuera de la Ley* (1965) with Pedro Armendáriz, Jr.; the triangle drama *Seis Días Para Morir* (1966) with Argentinean sex goddess Libertad Leblanc; Francisco Del Villar's impressive *Domingo Salvaje* (1966) with Kitty de Hoyos; and the domestic comedy *Don*

Juan '67 (1966) with the fast-rising Isela Vega and Mauricio Garcés. Next, unbelievably, he was cast in two abysmal low-budget features (perhaps the very worst films of his career) directed by the veteran Chano Urueta: *Blue Demon Contra Cerebros Infernales* (1966) and *Blue Demon Contra Los Diabólicos* (1966) opposite the equally wasted Ana Martín.

Reynoso starred in numerous Mexican *telenovelas* and recorded several albums. He made his theatrical debut in 1958 in *Amante en la Ciudad* and did not return to theater until 1971, in *Y Dios Hizo la Mujer* with Irma Lozano.

Reynoso's film career reflected the ebb and flow of the Mexican film industry. The 1970s brought him only two films of worth: Roberto Gavaldón's *Las Figuras de Arena* (1971) with Elsa Aguirre; and Alejandro Galindo's *El Juicio de Martín Cortés* (1973). Another mixed-quality film was José Estrada's satire *¡Maten Ellon!* (1975).

In 1985, he made his second U.S. film, playing an ex-convict who befriends a vengeful ex-convict (Burt Reynolds, who also directed) in *Stick*, based on Elmore Leonard's novel and costarring Candice Bergen and Puerto Rican playwright José Pérez.

Reynoso was married to Bertha Martinez in 1952 and they had four children.

David Reynoso died of throat cancer on June 10, 1994, in Mexico City.

JAIME SÁNCHEZ

Jaime Sánchez played one of the most prized Latino roles of the decade, that of Ángel in Sam Peckinpah's *The Wild Bunch* (1969, Warner Bros.).

He was born on December 18, 1938, in Rincón, Puerto Rico, and his family moved to New York City when he was in his teens. He worked odd jobs at night and studied during the day. He joined the Neighborhood Playhouse and studied under his first drama teacher, Wynn Handman. He would later recall, "I wanted to be an actor because I am a shy person. The words you are asked to say are not your own, so I can express myself fully without fear or shyness."[52] In 1965, he became a member of the Actors Studio.

He made his film debut in a small role in Frank Perry's *David and Lisa* (1962—Continental), a much-honored film about the plight of two mentally ill youths (Janet Margolin, Keir Dullea) who fall in love. He then played the doomed Puerto Rican youth, Jesus, in Sidney Lumet's powerful *The Pawnbroker* (1965, American International Pictures) about a Holocaust survivor, an emotionally damaged Jewish pawnbroker (Rod Steiger) in Spanish Harlem. For his performance Sánchez won the Screen World Award and Laurel Award. His third film role was as war-shocked soldier Colombo in the Cornel Wilde–directed and –produced *Beach Red* (1967, United Artists).

On the stage, Sánchez played Chino in the original production of *West Side Story* for two years. He was cast in *Oh Dad, Poor Dad, Mother's Hung You in the Closet and I'm Feelin' So Sad* and then played Puck in *A Midsummer Night's Dream* in the New York Shakespeare Festival. He also played a role in *Othello*.

For his stage work, he won the 1965 Most Promising Actor of the Season Award; in the same year, he won the Clarence Derwent Award. Sánchez stated of his awards, "I have been lucky as an actor. It's incredible, and I knock on wood for it."[53]

In 1969, director Sam Peckinpah cast him in the role of the Villista youth Ángel in *The Wild Bunch* (1969, Warner Bros.). Despite the international acclaim of the film and Sánchez's own powerful performance, no more lead roles were forthcoming after that. He was reduced to featured roles in films unworthy of his talent: *On the Nickel* (1980, RPP); *Invasion USA* (1985, Cannon); *Big Trouble* (1986, Columbia Pictures); and occasional roles on television and in theater.

He has had supporting roles in several television films: *Wings of Fire* (1967, NBC); and *Florida Straits* (1986, Home Box Office), among others.

One of his more recent roles was as a Puerto Rican mobster in Brian de Palma's *Carlito's Way* (1994). He was also seen in *Piñero* (2001) and *Lavoe* (2011).

LALO SCHIFRIN

Lalo Schifrin has enjoyed a prolific career for more than thirty years as a composer for film and the concert hall.

He was born Lalo Boris Schifrin in Buenos Aires, Argentina, on June 21, 1932. As a child prodigy, he studied under his father, himself a concertmaster at the Teatro Colón and the Buenos Aires Philharmonic. He became hooked on jazz and cinema from an early age.

In 1950, after dropping out of law school, he went to Paris to study classical music and jazz, later representing Argentina in the 1955 International Jazz Festival. He would later fondly remember those years: "I was living a double life. During the day I was studying classical music and at night I was playing jazz in the jazz cellars. That gave me a good musical scope. The musical education in France is incredibly tough, and you have to do it well."[54]

He returned to Argentina and formed his own jazz band. In 1958 he traveled to New York City as an arranger for Xavier Cugat, and during the period 1960–1962 he was a pianist-composer with the Dizzy Gillespie band. In 1964, he moved to Hollywood and soon won renown for the theme of the television series *Mission: Impossible*. He scored his first film, *Rhino,* in 1964. On scoring for film he stated, "The film is the style of the music. It not only dictates it, it is the style. There is a certain texture in the photography and the acting which dictates the style of the music: it's not becomes, not influenced, but is! You can teach the methods of synchronization, what to do, what not to do, but there are some things you cannot teach. This is, what you call it, a gift that is given by somebody."[55]

Schifrin has been nominated for an Academy Award six times: for *Cool Hand Luke* (1967); *The Fox* (1967); *Voyage of the Damned* (1976); *The Amityville Horror* (1979); *The Competition* (1981); and *The Sting II* (1983). He has won four Grammy Awards and many other awards and honors in his long career. His other well-known film scores include *The Cincinnati Kid* (1965); *Bullit* (1968); *Dirty Harry* (1972); *Enter the Dragon* (1973); *The Four Musketeers* (1975); and *Boulevard Nights* (1979). He has scored numerous episodic television shows and television films.

His international films include the Argentinean *El Jefe* (1957), the French *Les Felins/Joy House* (1965), and the Spanish *Berlin Blues* (1988). His U.S. films include *Blindfold* (1966); *The President's Analyst* (1967); *The Brotherhood* (1968); *Che!* (1969); *Kelly's Heroes* (1970); *The Beguiled, Pretty Maids All in a Row, THX-1138* (1971); *Prime Cut* (1972); *Charlie Varrick, Magnum Force* (1973); *Sky Riders* (1976); *The Eagle Has Landed, Telefon* (1977); *Return from Witch Mountain* (1978); *Serial, Brubaker, The Competition* (1980); *Caveman, Buddy, Buddy* (1981); *The Sting II* (music adaptation), *Sudden Impact, The Osterman Weekend*

(1983); *Tank* (1984); *The Mean Season* (1985); *The Ladies Club* (1986); *The Fourth Protocol* (1987); *The Dead Pool, Berlin Blues* (Spa), *Little Sweetheart* (1988); *Return from the River Kwai* (1989); *Naked Tango* (1990); *The Deadly Art of Illusion* (1991); *The Beverly Hillbillies* (1993); and *Rush Hour 2* (2007). He continues to perform and release albums.

He lives in Beverly Hills with his wife Donna and continues to score films and television and perform in concerts, as well as serve on various commissions.

RAQUEL WELCH

Raquel Welch became the preeminent film sex symbol of the 1960s, through clever public relations campaigns that emphasized her physical attributes at the expense of her Latina heritage and a desire to develop her acting skills.

She was born Raquel Tejada in Chicago, Illinois, on September 5, 1940, to Armand Tejada, a Bolivian immigrant engineer, and his U.S.–born wife Josephine (Hall) Tejada. Her parents would later divorce after having one son and another daughter and moving to La Jolla, a community near San Diego, California. She won her first of numerous beauty contests at the age of fifteen. At La Jolla High School she was the vice president of the senior class, a member of the drama club and a cheerleader. She married her high school sweetheart, James Westley Welch, on May 8, 1959, and had two children, a son, Damon, and a daughter, Tahnee (later an actress of a very modest career). The couple divorced in 1963.

After several odd jobs she made her film debut in a bit part: *A House Is Not a Home* (1964, Paramount) with Robert Taylor and Shelley Winters. She had another bit part in *Roustabout* (1964, Paramount) with Barbara Stanwyck and Elvis Presley. Upon meeting Patrick Curtis, a former child actor and then public relations man (they married on Valentine's Day in 1967) her career quickly picked up. She had a featured role in a forgettable teenage beach film, *A Swingin' Summer* (1965), in which she was noticed. Part of her build-up campaign concentrated on "de-ethnicizing" her high Native American cheekbones in a way similar to how Rita Cansino had been turned into Rita Hayworth. It included altering her nose through plastic surgery.

Film production company 20th Century–Fox signed her up for a five-year contract and gave her the female lead in Richard Fleischer's impressive science-fiction film *Fantastic Voyage* (1966, 20th Century–Fox), about a team of scientists who are reduced to microscopic size so as to enter the bloodstream of a sick man and cure him. The film costarred Stephen Boyd and Arthur Kennedy. It was one of the most commercially and critically successful of her films. The *New York Times* called the film "a dazzling, nifty hunk of science-fiction" and commented that "Raquel Welch is the most pneumatic-looking thing in a skin-diving suit that has yet to appear on the screen."[56]

She was then cast in the remake of the well-remembered Victor Mature–Carole Landis film *One Million B.C.* (1967). Regarding the film, she said, "Neither the producers nor I ever pretended that One Million B.C. was going to be an art film. The audiences bought a very lovely girl, a great-looking guy and a lot of prehistoric monsters. Furthermore, I am grateful for the opportunity to appear in the film."[57] Her husband, in the meantime, had made her "the most photographed woman of 1966." She made the cover of *Life* (August 26, 1966), and according to the cover story she appeared on a total of ninety-two European and sixteen U.S. magazine covers. Like Rita Hayworth and Betty Grable before her, Raquel Welch became the world's favorite pin-up girl. She followed this momentum with a series of films that established her as one of the top box-office stars, although the films were often met with critical hostility. According to *Screen World*, Welch was listed number 21 as a box-office draw in 1968; number 15 in 1969; number 15 in 1970; and number 19 in 1972.[58]

She played a loyal prostitute to Marcello Mastroianni in the limp comedy *Shoot Loud, Louder ... I Don't Understand* (1966); a super secret agent in *Fathom* (1967) with Tony Franciosa; a member of a bungling gang in *The Biggest Bundle of Them All* (1965) with Edward G. Robinson and Robert Wagner; and another prostitute in the droll Italian comedy *The Oldest Profession* (1968), about prostitution through history, with Elsa Martinelli and Jeanne Moreau. The only film from this period to acquire positive critical comment was *Bedazzled* (1967), a British satire on the Faust legend in which, as Lillian the Lust, she garnered excellent notices. *Newsweek* said it was "a fluffy and funny version of the Faust legend in mod dress" and noted that "Raquel Welch bountifully incarnates Lillian lust ... and she wiggles worse, or better than a dyspeptic python in a nest of nails." She commented, "I'm doomed to be a sex goddess in a generation of flower children.... It's necessary at some point to destroy your beauty. It's a distraction or it creates resentment."[59]

She joined Bob Hope and his Christmas tour in South Vietnam during 1967. Back in the movies, she played the Mexican-American female lead, Maria, in Andrew V. Mclaglen's *Bandolero* (1968, 20th Century–Fox) opposite James Stewart, Dean Martin and Jock Mahoney; and a murder suspect in the underappreciated detective yarn *Lady in Cement* (1968, 20th Century–Fox) with Frank Sinatra and Dan Blocker. She then traveled to Spain to film *100 Rifles* (1969, 20th Century–Fox), in which she played a fiery Yaqui Indian maiden, Sarita, in a story set in Mexico in 1910. Costarring with her were Burt Reynolds, Jim Brown, and Fernando Lamas. Making an attempt at a serious drama, she played a go-go dancer pursued by a killer in *Flareup* (1969, Metro-Goldwyn-Mayer), in which she was very good. The *Los Angeles Times* stated, "This modest, diverting little movie proves the lady can act as well as look sexy. Miss Welch has perhaps never before had a role so tailored not just to the dimensions but her ability and personality as well."[60]

She expressed her career disappointment: "I'm ambitious, but it's not money that drives me. I want to do solid work that will win the respect of my peers. Like all actresses, I'm a shattered personality, with lots and lots of people inside me crying to get out."[61] She played a cameo role as a galley slave driver in the offbeat film adaptation of *The Magic Christian* (1970, Grand), a dark comedy with Peter Sellers and Ringo Starr. A Reuters poll of world film exhibitors revealed that she was among the top box-office draws. Her reported salary called for $330,000 per film plus a percentage of the gross receipts.

She then had the misfortune to star in one of the most universally vilified films in film history: *Myra Breckinridge* (1970, 20th Century–Fox), based on Gore Vidal's controversial best seller about a man who becomes a woman through surgery. The film's producer Robert Fryer stated, "If a man were going to become a woman, he would want to become the most beautiful woman in the world. He would become Raquel Welch."[62] Other roles were played by Mae West and John Huston. The production was characterized by constant animosity between Welch and West, who walked out of the film for three days. However, after returning to the set she was still optimistic: "There's no way that this is not going to be a good movie."[63] The film would become a critical and commercial disaster.

Attempting to put distance between herself and that film fiasco, she starred in her television special *Raquel* (April 26, 1970) on CBS. The *New York Daily News* commented of her special, "She displayed an eagerness to please and an amiable TV personality." She stated to the press, "I consider all of the roles that I have done as camp. They have not been things of my choice. They've been things the studios have put me in. So I guess the best way to survive them is to play them to the hilt."[64]

Her private life remained private, unlike those of previous sex symbols. She lived with her husband and his two children (whom she adopted) and she reportedly neither drank nor smoked.[65] She stated, "I have never appeared in the nude. It is a very personal thing to take off your clothes. I refused to do a nude scene in *100 Rifles*, and for weeks the telegrams flew back and forth, arguing about who was going to get me to do it. Finally, they gave up and [had] some other girl strip."[66] She attempted to demystify herself: "The label sex goddess somehow eclipses everything about you. A sex goddess isn't a real thing. She's a plastic lady. She's superwoman. But she has not intellect, no emotions, no nothing."[67]

Indifferent films continued to mar her desire for better things: a drab western, *Hannie Caulder* (1971) with Robert Culp; the British melodrama *The Beloved* (1972), unreleased in the U.S.; and the mishap *Bluebeard* (1972) with the equally wasted Richard Burton. She was reunited on film with Burt Reynolds in the detective yarn *Fuzz* (1972). *Time* commented, "Most of the comedy stays at this slapdash level. Raquel Welch, looking as ever like a performer hired to entertain visiting conventioneers, plays a policewoman assigned to bag a rapist who is prowling the parks." On a more personal level, she divorced her husband Patrick Curtis in 1971 and managed her own career thereafter.

Raquel Welch (alias Raquel Tejada) was born of a Bolivian father and an English-origin mother. She became the preeminent Hollywood sex goddess of the 1960s and the 1970s. She earned acclaim for her roles in *Kansas City Bomber* (1972) and *The Three Musketeers* (1973), among others. She starred on Broadway in *Woman of the Year* in the 1980s.

In an interview during this period she expressed an important change in her life and career: "You have to stand up for yourself in Hollywood or you'll be stepped on. I used to do what everybody told me to do. But no more. When I first complained about something I didn't like I was surprised by the response and respect I got."[68]

She produced her first film, *Kansas City Bomber* (1972, Metro-Goldwyn-Mayer), about the ups and downs of a roller derby star, in which she also starred. For the first time, she received uniformly excellent notices. One publication commented, "Raquel Welch has gotten it all together." The *Los Angeles Herald-Examiner* stated, "Raquel Welch has found the role she was born to play."[69] *The Hollywood Reporter* called hers "a dazzling performance."[70]

She was also well-received in the mystery-comedy *The Last of Sheila* (1973, Warner Bros.) in which she competed for the acting honors with a formidable cast that included James Mason, Dyan Cannon, James Coburn, and Joan Hackett.

She was then cast in the role of Constance in Richard Lester's pair of excellent swash-bucklers *The Three Musketeers* (1974, 20th Century–Fox) and *The Four Musketeers* (1975, 20th Century–Fox) with a fine cast that included Charlton Heston, Richard Chamberlain, Faye Dunaway, Oliver Reed, and Geraldine Chaplin. The *Los Angeles Times* wrote, "To put it bluntly, who would have guessed that Raquel Welch, cast as D'Artagnan's equally klutzy lady love, could emerge as a light comedienne as graceful as Rita Hayworth?"[71] *Time* called it "an absolutely terrific movie."[72] Both films were commercial hits as well.

After this high point, she was once again plagued with routine films: James Ivory's uneven tale of 1920s Hollywood and a Fatty Arbuckle–like comedian immersed in scandal *The Wild Party* (1975); Peter Yates' mediocre *Mother, Jugs and Speed* (1976) about a down-and-out ambulance service, with Bill Cosby; Richard Fleischer's weak adaptation of Mark Twain's *The Prince and the Pauper* retitled *Crossed Swords* (1978) with Charlton Heston, Oliver Reed, Rex Harrison and George C. Scott; and a French film, unreleased in the U.S., *L'Animal* (1977) with Jean-Paul Belmondo. In 1981, MGM fired her from *Cannery Row* (1982), which effectively resulted in her disappearance from the screen and the innuendo that she was "difficult." In a prolonged countersuit she was successful when the courts awarded her a sizable sum for damages. The resultant film turned out to be a box-office disaster.

Branching out into other artistic mediums, she starred in a television film, *The Legend of Walks Woman* (1978), which chronicled the entire life span of one Native American woman. Welch stated, "We tried to be accurate in our portrayal of Indian life. We wanted to show the strong influence of customs in tribal life. At the same time, we tried not to be over-reverent about it. We didn't want it to be the old noble-savage portrayal."[73]

She won good notices as Lauren Bacall's replacement in the Broadway musical *Woman of the Year* and then developed a nightclub act which she went on to perform in Las Vegas and Paris. Years before she had said, "Well, I'm grateful for the success my attributes have brought me, but I can't be a decorative phenomenon for the rest of my career. It's a terribly destructive image; I know, because at one point, I began believing it myself."[74]

During the 1996–97 television season she was a regular on *Central Park West* on CBS.

Raquel Welch, alias Raquel Tejada, was the biggest film star of Latina ancestry to evolve in the 1960s. Her most important legacy may be that she put aside the old Hollywood stereotype of a film sex symbol, survived the onslaught of adulation and prevented her voluptuous film persona from destroying her private life. She survived and in the process exhibited more talent than many or most of her detractors ever expected. When asked by Dick Cavett what had helped her survive being a sex symbol, she stated, "I think I have to say that one really important factor ... was my children ... I think children are another stabilizing factor to a woman.... They give you a purpose outside of what people may perceive.... Children love you unconditionally."[75]

During June 1997, she replaced Julie Andrews in *Victor, Victoria,* a long-playing Broadway musical. During July 1999, she married restaurateur Richard Palmer. It was her fourth marriage.

During the 2000s, she appeared in juicy roles in several television shows. She also gave a touchingly dramatic performance in *Tortilla Soup* (2001) and a comedic performance in *Legally Blonde* (2001).

IV

The 1970s

The 1970s was a decade marked by the continuing ideological hostility of East and West. In Latin America, revolutionary insurgencies continued against predatory military juntas and cliques financed and bolstered by U.S. dollars and military advisers. For the first time in U.S. history, a president resigned from office. Latinos and other minorities continued to press for social justice and inclusion.

The United States finally made its withdrawal from Vietnam during March 1973. Expectations were high for the signing of the Strategic Arms Treaty, but it was forestalled by the Soviet invasion into Afghanistan in 1978 and the continuing insurgencies in Nicaragua and El Salvador. In Nicaragua, in July 1979, the Sandinistas toppled the forty-year-old Somoza dictatorship, which had been supported by the United States. In the meantime, OPEC (Organization of Petroleum Exporting Countries) raised oil prices, throwing industrialized countries into economic disarray. The installation of nuclear weapons by the United States in Europe further worsened East-West relations. During 1979, the Western client state of the Shah of Iran was overthrown.

In Latin America, popular movements challenged long-established military dictatorships. The United States continued to support the status quo of such military regimes as Stroessner's in Paraguay and Duvalier's in Haiti. In 1973, the democratically elected Salvador Allende was overthrown by a U.S.–sponsored coup led by Pinochet. The push and pull forces of capital attracted millions of Mexican undocumented workers into low-paying work, while the media accused them of "stealing jobs."

In August 1974, President Richard M. Nixon resigned from office in disgrace. The subsequent Watergate hearings confirmed his criminal wrongdoing. President Jimmy Carter's focus on human rights was a new shift into U.S. foreign policy.

The decade witnessed the withering of the federal government's commitment to affirmative action and resignation to a permanent underclass. The *Bakke* decision, decided in 1978, undermined the concept of "affirmative action." Chicanos and Puerto Ricans made modest progress in access to college education, but both communities continued to have high poverty rates. With regard to the Chicano community, Rodolfo Acuña wrote, "In the 1970s, Mexicans again became bandits, blamed for stealing jobs. They were made outlaws in order to criminalize them, to justify paying them less and hounding them like the bandits of old, while at the same time demonstrating the pseudo-need to appropriate more funds to the INS. Many poor and middle-class Chicanos 'believed' that the undocumented worker had invaded their land and taken their jobs."[1]

At the same time, Republicans courted Cubans and middle-class Chicanos like a possessive and jealous suitor. By the end of the decade, the Chicano and Puerto Rican civil rights movements had obtained some goals, among them university Chicano and Puerto Rican studies departments and bilingual education. The Latino cinema emerged midway through the decade, born out of the struggle for social justice. In mainstream films, however, in terms of filmic images, there were no gains, only qualitative losses.

Film Images and Film Stars

The 1970s saw the continued decline of film box-office receipts and the unchecked inroads of television. The Hollywood film industry nevertheless enjoyed a renaissance with the infusion of new talent and landmark films. For Latinos, their prevailing film images reflected those in the news media: illegal aliens, gang members, *narcotraficantes*, *cantineras* and violence-prone revolutionaries.

A box-office glut between 1969 and 1971 was a disaster for the Hollywood film industry. Numerous expensive films flopped, leaving many studios at the point of insolvency not experienced since the period of 1931 to 1932, at the height of the Great Depression. Desperate management changes by conglomerates to control studios were barely able to keep some of them in business. Inflation and the recession raised the average movie budget to seven million dollars, and by the middle of the next decade it had climbed to twelve million dollars.

Increasingly, the producer-director became more common and there were a growing number of independent maverick producers as well. Real film "stars" became an endangered species in the film marketplace. For example, Robyn Karney noted, "A star in the past was the incarnation of a particular stereotype. When the stereotypes were good of their kind there was much fun to be had in meeting them in as many situations as the ingenuity of the screenwriter could muster.... The old stars scarcely even acted. But the new stars act away as if their lives depended on it.... The lessons of Stella Adler and the Actors Studio had been taken to heart and interiorized. The 70's were a decade of studious professionalism."[2]

Regardless of the "studious professionalism," most of the Hollywood film fare of the 1970s was either escapist or true to the old Hollywood formulas. Much of it provided film-goers solace from the disenchantment of the Vietnam War, inflation, Watergate, and the energy crisis. Some of the key films of the 1970s included *Love Story* (1970, 20th Century–Fox), George Lucas' *American Graffiti* (1972, Universal), *The Exorcist* (1973, 20th Century–Fox) and Steven Spielberg's *Close Encounters of the Third Kind* (1977, Columbia). Later in the decade, there were sequels, remakes, and an increasing amount of self-indulgent film special effects that became increasingly repetitive, redundant, and oversaturated. Luckily, at periodic intervals the decade brought some offbeat and landmark films made by some new and visionary directors: Francis Ford Coppola's *The Godfather* (1972, Paramount) and *The Godfather II* (1974, Paramount) explored the fine line between free enterprise and criminal enterprise; Sidney Lumet's *Network* (1976, Metro-Goldwyn-Mayer) focused on the pervasive influence of television; Martin Scorsese's *Taxi Driver* (1976, Columbia) depicted the alienation and violence of the mean streets; Roman Polanski's *Chinatown* (1974, Paramount) examined the corrupted relationship between politics and economics; and Alan J. Pakula's *All the President's Men* (1976, Warner Bros.) questioned the ethics of business and a president's administration.

As for Latinos, they inevitably turned up as the usual suspects: illegal aliens, gang bangers, prostitutes, *narcotraficantes* and revolutionaries. One positive and welcome advent was the demise of the spaghetti western, which maintained its singular sense of style, as well as its unrepentant and reprehensible image of Mexicans as bandits and *cantineras*. In *The Mercenary* (1970, United Artists), a European-American hired gunfighter (Franco Nero) teamed up with a notorious Mexican desperado (Tony Musante) to rob banks and free revolutionaries. In *A Bullet for Sandoval* (1970, United Artists), an infamous Mexican bandit (Ernest Borgnine) is killed in a knife duel in a bull ring at the hands of a Confederate deserter (George Hilton), after the former went on a rampage in northern Mexico. In *A Town Called Hell* (1971, Brenmar), a priest and an ex-revolutionary (Robert Shaw) seek a desperate refuge in a town run by an evil and vicious Mexican bandit (Telly Savalas). Similar characters and geography were depicted in such spaghetti films as *Today We Kill ... Tomorrow We Die!* (1971, Cine); *Catlow* (1971, Metro-Goldwyn-Mayer); *Blindman* (1972, Fox); and *Compañeros* (1970, Trintone). In *Adios Sabata* (1971, United Artists), Sabata (Yul Brynner), a European-American soldier of fortune, joins a Mexican bandit, Scudo (Pedro Sanchez), and his motley crew in order to rob a gold shipment from Maximilian's occupation forces for Juaristas' nationalist forces. In the sequel, *Return of Sabata* (1972, United Artists), headlined by Lee Van Cleef, the cast was populated only by two types of Mexicans: bandits and *cantineras*. One of the genre's most ambitious efforts was Sergio Leone's *Duck, You Sucker* (1972, United Artists), set during the Mexican Revolution. It chronicled the tale of a fugitive Irish revolutionary, Sean Mallory (James Coburn), who is fascinated with explosives. He joins a cutthroat group of murderous bandits led by Juan Miranda (Rod Steiger). When the spaghetti western genre finally died, it had no Mexican mourners.

However, the portrayal of Mexican characters in domestic westerns was no better or less stereotypical during the decade. In *Barquero* (1970, United Artists), Marie Gomez played a promiscuous *cantinera*. In *Cannon for Cordoba* (1970, United Artists), General Pershing recruits the aid of a fearless intelligence officer (George Peppard) in order to put an end to the marauding band of Mexican bandits led by Cordoba (Raf Vallone). In *Machismo: 40 Graves for 40 Guns* (1979, BI), yet another Mexican bandit gang wreaks havoc, headed by Hidalgo (Robert Padilla). Mexican desperados and bandits were alive and well in *Macho Callahan* (1970, American Entertainment), played by Pedro Armendáriz, Jr.; in *Scandalous John* (1971, Disney), by Alfonso Arau; and in *El Condor* (1970, National General), by Patrick O'Neal.

In *The Magnificent Seven Ride* (1972, United Artists), the third and last sequel to *The Magnificent Seven*, Chris (Lee Van Cleef) commands a group of misfits to rescue several widowed European-American women from a band of murderous Mexican bandits. In *The Revengers* (1972, National General), an embittered Civil War veteran (William Holden) leads six convicts in order to track down one renegade European-American who has murdered his family and been granted refuge in a Mexican town, inhabited exclusively by robbers, bandits and murderers. In *Two Mules for Sister Sara* (1970, Universal), the technical and daring exploits of one European-American soldier of fortune (Clint Eastwood) turn the tide of battle for the Juaristas fighting the French Occupation. Eastwood replicated his role of mentor and liberator of Chicanos (Stella Garcia, John Saxon) struggling to recover their dispossessed land in *Joe Kidd* (1972, Universal), directed by John Sturges (of *The Magnificent Seven* fame). In turn, Howard Hawks' *Rio Lobo* (1970, National General) had something rare. It featured a Mexican Confederate officer, Cardona (Jorge Rivero), heroically aiding a colonel (John Wayne) who is tracking a fugitive who stole a shipment of gold. In *The Wrath of God* (1972, Metro-Goldwyn-Mayer), a defrocked priest (Robert Mitchum) is enlisted by a Mexican revolutionary to assassinate a villainous cacique (Frank Langella). Finally, in John Sturges' *Valdez Is Coming* (1971, United Artists), a humble Mexican-American sheriff (Burt Lancaster) heroically fights a wealthy rancher (Jon Cypher) who caused the death of an innocent African American man.

Latinos in contemporary settings in general had similar negative images. One new genre that sprang up in the decade was the Latino gang film. In *Trackdown* (1976, United Artists), a cowboy big brother (Jim Mitchum) embarks on a quest to find a country girl involved in the low life of Los Angeles, fighting off hordes of Chicano gang bangers in the process. In another simple-minded revenge film, *Assault on Precinct 13* (1976, TR), a multicultural gang lays siege to a police station for no apparent reason. Yet another film, *Walk Proud* (1979, Universal), focused on the purported rites of passage of Emilio (Robby Benson, with brown contact lenses and brown make-up), who falls in love with a rich European-American girl

Don Stroud and Stella Garcia in *Joe Kidd* (1970, Universal).

(Sarah Holcomb). Predictably, the interracial couple find true happiness only when Emilio discovers that his father is European-American, and he is therefore only half Chicano! In a more convincing and worthy film, *Boulevard Nights* (1979, Warner Bros.), a hard-working older brother, Raymond (Richard Yniguez) tries to help his younger brother Chuco (Danny De La Paz) leave the gang life.

Other films with contemporary settings included *Which Way Is Up?* (1977, Universal), in which an African American agricultural worker empathizes with the plight of Mexican farm workers (Daniel Valdez and El Teatro Campesino). A less positive image was the subject of *Up in Smoke* (1978, Paramount), in which Pedro de Pacas (Cheech Marin) and Man Stoner (Tommy Chong) are a pair of hard-pressed, marijuana-induced rockers. The film *Red Sky in the Morning* (1970, Universal) had a Chicano youth character (Desi Arnaz, Jr.) and was set in New Mexico; *Mr. Majestyk* (1974, United Artists) had Linda Cristal as a Chicana union activist battling racist growers assisted by Charles Bronson; and *The Last Movie* (1971, Universal), was set in the Andes and chronicles the odyssey of self-discovery of a stuntman (Dennis Hopper) and his relationship with a Peruvian *cantinera* (Stella Garcia) after a movie crew has left the location.

Latinos were on display in *Dog Day Afternoon* (1975, Warner Bros.), in which Chu Chu Malava portrayed the Puerto Rican boyfriend of the neurotic lead character; in *The Big Fix* (1978, Universal), Ofelia Medina turned up as a barrio suspect sought by a 60s radical-turned-detective (Richard Dreyfuss); in *Blue Collar* (1978, Universal), Jimmy Martinez played a union organizer; in *The Goodbye Girl* (1977, Metro-Goldwyn-Mayer), the two muggers were Latinos (Pancho González, Jose Machado); and in *Midway* (1976, Universal), the incidental Latino was named Chili Bean (Erik Estrada).

Two films during the decade depicted with depth and power the colonialism and neo-colonialism in Latin America. Gillo Pontecorvo's *Burn* (1970, United Artists), chronicled the revolutionary uprising on a Caribbean island during the colonial period. A second film, Costa-Gavras' *State of Siege* (1973, Columbia), dramatized the true story of a U.S. counterinsurgency adviser (Yves Montand) who was kidnapped by the Tupamaro guerrillas of Uruguay. A third but much lesser film, Sam Peckinpah's *Bring Me the Head of Alfredo Garcia* (1974, United Artists), attempted to capture the gradual corruption and moral ambiguities of the Mexican Revolution.

An important development in mid-decade was the emergence of Chicano and Cuban-

Evaristo Marquez (left) and Marlon Brando appeared in one of the most powerful indictments of colonialism in Latin America, Gillo Pontecorvo's *Burn* (1970, United Artists).

American cinema. In 1976, Efraín Gutiérrez became the first Chicano to direct (as well as write, produce and star) what is considered the first Chicano feature film, *Please Don't Bury Me Alive*. He followed it with two other films, *Amor Chicano Es Para Siempre* (1977) and *Run, Tecato, Run* (1977). In 1978 came Alejandro Grattan's *Only Once in a Lifetime,* and in 1979, Jesús Salvador Treviño directed the first Chicano/Mexican co-production, *Raíces de Sangre/Roots of Blood*. All five films were bilingual and finally placed the long overdue Chicano experience on screen. Unfortunately, all of these features have become "lost films." Gutiérrez sold the rights to his films to the Mexican company Azteca Films, which has not made his films available either in video or in film format. *Only Once in a Lifetime* is likewise unavailable either on film or video and has not been seen since its initial release. Finally, *Raíces de Sangre* is owned by the Mexican government, which has been impervious to repeated attempts by Treviño to have the film available on film and video. In 1978, Leon Ichaso and Orlando Jiménez Leal directed the first Cuban-American feature film, *El Super,* which depicted the experience of the Cuban exile, as well as that of the new generation born or raised in the United States.

The decade also marked the emergence of several Chicana filmmakers, specifically in the area of documentaries and short film. In 1979, Sylvia Morales' documentary *Chicana* presented a feminist critique of Luis Valdez' *I Am Joaquin*. Rosa Linda Fregosa noted, "The aesthetic discourse of Morales's film represents a rupture from that of the male-centered cultural nationalism, principally because the film critiques all forms of domination, including Chicano patriarchal lineage. Indeed, the ten year absence between the two films permits us to characterize *Chicana* both as the embodiment of the feminist critiques of cultural nationalist ideology and as a counterdiscursive tendency within the Chicano movement, never before articulated in a cinematic practice."[3] Lourdes Portillo and Nina Serrano's short film *Despues del Terremoto (After the Earthquake)* (1979) focused on the emigration of a Nicaraguan woman to the San Francisco area in the aftermath of the devastating 1976 earthquake in their homeland from a decidedly Third World feminist perspective.

If Latino filmmakers faced ethnic discrimination and economic adversity to make films, Latinas more often than not faced discrimination, class bias, and sexism as well in their creative efforts. They have been excluded from both mainstream and Latino feature films as directors. Their body of work has consisted of short films, documentaries, experimental films/videos, and television. As Rosa Linda Fregosa rightly points out, Latina filmmakers have been excluded from overdue recognition and scholarly study due to the emphasis on "bigness" and rampant sexism in society and the Hollywood film industry.[4]

An important venue for showcasing Latino shorts, videos, and feature films was the growing number of Latino-themed film festivals: the Chicano Film Festival in San Antonio (founded in 1975 and renamed the International Film Festival in the late 1970s, and finally called the CineFestival beginning in 1981); the National Film Festival in New York (1981 onwards); the Chicano Latino Festival; and the Latino Film Festival in Los Angeles beginning in 1999.

As for Latino film stars, they were increasingly rare during the 1970s. The one bona fide Latino "star" to emerge during the decade was the Chicano comedian Cheech Marin. He and Tommy Chong had begun their comedy team of Cheech and Chong in the late sixties in clubs, and later they recorded comedy albums. By the time they starred in their first feature film, *Up in Smoke* (1978, Paramount), they enjoyed a growing cult following, especially among the youth counterculture. Their films proved hugely successful commercially and they rose quickly to become one of the top box-office attractions during the late 1970s and early 1980s. Their humor, crude to some and drug-oriented to others, soon proved repetitive. The team broke up and Marin went on to write, direct and star in a key Chicano film of the 1980s, *Born in East L.A.*, as well as solo endeavors.

Other Latino film stars were equally talented, but their careers as leading men proved short-lived. One of these was the popular Mexican leading man Jorge Rivero, who was contracted to costar opposite John Wayne in Howard Hawks' western *Rio Lobo* (1970), but thereafter failed to get roles of equal prominence or films of similar commercial success. After infrequent roles in U.S. film, Rivero continued his career in Mexico. One of the most promising new Chicano leading men was Richard Yniguez, who began a prolific career on television and made an impact as the Chicano cop who kills the crazed sniper in *The Deadly Tower* (1975). He made further impact as the star of *Boulevard Nights* (1979) and *Raíces De Sangre/Roots of Blood* (1979). Thereafter, due to his efforts to improve the opportunities and images of Latinos he was blacklisted and his promising career received a mortal blow. Another young and promising talent was actor-singer Daniel Valdez, formerly of the famed Teatro Campesino, whose film debut was in *Which Way Is Up?* (1977). He waited another four years for a star-making role, in Luis Valdez' *Zoot Suit* (1981); however, like others, he found no other important roles to prolong his career as a leading man. Still other actors, like Pepe Serna and Henry Darrow, worked regularly in television and film, but never quite received the deserved opportunities to win star status.

Latina actresses met with similar fate. Here and there they won leading roles that brought them temporary prominence and even fame, but not the volume or quality roles on which to build a long career as leading ladies. Hollywood's obsession with Latinas as the "exotic other" resulted in the contracting of two already established Mexican film stars, Isela Vega and Ofelia Medina, and the Nicaraguan model-turned-actress Barbara Carrera. Isela Vega was in vogue briefly, with starring roles in Sam Peckinpah's *Bring Me the Head of Alfredo Garcia* (1974), *Drum* (1976) and *Barbarosa* (1982). However, by then her age caught up with her, as women beyond thirty-five are anathema in Hollywood, and soon thereafter she worked in Mexican films. Ofelia Medina's U.S. film career was even shorter—only one film, *The Big Fix* (1978). Barbara Carrera made her film debut in *The Master Gunfighter* (1975) as a Mexican señorita and soon thereafter was typecast as a dark lady of seduction in a series of films and in the very popular miniseries *Centennial* (1979). Her career was the most durable of the three, although it was not spectacular. Other Latinas making an impact as leading ladies included Stella Garcia, who scored in a pair of films: Dennis Hopper's *The Last Movie* (1971, Universal) and John Sturges' *Joe Kidd* (1972, Universal) with Clint Eastwood. Subsequently, her career was confined to television and she later faded into obscurity.

Representative Films

Boulevard Nights (1979, Warner Bros.)

The end of the decade saw the release of a series of youth gang–themed films, the best of which was *Boulevard Nights*. But the film gained controversy in the Chicano community.

The gang genre films produced a new ethnic stereotype, especially about Latino youth in the inner-city barrios. At times the films themselves contributed to the intergang rivalry in some communities. For example, Walter Hill's *The Warriors* (1979, Paramount), which focused on a New York City gang, became a *cause célèbre* when three gang murders occurred in theaters where the film was shown. The same year another film was released, *Walk Proud* (1979, Universal), which depicted Chicano gangs. The Hollywood film industry quickly jumped on the bandwagon with a series of other quickly made and low-budget films that perpetuated the new stereotype with gratuitous violence. Ironically, the films coincided with the rise of ethnic youth gangs which were caused primarily by cutbacks in social programs and the demise of entry-level jobs in manufacturing, which had left the U.S. in search of cheap labor abroad. James Diego Vigil noted, for example, "Traditionally, Mexican family and extended family ties are strong, and they foster respect for the authority of elders, especially older males.... However, the corrosive effects of economic hardship, social discrimination, and culture conflict on many barrio immigrant families have been noted ... the great majority of gang members interviewed for this study report family histories full of stress, and many of them explicitly maintain that they became involved in a gang ... to seek a kind of support they felt lacking from family sources."[5]

In 1981, Luis Valdez' *Zoot Suit* depicted the zoot suit riots and the Sleepy Lagoon case of 1942. With regard to *Boulevard Nights,* the film ranks above the others but below *Zoot Suit. Boulevard Nights* was shot in East Los Angeles and it was even more convincing because of its almost all–Chicano cast.

The narrative of *Boulevard Nights* revolved around the efforts of an older brother, Raymond Àvila (Richard Yniguez), to get his younger brother Chuco (Danny De La Paz) to break away from the gang life and abandon his preoccupation of cruising East Los Angeles' famed Whittier Boulevard. Raymond, an ex-serviceman, works in an auto shop and is about to marry Shady Landeros (Marta Du Bois). He gets his brother a job in the shop, but Chuco proves unable to be responsible, and is subsequently fired while under the influence. The experience further draws Chuco into the gang lifestyle. At Raymond and Shady's wedding, a rival gang member accidentally kills Mrs. Avila (Betty Carvalho) while trying to get to Chuco. Overcome with grief, both Raymond and Chuco swear revenge despite Shady's efforts to dissuade them. At a subsequent shoot-out, Chuco is mortally wounded as his brother attempts to rescue him. At the end, both Raymond and Shady are left in an empty house contemplating their troubled past and hopeful future.

The chemistry between Yniguez and De La Paz is especially touching. They convincingly depict the pain of codependency created among families when a member becomes caught up in the *locura* of *la vida loca*. However, the film failed to depict the long-established community efforts to work with gang youth and the importance of education as an alternative. The film's star, Richard Yniguez, tried to convince the studio to market the film as being about the love between two brothers, but the studio balked at the idea and promoted it as a gang film and emphasized the elements of violence. As a consequence, the film was the subject of pickets by some in the Chicano community and Yniguez was blackballed for a number of years by the film industry.

The film received mixed reviews. The *New York Times* noted that "it trivializes the Mexican-American experience by equating it with the melodrama of many other minor movies about gang wars. The film, written by Desmond Nakano and directed by Michael Pressman, is so busy trying to meet the needs of a conventional narrative that it appears to have no point of view about its characters.... With the possible exception of Mr. De La Paz, whose haunted looks suggest someone deeply troubled, the actors are not very good."[6]

The Los Angeles Herald-Examiner noted, "The movie is so fearful of its subject—gang warfare in East L.A.—that it gives 'responsibility' a bad name.... Chuco, in De La Paz's prehensible performance, almost matches DeNiro's Johnny Boy—and, perhaps, James Dean—as often as he echoes them."[7] Chicano journalist Frank Del Olmo wrote, "[The] cause of gang violence, barely touched on in *Boulevard Nights,* is another shortcoming in an otherwise well-intentioned effort. But perhaps the saddest exclusion is the film's failure to mention that there are people working, often very hard and at great sacrifice, to help real-life Chucos of East Los Angeles and other barrios."[8]

Burn! (1970, United Artists)

Burn! is one of the most powerful, incisive and uncompromising films ever made in its indictment of colonialism and neocolonialism. Although the film was only half-heartedly promoted by the studio that made it, it has acquired a well-deserved cult film status.

The film depicted the intrigues of Sir William Walker (Marlon Brando), an agent for the British government who works to foment a revolution in the Portuguese Caribbean island colony of Quemada. As part of his scheme, he recruits and trains an African dock worker, José Dolores (Evaristo Márquez), to lead a rural insurgency, while at the same time orchestrating a revolt in the capital led my a mulatto, Teddy Sanchez (Renato Salvatori). When the Portuguese finally leave and Dolores marches into the capital, he becomes aware of Walker's duplicity. Sanchez is chosen as president and Dolores disbands his army when he realizes that he lacks the education and skills to run a government.

Ten years later, another revolution erupts and Walker is recalled by the corrupt Sanchez administration to help develop a counterinsurgency against Dolores. As the repression becomes more brutal, Sanchez attempts to alter the war strategy, but he is arrested and promptly executed by clique of sugar growers. Dolores is ultimately defeated, captured and sentenced to die. Walker attempts to rescue him in order to deny him martyrdom, but Dolores sees through his plan and goes to his death.

The character of José Dolores was a composite of several Third World revolutionaries: Toussaint Louverture of Haiti, Augusto Sandino of Nicaragua, Patrice Lumumba of the Congo, Emiliano Zapata of Mexico, and Ernesto "Che" Guevara of Argentina. The film was directed by Gillo Pontecorvo, who had made the seminal *The Battle of Algiers* (1969). Pontecorro coscripted *Burn!* with Franco Solinas, who had begun by scripting spaghetti westerns and would later also write another key film about Latin American neocolonialism, *State of Siege* (1973). Another alumnus of spaghetti westerns, Ennio Morricone, composed the haunting music score. The film's star, Marlon Brando, was the prime mover of the film and he said of his motives, "You can say important things to a lot of people. About discrimination and hatred and prejudice. I want to make pictures that explore the themes current in the world today."[9]

The film, which was released at the end of the polemical sixties, was dismissed by some critics, who were obviously offended by its politics. But the fact remains that the film offered a deeply analytical and critical deconstruction of colonialism and neocolonialism in Latin America. The *Los Angeles Herald-Examiner* wrote, "'*Burn*' is a film to gaze and brood over. It is a film about idealism fractured by doubts, truth smeared by heroics. It is a film about freedom and inquisition, politics, economics, power and faith.... Brando has soured the plumpness of the voice he used in *Mutiny on the Bounty*. It matches well the pain of indifference, the knowledge of lack of understanding which dwells within Walker. He rivets our attention with the ache of his poise ... Evaristo Márquez has great presence ... yet he can only really symbolize the man struggling to make himself worthy of the myth which he knows will wing wide from his gallows."[10]

Duck, You Sucker (1972, United Artists)

Sergio Leone's *Duck, You Sucker*, set during the Mexican Revolution, was the director's last spaghetti western. Regrettably, it also proved that the old stereotypes about Mexicans survived intact for more than half a century.

The film is set in 1914 during the Mexican Revolution and it depicts the activities of a Mexican bandit, Juan Miranda (Rod Steiger), and his gang, which includes his aged father and six criminal sons. They run across Sean Mallory (James Coburn), a fugitive Irish revolutionary, who is haunted by the struggle in his homeland. The latter is an expert on explosives and Miranda persuades him to assist him in robbing an apparently impregnable bank. By coincidence, a revolutionary group takes the city the same day. Much to Miranda's surprise, the bank contains prisoners instead of gold and Miranda is quickly heralded as a new revolutionary hero and leader. After several military exploits, Mallory is killed in a battle, still haunted by his beloved Ireland.

Once again, the film exhibits the stubborn and unrepentant side of spaghetti westerns to portray Mexicans as violent, criminal and cruel. Juan Miranda is portrayed by Rod Steiger in the infamous Mexican bandit tradition, like Wallace Beery's Pancho Villa in *Viva Villa!* (1934); Eli Wallach's Calvera in *The Magnificent Seven* (1960); Paul Newman's Juan Carrasco in *The Outrage* (1964); and Wallach's Tuco in *The Good, the Bad, and the Ugly* (1968). Throughout the narrative, the film depicts Miranda's innate inability to control his violence and criminality. Upon first meeting Miranda, Mallory comments in surprise, "So, you can read!" Later, Miranda, despite expressing his sympathy for the revolutionary cause, reveals his opportunism by saying, "My country is me and my family." Even when he is made a leader, Miranda comments to Mallory, "I don't want to be a hero. All I want is the money." Once again, only a European, in this case an Irishman, possesses the technical skills and common sense to lead the Mexican revolutionary forces to victory.

Only Once in a Lifetime (1978, Sierra Madre/Esparza)

Only Once in a Lifetime holds a distinct honor of being one of the first Chicano film features ever made. Unfortunately for both scholars and the public at large, it has not been seen since its initial release.

It was the first film produced by Sierra Madre Productions (founded by Juan Silverio

González and Alejandro Grattan) and Moctesuma Esparza. It was directed by Alejandro Grattan, who also wrote the screenplay. However, the main driving force behind the film was Juan Silverio González (also known as Johnny D. González), who is listed as associate producer, along with Louis Dello Russo. González was one of the first Chicanos to do a mural (in 1969) in the advent of the Chicano movement. He was also the founder of the famous Goetz Art Gallery (1969–1981) in East Los Angeles, as well as a pioneer in the East Los Angeles rock and roll movement of the 1960s.

The narrative revolves around Francisco Domínguez (Miguel Robledo), a Mexican immigrant whose life takes a tragic turn when his wife Juanita (Socorro Swan) dies during childbirth, along with her child. Thereafter, Domínguez, a gifted artist, is consumed by his mourning and his failure as an artist.

Over the course of one day, his world is further reduced to meaningless existence. He is ordered by a zoning inspector (Frank Whiteman), not to sell his paintings and is also informed by the owner (Claudio Brook) of an upscale art gallery that if he doesn't make a drastic change in his painting style, he can no longer represent Domínguez. As he attempts to establish a livelihood, he is advised by a social worker (Elaine Partnow) that he should forget about his painting and become a more productive person.

He falls into a deep depression and decides to end his life. However, he puts his life in order, including finding a home for his aged mutt. He encounters an aging trollop (Sheree North), who fantasizes about old, romantic Mexican films. Despite her eccentric personality, she imbues Domínguez with a life force.

In the process of finding a home for his mutt, he falls for a spinster teacher, Consuelo (Estrellita Lenore López), who is also undergoing a life crisis. They discover, much to their pleasant surprise, that both have been deemed "failures." However, as they become closer, they realize the humanity and struggle of each other, as well as their worth. For Domínguez, it comes as an unexpected turn of events, for he had resigned himself that this kind of love came "only once in a lifetime."

Only Once in a Lifetime was met with warm and enthusiastic reviews. It premiered at the Chicano Film Festival in San Antonio, Texas. The National Council of La Raza sponsored a fundraising screening at the Kennedy Center in Washington, D.C. In addition, *Nuestro* magazine selected it as "The Chicano Film of the Year." The *Hollywood Reporter* commented that it was "spiced with liberal doses of humor" and "strong cast and story, which transcends ethnic concerns to embrace universal themes."[11] However, more recently, Christine List has noted, " The director merely uses the conventions of the love story genre to reproduce the structure of psychological dependency that contrasts Consuelo's actions, thereby circumscribing her agency within the traditional parameters of la familia.... The melodrama ends up directing the audience's desire towards fulfillment of Consuelo's character as a female subject through marriage and away from the social problem of assimilation initially proposed by the text."[12]

This evocative film, shot mostly on location in East Los Angeles, made use of the numerous murals and Chicano ambiance there. The role of Domínguez was intended for Gilbert Roland, the dashing Mexican star who had begun in films in the 1920s as a romantic leading man, but he was unavailable, and it was given to stage veteran Miguel Robledo, who played it touchingly and resembled Roland in both physique and acting style. Newcomer Estrellita

Lenore López played the female lead effectively, and veteran Sheree North is her usual excellent self as the slightly over-the-hill lady of the night. The music score (by Robert O. Ragland) and evocative cinematography (Turner Browne) were additional assets of the film.

Raíces de Sangre/Roots of Blood (1979, Conacine)

Jesús Salvador Treviño's *Raíces de Sangre* is the only film to focus on the common economic destinies of Chicanos and Mexicans. It also remains as the first and only Chicano/Mexican film co-production.

The film's narrative focuses on a Harvard-educated Chicano lawyer, Carlos Rivera (Richard Yniguez), who comes back to his hometown of Socorro, Texas, along the border with Mexico, to work one summer with the Barrio Unido Community Center. He reluctantly becomes involved in organizing workers along the border—Mexicans who work in a *maquiladora* and Chicanos in a factory owned by a multinational corporation. In time, Lupe (Roxanna Bonilla-Giannini) and Juan (Pepe Serna), both childhood friends, make him understand the similar socioeconomic factors that affect both groups of workers.

On the Mexican side of the border, Román Carvajal (Ernesto Gómez Cruz) is fired from the garment maquiladora for undermining the corrupt company union by organizing workers. Hilda Gutiérrez (Malena Doria) and Rosamaría (Adriana Rojo) work to organize

Roxanna Bonilla-Giannini and Richard Yniguez in *Raíces de Sangre/Roots of Blood* (1970, Conacine). The film was the first Chicano-Mexico co-production.

the women workers in unison with Juan and Barrio Unido's efforts. The union's efforts culminate with a rally in Socorro, which the police violently break up. It results in the death of Juan. Later, both the Mexican and Chicano workers hold a candlelight vigil along both sides of the border to commemorate their fallen comrades. From the Mexican side, Carvajal cries out, "Que viva la raza!" From the U.S. side, Rivera replies, "Que viva la raza unida!"

The film was shot in Mexicali, Baja California, Mexico. Ironically, the scenes of the U.S.–owned maquiladora were shot in an abandoned Mattel toy factory, which had closed when they found cheaper labor in Taiwan. The film was financed by the Mexican government film company Conacine. Director-screenwriter Jesús Salvador Treviño commented about the purpose of the film, "I made *Raíces de Sangre* to examine the question of who the Chicano is and who the Mexican is.... As I got more into the subject matter, I began to realize that a film like *Raíces de Sangre* could explain the Chicano reality to the Mexicans but could also explain the Mexican reality to Chicanos."[13]

The film received enthusiastic reviews in both Mexico and the United States. *Variety* called it "a solidly made call to political involvement and activism which effectively points up the problems of Mexican on the border in very human terms" and noted, "Writer-director Jesús Treviño stages that action simply and forcefully.... Richard Yniguez is significantly more effective here than he was earlier this year in 'Boulevard Nights.' ... Neo-realist and Third World cinema often seems somewhat remote from American concerns, but *Raíces de Sangre*, through its evenhanded considered polemics and sheer proximity, brings another culture's problems a lot closer to home."[14]

More recently, Rosa Linda Fregoso has pointed out about the film, "By portraying Mex-

Director Jesús Salvador Treviño (third from left) shooting *Raíces de Sangre* (1970, Conacine).

icans and Chicanos/as together, 'acting politically,' and 'pursuing common interests,' *Raíces de Sangre* critically challenges the legitimacy of the 'American' political-economic constitution of citizenship."[15]

State of Siege (1973, Columbia–Cinema 5)

Costa-Gavras' *State of Siege* focused uncompromisingly on the revolutionary conditions in Latin America and the U.S. role in maintaining the status quo of neocolonialism. The film is based on historical events. The lead character (Philip Michael Santore) was based loosely on Daniel Mitrone, an employee of the U.S. Agency for International Development (USAID), which trained and assisted Latin American police forces. Documents released after Mitrone's death evidenced his involvement in Uruguay's right-wing regime in the areas of counterinsurgency as an adviser.[16]

The film is set in the 1970s in Montevideo, Uruguay, and begins with the security forces' search for Philip Michael Santore (Yves Montand), who had been kidnapped by the Tupamaros (named after Tupac Amaro, one of the last Inca kings to die resisting the Spanish conquistadores). Santore's body is found in a car and the film flashbacks how this political act has resulted in a severe political crisis for the right-wing regime.

Mitrone had been kidnapped several days earlier and was interrogated by the guerrillas, who gradually unearth his dubious security activities, as well as his previous involvement in how he had participated in the overthrow of the democratically elected Juan Bosch in the Dominican Republic in 1965 and the Goulert government in Brazil. In the meantime, the administration attempts negotiations with the guerrillas after the latter offer to release Santore in exchange for 150 political prisoners. One of Santore's friends, Capitan López (Renato Salvatori), administers an intensive counterinsurgency operation.

The guerrillas finally confront Santore with evidence of his complicity and deeds with the state's apparatus and their policy of abduction, torture and assassination of political dissidents, to which Santore admits something. The guerrilla leader Hugo (Jacques Weber) concludes his interrogation of Santore: "You say you're defending freedom and democracy.... Your methods are war, fascism, and torture." Exasperated and frustrated, Santore lashes out, "You are subversives, Communists. You want to destroy the foundations of society, the fundamental values of our Christian civilization, and the very existence of the free world. You are an enemy who must be fought in every possible way."

The government is able to capture Hugo and some of the other leadership, which places the negotiations in an impasse. The guerrillas discuss whether their inability to carry out their threat of death will be seen as weakness by the regime. Only days after Santore's body is found, another USAID operative arrives. He is watched by the Uruguayans, some possibly Tupamaros, who understand what he represents.

The Latinos in this film articulate and act upon clearly designated political goals of self-determination. Director Costa-Gavras had already established himself as a progressive filmmaker by the time of *State of Siege*, having earned international recognition for such films as the political thriller *Z* (1969), about the Greek military junta of the 1960s, and *The Confession* (1970), which depicted the excesses of the left in Czechoslovakia. He commented about his work, "The cinema has never, or rarely, or insufficiently, tackled the reasons that are behind hunger or war. That's what the political film is trying to do today—define these causes and reasons. In my view, the cinema is a way of showing, exposing the political processes in our everyday life."[17]

State of Siege was shot on location in Chile under the administration of President Salvador Allende, who would shortly be overthrown in a C.I.A.-sponsored military coup in 1973.

The film received generally favorable reviews, although some suggested that it glorified political assassination. The *Los Angeles Herald-Examiner* wrote, "The film is documentary in tone, harsh but unflamboyant in both its visual and verbal statements.... The actors are kept deliberately low-key so that even such a star as Yves Montand is barely recognizable, displaying no qualities which might remind us that he has ever been featured anywhere else before. Denied gloss and gimmick, playing characters with no private lives and only political emotions, the actors triumphantly manage to create fully realized individuals."[18]

El Super (1978, New Yorker Films)

El Super was the first feature film of Cuban-American cinema. The depiction of the Cuban-American experience was another part of the Latino mosaic and complemented the Chicano cinema that emerged during the same decade.

The film revolves around Roberto (Raymond Hidalgo-Gato), a forty-two-year-old Cuban exile who has been an apartment superintendent and handyman in New York City for the last ten years. He lives with his wife Aurelia (Zully Montero) and his eighteen-year-old daughter Aurelita (Elizabeth Peña) in the drab and cold basement of the building. The couple's lives revolve around their nostalgic memories of Cuba and their present insecurities and difficulties in adapting to the cold weather, marginalization, and the growing independence of their Americanized daughter. Their small circle of friends includes a Cuban exile couple, Pancho (Reynaldo Medina), who constantly breaks into tirades against communism and recalls his exploits in the Bay of Pigs invasion, and his wife Ofelie (Ana Margarita Martínez Casado), who puts up with him. Roberto's only diversion is a weekly game of dominoes with another exile, Cuco (Efraín López Neri), and a Puerto Rican neighbor, Bobby (Juan Granda), with whom Pancho is at odds ideologically.

Roberto becomes increasingly despondent with the drudgery of his life, the city's crime, the snow and his desire for warmer weather. Things come to a head when Aurialita becomes pregnant and his mother dies in Cuba. The two events finally compel Roberto to leave New York with his family and go to Miami, where he gets a job at a factory.

The film powerfully captures the fracturing of the family and their identity in the face of the economic and cultural forces beyond their control. The father undergoes a loss of selfhood, clinging desperately to his memories, while his daughter, devoid of the memories of Cuba, is able to maintain a resiliency by becoming bilingual and bicultural. Like all immigrants, the adults dream of returning to their home country cognizant of the emotional and psychological losses incurred in their migration. The narrative documents the poignancy of misplacement and miscues of language, body gestures and way of thinking by Cuban-Americans in New York City.

The film was directed by Leon Ichaso and Orlando Jiménez Leal (who also did the impressive cinematography). The screenplay, by Leon Ichaso and Manuel Arce, was based on the play of the same name by Iván Acosta. The film marked the film debut of Elizabeth Peña. *El Super* remains the key film about the Cuban-American experience and over the years has earned a cult status.

The film received excellent reviews. Vincent Canby in the *New York Times* wrote, "*El Super*, a Cuban-American feature film shot in New York, ... [is a] funny, even-tempered, unsentimental drama about people in particular transit. The film was produced with care, intelligence and with a cast of marvelous Cuban and Puerto Rican actors.... Mr. Hidalgo-Gato gives a remarkably funny and touching performance that never slops over into sentimentality.... A performance and a movie to pay attention to."[19]

Latino Film Stars and Filmmakers

JOHN A. ALONZO

After a three-decade career, John A. Alonzo was one of the most highly respected and talented cinematographers in the Hollywood film industry. Later in his career he moved into directing as well.

He was born on June 12, 1934, in Dallas, Texas, to Mexican parents. He recalled later, "My father was picking beets in Wisconsin and my mother was working as a cook in a restaurant, hoping her husband would come back in time to take her back to Mexico to have her baby."[20] A short time later, the family moved to Guadalajara, Mexico. They moved back to Dallas when Alonzo was nine years old. An insatiable film buff since childhood, he later was employed at the Margo Jones Theater-in-the-Round and at FAA-TV in a variety of jobs: cleaning floors, camera pusher and director. Later, he took up photography, stage acting and had a television puppet show. In 1956, his puppet show ran for twenty-six weeks on KHJ-TV in Hollywood, California. He did bit parts on television and in two films: *The Magnificent Seven* (1960) and *Invitation to a Gunfighter* (1965).

He began as a cameraman in several short films for independent filmmakers: Bruce Curtis' *Rainbow in the Sand* and Robert Clause's *The Legend of Jimmy Blue Eyes*. He was employed by David Wolper for three Jacques Cousteau documentaries and numerous National Geographic documentaries. Two of his best-known documentaries were for film director William Friedkin, *The Thin Blue Line* (1966) and *Mayhem on a Sunday Afternoon* (1965).

In 1964, a shortage of union cinematographers in the Hollywood film industry meant there were not enough to meet the production needs. James Wong Howe, the legendary cinematographer, was then shooting the film *Seconds* for director John Frankenheimer and needed a camera operator. Alonzo was chosen and worked on the film for three consecutive nights. Impressed with the young man, Howe supported his entry into the union and as a consequence Alonzo got his IATSE card.

Alonzo's first feature film as a cinematographer was Roger Corman's gangster drama *Bloody Mama* (1969) with Shelley Winters and newcomer Robert De Niro.

Alonzo went on to lens some notable films in different genres. Some were artistic successes and some merely commercial ventures. Among his better-known films are the cult classic *Vanishing Point* (1971); the dark comedy *Harold and Maude* (1971); Martin Ritt's somber *Sounder* (1972); the melancholy and romantic biography of Billie Holiday, *Lady Sings the Blues* (1972) with Diana Ross; Roman Polanski's *Chinatown* (1974), which earned Alonzo an Academy Award nomination; the film noir *Farewell My Lovely* (1975) with Robert Mitchum; John Frankenheimer's thriller *Black Sunday* (1977); Steven Spielberg's *Close Encounters of the Third Kind* (co-photographer) (1977); Martin Ritt's union drama *Norma Rae* (1979) with Sally Field; the evocative western *Tom Horn* (1980), Steve McQueen's second-to-last film; the adventure tale *Zorro, the Gay Blade* (1981); the sensitive drama *Steel Magnolias* (1989); and the science-fiction drama *Star Trek Generations* (1994).

In 1978, he made his directorial debut with *FM*, the story of a disc jockey's attempt to save an FM radio station from overcommercialization by the parent company. On the difficulty of making the transition into directing, he commented, "Keeping your hands off the camera. Not forgetting the cinematography, but making it secondary, that's the most difficult, and I've managed to do that."[21]

With regard to what was the most difficult aspect of cinematography, he commented, "Trying to interpret what's in the director's mind. That's the most difficult because if a director is very knowledgeable about cinematography, he would probably do it himself. Trying to get that communication between the aesthetics and what the director has in mind indicated to me, the cameraman, who is technical as well as an artist, is the most difficult part."[22]

When asked what he looked for in a script he stated, "As I approach a script, I try to think in terms of what is going to be the most efficient way of photographing it, and also to give it some pizzazz, so to speak. If it's a very talky script you start looking for ways to make the camera move and angle so, in that case, I approach it from that kind of equipment, what kind of lenses I want to use, what kind of style I want to apply to it, along with conferences with the director to see if that's agreeable with him. I look for something new every time. To see if there's a way to do a scene differently than I've done before...."[23]

Regarding his motivation for becoming a cinematographer, he commented, "It was the challenge of a composition in motion. I love still photography because you can play with it and compose it. It's a fixed image and you can see the light just the way you want it to be.... Cinematography is lighting that you're seeing through its image, as opposed to a still which is opaque, and the light falls on it. The big challenges are lighting and composition."[24]

He once commented about an unrealized project, "Another project I'd love to do is a picture in Mexico. After all, I'm the only Mexican-American in the California I.A. [union] local ... and I'd like to work in the land of my forefathers. I'd love to take what I've learned about composition from the great Mexican artists Orozco, Rivera and Siqueiros and apply it to a film. Hey, and don't forget, I speak fluent Spanish!"[25] Alonzo partially realized his dream when he shot *Zorro, the Gay Blade* at the Mexico City Churubusco Studios.

Alonzo directed and lensed four television films: *Champions* (1979); *Portrait of a Stripper* (1979); *Belle Starr* (1980); and *Blinded by the Light* (1980).

His films include *Get to Know Your Rabbit* (1972); *Pete 'n' Tillie* (1972); *Hit!, The Naked Ape* (1973); *Conrack* (1974); *The Fortune, Once Is Not Enough* (1975); *I Will ... I Will ... For Now, The Bad News Bears* (1976); *The Cheap Detective* (1978); *Back Roads* (1981); *Blue Thunder, Cross Creek, Scarface* (1983); *Runaway, Terror in the Aisles* (1984); *Out of*

Control (1985); *Nothing in Common* (1986); *Overboard* (1987); *Physical Evidence* (1989); *Internal Affairs, The Guardian, Navy Seals* (1990); *Housesitter, Cool World* (1992); *The Meteor Man* (1993); *Clifford* (1994). Alonzo's last films were *The Prime Gig* (2000) and *Deuces Wild* (2000).

In 2001, Alex Schill, who had been one of his assistants and was later a director, made a feature documentary about Alonzo called *The Man Who Shot Chinatown: Cameraman John A. Alonzo.* By that time Alonzo was already a legend in cinema.

He died after a long illness in Brentwood, California, on March 13, 2001, survived by his wife and three daughters.

BARBARA CARRERA

Nicaraguan-born Barbara Carrera, a dark-haired beauty, burst upon the Hollywood scene in the mid–1970s and by decade's end had established herself as a star of middle rank. Quickly typecast as a Latina dark lady, she has been unable to completely break away from Hollywood's conventional perception of what Latina women are.

Barbara Carrera was born in Nicaragua and first became famous as a fashion model. She came to Hollywood in the 1970s. She starred in *The Island of Dr. Moreau* in 1977.

She was born on December 31, 1945, in Managua, Nicaragua, to an American father (who was an employee of the U.S. Embassy) and a Nicaraguan mother. Barbara was convent-educated in Europe and the United States, and became a high-fashion model at the age of seventeen. Her uniquely Latin American chiseled facial structure attracted the attention of various filmmakers at a fashion show in Cannes, France. It led to a lucrative modeling career. She later stated, "It is not where I come from that's important. It's who I am that matters. God, you can see the Indian in me. There are 200 kinds of Indians in Nicaragua—actually, I call myself a bouillabaisse of bloodlines. I have lived in so many countries and learned practically everything I know from living."[26]

It was actor Tom Laughlin who finally convinced her to test for the part of the señorita Eula in his film *The Master Gunfighter* (1975), a western set in 1836 in California. She won the part. She then played a beautiful creature born in a test tube and programmed by a scientist to be a super-intelligent super-lover in Ralph Nelson's interesting *Embryo* (1976). The *Los Angeles Times* wrote, "The ravishing Miss Carrera makes convincing the finally tragic and exquisite creature who sees herself as a sort of 'nonperson' who desperately wants to live and attain her rightful sense of identity."[27]

Another science fiction film followed, Don Taylor's *The Island of Dr. Moreau* (1977), in which a mad scientist (Burt Lancaster) transforms a young native girl (Carrera) into a puma. Carrera finished the decade with an impressive performance as an Indian maiden in love with a mountain man (Richard Chamberlain) in the excellent television miniseries *Centennial* (1979), based on James Michener's novel by the same name. The series had an all-star cast that included Clint Walker, Silvana Gallardo, Chad Everett, Sally Kellerman, David Janssen, and Henry Darrow.

Carrera also played effectively the role of a captive Jewish woman in the historical television miniseries *Masada* (1982), opposite Peter O'Toole.

These years of fame were her most rewarding and best remembered. She later stated, "I think I have broken the Hollywood stereotype image of Latin women.... I was a blonde Russian in *Condorman*, an Indian aging from 15 to 89 in *Centennial*. I feel *Masada* proved to people what I wanted to prove, that I am not just a glamor girl who wants to act but a real actress, and more an actress than a movie star."[28]

Her films thereafter became increasingly routine and obscure. She played the Tahitian Iolini in Irwin Allen's uneven disaster drama *When Time Ran Out* (1980), which was only partially redeemed by the stars, William Holden, Jacqueline Bisset and Ernest Borgnine. She played a blonde Russian spy in the mediocre *Condorman* (1981) with Oliver Reed; a murderous doctor in *I, the Jury* (1982), the weak adaptation of the detective novel by the same name, and she was wasted in the abysmal tale of Cold War zealots *Lone Wolf McQuade* (1983) with David Carradine and Chuck Norris. At this low point, Carrera scored one of her best roles as Fatima, a tongue-in-cheek villain in one of the better James Bond extravaganzas, *Never Say Never Again* (1983), opposite Sean Connery and Klaus Maria Barandaver.

Since then, her career has been cast adrift in the doldrums of inferior films: the disastrous *Wild Geese II* (1986) with the equally wasted Laurence Olivier; the mediocre *Love at Stake* (1988); the obscure *Loverboy* (1989); and *Wicked Stepmother* (1989) with Bette Davis. She also appeared in the television film *Sins of the Past* (1984, ABC), among others.

Her career appears as another example of a Latina player's unfulfilled promise and opportunity. At one time she stated, "I've been lucky enough to achieve star billing but not the salary that goes with it. That's going to come. I hope to work with people who value quality above money. But my life and career are my own."[29]

In 1996, she attempted a comeback in Renee Taylor and Joseph Bologna's dark comedy *Love Is All There Is*. Her most recent films include *Waking Up Horton* (1998); *Alec to the Rescue* (1999); *Coo Coo Café* (2000); *Panic* (2001); *Paradise* (2003); and *Don't Hurt Me* (2003). She has also guest-starred in several television shows: *The Rockford Files: Godfather Knows Best* (1996); *JAG* (1998); and *Judging Amy* (2004).

LYNDA CARTER

Lynda Carter won fame as television's *Wonder Woman* and went on to a brief career in films.

She was born on July 24, 1951, in Phoenix, Arizona, to an Anglo father and a Mexican-American mother. She would later recollect, "My family broke up when I was ten. I was lucky I was able to regain kind of family feeling with the musicians and people I worked with in show business when I was young."[30] Tall (5 feet, 9 inches), she began thinking of herself as an ugly duckling. She failed to make it as a cheerleader and was deemed too tall to be on the pep squad, and consequently became a member of the glee club. After high school graduation at seventeen she went on the road with a rock group and appeared at the Sahara Lounge in Las Vegas.

At her mother's suggestion, she returned to Arizona and entered a beauty pageant. In 1972, she won the title of Miss Phoenix and received wider media attention by winning Miss World USA representing Arizona. She was a finalist in the Miss World pageant in London.

Moving to Hollywood, California, she landed the coveted title role in *Wonder Woman,* beating out more than 2,000 auditioners. The show was a top-rated one (1976–1979) on ABC and CBS and she became a household word known for her statuesque frame and skimpy outfits.

She made her film debut in American International Pictures' *Bobbie Jo and the Outlaw* (1976), a crime drama about a pair of reckless and amoral drifters, with Marjoe Gortner. It received a mixed commercial and critical reception. The *Los Angeles Times* commented, "One of those rare films ... a tremendous vitality ... eliciting the most natural and spontaneous performance from its cast."[31] She later stated, "The nudity there wasn't really in bad taste.... It was a time in my career when I was confused—that's for sure. I was very alone out here."[32]

In the late 1970s, she became a spokeswoman for Maybelline.

She has hosted five television specials and starred in several television films: *Born to Be Sold* (1981); *Hotline* (1982); *Rita Hayworth, the Love Goddess* (1983); and *Stillwatch* (1987), which she also produced. She released a debut album entitled *Portrait* and a single, "Toto," which she composed. She has also performed a song-and-dance act in Las Vegas.

She withdrew from the film business in the late 1980s, but has made occasional returns. She once commented, "Being famous was the most important thing in the early years—even though I cared about being good. But I don't care about being famous anymore. I don't care how much money I'm making.... Professionally, I would like to be known as a good actress."[33]

Carter returned to television for the one-season series *Partners in Crime,* with Loni Anderson, during 1984. During 1994 and 1995, she starred in another one-season series entitled *Hawkeye,* which was inspired by James Fenimore Cooper's Leatherstocking Tales. The series was shot on location in Vancouver, British Columbia, Canada. She commented about the syndicated series, "When you have a network show, you get an order for six, and then [network executives] mess with it. Here, you get a guarantee, you don't have the interference of a network, you create the character, you collaborate with the writers, you tell them your ideas and then you get to do it."[34]

During 2005, she played Mama Morton in the West End London production of *Chicago.* She has recorded three albums and does concert tours. Her film career was reignited with several comedic roles in such films as *Super Troopers* (2001); *The Creature of the Sunny Side Up Trailer Park* (2004); *The Dukes of Hazzard* (2005); and *Sky High* (2005). She has made several television appearances.

She has married twice, to talent agent Ron Samuels (1977–1982) and to attorney Robert A. Altman in 1984 (they have one daughter). She and her family live in Washington, D.C., In 2008, she told *People* she was entering a rehabilitation clinic for alcoholism.

DANNY DE LA PAZ

The stage-trained Danny De La Paz gave a powerful and memorable performance as the self-destructive adolescent Chicano gang member yearning for love and acceptance in 1979's *Boulevard Nights*. Hollywood has failed to give him roles worthy of his considerable talent.

He was born on April 3, 1957, in Whittier, California, to Mexican parents. He graduated from Whittier High School.

He began acting in high school and worked thereafter in community and Equity-waiver theaters in Los Angeles. He honed his skills in such plays as *Spoon River Anthology, Dark of the Moon, Our Town* and *Under Milk Wood*. During a children's show at the Inner City Cultural Arts Center, Damon Evans of *The Jeffersons* television show spotted him and soon thereafter introduced him to various agents. De La Paz' diligence in attending casting calls paid off, and within a year and a half he landed a role in the short-lived television series *Popi,* which starred Héctor Elizondo.

He kept active in theater and by 1979 he had appeared in more than forty productions. In April 1978 he met casting director Vivian MacCrea, who had him read for parts. Later, he recalled, "I studied theatre in college and, at the time, I was working in a lumber yard in La Habra for $3 an hour. My agent called and asked me to audition for two films, *Boulevard Nights* and *Gangs*, which Robby Benson got."[35] The latter film was later renamed *Walk Proud* and received widespread criticism for its stereotypical portrayals of Chicanos.

In *Boulevard Nights*, Danny took the pivotal role of Chuco, the Chicano youth caught up in an East Los Angeles gang who yearns to be accepted on his own terms. Richard Yniguez played the older brother who tries to broker Chuco's departure from the gang life. The film, which was directed by Michael Pressman and scripted by Desmond Nakano, drew impressive performances from the predominantly Chicano cast. However, it drew ire from some quarters of the Chicano community who felt it exploited gang violence to the detriment of the community, but it earned the young actor critical praise for his sensitive performance.

The *New York Times* noted, "With the possible exception of Mr. De La Paz, whose haunted looks suggest someone deeply troubled, the actors are not very good."[36] On the other hand, *Variety* commented, "The acting throughout *Boulevard Nights* is first-rate, especially from Yniguez, de Bois and new-comer De La Paz."[37] The *Los Angeles Herald-Examiner* wrote, "Chuco, in De La Paz's prehensible performance almost matches De Niro's Johnny Boy—and, perhaps James Dean—as often as he echoes him."[38]

About the experience of working on the film, he stated, "For me it was one of the best experiences of my life. I don't expect to have that good a time again; but I really do hope so.... I always thought it felt like we were making ... well, maybe not a classic, but we were making a film that people cared about, something that was worth doing.... I see some very, very positive values in the film. I don't see it as condoning violence or glorifying gangs." So powerful was his performance that he would forever be identified with the role. Many years later he recalled, "I think it was my favorite role, because it was my cherry popping experience, so to speak. It was the first time that I did a film and I guess it's like the first time you fall in love, it's a very memorable experience."[39]

The film's executive producer Tony Bill, impressed with the young actor's talent, recommended him to director Richard Lester, who cast him in the role of a revolutionary student in 1958 Havana in his film *Cuba* (1979). The film starred Sean Connery as a soldier of fortune in love with a married woman (Brooke Adams). De La Paz' third role during 1979 was as a Mexican youth who comes to the United States in search of a better life, in *The Border* opposite Eddie Albert and Telly Savalas.

He commented on his success, "I've had some luck so far, but there are so many other sides for me that I want to show; I haven't gotten the opportunity to do so yet, but maybe in the future I can. In a way I'm not so lucky because if you're one of the few Chicano actors around who gets any work—what can you get? The parts are very unusual and sometimes limited."[40]

He was cast as a young Mexican firebrand in Jesús Salvador Treviño's evocative *Seguin* (1980, PBS), the story of Juan Seguín, who fought for Texas independence in 1836 and then sided with Mexico in the Mexican-American War. It was the first film to document the Mexican side of the conflict. The excellent cast included Edward James Olmos, A Martinez, Lupe Ontiveros, Rose Portillo, Alma Martínez, and Enrique Castillo. In a recent interview he recalled the film and working with such a cast: "I have a good experience working with him, Jesús [Treviño]. I didn't know him, prior to that and I had little or no education about the Movimiento, so I knew nothing about what [Seguín] had experienced or the contributions he had made, up to that point. But it was a good experience. It was an all Chicano or Latino cast and many of us knew each other from other projects. We may have worked together, but never so many of us, one project."[41]

De La Paz was again excellent in Fred Schepisi's unusual western *Barbarosa* (1982) with another stellar cast, headed by Gilbert Roland (in his final screen role), Isela Vega, Willie Nelson and Gary Busey. He played Eduardo, the tenacious youth who finally tracks down a legendary Anglo bandit. Danny recalls working with the legendary Roland very fondly: "I grew up watching him on television. So, to work with Gilbert was an honor and it was somebody that I knew, so it meant a lot to me, it was very meaningful. And I had my mom come out to Texas to visit us on the set. My recollections of Gilbert Roland, are that here is a guy, who at that time was maybe in his 70s, early 70s. He hardly ever sat down. He had to be in crutches on one leg throughout the film and for most of the time they were setting up the shots, he would remain standing on his one leg. I was just amazed at the man's fortitude and his strength. He was just a bull, in the best sense of the word."[42]

After this film, however, De La Paz' career languished. His roles became less significant and more limited. He was typecast as a Chicano gang member who does not permit Adam Baldwin to leave the gang in the television film *3:15—The Moment of Truth* (1984); he had a featured role in the futuristic *City Limits* (1985) with James Earl Jones, Rae Dawn Chong and Robby Benson; and he appeared in another youth-oriented television film, *The Broth-*

erhood of Justice (1986), in which a group of bright students form a vigilante organization to control the low-life elements in a school.

He was in a pair of films with the Bridges brothers. Beau Bridges headed the cast of *The Wild Pair* (1987), a drama about right-wing extremists. The cast included Lloyd Bridges and Raymond St. Jacques. It marked Beau Bridges' directorial debut. De La Paz was featured in *8 Million Ways to Die* (1986) with Jeff Bridges, about an alcoholic cop on the skids trying to rescue a prostitute in peril. The film was directed by Hal Ashby and was an excellent film noir set in Los Angeles.

He essayed the role of Carlos in a film about a brave cerebral palsy victim, *Gaby: The True Story* (1987), with Liv Ullmann, Norma Aleandro and Robert Beltran.

Looking back many years later, he talked about those years when his career had come to a virtual halt: "After *Boulevard Nights*, I never really got another role as full as that. I wasn't savvy about business at that time. All I did was a thing that was typical of young actors who weren't very good businessmen, was that I would just be going out, trying to get myself in other people's movies. That's the thing that separated me from Eddie Olmos. Eddie realized early on, I think too, that you have to get in a position where they come looking for you. Otherwise, you never separate yourself from the group; you'll always be looking for them, to get work. But, if I could give advice to young actors today, I would say, remember that it's show business, you know—business. Surround yourself with good business people."[43]

During these lean years, he kept busy in theater with plays such as *The Last Angry Brown Hat,* among others. He once stated, "I love the theatre; it's such a wonderful means of communication for me as an actor."

Two decades later, he has still maintained the close kinship to the theater: "Theater has always been fulfilling to me and it always will be fulfilling. And, no matter how many films I do or how successful I get making films, I'll never, ever stop doing theater. Those are my roots, that's where I come from and I always feel that, as long as I can get there, in front of an audience of 500 people and I can deliver truth live, when there's no chance to go back and do another take, then my skill will always be sharpened to the point, where I can easily make a film."[44]

De La Paz, like most Chicano and Latino actors, had developed a tenacious resourcefulness and philosophical reserves. He once commented, "It may all end tomorrow, and I'll be the first person to admit that. I'm not going to fool myself into believing this is going to be a pattern for the rest of my career because I know it's not. I'm just going to do what I can when I can, and the only goal I have right now is to be around in twenty years. I have no desire to be a movie star or make a fortune. The money is great, but the important thing is, I think, the work and how I feel about myself when I'm doing it."[45]

In 1992, he was cast by actor/director/producer Edward James Olmos in the film *American Me* in an overdue meaty role, playing Puppet, a Chicano gang member involved with the Mexican Mafia who mentors his younger brother's entry into the group. For this challenging role he earned rave reviews. The *Village Voice* wrote, "Danny De La Paz and Daniel Villareal stand out as brothers whose blood ties unravel from the pressure of the gang culture."[46]

When asked about what the film was trying to say and the controversy it generated in some quarters, he stated, "Well, that's exactly what Edward James Olmos wanted. He made the film to spark dialogue. He wanted to bring that problem out of the closet and into the open where we could look at it. From that point of view, the film was a success. I believe Olmos was trying to show the community that there's a cancer in the culture, you have to deal with it.... Well, you can change things, but not overnight. I think the single most important thing is to teach Latino parents to love their children by instilling them with a very strong sense of self-esteem.... I think Latino kids, especially, need to know that they can do anything they set their mind to. Their only true limit is their imagination."[47] (Since the early 2000s, De La Paz has made countless appearances and lectures on behalf of youth from grade school to the university level emphasizing positive thinking and self-esteem. He has been tireless and giving in these efforts that require unconditional patience and love.)

He had some reservations about the film himself. "*American Me* is a tough film to watch. It really basically just bludgeons its audiences over the head, making a point. My biggest problem with *American Me* is that it doesn't have any hope and I think that was intentional on Eddie's [Edward James Olmos] part, although I don't know how effective that was. I love Edward James Olmos, as a person. He's very respectful of me and of my talent and he gave me a lot of love, in that picture."[48]

During 1992, he worked as associate producer on the short film *Breaking Pan with Sol*, part of the Universal Pictures Hispanic Feature Project.

He has been twice married and divorced. He remains an indestructible optimist and advocate for the betterment of Chicano and Latino opportunities in the media: "Things are definitely changing—and for the better. It's taken a long time, but I feel there are a lot of talented people who are doing things now. Writers, directors, cinematographers, some producers and a lot of actors. What we really need are more writers and directors to get projects initiated and to get things done.... Latinos are going to change things by force of their buying power, which is ultimately the bottom line in Hollywood, just like any other industry."[49]

About the continuing Latino stereotypes, he commented, "I attribute it to the people who write these projects and who create them, to the fact that they're created by people outside the particular culture that [the films] are about. We have to make our movies, we have to write them, produce them, direct them, star in them, distribute them. That means for Latino businessmen to come together, pool their monies and make films."[50]

During 1997, he had a featured role in the independent film *Star Maps*. His recent films include *Suckers* (2001), *Taking the Westside* (2003) and *Moe* (2008).

STELLA GARCIA

One of the most promising Latina actresses at the beginning of the 1970s was the raven-haired beauty Stella Garcia.

She was cast by Dennis Hopper, fresh from his triumph in *Easy Rider* (1969), to play Maria, a Peruvian prostitute, in his directorial debut *The Last Movie* (1971, Universal). Shot in the remote Andes of Peru, it chronicled the adventure of a movie stuntman, Kausa (Hopper), who stays on in a film location site after the movie company has moved on and traces the impact of the filming upon the nearby Indian village. Among the numerous cameos were actors Julie Adams, Peter Fonda, Sylvia Miles, Kris Kristofferson, Rod Cameron, and Dean Stockwell, and directors Samuel Fuller and Henry Jaglom. The film would go on to win an award at the Venice Film Festival. In the United States, however, the film received mixed reviews and was a commercial failure. Stella Garcia's performance, however, was uniformly praised.

Variety wrote, "Film suffers from a multiplicity of themes, ideas, and a fragmented style with flash-forwards and intertwined and only suggested plot structure.... Stella Garcia is effective as the native girl. She is not moved by the dead she does not know, while Hopper has an American innocence tempered with violent rage when things go beyond his ken. Their lovemaking scenes are lucid, emotional and sexy."[51]

Impressed with her performance, Universal Studios signed her for a second film. She was cast as the female lead, Helen Sanchez, a Mexican-American activist involved in the struggle of dispossessed land in New Mexico, in John Sturges' *Joe Kidd* (1972) with Clint Eastwood and Robert Duvall. A film of mixed quality and less historical truth, it nevertheless was a commercial hit. Reviewers once again noted Garcia's performance. The *Los Angeles Times* noted, "Stella Garcia stands out as Chama's spirited aide."[52]

After these two promising performances, Stella Garcia disappeared from U.S. films. It was another example of how Latina players continue to be too expendable in Hollywood.

In 1996, she had a featured role in John Schlesinger's *Eye for an Eye* with Sally Field and Ed Harris and played a businesswoman in *Playing God* (1997).

ALEJANDRO GRATTAN

Alejandro Grattan played a historic role as one of the first Chicanos to direct a feature films in the 1970s.

He was born in El Paso, Texas, to a Mexican mother and a one-fourth-Irish and Mexican father. He and his brother Thomas grew up in dire poverty. Alejandro began to write from an early age, specializing in novels and screenplays. The latter provided him with a livelihood when he optioned them.

He directed several low-budget films in the late 1950s. In 1978, he wrote and directed *Only Once in a Lifetime,* about the tribulations of a Chicano artist in East Los Angeles. The film, along with those of Efraín Gutiérrez and Jesús Salvador Treviño, constitute the first Chicano films ever made. The title of the film came from the fact that his mother's favorite song had been "Solamente Una Vez" or "Only Once in a Lifetime."

Thereafter, however, Grattan concentrated on writing. In 1995, he published his first novel, *The Dark Side of the Dream* (Arte Público Press), a combination of two of his screenplays. His second novel, entitled *Breaking Even* (Arte Público Press) was published in 1997. He lives in Mexico, where he directs theater and also publishes an English-language newspaper.

EFRAÍN GUTIÉRREZ

The Chicano movement, the Mexican-American struggle for civil rights in the 1960s, was not only confined to politics but also generated a renaissance of Chicanos in the arts. In the process, Efraín Gutiérrez became the first Mexican-origin person to direct a feature film in the United States since Roberto Gavaldón, and the first Chicano to do so. However, his output was small and his time as filmmaker was short-lived.

Nevertheless, his impact and contribution has remained enduring and lasting. Gregg Barrios, for example, noted of his cinema, "He tells stories of weak, often well-intentioned Chicanos who get seduced by quick and tawdry experiences with women, drugs, booze, and revenge—things which all of us know about but somehow try to avoid. His anti-heroes are just that. Life offers no quarter. They learn (if they ever do) the hard way or die without redemption or the redemptive act that can make their lives and their existence meaningful to themselves or others. One can easily see the influence of the telenovela in his work, the icons of Chicano culture and el movimiento, the narcotic beat of our music, and the Brechtian commentary of our teatro."[53]

Efraín Gutiérrez was born in 1941, to Mexican parents, in San Antonio, Texas. As a child he traveled with his parents as an agriculture migrant worker. He graduated from Edgewood High School in San Antonio. Thereafter, he became very involved with Chicano *teatro* locally. He was an active participant in the Teatro Nacional de Aztlán (TENAZ) program with Luis Valdez. Subsequently, he won a Nosotros scholarship for acting classes. Empowered by these experiences, he attempted to break into U.S. and Mexican films. He was able to win bit parts in television shows, but no more. He later stated, "I found there was no future for Chicano actors, that the few good parts were going to the actors with a name and the only other parts for Chicanos were fakey. I remember a casting director once told me, 'We were forced to accept the blacks, but I'll be damned if we'll be forced to accept you all.'"[54]

He went on to earn a theater arts degree from Los Angeles City College in 1970, and then he joined the Mexican American Theatre in Los Angeles under the direction of Emilio Delgado. In 1971, he served as founder and director of the Chicano Arts Theatre, and the following year he traveled to Mexico City as a playwright student to work with Emilio Carballido. However, his desire to make films continued and in 1976 he served as founder and president of Chicano Arts Film Enterprises.

In 1976, Gutiérrez directed, produced, and co-scripted the first Chicano feature film ever made: *Please Don't Bury Me Alive*. He utilized a semiautobiographical idea and collaborated with Mexican poet and writer Sabino Garza in the screenplay. Gutiérrez played the film lead himself and cast his wife, Josefina Paz, as the protagonist's girlfriend. The cast included Abel Franco, Oscar Escamilla, and José Luis Garza. Gutiérrez invested $4,000 of his own money to start the film. He shot a four-minute segment and used it to convince the American Lutheran Church to grant him a $10,000 loan and then borrowed additional funds.

The film premiered at San Antonio's Century South Theater. He later recollected to *Hispanic*, "We shot the wad in San Anto [sic], man…. We had $12,000 to promote the film, and spent it all in San Antonio. It was make or break that weekend. We rented the theater for $4,000 for the week and then I spent the rest on advertising. There were fifty persons for the screening on Friday. By five o'clock, the house was sold out and people were in line for tickets for the late screenings."[55]

The film grossed $20,000 in its first showing and over $40,000 in three weeks, beating such blockbusters as *All the President's Men, The Godfather* and *Jaws. Please Don't Bury Me Alive* went on to gross more than $300,000 in some four months in Texas alone. Gutiérrez was approached by Rodolfo Echeverría, then head of Mexico's government-supported film corporation Conacine, to exhibit the film in Mexico and consider possible national and international release. During this time he also produced and directed a television show, *Lo Mejor Musica Tejana Con Efraín Gutiérrez,* about Tex-Mex music.

Many years later, he commented, "I was never able to fulfill my longevity as a filmmaker, because the first film made a lot of money and I quickly invested all of it into the next one. So we were never able to improve, and get good actors. That's one thing that bothers me, because after every film, we were back to square one."[56]

He then used some the earnings of *Please Don't Bury Me Alive* to direct, produce and co-script (along with Sabino Garza) his second feature film, entitled *Amor Chicano Es Para Siempre* (1977), a love story of a young Chicano couple. Once again, Gutiérrez played the film lead, and Tina González played the object of his desire. He commented about this film, "After *Please Don't Bury Me Alive,* I wanted to do something different, so I did a love story. I was trying to portray something that was real, about how we're never satisfied in relationships and always looking for someone else. *Amor Chicano Es Para Siempre,* but what is forever? Even though it was crudely and simply done, people liked it when it came out. Every age group could relate to it, the eternal love triangle."[57]

The cast included Henry Balderrama, Sylvia Garcia and Carolina Villalongin. Balderrama composed eight original songs for the film, including the theme song, "Amor Chicano Es Para Siempre." An album was released by Teardrops Records with the film. Also released with the feature film was a seventeen-minute documentary, *La Onda Chicana,* about a July 4th concert at Fort Lavaca. Featured in the documentary were such Tex-Mex stars as Little Joe y La Familia, Los Chachos, Snowball & Co. and La Fabrica.

Using the same marketing format that he had used successfully with his first film, Gutiérrez premiered the film in San Antonio and then other cities and towns. Tina González, Henry Balderrama and Gutiérrez toured different theaters, attracting even more media coverage. The film proved to be a commercial and critical success.

Gutiérrez's third film was *Run, Tecato, Run* (1979), a raw story about drug addiction in the Chicano community. The budget for the film was $60,000 and Gutiérrez once again played the lead. He told the *Lubbock Avalanche-Journal,* "I want people to get a look at the daily routine of a heroin addict—his problems, his feelings, whether they are inhuman or human."[58] About the purpose of the film, Gutiérrez told the *Laredo News,* "Los chavalitos [the kids] are important, and my movie is really aimed at them.... I hope that by watching the movie they can see what trying dope can do to you, then maybe they won't have to go through what many tecatos are experiencing right now."[59]

Regarding this film, Gutiérrez recalled, "*Run, Tecato, Run* has received some very interesting comments. I got a good response by the people in the religious community. I was invited to different churches and radio programs. And the tecatos really like it. They appreciated the fact that I told the story without exposing any more of the hurt that was already there. My movie deals with the daily life of a junky as a normal person and I used a lot of tecatos that were trying to clean themselves. San Antonio has been a center of heroin and tecatos for the last forty years."[60]

During 1978, Gutiérrez produced and directed a documentary entitled *El Juanito,* about paint sniffing among Chicano youth. For the film he utilized a budget of $6,000 and the energies of several barrio youth. He commented to the *Laredo News*, "The kids learned how to shoot film, lighting.... They helped plan the documentary, and choose the music. It was great to see such involvement."[61]

He was courted by major studios, but was leery of working under their control. He commented to the *Laredo News*, "I don't want to compromise my feelings. I'm not trying to make a political comment in my films, moreover, I'm trying to make a social comment. My films do not espouse one ideology, rather they paint the picture, and the audience is the one that decides on the action."[62] He commented about being an independent filmmaker to the *San Antonio Express-News*, "I could do what I wanted, the way that I saw it. You don't have the industry hanging over your head."[63]

In 1978, Gutiérrez was arrested and charged with possession of heroin, but the charges were later dropped. During 1982, he produced, directed and hosted a Texas-based television show, *Laredo Insight*. In the meantime, he sold the film rights to *Please Don't Bury Me Alive* to the Mexican film company Azteca, which had promised to distribute it in Mexico, but the film quickly vanished, presumably to keep it from competing with the declining number of Mexican films. He subsequently sold the distribution rights to his two other feature films and dropped out of the film world. Other planned projects, such as one about Gregorio Cortez, failed to come to fruition. He became increasingly disillusioned with the medium to which he had made a historic contribution. The time of the U.S. independent filmmaker was still in its embryonic stage.

He settled in Laredo, Texas, where he met and married his second wife. He went back to college and acquired a teaching credential, became a teacher and later served as a full-time representative of the Texas State Teachers Association. However, by the early 1990s, Gutiérrez's historic contributions were beginning to be widely acknowledged. Several of his films were screened at universities and forums. His first film, *Please Don't Bury Me Alive,* was added to the UCLA Film and Television Archive in 1997 and he was increasingly the subject of scholarly focus. *Filmmaker* magazine honored Efraín Gutiérrez as one of the fifty most influential independent filmmakers.

In 1996, Efraín Gutiérrez emerged from his self-imposed film exile and announced his new proposed film project, entitled *My Beloved República*. It is a historically based story about José Antonio Zapata and the short-lived Republic of the Rio Grande that was a buffer between the independent Texas Republic and Mexico during the 1840s. He is presently at work on acquiring funding and casting.

Whatever the future holds, Gutiérrez' contributions will remain undiminished. He was a visionary filmmaker who sought to document the Chicano experience. In the process of that struggle he laid down the marker, a place from which other Chicano and Latino filmmakers could go forth.

Reflecting back on his accomplishments, he stated, "I didn't lose interest in the movimiento and the movies, but personal life wasn't strong. I also thought that I had had a major disappointment about the end result of my career. A lot of people thought I was going to create a Hollywood in Texas and it just didn't happen."[64]

Gutiérrez returned to making films after a long absence with *A Lowrider Spring en San Quilmas* in 2000; he followed this up with another film, entitled *Barrio Tales: Tops, Kites and Marbles* in 2008.

ESTRELLITA LENORE LÓPEZ

Estrellita Lenore López had a very brief career as a film actress. Besides *Only Once in a Lifetime* (1979), she only appeared in *Police Story: Confessions of a Lady Cop*, a TV movie in 1980.

López is of Mexican ancestry and began in show business as a dancer. She began her acting career in theater. She performed in the Los Angeles Shakespeare Festival production of *The Comedy of Errors*. Among her feature films are *Scandalous John* (1971, Disney) with Brian Keith and the science fiction drama *Beyond Atlantis* (1973). She appeared in numerous television shows, including the top-rated *Police Story*.

She married and divorced actor Richard Mulligan.

JORGE LUKE

Mexican middle-rank star Jorge Luke was one of a diminishing number of young actors who attempted to cross over into U.S. films during the 1970s.

He was born in Mexico City in 1943. Trained as an architect, he practiced for several years before taking up acting. He debuted in a Mexican film entitled *Hay una Primera Vez* in 1969. Thereafter, he appeared in Mexican films, becoming a middle-rank leading man of mostly action films. He also appeared in several *telenovelas* and plays. He was married to Mexican actress Isela Vega for several years.

He made his U.S. film debut in Daniel Mann's *The Revengers* (1972), which starred William Holden and Susan Hayward. He made an impression as a young Mexican gunfighter named Chamaco. He was then cast for the third lead in Robert Aldrich's evocative and well-received *Ulzana's Raid* (1972) with Burt Lancaster. Luke received excellent notices and appeared headed for U.S. film stardom. The *Los Angeles Herald-Examiner* wrote, "The real star of *Ulzana's Raid* is Jorge Luke. The handsome Mexican actor gives complexity and humanity to the role of an Apache scout so long represented in Hollywood westerns as a mere stereotype. As Ke-Ni-Tay, Luke creates a convincing symbol of a race in transition and an individualized portrait of a man whose proud heritage survives, deep in his poetic soul, all the indignities of compromise."[65]

However, while he became a viable box-office star in Mexican action films, he met with limited success in U.S. films. He stated, "You think it is all going to be exceptional. They come down to talk to you about the film, drop big names like Holden, and you are full of hope."[66]

In subsequent U.S. films he played both featured and small roles: *Eagle's Wing* (1983) with Martin Sheen, in which Luke was another Indian brave; *The Evil That Men Do* (1984) with Charles Bronson; Oliver Stone's *Salvador* (1986) with James Woods; and *Pure Luck* (1991), among others. His Mexican film output declined substantially as well and was restricted to mediocre fare like *El Ansia De Matar* (1987).

Among his last films were *Eráse Una Vez en Durango* (2010) and *Borrar de la Memoria* (2010).

Jorge Luke died on August 14, 2012, in Mexico City.

Cheech Marin

Chicano comedian Cheech Marin acquired fame early in the 1970s as part of the Cheech and Chong comedy team. They made albums and appeared in nightclubs. Crossing over into films at mid-decade, they immediately became box-office stars. Thereafter, Marin embarked on a solo career with success that has been unabated.

He was born Richard Marin in Los Angeles, California, on July 13, 1945, the son of a middle-class Mexican-American family. His father was a police officer. When he was ten, Marin's family moved to the middle-class San Fernando Valley. Later, he recalled, "It served me well to see both sides of the tracks at that point of my life. As I got older, I began comparing the haves and have-nots ... but as a kid in the Valley it was just 'Wow! Swimming pools without 5,000 guys in them!'"[67]

Marin went on to study at California State University, Northridge, where he majored in English. Subsequently he ended up in Vancouver, British Columbia, Canada, where he met Tommy Chong. He recalled, "I had been involved with draft resistance ... and I had turned in my draft card so when they started hassling me I decided just to stay. My case went on to the Supreme Court and got thrown out because they drafted me illegally. Then they tried to redraft me but I got out on a 4-F because I had a badly broken leg. It's providence I was meant to go up to Canada and meet Tommy and do our thing."[68]

For the next sixteen years the comedy team of Cheech and Chong performed in nightclubs and made record albums and, ultimately, films. Tommy Chong would later recall, "Cheech wasn't the funniest guy I'd ever work with, but he was absolutely fearless. He'd do anything. On the spot. We were working four hours a night, six nights a week, for nine months solid. Total improvisation, no repeats."[69] Their first album was *Cheech & Chong*, released in September 1971, but it was their second album, *Santa Claus and His Old Lady*, released that November, that made them into top-selling record artists. They had three consecutive top-ranked albums in two and a half years and won one Grammy Award.

They made their film debut in *Up in Smoke* (1978, Paramount), which chronicled the adventures of two down-and-out band members. Chong later said, "*Up in Smoke* was the perfect counterculture movie of the early seventies. Cheech and I wrote it, I basically directed it."[70] The film was shot on a limited budget but it became an unexpected hit, grossing some $110,000,000. Their second film, *Cheech and Chong's Next Movie* (1980, Universal), grossed $95,000,000 and their third, *Nice Dreams* (1981, Columbia), some $85,000,000. Critics were not enamored of their films and many were especially hostile. Marin commented, "When critics call us lewd, racist, they're not really looking at what we do. Confront that kind of shit up front, you make it evaporate."[71]

The Cheech and Chong comedy team became a top box-office attraction. According to film industry sources, as tabulated by Quigley Publications, in 1980 they ranked number 13, in 1981 number 11 and in 1982 number 15.

Their fourth film, *Things Are Tough All Over* (1982, Columbia), featured them in dual roles as wealthy Arabs and as two buffoons engaged to drive a limousine stuffed with a cache of money. Their fifth and last film as a team was *Cheech and Chong's The Corsican Brothers* (1984, Orion), which recouped its cost but failed to reach the commercial success of its predecessors. Marin commented, "It was about the time we did *The Corsican Brothers* that

Tommy and I started to fall out—a classic case of creative differences. The problem with Cheech and Chong was that everybody wanted the same things from us every time, and when we deviated from that it was an abysmal failure ... we were at this point where we wanted different things."[72]

A new direction was expressed in Marin's first solo venture, *Born in East L.A.* (1987, Universal), about a Chicano who is deported to Tijuana by the immigration service. Written and directed by Marin, both the film and its theme song were big hits. Marin commented, "Usually, what happens is that, as a guy makes it, he moves more and more into the mainstream. But I've been in the mainstream for a long time. So in my first solo effort I've made a conscious effort to go back to my roots. I am more Chicano in this movie than I have ever been in any of my movies. I'm more concerned with the cares and troubles of the Chicano population."[73] When asked about the future direction of his film career, he responded, "I just wanna do social comedies. I don't find anyone out here in comedy doing this sort of social commentary. So I will."[74]

His second solo effort was entitled *Rude Awakening* (1989). It was about two activist hippies who have been living in a utopian commune somewhere in Central America and who uncover a plot by the United States to invade a certain Central American country. They return to reveal the plan but discover former friends are now uncaring, self-centered yuppies. The *New York Times* commented, "The idea is a good one, but *Rude Awakening* is otherwise short of ideas. It is a collection of occasionally funny scenes that play as black-out sketches."[75]

In reference to Chicano/Latino opportunities in film, Marin stated, "They're improving primarily by the fact there's precedence, because of *Born in East L.A., Stand and Deliver* and *La Bamba*, since they all made it commercially. There's a second-class mentality toward us. The backers give us low budgets and say, 'You gotta make it work.' Well, how many times you gotta make it work? That's a problem with any filmmaker, but you feel it a lot more when a poor subject is rejected. It's a struggle, but if it was easy, everybody would be doing it."[76]

Among Marin's 1990s films are a pair directed by Robert Rodriguez. The first, entitled *Desperado* (1995), starred Antonio Banderas and Mexican actress Salma Hayek. Marin played the sardonic bartender in a saloon located in a small northern Mexican town. Essentially, it was a remake of Rodriguez's independently produced and low-budget film *El Mariachi. Desperado* was given a medium budget and all the technical trimmings of a major Hollywood studio. Like its predecessor, it told the tale of a vengeful mariachi continuously mistaken for a notorious *narcotraficante*. The film was a commercial success but received a rather cool reception from critics.

The second Rodriguez-directed film was *From Dusk till Dawn* (1996) and was scripted by Quentin Tarantino, "hot" after his big success with *Pulp Fiction*. Marin played three roles in the film: a Mexican immigration officer, a sleazy cantina barker and a drug-money launderer. The tale, about a pair of bank robbers traveling to a Mexican border town to launder money, fell apart when the film noir transformed itself into a horror film. The latter part of the film was populated with droves of stereotypical Mexicans, especially women.

Marin played the role of the Chicano detective on the television series *Nash Bridges* with Don Johnson for CBS. The stylish show, set in San Francisco, began during the 1995–96 season and ran until 2001.

During June 1996, Marin was one of several Latino comedians participating in Show-time's *Latino Laugh Festival,* taped in San Antonio, Texas.

When asked about the dire status of Latinos on television he commented, "Blacks made progress by being loud and in-your-face with organizations like the NAACP.... Latinos don't have groups like that that are political allies. We need an all-encompassing voice. Sometimes the Latino voice is indistinguishable. But we're starting to populate shows around.... Rather than a full-frontal assault, now the move is to do these flanking maneuvers."[77]

Marin played the role of Romeo Posar, a Chicano caddie in the golf-centered feature *Tin Cup* (1996) with Kevin Costner, Rene Russo and Don Johnson. Marin remarked about his role, "Seventeen years I did Cheech and Chong.... Now I want to be taken seriously as an actor on my own."[78]

His recent films include *Luminarias* (2000); *Spy Kids I* (2001); *Spy Kids II* (2002); *Spy Kids III* (2003); *Once upon a Time in Mexico* (2003); and *The Perfect Game* (2010).

A Martinez

Chicano actor A Martinez has managed to maintain a gradually rising career amidst the vicissitudes of Hollywood.

He was born Adolfo Larrue Martinez III, on September 27, 1948, in Glendale, California, to parents of Mexican descent. Martinez is also one-eighth Cherokee. He was the oldest of six children. The A comes from Adolfo, which was the name of both his grandfather and his father. He attended Verdugo Hills High School in Tujunga and then studied acting at UCLA. He did Equity Theatre and also was a member of various rock and roll bands. While at UCLA he played rhythm guitar and sang for a band called Tujunga.

He was discovered by Fred Roos in a UCLA drama class. Roos was casting American International Pictures' *Born Wild* (1968) and gave Martinez a featured role. The film depicted a Mexican-American student strike in which most of the leads were non–Latino. Martinez scored thereafter in an episode of *Ironsides* playing a militant Brown Beret sympathetically. He was typecast in several roles as an assassin, pimp and pusher. He recalled later about these television roles, "I was the young Chicano street guy who was in the wrong place at the wrong time, and seemed to be guilty of a crime.... But somehow the hero of the show could sense that I had a good heart, then prove that it was circumstantial evidence and I was innocent. Occasionally I played the friend of the important guy."[79]

He acted in two television miniseries: playing the peasant Tranquilino in NBC's popular miniseries *Centennial* (1979) opposite Barbara Carrera, Richard Chamberlain and Silvana Gallardo, and essaying a featured role in *Roughnecks* (1980). Martinez later remarked, "I have a different kind of attitude than many Chicano actors. I don't reject the image. I'd like to play other parts. But this is how I got started and I'm certainty not ashamed to play these roles."[80]

His best role yet was that of Juan Seguín, a Mexican leader in San Antonio, Texas, who became embroiled on both sides of the Texas revolt of 1836 in Jesús Salvador Treviño's excellent *Seguín* (1981, PBS). Martinez later commented, "It was a watershed event for me. I got to actually demonstrate my heart for the first time. And it also was a chance to come together with the community of Chicano actors who normally don't get to work together."[81] It was a time fondly remembered by the actor: "I could not complain in those days, because I was working and I felt that my ethnicity was a benefit to me. I came on the scene with some training at the right time."[82]

In 1972, he played Cimarron, a substantial role in Mark Rydell's *The Cowboys,* starring John Wayne, a western tale of how a group of green youths complete a cattle drive after the cattle boss has been killed. Martinez referred to the film as "the linchpin of my career as an actor.... All of a sudden, I had a profile and I started to get offers for work. It really gave me momentum for the first time."[83]

However, after this important role his film career stagnated in rather undistinguished films. He had a featured role in the crime drama *The Take* (1974) with Eddie Albert and Billy Dee Williams; played Aquino in the film adaptation of Graham Greene's *The Honorable Consul,* retitled for film as *Beyond the Limit* (1983) with Michael Caine, Richard Gere and newcomer Elpidia Carrillo; and played support in the routine *Walking the Edge* (1985) with Nancy Kwan and Robert Forster. He played the Indian lead, Buddy Red Bow, in the evocative *Pow Wow Highway* (1989), a film which has now has acquired deserved cult status among Native Americans. Martinez had the supporting role of Garcia in the misfire *She-Devil* (1989) with Meryl Streep and Sylvia Miles.

He has costarred in numerous television films: *Hunters Are for Killing* (1970, NBC); *Mallory: Circumstantial Evidence* (1970, NBC); *Probe* (1972, NBC); *The Abduction of Saint Anne* (1975, ABC); *Death Among Friends* (1975, NBC); and *Exo-Man* (1977, NBC), among others. He played the lead as a cop tracking down a serial killer in NBC's *Search for the Night Stalker* (1989). Martinez commented, "There just aren't enough Latin roles to go around. You never get the chance to do the lead, and each one becomes so important. I've never been frustrated with the roles I've played, but like every other actor in town, you'd like to be doing great roles in film."[84]

Martinez established himself in the role of agent-turned-detective Cruz Castillo, one of a handful of Latino roles in the soaps in NBC's daytime soap opera *Santa Barbara* in 1984. The show lasted eight seasons and then went into syndication in more than forty countries. For his role he won the IMAGEN Award and an Emmy in 1990 after being nominated several times, the first Latino to do so. About the role he commented, "If you're going to do something like this, it's wonderful to play someone that you can respect."[85]

In 1992, he left *Santa Barbara* to play a regular on *L.A. Law* for two seasons. With regard to Latino roles, he commented, "I've played peasants and professionals. Occasionally you hear someone say that it is considered hot to be Hispanic now. I think that's a relative judgment, but it's certainly better now than it's ever been."[86]

During 1994, he played the title role of Tiburcio Vasquez in *Bandido,* directed by Luis Valdez, at the Los Angeles Mark Taper Forum. Martinez commented about the legendary character, "Tiburcio continues to be a heroic figure in the Mexican community.... When I was younger, I thought that he was like Robin Hood; he was a robber at a time when his culture was being trashed, and you could sort of understand it. And ... it becomes apparent to me that he was caught in a situation from which there was no graceful escape."[87] Director Valdez had nothing but praise for Martinez's performance: "I was very happy he accepted the role and equally happy to see he was as good an actor onstage as in film and TV, which isn't always the case. Some actors can't make the leap. But he trained in theater. It is a natural return for him."[88] Unfortunately, the play did not meet with either the critical or commercial success expected.

Martinez has continued to star in television films, among them *She Led Two Lives* (1994) with Connie Selleca and *Deconstructing Sarah* (1994) with Rachel Ticotin. He played the lead in the excellent HBO film about the plight of contemporary Native Americans entitled *Grand Avenue* (1996) and costarred in the sci-fi film The *Terminators* (2009).

Married since 1982, his wife Leslie and he have two children. About marriage he stated, "Having a family brings out a more efficient side of you."[89]

OFELIA MEDINA

Mexican film and television star Ofelia Medina was the only established Mexican actress to attempt a crossover into U.S. films in the 1970s.

Born on March 4, 1950, in Mérida, Yucatán, in Mexico to parents in professional fields, Ofelia Medina began as a dancer and then entered Mexican films and television (on which she starred in several *telenovelas*). She is the recipient of three Diosas de Plata Awards, considered the Mexican Academy Award.

She made her U.S. film debut in the role of Alora, a Chicana from the barrio and a murder suspect, in Jeremy Paul Kagan's *The Big Fix* (1978, Universal), which has gained a cult status since its release. The evocative film told the story of a sixties radical, Mose Wine (Richard Dreyfuss), who becomes a detective. The film was warmly received critically but was less than successful commercially. Medina stated of this film experience, "It's hard to make a profound relationship here. It's easy to find superficial friends but hard to find real intimacy in Los Angeles. It's a movie town, fantasy land."[90] During her stay in the United States, she enrolled in Lee Strasberg's Actors Studio.

A politically astute actress, she made some interesting observations of Chicanos in the United States: "I had an idea of how beautiful they are, and I found it was true. They're all fighting for unity.... Our roots would enrich American culture if we only knew how to make it known."[91]

When asked about Mexicans and Chicanos, she said, "There's an enormous difference.... We (Mexicans) haven't been discriminated against at home. That discrimination is what conditions Chicano behavior."[92] About Hollywood stereotypes of Latinos she commented, "You have to love to know what their features can be. If you have stereotyped vision you can't see a beautiful Indian and recognize him as beautiful. Instead they cast people they consider beautiful only by Anglo standards.... They haven't given those young people who want to be actors little roles so they can grown and get experience. That's their excuse now— the Chicanos have no experience."[93]

Medina's greatest film triumph occurred when she played renowned painter Frida Kahlo, who was married to famed Mexican muralist Diego Rivera, in Paul Leduc's *Frida* (1988). Both the film and Medina's performance earned international acclaim.

Among her other notable films are Alfonso Arau's *El Águila Descalza* (1969); Salomon Laiter's *Las Puertas del Paraíso* (1970) with Jorge Mistral and Isela Vega; and Alfredo Joskow-icz's *El Cambio* (1971) with Hector Bonilla. Her recent films include *Before Night Falls* (2000); *Valentina* (2004); *Innocent Voices* (2005); and *Las Buenas Hierbas* (2010).

She was married at one time to director Alex Phillips, Jr., and at another time to actor Pedro Armendáriz, Jr. More recently, she has been very active in support of indigenous rights in Mexico, especially in Chiapas.

TARYN POWER

Taryn Power, the daughter of matinee idol Tyrone Power and Mexican actress Linda Christian, flirted with film stardom in the 1970s.

She was born Taryn Stephanie Power on September 13, 1953, in San Francisco, California. She was the second child; her older sister Romina Francesca had been born in October 1951. Taryn was two years old when her parents divorced and five when her father died in Spain on November 15, 1958. Both girls lived with their mother in Italy and were educated in European boarding schools. Taryn played leads in school plays and later did a couple of plays in a Rome repertory company. She later commented, "It always frightened me, because I thought a lot more is expected of you then."[94]

At the age of sixteen, on the advice of family friend Sean Connery, she played the title role in the Mexican film adaptation of Jorge Isaac's famous romantic novel *María*. Shot in Colombia, directed by Tito Davison and with some impressive cinematography by Gabriel Figueroa, the film was released in 1970 and became a huge box-office hit in the Spanish-speaking world. She followed it with a less successful Argentinean musical comedy.

Power made her U.S. film debut in the NBC television film (released theatrically abroad) *The Count of Monte Cristo* (1975), which was sumptuously lensed in Italy. The cast was headed by Richard Chamberlain, Tony Curtis, and Trevor Howard. The film proved very successful. She was then cast in the role of Stephanie, who attempts to understand a disturbed Vietnam veteran accompanying a fallen comrade's body, in Henry Jaglom's evocative *Tracks* (1977).

She followed these successes with the excellent adventure *Sinbad and the Eye of the Tiger* (1977). While the reviews were mixed, the film proved to be a commercial hit. The *Los Angeles Times* commented, "*Sinbad and the Eye of the Tiger* is a fantasy laced with nostalgia and corn ... (Pat) Wayne makes a decent....Sinbad lacking romantic dash. Power exudes wholesome enthusiasm."[95]

As the decade ended, however, her career stalled. She recollected, "I was very fussy, very idealistic. I didn't want any violence or sex in my movies. I turned a lot of stuff down."[96] The memory of her famous father appeared intimidating: "I had the fear that I couldn't cut it. When I start the first day on a set, I have this feeling of everyone waiting to see what I can do. I don't find acting generally a breeze. It takes a lot of concentration for me."[97]

She continued to make infrequent stage appearances: *Night of the Iguana* in 1984; and *Jacki Charge!* in 1985. She made the film *The Sea Serpent* (1984) in Spain and guest-starred in a segment of the television show *Matt Houston*.

Her father's memory still looms large in her life. "I grew up with the idea of him as a legend and not as a person because I have no memory of him personally. And a lot of that was a very good picture, a very nice picture."[98] Asked about whether she felt intimidated by her father's career, she responded, "Actually, I felt it more an inspiration ... I know he was very proud of his work. He wanted to be recognized by his work, not by his looks."[99]

She appears to have retired from acting, having been seen most recently on screen in 1990's *Eating*, directed by Henry Jaglom. She married photographer Norman Seeff and the union produced a daughter, Tai, and a son, Tony. She had a daughter, Valentina, from a relationship with Tony Sales, son of Soupy Sales.

MARIA RICHWINE

The career of Colombian-born Maria Richwine typifies that of numerous Latina actresses, whose initial debut proves promising but who thereafter are unable to build their career due to a lack of worthwhile roles.

She was born María Agudelo on June 22, 1952, in Cali, Colombia. She arrived as a child with her family in New York City in 1962 and later moved to Los Angeles. Her first theatrical experience was as one of the Rockettes. Later, she recalled, "I was 9 and the stage seemed to cover me like the universe. I'd never felt such energy—I got rushes. I sat there afraid to blink because I might miss something."[100] She studied dancing and for a while worked as a Playboy Bunny. While visiting England she decided to become an actress.

She made her film debut as María Elena Holly, the Puerto Rican wife of pioneer rocker Buddy Holly (who died with Chicano rocker Ritchie Valens and the Big Bopper in an airplane crash in 1959) in Steve Rash's evocative *The Buddy Holly Story* (1978, Columbia). Gary Busey was nominated for an Academy Award as Best Actor for the title role. Richwine won good notices for her sensitive portrayal of the young lady caught between her love for Holly, her mother's preference for traditional courtship and her fear of the racism of the times.

Unfortunately, despite her promising start, her film career stalled. A decade later she had a featured role as Fatima in the routine action film *Ministry of Vengeance* (1989, Concorde). She had continuing roles as Michelle in the long-running television series *Magnum P.I.* and as Arda in *Star Trek: The Next Generation*. Her credits include guest appearances on the television series *Sisters, Walker, Texas Ranger,* and *Martin*. She played the lead in the Showtime/HBO cable film *Dead Badge*.

During 1999, she had an overdue lead role in the Chicana-themed drama *Luminarias*. Her recent films include *Dead Badge* (1994); *Midnight Heat* (1996, TV film); *Time Well Spent* (1996, TV film); *Trials of Life* (1997, TV film); *Picture of Priority* (1998, TV film); *McBride: The Chameleon Murder* (2005, TV film); *McBride: Murder Past Midnight* (2005, TV film); *McBride: It's Murder, Madam* (2005, TV film); and *Lone Rider* (2008, TV film), among others, and her recent television appearances include *That's Life* (2000); *The Division* (2001); *Law and Order* (2010); and *Bones* (2013).

JORGE RIVERO

Mexican film star Jorge Rivero has been Mexico's preeminent action star since the late 1960s. Most of his films emphasized his athletic physique. He has made several forays into U.S. film with limited success.

He was born Jorge Puos Ribe, on June 14, 1938, in Mexico City to Spanish parents who had emigrated to Mexico as a result of the Spanish Civil War. He graduated from college with a degree in chemical engineering. He competed on the Mexican national track team in the 1954 Pan-American Games, taking a second place in the 100 meters. At the 1960 Tokyo Games he took a sixth place in the 100-meter swimming competition.

He began his acting career with small roles in six different *telenovelas*. He made his film debut playing a masked wrestling hero, El Enmascarado de Oro, in two routine low-budget films: *El Asesino Invisible* (1964) with Ana Bertha Lepe and *Los Endemoniados del Ring* (1964). He played his first leads in a quartet of low-budget westerns: *Los Pistoleros* (1964); *Pistoleros de la Frontera* (1964); and *El Mexicano* (1965) with Elsa Aguirre, the latter two directed by veteran René Cardona, Sr.

Rivero moved up to "A" parts with a supporting role as Miguel Páramo in Carlos Vero's *Pedro Páramo* (1966) with Pilar Pellicer. He then played the romantic leading men in *Como Pescar Marido* (1966), with Maricruz Oliver, Fanny Cano and Joaquin Cordero, and *Arullo de Diós* (1966) with Libertad Lamarque. He returned to action films directed by René Cardona, Jr., with *Operación 67* (1967), with El Santo, and René Cardona, Sr.'s *El Tesoro de Moctezuma* (1968). By the end of the decade he had positioned himself as one of the top action stars of Mexican films.

He made his U.S. film debut as the Indian brave Spotted Wolf in Ralph Nelson's impressive *Soldier Blue* (1970), which recounted the U.S. Cavalry's massacre at Sand Creek. It costarred Candice Bergen, Peter Strauss and Aurora Clavel. *Variety* commented, "Mexican actor Jorge Rivero, as the Indian chief, makes the most of a very short time on screen."[101]

Howard Hawks cast him as the Mexican-French Captain Pierre Cardona in his perky western *Rio Lobo* (1970) with John Wayne and Jennifer O'Neill. Rivero recollected later, "Working with John Wayne made me a big man in Mexico. He's Mexico's favorite Hollywood actor. Being in a picture with Duke raises my status and my salary in Mexico City. Besides, it fulfills my dream of acting in a Hollywood movie."[102]

He made his third U.S. film appearance in the role of Cesar Menendez in Andrew V. McLaglen's sardonic western *The Last Hard Man* (1976), with an impressive cast that included Charlton Heston, James Coburn, Barbara Hershey, and Michael Parks.

Alternating in Mexican and U.S. films, he established his own production company with Carlos Vasallo.

Rivero's most ambitious U.S. film during the 1980s was Frank Zuniga's *Fist Fighter* (1989), released in English and Spanish. The *Los Angeles Times* said Rivero was "a likable action hero ... who projects rarely seen burly wholesomeness, like a matinee idol from a gentler, less cynical era."[103] Attempting to establish himself in Hollywood proved difficult. He stated, "In the United States there is a lot of competition. It's not like in Mexico where I'm a big film star. Here, there are a hundred Jorge Rivero types.... You have to remember, I'm coming from a Latin American country. I'm a foreigner, and some people are uncomfortable with this."[104]

Consequently, he was convinced to change his name to "George Rivero." He commented, "They told me it was hard to sell a movie with a Latin American guy playing the lead. It bothered me, but what could I do."[105]

His most recent films include a remake of the classic Mexican film *The Pearl* (2001). He has appeared in several Mexican *telenovelas*.

The muscular star has had limited success making the crossover into U.S. films, but in Mexico and Latin America he continues to be an important box-office attraction. More recently, he has starred in Mexican *telenovelas* and continues to seek financing for film projects he hopes to produce.

MIGUEL ROBELO

Miguel Robelo was born of Puerto Rican ancestry and became a well-respected actor in theater. However, it was in film and television that he made his mark.

During the 1970s, he won rave reviews in the role of Juan in Westwood Playhouse's *Short Eyes*. He later directed for the Los Angeles Actor's Theatre. He appeared in numerous television shows during this period and later, among them *Chico and the Man*, *Charlie's Angels*, *Kojak*, and *Falcon Crest*.

His most important role came as the tortured Chicano artist at the verge of suicide in Alejandro Grattan's *Only Once in a Lifetime* in 1978, for which he earned wide acclaim.

PEPE SERNA

For almost three decades the versatile Chicano actor Pepe Serna has been giving consistently good performances in theater, television and film.

Pepe Serna is a veteran performer and has worked in every type of role.

He was born on July 23, 1944, in Corpus Christi, Texas. He began acting when he was six. By high school he had won numerous awards in the National Forensic League. Sometime later he took up boxing at his godfather's boxing ring and became the welterweight Golden Gloves champion of the area. After serving six months in the Marine reserves, he headed for Los Angeles to become an actor.

He studied at Del Mar College in Texas and the University of the Americas in Mexico City. He was a resident actor in the Spanish Theatre in Mexico City, served two years with Mark Taper's Improvisational Theatre Project and six years with Synergy Trust Improvisational Theatre Project. He did theater in Los Angeles and Mexico before making his film debut in a bit role in Dalton Trumbo's antiwar drama *Johnny Got His Gun* (1971). During this time he also appeared in the racial prejudice drama *Red Sky in the Morning* (1970); Henry Hathaway's western *Shoot-Out* (1971); and Richard Fleisher's crime drama *The New Centurions* (1972). He made numerous television appearances.

Serna has worked continuously in feature films and television films. Usually, he has been cast in featured character roles in films and supporting roles on television. He is philosophical about it: "The piece is the star. That's why I work all the time because I don't believe in small parts. If the writer wrote it, then it's important. If I like it I'll do it."[106]

His television films include *The Gun* (1974, ABC); *The Last Angry Man* (1974, ABC); *The Deadly Tower* (1975, NBC); *The Desperate Miles* (1975, ABC); *McNaughton's Daughter* (1976, NBC); *Streets of L.A.* (1979, CBS); *City in Fear* (1980, ABC); *The Monkey Mission* (1981, NBC); *Three Hundred Miles for Stephanie* (1981, NBC); *White Water Rebels* (1983, CBS); *Best Kept Secrets* (1984, ABC); *Streets of Justice* (1985, NBC); and *A Year in the Life* (1986, NBC), among others. He had a supporting role in the television miniseries *Sadat* (1983).

His feature films include Henry Hathaway's *Hang-Up* (1974); *Day of the Locust* (1975) with Karen Black; Sidney Pollack's *Honeysuckle Rose* (1980) with Willie Nelson; Richard Donner's *Inside Moves* (1980) with John Savage; *Vice Squad* (1982); William Friedkin's comedy *Deal of the Century* (1983) with Sigourney Weaver and Chevy Chase; Brian De Palma's *Scarface* (1983) with Al Pacino; *Heartbreaker* (1983); *The Adventures of Buckaroo Banzai* (1984); the comedy western *Silverado* (1985) with Rosanna Arquette; *Fandango* (1985) with Kevin Costner; *Out of Bounds* (1986); and the comedy *Caddyshack II* (1988) with Robert Stack and Dan Aykroyd.

Serna has been especially memorable in a quartet of films based on the Chicano experience. He appeared in Jesús Salvador Treviño's powerful drama of the Chicano/Mexican labor struggle *Raíces de Sangre/Roots of Blood* (1979) in the role of Juan Vallejo; Treviño's chronicle of Mexico's dispossession of Texas, *Seguin* (1980, PBS), as a young firebrand; Robert Young's *The Ballad of Gregorio Cortez* (1983) in the pivotal role of Romaldo; and in Isaac Artenstein's *Break of Dawn* (1988) as the indomitable Primo.

In relation to his vocation, he has described himself as a "very broad actor but easy to direct. I'm not a tortured actor—in our heads, you know, we're all brilliant but the minute you try to put it together with your limbs it becomes another thing. For me a part is never finished. I find it thrilling to keep searching and finding within the routines of what the director wants."[107]

In 1979, he was honored by the Mexican-American Fine Arts Association in Montebello after a youth poll selected him as instrumental in inspiring young people to enter the performing arts.

He has returned to the theater often. He played Joy in Luis Valdez' play *Zoot Suit* (1977–78). In 1988, he returned to the theater after a ten-year absence in Milcha Sanchez' play *Roosters* at the Los Angeles Theatre Center to excellent notices.

Other films include Robert Towne's *Tequila Sunrise* (1989) with Mel Gibson and Kurt Russell, and Edward James Olmos' *American Me* (1992), in which he played a treacherous gang member. During the 1993–94 television season, he played a widowed Chicano father on CBS's *Second Chance*. The role was unusual not only in that it was a positive role but that it existed at all. Serna commented, "This is by far the best, most positive part I've ever gotten. It's the best thing seen in showing a Mexican American family that is strong, caring, intelligent and proud of their culture. Television always tends to exploit, and it has always exploited Latinos in the worst light."[108] He added that he was pleased "to show young Latinos that the possibilities are there for anything you can dream of. I love that I'm playing a positive guy ... Latino professionals from around the country call me and they think I'm a genius for writing all this brilliant stuff, for finally getting us up there on the screen...."[109]

Serna's most recent films include *The Virgin of Juarez* (2006); *Moe* (2008); and *Clean Sweep* (2012). He was a regular on the television series *American Family* (2002); *Justice League* (2003); *The PJs* (1999–2008); and *Criminal Minds* (2008). Serna has been married for twenty-two years to the former Diane Paton.

MARTIN SHEEN

By the beginning of the 1970s, Martin Sheen had established himself as the hottest and most enigmatic young actor in the tradition of James Dean. Since then, his social and political activism has taken center stage at the expense of his acting career.

He was born Ramón Estévez in Dayton, Ohio, on August 3, 1940, to a Spanish immigrant father and an Irish mother. His mother died when he was eleven, leaving his father to raise ten children. From high school he went directly to New York City and there began acting at the off-off-Broadway Living Theatre while working in the usual assortment of odd jobs. It was at this point that he changed his name to Martin Sheen, an act which he would subsequently regret. He said later, "When I was growing up, I wanted to be called Ramón, but everybody called me nicknames. They called me Ray, they called me Cactus Ray, they called me Eyes, and they called me Isaac. One of the reasons I changed my name was because no one would say it."[110]

He obtained his big break in theater when he landed the role of the returning soldier Timothy Cleary in Frank Gilroy's Pulitzer Prize–winning play *The Subject Was Roses* in 1964.

He made his film debut as one of two young punks who terrorize a group of hapless subway passengers in *The Incident* (1967, 20th Century–Fox) with Ruby Dee, Beau Bridges and Jan Sterling. He then appeared in the film adaptation of *The Subject Was Roses* (1968) with Patricia Neal, in which he repeated his role from the play. He earned rave notices and the film catapulted him to film stardom. He then played Lieutenant Dobbs in Mike Nichols' film adaptation of Joseph Heller's antiwar novel *Catch-22* (1970) with Orson Welles, Paula Prentiss, Tony Perkins, Alan Arkin and John Voight.

After these two notable films, however, he found himself in a series of routine films: *No Drums, No Bugles* (1971), in which he played a conscientious objector during the Civil War; *When the Line Goes Through* (1971), which was never released; *Pick-Up on 101* (1971); and *Rage* (1972) with George C. Scott (who also directed).

The film that returned him to prominence was Terrence Malick's dark and stark *Badlands* (1973), about the Starkweather-Fugate murder spree in Nebraska and nearby states in 1958. The film costarred Sissy Spacek and Warren Oates. The movie has acquired a cult status and Sheen gave one of his best performances. He was given the Best Actor Award at the San Sebastian Film Festival.

After this triumph he once more fell into a career doldrums with a slew of inferior films: *The Legend of Earl Durand* (1974); *The Cassandra Crossing* (1977) with Burt Lancaster; *The Little Girl Who Lives Down the Lane* (1977) with Alexis Smith; and the television movie *Sweet Hostage* (1978) with Jeanne Cooper and Linda Blair.

Robert Duvall (left) and Martin Sheen (alias Martin Estevez, right) in *Apocalypse Now* **(1979, United Artists/Metro-Goldwyn-Mayer).**

At this point, Francis Ford Coppola cast him in the pivotal role of Captain Willard, who is ordered to exterminate Colonel Kurtz (Marlon Brando), an American gone berserk during the Vietnam War, in *Apocalypse Now* (1979). He won wide acclaim for his powerful performance. During the arduous filming in the Philippines, he suffered a heart attack. He later commented, "The heart attack changed my life. I nearly died, and I realized I'd been dead all my life. I had not been responding to the spirit in me. I had thrown off Catholicism. My career had been of paramount interest all my life."[111] His political activism dates from that experience. He marched, protested and was arrested over involvement of the U.S. in Central America, homelessness, and nuclear weapons, among other issues. He has stated, "Not many of us are willing to change profoundly. Yet the kind of people who will change their lives are those that do. I don't want to change profoundly. I still love my cigarettes, my pool, my car, my image."[112]

His film career continued, but without many more great roles: the western *Eagle's Wing* (1979); the sci fi *The Final Countdown* (1982); a cameo in Richard Attenborough's excellent *Gandhi* (1982); *That Championship Season* (1982) with Robert Mitchum and Nick Nolte; *Man, Woman and Child* (1983); *The Dead Zone* (1983); *Enigma* (1983); *Firestarter* (1984); *Loophole* (1986) with Susannah York and Albert Finney; John Schlesinger's *The Believer* (1987) with Helen Shaver; *Siesta* (1987); *DA* (1988); *Judgment in Berlin* (1988); and *Beverly Hills Brats* (1989). He also did the narration for an Academy Award–winning documentary about Native Americans, *Broken Rainbow* (1985), and one about El Salvador, *The Name of the People* (1985). One of his better recent roles was in Oliver Stone's *Wall Street* (1987) with Michael Douglas and Martin's son Charlie Sheen.

During this period, his best roles were on television. He played the only U.S. soldier executed for desertion during World War II in *The Execution of Private Slovik* (1974); John Dean, of the Watergate scandal, in *Blind Ambition* (1981, CBS); and President John F. Kennedy, in arguably his greatest performance, in *Kennedy* (1983, NBC).

His other television films include *Then Came Bronson* (1960, CBS); *Goodbye Raggedy Ann* (1971, CBS); *Mongo's Back in Town* (1971, CBS); *Pursuit* (1972, ABC); *That Certain Summer* (1972, ABC); *Welcome Home, Johnny Bristol* (1972, CBS); *Catholics* (1973, CBS); *Crime Club* (1973, CBS); *Letter from Three Loves* (1973, ABC); *Message to My Daughter* (1973, ABC); *The California Kid* (1974, ABC); *The Story of Pretty Boy Floyd* (1974, ABC); *Sweet Hostage* (1975, ABC); *The Last Survivor* (1975, NBC); *In the Custody of Strangers* (1982, ABC); *Choices of the Heart* (1983, NBC); *The Guardian* (1984, HBO); *Consenting Adult* (1985, ABC); *The Atlanta Child Murders* (1985, CBS); *Out of the Darkness* (1985, CBS); *News at Eleven* (1986, CBS); *Samaritan: The Mitch Snyder Story* (1986, CBS); and *Shattered Spirits* (1986, ABC), among others.

He and his wife Janet have four children: Ramon, Renee and two well-known film stars, Emilio Estevez and Charlie Sheen.

Aside from his activism, acting continues to be an important passion: "Walking on a movie set, though, is paradise. And woe to anyone who screws up paradise. I still have a great passion for acting, and I take great joy in it, going into that undiscovered country, because then I discover myself. Acting is the creative expression I have for all the other parts of me."[113] During September 1998, he was honored at the 12th annual Hispanic Heritage Awards at the Kennedy Center in Washington, D.C.

His 1990s films include *Hear No Evil* (1994); a cameo in the spy spoof *Hot Shots! Part Deux* (1994) opposite his son, Charlie Sheen; and the epic *Gettysburg* (1994), in which he played General Robert E. Lee.

He was directed by his son, Emilio Estevez (who also costarred) in *The War at Home* (1996). The *Los Angeles Times* noted, "'The War at Home' offers a quartet of performances that are among the year's best."[114] The *New York Times* commented, "Mr. Sheen's stern but caring patriarch struggling to maintain his authority is the sort of fearsome domestic autocrat that a lesser actor could have made into a sitting duck."[115]

His more recent work includes *Truth or Consequences, N.M.* (1997) with Donald Sutherland; the HBO film *Hostile Waters* (1997) with Max von Sydow; and the television films *Storm* (1999, Fox) and *Forget Me Not* (1999, CBS). He starred as a fictional U.S. president on NBC's *The West Wing* (September 22, 1999–May 14, 2006). The show went on to become one of the most widely acclaimed and watched on television. More recently, he was directed by his son Emilio Estevez in the film *The Way* (2011), in which he plays a Catholic trying to recover his faith.

JESÚS SALVADOR TREVIÑO

Director and writer Jesús Salvador Treviño holds an honored place in the annals of Chicano cinema. He has served as a pioneer. He made his mark in historical documentaries that chronicled the Chicano movement experience. However, with the exception of two films, most of his output has been on television.

He was born on March 26, 1946, in El Paso, Texas, to Mexican parents. He recalled years later that his fascination with film began in childhood: "My earliest recollection of motion pictures was as a child of six or seven years of age. My stepfather worked at the Floral Drive-In in East Los Angeles and he would often take me to work with him. It was there that I saw my first films that made an impression on me. However, it wasn't until I got involved in the Chicano Movement as an activist in 1968 and began to film protests and rallies that the true power of film became evident to me. That was when I really began to perceive my role as a Chicano media activist who would work in all media, especially in film and television."[116]

He attended Occidental College on a minority scholarship and graduated in 1968 with a degree in philosophy. Upon graduation he enrolled in a government-funded program called New Communicators, where he acquired filmmaking skills. Upon the program's termination, he was employed in 1970 by Los Angeles public television station KCET for the nightly show *Ahora*, which focused on the Mexican-American community. He also produced a series of notable specials.

Regarding this period, he commented, "The experience was fundamental to my career and to my artistic development. It was baptism by fire. We produced 175 live half-hour programs that spanned the definition of what was television: we produced music shows, interview shows, remote broadcast, theater productions, telecast community protests and picket lines, as well as producing an original La Raza history series."[117]

The best of these specials was the documentary *Yo Soy Chicano!* which first aired in August 1972. It chronicled the past and contemporary history of Chicanos. *Yo Soy Chicano!* and Luis Valdez' *I Am Joaquin* remain the two most famous and acclaimed documentaries on the Chicano historical experience. About *Yo Soy Chicano!* Treviño stated, "This documentary was a key transition in my career and my development as a filmmaker and director. Prior to *Yo Soy Chicano!*, I had written and directed a number of Super–8 student films, notably *La Raza Nueva* (1968), which was my personal account of the six-day Los Angeles Board of Education sit-in [to reinstate teacher Saul Castro, who had been involved in the East Los Angeles High School walkouts] ... which I filmed ... as a participant. I had also written and directed a 16 mm student film, *¡Ya Basta!* and numerous *Ahora!* television programs, and the Siqueiros documentary *América Tropical*. I was obsessed with the notion of 'giving a face to our people.' At that time only Carey McWilliams' book *North from Mexico* was available. Rudy Acuña's *Occupied America* hadn't come out yet. I felt Chicanos needed to show our history. I felt that part of the drop-out was that kids felt inferior and did not know their rich history and traditions and the contributions Chicanos had made to the United States."[118]

Treviño himself was very much involved in the Chicano movement—the Chicano civil rights struggle: "I was very committed to the political activity that was going on in my community and I was committed to using the media as a way of expressing the concerns, aspirations, and strategies of that community."[119]

In 1976, he directed his first feature film, *Raíces de Sangre/Roots of Blood* (released in the U.S. in 1979), financed by Conacine, Mexico's national film corporation. It was the first

Mexican-financed film to be written and directed by a Chicano. *Variety* wrote that it was "a solidly made call to political involvement and activism, which effectively points up the problems of Mexicans on the border in very human terms" and said, "*Raíces De Sangre* is a refreshingly honest antidote to Hollywood's recent dalliance with Chicano problem pictures."[120] The film documented the unity of two labor struggles along both sides of the border: Mexican and Chicano.

Treviño explained the film's purpose: "Chicanos have also adopted a lot of American culture, we tend to be viewed as agringados—assimilated into the worst of American society ... the idea originally was to present Mexicans with a positive image of who we are. But once I got into the project, I saw the need to have it work both ways. To have the film deliver a message about Mexicans and Chicanos, as well as the other way around because we are no less guilty of prejudice against our Mexican brothers and sisters...."[121]

Treviño was very pleased with the film's reception. *Raíces De Sangre* had a short release in 1977 to Mexican audiences and received positive reviews. Treviño recalled, "Later, in 1979, we released an English subtitled version in the United States and it did brisk business here in both languages and revived a Mexican re-release of the film to favorable response. Whether everyone who sat [through] it got the message of cross-bordersolidarity and unity— who can tell? I know that on this side of the border, Cesar Chavez thought enough of it to attend the Los Angeles premiere and introduce the film. And I know that my filmmaker friends in Mexico got the message and I know that it set a precedent for Chicanos and Mexicanos dealing with one another."[122] The film unfortunately has not been released on video or DVD due to the Mexican government's intransigence and bureaucracy.

In 1980, Treviño directed *Seguín* (PBS), about Juan Seguín, who was involved in the 1836 Texas Rebellion against Mexico. Initially, Seguín had been involved with the Euro-American colonists' independence movement, but he ultimately regretted his involvement and then fought on the side of Mexico in the Mexican-American War. Treviño recollected about the film, "There are many versions to the Alamo myth and I tried to cut though some of the American precepts and give a version based on facts, some which Americans were not ready to hear. But Chicanos also had trouble with my version. I was criticized for my portrayal of Seguín, indeed for even including him in the film by some activists who had hoped for a more doctrinaire, politically correct version of the story. Some were critical [that I made] Seguín a hero since he was from the 'ruling class of that time.'"[123]

Concerning the extraordinary cast of Chicano and Latino performers in the film, which included Edward James Olmos, A Martinez, Henry Darrow, Alma Martínez, Rose Portillo, and Danny De La Paz, he noted, "By far the thing I remember most is the spirit of cooperation and unity that infused our work together. From the very beginning when all the actors agreed to be paid the same amount of money for their work, there was no jockeying for more pay the next day because I explained to them that the film was going to be made on a shoe-string budget."[124]

In 1985, he codirected along with Luis Torres the sequel to *Yo Soy Chicano!* which was entitled *Yo Soy.* He commented on the changing times, "Not many people are out on the streets these days.... Now there are Gloria Molina and other elected officials to carry the struggle. They deal with our problems within the system which means ... that the 60's were a success. Without the 60's there would never have been the people you see in *Yo Soy.* These times produced on a mass level, for the first time, the kinds of people who have come back to the barrio ... the politicians and the professionals."[125]

With regard to the image of Latinos and African Americans in the media, Treviño stated, "They have attempted to give their stories here and there or sprinkling the dialogue with some Black vernacular. That's not good enough. They inevitably come out looking like White films, which is what they are. The ethnic material must be integrated into the narrative. I'm confident I can do that because my point of view is fundamentally Chicano. That's who I am, and that's how I was raised."[126]

When asked about who encouraged him to keep working despite Hollywood's continued closed-mindedness about minorities, he said, "The success of the Cubans, the Brazilians and some of the younger Mexican filmmakers encourages Chicanos to keep trying to make their new films. We meet them at the film festivals in Latin America. We see their films and they see ours. The content is the same, the concerns are the same—social justice, lives as real people live them—and this gives us a sense of commonality of belonging."[127]

Trevino has continued working, primarily in television. One notable directing credit was a CBS Schoolbreak Special segment entitled *Gangs* (1986), about a Chicano youth's attempt to break out of a gang; and *The Eddie Matos Story* (1995, HBO), a true story about a teenage Puerto Rican drug dealer who ends up paralyzed. These two projects proved especially satisfying and rewarding for him: "*Gangs* was a particularly important project for me. I had all the character arcs and good drama. But the script was also full of misconceptions and stereotypes about the Chicano experience. Finally, I decided that I could not in good conscience direct the script as written. I thanked the producer and told him I couldn't accept the job. But, I also gave him a five-page single-spaced critique of the script, suggesting ways in which it could be improved and made more sensitive to our reality. To my surprise, Howard Meltzer (the producer) called me back and offered me the directing job on the condition that I sit down with the writer and help change the script to include my suggestions. I was dumbfounded! This never happens in Hollywood. Well, I did meet with the writer and I did direct the project and it wound up winning the Director's Guild Award for Best Daytime Drama as well as the Museo del Barrio's First Prize for Best Television Program in 1988. Since that time I have gone on to direct eight hours of television for Howard Meltzer, including *The Eddie Matos Story,* [a true story about] a Puerto Rican drug dealer of seventeen years of age crippled for life following a shooting. Matos has gone on to speak to high school students warning them [about] a life of drugs and crime."[128]

Among his other television credits are such shows as *NYPD Blue, Gabriel's Fire, Courthouse, Babylon, The Burning Season, SeaQuest, Space: Above and Beyond, Star Trek: Voyager, Nash Bridges* and *New York Undercover.* About directing for television, he commented, "It has given me the opportunity to learn and practice a variety of film styles and techniques, to work with a variety of actors and to try different approaches at someone's expense. I think all this helps me to become a better director and can only help me for the larger projects of my own [that] I will direct."[129]

Jesús Salvador Treviño is an indestructible optimist with the hindsight of history: "The key for me is not losing sight of why I originally became a filmmaker, or losing sight of the kind of world we can and should bring about. If your works are to help in liberating the human spirit, a little dirt on your wings is the price you sometimes have to pay."[130]

When I asked him about the sorry state of Latinos in film and television and what has kept him going, he replied, "What keeps me going is the firm conviction that our time is coming and the knowledge that you can't hit a home run if you never go up to bat or give up the game. By far the majority of Hollywood producers don't set out to consciously discriminate against Latinos by not hiring Latinos for a project he or she is producing. They merely go to the people they already know, or people on whom there is a good word of mouth. These people are often their friends, who have traditionally been white and not Latino."[131]

He directed the feature film *Resurrection* in 2000 for Showtime, which chronicled the trials and tribulations of a Chicano boxing family in East Los Angeles. It marked the first Latino-themed cable film. He commented, "Well, the creator of the show, Dennis Leoni, had been developing *Resurrection Blvd.* for quite a number of years. It had started off as Dennis' version of *Wonder Years* set in Tucson, Arizona. When he pitched to Showtime they suggested it be set in Los Angeles, so he went back and rewrote it and that is what came out as the pilot for *Resurrection Blvd.* Once he got the green light of making a two-hour pilot he interviewed several potential directions and settled on me."[132]

As the supervising producer, he stated about this role, "Early on, I approached Showtime and Dennis with the notion that we should see East Los Angeles in terms of visuals that America has not seen. So, one of the things I instituted was 'bumpers'—short scenes, short shots of East L.A. that we intersperse throughout the one-hour episode. To give a sense that you are there. Many of the bumpers reflect life in East L.A.: mariachis, playing soccer, *paleteros*, fruit vendors, and murals, everything that is rich life in East Los Angeles. All of this, I think, has given the show a certain richness."[133]

In reference to the significance of the show, he noted, "We're hoping it sets the precedent. We're hoping that other networks will look at it and say, 'There are not only interesting stories to be told, but there's also an audience that feels that they are telling our stories.'"[134]

Treviño is currently working on a documentary entitled *In Search of Aztlán* with the comedy trio Culture Clash and a feature film, *Heroes Street*. More recently, he published a book entitled *Eyewitness: A Filmmaker's Memoirs of the Chicano Movement*.

DANIEL VALDEZ

Actor-musician Daniel Valdez, the younger brother of director-writer Luis Valdez, has played a prominent role in the development of Chicano cinema. It is an important role that is not commensurate with his only modest fame.

He was born on April 7, 1949, in Delano, California, to a family of Mexican farm workers. He began working in the fields at a young age, and subsequently his schooling was interrupted as his family followed the crops throughout the San Joaquin Valley. He and his brother became involved in the Chicano movement that blossomed across the Southwest in the mid–1960s. Both were especially involved in the cause of the underpaid and impoverished farm workers and the efforts to organize the United Farm Workers Union (UFW) led by Cesar Chavez.

Luis founded El Teatro Campesino (the Farm Worker's Theater) to help educate and politicize union members and supporters. It consisted initially of a conglomeration of amateur musicians, actors, and writers, most of them farm workers. They performed in the open fields, on the back of pickup trucks, and at churches and community centers. Beginning in 1969, El Teatro Campesino began touring throughout the United States and Europe to enthusiastic crowds.

Daniel produced several solo albums, including *Mestizo* and *Songs of the Strike,* a collection of songs he wrote for the United Farm Workers. In 1978, he essayed the title role of Henry Reyna in Luis Valdez' play *Zoot Suit,* about the Sleepy Lagoon murder trial of 1943, which resulted in the incarceration of seventeen innocent Chicanos. The play opened at the Mark Taper Forum in Los Angeles and was performed thereafter in the Southwest. The play, whose music Daniel wrote, had a limited run on Broadway in New York City.

Daniel made his film debut in the title role of a farm worker union activist, Chuy Estrada, in *Which Way Is Up?* (1977, Universal) opposite Richard Pryor and Lonette McKee. His second film role was as the doomed sound man Hector Salas in James Bridges' *The China Syndrome* (1979, Columbia), about a Three Mile Island–like nuclear reactor breakdown. The film starred Jane Fonda, Jack Lemmon, and Michael Douglas (who also produced). In 1981, Valdez recreated his role of Henry Reyna in the film version of *Zoot Suit* (1981, Universal), which was directed by Luis Valdez. Daniel stated about the experience, "It was uncomfortable having to make the change to film, but I prefer it now because it can reveal what the stage can't. You can't see it all on the stage—the changes in expression and the other little things. And it's very frustrating to me because you can't reach that guy in the back row. I want to reach out to everybody."[135]

With regard to his most famous role, he commented, "The reality of Henry Reyna was me and in a lot of ways I feel very close to him. I understand the gangs, and I know what it's to grow up poor, but not to be surrounded by people who care about you. So much of what my brother writes about comes right out of our family life, which was a very hostile environment, and yet at the same time it was filled with love."[136]

In 1987, he was the associate producer of the Luis Valdez–directed and scripted *La Bamba* (Columbia), about pioneer Chicano rocker Ritchie Valens (Valenzuela) who died at the age of 17 in 1959. Daniel had hoped to play Valens, but it took ten years to put the film together and by that time he was too old for the part. He settled for the small role of Lelo, a friend of the Valenzuela family. In retrospect, Daniel was the ideal choice for the title role. Nevertheless, the film was a huge commercial success and earned some glowing reviews.

Since then, he has been involved in his brother's stage and television projects, like *Corridos* (1987), about the evolution of the *corridos* and Mexican/Chicano history. He has also performed with Linda Ronstadt in concert tours and albums.

He played the role of a farm worker in Silverio Perez's *Y No Se Lo Tragó La Tierra* (1996), and also appeared in *Silvio Prieto* (1999) and *Clon* (2005).

ISELA VEGA

For almost twenty years (from the late 1960s to the mid–1980s) the auburn-haired Mexican Isela Vega was one of the foremost box-office attractions in Mexico and Latin America. In two of her U.S. films (those directed by Sam Peckinpah), she contributed evidence that she was a considerable actress and not only a reigning witless sex symbol.

She was born Isela Vega Durazo in Hermosillo, Sonora, Mexico, on November 5, 1939. At the age of 18 she was crowned the princess of the carnival of Hermosillo. She soon branched out into singing and, inevitably, acting. In her late teens she set out for Los Angeles with the dream of making a career in fashion design. Her ambition took her into a variety of jobs: modeling, secretarial work, factory worker, cosmetician, and, finally, a professional singer in nightclubs and on television in Mexico City. She then underwent intensive training for acting under the late Seki Sano, a Japanese-born teacher of the arts.

She made her Mexican film debut in *Verano Violento* in 1960 and had a small role in the U.S. film *Rage* (1966). However, her first significant roles were in *Don Juan 67* (1966), opposite the popular Mauricio Garces and David Reynoso, and *SOS Conspiracion Bikini* (1966) with Julio Alemán, in which she had a more prominent role. Her career took off quickly after playing Cantinflas' leading lady in *Por Mis Pistolas* (1966).

She followed that film with leads in *Cámara de Terror* (1968) with Boris Karloff and *Tempora Salvaje* (1968) with Diane McBain and Armando Silvestre. She was quickly typecast in the role of exotic sexpot and earned the growing animosity of film critics. However, with a growing and devoted fan following, she soon evolved into one of the most bankable film stars in Mexico from the late 1960s to the 1980s.

In *El Deseo Llegó de Noche* (1968) she played a sheltered, frustrated young woman in love with an impotent doctor (Joaquin Cordero). However, her main film persona was that of a hard-bitten, independent, and assertive woman who was usually involved in illicit activities or a disenchanted gold-digger. For example, in *El Festín de la Loba* (1972), she played a manipulative painter who exploits a beautiful, naïve model (Pilar Pellicer). By the mid–1970s, she had made some 25 films. Her most popular Mexican films include *La Psicodélicas* (1968); *Las Golfas* (1969); *El Oficio Más Antiguo del Mundo* (1970); *El llanto de la Tortura* (1975); *El Hombre de los Hongos* (1976); *Las Sieta Cucas* (1981); *El Secuestro de Lola* (1985); *Salvajes* (1989); *En Legítima Defensa* (1992); *Fuera del Cielo* (2006); *Crepúsculo Rojo* (2008); and *Mas Allá del Muro* (2011).

She made her second U.S.

Isela Vega and Warren Oates in *Bring Me the Head of Alfredo Garcia* (1974, United Artists).

film appearance in the routine western *The Deadly Trackers* (1973, Warner Bros.), partly helmed by the cult director Samuel Fuller and starring Richard Harris, Rod Taylor, and Pedro Armendáriz, Jr.

She was cast in the dark and underrated Sam Peckinpah–directed *Bring Me the Head of Alfredo Garcia* (1974, Warner Bros.). She played Elita, a *cantinera* who takes up with a sardonic and cynical U.S. expatriate (Warren Oates) who becomes obsessed with a bounty reward that he wants to get so they can make a new life together. Isela described her character as "an anguished character of a woman who comes from the slums and works in a very expensive whorehouse, I would call it. She wants to retire from her violent life and settle down with this guy, this gringo.... It's her last chance. So she proposed to him ... I gave it all, you know, and whatever happens, I won't die of shame; I told the truth in the film."[137]

Of Peckinpah she said, "Actually, it is a fact the whole world thinks Sam is just a violent human being for what he portrays on the screen. But I find him like a sweet cake."[138]

For her performance, she received the best notices of her entire career. *Variety* noted, "Vega comes off well in the context of the story."[139] The *Los Angeles Times* commented, "The movie's discovery is Señorita Vega, a nightclub singer who has previously done bit parts in film. She had womanly warmth and sincerity in the tradition of Moreau and Mercouri."[140] The *Los Angeles Herald-Examiner* stated, "This woman [is] a lovely and warm companion playedg with soothing, engaging affection by Mexican actress Isela Vega."[141] *Newsweek* commented on the "extraordinary warm, wise performance from Vega."[142] *Films and Filming* wrote of "a fine performance form Isela Vega as Elita."[143] The *Hollywood Reporter* noted, "Isela Vega is a Mexican Jeanne Moreau whose mellowed beauty and knowledgeable fatalism creates a fascinating exception to Peckinpah's macho reputation."[144]

She was reteamed with Warren Oates in the critically lambasted but commercially successful *Drum* (1976, United Artists), the sequel to *Mandingo*. Isela played Marianna, a

Barbarosa (1982) brought together three generations of Mexican-American film stars: (left to right) Isela Vega from the 1970s, Gilbert Roland from the 1920s, and Alma Martínez from the 1980s.

promiscuous Cuban mistress. The cast included the popular Pam Grier and future heavy-weight boxing champion Ken Norton. She then played Josefina, a discarded señorita in love with a Euro-American outlaw (Willie Nelson), in *Barbarosa* (1982, Universal) with Gilbert Roland, Alma Martínez, and Danny De La Paz. The sensitive film disappeared unappreciated until years later when it won a cult status. She also costarred in two television films: *The Rhinemann Exchange* (1977, Universal) with José Ferrer; and *The Streets of L.A.* (1979, CBS) with Joanne Woodward.

She was married twice: once to Mexican actor Jorge Luke and once to Mexican singer Alberto Vasquez. Both marriages ended in divorce. She has two children and is raising three others, the children of her sister who was killed in a plane crash.

Regarding nudity on the screen she stated on one occasion, "Sex comes from the inside. I believe the sexiest scenes are with your clothes on."[145]

Over the years she has appeared in U.S. feature films and television films. She was in the television film *The Alamo: Thirteen Days of Glory* (1987) with Raúl Juliá, James Arness, and Alec Baldwin, in which she played the mistress of General Santa Anna. She has amassed more than 100 film and television credits. She has starred in several popular Mexican *telenovelas*. She has had meaty character roles in notable Mexican films such as in Luis Estrada's acclaimed *La Ley de Herodes* (1999) and *El Infierno* (2010). In 1986, she produced, wrote, and directed the film *Lovers of the Lord of the Night* and produced several other films. Isela Vega is a survivor and continues to contribute to cinema in many capacities.

RICHARD YNIGUEZ

Mexican American actor Richard Yniguez appeared to be the most promising Latino film star in the late 1970s. However, his career faded in the 1980s, another casualty of Hollywood intolerance of those who try to change the system.

He was born on December 8, 1946, in Firebaugh, California, and grew up in Sacramento. His mother died when he was still a child and for a while he moved in with his father in Guanajuato, Mexico, where he attended high school. He said of his early cinema images, "I was very impressed by Mexican cinema, at that time, because it was one thing my Dad would take me to and I would see these larger-than-life figures. I could identify with it. But there was still the other side of the coin, which was difficult for me because, watching films with John Wayne and all those other guys, I felt dehumanized. We were always the bad guy and to a great degree I was Indian."[146]

He joined the navy for a few years and upon his release performed with a band. It was while attending East Los Angeles College, where he majored in business administration, that he became attracted to acting. He began to study acting at Plaza de la Raza in Los Angeles.

In the late 1960s, Yniguez participated in the movement to improve and better the opportunities in film and television for Chicanos and Latinos. He started acting in 1968 in local theater and then television. He recollected later, "Back in the late 60's, I refused to do roles that I or others found demeaning. I still don't, but sometimes you have something that's borderline. My feeling now is that if I don't do it, they'll get another Latino actor who will. And maybe my experience will keep the role from being a stereotype—keep it from going over the line."[147]

He honed his acting skills in an extensive number of plays. His theater credits include

Nadine Vanderveld's *Queen Magnolia*; Federico García Lorca's *Blood Wedding*; Chekhov's *The Proposal*; Clifford Odets' *Waiting for Lefty*; and Tennessee Williams' *A Streetcar Named Desire*; and *Camino Real*.

Yniguez established his growing reputation as a handsome and excellent actor on television in the 1970s in such shows as: *Zorro* (2 episodes); *Midnight Caller*; *Supercarrier*; *The Flash*; *The New Lassie*; and *MacGyver*. He was a regular on several television shows: *Mama Malone* (1984, CBS); *Rituals* (1984–85, Fox); *O'Hara* (1987–88); and *Grand Slam* (1990, CBS).

He played second leads and leads in several television films during the 1970s and 1980s: *Tribes* (1970, ABC); *Fireball Forward* (1972, ABC) with Ricardo Montalbán; *Memories Never Die* (1972, CBS); *Man on a String* (1972, CBS); *Shark Kill* (1976, NBC); *Crash* (1978, CBS) with José Ferrer; *The Haunted Lady* (1977, NBC) with Donna Mills; *Crash* (1978, ABC) with Eddie Albert; *World War III* (1982, NBC) with Rock Hudson; and *Houston: The Legend of Texas* (1986, CBS) in which he played General Santa Anna.

Yniguez made several feature films: *Cancel My Reservation* (1972) with Eva Marie Saint and Bob Hope; *Together Brothers* (1974); and *Zandy's Bride* (1974) with Gene Hackman and Liv Ullmann. However, the role that brought him prominence and acclaim was that of the real-life Mexican-American policeman who killed Charles Whitman (portrayed by Kurt Russell) in the television film *The Deadly Tower* (1975). Whitman had killed thirteen and wounded thirty-three people from a tower at the University of Texas during August 1966. The film costarred John Forsythe and newcomer Pepe Serna. Yniguez would later state, "I thought *The Deadly Tower* would lead to bigger and better things ... but it didn't."[148]

Many years later, he commented about the importance of his role, "It was nice to see that we were bringing forward a positive Chicano who saved the day. It was a great experience for me and I think I grew a lot as a performer and it gave me a chance to really feel like I was starring in a project. So it was great fun."[149]

For a while, however, Yniguez did get good roles. He played three leads in the highly rated and respected television series *Police Story* on NBC. One two-hour episode entitled "River of Promise" won rave notices for its sensitivity and excellence. In it Yniguez played a Mexican-American policeman who goes undercover to investigate and apprehend a smuggling gang who exploit undocumented workers. The *Los Angeles Times* wrote, "That fine young actor Richard Yniguez plays the cop, Miguel Bataza, and he makes you feel the stomach-turning things he sees, watching his own people pick the bones of his brothers ... as this film attests, [he] is still a class act."[150] The episode costarred Jaime Sánchez and Edward James Olmos.

Yniguez then played Raymond Àvila, a former gang member attempting to convince his young brother (Danny De La Paz) to leave the gang life in Michael Pressman's *Boulevard Nights* (1979). The film was perhaps the best of the spate of gang films during the period, but it nevertheless met with controversy. However, there was no denying that both Yniguez and De la Paz gave brilliant performances, etching tender, yet, angry portrayals of two brothers. *Variety* commented, "While the acting throughout *Boulevard Nights* is first-rate, especially from Yniguez, du Bois and screen newcomer De La Paz, there is simply not enough to distinguish the pic from a number of [similar previous films.]"[151] Among Chicanos, however, the film has become a cult classic.

Yniguez had tried to persuade the studio to promote the film not as a gang film but as a story about the loving relationship between two brothers. The studio did not, and the film was picketed by some in the Chicano community. In reference to the controversy that resulted, Yniguez stated, "I accepted it [the film] with the grounds that they were going to promote this as either a love story between two brothers or a problem love story between a man and a woman, with a brother between them, some kind of triangle, because that would be defeating the purpose of the film. I got hurt by the film, literally in my pocketbook, as a performer, because I went against the marketing of the film, in that I didn't agree with the idea they market it as a gang film that was obvious and blatant."[152]

Yniguez had an important film role as the Harvard-educated and barrio-born Carlos Rivera in director-writer Jesús Salvador Treviño's *Raíces De Sangre/Roots of Blood* (1979, Conacine), the first and only Mexican-Chicano co-production (which was also shot bilingually). The film chronicled the union and political struggles of Chicanos and Mexicanos along the border. The *Los Angeles Times* commented, "They and the other characters are sympathetically drawn and involve the audience in personal—as well as ideological—conflicts."[153] *Variety* wrote, "A solidly made call to political involvement and activism, which effectively points up the problems of Mexicans on the border in very human terms ... Richard Yniguez is significantly more effective here than earlier this year in 'Boulevard Nights.'"[154]

Yniguez has very fond memories of this project: "I was very excited about the prospect of again doing a project about Latinos, with Chicanos and Mexicanos in this case, the two cultures basically colliding and in some cases coming together. And, it was also very good for me, because my wife, at the time (Roxanna Bonilla-Giannini), played my girlfriend. It gave us an opportunity to work together and grow. As far as the experience itself is concerned, as an actor I felt blessed having the opportunity to do it."[155]

After these three significant roles, Yniguez' career stalled. Later, Yniguez went on to direct one film shot in Costa Rica in 1983 and made an unsuccessful foray into television situation comedy. He continued to be an activist member of the Screen Actors Guild and the a screenwriters' guild. During 1987 and 1988, he was the president of Nosotros, the Latino media advocacy organization.

In more recent years, he made several television commercials for Spanish-language television. In 1996, he played the role of a Chicano mayor of Los Angeles in the HBO film *The Second Civil War* with a cast that included James Coburn, Elizabeth Peña, and Brian Keith. He continues to perform in theater, and was in the Nosotros production of *The Last Angry Brown Hat*. He is seen intermittently on television. Some recent film credits include *Meet Me in Miami* (2005); *B-Girl* (2009); and *Pretty Rosebud* (2011).

About changing the negative images of Latinos, he stated, "We need to invest in our own projects and be willing to lose money. For, in the long run, what you're doing is creating a catalogue of images that your children can appreciate and give them self-awareness, self-esteem, to go on to better and greater things, so that the community can also appreciate what our ancestors did."[156]

CARMEN ZAPATA

Carmen Zapata is a much respected actress who has performed on the stage and in film and television for more than thirty years.

She was born Carmen Margarita Zapata in New York City on July 15, 1927. Her father was Julio Zapata, a Mexican immigrant, and her mother, Ramona Roca, was from Argentina. She grew up in Spanish Harlem and thus was not well acquainted with her Mexican heritage until much later. As a child, she played the piano and sang in the school choir, as well as appeared in school plays. Carmen went on to study at the famed Actors Studio, as well as under Uta Hagen.

In 1947, she made her professional debut as part of the chorus in the Broadway hit *Oklahoma,* and she played the lead when it went on the road. Among her later Broadway roles are in such plays as *Stop the World, I Want to Get Off, Bells Are Ringing,* and *Guys and Dolls.* She performed in musicals for some twenty years. In between assignments, she worked in nightclubs performing her own singing and comedy act, *Marge Cameron.* At a low point in her career, she emceed at a strip club in Toledo, Ohio.

In 1967, after her mother's death, she moved to California to continue her acting career. She made her film debut in *Sol Madrid* (1968) as a prostitute. She commented to *Vista Magazine,* "I would try to play these roles with dignity, but I realized I was being boxed in. Although I made a lot of money and got a lot of visibility, people saw me only as a stereotype."[157] During this time she appeared extensively on television in such shows as *Marcus Welby, M.D., Flamingo Road,* and *Charlie's Angels.*

The limited opportunities and negative images of Latinos in film and television motivated her to become involved in efforts to change the situation. She was one of the cofounders of one of the first minority committees in the Screen Actors Guild and also became one of the original members of Nosotros, the Latino advocacy organization cofounded by Ricardo Montalbán.

In 1973, she and Cuban director Margarita Galvan cofounded the Bilingual Foundation of the Arts in the East Los Angeles barrio of Lincoln Heights. The foundation trained actors and performed plays (both bilingual and monolingual). She stated to *Vista Magazine,* "We had a hard time convincing people that we were capable and qualified because we were women; the fact that we were Hispanic made it twice as hard."[158]

Her visionary efforts earned her much admiration and many awards, including the Mexican-American Women's National Association Award for Exemplary Service and the National Council for La Raza's Rubén Salazar Award in Communications.

Zapata has been a regular in three television series: *The Man and the City* (1971–72, ABC) with Anthony Quinn; *Viva Valdez* (1976, ABC) with Rodolfo Hoyos; and *Hagen* (1980, CBS) with Chad Everett. She also played A Martinez' mother in the daytime soap *Santa Barbara.*

Her television films include *The Couple Takes a Wife* (1972); *The Girls of Huntington House* (1973); *My Darling Daughter's Anniversary* (1973); *Home of Our Own* (1975); *Winner Take All* (1975); *Shark Kill* (1976); *Flying High* (1978); *A Guide to the Married Man* (1978); *Leave Yesterday Behind* (1978); *Like a Normal Life* (1979); *Children of Divorce* (1980); *Homeward Bound* (1980); and *Not Just Another Affair* (1982).

Among her feature film credits are *Bad Charleston Charlie* (1973); *Hail, Hero!* (1977); *How to Beat the High Cost of Living* (1980); *Sister Act* (1992); *Point of No Return* (1993); *Sister Act 2: Back in the Habit* (1993); and *The Disappearance of Garcia Lorca* (1997). In 1985, she narrated *Las Madres de la Plaza de Mayo,* about a group of Argentine mothers attempting to uncover the fate of the "disappeared."

She was only married once, to Ron Friedman (1957–1973). She died January 5, 2014, in Los Angeles, California, of heart problems. She was 86.

V

The 1980s

The 1980s began with a series of U.S. military interventions in Latin America and the Middle East under the Reagan administration and ended with a historic thaw of United States–Soviet Union relations. Closer to home, the decade was deemed the "Decade of the Hispanic." The term was first used by the U.S. Census in 1980.

The decade began with tense East-West relations. The U.S.–orchestrated boycott of the Moscow Olympics in 1980 was seen as a sign of displeasure with the continued presence of Soviet troops in Afghanistan. The increasingly bellicose Reagan administration waged an intense eight-year covert war against Nicaragua and a counterinsurgency war in El Salvador. Reagan's gunboat diplomacy was capped by the invasion of Grenada. The lack of popular support for such policies of an imperial president induced Cold Warriors to establish a dual government apparatus which culminated with the Iran-Contra scandal. In the Middle East, the Palestinian question remained unresolved. Europe began the process towards a unified economy. Japan became the world's third most industrialized power. At the tail end of the decade, a new Soviet leader, Mikhail Gorbachev, initiated political and economic policies that contributed to fundamental changes in East-West relations.

In the meantime, the United States was the recipient of hundreds of thousands of Central American refugees fleeing the wars in their homeland, as well as Mexican workers responding to the U.S. economy's insatiable appetite for cheap labor. A pervasive jingoism and xenophobia began to assert itself. For example, ex–CIA director William Colby concluded in 1978 that Mexican migration was a greater danger and threat to the United States than the Soviet Union.[1] In California, in 1986, an "English Is the Official Language" proposition was passed. It was the beginning of several measures that would be instituted across the nation aimed against immigrants and Latinos.

Although the decade had been dubbed by some as "the decade of the Hispanic," politically and economically Hispanics continued to be at the bottom of the social scale and marginalized economically. During the 1970s, the number of Latinos and Hispanics had grown from nine million to some fourteen million, a spectacular increase of 61 percent, compared to 9 percent for non–Latinos. The projections indicated that by the year 2000, Latinos would become the nation's largest minority (if the estimated one to five million undocumented were counted), of which some 60 percent were Mexican-origin people. Other historical changes were occurring as well. Rodolfo Acuña noted, "In 1980 in California, the median age of Mexican-Americans was under 22; by the year 2000, the median age would be about 26. The majority of white North Americans were over 30 years in 1980, and, by the turn of the century, the majority would be over 35. The graying of 'America' in all probability will result in a greater reluctance on the part of society to pay for education, a policy change that would greatly affect Chicanos."[2]

Unfortunately, the increased Hispanic population made no impact on the negative film images of Latinos during the 1980s, but for a small body of work in Chicano, Cuban and Latino cinema.

Film Images and Film Stars

During the 1980s, Latinos were more in evidence in U.S. films than they had been in the 1960s and 1970s, but more was not necessarily better. What contributed to the increased visibility was the fact that Latinos were increasingly in the news due to Reagan's interventionist policy in Central America, especially in Grenada, Nicaragua and El Salvador. The growing news coverage was sparked by the specter of revolution and the mass migration of Central American refugees, as well as Mexican workers responding to the U.S. market of cheap labor. Consequently, the Hollywood film industry quickly dramatized these events on the screen in mainstream films. However, this critical mass of Latinos was important in the emergence of more Latino and Chicano cinema.

The Hollywood film industry itself underwent a major transition during the 1980s. Early in the decade, the advent of videocassettes created a technological and economic revolution in the motion picture industry, both in the U.S. and abroad. By the end of the decade, videos accounted for some 80 percent of movie receipts. The evolution of cable television was another new development. Some called it poetic justice, for both videos and cable television undermined network television, in a similar way that the last-named had done to motion pictures. Revenues from foreign markets increased during the decade due to the renaissance of U.S. films and their special effects, as well as to the faltering film industries in countries such as Mexico and others in Latin America.

By mid-decade, six studios accounted for 90 percent of domestic film receipts. In addition, two new studios emerged, Orion Pictures and TriStar Pictures (which proved to be short-lived). In 1986, they made 24 percent of the movies produced. The old and fabled studios of Hollywood's golden age were by now merely one of many holdings of vast conglomerates. Joel Finler, for example, noted, "The problems experienced by Fox and MGM/UA and changes in ownership of both, meant that the share of the six majors fell to an all-time low of only 64 percent in 1986."[3]

The film product of the 1980s was heavy on seemingly endless sequels, such as *Rocky III, Return of the Jedi, Rambo III,* and *Jaws II,* among others. As before, once a new trend or technology began, the Hollywood film industry was quick to overindulge in it. Thus, technological wizardry, special effects, Dolby sound and other gimmicks glutted the film market much as 1950s gimmicks had, as a way to induce and entice moviegoers. In this onslaught of technology, only some worthwhile films excelled on the basis of a story and character. They went against the grain. They included: *Ordinary People* (1980, Paramount); *Raging Bull* (1980, United Artists); *Reds* (1981, Paramount); *Gandhi* (1982, Columbia); *Sophie's Choice* (1982, Universal); *Terms of Endearment* (1983, Paramount); *Amadeus* (1984, Orion); *Wall Street* (1987, 20th Century–Fox); *Fatal Attraction* (1987, Paramount); and *Running on Empty* (1989, Warner Bros.).

Another historic occurrence was the passing of many of the great film stars and directors from Hollywood's golden age: George Raft, Duncan Renaldo, Mae West, and Raoul Walsh in 1980; Melvyn Douglas, Allan Dwan, Gloria Grahame, Ann Harding, William Holden, Robert Montgomery, Natalie Wood, and William Wyler in 1981; Ingrid Bergman, Henry Fonda, Henry King, Fernando Lamas, Eleanor Powell, and King Vidor in 1982; Luis Buñuel, George Cukor, Dolores del Río, David Niven, Pat O'Brien, and Gloria Swanson in 1983; Richard Burton, Jackie Coogan, Janet Gaynor, Carl Foreman, James Mason, Walter Pidgeon, and William Powell in 1984; Anne Baxter, Henry Hathaway, and Orson Welles in 1985; James Cagney, Emilio Fernández, Cary Grant, Ray Milland, Vicente Minnelli, and Donna Reed in 1986; Fred Astaire, Madeleine Carroll, Rita Hayworth, John Huston, Danny Kaye, Mervyn LeRoy, Robert Preston, Randolph Scott, and Raquel Torres in 1987; John Houseman and Trevor Howard in 1988. These unique talents had all flourished during Hollywood's golden age, and their absence could never be filled by the contemporary Hollywood film industry. This was even truer for Latino film stars and filmmakers, since Latino film stars and filmmakers had become an endangered species by the 1980s.

Latino images during the decade were on display in five identifiable types of films: one, mainstream films; two, the xenophobia/revenge genre; three, the *narcotraficante*/drug-theme genre; four, mainstream films that attempted to deal with the Latino experience in the United States or in Latin America in a more meaningful manner; and fifth, an emerging body of work identified as Chicano or Latino cinema.

Some mainstream films of the decade sometimes had Latino characters and infrequently Latino performers as Latino characters, but in either case they were typically incidental or negative roles. For example, in *9 to 5* (1980, 20th Century–Fox), Roxanna Bonilla-Giannini was the incidental secretary; in *Fort Apache, the Bronx* (1981, 20th Century–Fox) Rachel Ticotin was a Puerto Rican nurse; in *Whose Life Is It Anyway?* (1981, Metro-Goldwyn-Mayer), Alba Omsas was an incidental nurse; in *S.O.B.* (1981, Paramount), Bert Rosario played an ignorant Mexican gardener who is unable to discern his employer's attempted suicide; in *Death Wish II* (1982, Filmways), Silvana Gallardo portrayed a Mexican domestic who is raped and murdered; in *One from the Heart* (1982, Columbia), Raúl Juliá essayed the sleazy Latino gigolo; in *The Last American Virgin* (1982, Cannon), Louisa Moritz was a sex-starved older Mexican woman with a preference for white teenagers; in *Bad Boys* (1983, Universal), Esai Morales was a vicious Puerto Rican hoodlum; in *Stick* (1985, Universal), José Pérez was an inept cop who gets himself killed; in *Down and Out in Beverly Hills* (1986, Touchstone), Elizabeth Peña was a Mexican domestic who is unable to control her promiscuity; in *Colors* (1982, Orion), María Conchita Alonso was a Chicana who reverts back to *la vida loca*; in *Tequila Sunrise* (1988, Warner Bros.), Raúl Juliá was a corrupt Mexican cop caught up in drug smuggling; in *Moon over Parador* (1988, Universal), Raúl Juliá was a corrupt Latin American dictator; and in *Lust in the Dust* (1985, New World), Lainie Kazan was the proverbial Mexican *cantinera*.

Other mainstream films which featured Latino characters included *Zorro, the Gay Blade* (1980, 20th Century–Fox) with George Hamilton as the masked avenger and *caballero*; *Stir Crazy* (1980, Columbia), which featured Karmin Murcelo; *Seems Like Old Times* (1980, Columbia), which had Dolores Aguirre in an incidental role; *Barbarosa* (1982, Universal)—a rarity in that it had four important Mexican roles played by Mexican-origin performers,

Gilbert Roland, Isela Vega, Alma Martínez, and Danny De La Paz. In addition, there were *Heartbreaker* (1983, Miramax), which was unsuccessful in launching Mexican heartthrob Fernando Allende; *Paris, Texas* (1984, 20th Century–Fox), which had Socorro Valdez in an incidental role; *Let's Get Harry* (1986, TriStar),which featured Elpidia Carrillo; *The Penitent* (1988, Cineworld), which had Raúl Juliá; and *An Officer and a Gentleman* (1982, Paramount) with Tony Plana as a cadet.

During the decade, Hollywood began to document the Vietnam War experience in numerous films, most of which were conspicuously absent of Chicanos and Latinos, who in reality had made up one-third of the casualties in the war. Two of these features had identifiable Chicano characters, albeit incidental ones: in *Platoon* (1986, Orion), the Chicano was played by Francisco Quinn (Anthony's son); and in *Full Metal Jacket* (1987, Warner Bros.), the Chicano soldier was played by Sal Lopez.

The second type of films that featured Latinos, usually as the Other or as the perceived enemy, was the xenophobia/revenge genre. The genre had begun in the late 1970s with such inane fare as *Rambo* (1982, Orion) and *Missing in Action* (1984, Cannon). In fact, the stars of each film, Sylvester Stallone and Chuck Norris, became the cinematic poster boys of the Reagan and Bush administrations and their interventionist policies. The xenophobia/revenge genre represented the inner tension and frustration by unrepentant Cold Warriors unable to confront the defeat in Vietnam. The ethos of these films bordered on the edge of trauma and hysteria as a reaction to the revolutionary movements in Latin America, especially in Central America. This genre brought back into use two favorite Latino stereotypes: the docile ideological disciple and his counterpart, the Latino unable to control his ideology and violence. According to this predictable scenario, the fearless European-American hero needed to administer his benevolent mentorship or firm hand.

The xenophobia/revenge genre included *The Kidnapping of the President* (1980, Crown International), in which a Latin American guerrilla group fighting a right-wing military regime inexplicably takes the U.S. president hostage. In *Lone Wolf McQuade* (1983, Orion), Chuck Norris is a solitary Texas Ranger who single-handedly defeats a gang of gun runners who are stealing U.S. Army weapons and selling them to Central American guerrillas. In *Last Plane Out* (1983, New World), a "good ol' boy" (Jan-Michael Vincent) befriends the Nicaraguan dictator Anastasio Somoza, who is portrayed as a misunderstood family man who loves his country and is forced to destroy it only to save it. In *Red Dawn* (1984, Metro-Goldwyn-Mayer), the United States is invaded by ruthless and cruel Cuban, Nicaraguan and Soviet paratroopers; and in a similar geographic terrain, *Invasion U.S.A.* (1984, Cannon) has Chuck Norris as a messianic one-man army who resists the invaders. In *Heartbreak Ridge* (1986, Warner Bros.), a hard-drinking and broken-down Cold Warrior (Clint Eastwood) leads a squad of inner-city recruits (mostly Latino and African American) in a glorious invasion of Grenada, where the population is very much like the inner-city recruits.

The third type of Latino image on display in the 1980s was that of the *narcotraficante* or drug peddler in the *narcotraficante* film genre. These films perpetuated the notion that the evil of drugs and drug addiction was due to evil Latinos attempting to subvert the clean living of European-Americans. No mention was made of the sad fact that the United States had become the number one consumer of illicit drugs in the world. In an example of how the real and reel world criss-crossed each other, Chuck Norris in one interview stated that it was really the Soviet KGB that was responsible for the smuggling of drugs into the United States. The *narcotraficante* genre was born out of the increasing news coverage of the drug scourge and trade, especially with the advent of cocaine. Inevitably the news media focused on the Latin American connection, especially the Colombian drug cartels and the emerging Mexican ones. Instead of focusing on prevention and intervention efforts domestically, the news media emphasized the interception angles and thus created a new and convenient Latino stereotype, the Latino *narcotraficante* and drug peddler, or suspects, who attempted to undermine the moral fiber of the U.S.

Among the films that peddled the Latino stereotype as a *narcotraficante* were: *High Risk* (1981, AC); *Vice Squad* (1982, Avco); *Scarface* (1983, Universal); *Romancing the Stone* (1984, 20th Century–Fox); *Code of Silence* (1985, Orion); *Cocaine Wars* (1985, Concord); *Firewalker* (1986, Cannon); *Above the Law* (1988, Warner Bros.); and *Crocodile Dundee II* (1988, Paramount).

Also alive and well was the old Mexican bandit image in *The Three Amigos* (1986, Orion), in which three European-American film stars (Steve Martin, Chevy Chase, Martin Short) travel to Mexico to defend a town of hapless Mexican peasants and fight off a gang of despicable and barbarian-like Mexican bandits (Alfonso Arau, Tony Plana).

The fourth type of film to develop during the decade was mainstream film focusing on the Latino experience in the United States or Latin America. Many of these films focused on the revolution taking place in Central America, the moral ambiguities of U.S. foreign policy there, and the impact of the conflicts as regards refugees or immigration. Other films tackled the plight of undocumented Mexican workers pushed and pulled by globalization

Alfonso Arau in *The Three Amigos* (1986, Orion).

and the markets for cheap labor in the United States. *The Mission* (1986, Warner Bros.) was a strong indictment of colonization of indigenous peoples along the Argentinean-Brazilian border, as well as the duplicity and collusion between Spain, Portugal, and the Vatican. *Alsino and the Condor* (1983, Libra/Cinema 5), directed by Chilean director Miguel Littín, focused on the ordinary Nicaraguan peasant in the face of the U.S.–sponsored Contra war, and in the process humanized the struggle in a manner that the news media was unable to do. *Walker* (1987, Universal) in turn depicted the infamous exploits of U.S. filibuster William Walker (Ed Harris) and his attempts to make Nicaragua a U.S. slave state in the 19th century. Costa-Gavras' *Missing* (1982, Universal) chronicled the true story of the disappearance of Charles Horman (John Shea), who was murdered by the U.S.–supported Pinochet regime, and the efforts of his father, Ed Horman (Jack Lemmon), to find him. Similarly, the Argentine-made *The Official Story* (1985, Almi Pictures) depicted the plight of the families of the "disappeared" at the hands of the right-wing military junta as seen through the eyes of a disillusioned wife (Norma Aleandro), who is married to a fascist-minded officer.

The Emerald Forest (1985, 20th Century–Fox) focused on the fate and plight of Amazon indigenous people due to the unchecked deforestation of the Amazon forest. The Mexican-made *Frida* (1988, New Yorker Films) depicted the life of Frida Kahlo (Ofelia Medina), the famed but ill-fated Mexican feminist painter. Robert Redford's *The Milagro Beanfield War* (1988, Universal) had as its subject matter the efforts of a Chicano farmer (Chick Vennera) to hold on to his land in the face of an unscrupulous conglomerate. *Romero* (1989, Four Seasons/Vidmark) documented the struggle of Salvadoran Archbishop Romero (Raúl Juliá) for social justice during the raging civil war and his subsequent assassination by right-wing death squads. *Under Fire* (1983, Orion) focused on the beginning of the Nicaraguan Revolution, as witnessed by a three U.S. journalists (Nick Nolte, Joanne Cassidy, Gene Hackman). Oliver Stone's *Salvador* (1986, Helmdale) presented the strife of the Salvadoran civil war as lived by two down-and-out European-Americans (James Woods, Jim Belushi). Tony Richardson's *The Border* (1982, Universal) had as its central focus the plight of Mexican undocumented workers and the human toll on the border patrol. *The Kiss of the Spider Woman* (1985, Island Alive) depicted the fantasies of two Brazilian political prisoners (Raúl Juliá, William Hurt) and the woman (Sônia Braga) who was the subject of their dreams.

Other films that featured Latino settings included the mundane adaptation of Gabriel García Márquez's short story *Eréndira* (1984, Miramax); *Beyond the Limit* (1983, Paramount), the film adaptation of Graham Greene's novel *The Honorary Consul,* about the kidnapping of a British consul (Michael Caine) by Latin American guerrillas (Richard Gere, among others); a comedy set in Río de Janeiro, *Blame It on Rio* (1984, 20th Century–Fox); the lackluster *Menudo* (1983, Embassy) headlined by the titular rock group; and the equally dismal *Salsa* (1988, Vestron) which attempted to cash in on the salsa dance craze. Finally, there were a couple of Cheech and Chong entries, which chronicled the further marijuana-induced adventures of the pair, *Cheech and Chong's Next Movie* (1980, Universal) and *Things Are Tough All Over* (1982, Columbia).

Last but not least during the decade was the emergence of what is termed the Chicano, Puerto Rican, and Cuban-American cinemas. These ethnic cinemas can be defined as those cinemas that are written, directed, and produced by members of these communities; and that document the historical and cultural experiences, as well as the aspirations and hopes of the communities within the sociopolitical context of the United States. For example, Chon Noriega has noted, "'Chicano cinema' constructed itself in opposition to Hollywood and in alliance with New Latin American Cinema. Although framed as a matter of either/or choice, this strategy actually provided new terms within which access could be negotiated."[4]

Chicano cinema was a product of decades of evolution that began with the Spanish-language films of the 1930s and which was further defined by the premature Chicano cinema of 1949–1954. Later, it gained impetus during the Chicano movement of the 1960s with a series of documentaries of self-identity, beginning with Luis Valdez' *I Am Joaquin* (1967), as well as other key documentaries such as Jesús Salvador Treviño's *Yo Soy Chicano* (1973). Later, the first Chicano features, beginning with Efraín Gutiérrez's *Please Don't Bury Me Alive* (1976); Alejandro Grattan's *Only Once in a Lifetime* (1978); and Jesús Salvador Treviño's Chicano/Mexican co-production *Raíces De Sangre/Roots of Blood* (1978), established the foundations for Chicano films.

Nevertheless, Chicano cinema has often been remiss in its portrayal of women and its inability to develop fully developed images of Chicana characters. As of this writing, only a few Latino-themed feature films have had Latina leading roles. These include *Selena* (1997), *Luminarias* (2000), *Frida* (2000) and *Real Women Have Curves* (2002). Silvia Morales, for example, studied four key Chicano films, *Raíces de Sangre* (1978), *Zoot Suit* (1981), *Seguin* (1982), and *The Ballad of Gregorio Cortez* (1983), and concluded, "In summation, looking back over these four films, it is clear that Mexican women fare better in dramatic works by most Chicanos than they do in works by Anglos, as do Mexican men. But they do so, excepting perhaps in *The Ballad of Gregorio Cortez,* within a traditionally defined cultural context. Within this context, women follow the lead of men. Men are shown heeding their own dictates, regardless of whether their decisions end tragically or not. Women, on the other hand, are shown to have or little or no influence over decisions affecting their lives."[5]

In turn, Rosa Linda Fregoso has noted, "An additional reason for the marginalization of women derives from the fact that Chicana production is exclusively concentrated in short films, and Chicanas have therefore not benefited from the recognition that accompanies the production of feature films.... In other words, making Chicano 35-mm feature film translates into a certain prestige that virtually guarantees greater critical and scholarly attention as well as film reviews in the mainstream media."[6]

The critical mass of Chicano cinema came with Luis Valdez' *Zoot Suit* (1982, Universal), based on the play that he had written and directed. The film depicted the zoot suit riots and the Sleepy Lagoon case of the 1940s in Los Angeles. Other Chicano history was covered in Jesús Salvador Treviño's *Seguin* (1981, PBS), which documented for the first time the Mexican side of the Texas insurrection of 1835. Robert M. Young's *The Ballad of Gregorio Cortez* (1983, Embassy) told the tale of Gregory Cortez (Edward James Olmos), who had already been immortalized in Mexican *corridos* for decades. Gregory Nava's *El Norte* (1984, Island Alive/American Playhouse/Channel Four Films/Public Broadcasting Service/Independent Productions) chronicled the trek of a Guatemalan Maya brother and sister (David Villalpando, Zaide Silvia Gutiérrez) through Mexico and to a Chicano barrio in Los Angeles. *Latino* (1986, Orion) explored the moral choices of a Chicano military adviser (Robert Beltran) to the Nicaraguan Contras.

Luis Valdez' *La Bamba* (1987, Columbia) told the story of the first Chicano rocker,

Ritchie Valens (Valenzuela). Cheech Marin's *Born in East L.A.* (1987, Universal) was an overdue political satire on the whole issue of who was "American." *Stand and Deliver* (1988, Warner Bros.) depicted the story of a Bolivian-born teacher Jaime Escalante (Edward James Olmos) attempting to make a difference in an East Los Angeles high school and in the lives of its Chicano students. Lastly, *Break of Dawn* (1988, Cinewest) told the true story of the first Spanish-speaking radio broadcaster, Pedro González (Óscar Chávez), in Los Angeles in the 1930s.

In the meantime, two other Latino cinemas had evolved, namely the Puerto Rican and Cuban-exile cinemas. The former had begun on the Puerto Rican mainland in 1912, and had progressed with *Romance Tropical* (1934), which was the first Puerto Rican sound film. In subsequent years several independent Puerto Rican filmmakers continued to address critically the imposed relationship of Puerto Rico and the United States. Lillian Jiménez has noted, for example, "Puerto Rican cinema has grown from its infancy to toddlerhood with little guidance and parental direction. It emerged during the tumultuous era of the documentary form, characterized by a sense of urgency and expediency of the moment.... Although considerable time has elapsed since those early days, there is still a striking need for Puerto Rican and Latino filmmakers to produce and direct films and videotapes about the multiplicity of issues and concerns. Some of these concerns are directly linked to the status and conditions of the Puerto Rican and Latino communities in the United States, yet it would be a grave loss if the makers were to limit themselves—or be limited by cultural institutions and their gatekeepers—to just these themes."[7]

The Cuban-exile cinema was oriented politically in a different direction. It began with *PM* (1969), a short film about the night life in Havana from an exile perspective. The first feature film of Cuban-American cinema was *El Super* in 1979, which concerned itself exclusively with the Cuban experience in the United States. Later, both Puerto Rican and Cuban-American filmmakers synthesized their U.S. experiences with *Crossover Dreams* (1985, CF), which focused on the rise and fall of a Latino *salsero* (played by the Panamanian Rubén Blades) as he attempted to cross over into the elusive mainstream U.S. music scene. The different Latino cinemas often had much in common. Chon Noriega, for example, noted, "Hispanic cinema must embrace—not negate—our differences, if we are to discover the cultural glue that holds us together. As Chicanos, for example, we have a double consciousness: one of ourselves and another of the dominant culture. But the idea of a Hispanic cinema holds out the possibility of a third consciousness; one, in fact, that makes 'us' the majority in this hemisphere."[8]

Nevertheless, the expectations for a continuing body of work of these different Latino cinemas proved illusory, for as the 1990s dawned, Latino and Chicano, Puerto Rican, and Cuban-American cinema virtually disappeared.

Latino film stars and filmmakers made a slight increase in visibility during the 1980s, but it was negligible when compared to the dramatic demographics of the Latino community. For example, the *Los Angeles Times* noted, "According to the Screen Actors Guild, while Blacks, Latinos, Asians and American Indians account for about 22 percent of the nation's population, they made up 13 percent of the on-camera appearances in film, television and commercials in 1987.... According to a Screen Actors Guild study of hiring practices from 1982 to 1985, racial discrimination accounted for minorities making up only 2 percent of the writers employed each year in films and T.V."[9] But even more pathetic was the fact that Latinos made up some 10 percent of the national population and never represented more than 3 percent of film roles.

Television was even more negligent and narrow-minded. For example, in a study "examining more than 150 episodes of 30 network programs featuring minorities, the study found that [the spring 1989] network prime-time schedule contained nine Latinos, three Asians and one Indian in regular roles."[10] The world reflected on television was one that had nothing to do with the real world or the people who inhabited it. "As a result, TV's world of harmony does not present viewers with a picture of an ideal society where racism has been fought and overcome. Instead, it portrays an artificial universe where racial difficulties and realities are denied."[11]

A few Latino film stars and filmmakers transcended the obstacles and the odds, although most of them found their fame and success transitory. The most prominent of the Latino male stars who emerged during the 1980s were Edward James Olmos, Raúl Juliá, Andy García, Emilio Estevez, and his brother Charlie Sheen (Estevez). The star who came to symbolize Chicano cinema more than any other actor was Edward James Olmos. A former rocker, he worked his way up from television and film parts to the *pachuco* role in Luis Valdez' play *Zoot Suit* and then repeated his acclaimed role in the film version in 1982. He followed it with his role of General Santa Anna in Jesús Salvador Treviño's *Seguin* (1981), then the luckless lead character of *The Ballad of Gregorio Cortez* (1983), and then capped the decade with his Academy Award–nominated role in *Stand and Deliver* (1988, Warner Bros.). He would prolong his acting career with other successes in the next decades, as well as venture into directing.

The Puerto Rican–born Raúl Juliá had already established himself as a Broadway actor before beginning in films in 1971, and he rose from supporting roles to leads. His star-making role came with *Kiss of the Spider Woman* in 1985. Thereafter he played a series of diverse roles in both drama and comedy: *Moon over Parador* (1988), *Tequila Sunrise* (1988), and *Romero* (1989). His flourishing career was cut short with his death from cancer and a stroke in 1994. The Cuban-born Andy García began in films in 1983 and made his way from small roles to intense supporting roles such as the gangster in 1986's *Eight Million Ways to Die.* Thereafter, he built his career with such films as *The Untouchables* (1987); *Stand and Deliver* (1987); and *Godfather III* (1990), for which he received an Academy Award nomination for Best Supporting Actor. In the next decade his career somewhat tapered off, but he remained active.

Emilio Estevez and Charlie Sheen, the sons of Martin Sheen (Estevez) were of Spanish heritage and during this decade they enjoyed their greatest fame and success, although neither played Latino roles. Emilio began in films in 1982, and by 1984, with *Repo Man* he quickly won fame as a young leading man specializing in playing characters who refused to conform. In addition, he also became an able director and screenwriter. His successes include *The Breakfast Club* (1985), *Stakeout* (1987), *Young Guns* (1988) and *Men at Work* (1989), among others. Charlie Sheen made his film debut in 1984 and was catapulted to heartthrob stardom with 1986's *Platoon.* He followed this movie with such important films as *Wall Street* (1987), *Eight Men Out* (1988), and *Major League* (1989). In the 1990s, his increasing drug problem was the subject of media stories.

Other Latino male leads included Robert Beltran, a Teatro Campesino alumnus who scored with the lead role in *Latino* (1986) and *Scenes from the Class Struggle in Beverly Hills* (1989), but thereafter found no similarly prominent roles to maintain his leading man status. Still others included Daniel Valdez (playwright Luis' brother) who won temporary prominence with the role of Henry Reyna in *Zoot Suit* in 1982. The Cuban Esai Morales scored with *Bad Boys* in 1983 and *La Bamba* in 1987, but other than that he languished in lesser films. The Cuban-born Steven Bauer caused a sensation as the right-hand man of mobster Tony Montana in Brian De Palma's *Scarface* in 1983, but after *Thief of Hearts* in 1984, he was consigned to supporting roles and his promising stardom withered away.

There was other Latino talent that found only one good role to showcase their ability. Among these was Domingo Ambriz, who was especially impressive as the unhappy Mexican undocumented worker in Robert M. Young's *Alambrista!* (1983). Other capable and new Latino actors working during the 1980s in film (as well as television) were Trinidad Silva, Tony Plana, and René Enríquez, among others.

Latina film stars paralleled their male counterparts in terms of limited opportunities and shortened careers. The only two Latina film actresses to achieve full-fledged film stardom were the Brazilian-born Sônia Braga and the Cuban-born María Conchita Alonso. Braga first established herself in her native country in such films as *Doña Flor and Her Two Husbands* (1977) and *Gabriela* (1983). In the U.S. she had her greatest successes with *Kiss of the Spider Woman* (1985); *The Milagro Beanfield War* (1988); and *Moon over Parador* (1988). Thereafter, Hollywood's lack of roles for women after a certain age compounded her career's downward spiral. Alonso attained film stardom in 1984's hit comedy *Moscow on the Hudson* opposite Robin Williams. She fought the Latina sexpot typecasting with her roles in the comedy *Touch and Go* (1987), the futuristic *The Running Man* (1987), and the drama *Extreme Prejudice* (1987).

There were other talented Latina leading ladies during the 1980s. They included the Cuban-American Elizabeth Peña, who had made an impressive film debut in *El Super* in 1977, and then had a series of important roles in some key films of the decade: *Crossover Dreams* (1985), *Down and out in Beverly Hills* (1986) and *La Bamba* (1987). The Puerto Rican actress Rachel Ticotin began on a high note with the female lead in *Fort Apache, the Bronx* (1981) opposite Paul Newman, but was unable to get roles for a number of years. Her comeback films include *Total Recall* (1990) and *F/X* (1991). The Mexican-born Elpidia Carrillo played a series of roles that typically cast her as an uprooted Latina, a victim of the contemporary revolutionary upheavals in Mexico and Central America, in such films as *The Border* (1982), *Salvador* (1986) and *Predator* (1987).

Silvana Gallardo, an accomplished theater actress, scored in the films *Windwalker* (1980) and *Death Wish II* (1982), and in several television films, among them *Copacabana* (1985). Chicana actress Alma Martínez, a Teatro Campesino alumna, showcased her talent in such films as *Seguin* (1981), *Zoot Suit* (1982), *Barbarosa* (1982) and *Under Fire* (1983), among others. The Peruvian-born Jenny Gago made an impression in *Under Fire* (1983), *Best Seller* (1983), and *Old Gringo* (1989). Julie Carmen was similarly impressive in *Gloria* (1980), *The Milagro Beanfield War* (1989) and *The Penitent* (1987). Other Latina talents included Patricia Martínez, Lupe Ontiveros, and Carmen Zapata.

Latino directors and screenwriters who enjoyed several successes included Luis Valdez,

Leon Ichaso, Gregory Nava, Isaac Artenstein, Jesús Salvador Treviño and Emilio Estevez. Latino directors and screenwriters continued to be an almost extinct species in the Hollywood film industry. They had been few and rare throughout Hollywood history, beginning with Ramon Novarro (three films in the 1930s); Roberto Gavaldón (two films, one in 1948 and 1955); Hugo Fregonese (eleven films in the 1950s); and Efraín Gutiérrez (three films in the 1970s).

The following are some representative films of the 1980s.

Representative Films

The Ballad of Gregorio Cortez (1983, EM)

The Ballad of Gregorio Cortez was one of the rare U.S. films to celebrate a Mexican/Chicano hero. In the past, a few Mexican historical heroes had been depicted: Joaquin Murietta in *Robin Hood of El Dorado* (1936, MGM); Benito Juárez in *Juarez* (1939, Warner Bros.); Pancho Villa in *Viva Villa!* (1934, MGM); and Emiliano Zapata in *Viva Zapata!* (1952). Some of these films were well-meaning if not patronizing, while some were downright historically revisionist and stereotypical. In addition, the Mexican/Chicano characters were portrayed by non–Latino actors (with some exceptions), and many of the films were directed and scripted by non–Latino talent who were afflicted by a rigor mortis of ethnocentrism.

By contrast, *The Ballad of Gregorio Cortez* was directed by the progressive Robert M. Young, who had helmed the evocative *Alambrista!* (1977), a unique film which emphasized the universality of the human condition. *Ballad* was coscripted by the noted Chicano novelist Victor Villaseñor, whose novels included *Pocho* and *Rain of Gold*. To a large degree, the narrative was constructed from popular *corridos* about Gregorio Cortez which had been popular on the borderlands for decades. The film was further enriched by a talented Chicano cast.

The film had evolved and was funded under the auspices of Robert Redford's Sundance Institute and the Corporation for Public Broadcasting (PBS). Additional funding was obtained from the National Endowment for the Arts. *The Ballad of Gregorio Cortez* was originally scheduled to be a television film presented by American Playhouse. However, the film's star, Edward James Olmos, wanted a wider audience to see the film and felt that the Latino community, especially the Chicanos, could make it a commercial success. Olmos initiated an almost one-man marketing campaign, with English and Spanish-language television, radio and in-person presentations. The efforts paid off and the film went on to be a "sleeper," both commercially and critically.

The film depicted the true story (with some liberties) of Gregorio Cortez (Edward James Olmos), an indigent Mexican farmer who lived in San Antonio, Texas. On June 12, 1901, he and his brother Romaldo Cortez (Pepe Serna) were approached by a European-American sheriff and his deputy, who served as his translator but who in fact had limited proficiency in Spanish. The latter inquired whether Gregorio had bought a horse. The lawmen were unaware that in the Spanish language a distinction is made between *caballo* (male horse) and *yegue* (mare or female horse). Gregorio responded that he had not bought a horse;

he had bought a mare. The sheriff was told by his deficient translator deputy that Gregorio had stated that he would resist arrest. The sheriff then proceeded to mortally wound Romaldo, at which point Gregorio returned fire, killing the sheriff in what would be deemed self-defense. Aware of the rampant racism against Mexicans in Texas, Gregorio then decided to flee for his life.

The Texas Rangers, a notoriously anti–Mexican body of long standing, then launched the biggest manhunt in Texas history. The press anxiously followed the developments of the story. Cortez had initially planned to head towards the Mexican border, but when he heard that his family had been imprisoned he turned himself in. At the trial, he was found guilty of murder and nearly lynched by a vengeful mob. A Chicano activist, Carlota Muñoz (Rosanna DeSoto), organized an effort to free him. It is she who finally identifies the misunderstanding of language as a source of the conflict.

The real-life Gregorio Cortez was released from prison after several years. However, the experience had all but wrecked his life and in subsequent years he had several run-ins with the law. He was incarcerated once more. Later, a *corrido* about him became popular along the borderlands, highlighting both his courage and the great injustice perpetrated on him, as well as intertwining both fact and legend.

The critical response was excellent. *The Village Voice* wrote, "Eddie as Cortez neither speaks nor understands English. It is a remarkable performance, full of eyes, half-gestures, whispers—all without being ... dull. This is what underplaying is supposed to be about, the opposite of the flamboyance of El Pachuco called for. Eddie Olmos can do it all."[12]

The *Los Angeles Times* commented, "The performances are of a very high quality, Olmos' own as Cortez and, among the many others, Barry Crobin as Cortez's defense attorney, Rosanna DeSoto as the translator who, in Cortez's prison cell, evokes the truth of the tragic confrontation, and Tony Bauer as the monolingual deputies' chief pursuer.... The Latino audience alone is surely commercially viable at this point, and the appeals to pride, understanding and hope are considerable."[13]

According to Rosa Linda Fregoso, "The major work of the film ... is to discredit the verbal discourse of the Anglo-Texans. The neorealist codes of experimental documentary form, investigative journalism, interviewing, and active counterpointing in the text deconstruct verbal/spoken accounts, leading spectators to interrogate critically the process of constructing the 'truth.' This self-reflexive strategy underscores the limits of testimony and memory as a source of objective truth, particularly as it is written (newspaper) or spoken (witnesses) within existing configurations of power and privilege. By analyzing the processes by which judgments are made the filmmakers deconstruct offensive regimes of racism and call attention to the reconstructed nature of reality."[14]

La Bamba (1987, Columbia)

Luis Valdez' *La Bamba* was the first movie to celebrate a contemporary Chicano icon, in this case the first Chicano rock star, Ritchie Valens (Valenzuela) (1942–1959). In the process, the film became the highest-grossing Chicano film ever made.

Ritchie Valens was a Chicano rock pioneer who had scored three top-ten hits: "Donna," "Come On, Let's Go," and "La Bamba." He was only seventeen when he died on February

3, 1959, in a plane crash that also killed two other rock legends, Buddy Holly and the Big Bopper.

The film depicted the brief life of Ritchie Valens (Lou Diamond Phillips) from his early teen years, when he, his mother, Connie Valenzuela (Rosanna DeSoto), and two younger sisters are agricultural workers in Northern California. Ritchie's older half-brother Bob Morales (Esai Morales) is an ex-felon who deals in drugs. Nevertheless, Ritchie idolizes him until Bob seduces his girlfriend Rosie (Elizabeth Peña).

Ritchie's interest in music grows when he attends Pacoima High School and he begins taking guitar and singing lessons, as well as joins a band. He falls in love with a European-American girl, Donna Ludwig (Danielle Von Zerneck), whose parents make no effort to conceal their disapproval of the interracial romance. After he signs up with a small record label, his career quickly goes into high gear. He has three hits, does television appearances and makes an impression in a live performance for famed rock and roll promoter Alan Freed (Jeffrey Alan Chandler), in which other rock legends also performed—Eddie Cochran (Brian Setzer) and Jackie Wilson (Howard Hunstberry). He is on a winter tour in 1959 with two other popular rock stars, Buddy Holly (Marshall Crenshaw) and the Big Bopper (Stephen Lee), when he dies in a plane crash that stuns the nation.

The idea for a film about Ritchie Valens began fourteen years before the film was made, during 1978 when both Luis Valdez and his brother Daniel were involved in the Broadway production of the play *Zoot Suit*. Both later approached director/producer Taylor Hackford, who became "hot" after *An Officer and a Gentleman* (1982) and *Against All Odds* (1984). Hackford backed the project with a $6.5 million budget, with Luis as director and screenwriter and Daniel as associate producer. Daniel had initially planned to play the part of Ritchie, but by the time the film was made he was too old for the part and settled for a bit part as a family member. They obtained permission to make the film from the Valenzuela family, and Ritchie's sisters, Irma and Connie, even played small roles as workers in the farm camp. Their daughters were cast in the roles of their own mothers, while Ritchie's real-life mother and his brother Bob were also given small roles.

Some liberties were taken with the biography, among them that Ritchie's first album was released during his lifetime, when in fact it was only released eight days after his death. Some family members expressed mixed feelings, Ritchie's half-brother Bob among them: "Even though Luis Valdez ... used his own interpretation of what happened, it couldn't have been closer for me.... It was almost too close."[15] Ritchie's sister Irma, who was now a preschool teacher in Watsonville, felt that the film was an inspiration for Latino youth: "They don't have to be macho and mean or cuss or take drugs to be a man. They will also see that it's okay to be sensitive, tender and care for their families too."[16] One thing the film highlighted was that Ritchie Valens' version of "La Bamba" was the first Spanish-language song to make it to the top ten on the pop charts. Los Lobos re-recorded the song and actor Lou Diamond Phillips lip synced.

Luis Valdez expressed his feelings about the film: "I have always felt that the '50s, as they were portrayed on film, were not the full story.... Rock-and-roll gave focus to the emerging youth culture, the baby boom generation. At the same time it became a symptom for change. And the history of rock-and-roll is parallel to the history of integration in this country, and the fusion of rhythm and blues with the country western represents, as far as I'm concerned, the coming together of black and white people in this country. It is significant that Ritchie Valens was there as an Hispanic in 1959, and with one song, internationalized rock-and-roll."[17] About Ritchie Valens, Valdez commented, "It sort of sealed my teenage years. It ended them. I got involved in the civil rights movement and the Viva Kennedy campaign after that."[18]

La Bamba was a huge commercial and critical success. It grossed more than $100 million in its initial release, not including later video sales, cable and television revenues. Spanish-language versions made up some 10 percent of the gross receipts.

The following review was typical. *Variety* stated, "There haven't been too many people who died at the age of 17 who have warranted the biopic treatment, but 1950s rock n' roller Ritchie Valens proves a worthy exception in *La Bamba* ... *La Bamba* is engrossing throughout and boasts numerous fine performances. In Lou Diamond Phillips's sympathetic turn, Valens comes across a very fine young man, caring for those important to him and not overawed by his success. Rosanna DeSoto scores as his tireless mother, and Elizabeth Peña has numerous dramatic moments as Bob's distraught mate.... Most of the fireworks are Bob's and Esai Morales makes the most of the opportunities.... Musically, Valens' tunes have been covered by the contemporary band Los Lobos."[19]

Some critics, however, have felt that *La Bamba* is a traditional mythicized icon biography that only tended to complement the status quo. Christine List, for example, wrote, "In the process of taking a Chicano character and transforming him into a mythic rock 'n roll hero, ethnicity is relegated to the level of motif, ultimately having little to do with the thrust of the hero narrative. *La Bamba* is ultimately the story of how Ritchie transcends his ethnicity (embodied in Bob) to join the ranks of open minded American teenagers. Unlike *Zoot Suit*, where Valdez unfolds his hero in the cloak of a Chicano myth (a politicized pachuquismo), *La Bamba* is recognized by the anglicized 'American' music consensus myth. In the end, Ritchie turns out to be an American hero who happens to be a Chicano."[20]

Born in East L.A. (1987, Universal)

Born in East L.A. and *La Bamba* were released within months of each other. Never before had two films been released almost simultaneously that depicted the Chicano experience. They proved to be the most commercially successful Chicano films ever.

In a critical review of Cheech Marin's films, Christine List has written, "When we compare Marin's streetwise doper with [Luis] Valdez's pachucos, the differences in political messages of the two Chicano filmmakers become more apparent. Valdez created a character that was socially embedded in the Chicano community. Marin's street character, on the other hand, does not identify with the barrio or the gang.... His enemies and detractors, though obviously racist, do not stir up anger and violence in him, nor do they revive any primordial identity and consciousness."[21]

The film's narrative focused on Rudy Robles (Cheech Marin), a Chicano who works in an auto repair shop in East Los Angeles. When he goes to meet his Mexican cousin Javier (Paul Rodriguez) at the toy factory where Javier works, he forgets to carry his wallet and is caught in immigration raid carried out by "Body Count" McCallister (Jan-Michael Vincent). Rudy is deported along with other workers to Tijuana, Mexico.

Kamala Lopez and Cheech Marin in *Born in East L.A.* (1987, Universal).

In Mexico, he is jailed for vandalizing a public phone. In jail he fends off the machinations of fallen evangelist Feo (Tony Plana), and when he is finally released he is hired by Jim (Daniel Stern) as a doorman in a bar. In the process he meets a Salvadoran refugee, Dolores (Kamala Lopez), and her friend Gloria (Alma Martínez).

Rudy makes several unsuccessful attempts to cross the border: masquerading as a football coach and a moving bush, and even hiding inside a refrigerator. Increasingly hard-pressed, he joins a *norteño* group (Daniel Valdez, Steve Jordan, and David Silva). He finally develops a plan to cross the border with Dolores and several thousand others which proves successful.

Cheech Marin made his directorial debut with the film, which he also scripted. It marked his first solo film effort since his terminating his association with Tommy Chong. As a promotion for the film, Marin wrote a parody of Bruce Springsteen's song "Born in the U.S.A.," entitled "Born in East L.A." It became a hit. Often criticized for the pot-smoking characters he portrayed in the Cheech and Chong movies, Marin talked about the evolution of his film persona in *Born in East L.A.*: "Cheech (Rudy) today is more experienced, older, owns a body shop, been married, divorced, and owns his home. He's on his own. He's a lot hipper and wiser. But he is still has that same kind of younger heart. There's a bluer tinge to him now."[22]

Born in East L.A. is a film that makes an important social comment on the issues of borders and identity through the use of comedy.

Break of Dawn (1988, Platform)

Isaac Artenstein's *Break of Dawn* depicted the true story of Pedro J. González, a Mexican singer who became the first Mexican radio broadcaster in Los Angeles. In the process, the film also dramatized the era of the 1930s and several issues not previously on film.

The film begins with González (Óscar Chávez) and his wife María (María Rojo) immigrating to Los Angeles, California. On their arrival they stay with his cousin (Pepe Serna) and his wife (Socorro Valdez). Pedro begins to look for employment and is refused an audition at the KMPC station because the management feels that there is no audience for Spanish-language radio. Nevertheless, he perseveres and is given the opportunity to do commercials in Spanish, and finally he lands a 5:00 a.m. spot on radio. He quickly becomes a celebrity in the Mexican and Mexican-American community.

The politically ambitious and corrupt Captain Rodriguez (Tony Plana) convinces Pedro to help get out the Mexican-American vote for City District Attorney Kyle Mitchell (Peter Henry Schroeder), whose character is based on the true-life Los Angeles D.A. Buron Fitts, who was later removed from office for corruption. The advent of the Great Depression sparks xenophobia and an overt climate of racism against Mexican-origin people, and some 600,000 Mexicans and Mexican-Americans are deported. Pedro becomes involved in the Mexican community's efforts to fight against the deportations. Mitchell, however, who is a rabid bigot and opportunist, is angered by Pedro's involvement and in his own inability to corrupt him. Pedro himself succumbs to the allure of his celebrity status and becomes involved in an extramarital affair with a beautiful tango singer (Aixa Moreno).

Mitchell gets his revenge when he is able to blackmail a local beauty queen, sixteen-year old Linda (Kamala Lopez), to formally charge Pedro with statutory rape. Pedro refuses to plead guilty, but he is found guilty and sentenced to a long prison term. In the meantime, his wife, cousin and others organize a support committee. Subsequently, Linda retracts the charge and reveals the extortion plan to the authorities. Unable to halt an investigation into his own affairs, Mitchell fires Rodriguez. Mitchell is ultimately indicted and removed from office.

The real Pedro J. González was sentenced to one to fifty years in San Quentin for rape. However, he was released in 1940, after serving only six years, and was deported to Mexico. He lived in Tijuana (where he returned to radio broadcasting) for thirty years and was able to return to the United States in 1970. He was the subject of a documentary entitled *The Ballad of an Unsung Hero* in 1983 by KPBS. He died at the age of 99 in 1995.

Break of Dawn provides an uncompromising look at the state of Mexicans and Mexican-Americans during the 1930s in Los Angeles. The time period had previously been immortalized in the novels of Raymond Chandler and in the films based on them, as well as more recently in Roman Polanski's *Chinatown* (1974). However, the Mexican presence had largely been ignored. *Break of Dawn* depicted the mass repatriation, rampant racism and political corruption that were part of the history of Los Angeles.

The Mexican characters are flawed but three-dimensional. For example, Captain Rodriguez is an opportunist looking after his own self-interest who does not empathize with his community. Nevertheless, despite his relatively exalted position, he is often reminded of his ethnicity and of the ceiling that exists for his own ambitions. Mitchell keeps him in check by telling him, "Don't forget where you came from, and if you don't watch your goddamned mouth, I'll have you fired!" Predictably, when Rodriguez fails he gets no second chance: "It's all over, Gene, I should have known better than trust a goddamned greaser like you!" Rodriguez has betrayed the interests of his own people as a way to cement his place in the European-American world, but he realizes too late that he is expendable. The tango dancer is motivated to frame Pedro out of self-interest, rather than face a charge of pandering. The teenage girl Linda is willing to charge Pedro with statutory rape, rather than expose the fact that she lost her virginity to her molester father.

Pedro J. González himself is depicted as a tarnished man who succumbs to the allure of fame. It is only later, during his imprisonment, that he redeems himself and his dignity with the support of his wife and community. The film also acknowledges the importance of the Mexican community's efforts to release him (some 300,000 signatures were delivered to the governor of California's office).

Break of Dawn was directed and written by Isaac Artenstein, who was born in San Diego, California, to Mexican parents and later grew up in Tijuana. Artenstein had made a documentary about Pedro J. González entitled *Ballad of an Unsung Hero* (1983), which was aired nationally on PBS stations. The documentary went on to win various awards, including an Emmy, the CINE Golden Eagle, the Golden Mike Award, and the Blue Ribbon at the American Film Festival. The documentary was the basis for *Break of Dawn*.

The veteran Mexican folk singer Óscar Chávez played Pedro J. González. The acclaimed Mexican actress María Rojo played his wife María. Rojo was the veteran of several *telenovelas*. Her film credits included *Rojo Amanecer* (1988), the first Mexican film to focus on the 1968 student massacre in Tlatelolco. Newcomer Kamala Lopez played the young beauty queen Linda. She had previously made an impression in Cheech Marin's *Born in East L.A.* (1987) and Jesús Salvador Treviño's *Gangs* (1989, PBS). *Break of Dawn* was made on an $850,000 budget and shot on location in San Diego, California.

Break of Dawn premiered at the United States Film Festival, and it subsequently won top honors at the San Antonio Cine Festival and two Nosotros Awards. It went on to represent the United States at the Toronto Festival of Festivals, the U.S. Film Festival in Tokyo, and the Tashkent Film Festival. However, the film received limited exposure in the U.S. and was mostly restricted to art houses.

The film earned uniformly excellent reviews. *L.A. Weekly* wrote, "*Break of Dawn* is an eminently bi-national film. Óscar Chávez and María Rojo (who play Pedro and his wife) are both stars in Mexico—and do a fine job here. Actors of El Norte and El Sur meet in a bilingual script in which the dialogue for the Spanish-speaking actors flows in and out of both languages fluidly."[23] The *Los Angeles Times* noted, "Sometimes a story is so significant that it's worth trying to overlook the flaws in a the way in which it is told. This is the case with *Break of Dawn*, which has the awkwardness typical of some low-budget productions of a first-time director.... Óscar Chávez may be too old for González, but has a dignified presence and is a wonderful singer.... *Break of Dawn* evokes a sense of period with fewer anachronisms than films with much bigger budgets."[24]

Christine List in turn noted, "In *Break of Dawn* the importance of remembrance and its connection to identity formation are tantamount. The protagonist of the film established the link between the Mexican revolution and Chicano resistance.... By drawing connections between past acts of resistance and present situations Arenstein underscores his own commitment to the notion of agency in Chicano art and to producing a film which is informed by both a linguistic and class-based analysis of history."[25]

Crossover Dreams (1985, Crossover Films)

Crossover Dreams is an apt title for a film that sensitively explores the frustrations of a Latino *salsero*'s struggle to break into the mainstream music world of fortune and fame. The title of the film is symbolic of the hopes that Latinos have had for more than a century since they were incorporated into U.S. society, either through conquest or immigration.

The film's narrative focused on Rudy Veloz (Rubén Blades), a talented and ambitious Puerto Rican *salsero* who lives in Spanish Harlem and has dreams beyond the third-rate nightclubs where he and the seven members of his group play. He finally gets an opportunity to play his latest song to a sleazy record producer, Lou Rose (Tom Signorelli), but before they sign the contract the latter is arrested for the possession of controlled substances. Rudy is counseled by his mentor Chico Rabala (Virgilio Marti), who cautions him about moving away from his cultural and musical roots. Soon after, however, Rabala's own death on the stage of a third-rate nightclub reawakens Rudy's frustration and coiled ambition to break out of the cycle of failure and anonymity. At Rabala's funeral, Rudy confides to a friend, "I've seen our future in that church and it looks like shit! If we stay, we're dead!"

Rudy's initiative pays off when he finds another producer, Neil Silver (Joel Diamond), who takes a chance and signs a contract with him. Their first album is a big success. Rudy begins to make plans to marry his longtime girlfriend Liz Garcia (Elizabeth Peña). He feels he is at the point of his crossover dreams and he goes on a binge of material excesses: buying a vintage sports car and trendy clothes, renting an expensive high-rise apartment, getting involved in several loveless affairs, and using chemical substances with his schoolboy friend and horn player Orlando (Shawn Elliott).

Blinded by ambition, Rudy breaks up with Liz and fires Orlando at the advice of a "hip" producer, and replaces him with a bland European-American saxophone player. As he withdraws completely from his ties with Spanish Harlem, he begins to feel cultural and emotional isolation. He releases another album, but it receives only lukewarm reviews and little commercial success. As his drug habit escalates, he uses up all his income and more and is finally reduced to living in a run-down pad on Times Square. However, he is encouraged by his producer, who tells him that he will get a second chance, but Rudy knows otherwise: "People like me don't get a second chance.... We don't even get answers." Despondent and lonely, he visits Liz, who is now married to a European-American suburban dentist. Rudy finally decides to seek out his old friend Orlando, and the two decide to re-form their old band.

The character of Rudy Veloz is a composite of many Latino musicians, who at times feel compelled to de–Latinize themselves to cross over into mainstream success or live a life on the margins of their art. But the film explores whether the American dream is just that, one that never comes true, especially for Latinos and other people of color.

Crossover Dreams was directed by Leon Ichaso. The script was co-written by Ichaso, Marvel Arce and Rubén Blades. Ichaso and Arce had previously collaborated on *El Super*

(1979), which depicted the struggles of a Cuban refugee family and their adjustment to life in Spanish Harlem. Rubén Blades, the already well-known Panamanian-born *salsero,* played the role of Rudy, in what at times was an almost autobiographical part.

The film received excellent reviews and remains a key film of the Puerto Rican and Cuban experience in the United States. The *New York Times* noted, "As it turns out, Liz isn't very lucky nor, for that matter, is Rudy, but the movie that contains them is a winner. It's *Crossover Dreams,* and though small and made on a modest budget, it's a sagely funny comedy, both heartfelt and sophisticated, a movie that may well realize the crossover dreams that elude Rudy.... In Mr. Blades, who makes his film debut as Rudy Veloz, Mr. Ichaso and Mr. Arce have discovered who's also a screen natural, the kind of actor whose presence and intelligence register without apparent effort. The members of the supporting cast are almost as good, including Miss Peña, who was very funny as the cheeky Americanized daughter in *El Super.*"[26]

Latino (1985, Lucasfilm/Latino)

Latino was a very topical film that explored the common historical roots and destinies of Chicanos and the peoples of Latin America, especially during the time of the revolutionary insurgencies in Central America.

The film is set along the Honduran-Nicaraguan border in the early 1980s, soon after the Nicaraguan Revolution of 1979 that had overthrown the U.S.–supported Somoza dynasty. Two Chicano servicemen are sent to train the Nicaraguan Contras (counterrevolutionaries): Eddie Guerrero (Robert Beltran), a former Special Forces Vietnam veteran and East Los Angeles native; and Ruben (Tony Plana), a gung-ho veteran of various military conflicts. They are sent with CIA personnel in order to terrorize and recruit young Nicaraguan youths for the Contra forces, who plan to overthrow the Sandinista revolutionary government. In Honduras, Eddie meets Marlena (Annette Cardona), a widowed Nicaraguan exile and an agronomist who has a small boy. Her family members are Sandinistas. One day, at a debriefing session, a European-American CIA operative derisively refers to Nicaragua as another "spic country." Eddie disregards the comment, but it haunts him and slowly his loss of innocence begins. On one occasion, while carrying out a mission in Nicaragua, he happens across an old woman making tortillas whose son has just been abducted to join the Contra forces. He is reminded of his mother and the people of his own barrio back home.

He becomes increasingly disenchanted and confused about his activities. At one point Marlena tries to penetrate his motives and he responds, "I honestly can't say what's the truth and what a lie is anymore." Increasingly, he is unable to relate to Ruben's macho gung-ho attitudes. He tells him about the old woman that he saw: "And that old woman cursed me, Jesus, man, standing by her for a few minutes I thought I was in mama's kitchen." After returning from a trip to Nicaragua for her father's funeral, Marlena discovers the true nature of Eddie's mission and leaves him. Even more disillusioned with the ethical conduct of his activities and the ambiguity of the war, he reluctantly takes one more mission during which a Nicaraguan conscript (Luis Torrientos), whom he has mentored and trained, turns against him and his cause.

Latino was directed by the noted Oscar-winning cinematographer and director Haskell Wexler, who had made an impressive directorial debut with *Medium Cool* (1969), about the

1968 Chicago police riots. He went on to earn acclaim for his cinematography in *One Flew over the Cuckoo's Nest* (1975) and *Bound for Glory* (1976). He had also earned notice for a series of documentaries, including *Target Nicaragua*. He commented about the reason for making *Latino*, "I think the ability of the American people to make a dispassionate judgment about Nicaragua is more difficult. I'm hoping that *Latino* won't just make a statement about Nicaragua and Central America, but [will be a] film against violence, against war. You might call *Latino* pacifist ... although the word is not exactly in vogue nowadays."[27] The film was shot on location in Nicaragua during the first half of 1984.

But *Latino* also focused on the moral and historical dilemma of Chicano soldiers fighting against other Latinos with the same cultural roots and language, who are also the product of the same poverty and political marginalization. Eddie, for example, at one point tells him, "We're just niggers. We're the niggers of the world." Eddie has spent fourteen years in military conflict, beginning with three tours of duty in Vietnam, and now finds emptiness in his life. He comments, "It seems I've spent most of my life hiding in the bushes of countries." The choices and doubts pondered by these Chicano GIs, Eddie and Ruben, were not dissimilar to some real Chicano GIs who, when the wars were over, returned home only to realize that the racism against them made no allowances for their sacrifices and heroism in battle.

The critical response to *Latino* was mixed. Some critics were unable to fathom its relevance to the Chicano and Latino experience. *Variety* noted, "Although doubtlessly not intended as such, *Latino* comes off distressingly like a left-wing *The Green Berets*. A nobly conceived, on-the-scene look at the battle between the Sandinistas and the U.S.–backed Contras in Nicaragua, writer-director Haskell Wexler has woefully simplified a very complex situation that ill serves the cause of which he feels such sympathy ... Tony Plana stands out as a gung-ho U.S. Latin officer."[28]

The *Los Angeles Herald-Examiner* wrote, "Writer-director Haskel Wexler's *Latino* is a political film for people who like their politics ultrasalty, as in *Salt of the Earth*.... As a propaganda goes, *Latino* isn't convincing. It's shot in a semidocumentary style in actual Nicaraguan locations, but the story is rigged and acting is often awkward."[29] The *Los Angeles Times* stated, "Unlike most other American films this year, Haskell Wexler's *Latino* ... was obviously made without compromise: with passion and dedication.... Wexler falls into an old Hollywood trap by telling the story this way, letting the sexy, fine-boned Annette Cardona be Nicaragua's soul ... and building up Eddie, iconographically, as the classical American action-movie-star hero—handsome, bluff, boyishly cynical."[30]

The UCLA Chicano newspaper *La Gente* provided a different interpretation: "By the general audience, the movie will be seen as a movie about United States policy towards Nicaragua but for Chicanos, for the Mexican-American who watches the movie—it will be a movie about the essence of the Chicano. The movie will have a special significance because in real life, the history of the Chicano has been one of struggle with identity."[31]

El Norte (1984, Cinecom/Island Alive)

During the 1980s several films tackled the plight of Latino undocumented workers. The two most evocative and powerful were Robert M. Young's *Alambrista!* (1983) and Gregory Nava's *El Norte*.

The plight of Mexican and Latino undocumented workers has had a long trajectory in U.S. films, although not always an accurate or sympathetic one. The first films to deal with the subject were sensationalist and exploitive, like *The Fighting Edge* (1926, Warner Bros.), where a U.S. Secret Service agent (Kenneth Harlan) battled a ruthless gang who peddles passports for hordes of Mexican laborers; and *Human Cargo* (1936, 20th Century–Fox), which focused on the smuggling of Mexican laborers. It wasn't until Anthony Mann's *Border Incident* (1949), Joseph Losey's *The Lawless*, and William Wellman's *My Man and I* (1952) that U.S. films depicted the exploitative conditions under which Mexican undocumented workers worked and lived. In the late 1970s and 1980s, a number of films focused on the subject, the best of which were Jesús Salvador Treviño's *Raíces De Sangre/Roots of Blood* (1979) and Robert M. Young's *Alambrista!* (1983).

El Norte told the odyssey of a brother, Enrique Xuncax (David Villalpando), and a sister, Rosa Xuncax (Zaide Silvia Gutiérrez), Guatemalan Mayans who make a perilous journey from their homeland to Los Angeles, California. Their father, Arturo (Ernesto Gómez Cruz), is a worker on a plantation who is murdered because of his efforts to organize other workers. Subsequently, his wife Lupe (Alicia Del Lago) becomes "disappeared." After Enrique finds his father hanging from a tree, he and his sister decide to leave. They are enraptured by the seeming material abundance displayed in some old issues of *Good Housekeeping* and it is with these images of the United States that they set off on their trek.

When they arrive in Tijuana, Mexico, they are duped into crossing the border and robbed of their meager savings by an opportunistic *coyote* (smuggler). They eventually find a more reliable *coyote*, Raimundo (Abel Franco), who gets them across through an old sewage tunnel. They finally get to Los Angeles and decide to enroll in an adult education class in order to learn English. Enrique gets a job as a dishwasher at an expensive restaurant, while his sister Rosa, who is befriended by a kind older woman, Nocha (Lupe Ontiveros), is hired as a domestic at an affluent home. Over time, Enrique becomes so consumed in the pursuit of the materialism of the American dream that he abandons his sister when she is gravely ill. Nocha attempts to dissuade him: "Rosa is dying, but you're already dead!"

The film was directed by a new Chicano director, Gregory Nava, who had previously directed, written and produced *The Confession of Amans*. Nava belonged to the new generation of filmmakers who had learned their craft in film school, in this case the UCLA Film School. Nava, who coscripted *El Norte* with his wife Anna Thomas, spoke about his reason for making the film: "When you travel anywhere in Latin America, you're immediately struck by two forces: the lush, dreamlike beauty of the landscape—the people, colors, textiles, art, and the terrible social and political problems that are ripping these countries apart. There's an undercurrent of violence beneath this poetic beauty that can erupt at any moment, at any place."[32]

It took Nava several years to find financial backing for his film, and some of the delay was attributed to the ethnicity of the protagonists. "I kept hearing, again and again, that I should make Americans the main characters, that I'd never get it financed otherwise. I have nothing against films like *Missing* or *Under Fire,* but I wanted a film where Latin American people were the protagonists.... Everybody told me that audiences could never be able to cross that cultural and language barrier, but I thought that even though the cultural differences were great, if the film were done right, people would be able to cross that barrier and recognize human beings on the other side."[33]

Due to the nature of the story, only the opening scenes were able to be shot in Guatemala. Most of the on-location shooting was subsequently done in Chiapas, Mexico, until escalating political conflicts forced Nava to complete the filming in the state of Morelos, nearer to Mexico City.

El Norte opened to enthusiastic reviews and commercial success. The *New York Times* wrote, "A small, personal, independently made film with the sweep of *El Norte,* with solid, sympathetic performances by unknown actors and a visual style of astonishing vibrancy, must be regarded as a remarkable achievement.... Rosa and Enrique, who are played so plainly and touchingly (both Miss Gutiérrez and Mr. Villalpando are experienced Mexican stage actors making their film debuts) that the audience cannot help but empathize.... Mr. Nava makes *El Norte* real and involving throughout."[34]

The *Los Angeles Times* commented, "*El Norte* ... embodies an idea whose time has come: the dramatization on screen of the plight of the illegal immigrants. it is a subject that has been dealt with before in films, most notably in Robert M. Young's excellent *Alambrista!,* but young independent film maker Gregory Nava has attempted no less than an epic.... What ensues lays bare the treacherousness of the American Dream, where, in the struggle for survival, the individual is tempted increasingly to think for himself.... In plotting and movement ... [the film] recalls such epics of the poor and the dispossessed as Visconti's *Rocco and His Brothers* ... Gutiérrez and Villalpando convey genuine sweetness. By the end, Enrique has come full circle, confronted with the reality that his value to the world, like his father before him, lies only in the strength of his arms. Yet, at this moment, Enrique attains universality."[35]

However, more recent critique of the film has taken a different orientation. Christine List, for example noted, "*El Norte* constructs a patronizing vision of Mayan culture and the problem of poverty. On the one hand, the film valorizes the indigenous lifestyle where the ethos of family and community solidarity is held sacred. The filmmaker consistently gives us scenes pitting an idyllic Mayan culture against a corrupt mestizo one. At the same time, the trajectory of the narrative undermines the protagonist's potential as a self-determined indigenous subject. Enrique never speaks of going back home, never contemplates joining a Guatemalan human rights organization or resistance movement either in the U.S. or in Guatemala. Such an action would be a logical step for his character, given that his father tried to start a resistance movement himself.... Their only option, in terms of the narrative, is to head north towards economic opportunity. Embracing capitalism, not questioning its flaws, becomes an inevitable solution."[36]

Seguin (1981, PBS)

Jesús Salvador Treviño's *Seguin* was the first U.S. film to depict the Mexican side of the 1936 Texas insurrection. And like the film *Latino*, it explored the struggle of Chicano identity.

The film's narrative focuses on Juan Seguín (A Martinez), whose father, Don Erasmo Seguin (Henry Darrow), a landowner, had been a supporter of the Mexican government's policy to permit Stephen Austin in 1821 to allow European-Americans into Texas. One of the Mexican government's conditions was that they not bring slaves or attempt to establish the institution of slavery, as Mexico had banned slavery with the advent of its independence in 1821. Juan Seguín abhors slavery, and believes idealistically that the European-American settlers would abandon such an ignominious enterprise and abide by the laws and culture of Mexico. However, by 1836, the influx of European Americans has already outnumbered the Mexican inhabitants. Seguín initially sides with the immigrants and against General Santa Anna, who leads an army to put down the rebellion.

After Texas independence, Seguín is elected mayor. However, he becomes increasingly disillusioned with the establishment of slavery and the marginalization of and racism against Mexicans. During the Mexican-American War (1846–1848), Seguín fights on the side of Mexico. In 1849, Seguín is given a formal pardon by the U.S. government and he returns to San Antonio. Today, in his honor there is a town in south Texas with his name.

Initially, Seguín was supposed to be the first segment of La Historia, a six-hour mini-series that was to depict Chicano history from the Mexican-American War to the present. However, only *Seguin* was actually made and it aired during American Playhouse's first season. Director Jesús Salvador Treviño explained what happened to the rest of the project: "*Seguin* was funded by the National Endowment for the Humanities and the Corporation for Public Broadcasting during the Carter Administration. Then Reagan was elected, and he appointed William Bennett to head up the NEH. Bennett did a good job for his boss, complaining that too many NEH-funded projects were little more than propaganda for the Communists. He saw to it that there were substantial budget cuts and La Historia was one of the programs cut."[37]

Treviño, who was also the executive producer and writer, had done extensive research for some four years. "We're not distorting history," he said. "This is history that until now

Danny De La Paz and Alma Martínez in Jesús Salvador Treviño's *Seguin* (1982, PBS).

a few historians were aware of. I think Seguín and his family were among the first people to experience of the dual nature of bilingual-bicultural realities. Their conflicts and lives are prototypical of what all Latinos in the United States face."[38]

Seguin was the first U.S. film to tell the Mexican side of the Texas insurrection, and in a twist of irony it was shot in Bracketville, Texas, on the very sets left behind by John Wayne's ethnocentric and multimillion-dollar *The Alamo* (1960, United Artists). By contrast, *Seguín* was made on a $500,000 budget and filmed in twenty-one days.

Seguin was enhanced by a talented Chicano and Latino cast. It included A Martinez as Juan Seguín, Edward James Olmos as General Santa Anna, Henry Darrow as Erasmo Seguin, and Rose Portillo as Seguin's wife. Other roles were played by Alma Martínez, Danny De La Paz, Lupe Ontiveros, Enrique Castillo, and Julio Medina.

Over the years, however, *Seguin* has been subjected to criticism in its portrayal of the Seguin character. Rosa Linda Fregoso, for example, wrote, "In his effort to portray the Texas conflicts of the 19th century

Rose Portillo and A Martinez in *Seguin* (1982, PBS).

through the eyes of the protagonist, Juan Seguín, Treviño not only simplifies a historical period but also attempts to vindicate Seguín. The conflicts of the period are reduced to racism and the economic interests of the elite Tejano class are made to represent the interests of the entire Tejano population, seemingly homogeneous interests. Class conflicts are excluded. The film is critical, not of the economic structure that became the basis of human exploitation, but the ideological force (i.e., racism) that excluded Tejano landowners from partaking in the nascent transformation of economic relations in Texas. For when Seguín says, 'land I fought to defend,' he means 'my land' in the realistic rather that the metaphoric sense."[39]

Stand and Deliver (1988, Warner Bros.)

Ramón Menéndez's *Stand and Deliver* was released in the wake of the huge successes of *La Bamba* and *Born in East L.A.* It was the first film to focus on the most pressing issue for Latino families, their children's education.

The film told the true story of Bolivian-born Jaime Escalante, a math teacher at Garfield

High School in the East Los Angeles barrio. Upon his arrival at the school, it was overrun with drugs, gangs, an out-of-control dropout rate, and at the brink of losing its educational accreditation by the state. In 1982, he recruited a group of low-achieving students with low self-esteem who had limited math skills, and through a supportive and caring process of teaching turned their academic lives around. Eighteen of them went on to take the advanced placement calculus exam that is administered by the National Testing Service, which is mandated by the College Board. Although the advanced placement exam earns the students college credit, it is so rigorous that only 2 percent of all high school students take it. Nonetheless, all of Escalante's students took the exam and six of them earned perfect scores. Subsequently, the Educational Testing Service noted a similarity of incorrect answers among the students at Garfield School, and made the assertion that they may have cheated. In spite of Escalante's impassioned protest, his students were given only two choices, either to take the exam again or accept the Educational Testing Service's decision.

The students decided to take up the challenge and took the test again. At the end, they scored even higher and put to rest the stereotype about being low achievers. Their accomplishment was a source of inspiration to their teacher, the school and their families.

The film was directed by Cuban-born Ramón Menéndez, who became intrigued by the testing incident when the *Los Angeles Times* ran a story. Menéndez approached Escalante about the film project several times before he agreed. "He wasn't particularly blown away with the idea of a movie about his life and his commitment to kids and teaching them. What convinced him was my argument that if even one kid in any city across the country turned around by what we put on the screen, then we were essentially working toward the same goal."[40]

The film was financed by Public Broadcasting Service's *American Playhouse,* ARCO, the National Science Foundation, the Corporation for Public Broadcasting, and the Ford Foundation. It was distributed by Warner Bros. The film was shot at the real Garfield High School and around East Los Angeles in a short six weeks. Edward James Olmos, who had won an Emmy Award in 1985 for his role of Lieutenant Castillo in *Miami Vice,* was cast in the role of the teacher, Jaime Escalante. He was intrigued with the role and story: "The concept of false accusation was a theme I had dealt with in my earlier roles, both in *Zoot Suit* as well as in *The Ballad of Gregorio Cortez.*"[41] A meticulous actor, Olmos prepared arduously for the role, gaining forty pounds and having his hair cosmetically thinned to a few strands to resemble Escalante physically. In addition, he observed Escalante for dozens of hours. "Jaime and I spent extensive time together," he said. "I was lucky to have his commitment."[42] In the long run, his dedication to his craft paid off, as he received an Academy Award nomination for Best Actor for his performance.

The role of the gang member and student Angel was played by Lou Diamond Phillips, who had just played Ritchie Valens in the yet-unreleased *La Bamba,* and Rosanna DeSoto, who had just played Valens' mother in the same film, was cast as Escalante's wife Fabiola.

The film was an unexpected critical and commercial success. It received additional exposure when President Bush cited Escalante's work and the film as examples of what could be achieved in barrio schools. *Stand and Deliver* stressed several factors that resonated with the Chicano and Latino communities for academic success, such as self-esteem, initiative and self-sufficiency. As such, the film did much to also focus the media's attention on the troubled educational status of Chicanos and Latinos.

Most reviewers praised the film enthusiastically. The *Los Angeles Times* wrote, "You could remain, mesmerized, in Jaime Escalante's high school math class forever, the way you remain under the spell of Escalante himself as *Stand and Deliver* unfolds.... Olmos' self-effacing magnetism is at the center of a rousing true story of a man able to inspire a lethargic group of almost-dropouts at a school barely able to keep its accreditation—to galvanize them, give them pride in themselves and show them the road to earning it."[43]

Zoot Suit (1982, Universal)

Luis Valdez' *Zoot Suit* is a pivotal work in Chicano cinema. It documented the Chicano community's collective memory of two important events of its recent history, the Sleepy Lagoon case of 1942 and the zoot suit riots of 1943.

Mario Barrera has noted, "Luis Valdez has ... created in *Zoot Suit* an amazingly complex tapestry that interweaves two historical events, a courtroom drama, two love stories, several musical numbers, political messages, multiple resolutions, and myth. But the core of the story, the element that makes it hang together, is the inner transformation of the protagonist, his journey toward self-awareness."[44]

The film *Zoot Suit* was written and directed by Luis Valdez and based on his play of the same name. The play had first opened at the Mark Taper Forum in Los Angeles, in 1978, where it had galvanized both critics and audiences. After its Los Angeles run it had other successful engagements in Southwest cities and finally closed with a short run on Broadway, the first Chicano play ever to play there.

Luis Valdez spoke about the story that the film and play told: "History has different levels. In reality, there are seven, from the most personal to the cosmic, all spinning around the same axis. When it came down to exploring the Sleepy Lagoon murder case, I had all this documentation and historical material. I had to work my way through the mythic history. When I had started out with a naturalistic approach, I lost the Pachuco. Once you're confined to reality, there's a constraint. The way to contain the character was to put him in his setting, so I framed the film around the concept of a theatrical event. I feel the film captured a certain relevancy. We're entering a period of a new initiative and patriotic self-expression. I hope *Zoot Suit* will be a reaffirmation of America as a mix of many peoples."[45]

Valdez combined the two events of the Sleepy Lagoon case and the zoot suit riots into his narrative. Sleepy Lagoon was a reservoir in Los Angeles which youths used as a swimming hole and a romantic rendezvous spot. On August 2, 1942, a Chicano youth was found dead there, and soon thereafter some six hundred Chicano suspects were arrested. At the end, twenty youths went to trial before an obnoxious and prejudiced judge. Twelve of the defendants were given sentences of life imprisonment and quartered in San Quentin. The Chicano community organized a defense committee, and later, on appeal, the youths were released after serving eighteen months. The second event took place during the summer of 1943, when a fight between sailors and *pachucos* (Chicano barrio gang youth or youth who wore the zoot suit) escalated into a full-scale riot. The newspapers, especially the rabid William Randolph Hearst–owned *Los Angeles Herald-Examiner* and others, fueled the racist image of Mexicans and Mexican-Americans as violence-prone and uncivilized. The evening after the initial confrontation, hundreds of servicemen invaded the East Los Angeles barrio and vented their fury on every *pachuco* and zoot suit wearer that they came across. The "zoot suit riots" became an international incident and the Mexican government filed a formal protest to the U.S. government. At the very same time, hundreds of thousands of Chicano servicemen were fighting and dying abroad in the war against fascism.

The film focused on the experiences of Henry Reyna (Daniel Valdez), one of the twenty defendants who were sentenced to life imprisonment. In the process of his ordeal he undergoes two trials, a public and a private one. In the courtroom, he is defended by the European-American liberal lawyer George (Charles Aidman), who is aided by his dedicated assistant Alice (Tyne Daly). As he undergoes the trauma of incarceration, Henry breaks up with his girlfriend Della (Rose Portillo) and finds himself increasingly attracted to Alice.

Henry's second tribulation is between himself and his demons, represented by the mythical figure of the Pachuco (Edward James Olmos). The Pachuco represents the barrio and the street persona that Henry has appropriated. He tells the Pachuco, "I got you all figured out, carnal, you're the one that got me here. My worst enemy and my best friend. Myself."

Finally, upon his release, Henry is welcomed by his parents (Julio Medina, Lupe Ontiveros), his younger brother Rudy (Tony Plana) and sister (Alma Martínez). Although the story has a seemingly happy ending, it is noted that the real Henry Reyna endured two more prison terms, a drug addiction and a premature death in 1972. In the real end, the trauma of his experiences broke his life.

Daniel Valdez in Luis Valdez' *Zoot Suit* (1982, Universal). The film was directed by Luis Valdez and based on his seminal play of the same name.

The film *Zoot Suit* was shot in only thirteen days, mostly on sets at the Aquarius Theater, and it had a $1.3 million budget. Regrettably, the studio did a less than effective promotional campaign for the film. Later, after many years of effort by Luis Valdez, the studio finally released the film on video in 1991. Over the years, the film has earned a growing reputation on its own merits, and not just simply as a filmed document of a unique and historic play.

The reviews of *Zoot Suit* were generally positive, with some exceptions. The *Los Angeles Times* noted, "The film captures its pachuco swagger splendidly, not from the aisle seat struck safely back in the house, but from multiple angles and distances, as if reporting a sports event, which a show with this much jitterbugging is. The aim isn't necessarily to show how *Zoot Suit* looked at the Aquarius ... but to show how a typical performance felt. The ceremony and the story come through. Daniel Valdez and Edward James Olmos come through even more strongly than they did in the theater, which is saying something."[46]

Latino Film Stars and Filmmakers

NORMA ALEANDRO

Norma Aleandro is the first Argentinean actress to win international renown since Linda Cristal in the 1950s. Unlike Cristal, who was typecast as a sex symbol, Aleandro established from the beginning her credentials as a serious actress.

She was born in Buenos Aires, Argentina, on December 6, 1936, to a theatrical family. She began acting as a child in her parents' productions. Aleandro went on to become the most respected actress in Argentina, as well as an outspoken critic of her country's various military regimes. During the late 1970s and early 1980s she lived in exile, first in Uruguay and later in Spain due to persecution by the right-wing regimes.

In 1982, she returned to Buenos Aires and to both stage and film. During this time she also appeared on the New York stage, winning accolades. Aleandro's greatest success was her role of the wife married to an Argentinean general during the military dictatorship in *The Official Story* (1985). She shared the Best Actress award at the Cannes Film Festival for her superb portrayal and the film won an Academy Award as Best Foreign Film.

She was nominated for Best Actress for her role in Luis Mandoki's downbeat but inspiring *Gaby: A True Story* (1987), about a courageous palsy victim coping with her condition. The cast included Liv Ullmann, Robert Beltran and Danny De La Paz. She had another good role as the older bride Edie Costello in Joel Schumacher's popular comedy-drama *Cousins* (1989), bolstered by another good cast that included Sean Young, Ted Danson, and Lloyd Bridges.

In 1990, she costarred in two films, the Argentinean *Cien Veces no Debo* and the U.S. film *Vital Signs*, a not entirely successful medical school comedy with Jimmy Smits.

Recent films include *Carlos Monzón, el Segundo Juicio* (1995); *Sol de Otoño* (1996); *Una Noche con Sabrina Love* (2000); *Seres Queridos* (2004); *The City of Your Final Destination* (2007); *Música en Espera* (2009); and *Familia para Armar* (2010).

Aleandro found worthwhile roles in Hollywood film increasingly hard to find as a consequence of the film industry's obsession with youth and lack of roles for actresses beyond the age of thirty.

She kept busy with other pursuits, including collaborating on the screenplay of the Argentinean film *Los Herederos* and publishing short stories and poems.

MARÍA CONCHITA ALONSO

María Conchita Alonso was an established television and film star in Venezuela by the time she made her U.S. film debut in *Moscow on the Hudson* in 1984.

She was born in Cienfuegos, Cuba, in 1957. Her family left Cuba for Caracas, Venezuela, when she was five years old. There, she became a child star in films and television commercials. In 1971, she was selected Miss Teenager of the World, and in 1973, she won the title of Miss Venezuela. In the next few years, she went on to headline some ten *telenovelas* throughout Latin America. She later recalled about this period,

"What's fantastic is that for me that was like my school. I went for a little while to acting school. I think that the practice is what makes someone learn and be good at it. And that is what soap operas did for me. They taught me discipline and I learned slowly by working every day, by seeing myself, on the screen."[47]

Her U.S. debut occurred on U.S. television: the TV film *Fear City* (1984) with Rossano Brazzi and Melanie Griffith. After that, she made appearances in episodes of several television series. Her U.S. film debut came in the role of the Italian immigrant Lucia in Paul Mazursky's comedy-drama *Moscow on the Hudson* (1984, Columbia), for which she received excellent notices. She later recalled her departure to Hollywood: "My family and friends thought I was crazy to choose Hollywood. They said I would have a better chance in Mexico City where they make so many Spanish-language films because they use more foreign performers."[48]

She recounted how she got the role in *Moscow on the Hudson*: "I went to a party and my picture came out in the *Hollywood Reporter* in the society columns. And the people who were casting *Moscow on the Hudson* saw my picture and I looked like what they were looking for. So they called the Actors Guild to see whether I was an actress. And that's how they found me."[49]

Her next film roles were in Blake Edwards' misfire *A Fine Mess* (1986, Columbia) with Ted Danson; the Showtime film *Blood Ties* (1986) with Brad Davis; the excellent comedy-drama *Touch and Go* (1987, TriStar) with Michael Keaton; and then she played a Chicana in Walter Hill's drama *Extreme Prejudice* (1987, TriStar) with Nick Nolte and Rip Torn.

She scored another commercial hit in the role of Amber Mendez in Paul Michael Glaser's futuristic *The Running Man* (1987, TriStar) with Arnold Schwarzenegger and Jim Brown. She played a Chicana former gang member, Louisa Gomez, in Dennis Hopper's visually impressive but rather sensationalist account of Chicano and African American gangs in Los Angeles, *Colors* (1988, Orion), with Robert Duvall and Sean Penn. She played the mild-mannered secretary Alva Restrepo who is tormented by her vampire-influenced boss in

María Conchita Alonso grew up in Venezuela and first rose to fame in Mexican *telenovelas.* **Later she came to the United Sates and starred in television and film.**

Robert Bierman's excellent *Vampire's Kiss* (1988, Hemdale) with Jennifer Beals and Nicolas Cage.

Increasingly typecast as a sexpot, she commented, "In reality, I can play any foreign accent with a little coaching.... My accent is a good thing because it does set me apart from the others. But I have no doubts that I also lost parts because of it. It pleases me that not all my roles have been fiery Latin American women. And I have been given parts in both comedy and drama."[50]

She also embarked on a successful music career. She has eleven albums to her credit. In 1985, she was nominated for a Grammy as Best Latin Artist for her album *María Conchita,* which was certified international platinum. In 1988, she was given a second Grammy nomination for Best Performance for her song "Otra Mentira Más." Additionally, she has recorded four albums, including *O Ella O Yo,* which went gold. She wrote eleven of the songs in the album *Imaginane,* which was co-produced by María, K. C. Porter and Mark Spiro. The album was nominated for a Grammy for Best Latin Pop Album in 1993. She released another album, *Hoy y Siempre,* in 1996. She also sang the theme song for Brian De Palma's film *Scarface* (1983).

More recently, she played the lead in NBC's situation comedy *One of the Boys.* Her career geared up with *American Cousin* (1990). She played a tough cop, Leona Cantrel, in *Predator 2* (1990) opposite Danny Glover and Rubén Blades; top-lined the routine *McBain* (1991); and essayed the role of the courtesan in the film adaptation of Isabel Allende's novel *House of the Spirits* (1994) with Meryl Streep, Jeremy Irons, Glenn Close, and Antonio Banderas.

However, it was a pair of films directed by Robert M. Young that provided her with the meaty roles she had long deserved: an embittered sister in *Roosters* (1995) with Edward James Olmos and Sônia Braga, and the adulterous wife in Robert M. Young's *Caught* (1996) opposite Edward James Olmos. Both films revealed untapped dramatic talent and earned her her best notices, especially the latter film. The *Boston Globe* noted of her performance, "She projects a force of longing rarely encountered on screen, and there's desperation as well as heat."[51]

She has starred in Venezuelan films, one Dominican film and ten soap operas (*telenovelas*). She stated, "T.V. soaps are the best way for an actress to make a living in South America. But if you want to star in films you must go to Europe, Mexico City or Hollywood."[52]

During 1997, she made her Broadway debut as Aurora/Spider Woman in Hal Prince's *Kiss of the Spider Woman* at the Broadhurst Theatre. Alonso rose to the challenge by tapping into her accumulated reserves of talent and skill. She earned excellent notices from critics who had been ready to dismiss her foray into theater. Both the film *Caught* and the play reinvigorated her career, which had stagnated after several less than successful films.

She commented about performing on Broadway, "For me it was very important to do that play because it's very hard to get on Broadway. It's very hard, and also very competitive. It has nothing to do with Hollywood. In fact, my doing 'Spider Woman' did nothing for me, in Hollywood. But I obtained a certain respect out of those Broadway people that's not easy to get."[53]

She starred in the HBO film *Teamster Boss: The Jackie Presser Story* with Jeff Daniels and Eli Wallach; the NBC film *McShayne* with Kenny Rogers; the ABC film *Sudden Terror;*

the ABC miniseries *Texas*; and the USA Network film *Knockout* (1998). She also guest-starred on such top television shows as *The Outer Limits, The Nanny, Chicago Hope*, and *FX*.

Her 1990s and more recent films include *Black Heart* (1999) with Richard Grieco; *For Which He Stands* (1999); *Catherine's Grove* (1999) with Jeff Fahey; *The Hill Gang* (1999), about the life of John Dillinger; *Deadline* (1999); *Richard III* (2008); *The Art of Travel* (2008); and *Spread* (2009). However, it was the Spanish-language film *El Grito en el Cielo* (1998) that provided her with another rich and complex role.

An indestructible optimist of boundless energy, María Conchita Alonso has displayed an uncanny amount of reserves and talent. This has helped her survive the vicissitudes of the Hollywood film industry at a time when Latinos and especially Latinas are endangered species.

STEVEN BAUER

Among the Latino leading men of the 1980s was Steven Bauer. His performance as the drug dealer Manny Rivera in Brian De Palma's *Scarface* (1983, Universal) propelled him to film prominence.

He was born Esteban Echeverria on December 2, 1956, in Havana, Cuba, the elder son of a Cuban pilot and schoolteacher. His family left Cuba with their two boys when Steven was three years old. He attended the University of Miami and began acting in college plays. He later stated that he changed his name "because it was a real albatross. It immediately said, 'I am different. I'm not an American.'"[54]

After several television roles he was cast in the television film *She's in the Army* (1981) opposite Melanie Griffith, whom he married in 1982 and divorced in 1984. Both Bauer and Griffith studied acting briefly with drama coach Stella Adler.

Later he landed the role of Manny Rivera, the right-hand man of mobster Tony Montana (Al Pacino) in Brian De Palma's remake of *Scarface* (1983). While the film was a mixed commercial and critical success, Bauer earned rave notices for his performance and stardom seemed to beckon.

He was then cast in the title role of the ruthless womanizer in *Thief of Hearts* (1984), which generated good female audience response. He played two leads in the television series *Alfred Hitchcock Presents* (1985, NBC) with Melanie Griffith; and appeared in the HBO film *Sword of Gideon* (1986). He was then third billed as another thug, giving an effective performance in the fast-moving *Running Scared* (1986, Metro-Goldwyn-Mayer) opposite Billy Crystal and Gregory Hines. He played an Afghan rebel in *The Beast* (1988, Columbia), and then costarred in *Gleaming the Cube* (1989, 20th Century–Fox).

He had the lead as the slain DEA agent Kiki Camarena in NBC's *Drug Wars: The Camarena Story* (1990). He stated of the film, "I think *Drug Wars* will help get my career back on track because of the power of television and the power of the film."[55]

His most recent films include Brian De Palma's *Raising Cain* (1993) and *From Mexico with Love* (2011).

Presently married to former model Ingrid Anderson, he has two children (one from a previous marriage).

Robert Beltran

Chicano actor Robert Beltran began his film career in the 1970s and has gradually moved up to second leads and leads. Adept at comedy and drama, Beltran possesses the requisite physical resources for leading man status, but it remains to be seen whether Hollywood will continue to provide the necessary opportunities for him.

He was born and raised on November 19, 1953, in Bakersfield, California. A high school athlete, he broke into theater with initially some ulterior motives. He recalled later, "One of the reasons I joined the Drama Club in high school was to meet girls. I did end up meeting a lot of girls, but I also really started to enjoy acting."[56]

He gave up sports when he didn't acquire a scholarship to the college he wanted. In college, he became more serious about acting and averaged three to four theater productions per semester. He also worked in summer community productions, while sometimes coaching the football team or driving a tractor in the San Joaquin Valley fields. In 1975, he transferred to Fresno State University and continued acting, and also worked tutoring migrant workers.

After graduating in 1979, he was in a folk opera production, *David of Saasoun*, and during the run was nominated for the Irene Ryan Awards, a prestigious acting competition. He won the finals, held in Washington, D.C., and then toured with the California Shakespeare Festival for two years.

In 1980, he was cast in one of Luis Valdez' plays, and then he made his film debut in Valdez' adaptation of Valdez' play *Zoot Suit* (1981, Universal) in a bit part as a low rider in the audience. He was then cast in the title role of Paul Bartel's *Eating Raoul* (1982, 20th Century–Fox), a dark comedy about a middle-class couple who murder swindlers in order to make a living and then turn over the corpses to Raoul (Beltran) who sells them as dog food. He stated about getting the role, "They had been trying to cast the part of Raoul for months. They had even started filming the movie without the character. I was recommended for the film and they called me in Bakersfield. I thought it was a joke."[57]

After this noteworthy role, he was wasted in the one-dimensional role of Kayo, Chuck Norris' assistant, in the abysmal Cold War potboiler *Lone Wolf McQuade* (1983, Orion) with Barbara Carrera and David Carradine. He was in two television films: *Calendar Girl Murders* (1984, ABC), as a Chicano cop with the also excellent Silvana Gallardo and Tom Skerritt, and *The Mystic Warrior* (1984, ABC), in the lead role of the Sioux brave.

Robert Beltran in *Scenes from the Class Struggle in Beverly Hills* (1989, Cinecom Entertainment).

Beltran gave what is probably his best film performance in Haskell Wexler's evocative and powerful *Latino* (1986, Lucasfilm), which focused on a Chicano military adviser (Beltran) who is sent to Honduras to train counterrevolutionary forces fighting the Sandinistas in Nicaragua and who becomes involved with a Nicaraguan exile (Annette Cardona).

Beltran was again wasted in the small role of Luis in *Gaby: A True Story* (1987, TriStar) with Liv Ullmann and Norma Aleandro, and in another small role in Wayne Wang's effective film noir *Slamdance* (1987, IA) with Tom Hulce. At this low point, Paul Bartel cast him in the pivotal role of Juan in his *Scenes from the Class Struggle in Beverly Hills* (1989, Cinecrom) with Jacqueline Bisset. Beltran stated of his role, "I play a sort of man about the house, who works for Jackie, which means chauffeur, butler, gardener.... All of the other people from their lives converge and all kinds of crazy things happen."[58]

About his success he said, "I'm very happy that I gave up football for acting. If I was playing football, I would be in the twilight of my career. With acting, I feel like I'm only at the beginning."[59]

He had one of his best roles as a murder-plotting drifter in *Kiss Me a Killer* (1991) opposite Julie Carmen. The *Hollywood Reporter* commented, "As the soft-spoken, guitar-plucking Tony, Beltran's performance is well-calibrated and solid."[60]

Beginning in 1995, he had a regular role in *Star Trek: Voyager* on television. The popular series ran until 2001, when it was canceled. His films since the 1990s include the western *El Diablo* (1990); Oliver Stone's *Nixon* (1995), in which he played another covert military adviser; *Trekkies* (1997); *Luminarias* (1999); *Fire Serpent* (2007); and *Repo Chick* (2009). He was a narrator of the epic Native American documentary *500 Nations* (1995). He has guest-starred extensively on episodic television, including *Big Love* (2009–2010).

RUBÉN BLADES

Panamanian-born Rubén Blades has successfully managed two careers in music and films for more than two decades.

He was born in Panama City, Panama, on July 16, 1948, to Rubén Blades, Sr., a police detective and bongo player, and Anoland Blades, a Cuban radio actress, pianist and bolero singer. He was the second of five children and was raised primarily by his paternal grandmother, the Colombian-born Emma Bosques Laurenza. Blades was musically self-taught. After completing high school he began his law studies at the University of Panama. He sang with several Afro-Cuban bands, among them a group called Bush and the Magnificos, with whom he cut his first album.

In 1975, he began singing with Ray Barretto's band, and the next year became a songwriter and singer with the Willie Colón combo, a gig that lasted for five years. He performed on the "*cuchifrito* circuit" in the barrios of upper Manhattan and outlying boroughs and then internationally, with the Fania All Stars. In 1984, he signed with the mainstream American recording company Elektra/Asylum. During 1984 and 1985, he took time off his musical career to complete his master's degree in international law at Harvard University. His thesis concentrated on the historical differences between the concepts of justice and law.

Of his music, *Current Biography* in 1986 wrote, "With his bright, refreshing neo–Afro-

Cuban sound and his enlightened lyrics, Rubén Blades, the composer-singer from Panama, has revolutionized salsa, the dominant contemporary form of American Latin pop music, and universalized his appeal."[61]

Blades made his film debut in Leon Ichaso's *Crossover Dreams* (1985), playing Rudy Veloz, an East Harlem salsa singer who attempts to cross over into the mainstream music industry. He received excellent notices for his performance. The *New York Times* called Blades "a musical performer who's also a screen natural, the kind of actor whose presence and intelligence register without apparent effort."[62] That performance remains the best of his entire film career.

He went on to star or costar in several cable and feature films. They include the routine comedy *Critical Condition* (1986, Paramount) with Richard Pryor and Rachel Ticotin; the documentary *The Return of Rubén Blades* (1987); the flop crime-drama *Fatal Beauty* (1987, Metro-Goldwyn-Mayer) with Whoopi Goldberg and Sam Elliott; and the misfire *Disorganized Crime* (1989, Touchstone) with Lou Diamond Phillips.

Other than in his debut film, he also garnered good notices for his portrayal of Sheriff Montoya in Robert Redford's evocative, Capra-esque tale of a small Chicano rural town, *The Milagro Beanfield War* (1988, Universal).

Blades expressed a desire to become involved in Panamanian politics, in some elected office. He stated in 1985, "We will select an area that is considered impossible to correct and have its own people change it with the help of the private sector and the infrastructure being created right among students, young professionals, and others."[63]

His subsequent run for the presidency of Panama in 1994 proved to be unsuccessful and, stung by the magnitude of the defeat, Blades retreated into a period of reflection.

His 1980s films include the documentary *When the Mountains Tremble* (1983), for which he provided the music; *The Last Flight* (1983); *Beat Street* (1984), for which he co-wrote the music; *True Believer* (1988), for which he wrote the songs; *The Lennon Sisters* (1989); *Do the Right Thing* (1989), for which he wrote the songs; and *Chances Are* (1989), for which he wrote the songs. His 1990s films include *Q & A* (1990), for which he provided the music; *Mo' Better Blues* (1990); the dismal *Two Jakes* (1990) with Jack Nicholson (who also directed); and *Predator 2* (1990). He played a cameo in the Michael J. Fox comedy *Life with Mikey* (1994). More recently he was seen in *Once upon a Time in Mexico* (2003); *Greater Glory* (2011); and *Safe House* (2012).

SÔNIA BRAGA

Brazilian-born Sônia Braga began the 1980s as an internationally recognized sex symbol and ended the decade as a respected actress.

She was born in the small town of Maringa, in southern Brazil, on June 8, 1950. She was one of seven children and her father died when she was eight. She began acting on Brazilian television and doing film bits in order to help support the family while her mother labored as a seamstress.

She grew up idolizing some of Hollywood's legendary women: Garbo, Hayworth, Swanson and Monroe. She recalled later, "When I started to learn about actresses like that, I asked myself why they put them up on the pedestal.... They gave so much, Marilyn Monroe, for instance. I think she is an example we cannot forget."[64] About growing up, she commented, "Mine is the story about every girl as they grow up. They are so insecure about their sexuality, about their lives, about their body as it changes."[65] Her career went into high gear when she played the title role on the Brazilian television novella *Gabriela*. Gabriela was a country girl, barefoot, sensual and domestic, who marries the proprietor of the town bar. She discovers to her grief that he wants to remake her in order to conform to his selfish social ambitions. The novella became a sensation in Brazil, and she was well on her way to becoming a film sex goddess.

She was then cast for the lead in Bruno Barreto's 1977 film adaptation of Jorge Amado's *Doña Flor and Her Two Husbands*, which catapulted her to film stardom. She played Doña Flor, a beautiful woman whose lecherous husband suddenly dies. She remarries, only to be pursued by the ghost of her dead husband. Aside from being a huge commercial success, the film was instrumental in celebrating the rich mestizo mix of Brazil and in successfully challenging the rigid government censorship on films. Braga commented on the effect of the film, "All the movie stars are blonde and with blue eyes like Doris Day, all the woman have to dye their hair to look like Brigitte Bardot. But I decided I can be beautiful, that a Brazilian actress has to be how we are. So I started to transform myself. I look at myself, into my heart, into my eyes—beautiful!"[66]

Sônia Braga and Raúl Juliá in *Kiss of the Spider Woman* (1986, Island Alive).

Her next two films were Armaldo Jabor's *I Love You* (1982, Atlantic) and Neville d'Almedida's *Lady in the Bus* (1982, Atlantic). When asked about her acting technique, she said, "I never went to acting school. The best school is to be in the corner, sitting and drinking coffee and seeing what people do."[67] She added, "I never read theory about acting. I have no idea what acting is. I just try to understand that to be an actor or an actress is not to be special. It is just to be someone that others need, as they need a doctor. We all need the fantasy."[68]

In 1984, in the film version of *Gabriela* (Metro-Goldwyn-Mayer), she re-created her title role opposite Marcello Mastroianni. The film was directed by Bruno Barreto, and it met with enormous commercial and critical success.

She made her U.S. film debut in Hector Babenco's adaptation of the heralded Manuel Puig novel *The Kiss of the Spider Woman* (1985, IA). It told the story of two prisoners, one a revolutionary (Raúl Juliá) and the other a homosexual (William Hurt). Hurt tells fantastic stories drawn from his memories of old Hollywood movies. Parallels develop between the relationship of the two men and the character of their fantasies. Braga played a diverse number of characters: Julia's lover, a French chanteuse who falls in love with a Gestapo chief, and, ultimately, the Spider Woman. She said of the role, "I am the memory. Where I am is in their minds.... When you talk about life, your memory betrays you sometimes. You select and change the story. My characters were others' memories."[69]

The film earned her international recognition and acclaim. Jack Noll of *Newsweek* called her "the most life-enhancing movie star in the world."[70] Kevin Thomas of the *Los Angeles Times* said, "She combines a breathtaking sexiness with such wit, humor and intelligence that she can be uninhibited in front of the camera like no other serious actress of international renown."[71] When Braga was asked about working in Hollywood, she stated, "Any place is the same. I hope to do movies in beautiful places. But it is better for me in Brazil. My people I know better."[72]

She played Ruby Archuleta, a Chicana activist organizing to protect communal land threatened by reckless land developers, in Robert Redford's Capra-esque *The Milagro Beanfield War* (1988, Universal), which costarred Rubén Blades, Julie Carmen, and Freddy Fender. When interviewed about her involvement in the political message of the film, she stated, "From the time I was 17 to 27 I learned about political theory—I knew a lot of artists and intellectuals. But there was no chance to be active because of the military government. Besides, I come from a simple family. If your family is bourgeois, politics comes through your pores."[73]

In her third U.S. film she played Madonna, the mistress of a dictator who suddenly dies and is impersonated by a down-and-out actor (Richard Dreyfuss) under the coercion of an ambitious general (Raúl Juliá) in Paul Mazursky's dark satire *Moon over Parador* (1988, Universal). She was reunited with Juliá when they played a pair of German thieves in *The Rookie* (1989, Warner Bros.) opposite Clint Eastwood and Charlie Sheen.

Interviewed in 1989, the dark-haired and petite actress was candid about some future goals: "I have a lot of friends. But I'm not sure I'll marry. The qualities I look for in men are the same ones I like to find in women—for a man, coping with his fragility; for women, coping with virility. So fragility and virility cannot be used as weapons against each other. In terms of motherhood, I don't know. I wouldn't peer into a crystal ball. I'm ready and able. But the point is, I don't believe [in] independent production when it comes to maternity."[74]

As only the second Brazilian film star to become successful in Hollywood (after Carmen Miranda), Sônia Braga has been instrumental in internationalizing a new image of the contemporary Brazilian woman.

Her film career has slowed down of late. Her films include the inferior television production *The Last Prostitute* (1991); *The Burning Season* (1994); and Robert M. Young's drama *Roosters* (1995) opposite Edward James Olmos and María Conchita Alonso. She was excellent in the television miniseries *Larry McMurtry's Streets of Laredo* (1995, CBS), which wasted the talents of James Garner, Sissy Spacek, and Sam Shepard.

Recent films include *Angel Eyes* (2001); *Che Guevara* (2004); *Bordertown* (2006); and *Butterflies & Lightning* (2012). She has made numerous appearances on U.S. and Brazilian television.

JULIE CARMEN

A rising Latina leading lady of the 1980s was Julie Carmen, a talented actress with an extensive theater background.

She was born in Mount Vernon, New York, on April 4, 1954, to a father who was a retired salesman for a paper company and a mother who was a high school foreign-language teacher. Julie studied ballet for seven years and subsequently modern dance. She began acting in high school. She recalled later, "There were no Black students in Millburn High School and we were doing *The Crucible*; I was the closest to anyone who looked like a Barbados male so I was cast."[75]

At 15, she landed a role in the play *The Creation of the Universe* in New York, and thereafter she worked in some 20 experimental off–Broadway plays. She said of her experience, "I adore fine theatre and consider it a kind of Zen obstacle in a fresh way. It's such a deep challenge."[76]

She made her film debut in *Night of the Juggler* (1980, Columbia) opposite James Brolin. She was then cast in John Cassavetes' *Gloria* (1980) with Gena Rowlands. She played the doomed mother of a small boy. She said of the film, "I've never said this before but, as virgin actress, John Cassavetes broke me in. I'd done all the technical acting study groups up until then and John just said, 'Let there be all these pieces (of my performance) and I'm gonna put them together. Don't hold on in any way.'"[77] For her performance, she won the Gold Lion Award at the Venice Film Festival.

Her television film credits include *Can You Hear the Laughter?* (1979, CBS): *The Story of Freddie Prinze* (1979, CBS); *Fire on the Mountain* (1981, NBC) with Buddy Ebsen; *She's in the Army Now* (1981, ABC); and *Three Hundred Miles for Stephanie* (1981, NBC) with Edward James Olmos.

She had another important role as Nancy Mondragon in Robert Redford's magical-realist *The Milagro Beanfield War* (1989, Universal). Other films include *Last Plane Out* (1983, New World) in which she played a Sandinista; *Blue City* (1986, Paramount) with Ally Sheedy and Paul Winfield; *The Penitent* (1987, Cineworld) with Raúl Juliá; and *Fright Night II* (1989, New Century/Vista). She played the role of a 1937 brothel owner in love with Gary Busey in *Neon Empire* (1991), the most expensive miniseries Showtime has yet produced. It was slated for theatrical release in Europe. Her other film credits include *Cold*

Heaven (1992); *Drug Wars: The Cocaine Cartel* (1992-TV film); a starring role in John Carpenter's *In the Mouth of Madness* (1994); *The Omen* (1995-TV film); *King of the Jungle* (2000); *The Butcher* (2009); *Last Weekend* (2014); and *Dawn Patrol* (2014). She has also guest starred in several episodic television shows like *Touched by an Angel* (1999) and *City of Angels* (2000).

She costarred with Robert Beltran in *Kiss Me a Killer* (1991), inspired by James M. Cain's *The Postman Always Rings Twice*. She played an unhappy wife who falls for a drifter and subsequently plots to kill her husband. The film and performances earned excellent notices. The *Hollywood Reporter* noted, "The performances are terrific, especially Carmen as the passionate wife and barmaid. Her transformation from submissive slave to fiery motivator is credible and volcanic."[78] *Variety* commented on the "compassionate love scenes featuring Carmen and Beltran. Both performers do a fine job."[79]

Carmen has been outspoken about Latino stereotypes on film. She told *Newsweek* that she had played "ghetto ingenues" and "Maria characters" too long. She hoped the film "*La Bamba* is changing the quantity and quality of work for Hispanics."[80] Regarding her preferred roles, she said, "My favorite roles are psychological character pieces. I can work without direction but I love working with wonderful directors. I love to take risks and finally feel so centered I know there's a self to go back to."[81]

In addition to her acting career, Carmen works as a licensed psychotherapist.

ELPIDIA CARRILLO

Mexican-born actress Elpidia Carrillo was one of the most promising Latina actresses of the 1980s. She was usually typecast as a young and uprooted Latina, a victim of the contemporary political upheavals in the Latin American continent.

She was born on August 16, 1961, in the small village of Parácuaro, Michoacán, in southern Mexico, to a family of ten brothers and sisters. At the age of 12, she left for the larger town of Uruapan in order to live with her older sister and find employment. She began high school and supported herself by working as a waitress.

After several months, a model agency photographer saw her on the street and randomly snapped her picture, and got it to director-cinematographer Rafael Corkiki, who was casting for his film *Pafnucio Santo* (1974). Corkiki was so impressed with her that he brought her to Mexico City for a screen test and thereafter cast her in a small role in the film. She was then cast as the Virgin Mary in *El Nuevo Mundo* (1975), directed by Gabriel Retes, and within six months she was cast in a bigger role in *Al Filo del Agua* (1976). Other films followed: the routine remake of *Pedro Páramo* (1977), *Chicoácen* (1977), Gabriel Retes' *Bandera Rota* (1978), and *Winetoo* (1978). She followed these with three television movies, including *The Chess Player*, a French-American co-production directed by Juan Luis Buñuel (son of the famed director Luis Buñuel).

Elpidia stated of director Retes that he "has been a major influence on my life. He and all the people he regularly works with, a kind of repertory group."[82]

About actor-director-producer Jorge Santoyo she said, "He helped me to focus all my informed feelings and ideas. He's been father, teacher, brother, friend—*todo*."[83]

Carrillo made her U.S. film debut in Tony Richardson's *The Border* (1982, Universal). The film chronicled the story of two burned-out immigration officers (Jack Nicholson, Harvey Keitel), their hard-nosed boss (Warren Oates) and Nicholson's jaded marriage to his wife (Valerie Perrine). Carrillo played Maria, a young Mexican undocumented worker who is apprehended by Nicholson and subsequently becomes enamored of him. The film was one of several features released during this period about the plight of undocumented workers,

Elpidia Carrillo and Jack Nicholson in *The Border* (1982, Universal Pictures).

the best of which was Gregory Nava's *El Norte* (1984). *The Border,* however, was a well-meaning film that attempted to humanize the victimized workers. It was only moderately successful commercially and critically in the United States, but Carrillo garnered attention for her sensitive portrayal.

Richardson stated that she had been cast "literally out of hundreds of people. I went all over. At the end, there were five 'finalists,' all from Mexico City, and when we tested them, Elpidia was simply it. The girl had the quality we wanted."[84]

Nicholson, for his part, called her "a brilliant actress." She stated of the film, "It shows the problems of illegal immigrants, the dangers they run. Things I never really knew myself."[85]

Her second English-language feature was the adaptation of Graham Greene's novel *The Honorary Consul* entitled *Beyond the Limit* (1983, Paramount). She played Clara, a recently migrated Native American woman who marries an alcoholic British consul (Michael Caine), who is kidnapped by guerrillas who hope to liberate political prisoners. She develops an adulterous affair with a reluctant political activist (Richard Gere). The film was an uneven mix of political thriller and doomed love story and was met with indifference by audiences. Reviewers were enthusiastic, however, about the performances of Carrillo and Michael Caine. During this time she also had a costarring role in the CBS miniseries *Christopher Columbus* (1985) with Faye Dunaway and Gabriel Byrne.

She was then cast by Oliver Stone (who wrote, directed and co-produced) for his *Salvador* (1986), which documented the contemporary political upheaval in El Salvador, including the assassination of Archbishop Romero and the infamous death squads. Carrillo was cast in the role of Maria, a young uprooted woman with an orphaned brother who turns to prostitution when she encounters two misfit idealistic Americans (James Woods, Jim Belushi) and a photographer (John Savage), who is in search of his big scoop. The film was one of the first attempts by mainstream Hollywood to address the current Latin American reality with some critical thinking. It was a commendable effort by the independent-minded Oliver Stone. The film coincided with Carrillo's desire "to make movies of real social value. Movies are a wonderful way to communicate to people, if the film is good ... the media could help social change so much if they'd only show that more often. If I can't make such movies, I'd rather not work in the industry."[86]

Her next role was that of Veronica in the dismal action film *Let's Get Harry* (1986-TriStar) opposite Robert Duvall and Gary Busey. In her next role after that, she was cast as Anna, a Nicaraguan peasant abducted by U.S. Special Forces in the expertly crafted but Cold War–induced science-fiction *Predator* (1987, 20th Century–Fox) opposite Arnold Schwarzenegger and Carl Weathers. The film was a big hit commercially, but received lukewarm critical notices.

More recently, she scored impressively as the Salvadoran refugee who marries the *vato loco* (Jimmy Smits) in Gregory Nava's evocative *My Family/Mi Familia* (1995) with a cast that included Edward James Olmos, Esai Morales, Jennifer Lopez and Lupe Ontiveros. The *Los Angeles Times* noted, "And among the actresses mention should be made of .... especially Elpidia Carrillo, whose quiet performance as the Salvadoran immigrant Isabel is in some ways the emotional heart of the picture."[87]

Her recent films include *Tortilla Heaven* (2007); *Seven Pounds* (2008); and *Mother and Child* (2010).

ENRIQUE CASTILLO

Enrique Castillo was born in Calexico, Baja California, Mexico. His father was born in Jalisco and his mother in Baja California. As a child he joined his family to work in the fields of northern California.

He later recalled, "My father used to worry very much about that and the result was that I was the very first in my family that attended U.C. Berkeley. There, I met Luis Valdez and there I began my career as an actor with the Teatro Campesino."[88] Castillo went on to do a variety of roles in the theater, television and film.

He has been an active member of the Latino Theater Lab for a number of years. The lab, which is based in Los Angeles, is dedicated to nurturing, writing and producing plays that depict the Latino experience. In 1990, Castillo won the Los Angeles Dramalogue best actor award for his powerful performance in *August 29th*, which Castillo co-wrote with Evelina Fernández and which was produced at the Los Angeles Theater Center to commemorate the 20th anniversary of the killing of *Los Angeles Times* correspondent Rubén Salazar by Los Angeles County sheriffs.

Castillo's other theater credits include *A Burning Beach* and *Sarcophagus,* both directed by Bill Bushnell; *Corridos* and *Zoot Suit*, directed by Luis Valdez; *10 November,* directed by Steven Dietz; and three plays directed by José Luis Valenzuela, *Stone Wedding, Roosters* and *La Victima*. Additional credits include *Billy* at the Wallenboyd Center; *Black Hole* at the Met Theater; and *Working* at the Cast Theatre. He continues to write plays and screenplays, as well.

His television credits are numerous in top-rated shows like *L.A. Law*. He has costarred in such television films as *Fighting Back* (1980, ABC) with Bonnie Bedelia; *Small Killing* (1981, CBS) with Jean Simmons; Jesús Salvador Treviño's *Seguin* (1981, PBS); and *Stones for Ibarra* (1988) with Glenn Close.

His films include *Borderline* (1980) with Charles Bronson; *Losin' It* (1982); Gregory Nava's *El Norte* (1983*); Black Moon Rising* (1985) with Tommy Lee Jones; and Cheech Marin's *Born in East L.A.* (1987). His most important film role thus far has been that of Montana Segura, leader of the Chicano prison gang La Onda in Taylor Hackford's *Bound by Honor* (1993), which traced the crucial years of three Chicano youths. The *New York Times* noted, "Though they play at a fever pitch most of the time, Mr. Chapa, Mr. Bratt and Mr. Borrego are excellent, as are the members of the large supporting cast, notably Enrique Castillo, who appears as the leader of San Quentin's Chicanos."[89] His most recent film roles were in Gregory Nava's *My Family/Mi Familia* (1995); Oliver Stone's *Nixon* (1995); *The End of Violence* (1997) and *A Beautiful Life* (2008). From 2008 to 2012 he appeared in the role of Cesar in the cable series *Weeds.*

ROSANNA DESOTO

Perhaps the best-established of all Chicana character actresses in the 1980s was Rosanna DeSoto, who in the latter part of the decade scored with a pair of timely Chicano history–based films.

She was born on September 2, 1950, in San José, California. She studied Spanish and drama at San José State University, graduating with a bachelor of arts degree. She then joined the Northern California Light Opera Company and subsequently moved to Los Angeles. There, she performed in improvisational theater at the Music Center and appeared in the production *Remote Asylum.*

She made her television debut in the popular 1970s series *Barney Miller.* Her appearance led to a role in *A.E.S. Hudson St.* and numerous other roles. She made her film debut in Arthur Hiller's tale of CIA "dirty tricks," *The In-Laws* (1979, Warner Bros.) with Peter Falk and Alan Arkin. She then played the Chicana activist Carlota Muñoz, who struggles for the release of Gregorio Cortez (Edward James Olmos) in Robert M. Young's evocative *The Ballad of Gregorio Cortez* (1983, EM). She scored also in the comedic role of Diana the waitress in *The Redd Foxx Show* (1986, ABC).

She costarred in a pair of television films: *Three Hundred Miles for Stephanie* (1981, NBC) with Edward James Olmos and *Women of San Quentin* (1983, NBC) with Stella Stevens.

Other roles followed: that of Manuela in the underestimated crime drama *American Justice* (1985, Moe Sotre); and then the comedic role of Mrs. Lyons in *About Last Night* (1986, TriStar) with Demi Moore and Jim Belushi.

At this point, she won the most important role of her career, that of Connie Valenzuela, the mother of the pioneer Chicano rocker Ritchie Valens, in Luis Valdez' critical and commercial hit *La Bamba* (1987, Columbia). She stated of the film, "This film is about a family with hopes and dreams, rising up only to see their dreams shattered. Yet they manage to con-

Rosanna DeSoto and Elizabeth Peña in *La Bamba* (1987, Columbia).

tinue because they realize that life itself is nothing but a dream."[90] To prepare for the role while shooting on location in Hollister, California, she shared a motel room with Mrs. Valenzuela. She stated of the experience, "I thought Connie was tough—she suffered, but she's like this big beautiful old ship that has seen a lot of storms but remains a classic."[91]

DeSoto followed this with another good role as Fabiola Escalante in the very popular *Stand and Deliver* (1988, Warner Bros.), about real-life Garfield High School teacher Jaime Escalante (Edward James Olmos) who strives for the academic excellence of his Chicano students in the East Los Angeles barrio. Her follow-up role was that of Elaine McMullen in Sidney Lumet's weak comedy-drama *Family Business* (1989, TriStar) with Sean Connery and Dustin Hoffman.

When she is not acting, DeSoto writes poetry and plays music. She once commented, "I've had to work hard all my life and when I first came to Los Angeles to be an actress, I was all on my own ... I'm a survivor."[92]

Her other films include *Face of the Enemy* (1990, TCP) and *Once upon a Wedding* (2005). She continues to guest-star in episodic television.

RENÉ ENRÍQUEZ

For many years, the only positive Latino character on television was René Enríquez's Lt. Ray Calletano on NBC's popular *Hill St. Blues*.

He was born on November 4, 1933, in San Francisco, California, to influential Nicaraguan parents. He was educated in a Jesuit school in Nicaragua. Later, he returned to San Francisco to study international relations. His studies were interrupted by the Korean War when he was drafted. He then served in England for two years. After obtaining his bachelor of arts degree at San Francisco State University, he enrolled at the Academy of Dramatic Arts in New York City.

Within a year he was playing in off–Broadway theater under the noted Dominican theater director José Quintero. An important role was that of Sancho Panza in Tennessee Williams' *Camino Real*. In 1962, he costarred in *Marco Millions,* the initial season of the Lincoln Center Repertory Company of New York. In 1964, Enriquez founded the Artists Repertory Theater in New York City.

He made his film debut in *Girl of the Night* (1960) with Anne Francis and John Kerr. In the late 1960s, he debuted on television and appeared in numerous television shows: *The Defenders, The Nurses, Naked City, Charlie's Angels, Quincy,* and *Benson.* He appeared in several films, including Arthur Hiller's *Popi* (1969) with Alan Arkin and Rita Moreno; Woody Allen's *Bananas* (1971); Sidney Lumet's *Serpico* (1973) with Al Pacino; and Paul Mazursky's *Harry and Tonto* (1974) with Art Carney and Barbara Rhodes. His best role, however, was that of Nicaraguan dictator Anastasio Somoza in Roger Spottiswoode's effective *Under Fire* (1983) with Nick Nolte, Joanne Cassidy, and Gene Hackman.

He played roles in numerous television films: *Nicky's World* (1974, CBS); *Foster & Laurie* (1975, CBS); *Katherine* (1975, ABC); *The Call of the Wild* (1976, NBC); *High Risk* (1976, ABC); *It Happened at Lakewood Manor* (1977, ABC); *Rosetti and Ryan: Men Who Love Women* (1977, NBC); *Panic in Echo Park* (1977, NBC); *Gridlock* (1980, NBC); *Marathon* (1980, CBS); *The Return of Frank Cannon* (1980, CBS); *Choices of the Heart*

(1983, NBC); *Hostage Flight* (1985, NBC); *Dream West* (1986, CBS); and the miniseries *Centennial* (1979, NBC).

For many, however, his most popular role was that of Lieutenant Calletano, the taciturn police officer on *Hill Street Blues*. He said of the series, "I'm proud of the show. It made a powerful statement on the decay of cities and human isolation."[93]

An active member of Nosotros and other Latino organizations, he commented on the Latino film image, "Mexicans can identify with me and Puerto Ricans and Cubans. He (Calletano) is a man from a low economic status who speaks with little polish but who worked his way up."[94]

In 1989, Enriquez played the lead in *El Juez,* which aired over Univision.

René Enríquez died of pancreatic cancer on March 23, 1990, in his home in Tarzana, California.

EMILIO ESTEVEZ

One of the most multitalented young actors to emerge in the 1980s was Emilio Estevez, son of Martin Sheen and brother to Charlie Sheen.

He was born on May 12, 1962, in New York City. He attended Santa Monica High School and on the very day of graduation he was cast in the afternoon special *Seventeen Going On Nowhere*. He made his film debut in Francis Ford Coppola's *Apocalypse Now* (1979) starring Marlon Brando and his father, Martin Sheen. He followed it with a small role in *Tex* (1982), one of four films he has made based on the novels written by S.E. Hinton, and he played another role with his father in the television film *In the Custody of Strangers* (1982, ABC).

Estevez's big break came with the role of Two-Bit Matthews in Francis Ford Coppola's *The Outsiders* (1983, Warner Bros.), which was populated with a dozen future stars: Tom Cruise, Patrick Swayze, Matt Dillon, Rob Lowe, Ralph Macchio and C. Thomas Howell. He followed it with a starring role in the anthology film *Nightmares* (1983). He earned good notices as a punkish youth in the offbeat *Repo Man* (1984). A pair of 1985 films made him a teenage idol: *The Breakfast Club* and *St. Elmo's Fire*.

In 1985, he starred in and wrote *That Was Then ... This Is Now*, the film adaptation of another S.E. Hinton novel, in which he played a troubled young man whose father killed his mother and went to prison. In an attempt to break out of teen films he did an action film, *Maximum Overdrive* (1986); a detective yarn, *Stakeout* (1987) with Richard Dreyfuss; and a western, *Young Guns* (1988), in which he played Billy the Kid and which paired him with his brother Charlie Sheen for the first time.

At the age of 23, he became perhaps the youngest filmmaker to write, direct and star, in *Wisdom* (1986). When asked when he knew he wanted to be a filmmaker, he responded, "I started writing first—poems, short stories and that sort of thing. Then my parents brought Charlie and me a super 8 movie camera and sort of turned us loose. We would save our allowance and buy film. I think at that time it was $4 for a roll of film so it would take us a little while to scrounge up the change from whatever allowance we had."[95]

In reference to his triple duty in *Wisdom,* he said, "I made *Wisdom* for Gladden Entertainment ... and they were incredibly supportive. Their only stipulation was that I had to have a godfather on the set in the form of Robert Wise.... If I had problems or questions I was to go to him which I certainly did. Robert is a pretty fine filmmaker and a real gentleman."[96]

He repeated his role in the commercially successful *Young Guns II* (1990) with James Coburn and Lou Diamond Phillips, and then wrote, directed and costarred with his brother Charlie Sheen in *Men at Work* (1990), about a pair of restless garbagemen.

Estevez is a very independent-minded individual who has refused to be entirely "Hollywoodized" and has insisted on keeping his Latino surname. As to his creative preferences, he has stated, "You know what I think? I'm an actor first, a director second, and a writer third. I think if I have a weak area, it's in the writing."[97] About the skyrocketing costs of films, he said, "I'm glad I didn't make a $30 million movie. I don't think I ever want to direct a movie that has that kind of financial responsibility associated with it. I think that Hollywood has to get that sort of thing under control, as well. We've got to get back to making pictures for $10 to $15 million. I mean we've just got to."[98]

Following in his father's footsteps, Emilio has become active in a diverse number of social causes like homelessness, the sanctuary movement to help undocumented workers, and the farmworkers. Emilio Estevez is part of a new breed of filmmakers with a new creative vision.

His later films include *Freejack* (1992) with Mick Jagger, Anthony Hopkins and Esai Morales; *The Mighty Ducks* (1992); *National Lampoon's Loaded Weapon I* (1993); *Another Stakeout* (1993); *D2: The Mighty Ducks* (1994); the spoof *National Lampoon's Loaded Weapon 1* (1994); the crime comedy *Another Stakeout* (1994) with Richard Dreyfuss; the futuristic *Judgment Night* (1994); a cameo in the lethargic *Mission: Impossible* (1996); *The War at Home* (1996), director and producer; *D3: The Mighty Ducks* (1996); the TNT cable channel western *Dollar for the Dead* (1998); *Sand* (2000); *Culture Clash in America* (2005), director; and *Bobby* (2006).

He has guest starred in several episodic shows beginning in 1980, among them *The West Wing* (2003) with his father Martin Sheen and *Two and a Half Men* (2008) with his brother Charlie Sheen.

Another notable accomplishment was directing and costarring (with his father, Martin Sheen) in *The War at Home* (1996). The *New York Times* commented, "The anguished father-son relationship seems all the more authentic because of the striking visceral bond between Mr. Sheen and Mr. Estevez, who are father and son in real life."[99] The *Los Angeles Times* noted, "Estevez is a haunting Jeremy, and his ability to direct other actors (including his father) in highly complex and contradictory roles is formidable."[100]

His most recent film was *The Way* (2010), which starred Martin Sheen. Estevez directed and also costars in the film.

JENNY GAGO

One of the busiest Latina actresses at the end of the 1980s was the statuesque and brown-haired Jenny Gago, who made a successful transition from soaps into serious roles.

She was born on September 11, 1953, in Peru, and when she was six her family immigrated to the United States. The family lived in New York until Jenny was fourteen and then settled in Los Angeles. She graduated from UCLA with a degree in theater arts. Upon graduation, she received a full scholarship to study with the noted drama teacher Lee Strasberg.

She obtained her first television role in the daytime soap opera *The Young and the Restless*. She joined a local theater company called Twelfth Night Repertory which performed in schools throughout the country. She conceptualized a show which aired on KCET and won an Emmy Award. Her film debut came in the role of Miss Panama in the evocative *Under Fire* (1983, Orion), about the last chaotic days of the Somoza dictatorship in Nicaragua. The film led Gago to be cast in recurring roles in the popular television series *Dallas* and *Knots Landing,* in which she played the character Maria for three years.

Her film career continued with larger roles in Carl Reiner's *The Man with Two Brains* (1983, Warner Bros.) with Steve Martin and Kathleen Turner; *No Man's Land* (1987, Orion) with Charlie Sheen; *Best Seller* (1987, Orion) with James Woods; and *Valentino Returns* (1988, Skouros) with Frederic Forrest. She played the role of La Garduña in Luis Puenzo's flawed adaptation of the Carlos Fuentes novel *Old Gringo* (1989, Columbia). The *Los Angeles Times* wrote, "Jenny Gago seems a great find as La Garduna, the cheerful camp follower."[101]

Gago said of the film, "It's been very exciting because when you're working with Jane Fonda and Gregory Peck, they're megaforce! The whole story revolves around them and I never thought of my part being big enough to get this kind of attention. But, there you go. There are no small parts! ... I waited 10 years for a great part like La Garduña. I'm waiting for another 10!"[102]

She has costarred in several television films: *The Gun in the House* (1981, CBS); *Women of San Quentin* (1983, NBC); *Shattered Spirits* (1986, ABC) with Martin Sheen; and *Out on a Limb* (1987) with Shirley MacLaine, based on the book of the same name. She played a tough prison inmate in *Convicted: A Mother's Story* (1987) with Ann Jillian and an investigator for the state's attorney in *Unspeakable Acts* (1990) with Jill Clayburgh and Brad Davis. She was especially impressive as a struggling wife in PBS' Wonder series film, *Sweet 15* (1990) with Tony Plana, about a family applying for immigration amnesty and their daughter's symbolic quinceañera (a 15-year-old Mexican girl's social introduction as a young lady).

In 1990, she was cast as the undercover drug agent Teresa Robles in Fox's series *DEA* (1990–1991). She said of her role, "I got interested in the part because I hate drugs. I hate what they've done to our society. There's a big responsibility in being an actor now. Actors are right up there with politicians."[103] With regard to film stereotypes, she commented, "You can sit back and say, I'm Latino and they don't let Latinos play psychiatrists, or you can get pushy about reading for the part."[104]

She married an owner of a health club. Coincidentally, she had at one time been an aerobics instructor. She has been given the coveted CINE Golden Eagle Award as Most Promising Actress by Nosotros.

She has stated of her chosen profession, "When I was born, my mother said, 'Is it a boy or is it a girl?' The doctor said, 'It's an actress.' ... If I hadn't gone into acting, I probably would've been a psychologist. A lot of the problems we have as adults stem from the fact that we were stifled as children."[105]

Her recent film roles include that of the mother of a gang youth in Taylor Hackford's *Bound by Honor* (1994). She was most impressive as the indomitable mother in Gregory

Nava's evocative *My Family/Mi Familia* (1995). The *Los Angeles Times* noted, "The couple is equally well played by Eduardo López Rojas, one of Mexico's most respected actors, and Jenny Gago."[106] She gave a superb performance as a Native American in the excellent HBO film *Grandview Ave.* (1996). Recent films include *The Needs of Kim Staley* (2005) and *The Obama Effect* (2011).

SILVANA GALLARDO

Perhaps the most versatile and accomplished of all Latina actresses during the 1980s was the star of stage, television and film Silvana Gallardo.

She was born on January 13, 1953, in New York City's South Bronx, of Venezuelan, Italian and Cuban ancestry and the youngest of four children. She recollected later of her childhood, "I grew up in a neighborhood where ninety percent of the people died from unnatural causes. There were literally more drugs in our block than in all of England."[107] She would escape and dream of a better life in faraway places by performing dramatic skits of her own invention in her mother's living room to the delight of her neighborhood friends. She stated, "My mother and father were generous with us and encouraged us to express ourselves."[108]

Once in high school, she realized her true vocation of acting. She performed in such productions as *Bye, Bye Birdie.* After graduation, she attended night school at City College in New York and worked as a secretary. At this lean juncture she exhibited her characteristic resourcefulness and determination. She commented, "I traveled as a professional gambler. I made the money to support my acting by gambling. Gambling is a matter of discipline and I had wonderful experiences in Monte Carlo and Portugal.... I'm self-made as a gambler. You become aware of rhythms, aware of the flow and changes of circumstances. Like acting, it goes moment to moment and you try to capitalize on the moments. I still gamble. I do go to Las Vegas for a weekend. I like to do it as long as everybody is disciplined."[109]

Inspired by such acting role models as Viveca Lindfors, Katharine Hepburn, Montgomery Clift, and Marlon Brando, she honed her acting skills in several off–Broadway productions. From there, she then landed roles on Broadway in several productions, among them *Fathers and*

Silvana Gallardo (1953–2012) was an actress in film, television, and theater, as well as a renowned drama coach.

Sons and David Merrick's production of Tennessee Williams' *The Red Devil Battery Sign*, in which she had one of the lead roles. An important break came in the late 1960s, when she obtained a supporting role in the television soap opera *The Doctors*.

During this period, she began teaching drama, mostly in prisons and reform schools. She found it rewarding but frustrating with the array of cynical administrators: "People just didn't care. That's a real horrible thing because the problems escalate and the world is ... well, the world. I offered another possibility." [110]

In 1977, she moved to Los Angeles and began her television and film career in earnest. In 1977, she won wide recognition and acclaim in the title role in the PBS special *The People vs. Inez Garcia*. It documented a real-life highly publicized murder trial in 1974 of a young Puerto Rican woman who claimed she killed only because she was being raped. She was convicted of second-degree murder, but subsequently the conviction was overturned by the State Court of Appeals. She was given a new trial, and on March 4, 1977, she was found innocent by fact of self-defense.

Gallardo garnered rave reviews. She stated of the role, "I loved playing Inez Garcia. I actually met her. I like roles that have a social significance." [111]

She made her film debut in the leading role of Little Feather in *Windwalker* (1980, Pacific International), Keith Merrill's evocative tale filmed in the Cheyenne and Crow languages. In this film she played opposite Trevor Howard and Billy Drago, her future husband. She followed it with the strong role of a Latina cook who is raped and killed in Michael Winner's commercially successful sequel *Death Wish II* (1982, Filmways/Columbia) with Charles Bronson reprising his role as the vengeful engineer. She stated of the film, "*Death Wish II* was a very hard film to do. I did the role because I wanted to show people the reality of rape. Not a glorified, pretty rape, but a hard and disgusting and painful experience. I went to a crowded movie house to see it.... No one laughed.... No one said ugly things ... they saw a woman being victimized, brutalized. I think it was real and made a difference." [112]

In the meantime, she continued a busy television career with a role as a Spanish señorita in the epic miniseries *Centennial* (1979, NBC), adapted from James Michener's novel. In this role she played opposite Richard Chamberlain. She guest-starred in such television series as *Falcon Crest, Trapper John, M.D., Cagney and Lacey, Hill Street Blues, Hunter, MacGyver, J.J. Starbuck, Golden Girls, The Wizard, Adam 12,* and the "Cocoon" segment of *Monsters,* the last specifically written for her and Billy Drago. She also costarred in two television miniseries: *How the West Was Won* and *Born to the Wind*. As well, she was in a television pilot entitled *The Many Faces of Arthur*.

In 1985, she was honored with the Nosotros Golden Eagle Award for Most Promising New Star, and on December 3, 1985, she received a commendation from Mayor Tom Bradley on behalf of the City of Los Angeles. It read, "I am honored to join with other members of the community in commending your philanthropic activities, including the Mexico City Earthquake Relief Fundraiser, assisting in various Nosotros programs and volunteering for services with Cerebral Palsy and Variety Club Telethons. Your spirit and interest have made our city a better place in which to live."

Her television films include *The Calendar Girl Murders* (1984), playing a streetwise Chicana cop opposite Barbara Parkins, Tom Skerritt and Robert Beltran; the moving *Silence of the Heart* (1984), as a Latina high school counselor attempting to help a suicidal student opposite Mariette Hartley and Charlie Sheen; *Children of Times Square* (1986) with Joanna Cassidy, a film about homeless children; *If Tomorrow Comes* (1986); and *Deadly Care* (1987) with Cheryl Ladd and Jason Miller. In a departure, she played a Carmen Miranda–like character in the funny comedy *Copacabana* (1985) with Barry Manilow. The film was based on Manilow's hit song of the same name about the happenings in a famous nightclub. The film called for Gallardo to sing, dance and do comedy. She said of the character, "She is fun and outrageous and I had more fun doing the show than anything I have ever done. She uses her body when she talks and she has an accent."[113]

In 1988, she joined the cast of NBC's daytime soap opera *Days of Our Lives,* playing Rosa, a terminally ill cancer patient. She said of the character, "She died, so it didn't tie me up too long."[114] However, due to a strong positive response and fan mail, the character was resuscitated and this became a recurring role for Silvana.

She began an actor's workshop in Studio City with the hope of helping actors succeed. She commented of this effort, "The point is to strip away all the outside layers and leave yourself open to interpret any emotion. I believe everyone gets their shot.... It's important to be ready for it when it comes."[115]

She wrote, produced, directed and starred in a video about her acting workshop entitled *The Acting Class* (1988) with her husband Billy Drago that garnered an enthusiastic response.

Among her other films are the effective film noir *Out of the Dark* (1989, New Line Cinema), in which she played a tough New York cop, Lieutenant McDonnell, opposite Karen Black and Bud Cort; the $40 million futuristic *Solar Crisis* (1990) opposite Charlton Heston and Jack Palance; the television film *The Great Los Angeles Earthquake* (1990), in which she played a Latina mother searching for her son; and the HBO special *Women in Prison* (1991) with Rachel Ticotin.

A dark-haired and vibrant beauty, Gallardo was a multitalented woman who spoke four languages, taught acting and wrote. Her sister is a singer and her brother a playwright. Interviewed in 1991, she was optimistic about the future of Latinos in films: "I think times are changing for Latins in films and TV. It is opening up more. I've not been stereotyped as some have. Maybe because I've been fortunate in some of the roles I have had."[116] When asked about her experiences in dealing with stereotypical roles she commented, "At first, I didn't escape the stereotype. My first role, I was dressed in blue and yellow and orange, et cetera, and very pregnant. I have turned down roles now and then that I feel are demeaning to Latins. I have turned down maid roles ... not all ... but most.[117]

In response to the question of what she would recommend to young Latino actors and actresses in order to break into television and films, she noted, "This is a very hard business. You have to be willing to invest from your heart and soul with no guarantee of a payoff.... All young actors should study their craft and be very patient. It's a long distance run and there are no real short cuts. Do plays ... be seen ... get photos that represent them ... live a real life."[118]

Gallardo divorced actor Billy Drago in 1995. She continued as a drama coach and worked as a drama consultant/acting coach on Alfonso Arau's *A Walk in the Clouds* (1995, 20th Century–Fox) starring Anthony Quinn.

He television credits include *ER, NYPD Blue, The Trials of Rosie O'Neil, Equal Justice, Knots Landing, The New Adam 12,* and *Babylon 5.*

She died suddenly on January 2, 2012, at Jewish Hospital, in Paris, Kentucky, of undisclosed causes. She was a dear friend of this writer and her passing was a painful and personal loss.

ANDY GARCÍA

Among the handful of Latino stars at the end of the 1980s at the brink of stardom was the Cuban-born Andy García.

He was born in Havana, Cuba, on April 12, 1956. In 1961, his family moved to Miami Beach, where he excelled in sports. His father, a lawyer, developed a multimillion-dollar fragrance business.

García later recalled, "Once I got out of high school and basketball I realized basketball was no longer a real way to make a living. I had a slim chance of being a professional basketball player because of my height. I was in a period of limbo. The acting thing came on to me like a virus. It was something that I needed to do in order to maintain sanity."[119]

He went on to study theater at Florida International University in Miami, and after graduation he moved to Los Angeles. There, he worked for some four years with an improvisational theater group in the famed Comedy Store and also worked at various odd jobs.

He made his film debut in a bit part in *Blue Skies Again* (1983, Warner Bros.) with Harry Hamlin. He followed it with small roles in *A Night in Heaven* (1983, 20th Century–Fox) with Carrie Snodgress and Lesley Ann Warren; *The Lonely Guy* (1984, Universal) with Steve Martin; and *The Mean Season* (1985, Orion) with Kurt Russell. His turning point came with the costarring role of the brutal cocaine kingpin Angel Maldonado in Hal Ashley's sleeper crime drama *Eight Million Ways to Die* (1986, TriStar) with Jeff Bridges and Rosanna Arquette.

He then won the prized role of George Stone, the tough federal treasury agent, in Brian De Palma's critical and commercial hit *The Untouchables* (1987, Paramount) with Sean Connery, Robert De Niro and Kevin Costner. García said of the role, "First, his obvious talent is he's someone who is not intimidated by anyone; two, he's an untouchable, he can't be bought; and three, he is good with a gun. His function is to shoot well."[120] Of the director, De Palma, he commented, "He's such a visual stylist. A lot of the scenes felt like a dance, in a sense his camera was predetermined.... It was a challenge."[121]

Next came his role as the testing service investigator in the popular *Stand and Deliver* (1988, Warner Bros.) with Edward James Olmos, who earned an Oscar nomination for his performance. García then scored as the hard-boiled New York cop assisting Michael Douglas in tracking down a Japanese yakuza in Ridley Scott's fast-paced and visually stunning *Black Rain* (1988, Paramount). He followed it up with the ordinary *American Roulette* (1988).

García was Oscar-nominated for Best Supporting Actor for his performance of Sonny's bastard son in Francis Coppola's rather uneven *Godfather III* (1990, Paramount) with Al Pacino, Diane Keaton and George Hamilton.

In 1994, García directed the documentary *Cachao* about Cuban *salsero* Israel López. His 1990s films include *Hero* (1992, Columbia) with Dustin Hoffman and Geena Davis; the dismal *Steal Big, Steal Little* (1995) with Rachel Ticotin; *The Disappearance of Lorca* (1996), a film about the turbulent life of Spanish playwright and poet Federico García Lorca, opposite Edward James Olmos; and Sidney Lumet's crime drama *Night Falls on Manhattan* (1997) with Lena Olin and Richard Dreyfuss. He did an effective cameo as gangster Lucky Luciano in *Hoodlum* (1997) with Laurence Fishburne. He also appeared in *Just the Ticket* (1999).

In the 2000s he costarred in the franchise based on the original *Ocean's Eleven* (1960): *Ocean's Eleven* (2001); *Ocean's Twelve* (2004); and *Ocean's Thirteen* (2007). Other recent films include *The Arturo Sandoval Story* (2000), a cable film; *The Lost City* (2005), about the refugee perspective of the Cuban Revolution, which he both directed and starred in; *Across the Line* (2010); and *Greater Glory* (2011).

In reference to Latinos in the film industry, he once commented, "I think the industry is growing a bit ... I'm Hispanic, but I'm not a Hispanic actor. There's an element of racism still in the industry and the only way to crack that is through work. If ethnic actors train themselves to do a variety of things, then I think talent will always come through."[122]

LEON ICHASO

Director/writer Leon Ichaso belongs to the generation of Cubans who immigrated to the U.S. after the Cuban Revolution, grew to adulthood in the U.S. and constructed their own cinematic vision within the context of American film.

He was born in Havana, Cuba, and at the age of fourteen moved with his family to Miami. Subsequently the family moved to New York City. His father, Justo Rodriguez-Santos, was a well-known film and television director, as well as an honored poet.

Ichaso began his career in the advertising field, where he began writing commercials. He also made industrial and experimental films. In 1969, the Latino poetry magazine *La Nueva Sangre* sponsored an exhibition of his films at the Diaz-Balart Studio in New York City. In 1973, Ichaso's film short *Aluminum*, which was made in collaboration with Rene Fuentes-Chao, was presented at the first Cuban Cultural Festival organized by Iván Acosta, the author of *El Super*.

In 1979, Ichaso and Orlando Jiménez Leal codirected *El Super*, a dark and sensitive drama of a family of Cuban exiles adrift in alienation and nostalgia in a cramped New York City apartment. The film introduced a young Elizabeth Peña to film audiences. *El Super* was selected for competition at the Venice, Deauville and Miami Film Festivals. The film went on to win the grand prizes at both the Manheim and Biarritz film festivals.

In 1985, he directed and co-wrote (along with Marvel Arce and Rubén Blades) the film *Crossover Dreams*. The film explores the tribulations of a Puerto Rican musician and his efforts to find fame and fortune in the mainstream music world. Panamanian salsa star Rubén Blades played the lead role and Elizabeth Peña played his girlfriend. The *New York Times* wrote, "Though ... made on a modest budget, it's a sagely funny comedy, both heartfelt and sophisticated, a movie that may well realize the crossover dreams that elude Rudy."[123]

In 1994, he directed *Sugar Hill*, a film that traced the rise and fall of a drug lord (Wesley Snipes), and in 1996 he helmed another feature, *Bitter Sugar*. The latter film depicted the gradual disillusionment of an idealistic student (René Lavan) and his romance with a dancer (Mayte Vilán) in contemporary Cuba. The *Los Angeles Times* commented, "In contrast to the Cuban-made *Strawberry and Chocolate*, which strove to balance criticism and cautious optimism, *Bitter Sugar* is relentless in its depiction of present-day Cuba as oppressive to one and all and to young people in particular."[124]

On television, Ichaso directed two episodes of *Saturday Night Live,* five episodes of *Miami Vice* (one of which he also wrote) and the first five episodes of *Crime Story.* He directed *Table at Ciro's* for the Great Performances series on PBS and the acclaimed adaptation of Charles Fuller's Pulitzer Prize winner, *Zooman,* which aired on Showtime in 1995. His direction of *The Fear Inside,* which also aired on Showtime, earned him an Ace nomination for Best Director. His most recent films are *El Cantante* (2006), about salsa singer Hector Lavao, with Jennifer Lopez, and *Paraiso* (2009).

Bianca Jagger

Nicaraguan-born Bianca Jagger was a 1970s jet-setter turned 1980s political activist. During the latter decade, the striking Bianca also began a promising acting career.

She was born Bianca Pérez-Mora Macias, one of three children, in Managua, Nicaragua, on May 2, 1945. Her father was an apolitical businessman and a fervent anti–Somocista. Bianca attended the School of the Immaculate Conception, a convent school in Managua. Her parents' divorce in the early 1950s required her mother to return to work. Bianca recalled about this experience, "I saw the fate that women in countries like Nicaragua were condemned to have, to be second-rate citizens. I didn't want to have the same future that my mother had. I wanted to become a career woman, to have a profession, either as a politician or a diplomat."[125]

After graduation from high school, she continued her education at the local Alliance Française and then earned a scholarship to the prestigious Insitute d'Études Politiques in Paris, France. Initially, she became involved in university politics, but gradually drifted to the glamorous Parisian social scene. She met Mick Jagger, the famous lead singer of the Rolling Stones, at a party in late summer 1970. She stated of the meeting, "It sounds silly, but it was like a bolt of lightning."[126] They were married on May 12, 1971, in Saint-Tropez, France. In the following October, Jagger gave birth to a daughter, Jade.

Jagger worked to maintain her identity: "I'm not prepared to be just a part of someone's life. I will share my life if I can keep my own identity. I would like to do something on my own apart from Mick."[127] Possessed of a slim, finely chiseled bone structure, brooding dark eyes and a wide, full mouth, she became the darling of the jet set.

She made her film debut in Francoise Weyergan's *Couleur Chair/Flesh Color* (1978). She followed this with a U.S. film, William Richert's stylish *The American Success Company* (1980, Columbia), playing a high-class prostitute in love with a married man (Jeff Bridges).

Her increasingly strained marriage to Mick Jagger ended in divorce on November 2, 1979. She was awarded custody of her daughter, child support and a one-million-dollar settlement. She soon became more politically involved. On a visit to the earthquake-devastated Nicaragua in December 1972 she commented, "That's when I really became aware of the harm Somoza was doing to Nicaragua."[128] At her request in 1973, the Rolling Stones performed a benefit concert for earthquake victims that grossed $280,000.

In 1981, she headed a delegation for the Committee for the Defense of Refugees to Honduras and presented the report to the U.S. Subcommittee on Inter-American Affairs. She continued to work on a variety of Latin American issues, including human rights.

Bianca desired an acting career and took acting lessons from a teacher at the Royal Academy of Dramatic Arts in London and from the noted acting teacher Harold Buskin in New York. She played the sheik's sister in Hal Needham's commercial hit *Cannonball Run* (1981, 20th Century–Fox) with Burt Reynolds, Dean Martin, Farrah Fawcett and Roger Moore.

However, her political activities quickly overshadowed her acting ambitions. In the aftermath of the 1972 Nicaraguan Earthquake, she founded the Bianca Jagger Human Rights Foundation. Since then she has been involved in numerous social causes. She worked to oppose United States intervention in Nicaragua in the 1980s; organized to protect the rights of indigenous people and women in Latin America; collaborated with Amnesty International and the Human Rights Watch to monitor political abuses; during 2007 to 2009, was the chairwoman of the World Future Council; and during June 2012, in collaboration with the International Union for Conservation of Nature and Airbus, initiated an online campaign to recover some 150 million acres of forest by the year 2020. She has been hailed and recognized by many international organizations and groups for her dedication to all these social causes.

RAÚL JULIÁ

One of the most respected and versatile Latino actors to emerge in the 1980s was the stage-trained Raúl Juliá.

He was born Raúl Rafael Carlos Juliá y Arcelay in San Juan, Puerto Rico, on March 9, 1940, the eldest of four children of Raúl Juliá, a prosperous restaurateur, and his wife, Olga Arcelay. He grew up in the suburbs of San Juan and attended an elementary school run by American nuns. He graduated from San Ignacio de Loyola High School and then attended the University of Puerto Rico, where he obtained his bachelor's degree in liberal arts. He began performing in a theatrical troupe and then in nightclubs. In 1964, he moved to New York City where he enrolled in acting classes with Wynn Hanman, the artistic director of the American Place Theatre. He made his New York stage debut as Astolfo in the Spanish-language production of Calderon's *Life Is a Dream*, in March 1964. He joined Phoebe Brand's Theater in the Street, which performed Spanish and English plays in the barrios and ghettos.

He played a variety of roles, including Shakespearean ones, before making his Broadway debut in September 1968 as the servant Chan in Jack Gelber's *The Cuban Thing*. He followed it with *Paradise Gardens East, Conérico Was Here to Stay* and *The Castro Complex*. About the last-named play and his performance, Marilyn Stasio of *Cue* commented on his "strong presence" and stated, "He has a future—in better plays."[129] He would recollect of his theatrical experience, "I saw Broadway and the theaters and it was unbelievable! You could actually make a living doing theater, not just as a pastime. I wanted to work in New York, which is to me the theater Mecca. I don't know of any other place that has as much opportunity for doing plays. I just love the theater atmosphere."[130]

During a lull in theater roles, Juliá made his first screen appearances in three bit parts, in *The Organization Man* (1971, United Artists), a tale about an international drug-smuggling syndicate with Sheree North and Sidney Poitier; *Been Down So Long It Looks Like*

Up to Me (1971, Paramount), a weak adaptation of Richard Fariña's underground classic novel; and Jerry Schatzberg's powerful tale of a group of forlorn heroin addicts in New York City, *Panic in Needle Park* (1971, 20th Century–Fox), opposite Al Pacino in his own film debut.

In the latter part of 1971, Juliá returned to the stage in the role of Proteus in the musical version of Shakespeare's romantic comedy *Two Gentlemen of Verona*. In addition to wide acclaim, the role earned him his first Tony Award nomination as best actor in the play. Other notable stage performances were in the following plays: *Hamlet* (1972) with James Earl Jones and Stacy Keach; *As You Like It* (1973); *The Robber Bridegroom* (1974), which earned him his second Tony nomination; the Brecht-Weill masterpiece *The Threepenny Opera* (1976), in which he earned his third Tony nomination for his performance as the sinister and brooding Mack the Knife; *Othello* (1979) with Richard Dreyfuss as Iago; and *Nine* (1982), a musical about noted film director Federico Fellini. For his performance in *Nine*, Juliá was nominated once again for a Tony Award. He stated of these experiences, "Hispanic people have a certain culture that can bring new and interesting flavor to Shakespeare and other classics. Shakespeare played by an Englishman limits him, makes him smaller than he is. He was English but his work was universal."[131]

Juliá continued to pursue a film career, but for a while seemed trapped in inconsequential and routine roles. Among his credits is the forgettable comedy *The Gumball Rally* (1976, Warner Bros.), in which he played an Italian race-car driver opposite Michael Sarrazin; the interesting *Eyes of Laura Mars* (1978, Columbia), in which he was the embittered and parasitic ex-husband of a high-priced model (Faye Dunaway); Francis Ford Coppola's weak comedy *One from the Heart* (1982, Columbia) with Teri Garr, in which he essayed the role of the suave Lothario masquerading as a cocktail waiter; Paul Mazursky's imaginative retelling of Shakespeare's *The Tempest* (1982, Columbia) opposite John Cassavates, Susan Sarandon, Vittorio Gassman and Gena Rowlands, in which he played the Greek goat herder Kalibanos; and the modest comedy *The Escape Artist* (1982, Orion) with Teri Garr and Joan Hackett.

He starred in several television films: *McCloud: Who Killed Miss U.S.A.?* (1970, NBC); *Death Scream* (1975, ABC), with Tina Louise and Art Carney, in which he played a cop in a re-creation of the real-life Kitty Genovese murder; *Mussolini: The Untold Story* (1985, NBC) with George C. Scott; and the HBO film *Florida Straits* (1986). He appeared in *Aces High* (1974), a pilot for an unsuccessful CBS comedy series; made an appearance on the daytime soap opera *Love of Life,* and made numerous appearances in the role of Rafael, the fix-it man, on the Emmy-winning PBS series *Sesame Street*.

In 1985 Juliá played Lt. David Suarez, who teams up with an amateur sleuth (Susan Sarandon) in Frank Perry's comedy-mystery *Compromising Positions* (Paramount).

Juliá then won the best role of his film career, that of the political prisoner Valentín, who is imprisoned with a fantasy-filled homosexual (William Hurt) in Hector Babenco's film adaptation of Manuel Puig's famed novel *Kiss of the Spider Woman* (1985, Island Alive) opposite Sônia Braga. Both Juliá and Hurt were nominated for the Best Actor Academy Award, the latter being the recipient. Juliá said of the role, "I'm very happy with Valentín. As it turned out, after the research (Juliá met with several political prisoners) that I did and working on the part, I just love the part. It is important.... In fact, it was more of a challenge for me to have acted as Valentín than to have played Molina."[132] The film was shot on location in São Paulo, Brazil, well-known for the *favelas* or poor neighborhoods that surround the opulent tourist sites. He was moved to comment, "We seem to find poverty in other countries, but we don't see the poverty that's around the corner here. There are people going hungry in the cities in this country—elderly people, young people that are going hungry by the thousands every day."[133]

Juliá was next cast in the role of Adolfo in the first full-length film from Puerto Rico, Marco Zuringa's *La Gran Fiesta* (1987, Zaga Films). Several choice roles came his way: the strongman behind the presidency in Paul Mazursky's satire on Latin American military-meddling *Moon over Parador* (1988, Universal) with Sônia Braga and Richard Dreyfuss; the corrupt Mexican drug agent in Robert Towne's atmospheric and successful *Tequila Sunrise* (1988, Warner Bros.) with Mel Gibson, Kurt Russell and Michelle Pfeiffer; a participant in the love triangle in the weak *The Penitent* (1988, Cineworld) with Julie Carmen; and the tango dancer in another Puerto Rican film, *Tango Bar* (1989, Zaga Films).

He then gave another Academy Award–caliber performance as the martyred Archbishop Oscar Romero of El Salvador in John Duigan's *Romero* (1988, ESEV) with a cast that included Tony Plana and Richard Jordan. The precedent-making film was shot in Mexico and produced by Father Ellwood Kieser and partially financed by the Paulist order. Juliá said of the film, "It's important to make clear this is not a Catholic film. It's about a human being who grew. The archbishop evolved from an ordinary and quite timid person to a great popular hero.... The purpose is to show the way a human can reach the heights of humanity, and how one man can make a difference."[134] Of the role, he commented, "It's the ideal for an actor to be able to show that growth, the movements and the emotions, the mountains and the valleys. These days, we seem to have in the movies either unrealistic superheroes or bums who end up in jail. Here you have a man who was not a superhero but who did things far beyond his own small personal self."[135]

Juliá earned enthusiastic reviews for his performance. *Variety* wrote, "Raul Julia, in the central role of Romero, delivers a flawless and impassioned performance."[136] The *Los Angeles Herald-Examiner* noted, "With Raul Julia in the title role, 'Romero' is unquestionably a powerful film, but outside of Julia's performance, its power comes almost entirely from the source material—reality."[137] Robert Ebert, in the *Chicago Sun-Times*, said, "The film has a good heart, and the Julia performance is an interesting one, restrained and considered. His Romero is not a firebrand but a reasonable man who cannot deny the evidence of his eyes and conscience."[138]

In 1990, Juliá played the ace lawyer defending an assistant district attorney (Harrison Ford) accused of murder in Alan J. Pakula's big courtroom hit *Presumed Innocent,* opposite Bonnie Bedelia and Paul Winfield.

Raúl Juliá physically was an imposing figure, over six feet tall, with large, somewhat hooded gray eyes and black hair. In 1977, he married actress Merel Poloway. They did a musical together in Philadelphia and had two sons. (His first marriage ended in divorce in the late 1960s.)

Juliá was involved in a variety of interests and activities. He practiced the process of awareness and enlightenment developed by Werner Erhard. He was involved with the Hunger Project, an international organization devoted to the eradication of hunger, and with HOLA

(Hispanic Organization of Latin Actors), which is committed to the development of Spanish-language theater. He was also outspoken about Latino stereotypes: "There are still people out there—casting people, directors, producers—who see me as a stereotype. And one of my goals is to break these stereotypes.... What needs to be done is to transform people's way of looking at Latinos, and this goes beyond show business into policies and their attitude toward Latin America."[139]

He began the 1990s with a trio of mixed-quality films: *Frankenstein Unbound* (1990); the police drama *The Rookie* (1990) with Clint Eastwood, Sônia Braga and Charlie Sheen; and Sydney Pollack's ambitious misfire *Havana* (1990) with Robert Redford and Lena Olin. He then scored with a pair of comedy films: *The Addams Family* (1991) and its sequel *Addams Family Values* (1993). In both films he re-created the role of Gomez Addams, first played by John Astin in the popular 1960s television series of the *The Addams Family*. Anjelica Huston played his wife Morticia. In between these films he starred in the obscure *The Plague* (1992).

Despite his critical and commercial success in film, he preferred the theater. He commented about the two mediums, "To me the theatre is like standing on a mountain and shouting your confession.... And film is like being in the confessional whispering, 'I have done this, I have done this.'"[140]

His other television films include *Richest Man in the World: The Story of Aristotle Onassis* (1988) with Anthony Quinn and Jane Seymour, and a 1974 special of *King Lear* in which he played Edmund.

His last two films were aired on cable television. He played Chico Mendez, the Brazilian environmentalist who tried to save the Amazon rain forest and was subsequently assassinated, in John Frankenheimer's *The Burning Season* (1994, HBO) with a cast that included Edward James Olmos, Sônia Braga, Esai Morales, and Thomas Milan. Frankenheimer said of Juliá, "I think he is just a wonderful actor.... I think he is a compassionate guy. I don't see anybody else playing that part."[141] It was during the on-location shooting of this film that it was revealed that Juliá had cancer.

Juliá's final film was *Down Came a Blackbird* (1995, Showtime) in which he played a Latin American intellectual who falls in love with an American journalist (Laura Dern) while covering a revolution. The film costarred Vanessa Redgrave. The *Boston Globe* noted, "Julia died shortly after completing *Down Came a Blackbird,* and although his death was a surprise, he was obviously ill while making the film. Even with his beard, his cheeks are sunken. His magnificent voice almost seems to emanate from thin air, given the gauntness of his frame. But his eyes dance with light and mystery, concealing so well his character's secrets that when they are revealed, they are not merely shocking, but heartbreaking."[142]

Juliá had been scheduled to play the villain in Robert Rodriguez's *Desperado.* However, during mid–October 1994 he suffered a stroke. On October 25, he died at the North Shore Hospital in the Long Island community of Manhasset, New York, after slipping into a coma four days before and never regaining consciousness. Three days of mourning were officially declared in Puerto Rico and thousands of people attended the funeral there.

The *Los Angeles Times* eulogized him: "It is safe to say that Raul Julia made a difference to any young Latino actor dreaming of the stage, because his dignified presence effectively banished any lingering 'Bab-a-loo!' stereotyping. But he also radiated a great warmth and a straightforward modesty that, combined with his heavy-lidded grey eyes, translated into a powerful sexuality on stage and on screen.

"Theatergoers knew him first during his formative years in the late '60s and early '70s, when he trained on the stages of Joseph Papp's Public Theater. And for theatergoers, it's those elusive images, gone as soon as they are experienced, that will remain the most vivid."[143]

He left a rich legacy of his talent and of his humility.

He was survived by his wife, Merel Poloway, and two sons, Raul Sigmund and Benjamin Rafael.

ALMA MARTÍNEZ

Alma Martínez is representative of the richness of skill and talent possessed by many contemporary Latina actresses. She has performed extensively on stage, on television and in film in a diverse number of roles and always with a high degree of excellence and professionalism.

She was born on March 18, 1953, in Coahuila, Mexico, and moved with her family to the United States when she was one year old. She began acting in high school under the guidance of drama teacher Squire Fridell. She continued her acting and training at the University of Southern California, the University of Mexico, the Royal Academy of Dramatic Arts in London and at Whittier College (where she earned a B.A. in theater). She supplemented this training by studying with such noted teachers as Lee Strasberg and Jerzi Grotowski.

Her theater career began flourishing in the late 1970s. She played Rosalba in *Rosalba y los Llaveros* at the Bilingual Foundation for the Arts (in Lincoln Heights in East Los Angeles) and in 1977 she joined Luis Valdez' renowned El Teatro Campesino. She had lead roles in *La Carpa de los Rasquachis* and *El Fin del Mundo*, both of which toured the United States and Europe for one year. Upon her return, she won the role of Della, Henry Reyna's girlfriend, in the Luis Valdez–written and –directed play *Zoot Suit,* which ran for eight months at the Hollywood Aquarius Theater. When *Zoot Suit* was made into a film (1982, Universal) by Valdez, Martínez switched roles and played Lupe Reyna, Henry's sister.

Martínez has fond memories of working on the play: "*Zoot Suit* was an incredible phenomenon. Within the Chicano community nothing has matched it. For pure enthusiasm, excitement, artistry, *Zoot Suit* was unique. And of course, Luis, back then, Luis was the father of it all. He's incredible to work with. Because Luis just taps into, personally for me, everything that I love about theater, and love about life."[144]

Under Valdez' direction, she played La Rielera in the play *Corridos* in the Los Angeles run at the Variety Arts Theatre and the wife Connie in *I Don't Have to Show No Stinking Badges* in its Marine Memorial Theatre performance. She recreated the role of La Reilera in *Corridos* when it was aired as a PBS special in 1987, which earned the Peabody Award.

Other notable plays include *Joanne Akalitisis, Green Card, Bacon, Wait until Dark, House of Blue Leaves, Savages,* and *Burning Patience.* Of her latter performance in *Burning Patience, Variety* noted, "Performances are headed by Alma Martínez, strong and loving as the wary mother."[145] Alma performed Lope de Vega's *Fuente Ovejuna* in 1990 and also appeared in Octavio Solis' modern version of the Don Juan legend, *Man of the Flesh*. *Variety* wrote, "Alma Martínez nicely demonstrates the scope needed for the buffoonery of the rowdy maid and the ominousness of Death."[146] The *Los Angeles Times* commented, "These women all handle the translations smoothly, as does Alma Martínez in her triple role as the libidinous Downey maid, Juan's real mother who comes back to condemn him, as well as a third spirit who proves to be Joan's fatal attraction at the end of the play."[147]

On television, she played a wide variety of roles in numerous programs, including *St. Elsewhere, Twilight Zone,* NBC's pilot *Scamps* and several soap operas: *General Hospital, Santa Barbara,* and *Superior Court*. In 1990, she played the regular role of Sgt. Elizabeth Cruz, a Chicana cop, in the short-lived renewal of *Adam–12* opposite Ethan Wayne, son of John Wayne.

The striking brown-eyed and brown-haired Martínez has made almost a dozen films. She played a romantic lead in Jesús Salvador Treviño's evocative *Seguin* (1981, PBS), which documented the Mexican side of the 1836 Texas Rebellion, with a cast that included Edward James Olmos and A Martinez; and she played the lovelorn Juanita in Fred Schepisi's under-rated western *Barbarosa* (1982) with Gilbert Roland, Isela Vega and Willie Nelson. Being able to work with the legendary Gilbert Roland was especially memorable for her: "Gilbert was already in an advanced age. But, he was very proud of the fact, I remember him saying, see this waistline? The same as 40 years ago. There was majesty, and he was royalty. These are the maestros, this is the royalty. These are the people who set, who broke the road, opened the road before us and set the pace for certain things. So working with him, well, we all just treat him with the deepest respect and admiration."[148]

She was excellent in the role of Isela Cruz, a Sandinista, in Roger Spotiswoode's effective *Under Fire* (1983), about the last days of Nicaragua's Somoza dictatorship, opposite Nick Nolte, Joanna Cassidy and Gene Hackman.

She played the role of Gloria in Cheech Marin's box-office hit *Born in East L.A.* (1987). She also costarred in several television films: *Tough Love* (1985) with Lee Remick and Bruce Dern; *Dress Gray* (1986), a taut thriller with Hal Holbrook and Alec Baldwin; *Trial by Terror* (1986) with Kay Lenz; *The Boys* (1991) with James Woods; and a film pilot, *Murphy's Law* with Jerry Orbach.

Martínez is a dedicated and passionate advocate of a variety of issues, among them the Christian Children's Fund, the world's largest child sponsorship organization. She has also served on the board of directors of the Central American Refugee Center in Los Angeles. She wed Stephen Rothman, director of the Pasadena Playhouse, on March 3, 1988, but they were subsequently divorced.

She completed a doctoral degree program in theater arts at Stanford University. She has taught theater at the University of California, Santa Cruz, and is currently at Claremont University in Claremont, California.

With regard to the limited opportunities for Latino performers, she commented, "We just want to work and have equity in that. Just equity. We don't want Latinos, we don't want actors, only to play the roles of their ethnic origin like we don't want just actors to play white or to play Latino or to play Black. We want to be able to have actors to do everything: Shakespeare, classical theatre, Ibsen, to do different roles."[149]

During late 2000, she made a triumphant return to the stage with the lead in Luis

Valdez' *Mummified Deer* at the San Diego Repertory Theatre. The *Los Angeles Times* wrote, "The dying matriarch Mama Chu [is] played with grit and vitality by Alma Martínez."[150]

Her recent films include *Prozac Nation* (2001); *Most High* (2004); *Planting Melvin* (2005); *Crossing Over* (2009); *Greater Glory* (2012); and *Strike One* (2012). She continues to guest-star in episodic television.

ESAI MORALES

One of the several actors benefiting from the critical and commercial success of *La Bamba* was the stage-trained Esai Morales, who became one of the very few Latino leading men.

Esai Morales was born to Cuban parents on October 1, 1962, in Brooklyn, New York. He ran away from home at the age of 15 because his mother did not let him study acting. He attended the prestigious High School of Performing Arts in New York City while he lived as a voluntary ward of New York State in a group home. He later recalled, "I had to travel over an hour each way to school, which was a pain. And I split my eyebrow in a fight because I was always fighting for the underdog. I never graduated from school because I stopped going to my classes except my acting classes."[151]

On stage and screen he excelled at playing streetwise rebels and misfits. On the stage he performed in *Short Eyes* and thereafter made his film debut in Paul Morrissey's *Forty-Deuce* (1982, IA). On television, he played an Iranian in the miniseries *On Wings of Eagles* (1986) opposite Burt Lancaster. He appeared in the Emmy Award–winning Afterschool Special *The Great Love Experiment*. Other television appearances in the 1980s include *Miami Vice, Fame* and *The Equalizer*.

His film career went into high gear when he played Paco Moreno, a vengeful youth, in Richard Rosenthal's gritty *Bad Boys* (1983, Universal) opposite Sean Penn and Ally Sheedy. He followed it with the lead in *Rainy Day Friends* (1986, SP) with Carrie Snodgress, and another costarring role as another young tough in the popular *The Principal* (1987, TriStar) with Jim Belushi and Lou Gossett, Jr. Next came his most famous role yet, that of Bob Morales, the hard-drinking and rebellious brother of Chicano rocker Ritchie Valens in Luis Valdez' hit *La Bamba* (1987, Columbia). *Variety* noted of his performance, "Most of the fireworks are Bob's, and Esai Morales makes the most of the opportunities. Remembered as Sean Penn's opponent in 'Bad Boys,' [he] commands the screen whenever he's around, and makes the tormented brother a genuinely complex figure."[152] Morales commented later about the role, "Bob is cynical in that he is negative, but considers himself a realist. He knows that he's not the acceptable-looking type in this 1950s society, which was so 'Sandra Dee,'—he wasn't cut out to look like one of those 'nice guys.'"[153]

In 1987, he made his West Coast stage debut in William Mastrosimone's *Talked of Horses* at the Los Angeles Theater Center and obtained excellent notices. While he has continued to garner film roles, such as the misfire *Bloodhounds of Broadway* (1989, Columbia), his film career did not take off as expected despite his talent.

In reference to Hollywood film opportunities he has stated, "I've been told that if I make it big one day, I might get to be like Erik Estrada. Why doesn't anybody mention [Laurence] Olivier?"[154]

In 1995, Morales made another strong impression as a rebellious Chicano youth in Gregory Nava's evocative tale of three generations of Chicanos in East Los Angeles, *My Family/Mi Familia* (1995) with Edward James Olmos, Jimmy Smits and Jennifer Lopez. The critical and commercial success of the film did much to bolster Morales' career. For his next project, he chose a film about Argentinean revolutionary Ernesto "Che" Guevara.

He then played the role of Noro's rival in Kevin Reynolds' epic *Rapa-Nui* (1994), about the inhabitants of Easter Island before the arrival of the Europeans. Initially, he wanted the hero role that went to Jason Lee. However, he commented philosophically, "I like playing characters that are not necessarily evil, but they do things that piss people off or they have problems that don't jell well with others."[155]

His 1990s films include *The Disappearance of Lorca* (1996) and the NBC television miniseries *Atomic Train* (1999). The *New York Times* wrote, "This is a silly two-part miniseries that works surprisingly well on the level of formulaic action."[156]

His recent credits include *The Virgin of Juarez* (2006); and *Gun Hill Road* (2011). He played leads in several television series: *Resurrection Boulevard* (2000–02); *American Family* (2002); and *NYPD Blue* (2001–04).

BOB MORONES

The contributions of Latinos behind the cameras have been relatively anonymous and few in number, but increasingly their contributions in the collaborative art form of film have grown. An example is casting director Bob Morones.

Bob Morones was born to Mexican parents in Los Angeles, California. His father was a chef at the Universal commissary. Even as a child he was fascinated with movie stars and films. He attended Stevenson Junior High and Garfield High School. He served three and a half years in the U.S. Army. He subsequently earned a B.A. at California State University, Los Angeles. He learned filmmaking at UCLA and Columbia College of Film and Television. He got his film industry break at Universal Studios Television Casting during the period 1971–1975.

Morones began as a casting director in the early 1970s at Universal Studios with such television shows as *Night Gallery, Owen Marshall,* and *Faraday & Company.* In 1973, he was assigned to special projects and Movies of the Week, working on such shows as *Ellery Queen, Macmillan and Wife, McCloud, Holmes & Yoyo, Lannigan's Rabbi,* and *Night Stalker.*

Branching out on his own in 1976, Morones founded B.M.C. Inc., an independent casting company. His company filled an important void in the film industry by providing vital access for Latino actors working in film and television. Too often in the industry, casting companies perpetuated denigrating stereotypes by casting non–Latino actors in Latino roles which they were ill prepared to play. Over the next two decades, Morones' casting company earned industry respect and praise for providing talented actors for films and television, as well as non–Latino talent. He commented to *Drama-Logue,* "The best actor should play the role. However when the role calls for an ethnic actor, we like to see them first. If they don't work out, then we open up the field for everybody."[157]

Morones did the casting in some notable films over the next two decades, including Jesús Treviño's *Seguin* (1980), for which he was also associate producer; Brian De Palma's

Scarface (1983); Gregory Nava's *El Norte* (1984); Oliver Stone's *Salvador* (1986), on which he also served as associate producer; Haskell Wexler's *Latino* (1985); Oliver Stone's *Platoon* (1986); John Duigan's *Romero* (1989); Edward James Olmos' *American Me* (1992); and Severo Perez's ... *And the Earth Did Not Swallow Him* (1995).

Other film credits included: *American Pop* (1981); *Born American* (1986); *Shadow of the Wolf* (1986); *Magdalena* (1986); *HITZ* (1986); and *Beyond Desire* (1987).

His television film credits include *Juárez* and *Three Hundred Miles for Stephanie* (1981). He did the casting for Jesús Salvador Treviño's CBS Afterschool Special *Gangs,* PBS' *Much Ado About Sex* and the NAACP's *Up & Coming.* He was the associate producer of the television film *Twin of Hearts.* He produced *Laugh Your Nalgas Off,* a Latino comedy night at the Roxy Theatre, and served as associate producer of the Latino Comedy Olympics at the Improv, both events in Hollywood. In 1989, he directed Reynaldo Povod's play *Cuba and His Teddy Bear* at the Caliboard Theatre in West Hollywood. In 1990, he directed two Maxi-Care health commercials and one 35 mm film short, *Who Will Sing the Songs,* for the Hispanic Film Project.

Morones won the Casting Society of America Artios award for Best Casting for a Feature Film for *Platoon* (1987).

KARMIN MURCELO

The dark-haired and versatile Karmin Murcelo has worked in film and television for two decades.

Her film credits include *Walk Proud* (1979) with Henry Darrow and Robby Benson; the hit comedy *Stir Crazy* (1980) with Richard Pryor and Gene Wilder; *The Big Score* (1983) with Nancy Wilson and Richard Roundtree; and *Revenge* (1990) with Anthony Quinn and Madeleine Stowe. However, her most memorable film role remains that of the undocumented mother in *Borderline* (1980) with Charles Bronson and Enrique Castillo.

Murcelo has played costarring roles in several television films: *The Blue Knight* (1973) with William Holden and Lee Remick; *A Killing Affair* (1977, CBS); *Victims* (1982, NBC); *Best Kept Secrets* (1984, ABC) with Patty Duke Astin; *Right to Kill?* (1985, ABC); and *Seduced* (1985, CBS). She also costarred in the hit television miniseries *Centennial* (1979) with Richard Chamberlain. In addition, she has guest-starred on such series as *L.A. Law, Highway to Heaven, Cagney & Lacey, Shannon, Cannon,* and *Police Story.* She played the recurring role of Carmen Castillo, the mother of A Martinez' character, in the long-running daytime soap opera *Santa Barbara.*

More recent films include *Blood In, Blood Out* (1993); *Empty Cradle* (1993); and *Blasphemy the Movie* (2001), among others. She continues to appear extensively on episodic television.

She has performed on the stage at the Los Angeles Mark Taper Forum and at the New Mexico Repertory Theater.

GREGORY NAVA

Director Gregory Nava's *El Norte* in the 1980s seemed to herald the arrival of a major Chicano director, but in the ensuing ten years, his presence appeared to have dimmed—

until his return in the 1990s with two films that chronicled the Chicano experience, *My Family/Mi Familia* and *Selena*. It was a timely and impressive return.

He was born on April 10, 1949, in San Diego, California, to Mexican-American parents. He graduated from the UCLA film school. His thirty-minute dramatic film on the life of Spanish poet and playwright Federico García Lorca, which was titled *The Journal of Diego Rodriguez Silva*, won the Best Dramatic Film Award at the National Student Film Festival. In 1973, he won the Best First Feature Award at the Chicago International Film Festival for *The Confessions of Amans*, which he wrote, produced and directed. The film was budgeted at $20,000 and shot in Spain using leftover costumes from Anthony Mann's *El Cid*.

In 1979, he worked as a cinematographer on Anna Thomas' *The Haunting of M.* Nava later married Anna Thomas, a German filmmaker.

In 1984, he directed and co-scripted with his wife *El Norte*, a powerful tale documenting the odyssey of a Guatemalan brother and sister who migrate to the United States. Regarding the making of the film, Nava commented, "When you travel anywhere in Latin America, you're immediately struck by two forces: the lush, dreamlike beauty of the landscape—the people, colors, textiles, art, and the terrible social and political problems that are ripping these countries apart."[158]

Nava encountered difficulty in finding financial backing for the film because of the all–Mexican/Latino cast. "I kept hearing, again and again, that I should make Americans the main characters, that I'd never get financed otherwise.... Everyone told me that audiences could never be able to cross the cultural and language barrier, but I thought that even though the cultural differences were great, if the film were done right, people would be able to cross that barrier and recognize human beings on the other side."[159]

El Norte earned enormous critical and commercial success. The *New York Times* noted, "A small, personal, independently made film with the sweep of *El Norte*, with solid, sympathetic performances by unknown actors and a visual style of astonishing vibrancy, must be regarded as a remarkable accomplishment."[160]

The *Los Angeles Times* wrote, "*El Norte* ... embodies an idea whose time has come, the dramatization on screen of the plight of illegal immigrants. It is a subject that has been dealt with before in films, most notably in Robert M. Young's excellent *Alambrista!*, but young filmmaker Gregory Nava has attempted no less than an epic."[161] *El Norte* was nominated for an Academy Award for Best Screenplay.

His next film was the studio-financed *Time of Destiny* (1988) with William Hurt and Timothy Hutton, a conventional melodrama that failed to elicit a critical or commercial response.

Seven years went by before Nava was able to secure financial backing for another film, *My Family/Mi Familia* (1995), with a cast that included Edward James Olmos, Jimmy Smits, Esai Morales and Jennifer Lopez. The film chronicled three generations of Mexicans/Chicanos in the East Los Angeles barrio.

In reference to the status of Chicano and Latino players in the Hollywood film industry, he commented, "I think it's clear that the audience likes the Latino cast. I feel *The Perez Family* is miscast and certainly the Latino audience rejected it for that reason. If you make a Latino movie, it's really clear that the Latino audience doesn't like non–Latino casting. They want their own up there. So with Latinos rejecting a Latino film, you're in trouble. Of course you want to reach a non–Latino audience, but (Latinos) are the core audience. We're not in a world where there's an even playing field. We're not in a world where blonde parts are played by Latinos. We're in a world where the main Latino roles are played by non–Latinos."[162]

My Family/Mi Familia was lauded by the *Los Angeles Times:* "One of the reasons *My Family* is successful is that the simple concept of focusing on the real family, not the substitute gang family that many previous Latino films have latched on to, is a surprisingly effective one. And both the script and direction have taken care to give the film's characters what they themselves would consider essential: simple dignity."[163] The film proved to be a critical and commercial success.

Nava's next film project was about slain Tex-Mex music legend Selena Quintanilla. The film was entitled *Selena* (1997, Warner Bros.). The project was made with the full cooperation of Selena's family and the title role was played by Jennifer Lopez, her father by Edward James Olmos and her manager (and alleged assassin) by Lupe Ontiveros. The film was released in 1997 and received mixed reviews, but went on to become one of the highest grossing Latino-themed films of all time.

More recently, Nava directed *Why Do Fools Fall in Love* (1998), the story of early African American rock stars that was headlined by Lela Rochon, Halle Berry and Vivica A. Fox. The film proved to be only a moderate commercial success and earned mixed critical reviews. The *Los Angeles Times* noted, "Though Nava's soapy directing style makes *Fools* watchable enough in a campy way, the film's unsophisticated nature undermines its better qualities. Absent the kind of star performance Jennifer Lopez gave in *Selena* (and that film's cleaner, more direct story line), cornball dramaturgy can take audiences only so far and not one note further."[164]

Nava co-wrote the script for *Frida* (2004) and directed *Bordertown* (2007).

EDWARD JAMES OLMOS

The biggest Chicano film star to emerge in the 1980s was Edward James Olmos, who portrayed a remarkable number of Chicano/Mexican historical characters in socially oriented films.

He was born in the Boyle Heights barrio in East Los Angeles, California, on February 24, 1947. He attended Montebello High School and recollected of his experience, "I think we all had teachers who inspired us because we wouldn't have made it through school, but most of the time we were dealing with people who had spent so much time in teaching that they had gotten into a mode. They would say, 'You can either take advantage of this class or not, but either way shut up and no talking in class.'"[165]

In high school, he took up dance and music as two artistic disciplines. He formed a rock group called Eddie and the Pacific Ocean which became a long-term house band at the famed Gazzari's on the Sunset Strip in Hollywood during the 1960s.

In the late 1960s, he gradually gravitated to theater and television. An early role was that of an immigration officer in the *Police Story* segment "River of Promises" (1978), which starred Richard Yniguez and Jaime Sánchez. His film career began with a bit role in *Aloha Bobby and Rose* in 1975. His next role was as a wino derelict in Robert M. Young's evocative and powerful drama about the plight of Mexican undocumented workers, *Alambrista!* (1977), which went on to win the Golden Camera Prize at Cannes. Other films followed: the television film *Evening in Byzantium* (1978, Universal) with Glenn Ford and Shirley Jones; the U.S./Japanese co-production *Virus* (1980); and the television film *Three Hundred Miles for Stephanie* (1981).

He was effective in the role of General Santa Anna in Jesús Salvador Treviño's evocative *Seguin* (1981, PBS) about the 1836 Texas Rebellion; earned praise for his role in Michael Wadleigh's eerie thriller *Wolfen* (1981) opposite Albert Finney; and then essayed the role of Gaffe, a Los Angeles detective in Ridley Scott's impressive futuristic tale *Blade Runner* (1982, Warner Bros.) opposite Harrison Ford. About the multicultural role he played, he commented, "I went out to a Berlitz language school and learned pieces of languages. I wrote down

Edward James Olmos became the epitome of the Chicano actor in film, television, and theater.

my own dialogue, but instead of saying, 'I'm going to the police station' in English, I would say each word in a different language. I called it City speak. They couldn't deal with it. What I had done was beyond their wildest dreams."[166]

Olmos was cast in the role of the Pachuco in Luis Valdez' hit play about the Sleepy Lagoon case and zoot suit riots entitled *Zoot Suit*, which opened at the Mark Taper Forum in Los Angeles in 1978 and ended with a short run on Broadway. He said of the role, "There were people from the Royal Shakespeare Company who said my character was one of the few to come out of the American theater that was big enough to walk into the Shakespearean stage."[167] For his kinetic performance, he won the Los Angeles Drama Critics Award and earned a Tony nomination. When asked about how he researched for the role, he commented, "A lot of that came from the street. There's so much time spent checking people out. So much of the street is body language and attitude."[168] In 1982, he repeated his role in the film version of *Zoot Suit* (Universal), written and directed by Luis Valdez.

In 1983, he played the title role in Robert M. Young's fact-based and impressive *The Ballad of Gregorio Cortez* (Embassy), meeting with critical and commercial success. Olmos did extensive personal appearances and effective promotion for the film after distributors initially doubted the film's potential. He was reunited with director Young in the misfire *Saving Grace* (1986), about a fictitious pope who leaves the Vatican to mingle with his flock. The film costarred Giancarlo Giannini and Tom Conti.

In August 1984, Olmos replaced Gregory Sierra after he had done four episodes in the role of Lieutenant Castillo on the hit television series *Miami Vice*. He was given creative

**Edward James Olmos (left in top photograph, right in bottom) and Lou Diamond Phillips in
Stand and Deliver (1988, Warner Bros.). Olmos was nominated for an Academy Award for Best
Actor for his sensitive portrayal of real-life teacher Jaime Escalante.**

control of the character by executive producer Michael Mann. Olmos stated, "He allowed me that strength.... Basically, Castillo is probably the most disciplined character I've worked with in all my life. But that's what's extraordinary about him. He's able to survive doing close to absolutely nothing, except for thinking on camera."[169] He subsequently won an Emmy Award for his stoical portrayal. In one episode, entitled "Bushido," he made his directorial debut.

In 1988, he played an Italian fisherman in the television film *Fortunate Pilgrim* opposite Sophia Loren. He was nominated for an Academy Award as Best Actor for his performance as Garfield High School (in East Los Angeles) math teacher Jaime Escalante in Ramón Menéndez' *Stand and Deliver* (1988, Warner Bros.). Once more, he resorted to methodical preparation, which included gaining fifty pounds and having his hair thinned to a few strands. Olmos stated, "I demanded that they go in and set cameras and photograph a full day of classes.... I watched then six to eight hours a day, seven days a week."[170] Of his portrayal he commented, "If copying is the highest form of flattery then I've given one of the most flattering performances in my 27 years of studying the craft. But with all my craftsmanship I didn't get close to him. The man is too unique."[171] The film proved to be a huge popular and critical success.

In Robert M. Young's *Triumph of the Spirit* (1989, TRNI), he played a gypsy who befriends a Jewish boxer in their desperate attempt to survive a Nazi concentration camp. The role gave Olmos an opportunity to dance and sing once more. He was reunited with director Young for *Talent for the Game* (1991), in which he played an ex–baseball player turned talent scout. About his collaboration with Young, his favorite director, he noted, "Our collaboration involves the development of both in a way that I have not experienced with anyone. He is one of the greatest humanists that I've known and has a real sensitivity about the spirit and human condition."[172]

A long-term project came to fruition in 1992: a story of Chicano gang members and their entry into the Mexican Mafia at Folsom Prison that resulted in the film *American Me* (Universal). Olmos directed, produced and starred in the film. The film was the object of some criticism in some quarters of the Chicano/Latino community, but he stated, "There are those who say, 'If you can't say anything nice, then don't say it.' I think it's time for us to really understand where the cancer lies. This is a healing movie.... It's really necessary. Sixty-five percent of the kids in the L.A. County Juvenile Hall are Hispanic. Almost half are in for murder. These are kids from ages nine to eighteen."[173]

The film went on to be a critical and commercial success. In its review, *The Hollywood Reporter* noted, "In *American Me* Edward James Olmos has achieved several important goals, but one outweighs the rest; he has made a film that will scare the hell out of any inner-city youth not already lost to the hopelessness of gangs, drugs and prison.... Olmos' other achievements, not so incidentally, include a brilliant directorial debut and, arguably, his best screen performance to date."[174] The *Village Voice* wrote, "For as convincing an inspiration *Stand and Deliver* is to youth clinging to hope in the face of societal subjugation, *American Me* is a shot to the solar plexus of a people smothered in the darkness of a harsh reality."[175] *Variety* noted, "The criminal life is portrayed with all the glamour of a mug shot in *American Me,* a powerful indictment of the cycle of violence bred by the prisons and street culture.... Olmos makes for a mesmerizing, implacable Santana, one of the least romanticized film gangsters since Paul Muni's *Scarface.*"[176]

Olmos has been a tireless worker on behalf of many social causes, including farm workers, gang youth, anti-drug and stay-in-school campaigns and the betterment of Latino images in the media. On the third day of the Los Angeles riots in 1992 that followed the police beating of Rodney King, Edward James Olmos picked up a broom and began cleaning up the streets. Thousands emulated him. When asked about the riots, he stated, "I think that any time you have a disproportionate pain between people who have and the people who don't have, a tremendous amount of pressure is placed on the morality of society as a whole. For instance, most recently we've had Proposition 187, a very difficult issue to deal with. And once again it started to cause a moral imbalance within our society, as did the right-to-life issue."[177]

He worked with Robert M. Young once again in *Roosters* (1995) opposite Sônia Braga and María Conchita Alonso. It was a moderately successful film based on a play. Olmos then played the writer son and narrator in Gregory Nava's evocative *My Family/Mi Familia* (1995) with Jimmy Smits, Esai Morales and Jennifer Lopez. The *Los Angeles Times* wrote, "Holding it together is the extensive voice-over of Paco, the oldest son and an aspiring writer. Edward James Olmos, who plays Paco, does not have a great deal of screen time, but it's hard to imagine this film without his soothing narration and the Godfather-like quality of his voice."[178]

Olmos played the role of Piñheiro, who had a major influence on the slain Brazilian environmentalist Chico Mendez, in John Frankenheimer's *The Burning Season* (1994, HBO) opposite Raúl Juliá (in the title role and one of Juliá's last films). He was cast in the role of the father of the murdered Tex-Mex singer in Gregory Nava's *Selena* (1997).

In relation to the breakthrough of Chicano- and Latino-oriented films, he stated, "It's taken us a long time to get here, but it's also been done under our sense of values. Just 'cause its a Hispanic-themed film doesn't mean they're going to make money with it. Story means everything to making money in the Hispanic community."[179]

He commented on his Mexican culture in a multicultural world, "I never stop knowing that I'm Latino. I'm very much a part of the Latin experience. But I don't limit to one form or theory of being. I've being exposed to Russian culture, Asian culture, to Indian culture and Mexican cultures. I draw from all of them. I understand ... that the future involves a tremendous awareness of the world."[180]

Olmos played a cameo role in the directorial debut film of Paul Rodriguez, *A Million to Juan* (1995). He starred in the television film *Hollywood Confidential* (1997); Robert Altman's television miniseries *Gun* (1997); and the television remake of *The Taking of Pelham One Two Three* (1998) with his wife, actress Lorraine Bracco. He starred in the segment entitled *The Pencil Holder,* one of a trio in the Showtime cable film *The Wall* (1998). The *New York Times* noted, "Edward James Olmos is particularly good as the boy's widowed father, sad and carelessly disdainful of the boy's handmade gift, a tiny pencil holder."[181]

He earned good notices for his powerful performance in Robert M. Young's love triangle drama *Caught* (1996) with María Conchita Alonso. The *New York Times* noted, "Mr. Olmos lumbers through the film announcing salt-of-the-earth sturdiness and inviting sympathy for this cuckolded saint. Not until the film's heated finale, of which the title gives some indication, does he rise to give this story the surprise and fury it needs."[182] Other films include *The Disappearance of Lorca* (1997) with Esai Morales and Andy García; the HBO film remake of *12 Angry Men* (1997) opposite a strong cast that included Jack Lemmon and Ossie Davis; and the Showtime film *Bonanno: A Godfather's Story* (1999).

He continues to be a tireless Chicano community advocate. Since 1996, he has been instrumental in organizing a festival of books in Los Angeles, as well as a Latino film festival.

Recent film credits include *In the Time of the Butterflies* (2001) with Salma Hayek; *Walkout* (2006) about the 1969 high school walkouts, which he co-produced, directed, and played a cameo in; and *The Green Hornet* (2011). On television he guest-starred as a Chicano judge on the popular *The West Wing* (1999–2000); portrayed the patriarch in *American Family* (2002–03, PBS); and played Captain William Adams in *Battlestar Galactica* (2003–09) and Professor Gellar in *Dexter* (2011).

ELIZABETH PEÑA

By the end of the 1980s, one of the fastest-rising of the young Latina actresses was the versatile Elizabeth Peña.

She was born on September 23, 1961, in Elizabeth, New Jersey, and then moved with her parents to their homeland, Cuba. They lived there until she was eight and thereafter she grew up in New York City, where her parents went to administer the Latin American Theatre Ensemble in Spanish Harlem. Elizabeth made her theater debut at the age of eight in one of her father's productions. After attending the High School of Performing Arts in New York City, she went on to do Shakespeare, Spanish classics and avant-garde theater. She supplemented her income by doing numerous commercials.

She made her film debut in the independent production *The Super* (1977), an acclaimed tale of Cuban exiles who attempt to cope with life in New York City. She followed it with *Times Square* (1980, BVNV) with Trini Alvarado; Peter Bogdanovich's funny comedy *They All Laughed* (1981, 20th Century–Fox) with Audrey Hepburn; the television film *Found Money* (1981) with Dick Van Dyke and Sid Caesar; and *Fat Chance* (1985).

The turning point in her career was her lead role as the discarded girlfriend of Rubén Blades in Leon Ichaso's *Crossover Dreams* (1985, CF), a somber tale of a Latino musician's attempt to succeed in the mainstream music industry. She earned excellent notices for her role. Thereafter, she scored strongly in the role of Carmen, the radicalized Mexican domestic in Paul Mazursky's offbeat comedy-drama *Down and Out in Beverly Hills* (1986, Touchstone) with Nick Nolte, Bette Midler and Richard Dreyfuss.

She played Rosie, the former girlfriend of Chicano rocker Ritchie Valens (Valenzuela) in Luis Valdez' big hit *La Bamba* (1987, Columbia). *Variety* noted of her performance, "Elizabeth Peña has numerous dramatic moments as Bob's distraught mate."[183] She was then ill-used in a pair of routine films: the unfunny *Batteries Not Included* (1987, Universal) with Hume Cronyn and Jessica Tandy; and the silly *Vibes* (1988, Columbia) with Cyndi Lauper and Peter Falk.

During 1986, she was a regular on the short-lived CBS series *Tough Cookies,* and in 1987 and 1988, she starred in ABC's *I Married Dora,* playing a Salvadoran doctor reduced to being a nanny in the United States. During 1990 and 1991, she starred in another series, NBC's *Shannon's Deal.* She returned to the theater in 1987 in John Patrick Shanley's play *The Italian-American Reconciliation.*

Peña had a featured role in Kathryn Bigelow's taut police thriller *Blue Steel* (1990) opposite Jamie Lee Curtis and Ron Silver, and then she gave an exceptional performance in Adrian Lyne's psychological cult film *Jacob's Ladder* (1990, TriStar) opposite Tim Robbins. She had a small role in which she glowed in the Neal Jimenez–Michael Steinberg *The Waterdance* (1992, SGC).

In 1996, after a dearth of roles, she scored impressively as a Mexican-American widow in John Sayles' evocative tale of a small Texas town, *Lone Star,* opposite Kris Kristofferson, Chris Cooper and Miriam Colón. The *Los Angeles Times* noted, "As always, Sayles has assembled an expert cast.... The most notable newcomers are Peña, whose dance with Cooper to Freddy Fender's 'Desde Que Conosco' is a high spot."[184]

On the craft of acting, she stated, "If you are working with a bad director in a film or play, training helps you edit what you listen to. You have to learn how to give the people who hire you what they want without selling yourself out in the process."[185] In reference to the film image of Latinos, she commented, "I'm usually offered the roles of the whore, the junkie, the mother with seventeen children or the screeching wife getting beaten up. Now things are being developed for me."[186] About the future, she said, "There is a whole new breed of actor. They are just well-trained actors who just happen to be Hispanic. We're just playing people and not playing the results of people, especially negative people. We're not all whores and junkies."[187]

She commented to *La Opinión*, "I, with all honesty, don't see any progress, in general terms about what's happening with us. There are exceptions of course. There are the Andy García, the Jimmy Smits, the Cheech Marin and when I have some luck, the Elizabeth Peña. They are brief moments of consolation which have small duration, very small. And it's that there are very few Latinos who have the opportunity to work in Hollywood. There are thousands of Latino actors who would like to showcase their talents and there are only four or five who are working constantly."[188]

Her 1990s films include *Across the Moon* (1995); *Free Willy 2: The Adventure Home* (1995); and the HBO film *The Second Civil War* (1997) with Richard Yniguez and James Coburn. Of the last-named film, the *Los Angeles Times* wrote, "Director Joe Dante speeds the story along while pausing in spots to linger on the cast's good work, especially that of Bridges, Peña, Hedaya and Hartman."[189] Her more recent films include the action-comedy *Rush Hour* (1998) with Jackie Chan and *Tortilla Soup* (2001). She scored a critical triumph again during 2001, when she was cast as one of the leads in Showtime's cable series *Resurrection Blvd.*

Recent credits include *The Lost City* (2005) and *Off the Map* (2011). She appears extensively on episodic television.

MIGUEL PIÑERO

Miguel Piñero's jail experiences spawned the play *Short Eyes.* Starting as an off-off-Broadway play, it went on to win the New York Drama Critics Circle award for Best American Play in 1974, and left an indelible imprint of the Nuyorican experience.

Piñero was born in New York City, of Puerto Rican ancestry. Piñero had a troubled adolescence, which later led him to do time in jail for robbery and other offenses. He began writing *Short Eyes* while doing a sentence in Sing Sing. The play is set in the dayroom of a cell block and depicts how the prisoners treat a new inmate charged with the rape of a young girl.

Short Eyes opened in 1974 at the Riverside Theater as part of the Third World Project and then went on for a run at Lincoln Center. The film version of the play was made in 1976, directed by Robert M. Young, with a cast that included José Pérez, Bruce Davison and Freddy Fender.

Piñero followed *Short Eyes* with other plays, including *Straight from the Ghetto, The Sun Always Shines for the Cool, Eulogy for a Small-Time Thief,* and *A Midnight at the Great Spoon.* He was writing *Every Form of Refuge Has Its Price* when he died.

Joseph Papp called Piñero "the first major writer to come out of the large numbers of Puerto Ricans that came to New York in the 50's."[190] He was a mentor to other writers.

Piñero was also an excellent actor and had supporting roles in several films: *Fort Apache, The Bronx* (1981); *Breathless* (1983); *Exposed* (1983); *Deal of the Century* (1983); and *The Pick-up Artist* (1987).

He costarred in a pair of television films: *The Jericho Mile* (1979, ABC) with Peter Strauss; and *The Streets of L.A.* (1979, CBS) with Isela Vega.

He was also a poet and cofounder of the Nuyorican movement of Puerto Rican New York poets. He edited the timely anthology *Nuyorican Poetry.*

Piñero died of cirrhosis of the liver on June 16, 1988, in New York City. He was survived by his seven brothers and sisters.

In 2001, a film directed by Leon Ichaso was made about his life, entitled *Piñero,* in which he was played by Oscar-nominated actor Benjamin Bratt.

TONY PLANA

One of the most versatile and hard-working Latino actors during the 1980s and 1990s was the stage-trained Tony Plana.

He was born on April 19, 1952, in Cuba to a banker father. The family left with the coming of the revolution when Tony was eight years old and settled in Miami. They lived there for one year and then moved to New York, where they lived for several years before moving to Los Angeles, California. Plana began acting in high school and continued at Loyola University. He took a year off for intensive study at the Royal Academy of Dramatic Arts in London and then returned to complete his B.F.A. at Loyola. About his experience in London, he stated, "The most important thing I learned was the importance of voice, the craft of the acting. You know, José Ferrer said that the three most important skills for an actor to develop are first, voice, second, voice, and third, voice."[191]

He scored strongly at the PCPA/Theaterfest playing Sirhan in *Sirhan and RFK* at the Melrose Theater. He commented, "Then I played Sirhan, I played it with an accent—dialects was one of the things I studied in England and my ear got very attuned to listening and duplicating them.... They didn't realize I was Hispanic until I did *Zoot Suit.*"[192] With regard to the importance of this experience, he recalled, "I never really understood the Chicano Movement in a way that I started to understand it once I became involved with Luis Valdez. *Zoot Suit* opened my eyes politically and culturally and also it was the most powerful theatrical experience I have ever had, and probably will ever have."[193]

Plana turned professional in 1977, after some initial misgivings: "My concept of an actor was Robert Redford, a tall, blond Anglo man. At the time I never considered the whole genre of character actors like James Cagney or Edward G. Robinson or Peter Lorre, who were wonderful. Not tall, not blonde, not Anglo."[194]

In 1979, he was cast in the role of Rudy, Henry Reyna's kid brother, in Luis Valdez' hit play *Zoot Suit*. He stated of the role, "It opened me up. I'll always feel close to Luis Valdez. He's the guy who gave me confirmation of all my talents. I auditioned for *Zoot Sui* three times."[195] In 1982, he repeated his role in the film version of *Zoot Suit* (Universal).

Since then, his film work has been prolific and he has imbued every role with a singular dedication and skill. His film credits include *Teen Mothers* (1980, Cannon); James Toback's comedy thriller *Love and Money* (1981, Paramount) with Ornella Muti and Ray Sharkey; Taylor Hackford's critical and commercial hit *An Officer and a Gentleman* (1982, Paramount) with Richard Gere and Debra Winger, in which he played the Chicano cadet Emiliano; William Friedkin's *Deal of the Century* (1983, Warner Bros.) with Sigourney Weaver and Chevy Chase; Gregory Nava's evocative and powerful *El Norte* (1984, CIIA), about the plight of undocumented workers; *City Limits* (1985, Atlantic) with Rae Dawn Chong; *The Best Times* (1986, Universal) with Robin Williams and Kurt Russell; Oliver Stone's *Salvador* (1986, HFC), in which he excelled in the role of the murderous Major Max and which costarred James Woods and Elpidia Carrillo; and the lackluster *Three Amigos* (1986, Orion), in the role of Jefe.

Plana gave an outstanding performance as the swaggering Chicano Special Services officer, who trains Nicaraguan Contras in Honduras, in Haskell Wexler's impressive *Latino* (1986, CI) with Robert Beltran and Annette Cardona. *Variety* wrote, "Tony Plana stands out as a gung-ho U.S. Latin officer."[196] Plana commented on his acting, "I have a very technical approach to acting. It's not Actors Studio. I build a character, basically, from the outside in. I like to work with the character in terms of how he moves and how he dresses and work with that until I change from outside to inside. I've managed my career through different kinds of skills which I cultivated methodically when I first started."[197] This film also left Tony with a heightened sense of skepticism: "To hear stuff being said on American television or by American presidents or American politicians, and to look around and see that they were distorting the reality that was there, that was around me, was an eye-opener. I'll never look at a newspaper the same way. And also working with Haskell Wexler was really a wonderful experience. He gave me the freedom to improvise."[198]

His career took a comic turn with Cheech Marin's popular *Born in East L.A.* (1987, Universal); and in the rap-music comedy *Disorderlies* (1987, Warner Bros.). He was excellent as a corrupt Chicano cop who becomes expendable in Isaac Artenstein's fact-based *Break of Dawn* (1988, Cinewest) with Óscar Chávez and María Rojo. He played Father Morantes in the effective *Romero* (1989, FSEV) with Raúl Juliá in the title role of the slain Archbishop Romero of El Salvador. He recollected about Juliá, with whom he made four films, "He was really at the peak of his powers when he died. We never got to see him play those Anthony Quinn roles when he was in his 50s and 60s. We never got to see him play older roles. He was still in early middle age. So it was a tragic loss for us."[199]

He was a tireless advocate in the development and founding of the Latino Classical Repertory (now called East L.A. Classic Theater). It takes one-hour versions of Shakespeare plays to elementary schools and middle schools throughout the country. He noted about what it has accomplished, "I think we contribute to the students' perception of themselves and also help improve the possibilities they have in the world. Expanding their borders, so to speak. Expanding their limitations and whether they're self-imposed or externally imposed."[200]

Regarding stereotypes, he commented, "The roles I've been doing are mostly Hispanic. My frustration about playing such roles is that very often they don't represent us totally. They always present the more desperate aspects of our culture." He added, "Hispanic actors need to get out there and take chances. Unfortunately, a lot of them don't. I think it's comfortable for them to stay and just do film work. It's a very protective medium for the actor. You can screw up and they can fix it. You screw up in the theatre and no one can fix it."[201]

He has continued to play a diverse number of roles: a revolutionary in Sidney Pollack's *Havana* (1990) with Robert Redford and Raúl Juliá; a cop in *The Rookie* (1990) with Clint Eastwood, Raúl Juliá and Sônia Braga; a gangster in *One Good Cop* (1991) with Michael Keaton and Rachel Ticotin; a right-wing extremist in Oliver Stone's *JFK* (1991) with Kevin Costner; a servant confidante in Oliver Stone's *Nixon* (1995) with Anthony Hopkins; and an ambitious police officer in John Sayles' *Lone Star* (1996) with Elizabeth Peña and Kris Kristofferson.

He has costarred in several television movies: *Streets of L.A.* (1979, CBS); *Madame X* (1981, NBC); *Listen to Your Heart* (1983, CBS); and *Sadat* (1983, Columbia).

Other films include the comedies *Buy and Cell* (1989, TWE) and *Why Me?* (1990) with Christopher Lambert. He had a cameo in Paul Rodriguez' directorial debut film, *A Million to Juan* (1995). He also had a prominent role in a film about the slain Brazilian environmentalist Chico Mendez, *The Burning Season* (1994, HBO), with Raúl Juliá in the lead role.

In an interview, I asked him about continuing Latino stereotypes. He responded, "I think the reason why we're underrepresented is because in a sense we're underrepresented in mainstream culture. I think the reason why we are stereotyped is because we are marginalized in mainstream culture. We're not part of everybody's consciousness. And we're seen as foreigners, as not really part of the mainstream."[202]

During 2000, Plana scored as the patriarch of a Chicano boxing family in Jesús Salvador Treviño's *Resurrection* (2000) for Showtime. Recent film credits include *Man on Fire* (2004) and *America* (2011). He guest-stars on episodic television.

ROSE PORTILLO

Chicana actress Rose Portillo has worked with consummate craftsmanship in theater, television and film for the several decades. She was born on November 7, 1953, in Los Angeles, California.

She made her film debut in the role of the possessed Brazilian girl in *The Exorcist: The Heretic* in 1976, opposite Richard Burton and James Earl Jones.

She has displayed her acumen and skill as an actress in three costarring roles: as the strong-willed wife in Jesús Salvador Treviño's *Seguin* (1981, PBS) with A Martinez and Edward James Olmos; as Della, the supporting girlfriend in Luis Valdez' memorable *Zoot*

Suit (1982, Universal); and as the indomitable Florentina in Severo Perez' film adaptation of Tomas Rivera's ... *And the Earth Did Not Swallow Him.*

Of the last-named film, *The Hollywood Reporter* commented, "Rose Portillo and Marco Rodriguez create powerful impressions as his fretfully simple and devout parents."[203]

Portillo commented on the film to *La Opinión*, "The film is not a stereotype of poor immigrant workers, but it also does not negate the reality in which they live, [nor] the racism that impacts them or the lack of basic services."[204]

During 1992, a controversy erupted when Luis Valdez cast an Italian-American in the role of Mexican painter Frida Kahlo for a planned film. In a letter to the *Los Angeles Times*, Portillo expressed passionately what many Chicana/Mexican/Latina actresses experience: "My daily reality is that I can plead all I want but that I am not granted the privilege of reading for 'Italian' roles.... Italian and Italian Americans do not suffer the reverse situation.... I am a trained actor, but in order to play Roxane in *Cyrano* or Kate in *Other People's Money*, I had to go to Minneapolis."[205]

She has costarred in several television films: *Kill Me If You Can* (1977, NBC); *Victims* (1982, NBC); and *Best Kept Secrets* (1984, ABC). During May 1994, Rose played the lead role in the play *Know Your Place* at the Los Angeles Theatre Center.

In 1998, she was reunited with Edward James Olmos in a segment of the television show *Touched by an Angel,* in which she played his wife. Her film credits include *Breaking Through* (1996) and *Fathers and Sons* (2005), a TV film, among others. She continues to guest-star extensively in many popular television shows.

PAUL RODRIGUEZ

Other than Cheech Marin, the only other Latino comedian to rise to film prominence has been the equally irreverent Paul Rodriguez.

He was born on January 19, 1955, in Mazatlán, Sinaloa, Mexico, the youngest of five children. His family moved to the Boyle Heights barrio in East Los Angeles and found employment as migrant farm workers. He developed his talent for humor in elementary school. He recalled later, "It was a defense mechanism. If the other kids laughed, they wouldn't beat me up."[206]

He commented on a racial incident during his youth when his family visited Crystal City, Texas: "My dad had promised to stop at the next hamburger place and he did. He got out, talked to the man and then got back into the car with no burgers. We were all bitching and he never said a word. It wasn't until much later, I was nineteen or twenty, that I found out what had happened. My dad said, 'There was a sign, son. It said, No Blacks. No Mexicans. No dogs served in this establishment!'"[207]

Rodriguez graduated from Roosevelt High School and joined the air force (he was stationed in Iceland). After leaving the service in 1977, he attended Long Beach City College under the G.I. Bill to study engineering. Upon obtaining his A.A. degree, he entered California State University, Long Beach, to study pre-law. He took an elective theater course, during which his instructor became impressed by his quick wit and convinced him to perform in the amateur night at Hollywood's famed Comedy Store. In November 1980, at the age of twenty-five, Rodriguez was hired as both comic and doorman of the club. His career turn took his parents by surprise. "They never thought that being a performer or an actor was an attainable goal. Being farm workers, all they wanted was for their children to survive and find a steady job. But I knew I had to give it a chance ... although it took a while to work up the courage."[208]

His performances in colleges and clubs led to several television guest appearances. In 1983, he was cast in a short-lived ABC comedy, produced by Norman Lear, called *A.K.A. Pablo,* which was written for him. He costarred in a CBS series, *Trial and Error,* during 1988. He made his film debut as Xavier in the uneven but entertaining comedy *D.C. Cab* (1987, Universal), about a down-and-out cab company struggling for self-respect.

His films include *Quicksilver* (1987, Columbia), an urban western on wheels with Jami Gertz; *Miracles* (1986), about a pair of bumbling revolutionaries (Rodriguez, Christopher Lloyd) who accidentally kidnap a divorced couple (Teri Garr, Tom Conti); *The Whoopee Boys* (1986, Paramount), about a pair of hustlers (Rodriguez, Michael O'Keefe) trying to crash into high society in Palm Beach; and Cheech Marin's box-office hit *Born in East L.A.* (1987, Universal), about a Chicano (Marin) deported by the I.N.S. to Tijuana on his way to meet his Mexican cousin (Rodriguez).

He has made a multilingual comedy album entitled *You're in America Now, Speak English*; a video with Whoopi Goldberg called *Makin' Whoopie*; and had a one-man special which aired on HBO.

In 1990, he costarred in another short-lived comedy series for CBS, *Grand Slam* with John Schneider. He said of the role, "They allow me to ad-lib if I come up with a better line—which I do 90 percent of the time. It's wonderful because in other shows they're married to lines like 'Oh boy, it smells like bad tacos in here.' Like that's supposed to be funny. I've even had producers telling me how to do a Hispanic accent."[209] The series lasted one season and in the same year he hosted a short-lived talk show on Spanish-language Channel 34.

In 1994, he directed and starred in the low-budget *A Million to Juan.* Although it met with modest success, it presented something rare in U.S. films, a supportive Chicano father with a young son. He was able to get cameo appearances from Edward James Olmos, Cheech Marin, Rubén Blades, Pepe Serna, Tony Plana, and Evelina Fernández even though he had only a $500,000 budget. He said, "These people worked on scale. I called upon all my friends and reminded them that every time they asked me to be in one of their functions, parties, or quinceañeras I had been there and would continue to be there. So ... after this movie is out I'm booked: I'm going to host parties, I'll be sweeping floors and I'll be waxing Cheech Marin's car."[210] The *Los Angeles Times* noted of the film, "Paul Rodriguez, the comic actor and stand-up artist, is a funny man on TV and the stage. In *A Million to Juan,* he's trying to be touching. Very loosely based on Mark Twain's story The Million Pound-Note, it's not particularly funny and it's touching in the get-out-the-handkerchiefs mode."[211]

He played an overenthusiastic car salesman in Richard Benjamin's comedy *Made in America* (1994) with Ted Danson and Whoopi Goldberg.

On the content of his comedy, Rodriguez commented, "I'm not here to capitalize on white guilt. I live and let live. But my career is to stand on the stage and say one or two meaningful things."[212] About his goals, he stated, "I'm trying to become a film star and it's a difficult thing because the people in power don't see me or the Latino community as a whole, as a viable profitable option in spite of the numbers. They must be blind or something."[213]

His most recent films include *Price of Glory* (1998); *Melting Pot* (1999); *Tortilla Soup* (2000); *Ali* (2001); *Chasing Papi* (2002); *Beverly Hills Chihuahua* (2008—voice); *The Deported* (2009); and *Without Men* (2011). He continues to tour for comedy performances and appear in top-rated television shows.

María Rojo

Beginning in the 1990s, the Mexican-born María Rojo became Mexico's most respected and versatile actress of film, television and theater. It was during this period that she was contracted for one fact-based U.S. film.

María Rojo was born in Mexico City in 1944. She made her film debut at the age of 11 in Rafael Baledón's *Besos Prohibidos* in 1956. She appeared on Mexican television in *El Teatro Fantástico,* directed by Ernesto Alonso. She made her theater debut in a play entitled *La Mala Semilla* (*The Bad Seed*). She went on to study drama at the University of Veracruz.

She had her first adult role in the film *Los Recuerdos del Porvenir* in 1968, which was directed by Arturo Ripstein. She gradually worked her way from small roles to second leads and finally to starring roles while working with some of Mexico's best directors, like Jorge Fons, María Novarro, and Jaime Humberto Hermosillo.

Among her most important films are Felipe Cazals' *Las Poquianchis* (1976); Jaime Humberto Hermosillo's *Naufragio* (1977); *Intimidades en un Cuarto de Baño* (1990); *La Tarea* (1990) and *La Tarea Prohíbida* (1992); Paul Leduc's *Complot Petrolero: La Cabeza de la Hidra* (1981); María Navarro's *Danzón* (1990) and *Otoñal* (1992); Jorge Fons' *Rojo Amanecer* (1989); and *Callejón de Milagros* (1994).

She made her U.S. film debut in the role of Maria, the wife of Pedro J. González in Isaac Artenstein's *Break of Dawn* (1988, Platform). The film won critical praise at a number of film festivals and has become a key film of the 1980s in depicting Mexican/Chicano history. The *L.A. Weekly* commented, "*Break of Dawn* is an eminently bi-national film. Óscar Chávez and María Rojo (who play Pedro and his wife) are both stars in Mexico—and do a fine job here. Actors from El Norte and El Sur meet in a bilingual script in which the dialogue for the Spanish-speaking actors flows in and out of both languages fluidly."[214]

One of Rojo's more recent successes was the Mexican film *Esmeralda Viene de Noche/ Esmeralda Comes by Night* (1998), directed by Jaime Humberto Hermosillo, who had directed her in several other important films. The *Los Angeles Times* commented of her performance, "Last seen in the U.S. in *Danzón*, Rojo, a major star of the Mexican stage as well as its cinema and frequent Hermosillo collaborator, is clearly having the time of her life playing a lovely woman who gets away with a Marilyn Monroe wardrobe while admitting she's 42. Indeed, it was she who brought famed Mexican writer Elena Ponitowska's short story upon which the film is based to Hermosillo's attention in the first place. *Esmeralda Comes by Night* would be a treat any time of the day."[215]

Her films include *Los Cachorros* (1971); *El Castillo de la Pureza* (1972); *El Apando* (1975); *Nuevo Mundo* (1976); *Lo Mejor de Teresa* (1976); *La Aparencias Engañan* (1977); *Idilio* (1978); *La Víspera* (1982); *Confidencias* (1982); *Bajo la Metralla* (1982); *El Corazón de la Noche* (1983); *Robachicos* (1985); *Viaje al Paraiso* (1985); *Los Inocentes* (1986); *Lo Que Importa es Vivir* (1986); *Los Confines* (1988); *Día de Difuntos* (1988); *Me Llaman la Chata Aguayo*

(1988); *Morir en el Golfo* (1989); *El Otro Crímen* (1989); *Vai Tabalhar Vagabundo II* (1989); *La Sombra del Cipres es Alargada* (1989); *La Leyenda de una Máscara* (1990); *Encuentro Inesperado* (1991); *Tequila* (1992); and *Los Vuelcos del Corazón* (1993).

Her recent film credits include *El Atentado* (2010) and a hugely successful satire about the drug cartels, *El Infierno* (2011). She has appeared in numerous Mexican *telenovelas*. Not since Silvia Pinal has Mexican cinema had such a versatile actress of theater, television and film.

More recently, she entered politics as Partido de la Revolucion Democratica candidate. She was elected Senator of the Republic in the upper house of the Mexican Congress, serving from September 15, 2003, to September 14, 2006.

CHARLIE SHEEN

The second son of actor Martin Sheen (Estevez) to reach film stardom during the 1980s was Charlie Sheen. Blessed with matinee idol good looks, he has specialized in roles of troubled loners who are destroyed when they succumb to their dark side.

He was born Carlos Irwin Estevez in Santa Monica, California, on September 3, 1965. He is three years younger than his also famous brother, Emilio Estevez. He made his film debut at the age of nine in the television film *The Execution of Private Slovik* (1974), which starred his father, Martin Sheen. He played an extra in Francis Ford Coppola's *Apocalypse Now* (1979) with Marlon Brando, and his father once again. His first substantial role came in the low-budget horror film *Grizzly II* (1984). He was especially effective as a regret-filled youth whose best friend has committed suicide in the excellent television film *Silence of the Heart* (1984) with Silvana Gallardo and Mariette Hartley. He also appeared in another television movie with his father, *Out of the Darkness* (1985, CBS). His father advised him, "Look, Charlie, don't become a classroom actor. Don't do things by the book. As an actor, things just happen. You have to learn to trust yourself."[216]

On the big screen, he began to get costarring roles in a diverse assortment of films: the abysmal jingoistic Cold War fantasy *Red Dawn* (1984, Metro-Goldwyn-Mayer/United Artists) with Patrick Swayze; *The Boy Next Door* (1985, New World), in which he played a rebel without a cause; John Hughes' cult film *Ferris Bueller's Day Off* (1986, Orion), as another wayward youth, opposite Matthew Broderick; *Wisdom* (1986, 20th Century–Fox), written, directed and starring his brother Emilio Estevez and costarring Demi Moore; David Seltzer's *Lucas* (1986, 20th Century–Fox); and he played the lead in *The Wrath* (1986, NCP), a supernatural thriller.

At this juncture, he catapulted to stardom by playing the lead role of Chris, whose loss of innocence becomes a nightmare, in Oliver Stone's powerful and uncompromising tale about the Vietnam War, *Platoon* (1986, Orion). The film garnered four Academy Awards, including Best Picture. When asked about the changes that came with his stardom he stated, "Sometimes you just want to vanish ... to disappear in a puff of smoke one day or be shot out of the universe like a watermelon seed. You go through a weirdness stage, and then you settle down. Now I'm trying to make all the right decisions."[217]

His next films were Peter Werner's atmospheric crime drama *No Man's Land* (1987, Orion) and the comedy *Three for the Road* (1987, NCV) with Sally Kellerman. Oliver Stone cast him again for another important role, that of Bud Fox, a stockbroker corrupted by power and money, in *Wall Street* (1987, 20th Century–Fox), opposite Michael Douglas, Terence Stamp and Martin Sheen. The film was a huge critical and commercial success and further propelled him into the superstar realm.

He followed that movie with the role of a desperado in Christopher Cain's offbeat retelling of the Billy the Kid legend, *Young Guns* (1988, 20th Century–Fox), with his brother Emilio Estevez as the notorious Kid. The film was a commercial, if not a critical, success, as was his next film, John Sayles' evocative tale of a baseball scandal, *Eight Men Out* (1988, Orion). He returned to baseball in David Ward's contemporary tale of a rookie trying to survive in *Major League* (1989, Paramount) and then played a green cop being shown the ropes by a grizzled veteran in *The Rookie* (1990, Warner Bros.), opposite Clint Eastwood (who also directed) as they pursued a ruthless duo of thieves (Sônia Braga, Raúl Juliá). Asked about his experience of working with Eastwood, Sheen stated, "Well, Clint's a different story. 'Cause he's Clint, you know? He's directed sixteen movies. He's just a whole different level. It's really hard to explain. I haven't seen him panic on the show once about anything. He just grooves. He's already cut the sequence in his head. And he's great with actors because, you know, he's Clint. Clint Eastwood is the very definition of cool."[218]

About his famous father and brother, he commented, "We've always had this tremendously grounded family life. Yeah, family is very much what our family is about. We're very supportive of each other's work—even when we don't love the films."[219]

Charlie Sheen (aka Carlos Estevez) in *Wall Street* (1987, 20th Century–Fox).

In *Men at Work* (1990), he was reunited with his brother Emilio who wrote, directed and costarred. The film was about two Redondo Beach garbage collectors involved in a toxic waste dumping scam. Charlie noted, "We had a great time doing it. Emilio did a great job in all three departments. Which I don't know how he did, really. I don't have the capacity right now to write, direct and act in the same picture. I think I'm ready to direct, but I couldn't appear in it, too."[220] Sheen's next film, *Navy Seals* (1990), met with only modest success.

He was directed in *Cadence* (1991, Movie Group) by his father, Martin Sheen, who also costarred. Charlie played a young man pressured into joining the army by a discipline-minded father. The *Los Angeles Daily News* wrote, "Though *Cadence* offers the expected liberal and anti-military pieties, it does so lucidly and, for the most part, with convincing good humor and a minimum of hand-wringing." Charlie said of the role, "It's about locating some salvation and coming of age."[221]

His film stardom appears to have influenced him in a self-destructive manner, although he has made numerous efforts to rehabilitate himself. In a recent interview, he commented, "I thought there was an improvement physically. I think I looked a lot cleaner. I'm fortunate to recognize what may have been a problem and nip it, although I wasn't on the verge of checking into the Betty Ford Clinic, or any of that. You dabble in these negative areas, you exorcise certain demons, and you walk away."[222]

His 1990s films include *Courage Mountain* (1990); *Hot Shots* (1991); *National Lampoon's Loaded Weapon I* (1993); *Hot Shots! Part Deux* (1993); *The Three Musketeers* (1993); *Terminal Velocity* (1994, HP); *Major League II* (1994, Warner Bros.); *All Dogs Go to Heaven 2* (1996, Metro-Goldwyn-Mayer); and *The Arrival* (1996, Orion).

He had a surprise and long-overdue hit with the comedy-drama *Money Talks* (1997) with newcomer comic Chris Tucker. During 2000, he replaced the ailing Michael J. Fox in the popular television comedy *Spin City*. During the period 2003 to 2011, he starred in the CBS comedy *Two and a Half Men*. The show went on to become very successful and Sheen became the highest paid actor on television. However, during 2011, his increasing notoriety due to alleged sex scandals and alcohol and drug use led to his being fired from the show. In 2012, he made a successful return to TV with the lead role in the television comedy series *Anger Management*.

Recent film credits include *Scary Movie 3* (2003); *Scary Movie 4* (2006): and *Wall Street: Money Never Sleeps* (2010).

TRINIDAD SILVA

Chicano character actor Trinidad Silva was busy in the 1980s. He specialized in playing fast-talking, sleazy oddballs, small-time crooks and *veterano* homeboys.

He was born on January 30, 1950, in Mission, Texas. He moved to Los Angeles, California, in 1975, and the first time he visited a film set he found himself recruited as an extra.

On television, he won critical acclaim playing the recurring role of Jesús in the popular *Hill Street Blues*. His film credits included Robert M. Young's *Alambrista!* (1976), which chronicled the odyssey of a Mexican undocumented worker and his ultimate disillusionment with the American dream; *Walk Proud* (1979, Universal) with Robby Benson utterly miscast as a Chicano gang member, in which Silva's performance was the best thing; *The Jerk* (1979, Universal) with Steve Martin; *Second Thoughts* (1983, Universal) with Lucie Arnaz; Louis Malle's *Crackers* (1984, Universal) with Donald Sutherland and Sean Penn; Gregory Nava's *El Norte* (1984, CIIA), as a sleazy motel manager; and Robert Redford's *The Milagro Beanfield War* (1988, Universal) with Sônia Braga and Rubén Blades.

Silva played the *veterano vato loco* Frog in Dennis Hopper's controversial *Colors* (1988, Orion) about Chicano and black gangs. He earned his best notices in this role, and commented, "What I like about Frog is his redeeming love for his brother. He's not a hard-core criminal. He got into the gangs out of circumstances. And while he's loyal to his homeboys, he knows that you don't have to be in a gang to be somebody."[223]

His other films include the comedy *The Night Before* (1988, KRE) with Lori Laughlin and Keanu Reeves; *UHF* (1989, Orion) with Kevin McCarthy; and the television film *Stones for Ibarra* (1990) with Glenn Close.

Trinidad Silva was killed in an auto accident when he was hit by a drunken driver on August 2, 1988, in Los Angeles, California. He was survived by his wife Sofia and his son Samuel.

RACHEL TICOTIN

One of the few Latina actresses at the brink of film stardom at the end of the 1980s was the serene beauty Rachel Ticotin.

She was born in the Bronx, New York, on November 1, 1958, one of six children, to a Puerto Rican mother, the former Iris Torres, an employee of the Board of Education bilingual department, and a Russian Jewish father, a car salesman. She would recall later, "We all got interested in show business one summer when I was nine and our mother heard about a summer program called *Operation High Hopes!* with a free lunch. We loved it. Our appetites were whetted and we all wanted to keep taking lessons."[224]

Dance was the center of her life before acting and she became a member of New York's Ballet Hispanico. She attended the High School of Music and Art and became a member of Tina Ramirez' dance company.

She made her film debut in a small role in *King of the Gypsies* (1978) with Sterling Hayden and Shelley Winters on the recommendation of her mentor, choreographer Julie Arenal.

Rachel Ticotin and Paul Newman in *Fort Apache, The Bronx* (1981, 20th Century–Fox). Ticotin was born of Puerto Rican and Russian Jewish ancestry. She has had a long and prominent career in both film and television.

She was given another small role in the New York City gang film *The Wanderers* (1979, Orion) with Karen Allen and Ken Wahl. She worked as a "gofer" or production assistant on Martin Scorsese's *Raging Bull* (1980) and Brian De Palma's *Dressed to Kill* (1980).

In 1981, she landed the role of Isabella in Daniel Petrie's *Fort Apache, the Bronx* (1981), after attending an open casting call in which some 500 Latina-looking actresses also auditioned.[225]

She later said about the experience, "You go to open calls, all of the time thinking like it isn't fair, and nothing ever comes from these things. But they do."[226] In the film, she played a Puerto Rican nurse who is hooked on heroin and who has an affair with a down-and-out cop (Paul Newman). The cast included Pam Grier, Kathleen Beller, Edward Asner, and Ken Wahl.

She said of her role, "People complained that a person could not have a 9 to 5 job, and take drugs, which is an absolute lie. I did some research, and all the people that I talked to did that. You can be a very sane person and still destroy yourself."[227] The film proved controversial nevertheless in some quarters and was criticized and picketed as presenting stereotypes of Puerto Ricans and African Americans. The film was a moderate critical and commercial success. *Box-Office* noted, "Rachel Ticotin etches a memorable portrait of a tortured young woman who can't escape the curse of growing up in the streets."[228] *Playboy* commented, "Wahl registers like a rising star. So does newcomer Rachel Ticotin, vulnerable and credible as the Puerto Rican nurse."[229]

She was next employed by her mentor Julie Arena to serve as dance assistant in Arthur Penn's *Four Friends* (1981). Although she had made a strong impression in *Fort Apache, The Bronx,* no roles were forthcoming for almost four years. In 1983, she was cast as the part–Latina Corporal Grace Paulik in NBC's short-lived series *For Love and Honor,* about paratroopers in peacetime. She starred in two other short-lived series: *O'Hara* (1987–88, ABC); and *Crime and Punishment* (1993, NBC).

She has starred in several television films: *Love, Mary* (1985, CBS) with Piper Laurie; *Rockabye* (1986, CBS) with Valerie Bertinelli; *When the Bough Breaks* (1986) with Ted Danson; and *Spies, Lies and Naked Thighs* (1986). She was then cast in the female lead in Michael Apted's moderately successful comedy *Critical Condition* (1987, Paramount) opposite Richard Pryor and Rubén Blades.

In 1990, she costarred in HBO's trilogy *Doing Time: Women in Prison* opposite Silvana Gallardo. Also that year she played the female lead in Paul Verhoeven's adventure tale set in the year 2084 A.D. entitled *Total Recall* (1990) opposite Arnold Schwarzenegger and Sharon Stone. The $60–$70 million dollar blockbuster was shot in twenty-two weeks at Churubusco Studios in Mexico City. The film was honored with a Special Achievement Academy Award for the spectacular special effects. The film went on to become a huge commercial success. Ticotin said of the film role, "My character may not be as strong as his, but she's bright and capable of figuring out how to get out of a jam. All the running and jumping and shooting made me feel like a tomboy again."[230] Of her performance, *Newsweek* noted, "A lot of fun is provided by the two female leads, the good Melina (Rachel Ticotin) and the bad Lori (Sharon Stone)."[231]

Regarding Latinos in films, she stated, "Let's face it, there just aren't that many parts out there for my type of look, my color skin. Sometimes I think, 'Why can't they just cast a person? No one, for example, can tell me I can't play a Jew. When you go to Israel, you see a lot of Spanish people who are also not blonde and blue-eyed. There's so much typecasting that goes on. But if you're blond and blue-eyed, your range is limitless."[232]

Her 1990s films include the Canadian-lensed *FX 2* (1991, HP); the crime drama *One Good Cop* (1991, HP) with Michael Keaton; the somber *Where the Day Takes You* (1992, NLC); and John Schumacher's *Falling Down* (1993) with Michael Douglas and Barbara Hershey, in which she was excellent as the tough Chicana cop. She was ill-used in the mediocre *Steal Big, Steal Little* (1995) with Andy García and fared better in a supporting role in *Don Juan DeMarco* (1995, NLC) with Marlon Brando and Faye Dunaway. She was excellent in another supporting role as a Latina prison guard in the commercial hit *Con Air* (1997) with Nicolas Cage.

Recent film credits include *Full Disclosure* (2001); *Man on Fire* (2004); *The Eye* (2008); and *America* (2011). She has guest-starred extensively on television shows and has been a regular on *Law and Order: L.A.* (2010–11).

Ticotin was married and divorced from actor David Caruso and they have one daughter, Greta.

Luis Valdez

One of the key forces responsible for the emergence of a positive Chicano and Latino image in theater and film is the gifted playwright, actor, screenwriter, film director and social activist Luis Valdez.

He was born in Delano, California, on July 26, 1940, to a family of migrant farm workers. He has nine brothers and sisters. His younger brother is singer-actor Daniel Valdez. Luis began working in the fields at the age of six. His schooling was often sporadic in the San Joaquin Valley, but he completed high school and then obtained a scholarship to California State University, San José. He recalled how he was inspired to become a playwright: "I was six years old. I was a member of a migrant family. We were doing a play in school. And a week or two before we actually did the show we were forced out of the camp and we had to leave. We couldn't stay and I couldn't be in the play. So as I say, for more than 50 years I've been trying to fill an unfillable gap."[233]

At college, he wrote his first full-length play. He graduated with a B.A. in English in 1964 and then joined the renowned San Francisco Mime Troupe. In 1965, he went back to Delano to assist Cesar Chavez, who was in the process of forming a migrant farm workers union. Valdez founded El Teatro Campesino in order to organize and educate farm workers and supporters. It was made up of an assortment of amateur performers, musicians and union organizers, the majority of them migrant farm workers. They staged their actos (self-contained, short theater acts) in the back of trucks, in open fields, churches, community centers, and schools. He recollected later, "I had a vision of the farm workers' theater; I think when I was in San Francisco. It's an epiphany, you know, that one of those flashes can occur in your life. And I actually saw a truck. I remember the colors were yellow and brown, with lettering saying *Teatro Campesino*. The Farm Workers, Cesar [Chavez], and Dolores [Huerta] and their leadership and the strike, particularly the *huelga* [the famous grape strike of the United Farm Workers union] gave us a very clear focus. I mean it was, we had a subject matter. It was really a matter of just defining how we were going to go about it."[234]

Increasingly, Valdez injected other issues into his actos like racism, the Vietnam War, the emerging Chicano movement, education and the plight of undocumented workers. Among his early plays were: *Actos, Bernabé*, and *The Shrunken Head of Pancho Villa*. In 1966, El Teatro Campesino began touring throughout the United States. In 1969 and 1972, it performed in the World Theatre Festival in Nancy, France. El Teatro Campesino was instrumental in the creation and proliferation of Chicano *teatros* throughout the U.S. Southwest and in fostering cultural pride and social consciousness. For historic achievement, Valdez was honored with the 1968 Obie Award in New York for the founding of El Teatro Campesino and its demonstration of the politics of survival. In 1970, he was given the Los Angeles Critics Award for his *Actos* and *Mitos,* and in 1971 he won the Drama Critics Award for *Corridos.*

One of his early actos, *Los Vendidos,* was adapted into a PBS special in the late 1960s. In 1967, Luis and Daniel Valdez produced and narrated what became known as the first Chicano film, which was based on Rodolfo "Corky" González's epic poem of the same name, *I Am Joaquin*. In 1987, Luis played the omnipresent narrator in *Corridos,* which aired over PBS and featured Linda Rondstadt and Alma Martínez. Valdez said of the *teatro*, "It's about grounding. The *Teatro* is the roots of a tree. It's been important to me. Otherwise I would have been fried to a crisp by all the attention."[235]

In 1978, he wrote and directed the play *Zoot Suit* at the Los Angeles Mark Taper Forum to great critical and commercial success. The play earned him another Los Angeles Critics Award. The play subsequently had a short run on Broadway. In 1982 he scripted and directed the film adaptation of *Zoot Suit* (1983, Universal) with most of the stage cast repeating their roles. Valdez made the film in just thirteen days on a $1.3 million dollar budget.[236] When I asked him why he thought the play had resonated powerfully within the Chicano community, he stated, "There's something about the art, there's something about a play or a movie or a song or a painting that verifies reality. It is because people go along living their lives and they're not sure if they lived or not. They're not sure if they saw that or not. But if something comes along that registers the collective memory and then records it in a way that it can be reviewed and seen and talked about that that stuff is real. At least it's incorporated into the notion of reality. I think what happened with *Zoot Suit* is that it took the *pachuco* consciousness, part of the Chicano movement, but also made it part of the collective California experience, of the Los Angeles experience. So that in that sense the play justified its own experience as an American play."[237]

He had previously made his acting film debut in Michael Schultz' effective satirical comedy *Which Way Is Up?* (1977) opposite Richard Pryor and Luis' brother Daniel. He recalled in one interview about the experience, "We started talking about this project and he [Schultz] told me about a character he wanted to develop as a Chicano. And the character was basically a sidekick for Richard Pryor.... And so I was intrigued with the possibility and it was about campesinos and he showed me an early draft and they had a Cesar Chavez character in it as well.... I wrote some of the screenplay and it got down to casting and Michael asked me if I wanted to play the Cesar Chavez type. I said sure. I was glad to do it. We cast a number of the people of the Teatro."[238]

In 1987, he scripted and directed one of the most successful Chicano-themed films, *La Bamba* (Columbia). The film told the story of Chicano rocker and pioneer Ritchie Valens

(Valenzuela), who died in a plane crash at the age of seventeen with Buddy Holly and the Big Bopper. He said of this breakthrough film, "I understand that show business is a business, but it seems to me there is social responsibility no matter how much money is being made. *La Bamba* has proven that audiences will respond to the simple, honest truth about people, and if Hollywood has any decency and courage to represent Hispanics as human beings, there is a profit to be made."[239]

The film took almost ten years to get done. He recalled how he and his brother conceived the idea for the film: "The first idea for *La Bamba* was as a theater piece. Actually, I was sitting in Danny's dressing room on Broadway, before the *Zoot Suit* opening. And I was saying, we should come back with a musical. We've done the '40s, let's do the '50s. What can we do in the '50s? We can do rock and roll. Who can.... Well, Richie Valens. Right there on the spot. And then we can do a number, we can do *La Bamba* and do his story."[240]

Of his Hollywood experience, he commented, "I like Hollywood, you know, in its own way, because it is such a metaphor for American society as a whole ... [Hollywood] is just this concentrated swirl. I'm not particularly attracted to the frills, the fluff, showing up in the right places and being seen with the right people."[241]

He has continued to work with El Teatro Campesino and has talked of establishing a production company, "I couldn't turn around and kiss the *Teatro Campesino* goodbye without ruining my chances in Hollywood. My roots would dry up. I need to be true to what I set out to do. I set out to work on a problem twenty-five years ago in the theatre, to create an environment, a context for me to exist as a Chicano playwright. As it turns out, it wasn't just for me, it was for a lot of other people. And that's great."[242] When asked about what *teatro* was to him, he responded, "The *teatro* is the live art. It is in reality, the presence of the actors, the presence of our history, memories and images."[243]

Despite the overwhelming success of *La Bamba*, which grossed more than $100 million on a $6.5 million budget, he encountered reluctance from studios regarding financial backing for another of his film projects. He commented, "Producers are very cautious. You still hear too often the refrain: 'I don't know how to market this material.' Which is fine because it just opens up more opportunities for me and others. The Hispanic community in the U.S. spends $170 billion a year, $10 million a day in Los Angeles."[244]

In reference to Latinos and Hollywood, he commented, "Our culture is rich.... We have an enormous richness.... It is a universal value. What we are trying to do, those of us who work in Hollywood is to exploit this richness ... so that all of us enjoy it."[245]

Of his future goals, he said, "A lot of what I have been working on has to do with history. As a Latino I have been attempting to recapture those lost periods in American history that have to do with Latinos and that nobody knows anything about. *Zoot Suit* was about that. *La Bamba* was about that. And many of these projects are about that as well. I want to show that there's more to the Sunbelt than Southwest furniture and Mexican food."[246]

A proposed film about Mexican painter Frida Kahlo aroused a storm of protest in the Chicano community when an Italian-American actress was cast in the title role. The project was subsequently shelved. Later it would be resurrected by actress Salma Hayek and finally made into a critical and commercial success in 2002.

In 1994, Valdez directed a new version of *The Cisco Kid* for TNT with Jimmy Smits as the Kid and Cheech Marin as his sidekick. Valdez did an effective cameo as President

Benito Juárez. The *Los Angeles Times* noted about the film, "Without detracting too much from Cisco movie lore, this new 'kid' on the block shows true signs of the 90's. Director and co-writer Luis Valdez (*Zoot Suit, La Bamba*) has eliminated the bandido stereotype entirely. Like Batman, Cisco is independently wealthy and doesn't have to steal from anybody.... The plot bogs down toward the end; it is, after all, a 'Perils of Pauline'–like cartoon. But here, in a rare instance, is a TV movie for Latino families that Latino children can warm up to."[247]

The film was shot in the colonial towns of Zacatecas and Sombrerete, in Zacatecas, Mexico. Valdez commented, "I have thoroughly enjoyed interacting with Mexican crews.... This has been a watershed year."[248] Of his role as Benito Juárez, he said, "He is one of the great democratic heroes of the Americas ... I have identified with him since I was a kid.... At 18, I started to grow a mustache to emphasize my Mexican heritage.... It has become part of my permanent image. But now, I no longer need a mustache to affirm my Mexican heritage."[249]

Nevertheless, as with all Latino filmmakers, the Hollywood film industry continues to exclude his talent. He commented, "I'm willing to work still for low budgets if have to, provided I get the freedom. As other Latinos have discovered in Hollywood, I have casting problems, because there aren't enough established Latinos in Hollywood that can open movies for me. But the thing is that given my age, that I'm 59 years old, given the place where I started on the picket line for Cesar [Chavez] I'm not going to be making *What's New Pussycat*, you know what I mean? It's just in the works for me. I don't have to wait to be in a blacklist. I'm in a brown list, and the fact that I have a Latino last name already demotes me, just like it demotes every [Latino] actor, writer, producer, and designer, in Hollywood.[250]

"And so, let's be very clear, in your writing the book, that if I haven't made films it's not because I haven't wanted to. It is because I have not been able to. Which was, I think, Cesar's concern years ago when we talked about doing his life story. He asked, how are you going to pull it off? He knew what I was up against. He said, I don't think they'll let you tell the story. But my own solution is to continue writing scripts. And if I don't produce them maybe somebody else will. But don't be surprised if there's a little waiting period here, while people get used to the idea that you have been around okay. Chances are, by the time people really get hip to what I've done, I won't be on earth anymore. You know, I'll be gone by the time they say, okay, now he's safe, because he's dead."[251]

Sadly, Luis Valdez' creative energies have not translated into an enduring presence in film. His long-term project of making a film about labor leader and close friend Cesar Chavez did not come to fruition. Ultimately, the much-anticipated film about Cesar Chavez was directed by Mexican actor and director Diego Luna. It was released nationally in March 2014.

During October 2000, Valdez premiered his new play, *Mummified Deer,* at the San Diego Repertory Theatre to wide acclaim. He continues to write plays, screenplays, and television projects.

VI

The 1990s

The 1990s brought profound changes to the world at large, politically, economically, and culturally. The decade also marked two important historical events, the 500th anniversary of the European incursion or intrusion into the American continent and the advent of the millennium. Much was said and written about the rich diversity of the American fabric. All this notwithstanding, in U.S. cinema and television, Latinos had become an endangered species.

The Cold War came to an abrupt end early in the decade. The immediate impact of this pivotal event was the demilitarization and betterment of relations between the United States and the former Soviet Union. This was followed by the collapse of the socialist governments of Eastern Europe and the Soviet-backed Warsaw Pact. These events were cause for elation in the hearts and minds of many who trumpeted the triumph of the market economy. The end of the Cold War tension and nuclear buildups was cause for genuine celebration for most. However, even as the planet moved into the globalization of the world economy and the era of post-nation-states, most people in the Third World lived a marginalized and impoverished existence.

In Latin America, the market economy's failure was glaringly obvious from Haiti to Mexico to Brazil. Poverty, illiteracy, disease, malnutrition, unemployment, inflation, and recession ravaged all the Latin American nations. The 1990s brought the insurgencies in Nicaragua, El Salvador and Guatemala to an end. Some of the worst of the murderous and predatory regimes in Latina America, like Argentina and Chile, were compelled by the mass civil resistance and economic downturns to a political reconciliation and a democratic process. The year 1992 marked the 500th anniversary of Columbus's fateful voyage which in its wake brought genocide against the native people through disease, slavery and conquest on an unprecedented scale. When the long-anticipated First Continental Meeting of Indigenous Peoples took place at Quito, Ecuador, during the summer of 1990, one Guatemalan Native American delegate noted, "These 500 years have meant nothing but misery and oppression for our people. What do we have to celebrate?"[1] Others shared a similar historical assessment. For example, environmentalist Kirkpatrick Sale in his book *The Conquest of Paradise* wrote, "Columbus's landing and subsequent behavior [served] as the model for later explorers who plundered the New World for gold and set in place a civilization that committed genocide and 'ecocide' against the natives and their environment."[2]

Much of the latter part of the decade was focused on the pressing issue of "ethnic cleansing," especially the one taking place in Yugoslavia. Nevertheless, the same ethnic cleansing on an even greater scale in Latin America remained ignored until well after the tragedy of genocide had taken place. Such was the case in Guatemala, where an armed conflict had been taking place for some thirty-six years. The Truth Commission established under Guatemala's peace accords presented a 3,500-page report on human rights violations documenting that some 200,000 people had been killed. The document determined that some eighty-three percent of said victims were Mayans. It went on to state that the violence was "fundamentally directed by the state against the excluded, the poor, and above all, the Mayan people, as well as against those who fought for justice and greater social equity." According to the *Boston Globe*, "In presenting the report, Christina Tomuschat, the commission's coordinator, delivered a withering critique of the role played by the United States, particularly the CIA and the military, in contributing to the human rights violations detailed in the report."[3]

In the U.S., a series of exclusionary propositions that began in California and spread across the country were directed primarily at Latinos, especially Mexicans (both documented and undocumented) in an asphyxiating climate of xenophobia. Under the helm of George H. W. Bush, the conservative shift continued. Bush's vision of the "New World Order" included gunboat diplomacy and intervention in Panama and Iraq, as well as vetoing the extension of the Civil Rights Act. He postured as the "Education President." The trillion-dollar deficit remained unchecked. The subsequent Clinton administration jump-started the economy for almost a decade, but it became involved in a series of military interventions abroad.

In the meantime, the 1990 U.S. Census revealed that the Latino population was fast becoming the largest minority in the nation. In 1980, African Americans numbered 26.5 million, as compared to 14.6 million Latinos/Hispanics. By 1990, African Americans numbered just under 20 million, while at the same time Latinos had grown to 22.3 million. Some 70 percent of the Latino population lived in four states: Texas, California, Florida, and New York.[4] Notwithstanding the demographics, the data compiled by the American Council on Education noted the worsening condition of Latinos: "The study ... showed that the proportion of Latino students completing high school slid from 60.1 percent in 1984 to 55.9 in 1989.... In 1976, Latinos represented just 2.8 percent of all those earning bachelor degrees. In 1989, that figure has increased only to 3 percent—despite the doubling of the college-age Latino population during that time."[5]

Ironically, as Latinos became increasingly visible in every part of the nation, they virtually disappeared from films and television.

Film Images and Film Stars

The rising expectations of Latinos for a real and sustained breakthrough in U.S. films failed to take place. The emerging Chicano and Cuban-American cinema of the 1980s faltered badly during the 1990s. Not only did Latinos virtually disappear from film, but the few roles that remained were stereotypical and negative. The demographic changes taking place made no dent on the narrow and ethnocentric ethos of the Hollywood film industry.

The prevailing film images of Latinos during the 1990s closely mirrored the media news coverage about Latinos, which focused on four areas: immigration, drugs, welfare, and crime. Thus Latino male stereotypes were *narcotraficantes*/drug dealers, gang members, undocumented workers, or bandits. Latinas found themselves inevitably cast as prostitutes or *cantineras* whenever some inane summer movie featured the proverbial "rites of passage" scene for some cherubic European-American teenager, or when a "good ol' boy" contingent of marines wanted some sexual gratification.

Similarly, television reflected the same disdain for the reality in the nation. *Time* wrote, "Picture an America where friendly, funky, Cub-fan-fanatic Chicago is the only inhabited spot between New York City and Twin Peaks. Imagine that this mythical U.S. has become so awash in racial sensitivity and tolerance that even drug dealers practice affirmative action, yet, strangely enough, intergalactic aliens are a far more visible minority group than Hispanics."[6] An example of this was the new *Zorro* television series which premiered during January 1990. The character had been created by Johnston McCulley and had been first dramatized in film by Douglas Fairbanks in the 1920s in *The Mark of Zorro*. The new television Zorro was portrayed by Duncan Regehr, a non–Latino performer. The casting followed the well-worn proverb that the more things change the more they remain the same. The Zorro character was yet to be played by a Mexican-origin actor or a Latino.

An even more negative image of Latinos, specifically Mexicans, was in the NBC miniseries entitled *Drug Wars: The Camarena Story* (1990), which purported to depict the story of DEA agent Kiki Camarena, his 1984 kidnapping and eventual murder by a drug cartel. Although shot on location in Mexico, it portrayed all Mexicans as either corrupt government officials or as *narcotraficantes*. The Mexican government subsequently denounced the miniseries. Soon thereafter, NBC liberally substituted news for entertainment. *La Opinión* perceptively commented, "Without a shred of shame, NBC promoted *Drug Wars* like a chapter of the so-called war against drugs, in which Noriega had just been taken prisoner."[7] An NBC anchorman stated unequivocally that "in some cases we need to invade some countries." The message was not subtle: Latin American countries are incapable of governing their affairs of state and thereby the neighbor to the north must do it for them.

A refreshingly more accurate representation of the Chicano reality was on display in "Sweet 15" (1990), an episode of the children's show *Wonderworks*, which aired over PBS. The film portrayed the efforts of a hard-working Mexican father (Tony Plana), who is trying to legalize his undocumented status, while his daughter (Karla Montana) approaches a rite of passage with her quinceañera (fifteenth birthday party and social coming-out event).

Feature films displayed a no less reprehensible image of Latinos. In *The Rookie* (1990, Warner Bros.), two European-American cops (Clint Eastwood, Charlie Sheen) find Otherness in the guise of violent Chicano gang members. The *Los Angeles Times* commented, "The top cops' excursions into East Los Angeles are heavy on the Mexican xenophobia."[8] Meanwhile, Chicano/Mexican bandits and *cantineras* proliferated in the western *Bad Jim* (1990), a film whose only redeeming value was the film debut of Clark Gable's son, John Clark Gable. Elsewhere, *Shrimp on the Barbie* (1990) depicted the adventures of a footloose Chicano (Cheech Marin) in Australia. The *Los Angeles Times* wrote, "It's too bad that Marin didn't get to direct the film, for the gifts he displayed as a director (and writer) in 'Born in East L.A.' are just the ones needed here."[9]

Sidney Pollack's *Havana* (1990, Universal) was yet another film on the Cuban Revolution which failed to capture the ethos of the historical event. The *Los Angeles Times* commented that Pollack "seems torn between making a great, old-style, doomed lover's romance and a serious, politically committed epic, and he succeeds at neither."[10] Similarly, *A Show of Force* (1990), directed by Brazilian Bruno Barreto, allegedly portrayed the real-life story of the murder of two Puerto Rican *independistas* after they had been arrested by government forces in Cerro Maravilla, Puerto Rico, in 1978. The coverup that followed resulted in the downfall of the governor's administration. Predictably, the film trivialized the event by adding a contrived romance. The *Los Angeles Times* called it "a political thriller that spins giddily between fact and fancy, shocks and romance, politics and sex" and noted, "Sometimes it's difficult to guess whether the sex is there to sell the politics or vice versa."[11]

Hollywood's ethnocentric scenario of Latin Americans as *narcotraficantes*, corrupt government officials, and masses of childlike peasants seeking deliverance by clean-cut and stalwart European-Americans was put to service in *Delta Force II* (1990, Metro-Goldwyn-Mayer). The film was supposedly about a fictitious Latin American country, but it was really a composite of Panama and Colombia. However, the film was actually shot in the Philippines and was yet another example of Hollywood's utter disregard for cultural and ethnic accuracy. The film featured the perennial Cold Warrior Chuck Norris as the fearless DEA agent out to get a drug lord (Billy Drago). The most significant line of dialogue was uttered by the nation's dictator: "If the United States accuses us of being a country of drug pushers, we accuse them of being a country of drug addicts!" The *Los Angeles Times* wrote, "Characterizations are so cardboard and stereotypical and plotting so trite that there's not enough involvement."[12] By contrast, Paul Verhoeven's futuristic *Total Recall* (1990, TriStar) featured something unprecedented in the science-fiction genre: a bona fide Latina heroine (Rachel Ticotin)!

In *Kiss Me a Killer* (1991), which was obviously influenced by James M. Cain's *The Postman Always Rings Twice*, Julie Carmen and Robert Beltran portrayed an unhappy wife and a drifter, respectively, who plot to murder her European-American husband, the proprietor of a nightclub in East Los Angeles. *The Hollywood Reporter* wrote, "The performances are terrific, especially Carmen as the passionate wife and barmaid. Her transformation from submissive slave to fiery motivator is credible and volcanic.... As the soft-spoken, guitar-plucking Tony, Beltran's performance is well-calibrated and solid."[13]

Although Latino characters may not have been expected to appear as one of Julius Caesar's tribunes or as one of Robin Hood's merry men, common logic would dictate that they would be alive and well in the place where they existed in real life. Nonetheless, according to Hollywood's reel world, Latinos, especially Mexicans, were an extinct species even in Los Angeles! Regardless of the fact that Los Angeles was the second largest Mexican city after Mexico City, no Mexicans or Latinos existed in the Los Angeles where such films such as *L.A. Story* (1991, TriStar), *Doc Hollywood* (1991, Warner Bros.), *Grand Canyon* (1991, 20th Century–Fox) and *Terminator 2: Judgment Day* (1991, TriStar) were based. The latter film featured one Mexican character, but only when the story shifted to Mexico itself. However, it must be remembered that the original film *Terminator* (1984, TriStar), which was also based in Los Angeles, didn't even provide that courtesy. The fact that another futuristic film, *Star Trek VI: The Undiscovered Country* (1991, Paramount) featured a small role for a Latina (Rosanna DeSoto) was a galactic miracle.

Latinos were on display in several television films. Lynda Carter made a return after a long absence as the star of NBC's *Daddy* (1991), based on the Danielle Steel novel. She played a non–Latina role and stated about her comeback, "I had a star attitude before. I wasn't difficult or impossible, but I bought into the attitude that being an actress makes you special.... I'm anxious for the industry to know who Lynda Carter is today. I've grown up. Hopefully, I've put my ego aside!"[14] Rubén Blades portrayed a Mexican-American rancher moonlighting as a school custodian involved with the school principal (Christine Lahti) in the TNT television film *Crazy from the Heart* (1991). In reference to the state of Latinos in film and television, Rubén Blades commented, "They don't come to me if they are going to do a Custer movie and cast me as Custer. They are going to say, 'He is not a North American. How can he play Custer?' But there's no moment of hesitation that someone like William Hurt can play a Latino."[15] He felt that Latinos had a better chance if they "were closer to the Anglo ideal of a leading man.... My position is just cast the roles of talent and try to make it more representative of what it is all about."[16]

During 1991 and 1992, three other television films were afflicted with Latino stereotypes. In *The Last Prostitute*, Sônia Braga portrayed Leah, an allegedly legendary Latina prostitute who is retired from the profession. She is nevertheless doggedly solicited by two pubescent European-American youths for their sexual initiation. In *Lightning Field,* a pregnant woman (Nancy McKeon) is the victim of a violent, devil-worshipping, baby-stealing Latin American cult. The *Los Angeles Times* was compelled to write, "The closest thing to a surprise in this stupefying walk-through of a telepic is the somewhat anachronistic portrayal of anonymously Luciferian Latinos at this late, post-multiculturalist date.... Needless to add, ... *Lightning Field* won't be winning any Golden Eagle Awards from Nosotros."[17] In the NBC miniseries *Drug Wars: The Cocaine Cartel* (1992), Alex McArthur played a typical DEA "good ol' boy" convinced that he will topple the Colombian drug cartel almost single-handedly, reminiscent of the preposterous *The Magnificent Seven*.

During 1991, Cheech Marin produced a comedy for Fox Television entitled *Culture Clash,* which chronicled the tribulations of three Latino comedians (Richard Montoya, Herbert Siguenza, and Rick Salinas). Marin enthusiastically commented, "for one thing, you've never seen that many brown faces on the tube at the same time. We'll be the only Latino show on TV."[18] Not surprisingly, Fox promptly canceled the show even before its scheduled premiere!

In the meantime, ABC's miniseries *Texas,* which was based on the novel by James Michener, complemented the xenophobia and anti–Latino sentiment taking place across the country, especially in California. Howard Rosenberg noted in the *Los Angeles Times*, "From border to border, *James Michener's Texas* is weak storytelling and questionable history.... In this case [there is] an ugly side that, however inadvertently, subtly devalues Latinos and helps nourish an atmosphere of prejudice in which a loose tongue like Howard Stern believes he can get away with using the airwaves to demean the heritage of slain Latina singer Selena. All of this polarizing ethnophobia doesn't emerge in a vacuum, it has a history, a residue of ignorance that has thickened from generation to generation.... But *Texas* is history through the eyes of white people. 'Some day people will live and work and love and prosper in Texas ... your Texas,' Mattie promises Austin when he's in the dumps, the assumption being that the Mexicans and Native Americans already living there are not people. That sounds almost racist. Yet, what the hey, if they don't like it, let them make their own movie."[19]

Meanwhile, in Hollywood feature films it was business as usual. *The Mambo Kings*

(1992, Warner Bros.), based on the Pulitzer Prize–winning novel by Oscar Hijuelos, was undermined of much credibility when, with typical shortsightedness, Antonio Banderas and Armand Assante were cast as the two protagonist Cuban musicians. Similar casting logic was used on another film purporting to document another part of the Cuban-American experience. *The Perez Family* (1995, Samuel Goldwyn) focused on a group of disparate characters, 1980s Mariel boatlift refugees, but the film was totally undermined by a non–Latino cast. The *Los Angeles Times* wrote, "Whenever the performers take center stage, which is most of the time, the films turns into a play-act charade."[20]

In another example of historical amnesia and revisionism, Mexicans suddenly disappeared or became extinct overnight in the Southwest in a quartet of westerns: *Unforgiven* (1992, Warner Bros.), *Posse* (1993, Gramercy Pictures), *Tombstone* (1993, Hollywood Pictures), and *Wyatt Earp* (1994, Warner Bros.). Mexicans were also presumably an extinct species in other films: *Devil in a Blue Dress* (1995, TriStar), which took place in 1948 Los Angeles; *Waiting to Exhale* (1995, 20th Century–Fox), set in New Mexico; and *White Man's Burden* (1995, Savoy), set in Los Angeles. Other like-minded films included *Lethal Weapon 4* (1998, Warner Bros.), which was set in the heart of Los Angeles. But then, a similar pattern of the exclusion of Mexicans and Latinos had been established in *Lethal Weapon* (1987, Warner Bros.), *Lethal Weapon 2* (1989, Warner Bros.), and *Lethal Weapon 3* (1992, Warner Bros.), all of which were based in Los Angeles. Two futuristic films, *Star Trek Generations* (1994, Warner Bros.) and *Star Trek: First Contact* (1997, Paramount) were also seemingly set in a time when there were no Latinos in a single galaxy. In the lone futuristic film that did feature Latinos, *Escape from L.A.* (1997), they were all criminals, low-lifes and degenerates who had contributed to the decay and ruination of the city of Los Angeles.

A subgenre that had a vogue during the 1990s was high school–based films set in the barrio or the inner city. Many featured one solitary European teacher or cultural mentor who single-handedly proceeded to solve all the innate delinquent and dysfunctional behavior of Latino students, without addressing the socioeconomic conditions of their environment. In the film *Dangerous Minds* (1995, Hollywood Pictures), it was one European-American teacher, an ex–Marine (Michelle Pfeiffer), who creates this metamorphosis. Henry Giroux noted about the film, "*Dangerous Minds* functions mythically to rewrite the decline of public schools and the attack on poor black and Hispanic students as part of a broader project for rearticulating 'whiteness' as a model of authority, rationality, and civilized behavior. Racial politics in this film are such that black professionals come off as the real threat to learning and civilized behavior, and whites, of course are simply there to lend support."[21]

In *The Substitute* (1996, Orion), one ex–Special Forces Cold Warrior becomes a substitute teacher when his girlfriend is attacked by a youth gang. He then proceeds to uncover the fact that the African American principal is in league with the Latino students (affiliated with a gang) who are operating a drug ring! In *187* (1999), one traumatized African American teacher relocates to a Los Angeles barrio high school where all the Latino students are vicious gang members, including his best female student, who moonlights as a prostitute. The film's ending perfectly exemplified the simplistic stereotype mentality of the makers of the film. The teacher is compelled to play Russian roulette and kill himself in order to convince the gang members that he is as macho as they are and win their respect! The *Los Angeles Times* noted, "The most disheartening line in '187' is its last, written in bold type across the screen just before the credits roll: 'A teacher wrote this movie.' It's enough to make you weep, and not just because it's painful to think that this muddled and manipulative film was penned by someone in a position to mold impressionable minds."[22]

On a lighter note, *Dance with Me* (1998, Columbia) featured Chayanne (the Puerto Rican recording artist, making his U.S. film debut) winning the heart of a former dance queen (Vanessa Williams) through the body language of his salsa dancing. Meanwhile, in another example of historical revisionism, *Fear and Loathing in Las Vegas* (1998, Universal), which was based on the seminal book of the same name by Hunter S. Thompson, changed the real-life Chicano character Oscar "Zeta" Acosta to a "Samoan or something" named Dr. Gonzo. Acosta was legendary Chicano attorney, activist and writer of two cult books, *Autobiography of a Brown Buffalo* (1972) and *Revolt of the Cockroach People* (1973). One of the most bizarre and stereotypical films about Latinos during the decade was *Perdita Durango* (1999), which followed the criminal adventures of a *cantinera* (Rosie Pérez) and a desperado (Javier Bardem), whose Santería rituals include human sacrifice and sadism. By contrast, Steven Soderbergh's heist caper *Out of Sight* (1998, Universal) featured a Latina federal marshal (Jennifer Lopez) on the trail of an unrepentant thief (George Clooney).

Hollywood films continued with their obsession and stereotype of Latinas as promiscuous sexual objects. In *Money Train* (1995, Columbia), a Latina cop (Jennifer Lopez) is so unprofessional that she makes overtures to her new partner (Wesley Snipes) as soon as she meets him. Bob Rafelson's *Blood & Wine* (1997, Fox Searchlight) featured a duplicitous and scheming Latina (Jennifer Lopez) who drives three men to self-destruction in their desire for her. In *Fled* (1996, Metro-Goldwyn-Mayer), a widowed Latina (Salma Hayek) is unable to control her sexual appetite for an escaped convict (Laurence Fishburne) that she has met. Similarly, a one-night stand between a Mexicana (Salma Hayek) and a yuppie (Matthew Perry) in *Fools Rush In* (1994) results in her pregnancy. Elsewhere, *From Dusk Till Dawn* (1996, Dimension Films) featured only two types of Mexicans: prostitutes and criminals.

Latino criminal elements were alive and well in such film fare as *Falling Down* (1992, Warner Bros.), which featured a disturbed mild-mannered European-American businessman set upon by vicious Latino gang members; Brian De Palma's *Carlito's Way* (1993, Universal), which had a Puerto Rican ex-con (Al Pacino) unable to let go of his criminal habits; *I'm Not Rappaport* (1996, Greene Street), which featured a Latino park punk (Guillermo Díaz) who extorts money from elderly residents; *Con Air* (1997, Touchstone Pictures), which had a serial rapist (Danny Trejo) on board; and *Riot* (1997, Showtime), which showcased Latino looters during the Los Angeles riots of 1992.

Other films depicted the diversity of the Latino experience from other points of view. The yearnings of Chicano adolescence were the subject in three films. Joaquin Perea's independent film *Fish Outta Water* (1994) depicted the friendship between two boys in East Los Angeles, one Chicano and the other European-American. Paul Rodriguez' *A Million to Juan* (1995, Goldwyn/Crystal Sky) revolved around a down-and-out Mexicano trying to legalize his immigration status and provide for his eight-year-old son. A third film focused on the spiritual odyssey of a Chicano migrant youth during the 1950s, Severo Perez's *... And the Earth Did Not Swallow Him* (1995, Kino International).

The independent film *Follow Me Home* (1997), which was directed by first-time director Peter Bratt (brother of actor Benjamin Bratt), told the story of a group of muralists traveling cross-country to paint a mural at the White House. Their journey is cut short by the racial intolerance they confront along the way. *Latin Boys Go to Hell* (1997, Strand Releasing) was a tale about a shy Latino youth trying to determine his sexual orientation. Alfonso Arau's *A Walk in the Clouds* (1995, 20th Century–Fox) was a film about a Chicano wine-growing family in post–World War II California. *The Second Civil War* (1997, HBO) presented an apocalyptic vision of a United States balkanized by ethnicity. The *Los Angeles Times* commented, "This one emerges in a dysfunctional United States of splintered demographics, where the Los Angeles mayor addresses the city in Spanish, Rhode Island is largely Chinese, and Sioux Indians, the Nation of Islam, Crips, Bloods, Irish, Latinos, Sikhs and other groups seek to control the borders of the areas where they live."[23] By contrast, John Sayles' *Lone Star* (1996, Rio Dulce) focused on an ethnically diverse community in a border town in Texas with a more optimistic ethos

Paul Rodriguez has played comedy in all venues, and has played in both dramas and comedies in film and on television. He also directed *A Million to Juan* (1994).

of community. Other films including Latino characters in various degrees of misrepresentation were *Untamed Heart* (1993, Metro-Goldwyn-Mayer); *Made in America* (1993, Warner Bros); and *Super Mario Bros.* (1993, Hollywood Pictures).

A few films of the decade had Latin America as a backdrop. Roman Polanski's *Death and the Maiden* (1994, Fine Line) was based on the play of the same name by Ariel Dorfman, who became an exile from his native Chile after the coup against Allende in 1973. The film focused on what happens when a woman (Sigourney Weaver) turns the tables on the official (Ben Kingley) who raped and tortured her. Although an excellent film, it was undermined by the lack of Latino actors. The lack of Latino performers was a detriment to the muddled *The House of the Spirits* (1994, Miramax), which was based on the novel of the same name by Isabel Allende. The *Los Angeles Times* wrote, "Inert from its opening moments to its too-long-delayed close, this lackluster production is an example of international filmmaking at its least attractive, and a misstep in the careers of pretty much everyone involved."[24] A more conscientious film was John Frankenheimer's *The Burning Season* (1994, HBO), which chronicled the efforts of Chico Mendez (Raúl Juliá) to stop the ecological disaster in the Amazon due to the nexus of political corruption and economic greed. A film with an unexpected sense of political understanding of how U.S. drug policy towards Latin America often was compromised by political self-interest and corruption was *Clear and Present Danger* (1994, Paramount), which was based on Tom Clancy's best-selling novel. The *Los Angeles*

Times noted, "Though the expected thing for 'Danger' to do at this point is break down into a U.S. versus the drug lords scenario, what happens is more subtle. There turns out to be not one Colombian adversary but several, not necessarily on good terms with each other. And far from a single monolithic American presence, there are various power centers with different perspectives and antiethical agendas."[25]

Of Love and Shadows (1996, Betka Films), which was based on another novel by Isabel Allende, was set during the chaotic time of the Pinochet coup of the Allende government in 1973 Chile. *The Hollywood Drama-Logue* commented, "The intentions of ... *Of Love and Shadows* are admirable. Unfortunately, the filmmakers' awareness of the nobility of their enterprise weighs heavily upon it, crushing most signs of life and human detail out of the narrative."[26]

Leon Ichaso's *Bitter Sugar* (1996, First Look Pictures) depicted the disillusionment of a young couple with the Cuban Revolution. The *Los Angeles Times* commented, "In contrast to the Cuban-made *Strawberry and Chocolate,* which strove to balance criticism and cautious optimism, *Bitter Sugar* is relentless in its depiction of present-day Cuba as oppressive to one and all and to the young people in particular."[27] Ken Loach's independent feature *Carla's Song* (1998, Shadow Distribution), which was set in 1987, chronicled the odyssey of an unemployed Scottish bus driver (Robert Carlyle) and his Nicaraguan fiancée (Oyanka Cabezas) during the Contra war in Nicaragua. Robert Dornhelm's *The Break* (1998, Castle Hill Productions) revolved around the efforts of an Irish Republican Army fugitive to aid two Guatemalan refugees (Rosana Pastor, Alfred Molina) in the assassination of a notorious Guatemalan colonel and war criminal who lives in exile in New York City.

However, perhaps the worst and most stereotypical of all the Latin America–based films was the much-trumpeted *Evita* (1996, Hollywood Pictures), based on the Andrew Lloyd Webber and Tim Rice musical of the same name. This bloated, pompous, comic book history purported to tell the story of Eva Perón (1919–1952), wife of Argentine president Juan Perón and a genuine proletarian heroine in Argentina and elsewhere in Latin America. Both the play and film portrayed her as Hollywood's stereotypical Latina whore who climbs to political prominence. Surprisingly, even the film's star, Madonna, became aware of the film's appalling biases. She told the *Los Angeles Times,* "Lloyd Webber's point of view was that of the [Argentine] aristocracy of the time Eva was married to the president.... They were against her [and viewed her] as an opportunistic whore. I thought this was a male chauvinist point of view—that any woman who is powerful is a whore or slept her way to the top. There's that implication right through the [musical] and it's ludicrous."[28]

Late in 1999, *One Man's Hero* (Orion) told the true story of the St. Patricio Battalion. After the Potato Famine of the 1840s, many Irish had left their homeland for the U.S., where they had been promised citizenship if they enlisted in the army. Once enlisted, many of them encountered discrimination due to their Catholicism and national origin. Consequently, when the Mexican-American War came many went over to the side of Mexico, becoming part of the St. Patricio Battalion. Many of them who were captured by U.S. army authorities met with execution. The *Los Angeles Times* commented, "*One Man's Hero* is a deeply felt and engrossing period epic that not only presents the Mexican War of 1846–1848, in which Mexico lost more than half of its territory to the U.S., from the loser's point of view, but also spotlights the heroic role in Mexico's defense played by the San Patricios, Irish immigrant deserters from the American Army who cast their lot with the Mexicans."[29]

The latter part of 1999 saw the release of David Riker's pseudo-documentary Spanish-language black-and-white film *La Ciudad*. The film followed the lives of several Latinos in New York City. Made at a cost of $500,000, the film became a sleeper, especially in Latino neighborhoods. The *L.A. Weekly* noted, "Because contemporary American cinema so thoroughly lacks a social conscience, it's almost startling to see a film overtly political as *La Ciudad*.... Riker follows another tradition, one which accords a sense of dignity and grace to a working-class milieu by crafting images that are themselves stately and poetic."[30]

Elsewhere Latino film characters continued to be few and far between. In *The Cradle Will Rock* (1999, Touchstone) one noteworthy character was the famed Mexican muralist Diego Rivera, played by Rubén Blades. Two of Lupe Tovar's grandchildren (and sons of Susan Kohner), director Chris Weitz and producer Paul Weitz, met with a huge critical and commercial success with their comedy *American Pie* (1999). Richard Salazar's *Atomic Blue: Mexican Wrestler* (1999), an independent film, depicted the struggles of a Mexican wrestler on behalf of the downtrodden.

A group of films with varying degrees of flaws and quality attempted to depict a more accurate and genuine Latino reality. During 1992, two films portrayed the destiny of a group of Chicano youths involved in a gang and their evolution into a prison gang: Edward James Olmos' *American Me* (1992, Universal) and Taylor Hackford's *Bound by Honor* (1992, Hollywood Pictures). A third film, Allison Anders' *Mi Vida Loca* (1994, HBO), focused on Chicana/Latina gang youth. *El Mariachi* (1993) was a film set in the borderlands. It marked the directorial debut of a talented director, Robert Rodriguez.

Two films centered on another part of the Latino community: Darnell Martin's *I Like It Like That* (1994, Columbia) on the Puerto Rican and Ángel Muñiz's *Nueba Yol* (1995) on the Dominican American. Gregory Nava's *My Family/Mi Familia* (1995, New Line Cinema) told the history of three generations of Mexicans/Chicanos in Los Angeles. Miguel Arteta's *Star Maps* (1997, Searchlight Pictures) by contrast focused on the dark side of the same community and the margins of the film industry. Gregory Nava's *Selena* (1997, Warner Bros.) celebrated the short life of slain Chicana Tex-Mex recording star Selena Quintanilla. *The Mask of Zorro* (1998, TriStar) reincarnated the old Mexican masked hero, while John Sayles' *Men with Guns* (1998) chronicled the more contemporary masked men in indigenous Mexico.

Overall, however, the U.S. films of the 1990s appeared barely cognizant of the irreversible demographics taking place and the pronounced Latinization of the U.S. For example, a report by the Washington-based Center for Media and Public Affairs cited in the *Los Angeles Times* revealed that the number of Latinos in prime-time television programs had declined from 3 percent in 1955 to a dismal 1 percent in 1992.[31] In 1955, Latinos made up only some 4 percent of the U.S. population, while in 1995, by contrast, they constituted some 12 percent.

The information about Latinos in film and television was further supplemented by data documented by the Screen Actors Guild. According to the guild's Affirmative Action Department in 1992, Latinos constituted 3 percent of working actors, compared to 83 percent for Caucasians, 12 percent for Blacks, 2 percent for Asian/Pacific, and 0 percent for Native Americans. In 1993, these figures remained virtually the same, with Latinos at 3 percent; the only changes were the designation of 1 percent for Native Americans while Caucasians went down to 82 percent. The figures for 1994 remained identical to those of 1993.

For 1995, Latinos made up 4 percent, while Caucasians constituted 81 percent, Blacks 13 percent, Asian/Pacific 2 percent, and Native Americans 0 percent. In 1996, Latinos remained constant at 4 percent, Caucasians made up 80 percent, Blacks 14 percent, Asian/Pacific 2 percent, and Native Americans 0 percent. Making things worse for the Latino actors was the fact that the bulk of Latino roles were incidental or small. On television, Latinos fared even worse. During the 1995–96 season, for example, only 2 percent of prime-time characters were Latinos.[32]

In yet another study, undertaken by the Tomas Rivera Policy Institute at Claremont College, the results were the same. In reference to this study, Harry Pachon and Manuel Valencia in an op-ed piece for the *Los Angeles Times* concluded, "More alarming than the pigeonholing of Latino actors and actresses, the stereotyping and the TV industry's denial of the nation's demographics, is how efficiently television makes minorities non-existent, a kind of ethnic whitewashing. Many metropolitan regions, including L.A., are polarized between the haves and have-nots. TV contributes to this by deciding who will exist and who won't on TV. If a group doesn't exist, then neither do its problems with education, health care and jobs."[33]

The television networks remained incorrigible and recalcitrant in diversifying their 1999 fall season. The twenty-six new shows being premiered by NBC, CBS, ABC, and Fox contained not a single Latino, African American, Asian American, or Native American in a leading role. Various minority advocacy groups rallied to protest their continued exclusion. Their activities included boycotting television for two weeks to call attention to the "brown-out." Actor Edward James Olmos told the *Los Angeles Times*, "If I were in the hierarchy of any of these networks, I would hang my head in shame for the rest of my life."[34] At the 1999 Emmy ceremonies, John Leguizamo commented to the *Los Angeles Times*, "The roles [Latinos] get are not breakthrough.... They're not the upscale Latino people I meet in my life. They don't represent the doctors, the lawyers, the writers.... It's changing gradually. But I think Latino people have to do that themselves."[35]

One of the great ironies about this contemporary exclusion was that this often-liberal industry has been based for almost a century in Los Angeles, which has the nation's largest concentration of Latinos (the majority Mexican), but nevertheless continues to exclude them. But some of this criticism has also been leveled at the booming Spanish-language television world.[36] For example, Cindy Rodriguez in an editorial for the *Boston Globe* noted, "The problem isn't with the Christinas and Walters of the Latin American world, it's the lack of faces any shades darker. The majority of the TV news anchors and novella stars have European features, a misrepresentation of the majority of Latinos. Most of us are mestizo; we come in some form of beige or brown. A good number of us have African or indigenous features. Watching Spanish-language TV, I sometimes feel I have stepped into an episode of *Twilight Zone,* where everything is reversed; the majority becomes the minority. If the characters weren't speaking Spanish, anyone stumbling across one of these shows would swear it was a broadcast from Europe."[37]

In conclusion, during the 1990s, despite the fact that Latinos had become the nation's largest minority, both film and television remained European-American preserves and industries of exclusion. Whatever roles were available for Latino performers were typically limited, incidental, and stereotypical.

Latino Film Stars and Filmmakers

All this notwithstanding, during the 1990s a few Latino film stars and filmmakers managed to break through against all odds and adversity. The three Latino-origin film stars who enjoyed the most spectacular success were three women, Salma Hayek, Jennifer Lopez, and Rosie Pérez. They were the first major Latina stars since Raquel Tejada, alias Raquel Welch. The Mexican-born Hayek had earned fame in her native country in two *telenovelas* before embarking on her U.S. film career. Once in the U.S., however, she had to begin again, doing bit parts in films, as well as television. Her breakthrough came in Robert Rodriguez' *Desperado* in 1995, and her fortunes soared with lead roles in *Fools Rush In* (1997), *54* (1998) and *The Wild, Wild West* (1999). The Nuyorican Lopez had a similar trajectory. She began with bit parts on television and later landed a costarring role on a one-season television series. She made an impact in Gregory Nava's *My Family/Mi Familia* in 1995 and her career went into high gear with the title role in *Selena* in 1997. Oliver Stone's *U-Turn* (1997) and Steven Soderbergh's *Out of Sight* (1998) cemented her stardom. Both Hayek and Lopez endured Hollywood typecasting as sex symbols. But both by the end of the decade were making concerted efforts to become serious actresses.

A third Latina enjoyed briefly both fame and fortune on a scale similar to Salma Hayek and Jennifer Lopez, the Nuyorican Rosie Pérez. She began on television as a dance coordinator, and made a strong film debut in Spike Lee's *Do the Right Thing* in 1989. She consolidated her stardom with roles as strong-willed Latinas in *White Men Can't Jump* (1992), *Fearless* (1993), and *It Could Happen to You* (1994). However, thereafter her film efforts were confined or reduced to obscure independent films. Nevertheless, Rosie Pérez was the first Black Latina to win Hollywood film stardom. This, coupled with her strong independence and candor, earned her the enmity of a few in the film industry who were not ready for such a unique life force. Consequently, her career suffered, but she has persevered.

Other Latina film stars include Lumi Cavazos, Constance Marie, Annette Murphy, Julieta Rosen, Valentina Vargas, Lauren Vélez, Leonor Varela and two Spanish-born actresses, Trini Alvarado and Aitana Sánchez Gijón. Lumi Cavazos earned worldwide fame and acclaim in Alfonso Arau's *Like Water for Chocolate* in 1991. After a pair of Mexican *telenovelas*, she embarked on a U.S. film career beginning with *Land of Milk and Honey* in 1994. Since then, she has made several independent films, including Wes Anderson's *Bottle Rocket* (1995), Francisco Athié's *Fiber Optics* (1999) and Allison Anders' *Sugar Town* (1999). Constance Marie made a strong impression in two films directed by Gregory Nava, *My Family/Mi Familia* (1995), in which she played the novice, and *Selena* (1997), in which she played Selena's mother.

The stage-trained Annette Murphy turned in a powerful performance in Miguel Arteta's *Star Maps* (1997), but since then has been less visible. Julieta Rosen built her career with leads in five popular *telenovelas* in her native Mexico before her U.S. film debut in 1997's *Wind Runners*. However, it was her role of the ill-fated wife of Zorro in *The Mask of Zorro* in 1998 that won her wide attention. The Chilean-born Valentina Vargas made an impressive debut in 1986's *The Name of the Rose*, but her career faded out except for a few roles in low-budget films during the 1990s. The Nuyorican Lauren Vélez earned raves in Darnell Martin's *I Like It Like That* in 1994 and later played the female lead in the popular television series

New York Undercover. Finally, the Chilean-born Leonor Varela made an impact in the ABC miniseries *Cleopatra* during 1999. Trini Alvarado was one of two Spanish leading ladies who emerged during the 1990s. She first gained notice as a child star beginning in 1979, and during the 1990s she costarred in such diverse fare as *Stella* (1990), *Babe* (1992) and *The Perez Family* (1995). Thereafter, her career began to slow down. Her compatriot Aitana Sánchez Gijón made her U.S. debut in *A Walk in the Clouds* in 1995. Her career moved into high gear with *Boca a Boca/Mouth to Mouth* (1997) and *The Chambermaid* (1998). During late 1999, Mexican *telenovela* star Daniela Romo made her U.S. film debut in *One Man's Hero* (Orion).

Other Latina actresses visible during the decade included Yareli Arizmendi, Angel Aviles, Seidy López, and Lupe Ontiveros.

The most prominent Latino leading men to emerge during the 1990s were Antonio Banderas and Jimmy Smits. Banderas had already earned fame and fortune as a leading man of satirical comedies in his native Spain, especially those directed by Pedro Almodóvar. He made his U.S. film debut in 1992's *The Mambo Kings*. However, it wasn't until *Desperado* in 1995 that his career as a heartthrob leading man took off. Banderas cemented his stardom with *The Mask of Zorro* (1998) and *The 13th Warrior* (1999). He became only the second Spanish-born actor to become a major Hollywood film star since the days of Antonio Moreno in the silent period. Smits had played leads in two popular television series but had been unable to jump-start his film career early in the decade, beginning with *Old Gringo* in 1989. It was not until *My Family/Mi Familia* in 1995 that he appeared poised to make a successful transition into a movie leading man.

Several talented Latino actors emerged during the decade. They included Jesse Borrego, Benjamin Bratt, Raymond Cruz, Michael DeLorenzo, Benicio Del Toro, Héctor Elizondo, Efrain Figueroa, Mike Gomez, John Leguizamo, Sal Lopez, Jon Seda, and Douglas Spain. A few of them starred or costarred in their own television series: Bratt in *Law & Order*, DeLorenzo in *New York Undercover,* and Elizondo in *Chicago Hope*, among others. Of this group of talented actors only Benjamin Bratt, nominated for Best Actor for the film *Pinero* in 2001, was able to become a leading man in feature films. This was despite the fact that several of them had played leading roles in movies. Borrego, for example, attracted notice in *Bound by Honor* (1992); Del Toro in *The Usual Suspects* (1995) and *Fear and Loathing in Las Vegas* (1998); Figueroa in *Star Maps* (1997); Leguizamo in *To Wong Foo, Thanks for Everything, Julie Newmar* (1995) and *Spawn* (1997); Lopez in *American Me* (1992); Seda in *I Like It Like That* (1994) and *Selena* (1997); and Spain in *Star Maps* (1997). During 1999, the Puerto Rican recording star Chayanne made his film debut in the leading role in *Dance with Me* with only modest success. Yet, full-fledged stardom eluded them. New Latino character actors during the decade included Danny Trejo, Jacob Vargas, Eddie Velez, and Del Zamora.

In spite of the declining visibility of Latinos before the camera, a group of new and talented Latino directors carved out a place for themselves in U.S. films behind the camera. They included: Miguel Arteta (*Star Maps,* 1997); Alfonso Cuarón (*Great Expectations*, 1997); Guillermo del Toro (*Mimic,* 1997); Severo Perez *(... And the Earth Did Not Swallow Him*, 1996); Robert Rodriguez (*El Mariachi*, 1992); Raúl Ruiz (*Dark at Noon*, 1994); and Richard Salazar (*Atomic Blue: Mexican Wrestler,* 1999).

Latina directors of feature films had yet to make their appearance. However, the new Latino directors of the 1990s brought a new vision and energy from the Latino experience that did much to enrich and diversify the U.S. cinema of the 1990s.

Representative Films

American Me (1992, Universal)

American Me, along with *Zoot Suit,* remains one of the two most authentic and evocative film ever made about the Chicano gang experience. While *Zoot Suit* documented the world of the zoot suiters and *pachucos* of the 1940s, *American Me* depicted the world of the *vatos* and homeboys of contemporary times.

The film revolved around the friendship developed by three youths, two of them Chicano: Santana (Edward James Olmos) and Mundo (Pepe Serna); and one European-American, J.D. (William Forsythe). The association begins with their membership in an East Los Angeles gang. Their activities lead to their confinement in Juvenile Hall, where Santana kills another youthful inmate who rapes him. Later, in Folsom Prison, they cofound La Eme, or the Mexican Mafia, as a means to protect themselves with a primitive sense of ethnic nationalism, but also as a means to control the drug trade in the barrios.

After many years in prison, Santana is finally released to a society he barely knows. Once outside, Santana comes to terms with his long-estranged father (Sal Lopez), whose detachment is based on his lifelong suspicion that Santana might not really be his son, as his wife (Vira Montes) had been raped by U.S. servicemen during the Zoot Suit Riots of 1943. Santana becomes increasingly disillusioned with his former life, as he becomes involved with a barrio single mother (Evelina Fernández). His growing love for her gradually tempers his ruthlessness to the degree that the gang ultimately finds him expendable and murders him on his return to prison.

American Me marked Edward James Olmos' directorial debut (he also co-produced with Robert M. Young). The film was based on Floyd Mutrux's original script (which at one time was to be a project for Al Pacino), and both Mutrux and Desmond Nakano received coscripting credit. The film crew received unprecedented access to shoot inside Folsom Prison.

However, what makes *American Me* especially memorable is the evocative direction of Olmos and the largely Chicano cast who bring sensitivity, power and passion to the characters. Unlike with other Chicano gang films, the viewer is seeing this Chicano world from the inside looking out and not the contrary. The feel, the look, and the East Los Angeles barrio are genuine and real, as is the human vulnerability behind the gang personae.

The Village Voice wrote, "For as convincing an inspiration as *Stand and Deliver* is to youth clinging to hope in the face of societal subjugation, *American Me* is a shot to the solar plexus of a people smothered in the darkness of a harsh reality. In *American Me*, the pencils and slide rules of *Stand and Deliver* have been replaced by cold steel and sharp blades; these kids are struggling with problems that refuse to add up."[38] *Variety* commented, "The criminal life is portrayed with all the glamour of a mugshot in *American Me,* a powerful indictment of the cycle of violence bred by prisons and street culture.... Olmos makes for a mesmerizing, implacable Santana, one of the least romanticized film gangsters since Paul Muni's *Scarface* ... Daniel Villareal is a particular standout as Little Puppet."[39]

The Hollywood Reporter stated, "In stark contrast to *Stand and Deliver*, Olmos has made a film with little hope.... In playing a character who has lost all feelings of human compassion, Olmos projects a dignity and sense of warmth that still might be reclaimed were it not to meet a tragic end.... Reynaldo Villalobos' icy, nearly black-and-white cinematography makes Folsom Prison a treacherous landscape and gives colorful East L.A. a shadowy, film-noir look."[40]

Over the years, *American Me* has become a cult film. Similarly, the film has come in for some strong criticism because of its representation of women. Christine List, for example, noted, "*American Me* traces Santana's downfall to a primal rape scene: his mother's rape by U.S. servicemen during their invasion (conquest) of East L.A. Racial domination of East L.A. Chicanos is here figured symbolically in the mother's rape, propelling Santana's criminality.... Chicanos inherit the legacy of 'La Malinche,' originating in this case the downfall of Chicanos in the barrio.... The effects of this 'original sin,' the violation of a passive woman's sexuality, continue to inform the internal logic of the film's narrative: rape, violations of masculine sexuality, serves as the primary mechanism for shocking retaliations on the part of Chicano males."[41]

Blood In, Blood Out/Bound by Honor (1992, Hollywood Pictures)

Blood In, Blood Out, another film dealing with the friendship of three youths in East Los Angeles and their association with street and prison gangs, was released some forty days after *American Me*. Although ambitious and featuring an excellent and almost exclusively Latino cast, it came in a distant second to *American Me*.

The script for *Blood In, Blood Out* had its genesis when producer Jerry Gershin hired novelist Ross Thomas to write a script, which subsequently went into development under director Harold Becker. Later, Floyd Mutrux (who had written the original script for *American Me*) did a rewrite. The screenplay is credited to Jimmy Santiago Baca (the New Mexico poet), Jeremy Iacone, and Floyd Mutrux.

The films share similarities. Three youths, two Chicano: Cruz (Jesse Borrego) and Paco (Benjamin Bratt); and one, part European-American and part Chicano, Miklo (Damian Chapa), begin their friendship in an East Los Angeles gang. Of the three, Miklo becomes the most *loco*, motivated in part by his lack of acceptance by other *vatos locos* due to his mixed ethnicity. Paco, initially the most into the *vida loca,* undergoes an off-screen metamorphosis when his young nephew overdoses in the proximity of Miklo. He becomes a marine and subsequently a police detective.

In the meantime, Cruz, a talented painter, becomes a drug addict, shunned by his family. Miklo is incarcerated for a crime, but upon his release, he is unable to make a go of it as an ex-con. He becomes involved in a holdup of an armored truck, during which he is wounded by Paco and loses his leg. Returning to prison, he eventually becomes the leader of a notorious Latino gang, La Onda, after he ruthlessly removes its founder

Montana (Enrique Castillo). At the end, Paco and a rehabilitated Miklo are left to ponder their different destinies in the outside world.

Blood In, Blood Out was directed and produced by Taylor Hackford, who had also produced *La Bamba.* The film's main assets were the striking cinematography by Gabriel Beristain and the talented Latino cast that included Jesse Borrego, Benjamin Bratt, Damian Chapa, Enrique Castillo, Jenny Gago, Raymond Cruz, and Lupe Ontiveros, among others. However, Hackford's direction tended to be overly melodramatic and the effect is of a film depicting the Chicano gang experience from the outside looking in, whereas *American Me* had the opposite vision. Consequently, *Blood In, Blood Out* draws rather than evokes that part of the Chicano experience.

The reviews tended to reflect the above-mentioned aspects. The *New York Times* wrote, "*Bound by Honor,* Taylor Hackford's ambitious melodrama about the Chicano experience in and around East Los Angeles, is like one of those huge wall murals that give bold, defiant color to an urban landscape that otherwise looks passive and drab.... Mr. Hackford has cast the film well. Though they must play at a fever pitch most of the time, Mr. Chapa, Mr. Bratt and Mr. Borrego are excellent, as are the members of the large supporting cast, notably Enrique Castillo, who appears as the leader of San Quentin's Chicanos."[42] The *Los Angeles Times* noted, "The Olmos film is largely unsentimental and inescapably earnest, a kind of wake-up call to the Latino community, while Hackford's, for all it fervor, is thoroughly slick and commercial, a potboiler more concerned than not with getting an exploitative rise out of the audience."[43]

I Like It Like That (1994, Columbia)

I Like It Like That marked the directorial debut of African American director Darnell Martin. The film was a long overdue look at the Puerto Rican or Nuyorican experience, one different from the proverbial Hollywood stereotype.

The film focused on Lisette (Lauren Vélez), a Black Puerto Rican wife, who struggles between self-sufficiency and her love for her irresponsible husband Chino (Jon Seda). Her life is further complicated by the nagging of her mother-in-law (Rita Moreno), the eccentricities of her cross-dressing brother Alexis (Jesse Borrego), the care of her two young children and her ambition to become a businesswoman.

The film was directed and written by Darnell Martin, herself of mixed lineage (of an Irish mother and an African American father). A graduate of New York University film school, she was touted by Columbia Pictures as the first African American woman to direct a major motion picture. Martin made the film on a $5.5 million budget and a nine-week shoot. Martin had grown up in a Puerto Rican section of the Bronx, where *I Like It Like That* was shot. The film marked the debut of Lauren Vélez as the resilient Lisette; and it also provided the first lead for Jon Seda, a former boxer.

I Like It Like That received a warm critical and commercial reception. *Variety* wrote, "A thick veneer of happening music, multi-ethnicity, tough hood attitude and sexual frankness gives a hip feel to what is actually an old-fashioned and conventional story of a bickering family.... Darnell Martin ... displays plenty of energy and an adeptness at staging scenes vividly."[44] The *New York Times* commented, "Ms. Martin's terrifically buoyant debut feature is as scrappy and alluring as its heroine."[45]

Drama-Logue noted, "*I Like It Like That* is a happy surprise, bracingly vital and smart and funny ... a refreshing change from a slew of recent releases that depict ghetto residents as one step up from brain-damaged."[46] The *Los Angeles Times* wrote, "Lively, assured and practically vibrating with color and excitement, *I Like It Like That* marks the emergence of a passionate new film voice."[47]

El Mariachi (1993, Columbia)

El Mariachi was a stylish, low-budget, independent film that marked the directorial debut of Chicano director Robert Rodriguez. It also signaled the emergence of a new generation of filmmakers trained in film schools and the growing importance of independent films.

El Mariachi was made on a $7,000 budget and ran only 82 minutes. Robert Rodriguez and Carlos Gallardo (who also played the lead role) co-produced and co-wrote the screenplay. The film was made on a fourteen-day shoot in Acuña, Mexico. Columbia Pictures then spent one million dollars to publicize the film for a wider release. The film's critical and commercial success earned the twenty-four-year-old director a two-year deal with Columbia. Ironically, one of the films that he would subsequently would make was *Desperado* (1995), a remake of *El Mariachi* with a bigger budget and different cast.

Director Robert Rodriguez came to fame with *El Mariachi* (1992).

The film revolved around a wandering *mariachi* (Carlos Gallardo) who travels to a Mexican border town where he is mistaken for drug cartel hit man Azul (Reinol Martinez). Both carry an almost identical guitar case and by coincidence *el mariachi* is helped by Domino (Consuelo Gómez), the girlfriend of the local drug lord (Peter Marquardt). The latter is the hit man's main target. *El mariachi* himself, however, has his own score to settle with the drug lord.

El Mariachi was a mixture of spaghetti western and Mexican low-budget *narcotraficante* movie. But Rodriguez infused it with his own energy and vision laced with elements of tongue-in-cheek humor and sardonic melodrama. The film garnered enthusiastic reviews. *Variety* noted, "Rodriguez has pulled off a good deal more than that, since he has created a solid genre piece with a sense of style that is partly original, partly dictated by economic necessity and partly a smart wedding of such influences as Sergio Leone, George Miller and south-of-the-border noir."[48] The *New York Times* commented, "It goes without saying that Mr. Rodriguez, having made such a clever and inventive debut, is prepared for a big future of his own."[49]

The Mask of Zorro (1998, TriStar)

The Mask of Zorro brought back an old cinematic hero. The character of Zorro was one of only two (the other is the Cisco Kid) Mexican U.S. film heroes. The film marked the first appearance of Zorro since 1981's *Zorro, the Gay Blade.*

The film begins in 1821 Los Angeles, when Mexico has won its independence and the Spaniards are beating a hasty retreat. Even at this late date, however, the governor, Don Rafael Monteros (Stuart Wilson), is bent on the execution of several men who have battled his tyranny. Zorro (Anthony Hopkins) comes to their rescue, but Monteros comes looking for him at his hacienda where he lives as Don Diego de la Vega. In the ensuing struggle, Vega's wife (Julieta Rossen) is killed. Don Diego is imprisoned and his small daughter is abducted by Monteros to be raised as his own.

The film shifts to 1841, when Monteros and other *caballeros* have made a secret pact with General Santa Anna to get their real estate back. He is aided by Captain Love (Matt Letscher), who had tracked down two bandit brothers, Alejandro Murietta (Antonio Banderas) and Joaquin. He managed to kill and behead the latter. Don Diego is able to escape and becomes aware of Monteros' plans, as well as the fact that Elena (Catherine Zeta-Jones) thinks she is Monteros' daughter. Don Diego runs across Alejandro, whom he trains to carry on his ideals. In the process Alejandro falls in love with Elena. At the end, Don Diego, Alejandro and Elena thwart Monteros' plans, although Don Diego is killed and dies in the arms of his daughter.

Shot on location in Mexico, the film boasted some stunning scenery, excellent swordplay and fine performances from Hopkins, Banderas, and Zeta-Jones. Unfortunately, the film has no Mexican or Latino actors in any of the major roles. Initially, the film was to have been directed by Robert Rodriguez and to have starred Banderas and Salma Hayek. Due to creative differences, both Rodriguez and Hayek left the project. One can speculate that their services would have brought more truth to the history depicted. The fact remains, however, that *The Mask of Zorro* is filled with historical inaccuracies that perpetuate an undervaluing of both Mexican and Chicano history. First, the character Joaquin Murietta was a real Mexican who during the early 1850s battled against the blatant European-American injustices against Mexicans in the aftermath of the Mexican-American War (1846–1848). This film cast him as a mere bandit and sets him in 1821, thus totally removing the historical context and the cause to which he was committed. In addition, Captain Love, another character that the film has set in 1841 (instead of the 1850s), is the alleged assassin of Murietta. There has long been speculation that Love never captured the real Murietta, but rather that he seized an innocent Mexican, cut off his head and took that as evidence to receive the state's reward. Again, the real-life Love exemplified the nefariousness and lawlessness that came with the takeover of California.

The Mask of Zorro received a warm critical reception and was a commercial hit. The *New York Times* wrote, "*The Mask of Zorro* extends a tempting invitation: travel back to the days when swashbuckling was serious business, when boyish adventure films still had their innocence, when the bravado of thrilling stunt work was all a movie needed in the way of special effects. With a wealth of charismatic Zorros (two), a smashing heroine and a dauntless love of adventure, this hot-weather escapism is so earnestly retrograde that it seems new."[50] The *Boston Globe* commented, "Zorro is back, with more swashbuckling panache than ever. *The Mask of Zorro* proves that Antonio Banderas can hold his own with the long, honorable line of Zorros that began with Douglas Fairbanks, Sr. in 1920 and included Tyrone Power."[51]

Men with Guns (1998, Sony Pictures)

John Sayles' *Men with Guns* is a rare and unique film, one that focuses on the contemporary and continuing genocide against the indigenous people in Latin America.

The film tells the story of Humberto Fuentes (Federico Luppi), a wealthy doctor in Mexico City, who caters to an upscale clientele. He is a widower whose grown children offer him little empathy. He decides to embark on a journey to discover what happened to the young doctors he trained under an international health program. In the impoverished outskirts of the city, he finds Bravo (Roberto Sosa), who had been his best student and now operates a black market of medicine. He makes his way to the poorest state of the republic Chiapas in search of his other students. Along the way he meets Conejo (Dan Rivera González), a young boy who is a product of his mother's rape and has now been abandoned. It is through the boy that the doctor becomes aware of the army's murderous campaign of intimidation, torture and murder against the indigenous peoples.

The doctor and the boy then run across Domingo (Damián Delgado), an embittered indigenous young man and army deserter who further confirms the army's atrocities. As the three continue their journey, they meet Portillo (Damián Alcázar), a former priest traumatized by his inability to practice what he preached. They are detained by an army barricade and Portillo is taken away, perhaps to be "disappeared." In the camp, they find hundreds of indigenous people who have been forced out of their villages and Fuentes puts to use some of his medical skills. Leaving the camp, they encounter a young Indian woman, Graciela (Tania Cruz), and make their way to Cerca del Cielo, a haven for landless Indians high in the mountains where one of his former students may be.

When they arrive at the summit, Fuentes discovers that his student has been killed by the army. Heartbroken and disillusioned by his previous ignorance and his loss of innocence, he states, "It's my legacy." The doctor's death makes Domingo finally withdraw from his cynical apathy and he commits himself to working with the refugees.

John Sayles, an independent director with impeccable progressive credentials who made such films as *Matewan* (1987) and *Lone Star* (1996), commented about why he made the film, "One of the things the movie is about is about the responsibility to know.... What is your police force doing? What is your government doing? What is your company doing? And not to pretend that you can't know. And there is that point between ignorance and willful ignorance."[52] The film was shot on location in the Mexican states of Veracruz and Chiapas, and in Mexico City, and except for a few scenes in English, most it was in Spanish or in the Mayan dialects of Nahuatl, Tzotzil, and Kung. Cast in a small role was David Villalpando, who had played the Mayan youth so memorably in Gregory Nava's *El Norte*.

Men with Guns is a remarkable film in many ways. Using the metaphor of a quest for the meaning of a life lived, the film places the protagonist in a netherworld of unexpected challenges and conflicts that adds powerfully to the narrative. The characters are complex, compelling and convincing and they propel the narrative. Lastly, the film presents an evocative look into the contemporary plight of indigenous peoples with sensitivity and depth.

The film received enthusiastic reviews, although commercially it was restricted to art houses. *The Hollywood Reporter* commented, "The film title refers to the native population's classification of all foreign invaders—from Hernando Cortez's to the current military brigands—as 'men with guns.' They are to be feared and avoided.... The players are well-chosen, especially Luppi as the regal doctor and Damián Delgado as the brutal-and-brutalized soldier. Dan Rivera González is aptly feisty and resourceful as the Indian boy.... A particular highlight is Mason Daring's spicy sounds and Slawomir Idziak's wide-eyed framings."[53] The *New York Times* noted, "To the extent that artists are defined by their goals, John Sayles is the most courageous and decent storyteller working in American films today. He proves that again in *Men with Guns*, which brings the quiet integrity of Mr. Sayles' *Lone Star* to bear upon even more uncompromising material. Set in a nameless Latin American country, this is an allegory about war and responsibility, confronting the burden of history as hauntingly as this director's films so often have.... It is rendered with great vividness by varied and evocative settings, by meticulous attention to detail, and by a large cast of indigenous nonprofessional actors."[54]

Mi Vida Loca (1993, HBO)

Allison Anders' *Mi Vida Loca* was the first Hollywood film to focus entirely on the Latina gang lifestyle. However, despite an ambitious vision it is a flawed film and does not ultimately ring true.

The film is set in the predominantly Chicano/Latino northeast part of Los Angeles, in a barrio named Echo Park. The narrative tells several interconnecting stories of Chicana gang members. There is the story of Mousie (Seidy López) and Sad Girl (Angel Aviles), who lives on welfare, and who almost become adversaries when they discover much to their disappointment that they have been seduced by the same homeboy.

Another home girl, Whisper (Nélida López), is trying to join Ernesto (Jacob Vargas) in his drug-dealing enterprise. Sad Girl's sister, La Blue Eyes (Magali Alvarado), a college student, becomes involved in a love affair through letter-writing with a prison inmate although she has never met him. Finally, there is Giggles (Marlo Marron), who has just come out of prison and carries on a romance with Big Sleepy (Julian Reyes).

The lifestyle of Chicana gang members has been long overlooked in both research and literature. In films, they have been incidental characters without depth or context. It has only been recently that Chicanas in gangs have been the subject of study. Joan W. Moore, who has done extensive research on Chicano and Chicana gangs, wrote, "Even though most of the women (65 percent) also claimed to live in the gang neighborhood during their early teens, the pattern of being 'raised into the gang' because of living in the neighborhood was less common among the girls. They were more likely to join through relatives and close friendships, including, occasionally, boyfriends. Women were also more likely to mention problems at home when they talked about joining the gang."[55]

The main virtue of *Mi Vida Loca* is that it attempted to depict their experience as a central focus. Allison Anders, a talented feminist director who had just earned widespread acclaim with *Gas Food Lodging* in 1992, and who actually lived in the Echo Park barrio, was unable to imbue the film with the feel of "from the inside looking out" that *American Me* so evocatively captured. *Mi Vida Loca* ultimately resembles *Blood In, Blood Out* in its pseudo-authenticity of the barrio. Although *Mi Vida Loca* is well-meaning, both Anders' screenplay and narrative fail to provide the societal context of the Chicano and Latino historical experience. *Mi Vida Loca*'s main strength lies in its young and talented Chicano/Latino cast and the cinematography of Rodrigo García (the son of novelist Gabriel García Márquez, who had previously lensed *Danzon*) and less on the often contrived screenplay.

Mi Vida Loca received mixed reviews. *Variety* wrote, "A portrait of young Latino women in the Los Angeles barrio, Allison Anders' *Mi Vida Loca* is a particularly disappointing follow-up to *Gas Food Lodging*. Dramatically fuzzy and very flat visually."[56] The *New York Times* noted, "Ms. Anders ... is neither condescending nor arrogantly intimate in her approach to these characters. Maybe that position, neither inside nor outside, contributes to the film's problems.... Smart though it is, too much of *Mi Vida Loca* elicits a response from the head, rather than a heartfelt reaction to the energy of the lives on screen."[57] The *Los Angeles Times* commented, "With all good intentions, Anders has ended up confirming a decidedly negative stereotype of young Latinos as aimless, dangerous, and incapable of thinking for themselves, not to mention welfare-dependent. As a result, *Mi Vida Loca* is downright offensive.... *Mi Vida Loca* desperately needs to suggest the impact of the historical, social, economic, religious and cultural forces that shape the lives of these young women and their behavior and values. It isn't enough to depict their touching loyalty to each other and their loving devotion to their children."[58]

My Family/Mi Familia (1995, New Line Cinema)

Gregory Nava's *My Family/Mi Familia* told the story of three generations of a Mexican family in Los Angeles, and in the process also celebrated the indigenous roots of Mexican people in the Southwest. It also marked the return of director Gregory Nava, who with the exception of one other film had not directed since his memorable *El Norte* in 1984.

The film told the story of a young man, Jose Sanchez (Jacob Vargas), who leaves his village in Michoacán, Mexico, and makes his way to Los Angeles in the early part of the 1920s. There he is helped by his only relative, El Californio (Leon Singer). When he dies his epitaph reads, "When I was born, this was part of Mexico, and where I am buried is still Mexico!" Soon after his relative's passing, Jose falls in love with and marries Maria (Jennifer Lopez) and they settle down to have a family in East Los Angeles.

The film then shifts to the 1950s and 1980s, as Jose (Eduardo López Rojas) and Maria (Jenny Gago) see their children reach adulthood and make a life of their own. They are Paco (Edward James Olmos, who also serves as the narrator of the film), who becomes a writer; Irene (María Canals, Lupe Ontiveros), who becomes a businesswoman; Toni (Constance Marie), a nun who later becomes a community activist; Chuco (Esai Morales), whose gang lifestyle leads to an early death; Memo (Enrique Castillo), who becomes an attorney; and the youngest, Jimmy (Jimmy Smits), who ends up in prison.

The film received an Academy Award nomination for the excellent make-up by Mark Sanchez and Ken Diaz. This evocative film resonated especially with Mexicano/Chicano audiences to a large degree because it centered on one single barrio family across three generations and time periods. It dramatized the cultural and economic stresses, as well as the bilingual and bicultural experiences, in a historical context that was both compelling and powerful. The film was released at the same time as *The Perez Family,* a film that was fatally undermined by its non–Latino cast.

My Family/Mi Familia received a warm critical and commercial reception. Indicative of the reviews was the *Los Angeles Times':* "One of the reasons *Mi Familia* is successful is that the simple concept of focusing on the real family, not the substitute gang family that many previous Latino films have latched onto, is surprisingly effective. And both the script and direction have taken care to give the film's characters what they themselves would consider essential, simple dignity."[59]

Nueba Yol (1995, Cigla/Miramax)

Nueba Yol was the first U.S.–made film to depict the Dominican-American experience. Itmarked the directorial debut of Ángel Muñiz, who also scripted the film.

The film's narrative revolved around Balbuena, a native Dominican who dreams of making a lot of money and returning to his homeland. At the urging of a friend (Raul Carbonell), he mortgages his house in Santo Domingo and leaves for New York. There, he rooms with his cousin Pedro (Rafael Villalona) in his overcrowded household. He soon learns that he is despised by Pedro's children, who are ashamed about their Dominican background.

Balbuena embarks on an odyssey of trying to find employment but is thwarted at every turn by his undocumented status, drug dealers who do not recognize him as part of the barrio, racism and the proverbial New York City rudeness. When he is about to give up, he finds romance with an attractive younger woman, Nancy (Caridad Ravelo), who values him. Balbuena ultimately finds employment in a Mexican restaurant.

The Dominican community in the United States has recently experienced dramatic growth. Dominicans now constitute the second-largest Latino population in New York City. The New York City Dominican community has become so important that politicians make it a focus for campaigning and raising money. For example, the current president of the Dominican Republic was actually born and raised in New York. The Dominican community was overdue for a movie that depicted their experiences. Director Ángel Muñiz, a Dominican himself (and a graduate of a film school in San Francisco), was given a budget of only $350,000, but as of March 1999 the film had grossed some $3.3 million in the United States alone. In the Dominican Republic, the film grossed $700,000 in only four months. A sequel, entitled *Nueba Yol 3,* was made on a budget of $550,000 and went on to make $2.1 million in the United States. Muñiz stated to *La Opinión,* "I think that the Latin American film can be reborn. We have the product, we make good films, but what need is the mechanism of promotion, of publicity."[60]

Nueba Yol greatly benefited from its talented Latino cast. Luisito Marti, who played the title role of Balbuena, is popular on Dominican television and also in Miami and New York. The cast included Cuban actress Caridad Ravelo, the Puerto Rican actor Raul Carbonell, and Mexican actors Alfonso Zayas and Joel Garcia.

Nueba Yol received enthusiastic reviews. The *New York Times* noted, "The movie ... is a crude but engaging combination of humorous star vehicle, social-realist commentary and lighthearted farce."[61] The *Los Angeles Times* wrote, "It's no wonder writer-producer-director Ángel Muñiz made such an instant connection with Latino audiences in New York in bringing a beloved *telenovela* character to the big screen. Muñiz knows how to offset the harshness of an immigrant experience with comedy, melodrama, a little silliness and lots of heart. Most important, he does it with much affection and no condescension. The distributor isn't going for crossover audiences, but *Nueba Yol*, slang for New York, actually possesses universal appeal—and its score has an irresistible Caribbean beat."[62]

Selena (1997, Warner Bros.)

Selena celebrated the short life of Tex-Mex singing star Selena Quintanilla Perez (1971–1995), who was murdered as she was about to cross over into the mainstream U.S. music industry. It also marked the first time in Chicano cinema that a Latina was the central focus of the movie.

The film begins with Selena's big concert at the Houston Astrodome that took place just a few weeks before her death. It flashes back to 1961, when her father, Abraham Quintanilla (Panchito Gómez), and his own doo-wop group called the Dinos played in Corpus Christi, Texas. However, he finds his desire for music success thwarted by discrimination against Mexicans, and also by the monolingual desire of some in the Mexican community for Spanish-language music.

The film then moves to 1981, by which time Quintanilla (Edward James Olmos) is married to Marcela (Constance Marie). They have three children, one son and two daughters, including Selena (Becky Lee Meza), and Quintanilla pushes and exhorts them to begin a second doo-wop group also named the Dinos. Once grown, Selena (Jennifer Lopez) and her two siblings (Jacob Vargas, Jackie Guerra) continue to play with only modest success. However, Quintanilla continues to persevere, sometimes with a seeming obsession for their success. He convinces Selena to sing in Spanish and gradually the group gathers a strong following after they play in Monterrey, Mexico. She wins a Grammy a short time later. During this time she falls in love with a heavy metal guitarist, Chris Ferrer (Jon Seda), much to the dismay of her father. They marry and her father finally acknowledges the fact that she is a grown woman.

As her popularity soars, she develops boutiques and a fan club, the latter of which is managed by Yolanda Saldívar (Lupe Ontiveros). However, Quintanilla uncovers evidence that Saldivar is embezzling money and they confront her. Saldivar requests that she be permitted to rectify the situation. However, a short time later, on March 25, 1995, she fatally shoots Selena.

The film was budgeted at $20 million and it also marked the first time that a Latina actress earned a million dollars in a film, in this case Jennifer Lopez, who played the title role. A nationwide search was made by Gregory Nava for both the young Selena and the adult Selena. The search landed the young Becky Lee Meza, from Harlingen, Texas, the role of Selena from ages six to ten. Producers Moctesuma Esparza and Robert Katz settled on actress Jennifer Lopez, who made an impression in Nava's *My Family/Mi Familia*, for the adult Selena. However, some in the Mexican/Chicano community expressed dismay that a Puerto Rican–origin actress would play the Mexican-origin Selena. Director Nava commented, "Casting Jennifer Lopez gave me a head start as a director. She already has the heartbeat. Preview audiences love her for the same reason audiences loved Selena. It's because she's wonderful, her talent and humanity shine through—not because she's Latin."[63]

For her part, Jennifer Lopez said she did feel a lot of pressure, but didn't focus on it. She commented to *People*, "It's the most difficult role I've had, because Selena isn't a fictional character—and her family is sitting right in front of me while I'm acting."[64] Lopez lip-synced Selena's songs, was effective, and contributed greatly to the feel of the film. The film was made in close cooperation with Selena's father, Abraham Quintanilla, who was also a co-producer and advisor on the set. Some feel that this fact contributed to a sanitization of the film, as well as the toning down of his alleged controlling personality.

The film received mixed reviews, but it was a box-office success (it grossed $27.7 million in only three weeks). The *New York Times* wrote, "Gregory Nava's bland, upbeat hagiography of Selena Quintanilla Perez (Jennifer Lopez), the Mexican-American pop star ... doesn't contain a single world or image that suggests the Queen of Tejano music was ever anything less than a perfect angel."[65] *The Boston Globe* commented, "Two-dimensional iconography doesn't get any richer-looking than *Selena*, Gregory Nava's film based on the tragically brief life of the Latina singer.... As Selena, Jennifer Lopez projects a lot of sweetness to go with Selena's extroverted performer's sass."[66]

Star Maps (1997, Fox Searchlight Pictures)

Star Maps documented the harsh realities and consequences of a dysfunctional Latino family in Los Angeles. It was set against the backdrop of the seamier side of the Hollywood film industry. The film also marked the directorial debut of a new and talented Latino director, Miguel Arteta.

The film's narrative is driven by the disparate members of the same family. The father, Pepe (Efrain Figueroa), is a pimp whom even his own father disowned. Now, he convinces his own son Carlos (Douglas Spain), who dreams of becoming a film actor, to prostitute himself (by selling star maps) as a way to establish valuable contacts in the film business. Carlos manages to do that when a popular television star, Jennifer (Kandeyce Jorden), becomes one of the clients and manifests an insatiable appetite for extramarital sex with marginalized Latinos. Carlos is taught the tricks of the trade by Letti (Annette Murphy), the prostitute girlfriend of his father, who is under the delusion that he will marry her.

Meanwhile, his mother, a victim of a nervous breakdown, maintains hallucinatory discussions with the ghost of the Mexican comedian Cantinflas (played by Culture Clash's Herbert Siguenza). His brother Juancito (Vincent Chandler) is a vegetable who watches television day and night, while his sister Maria (Lysa Flores, who also did the film's soundtrack) remains the only one holding the family together.

Miguel Arteta, a graduate of the American Film Insitute, made his directorial debut with *Star Maps*. He also wrote the screenplay, which was based on a screenplay by Arteta and Matthew Greenfield. The film was enriched by the talented Latino (especially Annette Murphy and Efrain Figueroa) and non–Latino ensemble cast, the evocative cinematography by Chuy Chávez and the soundtrack.

Star Maps received excellent reviews. The Los Angeles Times commented, "A word-of-mouth success at this year's Sundance Film Festival, Star Maps is balanced between con-trivance and reality. Heavy on melodramatic elements, it nevertheless exerts a powerful emotional pull.... Writer-director Miguel Arteta has given this story both sweetness and edge, as well as an explosive father-son relationship that is a considerable strength."[67]

Latino Film Stars and Filmmakers

TRINI ALVARADO

Latina child stars have been rare in U.S. films, and as such, the case of Trini Alvarado is unique. She was a child star in the 1980s who went on to become an adult star in the 1990s.

Trini Alvarado was born on January 10, 1967, in New York City, to a Puerto Rican mother and a Spanish father. She began dancing flamenco at the age of seven in her parents' troupe. She made her theater debut at the age of nine in the musical *Becca*, and two years later made her Broadway debut in Joseph Papp's *Runaways*.

She made her film debut in 1979 in the film *Rich Kids*. She followed it with a role in the television film *Times Square* (1980) with Silvana Gallardo; played the daughter of Diane Keaton in *Mrs. Soffel* (1984); and then played the daughter of Bette Midler in *Stella* (1990). She had other roles as daughters in two other films: Susan Sarandon's in *Little Women* (1994); and Anjelica Huston's in *The Perez Family* (1995).

Other films include *Dreams Don't Die* (1982, ABC); *Jacobo Timerman: Prisoner Without a Name, Cell Without a Number* (1983, NBC); *Sweet Lorraine* (1987); *Satisfaction* (1988); and *American Blue Note* (1991, P.E.). She moved into adult roles playing the wife of Babe Ruth in *The Babe* (1992). She also appeared in *Fringe* (2009) and *All Good Things* (2010).

YARELI ARIZMENDI

Yareli Arizmendi was born in Mexico and came to the United States in 1981.

She earned wide acclaim in the role of Rosaura, the overweight bride in Alfonso Arau's commercial and critical hit, *Like Water for Chocolate* (1991).

She played Marbelly Morales in Disney's *The Big Green* (1995) with Steve Guttenberg and had a featured role in *Gunfighter's Moon* (1996).

She played the lead role in the play *Nostalgia Maldita: 1-900-Mexico,* which opened at the Los Angeles Theatre Center during June 1995.

Her most recent roles were in *Up Close & Personal* (1996) with Robert Redford and Michelle Pfeiffer; Sergio Arau's *A Day without a Mexican* (2005); and *Naco Es Chido* (2010). She has made appearances in numerous television episodes.

She is married to Sergio Arau (the son of Mexican director Alfonso Arau).

MIGUEL ARTETA

Although the 1990s saw a diminished Latino presence in film, some Latino actors and filmmakers began to use independent film as a vehicle for entry. Such was the case of director/screenwriter Miguel Arteta.

Miguel Arteta was born in 1965 in San Juan, Puerto Rico. He grew up in Puerto Rico before going to the United States to attend college. In 1989, he graduated from the film program at Wesleyan University. He enrolled in the documentary program at Harvard University, but subsequently left due to a dispute over curriculum. In 1993, he obtained a master of fine arts degree from the director's program at the American Film Institute.

In 1990, his musical satire *Every Day Is a Beautiful Day* was nominated for the Student Academy Award, and it was showcased at the Berlin Film Festival the same year. In 1995, his American Film Institute thesis, *Lucky Peach,* was selected for the Chicago Latino Film Festival. In 1996, he attended the Sundance Institute Writer's Lab to work on *Ball and Chain*, a screenplay he co-wrote with Ron Nyswaner. He supplemented his filmmaking experience by working on Sidney Lumet's feature film *Q & A* (1990) and Jonathan Demme's documentary *Cousin Bobby* (1991).

In 1997, he directed and scripted the independent film *Star Maps*, a tale of the dark side of a Latino family at the margins of the American dream. He stated about his intent in making the film, "My goal was to make a personal film about the insane world of Hollywood. I wanted to show how extreme this culture really is from the point of view of people's dreams, expectations and sexual perversions. These are dysfunctional people living in a melodramatic world. Their dreams and the themes I am exploring are real, but the world around them is so twisted they have little chance for self-awareness. The film needed to be larger-than-life and metaphoric. Normalcy has been thrown out and different cultures and people clash and come together in absurd ways."[68]

When I asked him how he conceived the idea for the film, he commented, "I was at AFI [American Film Institute]. I was driving to school through Sunset Boulevard and watching the kids stand at the corner and sell maps and there was something kind of beautiful about that image. You know, as a Latino trying to get into the business somehow, I could identify with the image, by trying to sell little bits of dreams. And I knew I wanted to make a movie about how far you should go to make a dream come true, should you be willing to hurt yourself or not? This metaphor of prostitution seemed to be something that could be interesting. We [Arteta and producer Matthew Greenfield] started writing the script while I was finishing my short film at AFI and it took about a year to develop the script."[69]

It took Arteta and Greenfield some four and a half years to get their project to the screen. Arteta and Greenfield raised the money in bits and pieces, and shot the entire film in 29 days. They worked on a budget of $200,000 and then raised more money for editing and printing. He commented, "We turned down money left and right for this movie.... Actors would be interested because they wanted to play these risky roles, and a lot of them came with money. But they also came saying that they had to have some say in casting or they wanted final cut. We would suffer for three nights, lose a lot of sleep and then say no."[70]

The film opened at the 1997 Sundance Film Festival to universal acclaim.

At first, Arteta was anxious about the response of Latino actors due to the film's offbeat story. "We were trying to do a Latino film, that was, I think, in some ways challenging, what people expect from a Latino to do. I mean, I think there have been a few Latino filmmakers that opened the doors for more artistic vision and made it easier for us to do this. Alfonso Arau, I think, with *Like Water for Chocolate*. And Robert Rodriguez, I think, went a long way to sort of say, you know, Latinos can have different kinds of stories. Once we showed the script around the Latino acting community, which we were nervous, but rather than getting criticized, what we got, we got tons of encouragement, like it was wonderful; the Latino acting community really came out and supported the script."[71]

Star Maps opened during July 1997, earning widespread and commercial success. The *Los Angeles Times* noted, "Part of what makes *Star Maps* different is its potentially exploitative subject matter, its fictional thesis that some of those cute young people out there selling maps on our streets are in reality male prostitutes on call to potential customers of both sexes. Writer-director Miguel Arteta has given this story both sweetness and edge, as well as an explosive father-son relationship that is a considerable strength."[72]

Arteta spoke of the film's content: "As a Latino artist it is hard to live in Los Angeles without satirizing Hollywood and the racism inherent within ... I have noticed that because I am Latino, people generally expect me to make one of two types of films: either the gang banging, drug dealing, hustling film with one-dimensional characters or the film that deals strictly in positive images of Latinos. While I support the value and need for films with positive images, I wanted to go beyond this expectation."[73]

I asked him whether he would continue making independent films or prefer to work within the studio system in the future. He responded, "I'd like to do both. Jonathan Demme is a good role model for me. He will do a documentary, he will do quirky comedies, he will do a thriller, he will do *Philadelphia*, and he just moves back and forth, including doing music videos. I'd like to go back and forth, just make different kinds of stories."[74]

Arteta's second feature film, *Chuck and Buck*, was released in 2000. His other recent films include *The Good Girl* (2002), *Youth in Revolt* (2010), and *Cedar Rapids* (2011). He has directed several television films and TV series episodes. Miguel Arteta continues to write prospective film projects.

ANGEL AVILES

Angel Aviles is part of a new emergence of Latina and Latino actors and actresses enriching U.S. cinema.

She was born in New York City to Puerto Rican parents. She attended the High School of the Performing Arts in New York., She had originally planned to be a dancer, but a leg injury altered her course into acting.

She made her film debut in *Chain of Desire* in 1993, but the dark-haired actress made a strong impression in the role of a waitress in Alan Rudolph's acclaimed *Equinox* (1992).

During 1994, she starred in the ABC Afterschool Special *Flower Babies,* which was directed by actress Linda Lavin.

Her big break came with the role of Sad Girl, the jaded Chicana gang girl in Allison Anders' flawed but well-intentioned *Mi Vida Loca* (1993). The acting of Angel and the other young Latinas and Latinos in the cast was the best thing about the film.

Aviles' subsequent films include Robert Rodriguez's *Desperado* (1995) with Salma Hayek and Antonio Banderas; Brian Cox's *Scorpion Spring* (1996); Alan Castle's *The Edge of Innocence* (1996) and *Somebody to Love* (1996) with Anthony Quinn and Rosie Pérez; *Stir* (1997); and *Deliverance from Evil* (2011).

She has a brother who is also an actor, Rick Aviles.

ANTONIO BANDERAS

Hollywood's nostalgia for an old-fashioned romantic leading man during the 1990s contributed to Antonio Banderas' rise to stardom. He was the first Spanish-born leading man since Antonio Moreno in the 1910s to acquire major Hollywood stardom.

He was born in Málaga, Spain, on August 10, 1960, to a father who was a policeman and a mother who was a teacher. He studied acting at the School of Dramatic Arts in Málaga and performed with the city's independent theater company. By the age of 21, he had moved his acting career to Madrid, where he worked in theater and television.

In 1982, director Pedro Almodóvar selected him for the lead in his film *Laberinto de Pasión/Labyrinth of Passion*. The film gave Banderas both a matinee idol and a serious actor status overnight. Banderas consolidated his stardom in several other films directed by Almodóvar, usually in filmic tales of the confusions of desire and fetishes of the generation who came of age after Franco's regime: *La Ley del Deseo/The Law of Desire* (1987); *Mujeres al Bordo de un Ataque Nervioso/Women on the Verge of a Nervous Breakdown* (1988); and *Átame/ Tie Me Up! Tie Me Down!* (1990).

Banderas' other films during this period included: *Pastaña Postizas* (1982); *El Señor Galindez* (1983); *El Caso Alomeria* (1984); *Los Zarcos/The Stilts* (1984); *Casa Cerrada* (1985); *La Corte de Farón* (1985); *Requiém por un Campesino Español* (1985); *27 Horas* (1986); *Así Como Habían Sido* (1987); *El Placer de Matar/The Pleasure of Killing* (1987); *Baton Rouge* (1988); *Si Te Dicen Que Caí* (1989); and *Contra el Viento* (1990).

In 1992, director Arne Glimcher cast him as the second lead, a Cuban *salsero*, opposite Armand Assante in his film *The Mambo Kings*. The film was only a moderate success but it helped introduce Banderas to mainstream U.S. audiences who did not frequent art house theaters that played Almodóvar films. Soon thereafter, director Jonathan Demme cast him as the gay lover of the AIDS victim (Tom Hanks) in his ground-breaking film *Philadelphia* (1993). Banderas commented later to the *Los Angeles Times*, "I came here because [Glimcher] trusted me.... He took the risk. And from that film Jonathan Demme calls me and it's impossible to say no to a name like Jonathan Demme. And then—boom."[75]

Banderas was third-billed in Neil Jordan's uneven *Interview with the Vampire* (1994), which was headlined by Tom Cruise and hot newcomer Brad Pitt. Banderas was eighth billed in Belle August's adaptation of Isabel Allende's novel *The House of the Spirits* (1995) after Jeremy Irons, Meryl Streep, Glenn Close, Winona Ryder, Vanessa Redgrave, María Conchita Alonso, and Armin Mueller-Stahl. The film was reviled and picketed by the Latino community for the absence of Latino actors in the main roles.

For Banderas' U.S. film career, however, the banner year was 1995, during which he starred in four films: the comedy-drama *Miami Rhapsody* with Mia Farrow and Sarah Jessica Parker; a cameo in the Robert Rodriguez–directed segment "The Misbehavers" in *Four*

Rooms; the maudlin thriller *Never Talk to Strangers* with Rebecca De Mornay; and Robert Rodriguez's more expensive remake of his previous *El Mariachi,* retitled as *Desperado* with hot newcomer Salma Hayek and veteran Cheech Marin. *Variety* commented, "Banderas cuts a devastatingly attractive figure, which will help somewhat to draw women to the pic."[76]

During 1996, he paired with the declining Sylvester Stallone in the weak action-drama *Assassins* and with Melanie Griffith and Daryl Hannah in *Two Much.* It was during the making of the latter film that Griffith (divorced from actor Don Johnson) and Banderas began a romance that made them the darlings of the paparazzi. Banderas separated from his wife, Spanish actress Ana Leza, and moved in with Griffith.

Banderas was then cast in the lead role in Betty Kaplan's uneven adaptation of another Isabel Allende novel, *Of Love and Shadows* (1996), with Jennifer Connelly and Stefanie Sandrelli. The *Los Angeles Times* noted, "Banderas and a few other actors have some good moments, but on the whole *Of Love and Shadows* is as terrible as it is well-meaning."[77] Banderas played (or rather sang) in the role of Ernesto "Che" Guevara in Alan Parker's atrocious and stereotypical film based on Andrew Lloyd Webber's equally historically distorted *Evita* (1996). The bloated, pompous and dull film was further sunk by the totally miscast and anemic Madonna in the lead role. The overbudgeted and overpublicized film came and went as the audiences stayed away.

Banderas had a cameo in Madonna's bizarre 1991 tour documentary *Truth or Dare* (1996).

One of Banderas' dream projects is a new film version of the Don Juan story (the don has previously been played memorably on the screen by John Barrymore and Errol Flynn). He told the *Los Angeles Times,* "I've always dreamed of doing the classic version, in Spanish, with a Spanish crew, the whole thing in verse.... The British, they put Shakespeare, their ancient culture, up on the screen. Spain never did that, and I would like us to bite the cake, and see if it is possible ... I don't feel freaked out ... I don't feel fear. I've been in this profession twenty years ... I believe exactly when they say to me 'action' and 'cut.' That's where I want to focus all my energy, in the moment. That's what I'm looking for my whole life."[78]

More recently, he was cast in the title role of *The Mask of Zorro* (1998) opposite Anthony Hopkins. Unfortunately, the spirited film was tainted with careless disregard of Mexican and Chicano history, as well as the casting of non–Latinos in the main roles. The film benefited from the location shooting in Mexico, the cinematography and the dashing swordplay. Banderas was the first Spaniard to play Zorro in a U.S. film. Nevertheless, the film proved to be the first commercial and critical hit that really depended on Banderas' box-office appeal.

During 1999, Banderas made his directorial debut with the drama *Crazy in Alabama,* which starred his wife Melanie Griffith. The film was only a modest success. The *New York Times* noted, "Mr. Banderas directs capably enough to keep the film lively."[79] He was more successful in front of the camera with Woody Harrelson and Lolita Davidovich in Ron Shelton's evocative drama *Play It to the Bone* (1999, BV/Touchstone) which focused on two journeyman middleweight boxers getting their big chance. The *Los Angeles Times* commented, "Antonio Banderas [plays] what is arguably his most challenging role ever and perhaps the richest since his collaborations with Pedro Almodóvar."[80]

In 2003, he starred in Maury Yeston's musical *Nine* on Broadway to notable acclaim.

The play was based on Federico Fellini's film *8½*. Banderas won the Drama Desk Award and the Outer Critics Circle Award. He was also nominated for a Tony Award.

His film career has continued to flourish with such films as the Robert Rodriguez Spy Kids franchise: *Spy Kids 1* (2001); *Spy Kids 2* (2002); *Spy Kids 3* (2003); and *Spy Kids 4* (2011). In 2002, he was reunited with his most frequent costar, Salma Hayek, for the critical and commercial success of *Frida*. In addition, he has been in another Rodriguez film, *Once upon a Time in Mexico* (2003), and appeared in *The Legend of Zorro* (2005). In 2011, he was reunited with director Pedro Almodóvar for the film *The Skin I Live In*.

JESSE BORREGO

Jesse Borrego was born on August 1, 1962, in San Antonio, Texas, to Mexican parents. He honed his acting skills as a student at the Incarnate Word College and later had roles at the Sol/Sun Experimental Theater in Texas. He continued his study of acting at the California Institute of the Arts.

Borrego is also an accomplished dancer and it was in an audition for the television series *Fame* that he won the role of Jesse Velasquez, the Mexican national enrolled at the dance school in the series. He later said that *Fame* "really allowed me to economically settle myself."[81] During 1993, he played the title role in the New York Shakespeare Festival's new production of *Woyzeck,* which was directed by JoAnne Akalaitis.

Borrego earned rave reviews and Akalaitis commented, "He belongs in great roles.... He is not afraid to go to those emotions that are painful."[82] Borrego, who grew up in a music-oriented family (his father, Jesse, Sr., is a professional accordionist in San Antonio) has often felt constrained by typical roles in both film and television. Borrego commented, "Some people do dinner theater after television. The first thing I did was an ensemble, avant-garde piece.... When I did it, I thought, 'Yeah, this is where I'm from. This is it, baby.'"[83]

He made his film debut in Martin Scorsese's "Life Lessons" segment of *New York Stories* (1989) opposite Nick Nolte and Rosanna Arquette. Other films include *I Like It Like That* (1994); Allison Anders' *Mi Vida Loca* (1993); Peter Bratt's *Follow Me Home* (1995) with Salma Hayek and Benjamin Bratt: John Sayles' *Lone Star* (1996) with Elizabeth Peña; and *Con Air* (1997) with Nicolas Cage and Rachel Ticotin. His most important film role remains that of Cruz, the gifted Chicano painter who becomes a drug addict in Taylor Hackford's *Blood In, Blood Out/Bound by Honor* (1993), for which Borrego and the cast received excellent notices, despite the film's negative reviews.

His stage credits include *Green Card* at the Mark Taper Forum; *'Tis Pity She's a Whore* at the Chicago Goodman Theater; *Cymbeline* and *American Notes* at the Public Theater; *Widows* at the Williamson Theater Festival; and two plays at the Guthrie Theater, *The Screens* and *Leon, Lena & Lenz*. Borrego is also a member of the Tribal Players, which performed an ensemble adaptation of Shakespeare's *Hamlet* during the spring of 1992.

Among his numerous television appearances is a recurring role in ABC's *Under Cover* and guest roles in *Miami Vice*; *China Beach*; *Married with Children*; and *Midnight Caller*.

In 1990, he began Lupita Productions, and has produced several plays, concerts, and short films. His most recent films include *La Mission* (2012) and *Colombiana* (2011).

BENJAMIN BRATT

During the 1990s, Latinos and Latinas on television were nearly extinct. One of the few Latino regulars was Benjamin Bratt, who played Rey Curtis, the half–Peruvian Native American and half–European police detective on *Law & Order*.

He was born on December 16, 1963, in San Francisco, California, to a Peruvian Indian mother and a German-American father. He began acting as an undergraduate at the University of California at Santa Barbara. He completed a master's degree at the San Francisco American Conservatory Theater. His classical training includes lead roles in productions of *Picnic* and *Terra Nova*.

He made his professional debut as an actor at the Utah Shakespeare Festival, later returning to the conservatory to continue his studies and training. Soon thereafter, he won a leading role in the ABC pilot *Juarez*. Lead roles in two other short-lived series followed: ABC's *Nightwatch* and *Nasty Boys*. He had a leading role in the ABC miniseries *Texas*.

Bratt began his film career in earnest playing an inexperienced detective in *One Good Cop* (1991) opposite Michael Keaton and Rachel Ticotin, and he followed this part with roles in *Bright Angel* (1991) with Sam Shepard and *Chains of Gold* (1991) with John Travolta.

His biggest film break came with Taylor Hackford's *Bound by Honor* (1993) aka *Blood In, Blood Out*, which followed the crucial years in the lives of three Chicano youths in East Los Angeles. While the acting was praised by the critics, the film suffered in comparison to Edward James Olmos' *American Me*. The *Los Angeles Times* wrote, "The Olmos film is largely unsentimental and inescapably earnest, a kind of wake-up call to the Latino community, while Hackford's, for all its fervor, is thoroughly slick and commercial, a potboiler more concerned than not with getting an exploitive rise of an audience."[84] The *New York Times* wrote, "Mr. Hackford has cast the film well. Though they must play at a fever pitch most of the time, Mr. Chapa, Mr. Bratt and M. Borrego are excellent."[85]

Bratt had supporting roles in *Demolition Man* (1993) with Sylvester Stallone; *The River Wild* (1994); and *Clear and Present Danger* (1994) with Harrison Ford.

Bratt's casting in *Law & Order* was timely. In the wake of actor Chris Noth's departure, executive producer and creator Dick Wolf called Bratt. They had worked previously on *Nasty Boys*. Bratt later recalled, "He ... flattered me with offers on other series, but I focused on my film career ... it was an opportunity to mix things up a little on a show that was well-written and smart and worth watching and endured despite the cast changes."[86] In the show, Bratt played a conservative, happily married detective with three daughters who often clashes with the older, liberal detective Briscoe (Jerry Orbach).

About the significance of his role, he stated, "As a person of color, every role I play, I carry a certain amount of responsibility to my community. There's no denying the fact, whether you want to or not, you're forced into being a role model because there are so few to look to. Today, there's a real sense of pride that runs through the community when one of our own makes it."[87]

In 1995, Bratt was reunited with Jesse Borrego to headline an independent film directed by his brother Peter Bratt (in his directorial debut) entitled *Follow Me Home*. The film told the story of four ethnic men who embark on a spiritual cross-country odyssey of self-discovery.

In the early 2000s he appeared in the comedy *Miss Congeniality* (2000) with Julia Roberts and the drama *Traffic* (2000) with Michael Douglas. He played the lead role of Puerto Rican poet and playwright Miguel Piñero in *Piñero* in 2001, for which he was nominated for an Academy Award as Best Actor. Later in the decade he was in *Catwoman* (2005); *The Great Raid* (2005); *Tucker* (2008); and *La Mission* (2010), directed by his brother Peter Bratt.

LUMI CAVAZOS

During the 1990s, three promising Mexican actresses attempted to cross over into U.S. films. One of these was Lumi Cavazos, who honed her considerable acting skill in theater and who had just scored a widely heralded success with *Like Water for Chocolate*. (The other two were Salma Hayek and Julieta Rosen, both well-established in *telenovelas*.)

She was born Luz María Cavazos Aguirre on December 21, 1968, in Monterrey, Nuevo León, Mexico. She was initially interested in music but failed in her attempt to enter a school of music. She began acting at the age of fifteen in a theater group at the University of Guadalajara and thereafter traveled to Mexico City to further develop her craft. She later recalled, "I think the most important thing that I learned in theatre was to learn to work in a group, and the discipline that theater gives you. The theater experience helps you to concentrate, the analysis of the text and the characters. All those have been tools that now, in my film career, have been useful to me because I learned that the more you study, research and work a character, the better your performance will be. And you will be more secure as an actor."[88]

In Guadalajara, she did numerous plays, among them: Ann Jellicoe's *El Knack Y Como Lograrlo;* Franz Kafka's *Metamorphosis;* Lorenzo Villalanga's *La Tuta y La Ramoneta*; Dario Fo's *No Puede Pagar? No Pague;* Peter Weiss' *La Pasión de Pentesilea*; Molière's *Las Mujeres Sablas;* and in Los Angeles in 1998 she did *Tina*.

She made her film debut in 1988 in a Mexican film, Busi Cortés' *El Secreto de Romelia*. In 1991, she came to the attention of Alfonso Arau, who was conducting interviews and auditions for the role of Tita in the film adaptation of Laura Esquivel's novel *Como Agua para Chocolate* (Like Water for Chocolate, 1991). After her interview, she told the *Los Angeles Times*, " I ran to a bookstore to get the novel ... and read it several times to imbue myself in the character. I real-

Lumi Cavazos was born in Mexico and became an international hit with *Como Agua para Chocolate* (*Like Water for Chocolate*) in 1993.

ized how much Tita was like me, coming from a conservative family and all."[89] Cavazos won the prized role and went on to give a memorable performance.

When I asked her how she prepared for the role, she commented, "Laura Esquivel would organize dinners at her house and we spoke a lot. One time we prepared mole together, from toasting the almonds and nuts and everything. For me that was really important because it was creating the intricacies of my character and directly with the author of the novel. Also, on one occasion she showed me photos of the real Tita. She wrote the novel in honor of her great-aunt, who like Tita was not able to marry."[90]

The film became an international commercial and critical hit and launched Cavazos and her co-star Marco Leonardi into overnight fame. In the United States the film earned more than $22 million and became the highest-grossing foreign film of all time. *Time* noted, "Acted with subtle ferocity, directed with expansive tenderness, *Like Water for Chocolate* is a story of passion in bondage and death in a fire storm of desire too long withheld. Viewers need not feel so constrained; they can enjoy the emotional splendor, gasp at the ghosts, cry with as much good cause as Tita. By comparison with this banquet of feelings, most other movies are trail mix."[91] Lumi went on to win the Best Actress award at the Tokyo International Film Festival, as well as the Festival of Granada in Brazil and the Festival in Cali, Colombia. In Mexico, she was nominated for the Ariel as Best Actress.

With regard to the importance of *Like Water for Chocolate,* she stated, "I think it is a very important film that opened, once again, the door for Mexican cinema to the outside world—internationally. After this movie, it is more possible for people to give credit to a movie that comes from Mexico."[92]

In 1991, she starred in a Mexican television series, Guillermo del Toro's *La Hora Marcada.* Soon thereafter, Televisa contracted her for a *telenovela,* Jose Fons' *El Vuelo del Águila;* and the rival Telemundo garnered her services for their *telenovela Tres Destinos* (1994), which was shot in Puerto Rico. In an unprecedented coincidence, both *telenovelas* played simultaneously in 1994.

Soon thereafter, Alfonso Arau asked her to audition for the female lead in his U.S. directorial debut film, *A Walk in the Clouds,* but she failed to get the role when the project went to a different studio. In 1991, she made her third Mexican film, Busi Cortés' *Serpientes y Escaleras.* She made her U.S. film debut in Joe Land's *Of Milk and Honey* (1994) and followed it with Wes Anderson's *Bottle Rocket* (1995) and the TNT western film *Last Stand at Saber River* (1996) with Tom Selleck.

She is philosophical about her transition into U.S. film: "You never know how hard it's going to be, and what's more, like I never had a Hollywood dream. But ... thanks to *Like Water for Chocolate* there was interest from the talent agencies to sign us [Cavazos and Marco Leonardi] and we decided to stay. And it was like starting again."[93]

A by-product of *Like Water for Chocolate* was working with Italian actor Marco Leonardi (star of *Cinema Paradiso*). The two fell in love. When she left for Hollywood he accompanied her to try his luck in U.S. films as well. She commented to the *Los Angeles Times,* "I came here because I wanted to be with Marco and he wanted to be with me.... One day, we were friends, and the next, we were in love.... Our romance didn't affect our performance in the film ... but the chemistry between us made our love scenes much better."[94] In 1995, the couple costarred in the Italian film *Viva San Isidro!,* shot on location in Mexico.

In 1996, both Cavazos and Leonardi starred in three films: the independent film *Manhattan Merengue,* Alessandro Cappelleti's *Viva San Isidro!,* and Stefano Mignucci's *Anime Ribelli/Rebel Souls.* When asked about the status of Mexican cinema by *La Opinión,* she commented, "I look at it with hopeful eyes, because I have seen very good work and the people in it have contributed to its renaissance. There is much interest in people to improve its quality. There are many well-trained actors. And I am committed to working in Mexican films."[95]

During 1997, there were reports that she had been cast as Emiliano Zapata's wife in a film to be directed by Alfonso Arau and shot on location in Mexico. However, problems plagued the production. Arau later made the film but without her participation. She broke up with Leonardi and returned to Mexico in 1999. She continues to hone her acting skills and studies acting and singing performance under Carole D'Andrea.

Her more recent films include a Mexican short film, Carlos Cuarón's *Sístole, Diástole* (1998); Francisco Athié's *Fiber Optics* (1999); Linda Kandel's *Máscara* (1999); a cameo in Wayne Wang's *Anywhere but Here* (1999; and Allison Anders' *Sugar Town* (1999). Her most recent roles include the film adaptation of the Julia Alvarez novel *In the Time of the Butterflies* (2001); *Exposed* (2003); and *Las Buenasrostro* (2005). She has appeared on both Mexican and U.S. television.She has appeared in several Mexican *telenovelas*: *La Ley Del Silencio* (2005); and *Gritos de Muerte Y de Libertad* (2010), among others.

CHUY CHÁVEZ

Chuy Chávez was born in Mexico City. He grew up on Mexican movie sets starting at age twelve. His father was a cinematographer in Mexican films.

After attending film school in Mexico City, he quickly established himself as one of Mexico's best cinematographers in the early 1990s. Among the notable Mexican films that he has lensed are *El Bulto* and *Gringito*. In 1995, he won the Ariel Award for best cinematographer for the film *Bienvenido Welcome.*

In 1997, he worked on his first U.S. film, as cinematographer for Miguel Arteta's *Star Maps.* His most recent film credits include *Daniel and Ana* (2009) and *Cedar Rapids* (2011).

CHAYANNE

The popular Puerto Rican–born recording artist made his U.S. film debut in the 1998 film *Dance with Me.*

He was born Elmer Figueroa Arce in San Lorenzo, Puerto Rico, in 1968. Musically inclined since an early age, at the age of ten he joined Los Chicos, a group that went on to rival Menudo in popularity. By the age of seventeen, Chayanne had recorded his first of seven solo albums. His albums have sold some four million copies, thirteen of which have become Top 10 Spanish-language hits. One of them earned a Grammy nomination. He has acted in one *telenovela* and one Spanish-language television series.

He made his U.S. film debut in *Dance with Me* opposite Vanessa Williams, which met with modest success.

RAYMOND CRUZ

Chicano actor Raymond Cruz has done diverse roles in theater, television and film. However, Hollywood more often than not has typecast him as either a *vato loco* or a gung-ho macho soldier.

He was born on July 1, 1961, in East Los Angeles, California. He earned the Los Angeles Drama Critics Award for his powerful performance in *Buck*. His other notable theater appearances were in *The 4th Club* and *American Buffalo*, among others.

On television, he was memorable as the strung-out *vato loco* in Jesús Salvador Treviño's evocative Afterschool Special *Gangs*. His television credits include *Working and Living in Space* and *Vietnam War Stories*, among others.

His most prominent film roles remain those of the drug-adducted *vato loco* in Taylor Hackford's *Bound by Honor* (1994), aka *Blood In, Blood Out*, and the gung ho soldier in the popular *Clear and Present Danger* (1994). His films include *Gremlins 2: The New Batch* (1990); *Dead Again* (1991); *Man Trouble* (1992); *Under Siege* (1992); *Broken Arrow* (1996); *Up Close & Personal* (1996); *The Substitute* (1996); *Last Stand at Saber River* (1996); and *Alien: Resurrection* (1997); among others. Cruz is overdue for leading roles.

He was offered better opportunities on television. He costarred as a regular on several television series: *Nip/Tuck* (2003–05); *CSI: Crime Scene Investigation* (2003–08); *My Name Is Earl* (2007–08); *CSI: Miami* (2003–11); *The Closer* (2005–11) and *Major Crimes* (2012–). He played a brief but memorable role as Tuco in *Breaking Bad* (2008–09).

ALFONSO CUARÓN

During the 1990s, among the new generation of Mexican directors contributing to the renaissance of Mexican cinema was Alfonso Cuarón.

Alfonso Cuarón was born on November 28, 1961, in Mexico City, Mexico. He learned filmmaking at the Centro de Capacitación Cinematográfica (CCC) in Mexico City. In 1993, he made his directorial film debut with the funny comedy *Sólo Con tu Pareja,* which earned worldwide acclaim. Hollywood quickly came calling and he was contacted to direct *A Little Princess* (1995). Cuarón enlisted the services of Mexican cinematographer Emmanuel Lubezki, who had lensed his first film. Although the film was not a great commercial or critical success, Cuarón's undeniable filmmaking talent did not go unnoticed.

In 1997, he directed his second U.S. film, the contemporary version of Charles Dickens' *Great Expectations* with Robert De Niro and Anne Bancroft. He hit greater renown with *Y Tu Mamá También* in 2001 and *Harry Potter and the Prisoner of Azkaban* in 2005. His most recent film is *Gravity* (2013), which earned him a Best Director Academy Award.

MICHAEL DELORENZO

Michael DeLorenzo had the unique distinction in the 1990s of starring in a popular television series in which the two leads were Latino and African American.

He was born on October 31, 1959, in New York City, the son of a Puerto Rican father and an Italian mother. He began in show business at the age of six as the youngest boy in a Rita Moreno Christmas special.

Due to the tough barrio environment in which he grew up, his mother had enrolled him in dance classes to keep him out of trouble at the age of six. He started out with the flamenco with the Ballet Hispánico in Manhattan and by the age of seven, he won a scholarship to the School of American Ballet. Later, he went on to study at the New York School of Ballet with Richard Thomas and Barbara Thallus and then to the High School of the Performing Arts (the school in Manhattan on which the television series *Fame* was based).

By the age of seventeen, he was cast in the role of Chino in Jerome Robbins' Broadway revival of the musical *West Side Story*. In 1993, he won the Los Angeles Drama Circle Award for his powerful performance in the play *Stand Up Tragedy*. In the play, he portrayed five different characters, which required him to deliver fifteen-page monologues.

In the late 1970s, he worked as a dancer on the popular television series *Fame*. Subsequently, he also appeared in the film version in 1980 with Irene Cara. He appeared in more than twenty films, including the Vietnam drama *Platoon Leader* (1988); *A Few Good Men* (1991); *Diggstown* (1992); *Judgment Day* (1993); and Gregory Nava's evocative *My Family/ Mi Familia* (1995).

In 1993, he won the plum starring role of the Puerto Rican detective Eddie Torres in the Fox television police drama *New York Undercover*. DeLorenzo and his costar Malik Yoba headlined the only show with Latino and African American leads, and the show quickly became the most popular prime-time series in Latino and African American homes. However, by the end of the third season conflicts arose. According to the *Los Angeles Times*, "The furor on the show erupted when DeLorenzo and Yoba, who were both largely unknown before the program's premiere, failed to report for work on July 22, the first day of production. Statements released ... said that one of the actors was seeking $75,000 an episode. Each lead makes between $20,000 and $30,000 per episode."[96]

For his part, DeLorenzo stated, "I wanted to explore the opportunities to direct. Everyone else on dramas gets to direct.... This was a matter of broken promises and giving people respect."[97] Both stars subsequently returned to the series with none of their demands met. During the 1996–97 season, a white character role was added to the cast, which did much to undermine Fox's contention that the show's budget could not meet DeLorenzo and Yoba's demands. The show was soon thereafter dropped by Fox.

DeLorenzo appeared in the comedy *Someone to Love* (1996), a disappointing film considering the cast, which included Anthony Quinn, Rosie Pérez and Harvey Keitel. During 2000, he won the prized role of a problem-plagued Chicano boxer in the Showtime cable series *Resurrection Blvd.*

He has branched out into directing in both film and television, and is a musician and composer. His most recent film is *The City of Gardens* (2010).

BENICIO DEL TORO

Among the handful of young Puerto Rican actors at the brink of film stardom at the tail end of the 1990s was the stage-trained Benicio Del Toro.

He was born on February 19, 1967, in Santurce, Puerto Rico, and was raised in Pennsylvania. He trained as an actor at the Stella Adler Conservatory and Circle in the Square, as well as the Actor's Circle Theatre in Los Angeles. He had originally signed up at the University of California, San Diego, to major in business and planned eventually to study law like his father, mother, grandmother, godfather and an uncle. However, once he tooled his skills in an acting class as a freshman he was hooked on acting. He recalled later, "I knew this what I wanted to do for the rest of my life."[98]

It was while at the Stella Adler Conservatory that he began appearing on television in such series as *Miami Vice* and *O'Hara*. Other television credits included *ShellGame* and *Hard Copy*. He won the plum role of Mexican *narcotraficante* Rafael Caro Quintero in the television miniseries *Drug Wars: The Camarena Story* (1990) opposite Elizabeth Peña and Steven Bauer.

His film debut came in the James Bond film *Licence to Kill* in 1989. He had featured and supporting roles in the following films: *Big Top Pee-Wee* (1989); Sean Penn's *The Indian Runner* (1991) with Charles Bronson; Peter Weir's offbeat *Fearless* (1993) with Rosie Pérez, in which he played her husband: and a small role in *Money for Nothing* (1993) with John Cusack.

However, it was the role of the conniving Lamar Dickey, the corrupt cop in John Bailey's film noir sleeper *China Moon* (1994), that tagged him as a future star. He won excellent notices along with his costars Madeleine Stowe and Ed Harris. He followed this with a role in George Huang's independent film *Swimming with Sharks* (1995), about the tribulations of an aspiring screenwriter (Frank Whaley) at the hands of an abrasive executive (Kevin Spacey).

He scored in Bryan Singer's sleeper of the year *The Usual Suspects* (1995), an offbeat and dark tale of a group of small-time thieves trying for the big time. The ensemble cast included Kevin Spacey (who won the Academy Award for Best Supporting Actor for his performance), Gabriel Byrne, Stephen Baldwin and Chazz Palminteri. Del Toro won raves for his portrayal of Fred Fenster, the enigmatic gay thief. *Newsweek* noted, "Del Toro played Fred Fenster, a con man with cool threads and the most marvelously slurry voice anyone had heard (or misheard) in years."[99] He stated, "I like anything that's three-dimensional, anything I can believe in—even if it's fantastic, surreal or from another planet."[100]

About the state of Latinos in the media, he told the *Boston Globe*, "It's hard for anybody to make it.... It's harder if you're a woman, an African American, a Latina—to make it in anything. But it'd probably be less [difficult] if I'd had a different first and last name. If people like me—good, if not, I do bits all my life and I'll open a theater company. As an actor you're a gun for hire.... It's all beyond your control. Hopefully there will be more Latino writers and directors. Young writers and directors will take chances, like Robert Rodriguez [of *El Mariachi* and *Desperado*]."[101]

More recently, he played the lead in the comedy *Excess Baggage* (1997) opposite Alicia Silverstone; the legendary Chicano activist/attorney Oscar Zeta, alias the "Brown Buffalo," in *Leaving Las Vegas* (1998); and an embattled Mexican cop in *Traffic* (2000). For his role as the honest Mexican cop battling the drug cartels, Del Toro won an Academy Award for Best Supporting Actor.

In 2008, he played the Argentine revolutionary Ernesto "Che" Guevara in the two-part film called *Che,* for which he won numerous accolades and awards. His recent films include *The Wolfman* (2010), *The Iceman* (2011), and *Savages* (2012).

GUILLERMO DEL TORO

One of the new generation of talented Mexican-born directors who made the crossover into U.S. film in the 1990s was Guillermo del Toro.

He was born on October 9, 1964, in Guadalajara, Mexico, and from an early age became fascinated with film, especially the horror genre. In 1992, he directed the Mexican horror classic *Cronos*, which went on to become an international success. Among the several awards that the film earned was that of Best Picture at the Cannes Film Festival. On the strength of that one film, he was courted by most of the major Hollywood studios.

Del Toro made his U.S. directorial debut with the film *Mimic* (1997), which he also co-scripted. The *Los Angeles Times* wrote, "As those familiar with Del Toro's previous work, the haunting Mexican vampire film *Cronos,* already know, that gift is a disturbing thing to observe. Del Toro is an expert at the ominous, using a striking visual sense to drench his films with an atmosphere suffocating thick with undefined menace."[102]

His recent film credits include *The Devil's Backbone* (2001), *Hellboy* (2004), *Hellboy II* (2008), and *The Pacific Rim* (2012). He is a screenwriter, producer, and director. Del Toro currently has several film projects in different stages of development.

HÉCTOR ELIZONDO

One of the few Latinos to costar in a television series during the 1990s was Héctor Elizondo, who played the Emmy-nominated role of the chief of staff on CBS' *Chicago Hope.*

He was born on December 22, 1936, in New York City, of Puerto Rican parents. He obtained his training at the Ballet Arts Company of Carnegie Hall and at the Actors Studio.

He began his career at the age of ten, appearing on radio's *The Okey-Dokey Ranch House*, and he appeared on *The Wendy Barrie Show* on television in 1947. He later recalled, "Then I did radio as part of the Frank Murray Boys' Choir. I did that for a year and then finally decided after school I didn't want to go to rehearsals any more. I wanted to play ball." A decade later he returned to performing, and had this to say: "My father was a proud man and one who identified strongly with his culture. When he finally accepted the idea that I was going into this profession, he said, 'Change your name.' I said, 'Dad, it's a lovely name. You cannot mispronounce Elizondo.'"[103]

Elizondo went on to the Off-Broadway stage, where he earned fame and respect as a versatile actor. In 1971, he won an Obie Award for his role of God in the comedy *Steambath*.

He made his film debut in *The Vixens* in 1969 and over the next three decades played villains and good guys in both comedy and drama. He won acclaim for his role of the supportive hotel manager in the comedy-drama *Pretty Woman* (1990) with Julia Roberts and Richard Gere. When queried about the lack of Latino roles in his career, he commented, "I never get sent Latin scripts. The ones I'm sent stink and I wouldn't do them. I never play Latinos because usually what I'm sent is 'this guy's a drug dealer, this guy's a killer.' Those are caricatures, that's nobody I knew growing up. I don't want to be ethnocentric. To be the only Latin ... I'm somewhat bemused by it because there should be more of use and that's too bad.... I didn't know that there was a category, which I oppose, of Latin actor. Is there a category of Latin actor, or Irish actor? My nationality is American. I didn't have [the Latin] category till I came to Los Angeles. In New York I was an actor. I did everything. I came from the theater: I did Off Broadway, I did movies, I did television, and then I came here and read scripts. 'Fulano, matón, drugita.' I went back to New York to be an actor, here I was a Latin actor, and there I was an actor who happened to be Latin.'"[104] When asked how he escaped stereotypes, he stated, "I've dodged a bullet because of an accident of birth. I was born in New York City and am bilingual. I met a lot of Latinos here who didn't speak Spanish. My dad wouldn't let me speak English at home until I went to school because he thought, wisely I think, to have another language is to have another soul. [The other reason] is that I'm a white guy. Do you think if I was mestizo or a mulatto I would have the same opportunities? No way." In another interview he noted, "I have also been stubborn in refusing to do certain types of roles that feed into that distortion, that feed into that horrible misrepresentation [of Latinos]—the drug dealer of the month. That kind of garbage. I don't know if I wouldn't have done those [roles], if I had been starving, but it never quite came to it."[105]

Elizondo also feels strongly about not wanting to be a traditional leading man. He remarked, "I've been offered leads in shows and movies, I usually turn them down. It's too much trouble. What I look for is a good role that I can find the humanity in."[106]

Before his successful turn in *Chicago Hope*, he had played in scores of television shows. During 1992, he costarred with Brian Dennehy in the ABC miniseries *The Burden of Proof*. The film was a sequel to Scott Turow's *Presumed Innocent*, the 1990 film with Harrison Ford and the late Raúl Juliá (with Elizondo as a replacement). The long-running success of *Chicago Hope* began in 1992 and extended to 2000.

He has costarred in several television films: *The Impatient Heart* (1971, NBC); *Wanted: The Sundance Woman* (1976, ABC); *The Dain Curse* (1978, CBS) with Jean Simmons; *Honey Boy* (1982, NBC); *Women of San Quentin* (1983, NBC); *Murder: By Reason of Insanity* (1985, CBS); *Out of the Darkness* (1985, CBS); and *Courage* (1986, CBS) with Sophia Loren.

His films include *The Landlord* (1970); *Valdez Is Coming* (1970); *Born to Win* (1971); *Pocket Money, Deadhead Miles* (1972); *The Taking of Pelham One Two Three* (1974); *Report to the Commissioner* (1975); *Thieves* (1977); *Cuba* (1979); *American Gigolo* (1980); *The Fan* (1981); *Young Doctors in Love* (1982); *The Flamingo Kid* (1984); *Nothing in Common* (1986); *Leviathan* (1989); *Taking Care of Business* (1990); *Necessary Roughness* (1991); *Frankie and Johnny* (1991); *Pay Dirt, Final Approach* (1991); *Being Human* (1994); *Beverly Hills Cop III* (1994); *Exit to Eden* (1994); and *Dear God* (1996).

Elizondo continues to keep a busy schedule. During 2008, he took up the role of the therapist Dr. Nevel Bell in the award-winning series *Monk* (USA Network). His most recent film credits include *The Princess Diaries* (2001) and *The Princess Diaries 2* (2005); *Love in the Time of Cholera* (2007); *Valentine's Day* (2007); and *New Year's Eve* (2011).

Moctesuma Esparza

Moctesuma Esparza is the most successful Chicano producer in mainstream films today. His survival in Hollywood can perhaps be attributed to his long history of activism, as well as his uncanny ability to navigate the shark-infested waters of the Hollywood film industry.

He was born on March 12, 1949, in East Los Angeles, to Mexican parents. His mother Esther died giving birth to his only brother, Jesus. He graduated from Abraham Lincoln

High School in 1967 and attended UCLA that fall, majoring in theater arts. There, along with other Chicano activists he cofounded the Young Chicanos for Community Action, from which later the Brown Berets and the United Mexican-American Students developed.

During 1968, he and others helped to organize the high school walkouts in East Los Angeles, which focused government and media on the plight of Mexican-Americans in education. After this activity, Esparza and others were charged with 15 counts of conspiracy to disrupt schools, each a felony which carried three years of prison. They were acquitted after two years of legal battle on an appeal. Soon thereafter, he was charged with arson, burglary and tampering with electrical wiring during a speech by Governor Ronald Reagan at the Biltmore Hotel in Los Angeles. If convicted, he faced life imprisonment. The case became well known as the Biltmore Seven in the Chicano community. Once again, due to widespread community support and a spirited defense during a two-year court battle, the charges were dropped.

At age twenty-two, he entered the UCLA film school, where he focused on producing. His senior thesis was entitled "Cinco Vidas/Five Lives." It was aired on NBC and earned a local Emmy Award. After graduation, he became an independent producer, mostly in documentaries. One of them was *Borderlands*, which aired on PBS in 1973. The first feature film that he produced was *Only Once in a Lifetime* in 1978.

In the next twenty years he produced documentaries, independent films and studio-backed films, usually in association with his partner Robert Katz under the banner of Esparza/Katz Productions.

His productions include *The Milagro Beanfield War* (1989, Universal); *American Me* (1992, Universal); *Gettysburg* (1993, Turner); Luis Valdez' *The Cisco Kid* (1994, TNT); *Rough Riders* (1997, TNT); *The Disappearance of Garcia Lorca* (1997); *Selena* (1997, Warner Bros.); *Introducing Dorothy Dandridge* (1999, TNT); and *The Price of Glory* (1999).

His other projects include *Caliente y Picante* (1990), a Latino musical television special, and *Chicano! The History of the Mexican-American Civil Rights Movement* (1996).

He continues to be an advocate for more opportunities for Latinos in the media, as well as for the eradication of stereotypes. In an interview, he stated, "It is now vital that everyone in our community understand we can create our own lives.... Even though there is still institutional racism and external barriers, we now have the power to overcome them and achieve our goals."[107]

In 2005, he opened the first multiplex in Salinas, California, the Mayan Cinemas. Thereafter, he opened 16 more cinemas and scheduled 26 more in California. The chain of theaters screened first-run Hollywood films, as well as Latino-themed and Spanish-language films.

His recently produced films include the cable film *Walkout* (2006); executive producer; *Moe* (2008), executive producer; *Harlem Hostel* (2010), executive producer; and *Taco Shop* (2012).

He married his wife Esperanza in 1977, and the union has produced four children.

EVELINA FERNÁNDEZ

One of the characteristics of new Latino talent has been its versatility. One of these exemplifying this trend has been Evelina Fernández.

She obtained her B.A. degree from California State University, Los Angeles. She became active in Chicano teatro during her college years early on began to write plays on her own. Her better-known plays include *"Luminarias"*; *"Premeditation"*; *"August 29"*; and *"How Else Am I Suppose to Know I'm Still Alive."* She has been an active member of the Latino Lab, a group of Latino performers who have written and performed plays in Los Angeles for almost two decades.

Her film credits include *Sparks* (1990), *Postcards from the Edge* (1990), *American Me* (1992), and *A Million to Juan* (1995). She has appeared in such television shows as *The Larry Sanders Show*, *Roseanne,* and *Women.* She also costarred in the television film *Hollywood Confidential* (1995) with Edward James Olmos.

During 1999, her long-term project of a film adaptation of her play *Luminarias* came to fruition. Both the play and film focus on the ups and downs of four Chicana girlfriends who frequent a popular East Los Angeles nightclub. The independent film received some glowing reviews and went on to become a moderate success. Fernández both costarred and wrote the screenplay, and her husband José Luis Valenzuela directed.

Her most recent films include *Gabriela* (2001); *Moe* (2008); and *A Clean Sweep* (2012).

EFRAIN FIGUEROA

Efrain Figueroa was the epitome of the Latino actor of the 1990s who had been honing his craft diligently for years in theater and was ready when the great film role came. For Figueroa, it was in *Star Maps.*

Efrain Figueroa was born in New York City to Puerto Rican parents. He established a

Efrain Figueroa played the ruthless and amoral father in *Star Maps* (1997).

successful career as a marketing manager for international airlines, but he held a long-term desire to become an actor. He made the move into acting in his late 30s. His first acting employment consisted of making seventy-five bilingual commercials in English and Spanish. He subsequently wrote, produced and codirected several corporate films.

However, it was in the New York and Los Angeles theater that Efrain fine-tuned his acting talent. Among his most distinguished roles was that of Josefino in Mario Vargas Llosa's play *La Chunga*, for which he won the 1995 Drama-Logue award for Best Performance in a Theatrical Performance.

Moving into television, he scored a starring role in the short-lived CBS series *Houston Knights*. His television credits include *NYPD Blue*, *JAG*, *Cagney & Lacey*, *Dallas*, *Murder, She Wrote,* and *Diagnosis Murder.* He had a costarring role in the television miniseries *Drug Wars II: The Cocaine Cartel.* During the 1996–97 season, he played the recurring role of Jesse Rodriguez on the CBS series *Walker, Texas Ranger.* He earned critical accolades for his performance as Padrino in the Hudlin brothers' HBO series *Cosmic Slop.*

His film credits include *Fort Apache, the Bronx* (1981); *Ragtime* (1981); *Tequila Sunrise* (1988); and *Pretty Woman* (1990). The film role that propelled him to widespread acclaim and fame was that of Pepe Amado, the sleazy father whose business of selling maps to movie stars' homes is a front for a prostitution ring in Miguel Arteta's dark *Star Maps* (1997). The *Los Angeles Times* noted that he was "the film's most frightening and most involving character."[108] The film signaled the arrival of a truly major talent.

Figueroa's next role, however, proved to be anticlimactic and incidental in *Desperate Measures* (1998), headlined by Michael Keaton and Andy García. All this notwithstanding, he continues to keep busy. He completed a short entitled *Homers & Clinkers*, as well as several television pilots. In the late 1990s and early 2000s, he appeared in several television series: *JAG* (1997–2001); *NYPD Blue* (1997–2002); and *The Shield* (2002–2004). His most recent film was *Stiletto* (2008).

MIKE GOMEZ

Chicano actor Mike Gomez has enjoyed a versatile career in theater, television and film for the many years.

He was born on April 18, 1951, in Dallas, Texas. He made his Broadway debut in the role of Joey Castro in Luis Valdez' *Zoot Suit* at the Winter Garden Theater. Another highlight is his role of Jojo in *The Last Angry Brown Hat* at Plaza de La Raza in Los Angeles. Other plays include *August 29, Father & Sons, Death & the Blacksmith,* and *La Fiaca.*

His television credits include *The X-Files, Star Trek: The Next Generation, T.J. Hooker*, and *Yellow Rose,* among others.

His film credits include *Zoot Suit* (1981); *The Border* (1982); *El Norte* (1984); *The Patriot* (1986); *Heartbreak Ridge* (1986); *Born in East L.A.* (1987); *The Milagro Beanfield War* and *Colors* (1988); and *American Me* (1992).

His more recent films include *Dance with Me* (1998); *Luminarias* (2000); and *Yes Man* (2008). He continues to appear in numerous television series episodes.

RUBÉN GONZÁLEZ

Among the new generation of talented Latino actors is Rubén González, who has honed his acting skills in the theater.

He was born in Jalisco, Mexico, and came to live with his parents in Los Angeles, California, at a very young age. He graduated from Bell Gardens High School, and obtained his B.A. degree in speech and communication at California State University, Los Angeles. During the same time, he began taking acting classes at East Los Angeles College. He recalled later, "After that, it was kind of like fate, the acting bug, it bit me. And so that's where I started."[109]

Subsequently, he studied drama during one summer in London. He was selected to be part of the Circle in the Square Theatre School, where he did numerous plays. In New York, he further honed his acting skills. He recollected about this period, "You become Hispanic, and then you're not Mexican anymore. And I think that's where the challenge is and that's the hard part. Because you're trying to find who you are, in this place where no one knows who you are. And so you make your own way."[110]

After a series of commercials, he landed a substantial supporting role as a member of Selena's band in Gregory Nava's *Selena* (1997, Warner Bros.). He recalled about the experience, "What I liked about Gregory Nava is that he lets the actors do the actor's work. He's the type of director, like a choreographer, and you're welcome to say, hey Greg, can I look at the camera and see how it looks? If there's a line that we don't think is something the character would say, he would go like, well, change it. I think Selena will be an important film. You have this woman—I mean when have you ever seen a Latino woman as the star of the movie? You had *La Bamba* and all these other movies, but now it's a woman in the lead role, it's a different experience."[111]

Rubén González is an actor in film and television, and is currently with Luis Valdez' Teatro Campesino.

Since 2006, he has been a guest star at the Black and Latino Playwright Conference at Texas State University.

His theater credits include *La Virgen de Tepeyac* (2000–2012); *Mundo Mata* (2001); *Rhinoceros* (2003); *The Messiah Complex* (2003–08); *Between Us* (2005); and *La Esquinita* (2010–present). He has also done a solo show, *Diary of a Mad Mexican*. His television credits include *The Minor Accomplishments of Jackie Woodman* (2005); *Veronica Mars* (2005); and *Medium* (2006).

His recent films include *Barrio Murders* (1998), director; *Perfect Game* (1999); *Suckers* (1999); director; *The Fourth Corner* (2004), director (short); *La Mission* (2008), director; *Food Stamps* (2009), director; and *Oscar* (2011), director/writer.

SALMA HAYEK

The arrival of the dark-haired, brown-skinned Mexican-born beauty Salma Hayek in Hollywood in the early 1990s was eagerly awaited by the film industry, which quickly put out the "Latina sex symbol" welcome mat. However, while her physical attributes are undeniable, she earned a reputation as a talented actress in Mexico.

Additionally, she possesses the requisite "star potential" that could propel her into the top-rank stardom of Dolores del Río, Lupe Vélez, Maria Montez or Rita Hayworth (Cansino).

Salma Hayek was born on September 2, 1966, in Coatzacoalcos, Veracruz, Mexico. Her father was in the oil industry in Veracruz and her mother was an opera singer. Regarding her interest in acting, she stated to the *Los Angeles Times*, "I always was a spoiled brat; I never committed to anything until acting.... In Mexico an acting career is frowned upon, especially if you're a girl. I come from a conservative, Catholic family."[112]

She made her Mexican television debut in the *telenovela Nuevo Amanecer* in 1988, for which she won the TV Novela Award for Best Newcomer. She reached even greater fame when she played the title role in the *telenovela Teresa* in 1989, for which she earned the TV Novela Award as Best Actress.

At this point she decided to move to Los Angeles to redirect her career. She focused on perfecting her English, but after almost a year and a half she was unable to find any significant roles. She landed a bit part as a Chicana *chola* (gang member) in Allison Anders' ambitious but seriously flawed *Mi Vida Loca* (1993), about Chicana gang members.

She did manage a number of guest roles on U.S. television: in *Dream On* (1992), as a Mexican maid; in *Street Justice* (1992) as a gang member's wife; in the unsuccessful Roseanne/Tom Arnold–produced pilot, *Cherry Street, South of Main* (1993); and in *Sinbad* as a series regular. Optimistic by nature, she remarked, "I had to capture the American humor and timing, but I did it."[113]

At this juncture, she wisely took the lead role of a girl struggling to escape a poor barrio in Jorge Fons' excellent Mexican film *El Callejón de los Milagros* (1994). It was based on a novel by Nobel laureate Naguib Mahfouz and the film earned numerous international awards. She followed it with the Mexican historical miniseries *Don Porfirio* in 1994.

Upon her return to the United States, she starred in the Showtime cable movie *Roadracers* (1994). The film began her prolific association with Chicano filmmaker Robert Rodriguez, who had scored a personal triumph with *El Mariachi* in 1992. Rodriguez had spotted Salma on a Latino talk show and thereafter cast her in all his subsequent films.

Hayek's next role was a cameo in the Rodriguez-directed segment in *Four Rooms* (1995). Soon thereafter, she made her biggest impact as the earthy Carolina in Rodriguez' stylish *Desperado* (1995) opposite Antonio Banderas and Cheech Marin. It was a partial remake of *El Mariachi* (with a six-million-dollar budget) and it was a commercial success. She dismissed accounts

Salma Hayek in *Desperado* (1995, Columbia). She was the first Mexican actress to be nominated for an Academy Award for Best Actress, for *Frida*, in 2003.

of a romantic involvement with Banderas: "Yeah, but *Desperado* is not so much about Antonio. My biggest passion, the love of my life, is my work."[114]

She did a cameo role in Rodriguez' *From Dusk till Dawn* (1996), an exploitation film that alternated unsuccessfully between film noir and horror. She performed a seductive dance with a snake in her role as a vampire woman. The film unfortunately was replete with Mexican stereotypes of *cantineras* and drunken Mexicans. She did another cameo in the independent feature directed by Peter Bratt, *Follow Me Home* (1995), about an odyssey of two Chicanos, a Native American and an African American from San Francisco to Washington, D.C. It costarred Benjamin Bratt and Jesse Borrego.

Hayek essayed the role of the gypsy girl Esmeralda in the seventh film version of *The Hunchback of Notre Dame* (1997), which aired on the TNT television network. The film was shot in France and costarred Mandy Patinkin as Quasimodo and Richard Harris as Zollo. The film was generally panned by critics. The *Boston Globe* called it "the most embarrassing adaptation."[115]

Her next theatrical film was *Fled* (1997, Metro-Goldwyn-Mayer), a rather routine film, faintly reminiscent of *The Defiant Ones*, in which two convicts, one white (Stephen Baldwin) and one black (Laurence Fishburne), make an escape. Due to Hayek's performance and that of her costars, the film was a moderate commercial success. The *Los Angeles Times* commented, "Piper and Dodge are given shelter in Atlanta by a gorgeous, witty Salma Hayek, who plays the ex-wife of a cop who conveniently left behind a key that just happens to unlock her guest's chains."[116]

However, it would be her next film which would launch her into full-fledged stardom. In *Fools Rush In* (1997, Columbia), she played a Mexican photographer who falls for an Anglo yuppie in Las Vegas. The studio wisely released the film with Spanish subtitles in eleven theaters nationwide—nine in Southern California and two in Texas. Sony Pictures Releasing President Jeff Blake commented, "We think one of the real positive elements of the film is the sort of culture clash between Matthew Perry's WASP family and Salma Hayek's traditional Mexican family.... We felt it was a fun interchange and that there definitely would be appeal in the Mexican-American community."[117] The subtitled version outgrossed the nonsubtitled version. The film became a commercial hit beyond expectations.

Two of her films met the fate of obscurity. *Breaking Up* (1997) with Russell Crowe went straight to video. In turn, *Who the Hell Is Julieta?* (1997), which was written, produced, and directed by Carlos Marcovich and was a Mexico-Cuba co-production, was so bad that it also went to video. Hayek had a cameo in this latter film.

She realized the importance of *Fools Rush In*'s success and had expressed apprehension: "I try to be very strong and look like I'm not nervous about having the movie coming out that could represent a big chance in my life. The truth is, part of you is always scared."[118] Salma earned rave reviews. The *Boston Herald* wrote, "The film retains dignity primarily because Hayek (*Desperado*) gives a sweet, charismatic performance that shows she's more than the proverbial pretty face."[119]

Both Hayek and Jennifer Lopez were invited to be presenters at the Academy Awards in April 1997. They brought a fresh and welcome Latina presence to the proceedings.

Soon thereafter, it was announced that Hayek would portray Mexican painter Frida

Kahlo in a biopic for Trimark Pictures to be directed by Robert Sneider, based on the book *Frida: A Biography of Frida Kahlo* by Hayden Herrera. Hayek would also be a co-producer, but the film would be a long time in the making.

Meanwhile her next role was that of a Latina check girl and aspiring singer in the 1970s nostalgia film entitled *54* (1998), about the famous New York City club Studio 54. The film was a moderate commercial success, but earned less than glowing reviews. The *Los Angeles Times* commented, "If you never understood why people begged, wheedled and pleaded to get past the velvet rope and into the celebrated discos of the 1970s, don't look to *54* to enlighten you."[120]

She had a cameo in Robert Rodriguez' pulp horror film *Faculty* (1998), which was a moderate critical and commercial success. However, her next two films for which she had high hopes proved to be a mixed lot. She played the female lead in the film version of the popular 1960s television show *The Wild, Wild West* (1999, Warner Bros.) opposite Kenneth Branagh, Will Smith (who was totally miscast) and Kevin Kline. The film, directed by Barry Sonnenfeld, represented what too many Hollywood blockbusters were: mindless, cartoonish and oversaturated with special effects that had more affinity with an amusement park than a motion picture. The official budget for the film was allegedly $105 million. However, the *Los Angeles Times* noted, "Other reports go as high as $180 million."[121] The studio trimmed Hayek's part to an incidental role of no consequence or purpose. Touted as a Will Smith film (though Smith had never carried a film himself), *The Wild, Wild West* quickly became a disaster on the level of such legendary big-budget flops as *Heaven's Gate* (1980) and *The Last Action Hero* (1993). When the film bombed, the studio's advertising campaign quickly began to feature Hayek's face (having previously highlighted Smith's and Kline's images). It was projected that the film would gross barely $100 million of its bloated budget.[122]

Reviews for the film were scathing. The *Los Angeles Times* wrote, "As clumsy and top-heavy as the 80-foot tarantula that is a prize special effect, the film sacrifices playfulness and humor to concentrate on a relentless display of elaborate but ho-hum gadgets and gizmos.... A popular ingénue these days, Hayek is capable enough in what may be an abbreviated role ... but her character is used mainly as an excuse for tired double-entendre jokes and peek-a-boo glimpses of her body."[123]

At the same time, the low-budget independent film *The Velocity of Gary* (1999), which was co-produced by Hayek's own Ventanarosa Productions, met with equally negative reviews. The film, which was directed by Dan Ireland, focused on the unconventional triangle of a bisexual (Vincent D'Onofrio), a homosexual (Thomas Jane) and one woman (Hayek). The *New York Times* wrote, "At least *The Velocity of Gary* isn't afraid to be pretentious."[124] The *Los Angeles Times* noted, "The gritty locales serve only to make the material seem all the more artificial. There is almost nothing going on to anchor these people to everyday existence.... Hayek has been asked to throw hysterics almost continually. In committing herself to her role and in trusting her director she gives a screeching, over-the-top performance that is just plain awful."[125] All this notwithstanding, Salma's role was an example of her willingness to take a risk and break away from some of her one-dimensional Hollywood mainstream films.

Not ironically, at the same time that these two previous films were being slammed, her third new film was playing to capacity crowds in Mexico City and Paris, as well as earning raves. It was a Mexican film (which Hayek co-produced) called *El Coronel no Tiene Quien le Escriba,* based on the novel by Gabriel García Márquez and directed by the veteran Arturo Ripstein.

Hayek's next film was *Dogma* (1999) with Matt Damon and Ben Affleck, a comedy about two misguided angels attempting to undermine God. Despite promise and style, and a good cast, it felt apart at the end in self-indulgence. The brightest performance was given by Hayek in the role of the Muse. The *Boston Globe* commented, "It's a sweet, clunky film that's so eager to air its theological ponderings that it isn't afraid to seem a bit of a bore."[126]

During Thanksgiving in 1999, Salma traveled to Kosovo to entertain U.S. troops. Her trip drew a firestorm of wrath by some ultra-conservatives in the Mexican Congress, who even threatened to strip her of her Mexican citizenship (which was clearly unconstitutional).

In 2000, Hayek played the lead in the film adaptation of Julia Alvarez' novel *In the Time of the Butterflies*. Her next film would be a crowning achievement. She became the first Mexican actress to be nominated for an Academy Award for Best Actress (previously Katy Jurado had been nominated for Best Supporting Actress for *Broken Lance* in 1954), for the title role in *Frida* (2002), which she co-produced. She was the guiding light behind the film, ultimately directed by Julie Taymor. In 2003, she produced and directed *The Maldonado Miracle,* a Showtime cable film. She was the executive producer of the award-winning television series *Ugly Betty* (2006–2010). She also produced the Mexican romantic comedy *La Banda* (2011).

Her film career continued with Robert Rodriguez's *Spy Kids 3-D: Game Over* (2003) and *Once upon a Time in Mexico* (2003); *After Sunset* (2004); *Bandidas* (2006); *Lonely Hearts* (2006), for which she was nominated at the San Sebastian International Film Festival for Best Actress; *Across the Universe* (2007); a cameo in *Grown-Ups* (2010); her voice in the animated feature *Puss in Boots* (2011); *Americano* (2011), for which she was nominated again at the San Sebastian International Film Festival for Best Actress*; La Chispa de la Vida* (2011), for which she was nominated for the Spanish Goya Awards for Best Supporting Actress; and *Here Comes the Boom* (2012). She played an offbeat drug cartel queen in Oliver Stone's *Savages* (2012) opposite Benicio Del Toro.

Hayek married French billionaire Francois-Henri Pinault on Valentine's Day, 2009.

JOHN LEGUIZAMO

One of the most multitalented Latino newcomers of film, television and theater in the 1990s was John Leguizamo. Despite his considerable talent, he has yet to find the great film role that can showcase the full range of his comedic and dramatic skills.

He was born in Bogotá, Colombia, on July 22, 1965, but he grew up in New York City from a very young age. He studied drama at the famed Lee Strasberg Studio and later at New York University. His stage credits include *Sueño de una Noche de Verano* and *La Puta Vida* at the Public Theater and *Parting Gestures* at INTAR.

However, it was on HBO cable that he won accolades for his biting and satirical depiction of Latino stereotypes in two comedy specials, *Mambo Mouth* and *Spic-o-Rama*. He portrayed multiple characters and wrote the long satirical monologues brilliantly. For the latter show, he won the Hull-Warriner Award, the Lucille Lortel Award for Best Performance Off-

Broadway, Theater World's Most Promising Talent and the Drama Desk Award, among many others.

During 1995, he wrote and starred in Fox's *House of Buggin'*, the first national television show produced completely by Latinos. However, despite good reviews the show was canceled before the end of the season.

Next, Leguizamo focused on building a film career. He debuted in *Out for Justice* in 1991, opposite Steven Seagal. Over the next few years he began to make a growing impression in costarring roles in feature films in both comedy and drama: Joseph B. Vasquez' independent film *Hangin' with the Homeboys* (1991); Mike Nichols' dark comedy *Regarding Henry* (1991) with Harrison Ford and Annette Bening; Tony Scott's uneven *Revenge* (1991) with Anthony Quinn; the mega-hit *Die Hard 2* (1991) with Bruce Willis; the routine low-budget *Street Hunter* (1991); the somber *Whispers in the Dark* (1992) with Jill Clayburgh; the fiasco *Super Mario Bros.* (1993) with Bo Hoskins; Brian De Palma's stereotypical *Carlito's Way* (1993) with Al Pacino; and the obscure A *Pyromaniac's Love Story* (1995) with Erika Eleniak.

He earned good notices for the bizarre *To Wong Foo, Thanks for Everything, Julie Newmar* (1995) about three transvestites (Leguizamo, Patrick Swayze, and Wesley Snipes) stranded in the midwest. He co-wrote and played the lead in *The Pest* (1997), a comedy which failed critically and commercially. About this, he stated to the *Los Angeles Times*, "You can't compromise your vision. I thought it was a collaborative art form, then all of a sudden it's not your vision anymore and it's a children's movie. There are great moments I'm proud of, but great moments do not a movie make."[127] On the problems in the film industry, he commented, "Big studios are giant amusement rides—very little content, and I don't think they care.... Independent films. That's gonna be the saving grace of American cinema. That's where everyone can take more chances.... We'll eventually have few blockbuster movies, a lot of independent films and almost nothing in between."[128]

Leguizamo divides his time between homes on New York's Lower East Side and Los Angeles' Echo Park. He stated, "I hate being in the Hollywood ghetto where everyone's rich and deep in mortgages and Mercedeses. In Echo Park you have Silver Lake and Chinatown and Thai Town nearby, the best of everything where all cultures meet."[129]

His 1990s films include the comic book–inspired *Spawn* (1997) with Martin Sheen; the independent film *A Brother's Kiss* (1997) with Rosie Pérez; the action film *Body Count* (1997); and *Dr. Doolittle* (1997). During 1997 and 1998 his one-man show *Freaky* saw a long and successful run on Broadway.

His more recent films include Spike Lee's *Summer of Sam* (1999), which focused on the impact of infamous serial killer Son of Sam upon a community in New York City; *Love in the Time of Cholera* (2007); *Ice Age 3: Dawn of the Dinosaurs* (2009); *The Lincoln Lawyer* (2011); and *Chef* (2014).

JENNIFER LOPEZ

During the 1990s, only three full-fledged Latina stars emerged: the Mexican-born Salma Hayek, the Nuyorican Rosie Pérez, and Jennifer Lopez.

Jennifer Lopez was born in the Bronx borough of New York City, on July 24, 1970, of

Puerto Rican parents. She began in show business as a dancer. She moved to Los Angeles in 1991, after being cast as a "fly girl" on Fox TV's *In Living Color*.

She later stated, "I was going back, that was always my attitude.... But some opportunity, some possibility, always kept me here ... I know I'm incredibly lucky and just can't help but think there's something besides talent guiding me. I guess that's just my Catholic upbringing."[130]

She made an impression as the Chicana daughter of Pepe Serna in the short-lived CBS series *Hotel Malibu* (1994–95). She told *La Opinión*, "Any actor or person of Latino origin who has an opportunity to watch this program will be glad and proud of the positive Latino image."[131] During this time she also costarred in the television film *Nurses on the Line: The Crash of Flight 7* (1994).

Director Gregory Nava was impressed enough to cast her in the pivotal role of the young Mexican mother in *My Family/Mi Familia* (1995) opposite a stellar cast that included Edward James Olmos, Jimmy Smits, and Esai Morales. The critical and commercial success of the film showcased her dramatic talent. She followed it with the role of a Puerto Rican transit cop in the only lukewarm *Money Train* (1995) with Woody Harrelson and Wesley Snipes, which received generally negative reviews. Next came the role of a fifth-grade teacher in Francis Ford Coppola's *Jack* (1996) opposite Robin Williams, which was only moderately successful.

The turning point of her film career came in 1997, a year in which she had lead roles in four films. First came the role of Gabriela, the sultry Cuban femme fatale in Bob Rafelson's evocative film noir *Blood & Wine*, opposite Jack Nicholson and Michael Caine. The *Los Angeles Times* commented, "Let's just say that Lopez, high-heeled and high maintenance, simmers volcanically while providing the catalyst for the Alex-Jason meltdown."[132]

She was then selected by director Gregory Nava to play the slain Tex-Mex singer Selena Quintanilla after a national casting search in the film entitled *Selena* (1997, Warner Bros.). Nava told *Buzz*, "I have always fought very hard to cast Latinos in Latino roles.... And Jennifer was the best choice for the part. Her resemblance to Selena is uncanny, and at the audition she was

Jennifer Lopez in *Money Train* (1995, Columbia). She came to prominence playing the title role in *Selena* (1997).

head and shoulders above everyone else. Her acting was marvelous, her dancing was great, and she hit all the emotional notes."[133] The casting of a Puerto Rican actress as the Chicana singer, however, aroused the ire of some in the Chicano community. Lopez responded to the reaction, "I got this role because I could sing, I could dance. The last thing I expected was for people to go, 'She's Puerto Rican. Why is she playing Selena?' When that happened, I was hurt that my own people were rejecting (me)."[134]

Selena opened during March 1997 and within three weeks had grossed $27.7 million. The film's strong opening gross of $11 million in its first week exceeded the expectations of many, including Warner Bros., which had doubted the crossover appeal. The film's success validated the $20 million film budget and Lopez' $1 million salary.

Her performance earned her some glowing praise from critics. The *Los Angeles Times* wrote, "Though Lopez lip-syncs to Selena's voice, she makes use of her background as a dancer ... to project an irresistible joy in a performance that both does justice to Selena's appeal and helps turn away the film's saccharine haze."[135] The *New York Times* stated, "Ms. Lopez, much more at home here than in the recent *Blood and Wine*, cavorts and dances about the stage with un-self-conscious glee of a seasoned concert performer basking in the limelight."[136] The *Boston Globe* noted, "There's a real dazzle and pizzazz in Lopez's performance, right through the double irony when she sings, *I Will Survive.*"[137] *Time* wrote, "Lopez ... gives a feisty, buoyant performance that could set her on a star path similar to the singer's."[138]

Director Oliver Stone rescheduled his production of his film *U-Turn* (1997), so that Lopez could costar in the film noir tale of a hapless drifter (Sean Penn) and fatal dark lady (Lopez). The film costarred Jon Voight, Nick Nolte and Billy Bob Thornton.

She married a Cuban model and aspiring actor, Ojami Noa, in early 1997, but they were divorced by June of the same year. Her second marriage was to a backup singer, Cris Judd, on September 29, 2001, but it quickly unraveled during June 2002.

In another change-of-pace role, she played an FBI agent tracking down an amoral bank robber (George Clooney) in Steven Soderbergh's crime caper *Out of Sight* (1998, Universal), which costarred Michael Keaton and Samuel M. Jackson. The *New York Times* noted, "Ms. Lopez has her best movie role thus far, and she brings it both seductiveness and grit; if it was hard to imagine a hard-working, pistol-packing bombshell on the page, it couldn't be easier here."[139]

She commented to *Vibe*, "I'm aware that I'm becoming more known and I want to set a good example for my people.... Being a role model is okay with me—you have that responsibility when you're in the public eye. That's an attitude Selena had too."[140]

Inspired by her role in *Selena*, she made a debut album titled *On the 6*. She told the *Los Angeles Times*, "The idea to do an album is not a gimmick.... When I did *Selena*, it all came back again, having the interaction with the fans and the public, which you don't get in movies. I missed that very much. I missed the excitement of the stage, which I had early in my career with the musical theater."[141] The *Los Angeles Times* noted of her album, "While Lopez's light, tangy voice isn't exactly a technical wonder; her singing is as seductively emotive as her work on screen."[142]

More recently, she provided one of the voices in the animated feature *Antz* (1998) and starred in the feature films *The Cell* (2000); *The Wedding Planner* (2001); *Angel Eyes* (2001);

Maid in Manhattan (2002); *Enough* (2002); *Shall We Dance?* (2004); *An Unfinished Life* (2005); *Monster-in-Law* (2005); *Bordertown* (2006), which reunited her with director Gregory Nava; *El Cantante* (2007) with singer Marc Anthony; and *What to Expect When You're Expecting* (2012). She suffered a major bomb with *Gigli* (2003) with then-boyfriend Ben Affleck.

She married Marc Anthony on June 5, 2004, but they would divorce in 2011. On February 22, 2008, she gave birth to a set of fraternal twins. More recently, she signed on as one of the judges in the highly rated television show *American Idol.* She continues as a music recording artist and performer.

SAL LOPEZ

One of the most highly respected Chicano actors of the 1990s who blossomed towards the end of the decade was Sal Lopez. That esteem by both peers and critics was based on some seventeen years of theater, television and film acting.

Sal Lopez was born on November 8, 1954, in Tijuana, Baja California, Mexico, to a working-class Mexican family who immigrated during his childhood to Los Angeles. He attended Huntington Park High School and studied dancing and acting at Los Angeles City College, East Los Angeles College and California State University, Los Angeles.

It was his dancing skills that earned him the role as a dancing zoot suiter in Luis Valdez' stage success *Zoot Suit* at the Aquarius Theater in Hollywood, California, during 1979. It was a role he repeated in the film version in 1982. He later said that doing the play and film made him decide that acting would be his lifelong profession.

He honed his acting skills in many stage productions, including *Wanted Experienced Operators* at the Los Angeles Bilingual Foundation of the Arts; Luis Valdez' *Corridos* at San Diego's Old Globe Theater, for which he won the Bay Area Critics Best Supporting Actor Award; *Green Card* at the Mark Taper Forum; *Lorca Child of the Moon* and *Young Lady from Tacna* at the Los Angeles Bilingual Foundation of the Arts; *A Victima* at the Minskoff Theater on Broadway; the Teatro Campesino's *La Virgen del Tepeyac*; *August 29* at the Los Angeles Theater Center, for which he won a Drama-Logue Award; Luis Valdez' *Bandido* at the Mark Taper Forum; *Blade to the Heart* at the Mark Taper Forum; and *Latinos* (based on the book) at the Mark Taper Forum during 1997.

His growing list of television credits includes Luis Valdez' *Corridos* (*Tales of the*

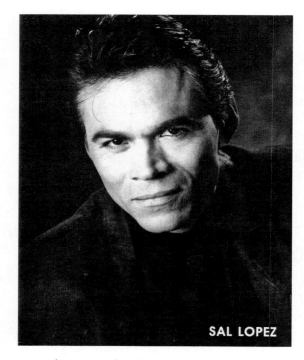

SAL LOPEZ

Sal Lopez is a highly respected actor in film, television, and theater.

Revolution); *Chips*; *Benson*; *T.J. Hooker*; *Hill Street Blues*; *Wise Guy*; *Hunter*; *Matlock*; *Eddie Dodd*; and *Reasonable Doubts*. His television films include *The Rockford Files* (1984) with James Garner and *Breaking Free* (1996). He has had featured roles in two television mini-series: *The Fire Next Time* and *Intruders (They Are Among Us)* for CBS.

He began his film career with a small part in Luis Valdez' *Zoot Suit* (1982) and has gradually worked his way through featured, supporting and costarring roles that have displayed his versatility in both comedy and drama. His films include *The Glitter Dome* (1985) with James Garner and Margot Kidder; *Million Dollar Mystery* (1987); Cheech Marin's *Born in East L.A.* (1987); and Stanley Kubrick's powerful tale about the Vietnam War, *Full Metal Jacket* (1987), in which he played a Chicano marine. He recalled about the film, "Well, that's another one of those flukes, or things that I've been fortunate with. I remember the day we wrapped, it was my last day. I remember hearing talk that Oliver Stone was casting a movie called *Platoon*. So that's how long it took Stanley to finish his movie and get it out. So I think if Stanley would have released his movie first it would have been another landmark film by Stanley Kubrick, because all of his films have been so significant in the industry."[143]

He was cast in Sévero Pérez's evocative film adaptation of Tomas Rivera's novel ... *Y Se No Lo Tragó la Tierra* (1996), as a luckless boarder; and Gregory Nava's *Selena* (1997), a film about the slain Tex-Mex idol with Edward James Olmos and Jennifer Lopez. However, his most memorable film role remains that of Pedro, the flamboyant zoot suiter who fathers the Mexican Mafia kingpin Santa (Edward James Olmos) in the powerfully moving *American Me* (1992). It was a role in which he aged twenty years, perfectly capturing the swagger and passion of youth and the weariness and disillusionment of old age.

He recollected about getting the role of Pedro, "Eddie [James Olmos] knew I could play him when he was young. But they decided to try to doing the makeup on me just for the heck of it, to see if I could play the older man. And Ken Diaz, who was nominated for an Oscar in that, he did the makeup on me. I ended up getting the role. So it was a phenomenal challenge and experience. Because you know, to play the age range was a challenge."[144]

He is a member of the Latino Theater Company, which is based in Los Angeles. He commented, "I think that's the most satisfying, and the most challenging theater I've done. The Latino Theater consists of six actors and has been together for twelve years now. We've always dedicated ourselves, our mission; our vision has always been to create work that reflects the Chicano experience. Nobody does that anymore."[145]

He possesses both charisma and talent, requisites for film stardom and longevity.

He is married and has two children. More recently, he co-produced and costarred in the film *Luminarias* (2000). Other recent film credits include *The Price of Glory* (2000), *Boyle Heights* (2010), and *Wake* (2011). He continues to guest-star in numerous top-rated television series.

FEDERICO LUPPI

Federico Luppi has enjoyed a long career as a leading man and serious actor throughout Latin America. He made his U.S. film debut in John Sayles' evocative *Men with Guns*.

He was born on February 3, 1934, in Buenos Aires, Argentina. He made his film debut in 1965 in Rodolfo Kuhn's *Bird Gomez* and has gone on to make some forty films. His stardom came with *Kuhn's Terrible Night* in 1967. The same year, he won the Best Actor award from the Argentine Association of Cinematographic Chroniclers (AACC) for his role in *The Romance of Aniceto and Francisca*. Other successes during this time included *Chronicle of a Woman* (1971); *The Revolution* (1973); *The Vengeance of Beto Sanchez* (1973); and *The Rebellious Patagonia* (1974). His role in this last film, as well as his progressive politics, angered the Argentine military government and they did not permit him to make films for five years, from 1975 to 1980.

He made his comeback in 1981 in Adolfo Aristarian's *Time for Revenge*, a role for which he won his second Best Actor award from the AACC, as well as the Best Actor prize from the Chicago International Film Festival in 1982. Luppi worked with Aristarian in several more films: *The Last Days of the Victim* (1982); *A Place in the World* (1992); *The Law of the Frontier* (1995); and *Martín Hache* (1997).

His films include *Sweet Silver* (1982); *The Settlement* (1983); *Passenger from a Nightmare* (1984); *Funny Little Dirty War* (1984)—Silver Bear award, Berlin Film Festival; *The Old Music* (1985); *Cocaine Wars* (1985, a U.S./Argentine coproduction); *Les Longs Manteaux* (1986, French); *The Tombs* (1991); *My Dear Tom Mix* (1992, Mexican); *Killing Grandpa* (1993); *Nobody Will Speak of Us When We're Dead* (1995); *Wild Horses* (1995); *Extasis* (1996); and *Sol de Otoño* (1996). He scored a notable success in Guillermo del Toro's brilliant *Cronos* in 1992.

In 1998, he played the lead role as the disillusioned doctor in John Sayles' *Men with Guns*. Sayles said of Luppi, "I had seen a number of his films and I always had him in mind when I wrote the screenplay.... In addition to being a good actor, he has the kind of bearing, dignity and intelligence I needed for the movie."[146] In turn, Luppi commented about *Men with Guns*, "I thought the script was beautifully written.... My character develops in a realistic way, the way a human being does, without political speeches or an obvious 'message.' And I found John Sayles to be a man who loves cinema deeply and loves the feeling of truth that cinema has. Also, he's very sympathetic, patient and prepared—something that the actors are very grateful for."[147]

Luppi won more accolades with his portrayal of an aging Spanish Republic loyalist in Guillermo del Toro's *The Devil's Backbone* (2001), set during the Spanish Civil War; and *Pan's Labyrinth* (2006). His other recent films include *Verano Amargo* (2010); *Sin Retorno* (2010); and *Phase 7* (2011). He continues to appear on Latin American television.

CONSTANCE MARIE

One of the bright Latina newcomers in the late 1990s was the vivacious Constance Marie.

She was born on September 9, 1965, in East Los Angeles, California. She made her film debut in *Body Rock* (1984) opposite Lorenzo Lamas.

Her early film credits include *Back to the Beach* (1987) with Annette Funicello and Frankie Avalon; and *Salsa* (1988). However, she made her biggest impact in the role of the raven-haired social activist Toni in Gregory Nava's *My Family/Mi Familia* (1995). Later, she played the mother of Tex-Mex singer Selena in Nava's *Selena* (1998), in which she aged some twenty years.

Her television credits include roles in the daytime soap operas *Santa Barbara* and *Dirty Dancing*. Her television guest-star appearances include *Jake and the Fatman* and *Reasonable Doubts*. She was cast as a series regular on NBC's *Union Square* during the 1998–99 season.

Her recent films include *Tortilla Soup* (2001) and *Puss in Boots* (2011). She costarred as a regular in the television series *American Family* (2001), and appeared on *The George Lopez Show* (2002–2007); *CSI: Crime Scene Investigation* (2008); and *Switched at Birth* (2011).

ANNETTE MURPHY

Important roles for Latinas in the 1990s were endangered species. Only sporadically did a Latina actress break through with a complex role that gave her the opportunity for a memorable performance. One of those rare opportunities came for Annette Murphy in the independent film *Star Maps*.

Annette Murphy was born in 1963, in San Diego, California, to an Irish father and a Mexican mother. At an early age she was fascinated with photography, but went on to study pre-law and women's studies at Duke University in North Carolina.

Although she has a sister in films and a brother in a band, Annette drifted into acting by coincidence. She began acting in Los Angeles and studied the Meisner technique under Bob Carnegie and actor Jeff Goldblum.

Annette Murphy

Among her theater credits are *Marriage Is Forever*, at the San Diego Repertory Theater; *Dominion* at the Mark Taper Forum; *The Seagull* at the Attic Theater; *The Rose Tattoo* at the Long Beach theater; *Virtue Rewarded* at the North Coast Repertory; *No. Spic. English* at the Ice House Comedy Club; and *This Is LA?* at the L.A. Teatro/Glaxa Studios.

Her television appearances include *One Saturday Morning, Days of Our Lives* and *Unsolved Mysteries*.

She made her film debut in *Eddie Presley* (1991). She had featured roles in a trio of films: *American Son* (1992), *The Proof* (1992), and *Twenty Bucks* (1993). However, it was in the role of Letti, the streetwise prostitute who is vulnerable to love, in Miguel Arteta's dark drama *Star Maps* (1996) which provided her with the role of a lifetime. She responded by turning in a richly textured and powerful performance, which earned her the accolades of critics and the public alike.

Annette Murphy came to prominence in *Star Maps* (1997), an independent film documenting the margins of the Hollywood film industry.

I asked her if she felt that independent films provide more access to Latino talent. She replied, "Yes, definitely. Because if we didn't have *Star Maps*, I would still be doing theater in little bits and pieces here and there. And always playing the young and pregnant mother, you know what I mean. I don't think studio films have a pulse in any sort of reality. I think independent films, because they're independent, are usually made by people that really care about the subject matter."[148]

Her more recent films include the female lead in Tom Musca's *Melting Pot* (1998) with Paul Rodriguez; the short film *Disco Man* (1998); *Race* (1998); *Chuck and Buck* (2000); and *Temptation* (2004). She has branched out as a producer and writer as well.

LUPE ONTIVEROS

Chicana actress Lupe Ontiveros created a versatile body of work in film, theater and television for several decades. She played sympathetic mothers, twisted villains and strong-willed women. Her characters' trademarks have been resourcefulness and a sense of humor.

She was born on September 17, 1942, in El Paso, Texas, the only surviving child of Juan Moreno and Lucia Castañon. She was named for the Virgin of Guadalupe, after her parents' loss of two sets of twins due to inadequate medical assistance and premature birth. Her parents promised to name her for the Virgin if she survived. Her parents were working-class people who toiled incessantly to give her a better life.

She earned a bachelor of science degree from Texas Women's University and planned to become a nurse. However, after she married she moved to San Diego in 1968, and subsequently to Los Angeles, where she worked as a social worker in East Los Angeles and Compton for the next sixteen years. In the latter part of her career as a social worker, she auditioned and won a role as an extra in a film. Her complete transition into a full-time actress took place when she won the role of the Mexican mother in Luis Valdez' play *Zoot Suit*, which had a long run in Los Angeles and later went on to Broadway. She commented about her transition into acting, "My background as a social worker helped me in acting. My training in one to one, put me in a very, very unique position to be able to understand human nature, through the course of interviewing, through the course of working with people. So I would say that that social work was very instrumental in allowing me also in expression."[149]

In reference to the being part of the cast of *Zoot Suit*, she recalled, "I loved seeing the grandfather and the grandmother and the papa and the mama, and the children, and all of these three or four generations sitting there watching us. Not watching us, watching ourselves. Because it was the first time in history we were seeing ourselves up there, in all our glory and all our shame, and all our beautiful and emotional selves. We've never seen that again. So I say, as you said, what has been the most influential and I would say, *Zoot Suit* started it all for me."[150]

She was one of the cofounders of the Latino Lab, a theater company in Los Angeles whose productions document the Chicano/Mexican experience. Ontiveros' theater credits include *Plaza Suite* at the Nosotros Theatre and Latino Lab productions such as *La Víctima, Roosters, Stone Wedding, August 29,* and *How Else Am I Supposed to Know I'm Alive* at the Margo Albert Theatre. When I asked her what medium she found more satisfying, she stated, "I would say in order of preference it has to be the theatre, and then film. I've been equally comfortable in one as the other. Of course, I prefer the theatre because in the theatre there are no compromises made the way they are in film. Because film is affected by money and the commercialism, and the need to make money on a film that a writer is often made to make concessions either in the casting or in his piece."[151]

Her numerous television credits include several roles as a series regular for CBS: *Dudley* with Dudley Moore, during 1993; *Grand Slam*; and the pilot *George*. She was in *Tales from the Crypt* on HBO; Luis Valdez' *La Pastorela* on PBS; Jesús Salvador Treviño's *Gangs*, a CBS Afterschool Special; *Who's the Boss*; *Shell Game;* Jesús Salvador Treviño's *Mariposa* on American Playhouse; and *Chicken Soup*; and she had recurring roles on *Grand Slam* and *I Married Dora*.

She repeated her stage role in Luis Valdez' film version of his play *Zoot Suit* (1992). Her films include *Bad News Bears in Breaking Training* (1977); *The World's Greatest Lover* (1977) with Gene Wilder; *California Suite* (1978) with Jane Fonda; Gregory Nava's *El Norte* (1984); *Born in East L.A.* (1987) with Cheech Marin; *Show of Force* (1990); *Blood In, Blood Out/Bound by Honor* (1993); *And the Earth Did Not Swallow Him* (1995); and Gregory Nava's *My Family/Mi Familia* (1995) and *Selena* (1997). Her television films include *Daddy* (1987) and *Stones for Ibarra* (1988) with Glenn Close. When I asked her what her most satisfying role was thus far, she replied, "My role in *El Norte* will always remain for many, many reasons. One being that it was the opportunity of a lifetime through that piece, that masterpiece that I call, masterpiece of a look at humanity, and the most honest look at what the undocumented goes through."[152]

Ontiveros studied acting with renowned drama mentors such as José Quintero, David Alexander and John Post.

She was a producer of an award-winning educational film, *Una Vez al Año Para Toda una Vida*, a call to awareness about breast cancer among Latinas. She was involved in the struggle to improve the images and opportunities of Latinos in the media through such organizations such as Nosotros.

She was a regular on *Veronica's Closet* with Kirstie Alley beginning in the 1997–98 season. Another film role was in the Oscar-winning comedy *As Good as It Gets* (1997) with Jack Nicholson and Helen Hunt. Her other roles include Alfonso Arau's *Picking Up the Pieces* (1999), a comedy with Woody Allen, Cheech Marin and Sharon Stone; Miguel Arteta's *Chuck and Buck* (1999); Tim Disney's *Blessed Art Thou* (1999); and Enrique Berumen's short film *La Olla/The Pan* (2001), about Latina stereotypes.

Lupe Ontiveros (1942–2002), a gifted and versatile actress.

She was a dedicated advocate for the improvement of opportunities for Latinos in the media, as well as images. When asked to what she attributed the negative images, she commented, "I think it's just plain ignorance, and to some degree a great deal of insensitivity. We have become a commodity to be used as they see fit."[153]

Her recent films include *Real Women Have Curves* (2002) and *Our Family Wedding* (2010).

Lupe Ontiveros succumbed to liver cancer on July 26, 2012, after a long fight with the disease. She was survived by her husband and children.

ROSIE PÉREZ

Rosie Pérez was only one of three Latinas to rise to film stardom in the 1990s, the others being the Mexican-born Salma Hayek and Pérez' fellow Nuyorican Jennifer Lopez.

She was born on September 6, 1964, in Brooklyn, New York, to Puerto Rican parents. She was one of ten children and had a troubled childhood. At the age of twelve, she was removed from school for attacking a woman but later returned to finish high school. She attended Los Angeles City College, where she majored in marine biology.

One night, the dance coordinator of television's *Soul Train* spotted her in a Latino club and offered her a job as a dancer. After a stint of eight months, another executive asked her to choreograph a video for singer Bobby Brown. Pérez recalled later, "At first I told him I couldn't do it—I didn't know how.... He told me I could. He presented the challenge, and I just had to take it."[154] Her work proved successful and she went on to choreograph videos for Diana Ross, L.L. Cool J and Heavy Dm.

She was spotted by director/writer Spike Lee at a nightclub and approached about playing the role of Tina in his upcoming *Do the Right Thing* (1989). She commented of the experience, "I was scared.... But at the same time I wasn't going to say, 'Well, no, Spike. I'd rather not do the film.'"[155] The film went on to become a huge commercial and critical success and Pérez earned glowing reviews for her performance of the strong-willed Tina.

On television, she guest-starred in such shows as *21 Jump Street* and *WIOU*. She also worked briefly as the choreographer for Fox's *In Living Color*. She won accolades for her role of Denise, a young Latina drug addict, in the HBO film *Criminal Justice* (1992).

When she initially read for the part of the girlfriend who dreams of one day winning as a *Jeopardy!* contestant in *White Men Can't Jump* (1992), the part had been written for a white actress. She confided to the *Long Beach Press-Telegram*, "I knew that getting the part was going to be a long shot.... But when I saw Rosanna Arquette sitting there, I started bugging out. I said a prayer. I thought, 'I survived the social welfare system of New York City. Surely I can survive one audition.' Unfortunately, all the quality work caters to white actors. I just want a chance at good parts. I said I wanted to play Jessica Lange roles. I would love to play a Hispanic...."[156] *White Men Can't Jump* proved to be another critical and commercial success for all involved, including Pérez and her costars Woody Harrelson and Wesley Snipes. She told *Newsweek*, "I finally played someone ... who had it together, who wasn't a victim or messed up by the ghetto."[157]

Her next role came in Tony Bill's *Untamed Heart* (1993) opposite Christian Slater and Marisa Tomei. Tony Bill stated to *Newsweek*, "She has such a naturalness and a genuineness about her ... that her way of doing something becomes a right way, the only way."[158] Pérez followed this with Jim Jarmusch's dark comedy *Night on Earth* (1992), about the accidental encounters between passengers and cabdrivers.

She then played a woman who develops an unusual attachment for a fellow passenger (Jeff Bridges) after they survive a plane crash in Peter Weir's highly praised *Fearless* (1993) with a cast that included Oscar nominee Tom Hulce and Isabella Rosselini. The *Los Angeles Times* wrote, "It is no accident that the scenes with her are almost uniformly *Fearless's* most solid and affecting. Carla, acutely played with a fine-tuned sadness by the usually rambunctious Rosie Pérez, has never gotten over the death of her baby in the crash."[159] *Time* noted, "Together, the filmmakers have given Bridges a singular figure—beamy, spooky, secretive— to play and provided Pérez, a ferociously real, marvelously touching actress, with a role that should make her a star."[160]

She won more accolades in the comedy *It Could Happen to You* (1994) about a cop (Nicolas Cage) who promises to give a waitress (Bridget Fonda) half of a winning lottery ticket, despite the protestations of his social-climbing wife (Pérez). The *Los Angeles Times* noted, "Perez's life-of-the party spiritedness and rat-a-tat locutions give the film a buzz. Post-lottery, she twinkles like a 44-carat diamond, and she's just about as hard."[161]

About her success, she commented, "It's exciting, but it's scary to be responsible for some projects.... It has made me grow up a lot. I'm learning to be softer and cool out, and finally I'm letting people get closer to me. There's nothing wrong with wanting better—so long as you can enjoy it with others." About racism, she commented in the same interview, "Sure, being the recipient of racism makes me angry and bitter ... but it's really important to overcome the bitterness. If you don't, you can begin to reciprocate that attitude. On the other hand, I think it's a good to stay angry, so you stay aware of the problem of racism. Only then can you do something to change it."[162]

She had high hopes for Alexandre Rockwell's *Somebody to Love* (1996), a bittersweet comedy that failed commercially despite the cast that included Anthony Quinn, Harvey Keitel and Michael DeLorenzo. Nevertheless, she earned excellent reviews. The *Los Angeles Times* wrote, "*Somebody to Love* is a valentine to Rosie Perez, whose career includes numerous bigger and more prestigious pictures but who surely must cherish this modest and amusing little heart-tugger for the way in which it showcases her unique beauty, talent and personality."[163]

A better film was Seth Zvi Rosenfeld's *A Brother's Kiss* (1997), about two brothers, one of whom becomes a cocaine dealer and addict, and the love that survives. Pérez played the abandoned young wife. The *New York Times* noted, "Limning the demise of a doomed marriage, Mr. Chinlund and Ms. Perez strike some hot, nasty sparks."[164] It was Rosenfeld's directorial debut (he had also written the screenplay).

During 1999, she starred in two independent films. In *The 24-Hour Woman*, she played a harried television producer. The *Boston Globe* wrote, "It's heartening to see a film sympathetic to the meat-grinding lives of working moms.... But because the frenzy is nonstop, the film loses its way as it goes the sitcom route."[165] *Perdita Durango* was a rather stereotypical tale about a pair of amoral santería adherents and cruel lovers on the run. However, critics were impressed with Pérez' performance. The *Boston Globe* wrote, "Even though Pérez's character is forced to go unbecomingly soft, ... *Perdita Durango* runs on her spitfire energy, and a lot of the time it's enough. It's the film we knew she had in her ever since *White Men Can't Jump*. It takes the view that there are other things white men can't do, too, although killing is not among them."[166]

During 2000, she played one of the leads in the play *The Vagina Monologues* in Los Angeles. Her recent films include *The Road to El Dorado* (2000), *The Take* (2007), and *Small Apartments* (2011). She has been a regular in *Go, Diego, Go!* (2005–2008) and appeared in other television series including *Frasier* (1995, 2004) and *Lipstick Jungle* (2008–2009).

SEVERO PEREZ

Chicano director/writer Severo Perez honed his skills for almost twenty years in the medium of television before he made his directorial film debut in 1995.

He was born in San Antonio, Texas, to Mexican parents. He earned a B.A. degree in American literature and contemporary history at the University of Texas, Austin.

In 1972, he moved to Los Angeles in order to pursue a career in motion pictures. During 1972 and 1976, he worked as a freelance production manager on feature film and educational productions. He is credited with reorganizing Learning Garden, Inc., a production company which produced animated and live action medical, scientific, documentary, and educational and entertainment programs. Subsequently, his productions earned more than fifty awards, including the CINE Golden Eagles. Later, as a producer and head of production for Learning Garden, Inc., from 1976 to 1981, he was in charge of creating programming for HBO, CBS, and the Disney Channel.

In 1980, he was instrumental in MCA Universal acquiring Luis Valdez' *Zoot Suit,* which the studio subsequently made into a film. During the same year, he was the line producer for Jesús Salvador Treviño's *Seguin*. In 1982, he served as the playwright-in-residence at Teatro Campesino, which culminated in the play *Soldier Boy*, co-written with Judith Perez and directed by Luis Valdez.

He subsequently directed and co-wrote three award-winning half-hour films chronicling the Chicano experience: *Yolando Nuevo* (1988), *Dreams of Flying* (1989) and *Between Friends* (1990).

In 1995, Perez made his feature film directorial debut with the adaptation of Tomas Rivera's coming of age novel ... *And the Earth Did Not Swallow Him*. The excellent cast included Rose Portillo, Daniel Valdez, Sal Lopez, Lupe Ontiveros, Marco Rodríguez and Jose Alcala as the boy Marcos.

The *Miami Herald* noted, "Written and deftly directed by Severo Perez, produced by Paul Espinosa and acted by a talented cast ... *And the Earth Did Not Swallow Him* is an artistic contradiction—a beautiful story about a hard life. Happily, the filmmakers tell us that author Rivera grew up to become chancellor of the University of California in Riverside. All children's heroes should be so fortunate."[167]

The film went on to win awards at the Santa Barbara International Film Festival, the Minnesota International Film Festival, and the San Antonio CineFestival, and the director was honored with the Jury Award for Artistic Achievement by Director.

Perez is currently working on several screenplays which he hopes to direct as well.

ROBERT RODRIGUEZ

The most heralded Chicano director of the 1990s was Robert Rodriguez. His directorial debut with *El Mariachi* in 1993 boosted both independent films and ushered in a new generation of Latino filmmakers.

He was born on June 20, 1968, in San Antonio, Texas, to a working-class Mexican family who had nine other children. He began dabbling in film at the age of twelve. His first success took place when his short comedy *Bedhead* won awards at some fourteen festivals.

It was while still a student at the University of Texas, Austin, that he and classmate/friend Carlos Gallardo co-produced and co-wrote *El Mariachi* in 1992. The film was budgeted at $7,000 and chronicled a tale of mistaken identity between a *mariachi* and drug lord along the Mexican border. Rodriguez also directed, edited, lensed and did the sound. Gallardo did extra duty by playing the title role of the *mariachi*. Everyone in the cast, except for the leading lady (Consuelo Gómez), worked on credit. The film had a fourteen-day shoot in Acuña, Mexico, and utilized only a hotel, two bars, a school bus, a motorcycle and a pit bull. When Columbia Pictures purchased the film, they transferred it to 35mm from the original 16mm and refurbished the soundtrack. Upon wider release the film earned $5 million in profits.

Critics heralded the coming of a new and important filmmaker. *Time* commented, "One of *El Mariachi*'s zestful pleasures is that you can enjoy it without awarding affirmative-action points. It's a real movie, high, not woozy on its own cinematic verve, and Rodriguez is the goods—not just for what his career promises but for what his film delivers."[168] The *Los Angeles Times* called the film a "tall-tale shoot-'em-up that draws on a whole arsenal of styles, including those of Peckinpah, Scorsese, Spielberg, Leone and Hill. It's a movie made by a talented tyro who, judging from what's on the screen, hasn't yet lived much of life."[169]

The *New York Times* stated, "*El Mariachi* is a skillful, familiar-feeling hybrid of film noir and western conventions, with a hint of futuristic nihilism in its final scenes. It is also visually primitive, with a home-movie look that would be distracting if Mr. Rodriguez's storytelling skills were not so keen. While rough around the edges, *El Mariachi* displays a textbook knowledge of Hollywood trademarks: stock characters (the soigné villain, the decorative moll), well-staged shootouts, showy camera work (fisheye, slow-motion and zoom flourishes), dream sequences and broad humor."[170]

Rodriguez later recalled about the making of the film, "I didn't want the cast working too hard, so we wouldn't rehearse the script. I'd feed them a few lines, they'd say it back to me, we'd shoot one take. I'd tell them to forget that line, and we'd go on to the next. I shot it all silent and then synchronized the sound by hand. It was a tremendous amount of work. But I'd rather work hard and have a movie than have nothing.... They love me out there.... They know they can save money with me.... I told Columbia I'd sign with them if they let me stay in Texas.... I wanted to be near my family. Near my inspiration."[171]

Columbia signed him for a two-picture deal, the first being a medium-budgeted remake of *El Mariachi* entitled *Desperado* (1995), with the fast-rising Antonio Banderas as the luckless title character, and the sultry new Mexican star Salma Hayek. Rodriguez commented to the *Los Angeles Times*, "I wanted to make another movie with a Latin hero ... that was bigger [than *El Mariachi*,] that would go around the world and be seen. And it just seemed easier for me, because there were no scripts around like this, to just use this character again to accomplish that.... But I think if [*Mariachi 2*] would be successful enough, if it made enough money, other Latino movies would be made. It's like with African American films. As soon as Spike Lee made his movies, everyone was giving checks for other black filmmakers to come up."[172] Antonio Banderas stated, "This guy has incredible energy.... It reminds me of the first films I did with [Pedro] Almodóvar. Not in his style of course. But it's like, you know, the same thing, when you don't have any money and you're working outside the studio, with no trailer, no nothing, just waiting on the corner to do the shot. And I thought, 'Wow! That's the kind of cinema I would like to do again.'"[173]

Desperado received mixed reviews, but grossed $25,540,000 in its first release (according to *Screen World 1996*). The *Los Angeles Times* commented, "Seeing *Desperado* makes obvious what was only implicit in the fuss over *El Mariachi.* What the suits saw in Rodriguez was not necessarily the next Orson Welles but, rather, someone with a clear facility for action, the one genre that can be counted on to sell tickets worldwide."[174] *Daily Variety* wrote, "The young Tex-Mex director's much-anticipated follow-up to his wildly inventive no-budget 1993 debut *El Mariachi* could scarcely be more dazzling on a purely visual level, but it's mortally anemic in the story, character and thematic departments."[175]

His third theatrical film, *From Dusk Till Dawn* (1996), a mixture of the film noir and horror genres, was blasted by critics, but went on to be a modest commercial success. Especially disturbing was the film's perpetuation of the Mexican stereotypes of *cantineras* and

Steve Buscemi and Antonio Banderas in Robert Rodriguez' *Desperado* (1985, Columbia).

drunkards. The film's screenplay was written by Quentin Tarantino (who also costarred), and the cast included Salma Hayek (in a cameo role), Cheech Marin, and George Clooney.

Rodriguez directed the segment called "The Misbehavers" in the film *Four Rooms* (1995) which featured Antonio Banderas and a cameo role by Salma Hayek. Other segments were directed by Quentin Tarantino, Allison Anders and Alexandre Rockwell. The film received lukewarm reviews and was a commercial flop. During June 1996, Rodriguez pulled out of directing a new version of the Zorro story (later titled *The Mask of Zorro* and released in 1998) that was to star Salma Hayek and Antonio Banderas and be shot on location in Mexico. He stated that he had creative differences with producer Steven Spielberg. Hayek subsequently withdrew from the project as a gesture of loyalty and support. Predictably, a non–Latina was cast in her role, and the other leading roles had non–Latinos as well.

In the meantime, Rodriguez had directed the Showtime cable feature *Roadracers* which starred his frequent leading lady, Salma Hayek.

When asked by *Profile* what distinguishes a Robert Rodriguez film, he stated, "Energy. The crew is small, fast, and we shoot with the camera on. So the film looks rougher, more fluid. I grew up in a family of ten. I'm used to seeing everything rushing around. That's why my movies are so frantic. It's very much the way I see things."[176]

His most recent films include *Frantic* (1998), in which Salma Hayek plays a cameo role; *Spy Kids* (2001); *Spy Kids 2* (2002); *Spy Kids 3* (2003); *Once upon a Time in Mexico* (2003); *Sin City* (2005); *Machete* (2010); and *Spy Kids 4* (2011).

JULIETA ROSEN

Julieta Rosen belongs to the new generation of Mexican actresses (which includes Salma Hayek) attempting a crossover career in the United States having honed their acting skills primarily in very popular Mexican *telenovelas*.

Julieta Rosen was born on November 8, 1962, in Mexico City to a Mexican father and a Swedish mother. Even as a child she dreamed of becoming an actress and she played her first lead in a play at the age of sixteen at the University Theatre. At the theater she received training in acting, dancing and singing.

She made her professional acting debut in *Don Juan Tenorio* at the Teatro de la Ciudad in Mexico City. Other plays soon followed, such as *With Love Eyes Filled* on a national tour; *Cactus Flower* at the Arlequin Theatre; *My Girlfriend, Your Wife, My Lover*; *Selfish Woman*; and *High Seduction*. The last three plays were performed on an extended national tour. I asked her if she had a preference among the different mediums of acting, and she commented, "Well, it's a different thing. You know, there's a lot of people that criticize television and that really makes me mad, every area is respectable. I respect very much all these actors that are forever and ever in a play. I like to do that and I enjoy it very much. But I need a change. It takes a lot of energy. What's very interesting is that your performance varies almost every day. And that's the magical part. On television, you are working with your own tools, and you rely a lot on the other actors, the director, and the working in conjunction."[177]

In 1983, she made her *telenovela* debut playing the lead in Televisa's *Un Solo Corazón*, which earned her the Golden Rose Award for Best Actress of 1984. Her second *telenovela*, *Senda de Gloria* (Televisa) won her the Golden Sun (Historical Series Award) for Best Actress

Anthony Hopkins and Julieta Rosen starred together in *The Mask of Zorro* (1998, TriStar Pictures).

in 1987. Her third *telenovela, Encadenada* (Televisa) earned her the Golden Palms Award for Best Actress in 1989. She starred in two other *telenovelas* for Televisa, *High Mothers* and *Lighting Torch.* In 1994, Rosen cohosted an entertainment program entitled *En Vivo* with Ricardo Rocha. Asked which was her favorite role in a *telenovela,* she stated, "I think the one in which I was the bad girl [*Infierno en el Paraiso,* 1999]. I just had such fun. You know, because you're supposed to be the leading actress. And that can be kind of horrid. They can be so good, so good they can be stupid."[178]

She made her film debut in the French-Mexican co-production *The Goat* (1978) with Gerard Depardieu. She went on to play leads in fourteen Mexican films of mixed quality: *Agreement with Death* (1984); *Enemies Till Death* (1984); *The King of the Neighborhood* (1985); *I Am the Law* (1986); *Edge of Terror* (1986); *Cops II* (1987); *The Face of Death* (1987); *Cop or Criminal* (1988); *Fangs* (1988); *Trapped* (1988); *Prison Murder* (1989); *My Dear Old Man* (1989); *Bloody Roulette* (1989) and *Love in the Right Measure* (1990). The best of these films, *The King of the Neighborhood,* earned her the Heraldo Award for Best Actress.

She made her U.S. television film debut in *Wind Runner* (1997) and followed it with the lead in the HBO film *Perfect Target* (1997) with Robert Englund. However, it was her role as the beautiful and ill-fated wife of Zorro (Anthony Hopkins) in the critical and commercial hit *The Mask of Zorro* (1998) that earned her wide commendation and a foothold in U.S. films.

She has starred in several Mexican *telenovelas*: *Viva Vegas* (2000); *El Amor No Tiene Precio* (2004); *Mi Vida Eres Tú* (2006); *Bajo las Riendas del Amor* (2007); *Amor de Casa Desesperadas* (2008); *El Show de Julieta Rosen* (2008); and *Cuando me Enamoro* (2010).

Raúl Ruiz

Director Raúl Ruiz has worked in four national cinemas, those of his native country Chile, France, Italy, and more recently in the United States.

He was born on July 25, 1941, in Puerto Monti, Chile, the son of a ship's captain. He studied law and theology at the University of Chile, in Santiago. Later, under a Rockefeller Foundation scholarship, he wrote numerous plays. After a short stint of film studies in Santa Fe, Argentina, he worked as a technician and writer in both Mexican and Chilean television programs for the next few years.

He borrowed money from family and friends to produce and direct his first feature film, *Tres Tristes Tigres/Three Sad Tigers* in 1968. The film went on to win the Grand Prix at the Locarno Film Festival and it quickly established him as one of the most important national filmmakers. Politically conscientious, as well as cinematically gifted, he utilized the art form to chronicle the tumultuous times taking place in Chile during the late 1960s and early 1970s in such films as: *Qué Hacer* (1970, codirector); *La Colonia Penal* (1971); *Nadie Dijo Nada* (1971); *La Expropiación* (1972); *El Realismo Socialista* (1973); *Palomilla Brava* (1973); and *Palomita Blanca* (1973), which he codirected. The last-named film remained unfinished when General Pinochet overthrew the democratically elected Salvador Allende in Chile in 1973. As a vocal critic of the new military regime, Ruiz was forced to flee into exile in Europe, where he lived in different countries.

During these years of exile, he resided most of the time in France, but worked throughout Europe in film and television. His first feature focused on the plight of Chilean exiles, *Diálogo De Exiliados* in 1974. In the following years, he directed a prolific output of widely acclaimed films. Film historian Ephraim Katz wrote of him, "His bold narrative style and innovative use of lighting and camera techniques earned him the admiration of the Paris avant-garde."[179]

His films during this period included *Mensch Versreat Und Verkekehrt* (1975, Germany); *La Vocation Suspendue* (1977, France); *L'hypothese du Tableau Volé/Hypothesis of the Stolen Painting* (1978, France); *De Grands Evénéments et des Gens Ordinaires* (1979, France); *Le Borgne* (1981, France); *The Territory* (1981, Portugal); *On Top of the Whale* (1982, Holland); *Les Trois Couronnes du Matelot/Three Crowns of the Sailor* (1983, France); *Berenice la Ville des Pirates* (1984, France/Portugal); *L'Eveille du Pont de L'alma* (1985, France); *Les Destins de Marcel* (1985, France); *Régime sans Pain* (1986, France); *Rihand lii L'Île au Tresor/Treasure Island* (1986, France/U.S.); *Mammame* (1986, also design; Chile/France); *Memoire des Apparences/La Vie Est un Songe/Life Is a Dream* (1987, France); and *La Chouette Aveugle* (1987, France/Switzerland).

He often both directed and wrote his own screenplays. He also collaborated with his director wife Valerie Sarmiento on such films as *Notre Mariage* (1985) and *Amelia Lopes O'Neill* (1991). He also was an actor in *Palombella Rossa* (1989).

In 1990, he directed *The Golden Boat*, which was shot in New York City in black-and-white 16 mm. This was his U.S. film debut. In 1994, he directed and wrote the film *Dark at Noon* with John Hurt and met with notable success, and in 1996, he scored another hit with *Three Lives and Only One Death*, one of Marcello Mastroianni's last films.

Ruiz directed two full-fledged U.S. feature films, *Shattered Image* (1998) with Alec Baldwin and Anne Parillaud, and *A Closed Book*, aka *Blind Revenge* (2010) with Daryl Hannah. He continued to direct important films: the star-studded Marcel Proust adaptation *Time Regained* (1999); *Comedy of Innocence* (2000) with Isabelle Huppert; *Savage Souls* (2001); *That Day* (2003); *Klimt* (2006); and his final film, *Night Across the Street* (2012). When he died in 2011 he was preparing to film the Napoleonic epic *Lines of Wellington* (2012). His widow, Valerie Sarmiento, was often his collaborator and an editor in her own right.

MARK SANCHEZ

Latinos have had a long presence in films in a variety of capacities. Some, including Mark Sanchez, are make-up artists.

Mark Sanchez was born in 1955, in the barrio of East Los Angeles, California. He became immersed in art at an early age. He drifted into make-up as an extension of his art vocation. He began as a make-up man on television and won an Emmy for *The Joan Rivers Show*.

In 1994, he worked on Luis Valdez' TNT film *The Cisco Kid* (1994) with Jimmy Smits, with whom he subsequently worked in *NYPD Blue*. Branching out into films, he did the make-up for Edward James Olmos' *American Me* (1992) and Gregory Nava's *My Family/Mi Familia* (1995). In the latter film, he worked with Ken Diaz and both were nominated for an Academy Award for their impressive work. His most recent film credits include Gregory Nava's *Selena* (1997).

Sanchez continues to do art work. In 1996, he held an exhibit along with other Chicano artists at the Galeria Self-Help Graphics entitled "Chicano Beloved."

AITANA SÁNCHEZ GIJÓN

After the film success of Antonio Banderas, Hollywood continued to scout for other Spanish talent. One of those who heeded the call was the actress Aitana Sánchez Gijón.

She was born on November 8, 1968, in Rome, Italy, to Spanish parents. She is a descendent of the great Spanish poet Rafael Alberti. She began and honed her acting talent in Spanish theater.

She made her U.S. film debut playing a Mexican-American in love with a GI in Alfonso Arau's romantic drama *A Walk in the Clouds* in 1995. Although the film was a modest success, her stock in film went up, especially in Spain. Among her successes is Adolfo Aristarian's *La Ley de la Frontera* (1995).

One of her 1990s films is Javier Bardem's farce *Boca a Boca/Mouth to Mouth* (1997). The *Los Angeles Times* noted, "*Mouth to Mouth* is a gloriously giddy Spanish face of consistent humor and invention that embraces romantic comedy, a thriller, a sharp satire of Hollywood pomposity and even a nudge to gays to get out of the closet.... Sánchez-Gijón's Amanda is herself formidably sexy, gorgeous yet vulnerable."[180]

She scored another critical and commercial hit playing a chambermaid caught up in the

Titanic disaster in Bigas Luna's *The Chambermaid* (1998). The *Los Angeles Times* wrote, "This light, consistently original and delightful period fable is the kind of film in which sophisticated European filmmakers excel, but they don't come along as frequently as they once did."[181]

Her recent films include *Sus Ojos Se Cerraron* (1998); *I'm Not Scared* (2003); and *The Machinist* (2004); *El Genio Tranquilo* (2005); *Oviedo Express* (2007); *The Frost* (2009); and *Maktub* (2011).

Jon Seda

Jon Seda was born on October 14, 1971, in Clifton, New Jersey, to Puerto Rican parents. Involved in sports since a young age, he focused on boxing and went on to win twenty-one fights, five of them in the 1990 Golden Gloves competition. At his mother's urging, he began taking acting lessons, and won the supporting role of the boxer Romano in the film *Gladiator* in 1992.

He subsequently made an impression in supporting roles in *Carlito's Way* (1992) with Al Pacino and in *Zebrahead* (1992). He won the role of Chino, the young Puerto Rican husband married to Lauren Vélez, in Darnell Martin's sleeper *I Like It Like That* (1994) after an unexpectedly arduous audition. He recollected later, "Before that, I knew nothing about acting. All I did was go to the movies and watch them. If you had said to me five years ago, 'You're going to be an actor, you're going to be in this position,' I would have laughed at you. I would have said, 'What, me?'"[182]

Both the film and the cast earned rave reviews. *Variety* stated, "Seda is fine as the temperamental young father."[183]

Seda's 1990s films included *12 Monkeys* (1996) with Bruce Willis and Brad Pitt; *Primal Fear* (1996) with Richard Gere; *Boys on the Side* (1996) with Whoopi Goldberg; *Sunchaser* (1996); *Dear God* (1997) with Greg Kinnear; and the meaty role of Selena's wayward boyfriend in Gregory Nava's *Selena* (1997). His most recent films include *The Price of Killings* (1997); *Little Pieces* (1998); *Love the Hard Way* (2001); *Double Bang* (2001); *Larry Crowne* (2011); and *Bullet to the Head* (2013).

Seda has guest-starred in numerous top-rated television series like *Ghost Whisperer* (2006); *CSI: Miami* (2008); and *Hawaii Five-O* (2011–13). He has been a regular on *Chicago P.D.* since 2013 and had a regular role in *Treme* (2011–2013).

He was nominated as Best Actor for his performance in *I Like It Like That* in the fourth annual Desi Awards, which are named for the late Desi Arnaz and dedicated to honoring Latino contributions in film and television.

His most memorable role thus far as is as one of the sons of Jimmy Smits aspiring to boxing glory in the excellent boxing drama *Price of Glory* (2000). His recent films include *Bad Boys II* (2003); and *Larry Crowne* (2011). He has made numerous television appearances in both series and films.

Jimmy Smits

One of the most visible and popular Latino film stars of the 1990s was the dark and tall Jimmy Smits, who starred in two hit television series and several films.

He was born in Brooklyn, on July 9, 1955, and educated at Brooklyn College, where he majored in education, and at Cornell University, where he studied theater arts. He appeared with the New York Shakespeare Festival and numerous productions.

About his mixed ethnic heritage, he told *Playboy*, "My mother is from Puerto Rico and my father is from Surinam, a former Dutch colony in South America. His father was from Holland. Smits is Dutch derivative, a common name in Holland—kind of like Smith.... When I was ten we moved to Puerto Rico to live for a couple of years. It was one of the most traumatic things that ever happened to me. I spoke no Spanish. But I had to go to school there, and there was a point when I was lost. But looking back, it was also one of the greatest things that happened to me. It really defined who I am. It formulated my cultural identity."[184]

His big opportunity came when he was cast as the Latino attorney Victor Sifuentes in the hit television series *L.A. Law* from 1986 to 1992. He had a small role in the television film *Rockabye* (1986, CBS) with Rachel Ticotin. Previous to this he had featured roles in two popular films that brought him to the attention of casting directors: *Running Scared* (1986) with Billy Crystal and Gregory Hines, in which he played a wisecracking police detective, and *The Believers* (1987) with Martin Sheen and Helen Shaver, in which he played the persecuted victim of a voodoo cult.

Once established as a television star, he starred in a series of disappointing films that failed to make use of his particular talent and personality: *Old Gringo* (1989) based on the

(Left to right) Gregory Peck, Jimmy Smits, Jane Fonda, director Luis Puenzo, and Carlos Fuentes (the author of the novel being filmed) on the set of *Old Gringo* (1989, Columbia).

novel by Carlos Fuentes, with Gregory Peck and Jane Fonda, in which he played a Mexican revolutionary; the medical school comedy *Vital Signs* (1990), in which he played a doctor; Blake Edwards' *Switch* (1991) with JoBeth Williams, Lorraine Bracco and Ellen Barkin; and *Fires Within* (1991) with Greta Scacchi.

About his departure from television, he told *Los Angeles Times TV Times*, "I left *Law* because my five-year contract was up, and I felt that everything that I had to say about that character had been said. I wanted to do different things. But I never said anything to any interviewer about wanting to be a movie star. I did not leave a three-picture deal at Columbia. There are a lot of people who are snobbish about where you fit into this business. I'm not one of them."[185]

In 1994, he replaced actor David Caruso in the hit television series *NYPD Blue* on ABC. He played police detective Bobby Simone, partner to detective Sipowicz (Dennis Franz). Smits told *Los Angeles Times TV Times*, "I know there's going to be a lot of scrutiny, but I'm trying not to think about it ... I hope people really give me a chance to just slip in there.... I know the show has loyal fans, and that's not going to happen overnight. It's going to take a while. I just hope people are patient. In the best possible world, the work will speak for itself."[186] Smits' worries proved unwarranted and *NYPD Blue* continued to be a top-rated and critically acclaimed show. Smits earned several Emmy nominations for Best Actor (he had previously won a Best Supporting Actor Emmy for *L.A. Law*).

When interviewed by *Playboy* (October 1996) about the controversial California Proposition 187 regarding illegal immigration he stated, "At base, don't forget the principle upon which this country was started. We are a collection of different peoples from lots of different places. It's convenient for the U.S. to have an open-door immigration policy when it benefits growers, because there's a better harvest. But on the other hand when times get tough, there has to be a scapegoat."[187]

When he was asked to name some Latino heroes, he commented, "First, Cesar Chavez. He's our Martin Luther King, Jr. Then, Simon Bolivar, because his ideal was that there would be a unified Latin America. That means so much, because that's the only way Latinos are going to make inroads in this country.... To become a viable economic and political bloc, we need to show a unified front."[188]

In the same interview he talked about the status of Latinos in the film and television industry. "Hispanic actors have always had difficulty finding work, and it's worse now than it was in the Fifties. If our percentage of the population has increased, why isn't that reflected on film? But that said, I would like people to think of me as an actor who happens to be Hispanic, in the same way they think of Al Pacino as an actor who happens to be an Italian American."[189]

In 1994, he essayed the title role in Luis Valdez's *The Cisco Kid* for TNT, which costarred Cheech Marin and was shot on location in Mexico. He was the fifth actor to play the role in various versions (the others are Warner Baxter, Cesar Romero, Duncan Renaldo, and Gilbert Roland). In 1995, he garnered excellent notices for his performance in Gregory Nava's *My Family/Mi Familia*. The critical and commercial success of the film boosted Smits' status as a leading man and serious actor.

In 1998, Smits announced his departure from the cast of *NYPD Blue*. Soon, he appeared again in films. He was excellent as a former boxer training his sons in the excellent underappreciated boxing drama *Price of Glory* (2000). Other recent films include *Stars Wars: Episode II: Attack of the Clones* (2002); *Star Wars: Episode III: Revenge of the Sith* (2005); and *Mother and Child* (2010). He continues to guest-star in television shows and has played a regular role in *Sons of Anarchy* since 2012.

DOUGLAS SPAIN

Douglas Spain is one of the young Latino actors who made a notable impression at the end of the 1990s in the independent film *Star Maps*. He was born of Guatemalan ancestry on April 15, 1974, in Los Angeles, California. Spain began acting at a young age. His television credits include TNT's film *Tecumseh! The Last Warrior* and HBO's *Flash Fires*. He performed the play *Gunplay: La Familia* in Los Angeles.

His 1990s credits include William Friedkin's remake of *Twelve Angry Men* (1997) on Showtime; the independent film *Happy Together* (1997); and Showtime's *Riot* (1997).

However, it was the role of Carlos, the young Latino consigned to prostitution by his dysfunctional father, in Miguel Arteta's *Star Maps* (1997) that won him wide recognition.

His most recent films include *Walkout* (2006); *Without Men* (2011); and *Line of Duty* (2013). He has appeared on television frequently.

Danny Trejo

Chicano actor Danny Trejo has used his muscular, tattooed build to play scores of *veterano vatos locos*, small-time hoods, and unremorseful villains, such as his role in *Blood in, Blood Out*, aka *Bound by Honor* (1993).

He was born on May 6, 1944, in the Echo Park area in Los Angeles. He lived in the barrios of Echo Park and later in Pacoima and became involved in gangs and drugs. Later, he was arrested on drug and robbery charges. While incarcerated, he earned his high school diploma. He was finally released in 1969, and upon his release he went to work with the Narcotics Prevention Project and Western Pacific Rehab. He later recalled to *Latin Style*, "I thought the entire world was my barrio. For most young Chicanos growing up in the barrio it's so hard to get a broader scope.... My life before was like I was in a nightmare; then I got sober and clean and I'm no longer in that nightmare. All I've ever done since I've been out of the joint is to try help people. The only failure is not trying."[190]

He made his film debut in *Runaway Train* (1985) with Jon Voight, in which he played a convict. He was asked initially to train actor Eric Roberts to box, but soon he was convinced by the film's director and actor Jon Voight to take an acting role. Among his best roles are the down-and-out drug addict who loiters in the park in Allison Anders' *Mi Vida Loca* (1993) and the knife-wielding Navajas in Robert Rodriguez's *Desperado* (1995).

His films include *Death Wish IV* (1987) with Charles Bronson; *Penitentiary III* (1987); *Kinjite* (1990) with Charles Bronson; *Lock Up* (1990) with Donald Sutherland and Sylvester Stallone; *Marked for Death* (1990) with Steven Seagal; *Guns* (1990) with Erik Estrada; *Homicide* (1991); *Heat* (1995) with Robert DeNiro and Al Pacino; and *Con Air* (1997) with Rachel Ticotin and Nicolas Cage.

He has become a cult figure, especially with the films directed by Robert Rodriguez such as *Desperado* (1995); *From Dusk Till Dawn* (1995); *Spy Kids 1* (2001); *Spy Kids 2* (2002); *Spy Kids 3* (2003); and *Machete* (2011) in which he played the title role. He has appeared extensively on television.

He contributes much of his time as a drug, suicide and gang intervention counselor.

LEONOR VARELA

Leonor Varela was born on December 29, 1972, in Santiago, Chile. At the age of two months, she and her parents fled after the military coup by General Pinochet in 1973. They first settled in Costa Rica and later in Boulder, Colorado. Eventually, they moved still another time, this time to Paris, France, where she began acting.

She made her U.S. debut in 1998's *The Man in the Iron Mask* opposite Gerard Depardieu, Gabriel Byrne, and Leonardo DiCaprio. She was then cast in the title role of the multimillion-dollar miniseries *Cleopatra,* which aired on May 23 and 24, 1999. Although the television miniseries earned less than kind reviews and ratings, it brought Varela to the notice of Hollywood film producers. The miniseries was shot in Morocco and London during a three-month shoot. She told *People*, "I wanted to be a 90's Cleopatra, to make her as women are today.... A woman of power."[191]

Her recent films include *The Tailor from Panama* (2001); *Texas Ranger* (2001); and *Human Target* (2010). However, her most important role has been that of the distraught Salvadoran mother caring for her children in civil war–torn El Salvador in *Innocent Voices* (2004). She has appeared extensively in television shows and movies.

JACOB VARGAS

One of the busiest young Latino actors of the 1990s was the dark-haired Jacob Vargas.

He was born on August 18, 1971, in Los Angeles, California, to Mexican parents. At an early age he began to breakdance, and soon, at age 14, he was signed for a television role on *Diff'rent Strokes*. Other appearances on television shows followed: *Hunter, The Tracey Ullman Show, The Last Resort,* and Disney's *Hard Times on Planet Earth*. He also had featured roles in several television films: *Miracle of the Heart: A Boy's Town Story* (1986) with Art Carney; *The Children of Times Square* (1986) with Silvana Gallardo; *Drug Wars:The Camarena Story* (1990) with Steven Bauer; and *The Great Los Angeles Earthquake* (1995) with Silvana Gallardo. During the late 1980s, he had a continuing role in the short-lived series *The New Gidget*.

He made his film debut in *The Last Resort* in 1986. His other theatrical film credits include *Ernest Goes to Camp* (1987); *The Principal* (1987), for which he was nominated as Best Young Actor in a motion picture at the 1987 Youth in Film Awards; *Little Nikita* (1989) with Sidney Poitier; *Crack House* (1990) with Jim Brown; *Airborne* (1993); *Fatal Instinct* (1993) with Kate Nelligan and Sean Young; Allison Anders' *Mi Vida Loca* (1993); *Crimson Tide* (1995) with Gene Hackman; and *Get Shorty* (1995) with John Travolta. Despite his overall good work, his best roles have been in a pair of Chicano-themed films: Edward James Olmos' *American Me* (1992), in which he played a young gang member; and Gregory Nava's *My Family/Mi Familia* (1995), in which he played a hardworking Mexican father. He had another well-received role, as a young man who brings a glimmer of hope to the characters, in *Gas Food Lodging* (1992); and he played a Mexican cop in *Traffic* (2000).

Vargas is an accomplished dancer and singer. He is a member of the L.A. Breakers and Street Motion Breakdance Crew. His recent films include *Dragonfly* (2002); *The Virgin of Juarez* (2006); *Bobby* (2006); *Devil* (2010); and *Cesar Chavez* (2014). He has guest-starred on many television shows.

VALENTINA VARGAS

Valentina Vargas was born on December 4, 1964, in Chile. She studied drama, music and dance at a conservatory. Her family sent her to finish her studies in France three years later, and there she became fluent in English, French, and Italian.

It was in France that she made her film debut. She appeared in an episode of the televison series *Le Petit Docteur* directed by Marc Simenon and the film *Strictement Personnel*, which was directed by Pierre Jolivet. She also cut two records.

In 1985, she met director Jean-Jacques Annaud, who was preparing to direct the film version of *The Name of the Rose* (1986), which was based on the best-selling novel by Umberto Eco and set in the 14th century. Vargas auditioned for the role of The Girl, and eleven months later won the part, a peasant maiden who helps monk William of Baskerville (Sean Connery) and his assistant Severinus (Christian Slater) find a murderer. The film became a big commercial and critical success and Vargas was also singled out for her sensual performance.

Despite the impression she made in *The Name of the Rose*, Hollywood did not know what to do with the dark-haired, brown-skinned actress. She was subsequently cast in three films, Luc Besson's *The Big Blue* (1988) with Rosanna Arquette; *Street of No Return* (1992) with Keith Carradine; and *Hellraiser: Bloodline* (1996). Thereafter, like many Latinas in the Hollywood film industry, her career stalled.

Her most recent films include *Southern Cross* (1999); *Bloody Mallory* (2002); and *Faces in the Crowd* (2011). She has appeared frequently on French television.

EDDIE VELEZ

Eddie Velez is one of the many Latino character actors who have weathered the good and bad times of being a working actor for decades years.

He was born on June 4, 1958, in Manhattan, New York, to Puerto Rican parents. He attended the High School of Art and Design and the School of Visual Arts, but unable to find employment, started a career as a stand-up comic. After a stint in the air force he headed for Los Angeles where he did theater. He continued his drama training at the Estelle Harman Actors Workshop and with the renowned José Quintero at the Mark Taper Forum.

He has had a growing number of credits on the stage. He played in the world premiere production of *Delirious* at the Matrix Theatre, which won the Drama-Logue Award for Best Ensemble. He also appeared in the acclaimed West Coast premiere production of *Balm in Gilead* at the Coast Theatre. Other plays include *The Odd Couple*, *Steambath*, *The Petrified Forest*, *The Threepenny Opera*, *Dracula*, and *Barefoot in the Park*.

He has had recurring roles in five television series: *Berrenger's* (1985, NBC); *The Charley Weaver Show* (1985–86, CBS); *The A-Team* (1986–87, NBC; *Trial and Error* (1988, CBS); and *True Blue* (1989–90, NBC).

Additionally, he has guest-starred in numerous other television shows: *Murder, She Wrote, Empty Nest, The Flying Nun, The Trials of Rosie O'Neill, Midnight Caller, Tour of Duty, Cagney and Lacey* and *Hill Street Blues*. His television film credits include *For Love and Honor* (1983); *Shannon's Deal* (1984) with Elizabeth Peña; *Summer Fantasy* (1984, NBC); *Children of the Night* (1985, CBS); *C.A.T. Squad* (1986, NBC); and *A Jury of One* (1994). He costarred in the NBC miniseries *Drug Wars: The Camarena Story* (1990).

His film credits include *Repo Man* (1984) with Emilio Estevez; Robert Wise's *Rooftops* (1989); *Romero* (1989) with Raúl Juliá; and *A Rainy Day* (1994).

Regarding the status of Latinos in the media, he told *Drama-Logue*, "I think being a Latin, and being who I am, is why I am working. It's tough for any actor in the business but I think I've learned to work within the system and I've used whatever it is about me that is complementary to me.... I'd like to play a hero.... It's been a long time since the days when there was a romantic Latin hero. Someone the entire country wants to see, not just Latins. I think [this is] the right time that it can happen."[192]

His most recent films include *Traffic* (2000); *White Chicks* (2004); and *Repo Chick* (2009).

LAUREN VÉLEZ

Lauren Vélez played one of the key Latina roles of the 1990s in film, that of Lisette, the resourceful and struggling Puerto Rican mother in *I Like It Like That*. It was a rare good role for Latinas.

She was born on November 2, 1964, in Brooklyn, New York, one of eight children of Puerto Rican parents. Her father, a policeman, wanted her to follow in his footsteps. However, she took dancing classes with Alvin Ailey and then acting classes.

Her acting career blossomed first in theater and then television. She had roles in such Broadway plays as *Into the Woods* and *Dreamgirls* and off-off Broadway productions such as *Much Ado About Nothing* and *Little Shop of Horrors*. On television, she had roles in *True Blue* and *Ryan's Hope*.

Her opportunity to play the lead in Darnell Martin's directorial debut, *I Like It Like That* (1994), an independent film about a young, separated Puerto Rican mother, came as a surprise to Vélez. She had just taken off a year from acting. She later recalled, "It was just luck, getting this role, because I had been out of the business for a year. Once I decided to get back into the business, I sent a picture to an agent, who happened to be casting for this film, and they sent me in. And the role just fit like a glove. I totally knew this character."[193]

She found acting on film a challenge of a different sort: "Making a film is just so different. I'm mostly a stage actress, so to me it was quite a different experience. I thought I would dislike it a lot more—the idea of stopping and starting, setting up and then coming back in a half-hour—and not living through something all at the same time. But I found that I really like it a lot."[194]

She also liked the positive aspects and nuances of the film: "I hate seeing these films about these ethnic families being portrayed as all growing up with drug dealers and hearing gunshots in the distance, and that sort of thing. It's like they've become the definitive portrayal of ethnic families living in a certain economic status—and it's not true.... This is just a normal family—they're funny, and they try to make a living, and it's not tragic."[195]

Vélez earned wide acclaim for her performance in *I Like It Like That*. The *New York Times* wrote, "It is Ms. Velez who is in almost every scene, holding the movie together and carrying off a flamboyant role with bright, scrappy style. She and Mr. Seda are touchingly matched, both of them outwardly bold and secretly delicate, trying hard to live up to their own ideas of what adulthood is supposed to be."[196] *Variety* noted, "Velez convinces as she manages to cope while being on the brink most of the time."[197]

In 1995, she was cast as one of the leads in the Fox television hit *New York Undercover*, which chronicled the efforts of two young detectives—one Latino (Michael DeLorenzo) and one black (Malik Yoba). Lauren and DeLorenzo played a couple, the only Latino couple on television. She commented about the show, "Coming into what was their show was difficult ... I love this couple. They're fiercely independent, but they love each other. And having [Puerto Rican] culture in common, it's so comfortable."[198]

During 1996, she played the widow of a policeman in the film *City Hall*, opposite Al Pacino. Her second film during the year was a Spanish-language film entitled *En Busca de un Sueño (In Search of a Dream)*, about two women involved in green-card marriages with Dominican baseball players.

In 1998, the series *New York Undercover* was canceled. Lauren landed a role as a series regular in HBO's *OZ*, about the daily life in prison. She played the prison doctor. Her recent films include *Taino* (1999); *Medium* (2006); and *Serial* (2007). She was a regular on the hit television series *Ugly Betty* (2009–10) and *Dexter* (2006–12).

DEL ZAMORA

Chicano actor/writer Del Zamora has appeared in some fifty-four films, forty-eight television programs and sixty-eight plays in a career that has spanned more than fifteen years.

He has displayed his intense versatility in theater, television and film. On the stage, he created the role of Rude Boy in *The Last Angry Man* at the California Plaza. Other important roles have been in *Out in Front: Otra Vez* at the Mark Taper Forum; *El Luchador Chicano* at the San Antonio CineFestival; *Romeo and Juliet* at the CBS Studio Center; and *Banana* at the Los Angeles Theatre Center.

His television credits include *NYPD Blue, Murphy Brown, Cybill, My So-Called Life, In Living Color, Saturday Night Live, Hill Street Blues, Miami Vice, In the Line of Duty, Heathcliff & the Catillac Cats* (cartoon voices), and *ASCO Is Spanish for Nausea* on PBS.

Among his film credits are *Robocop* (1982); *Repo Man* (1984); *Born in East L.A.* (1987); *The Fabulous Baker Boys* (1989); and *The Killing Time* (1987).

An articulate and conscientious activist for the improvement of opportunities for Latinos in the media, he penned an article for the *Los Angeles Times* that spoke strongly for that concern: "As a Chicano actor-writer-director with more than 14 years of experience, I can provide firsthand knowledge of the dearth of Latino roles in the film and television industry. The irony of the situation is as thick as the smog that hangs over the city of Nuestra Señora de Los Angeles (named by Latinos in the 18th century). The United States has close to 30 million Latinos. Many of this population ancestors lived in and pre-dated the Anglo takeover of the Southwest. Just take a look around at the names of the states, cities, streets, etc. In modern time, Latino audiences have purchased enormous amounts of tickets to Hollywood movies (as shown by several studies and surveys), yet Latinos hardly ever portray lead characters in these movies. A sort of financing of their own exclusion.... Much talk is made of qualifications and merits of the actors. Tell me, who is more qualified to portray Latinos? A Latino actor who has knowledge of the culture, language, history, etc. or a non–Latino who has, at best, cursory knowledge of what a Latino really is? To this date, I have not seen one portrayal of a Latino by a non–Latino that was even in the ballpark. This is not a legacy of Hollywood or these non–Latino actors to be proud of."[199]

His most recent films include *Town and Country* (2001); *Tortilla Heaven* (2007); *Repo Chick* (2009); *American Flyer* (2010); and *Thursday's Speaker* (2011). He continues to guest-star in top-rated television shows.

VII

The 2000s

The 2000s brought many profound sociopolitical and economic changes to the United States and the rest of the world. As the Cold War receded into history, the specter of terrorism and narcoterrorism (especially in Mexico) dramatically changed the national security and civil liberties of millions around the world. A worldwide recession (the worst economic meltdown since the Great Depression) buckled the foundations of the majority of nation states in the First World. Conversely, these twin calamities fueled xenophobia and the demonization of the darker peoples of the world. The popular media became the major venue for demagoguery, intolerance, and stereotypes.

The United States had begun the decade with the longest term of economic expansion and prosperity in its history under President Clinton. A federal budget surplus and the implementation of the North American Free Trade Agreement (NAFTA) further bolstered the hopes and dreams of many. However, on September 11, 2001, that tranquility and security was shattered forever by the terrorist attacks on the Twin Towers and the Pentagon. There had been acts of terror abroad for decades, but never in such magnitude in the United States. The shock and trauma of the attack was incalculable psychologically, politically, and economically. There were those who commented that the "chickens had come back to roost," a phrase that implied the attacks were the consequence of centuries of exploitation of the Third World by the First World. The direct effect on the United States was the militarization and heightened security of all governmental institutions, ports, and airports. The U.S. Congress passed the USA Patriot Act, which essentially made it legal for the government to deny or restrict constitutional rights for purposes of national security.

President George W. Bush and his administration quickly capitalized on the nation's trauma by becoming involved in two foreign military ventures, which provided a catharsis for some. The first was an invasion of Afghanistan, which had harbored the presumed perpetrators of the 9/11 attacks, and the second was an invasion of Iraq (which had the world's second-largest reserve of oil) under the excuse that that nation harbored "weapons of mass destruction." The latter assertion proved to be utterly false, but the millions of dead, maimed, and refugees were completely true.

Then, midway through the second Bush term, a deep-rooted recession (which began in the housing market and quickly spread to other sectors of the national economy) brought economic ruin, unemployment, homelessness, and suffering not seen since the Great Depression. The recession, which began in the United States, quickly spread throughout the rest of the world. The interdependent nature of all the world's economies through globalization brought the First World to its very knees. The Third World, which lived under a perpetual depression, felt the economic consequences as well.

Closer to home, in Mexico, a series of vicious and violent drug cartels grew dramatically to challenge the national government's authority and sovereignty. The rise of these cartels had several causes. One was the fact that the United States remained the world's biggest market for illicit drugs. Another was the worsening poverty and marginalization of millions; and yet another was the continuing political corruption.

In the rest of Latin America, a growing number of left-of-center movements challenged United States hegemony in the region, the neoliberal policies which had left many countries in bankruptcy, and the growing revulsion against the abusive and unethical practices of the World Bank and the International Monetary Fund. For the United States media, Hugo Chávez (the democratically elected president of Venezuela in 1998 who was subsequently reelected in 2000 and 2006) became persona non grata and the bogeyman of the region. However, democratically elected and left-of-center leaders marked the trend, rather than the exception. A new era began in Latin America. There was Evo Morales (2005–2009, 2009 to present), the first Native American president elected in Bolivia; Lula Da Silva (2003–2010) in Brazil; Rafael Correa (2007–2011, 2011 to present) in Ecuador; Cristina Fernández de Kirchner (2007–2011, 2011 to present) in Argentina; and the old U.S. nemesis Daniel Ortega (2007–2011, 2011 to present) in Nicaragua.

In the U.S., local, state, and federal legislation was proposed or passed that reflected the growing xenophobia, racism, and intolerance for "otherness" and difference. These included English Only laws, racial profiling (as in Arizona's SB 1070),[1] and proposals to deny citizenship to U.S.–born children of undocumented workers to add to the woes of minority communities and working-class folk. The state of Arizona in 2012 also outlawed the Tucson Unified School District's Chicano (or Mexican-American) studies program based on an obscure 2000 law that took effect in 2011. Said law prohibits any program that "promotes resentment toward a race or class of people or that promotes "the overthrow of the U.S." or that encourages "ethnic solidarity instead of the treatment of pupils as individuals."[2]

The economic crisis further fueled a movement towards the privatization of public education supported by corporations, corporate sponsors, and opportunistic politicians. Many saw it as a blatant effort to destroy the last public service unions (national labor union membership was down to only 8 percent from a high of 36 percent in 1945). A proliferation of corporate and billionaire benefactors flooded the media, demonizing teachers and pledging to help minorities. Diane Ravitch wrote, "In Hollywood films and television documentaries, the battle lines are clearly drawn. Traditional public schools are bad; their supporters are apologists for the unions. Those who advocate for charter schools, virtual schools, and 'school choice' are reformers; their supporters insist they are championing the rights of minorities."[3]

The 2010 U.S. Census provided a revealing snapshot of the United States. The population of the nation had increased to 308,745,538. Latinos remained the nation's largest ethnic minority, with 46.9 million (15.4 percent of the nation's population in 2008). This is an increase from 35.3 million in the 2000 U.S. Census. The census also revealed that 62 percent of Latinos were born in the United States, while 38 percent had been born outside of the nation.

The states with the largest number of Latinos were California, Nevada, Texas, New Mexico, Florida, and Colorado. The post–World War II trend of Latinos outside the Southwest continued. States registering a significant growth of Latinos included North Carolina, Virginia, Oregon, Idaho, Illinois, Pennsylvania, New York, Connecticut, Rhode Island, and Massachusetts. Minorities made up some 35 percent of the national population. According to the 2010 U.S. Census, the different Latino communities were as follows: Mexicans, 29.3 million; Puerto Ricans, 4.1 million; Cubans, 1.5 million; Salvadorans, 1.5 million; and Dominicans, 1.2 million. Latinos from Central America added up to 3.6 million and from South America 2.5 million. Minorities were projected to be the majority in the nation by the year 2050.

Despite the indisputable fact that Latinos had an increased national presence, they continued to be almost invisible in both films and television. Both film and television continued to be preserves of amnesia, and remain predominantly white and black. According to the Screen Actors Guild Report 2009, for the year 2008, Latinos made up only 6.4 percent of roles in film and television (the majority in incidental roles); Blacks, 13.3 percent; Asian–Pacific Islander, 3.8 percent; and Native American, 3.8 percent.

For Latinos in film, the more things changed, the more they remained the same in the 2000s.

Film Images and Film Stars

Latino film images of the 2000s remained mostly negative with a handful of exceptions. The number of Latino film stars and actors remained minuscule, even as the Latino community grew dramatically in numbers across the U.S. and consolidated itself as the largest ethnic community in the United States.

Latino images and representations during the 2000s were a continuation of long-established stereotypes and new ones created by the rise of the drug cartels and xenophobia fueled by the 9/11 events. The majority of Latino film parts were incidental roles and to a lesser extent supporting roles (with a few lead roles).

The Latino drug cartel thug was alive and well in a series of action films which pitted an invincible, testosterone-fueled white or black hero who single-handedly battled Latino drug cartels. In *A Man Apart* (2003, New Line Cinema), Vin Diesel and his sidekick (Lorenz Tate) hunt down every single member of a Mexican drug cartel after they kill his wife (Jacqueline Obradors). In *Bad Boys 2* (2003, Columbia Pictures), which was a sequel to the 1995 film *Bad Boys*, Will Smith and Martin Lawrence play DEA agents who uncover drug smuggling from Cuba to Miami. The two DEA agents and a SWAT team then proceed to invade Cuba in pursuit of a Cuban drug lord, Johnny Tapia (Jordi Molia). There they single-handedly annihilate the cartel and the Cuban military. Unscathed, they then seek asylum in the U.S. military base at Guantánamo Bay. The film was soundly criticized for its misogynistic depiction of women, as well as its mindless brutality. Many critics also voted it as the worst film of 2003 (even more awful than *Gigli*!).

In *Proof of Life* (2004, Castle Rock Entertainment), Russell Crowe played an Australian ex-soldier hired to rescue a U.S. technician (David Morse) kidnapped by a leftist guerrilla army (and drug traffickers) while building a dam in a South American country (in reality Colombia, but the film was shot in Ecuador). The Aussie and a handful of associates then take on the entire guerrilla force and decimate it.

In *Man on Fire* (2004), a disillusioned ex-CIA agent, John W. Creasy (Denzel Washington), is hired by a businessman (Marc Anthony) to guard his nine-year-old daughter (Dakota Fanning). When the girl is kidnapped, the monolingual Creasy goes on a violent rampage whose victims include kidnappers and Mexican government officials. The film supposes that all Mexicans are corrupt, criminally inclined, and inept. Some critics asserted that Creasy would not last one hour in the underworld of Mexico City without being killed.

Another film, *Traffic* (2000), presented another side of the drug cartel scourge: the insatiable demand in the United States for illicit drugs and the Third World marginalized people who supplied it. Another, *Maria Full of Grace* (2004), depicted the odyssey of a young Colombian woman (Catalina Sandino Moreno), who becomes a drug mule and smuggles cocaine into New York City. Elsewhere, *Training Day* (2001) dramatized the corruption and fall of an LAPD officer (Denzel Washington) amid the drug trade. The film dramatized twenty-four hours in the life of two narcotics detectives (Washington and Ethan Hawke) in two low-income neighborhoods, East Los Angeles and South Central. Denzel Washington won an Academy Award as Best Actor for his sensitive portrayal of a crooked cop. Unfortunately, all Mexican characters (with the exception of one cop) are bleakly portrayed as harlots and criminals.

The issue of immigration was prominent in many of the decade's films that had Latino characters. In *Casa de Los Babys* (2003), six Euro-American women travel to an unnamed South American country to adopt children. The documentary *Balseros* (2003) tackled the plight of Cuban immigrants. The previously mentioned *Maria Full of Grace* (2004) explored the underclass of undocumented Colombians in New York City. *Silver City* (2004) featured a Mexican-American character, Vince Esparza, who specializes in smuggling Mexican undocumented workers into Colorado. *The Gatekeeper* (2004) focuses on a Mexican who passes for white and is a member of a right-wing group that ambushes Mexican undocumented workers coming in from Baja California. *A Day Without a Mexican* (2004) satirized the economic calamity that would befall California if Mexican gardeners, nannies, dishwashers, hotel workers, maids, farmworkers, and other low-wage workers disappeared all of a sudden. The sci-fi film *The Day After Tomorrow* (2004), which warned about global warming and its consequences, depicted the mass illegal entry of U.S. residents into Mexico to escape the various natural disasters.

Another type of film seen during the decade was based in the Southwest yet had zero Latino presence or only incidental Latino roles: *Crocodile Dundee in L.A.* (2001); *Laurel Canyon* (2003); *Terminator 3* (2003); and *Hollywood Homicide* (2003), among others. One film, *The Perfect Game* (2010), celebrated the Monterrey (Mexico) Industrials baseball team that won the Little League World Series in 1957. The *Los Angeles Times* wrote about the film, "*The Perfect Game* is ... sweet and disarming in its belief that something like a baseball game can make a bigger difference."[4] Two films depicted the nation's largest Mexican barrio, East Los Angeles: *Eastside* (2000), a crime drama about an ex-con (Mario López); and *From Prada to Nada* (2011), a comedy that focused on two spoiled sisters (Camilla Belle, Alexa Vega) who are left penniless and move along with their aunt (Adriana Barraza) to East Los Angeles. A third film, *Tortilla Soup* (2001), set in the same barrio, explored the life of hardworking ordinary Mexicans.

Three films dealt with the turbulent lives of three Latino artists: *Before Night Falls*

(2000) was about Cuban gay poet and novelist Reinaldo Arenas; *Piñero* (2001) focused on Puerto Rican playwright Miguel Piñero; and *Frida* (2002) dealt with the passionate and creative life force of Mexican painter Frida Kahlo. Two films were made about Argentine revolutionary Ernesto "Che" Guevara during the decade. *The Motorcycle Diaries* (2004) chronicled the travels throughout South America of a young Guevara (played by Gael García Bernal) when he was still a medical student. *Che, Part One* (2008) and *Che, Part Two* (2008) documented Guevara (played by Benicio Del Toro) as a revolutionary in both Cuba and Bolivia. Mexican-American history was revived in two films: *The Alamo* (2004), about the 1836 uprising of Euro-Americans in Mexican Texas, and *Walkout* (2006) about the Chicano high school walkouts of the 1960s. The recent history of the Salvadoran civil war of the 1970s and 1980s was depicted in *Innocent Voices* (2004).

In the western genre, Penélope Cruz played a Mexican señorita who falls for Matt Damon in *All the Pretty Horses* (2000); Diego Luna played a young Mexican gunslinger in *Open Range* (2003); and a romanticized view of the outfit *Texas Rangers* (2001) featured Leonor Varela as another Mexican señorita.

Dramas with Latino characters included *Angel Eyes* (2001) with Jennifer Lopez and Sônia Braga; *Original Sin* (2010) with Antonio Banderas and Pedro Armendáriz, Jr.; *Sidewalks of New York* (2001) with Rosario Dawson; *Hunted* (2003) with Benicio Del Toro; *Raising Victor Vargas* (2003), which focused on the life of a teenager in the Lower East Side of New York City; and *Jersey Girl* (2004) with Jennifer Lopez. *Ladder 49* (2004) celebrated the firefighting profession in Baltimore and featured Jay Hernandez; and *Shall We Dance* (2004) featured the busy Jennifer Lopez as a dance instructor in Chicago. Crime dramas that featured Latinas and Latinos included *Fast and Furious* (2001) and *Fast and Furious 2* (2003) with Michelle Rodriguez as a highjacker of fuel tankers; *Ocean's Eleven* (2001), a remake of the Sinatra classic, which featured Andy García as a slimy casino manager; and *Price of Glory* (2000), which depicted the passing of boxing glory from a father (Jimmy Smits) to his children and the corruption in the boxing game. *Girlfight* (2000) documented the odyssey of an angry Latina teenager and her quest for boxing recognition. *Real Women Have Curves* (2002) told the story of another young Latina who aspires to be the first in her family to attend college.

Comedies featured some prominent Latino roles. Jennifer Lopez was a hard-pressed San Francisco *Wedding Planner* in the 2001 film; Héctor Elizondo essayed the head of security in *Princess Diaries* (2001) and *Princess Diaries 2* (2004), about a teenager who is an heir to a throne; and Freddie Prinze, Jr., headlined a couple of romantic comedies, *Head Over Heels* (2001) and *Summer Catch* (2001). The flat *Charlie's Angels Full Throttle* (2003) featured Cameron Diaz but was best remembered for the ageless Demi Moore. The romantic comedy *Something's Gotta Give* (2003), headlined by Jack Nicholson and Diane Keaton, featured Rachel Ticotin, and *Dirty Dancing: Havana Nights* (2004) featured Diego Luna as a hotel worker who romances a spoiled Euro-American girl right before the Cuban Revolution. *Nacho Libre* (2006) explored the struggles of a Mexican/Euro American wrestler to raise money for orphan children.

The second decade of the new century saw a diverse group of films depicting Latino images. The film *Colombiana* (2011) was produced and written (with Robert Mark Kamen) by French action film director Luc Besson and directed by Oliver Megaton. Zoe Saldana played a hit woman who is obsessed with wiping out a Colombian drug lord and his organization for the murder of her father. Some praised the film because it had a Latina action star. However, the far-fetched and violent film was criticized for being stereotypical and defamatory of Colombia. The film used the slogan "Revenge is beautiful," and some critics turned it around to say "Colombia is beautiful."[5] *The Expendables* (2010, Lionsgate) focused on a group of over-the-hill mercenaries (among them Sylvester Stallone) whose mission is to overthrow an evil Latin American dictator (David Zayas).

Casa de Mi Padre (2012) was a Spanish-language spoof headlined by popular comedy star Will Ferrell, which purported to be shot in "Mexicoscope." It told the story of Armando (Ferrell), whose rancher father (the late Pedro Armendáriz, Jr., to whom the film is dedicated) is facing severe economic difficulties. Diego Luna played the irresponsible younger brother and Gael García Bernal played a drug lord. The *Los Angeles Times* wrote, "The picture also plays on cross-border paranoia by pushing stereotypes to ridiculous extremes."[6] The film *For Greater Glory* (2012) chronicled the Cristero uprising (the armed resistance of some Catholic elements in central Mexico during the 1920s). The uprising according to some was sparked by President Elías Calles' anticlerical laws, while others have argued that the all-too-powerful Catholic Church had compelled fanatics to challenge federal laws that limited the power of the church. The film purported to say that more people were killed in the Cristero uprising than in the entire Mexican Revolution (1910–1920), which claimed more than one million lives. This is patently untrue. The film was headed by Andy García as General Gorostieta, television star Eva Longoria as his wife, Catalina Sandino Moreno as an ammunition smuggler, and Peter O'Toole as a priest. The *Los Angeles Times* wrote of the film, "*For Greater Glory* is mostly single-minded, dying-for-the-cause fodder, catnip for crusaders but not so interesting to those looking for a deeper view into how politics and religion can tragically clash."[7] Oliver Stone's *Savages* (2012) focused on the struggle of the Baja drug cartel and its expansion into a lucrative drug market in Southern California. The uneven crime drama provided some meaty roles for Salma Hayek, Benicio Del Toro, and Demián Bichir.

The old practice of casting non–Latinos in clearly Latino roles, even as historical characters, was in evidence in *Argo* (2012, Warner Bros.). The political thriller was loosely based on the efforts of Tony Mendez, a CIA agent who organized and carried out the rescue of six United States diplomatic employees from Tehran, Iran, in 1979. In real life, Tony Mendez was a Mexican American. However, in the film the role is played by Ben Affleck (who also directed). *The Last Stand* (2012, Lionsgate) featured the return of Arnold Schwarzenegger (after his disastrous California governorship) as a lawman in a small town in the Southwest who single-handedly destroys an entire Mexican drug cartel.

At times, some films go against the grain of Hollywood filmmaking. Such was the case of *Bless Me, Ultima* (2013, Tenaja Productions). The film was based on the 1972 novel of the same name by Rudolfo Anaya. The book has become a key work in Chicano literature. The novel was the first of a trilogy that included *Heart of Aztlán* (1976) and *Tortuga* (1979). Filmmakers had come and gone, promising Anaya to make it into a film. As time went on, no major film studio would consider doing it. At some point, Christy Walton, an heir of the Wal-Mart fortune, stepped in to make the film. Walton stated, "One of the things I wanted to do before I died was to see this book made into a movie.... It's the only book I've felt that way about."[8] The novel is set in northern New Mexico after World War II and depicts the coming of age of a young Mexican-American boy. A *curandera* (or Native American shaman) helps him navigate through his unfolding life and the bicultural world in which he lives. The film opened to warm reviews, but received only limited screenings. Author Rudolfo Anaya (who is now a retired professor from the University of New Mexico) commented, "I keep complaining that the producers, directors and actors in the Hollywood area all seem to be blind.... My God, these people walk around Los Angeles and the entire California area surrounded by the Mexican-American community. Don't they see them? There's so many beautiful, tender, dramatic stories out there. I hope that *Bless Me, Ultima* opens a few of those blind eyes."[9]

No (2012, Sony Picture Classics) focused on the efforts of an advertising man (Gael García Bernal) to utilize advertising tactics in a political campaign. The campaign was for the 1988 plebiscite in Chile to determine whether General Pinochet (who had launched a military coup against the democratically elected Salvador Allende in 1972) should have another eight-year term as president. The film went on to be nominated for an Academy Award for Best Foreign Film.

Finally, one film franchise refuted the Hollywood film industry mindset that Latino-themed films didn't make money. During the decade, Robert Rodriguez' quartet of films about a Latino family, *Spy Kids I* (2001); *Spy Kids 2* (2002); *Spy Kids 3* (2003); and *Spy Kids 4* (2011), made more than $348 million at the box office.[10]

One long-overdue film project that finally came to fruition was *Cesar Chavez* (2014, Canana Films). The film focused on Mexican labor and civil rights leader Cesar Estrada Chavez (1927–1993) and documented the pivotal period in his struggle to co-found the United Farmworkers Union (UFW), along with Dolores Huerta, in the late 1960s and 1970s. The film included the great grapes boycott, the Salad Bowl Strike (or *huega*), and the farm worker march to the capital of California, Sacramento.

At various times, different Latino filmmakers and others had tried to make the film, but Hollywood studios would not green light the project. Finally, Mexican actor and director Diego Luna was able to get financing from Mexico to make the film. The film was shot entirely in Mexico due to lower production costs; the similarity of the rural areas of California of the 1960s (especially those in the Mexico's northern state of Sonora); and the fact that all the financial backers lived and worked there. The makers of the film strove for historical accuracy. In addition to the geographic similarity, actors were coached to speak the *Chicano* dialect of the 1960s and 1970s.[11]

Cesar Chavez was Diego Luna's first English-language film, and he expressed anxiety with the challenge. Mexican-American actor Michael Peña was cast as Cesar Chavez; America Ferrera played his wife Helen; Rosario Dawson was Dolores Huerta; and Jacob Vargas (who at one time was considered to play Cesar Chavez) played his brother Richard Chavez. Keri Pearson was assigned to write the screenplay (he had received an Academy Award nomination for his screenplay of the film Hotel *Rwanda* in 2004). The film was made for $10 million, a fraction of current Hollywood A-films.

The film received mixed positive reviews, but little promotion. The *Los Angeles Times* wrote, "It is a very difficult role for Pena, and not just because the weight of the film rests on his shoulders ... Chavez is emotionally isolated in the extreme. The actor certainly captures that, but it also serves to throw up a barrier between the character and the audience."[12] The

New York Times wrote, "What the film struggles to depict, committed as it is to the conventions of hagiography, is the long and complex work of organizing people to defend their interests. You are invited to admire what Cesar Chavez did, but it may be more vital to understand how he did it."[13]

Latino Film Stars and Filmmakers

The number of Latino film stars and filmmakers in the 2000s remained small in proportion to the 50-million-plus Latinos (not including the traditionally undercounted millions of undocumented Latinos). A very small number of Latino performers managed to break through in a few films. However, the challenge remained: how to prolong their film careers when so few roles were actually written for Latinos and the stereotypical images continued to be perpetuated.

Remarkably, the decade witnessed the infusion of many Latin American filmmakers and actors as the film industry became more and more globalized. The Latino film stars and filmmakers of the 2000s were incredibly ethnically diverse and increasingly of mixed heritage. It made for a rich and fascinating group of talent. From Mexico came actors Gael García Bernal, Demián Bichir, Laura Harring and Diego Luna and directors Alejandro González Iñárritu and Luis Mandoki. From Spain arrived Penélope Cruz and Javier Bardem. Actress Catalina Sandino Moreno is from Colombia and director Walter Salles from Brazil. Home-grown talent included Mexican-American actors Michael Peña, Jay Hernandez, Mario López, and Jessica Alba and directors José Luis Valenzuela and Carlos Ávila. Puerto Rican talent was represented by Luis Guzmán, Rosario Dawson, and Michelle Rodriguez; Honduran by America Ferrera; and Mexican and Salvadoran by Efren Ramirez.

Latinos, who now make up more than 16 percent (or more than 50 million persons) of the United States population, bought more movie tickets per capita than any other ethnic group, according to the Motion Picture Association of America.[14] However, the Latino community has been rightly disappointed by having few of their own either in front of or in back of the camera. Alex Nogales, president of the Coalition of Hispanic Media, indicated in July 2011 that Latinos constitute less than 2 percent of actors in films and less than 1 percent behind the camera.[15]

Part of the challenge for Latinos and other minorities is that the Hollywood film industry is overwhelmingly controlled by people who are not like them. The Academy of Motion Picture Arts and Sciences, for example, is 94 percent white and 6 percent other; 77 percent male and 23 percent female. The statistics correspond to the lack of diversity in films and people in decision-making positions.[16] Statistics of those who control film studios, talent agencies, and other entities of the film and television industry are not available, but one can assume they are not ethnic minorities or women.

The new millennium also brought about a quantum leap in technology and the way consumers will see motion pictures in the future. By 2012, the once-profitable DVD business had dropped about 40 percent in home entertainment revenues. Internet-connected television, streaming, smartphones, and Facebook enticed consumers with more convenience. "The days of baby steps on the Internet are over," commented David Bishop of Sony Pictures

Home Entertainment.[17] Another technology was special effects, marked by out-of control spending. Ben Pritz commented, "The star now is the spectacle. Studios can spend more than $100 million just on the special effects necessary to make *Spider Man* swing through New York."[18] The special effects mania was fueled by the fact that box-office receipts abroad have grown 35 percent during the years 2007 to 2011. During 2011, the receipts abroad accounted for $22.4 billion, in contrast to the $10.2 billion generated in the United States and Canada.

Despite the enormous technological developments, however, the sad fact remains that Latinos in particular continue to be grossly underrepresented in every capacity of filmmaking in the Hollywood film industry. The irony is that the United States will be more than 50 percent people of color by 2050 (if not sooner). This nation makes up only 6 percent of the world's population. Nevertheless, the U.S.–based film industry continues to perpetuate a white and black race and ethnicity construct.

The story of contemporary Latino film stars and filmmakers informs us too often that the Latino infusion into U.S. cinema has occurred only infrequently. In recent decades, there have been clusters of Latino talent and Latino-themed films, but the trends were not sustained. The United States for the most part remains a white and black world when it comes to media, race, and politics. It remains to be seen whether that will alter as the Latino presence becomes more and more pronounced and irreversible, and whether the creative space will become truly diverse.

Representative Films

The following representative films have been selected as a cross-section of the different visions and interpretations of the Latino experience in the United States. As in previous decades, a cluster of Latino-themed films was produced during the decade that focused on the Latino experience within the United States or in Latin America. These films are not necessarily the best or the worst. However, some of the best films that depicted the Latino more truthfully and honesty are listed here.

The Alamo (2004, Touchstone Pictures)

This version of *The Alamo* was the first feature film (not counting several television films) to focus on the Battle of the Alamo (of 1836) since John Wayne's epic version of the same name in 1960. However, unlike the John Wayne version, which earned moderate critical and commercial success, *The Alamo* film of 2004 proved to be a major commercial and critical disaster. Despite the rampant xenophobia of the times, the film found few who were interested in the history it told or from what viewpoint.

The film was directed by John Lee Hancock and scripted by Leslie Bohen, John Lee Hancock, John Sayles, and Stephen Gaghan. It was produced by Ron Howard and Mark Johnson, released by Imagine Entertainment and distributed by Touchstone Pictures.

The film purported to tell both the Mexican and the Euro-American perspectives. The film starts with a scene of the bodies of the dead in March 1836 in the former Alamo mission, in San Antonio de Bexar, Texas. There is a flashback to a year earlier, a party where Sam Houston (Dennis Quaid) tries to convince people to migrate to Texas. One of them is the recently defeated congressman Davy Crockett (Billy Bob Thornton). However, the institution of slavery had spread as far west as Louisiana by 1835 and in order for it to continue to grow, Texas was the next area of expansion. In addition, the ethos of Manifest Destiny, the idea that the United States was destined by God to spread from coast to coast, was deeply rooted.

The film then shifts to San Felipe, Texas, where the Opposition Party, mostly made of recently arrived Euro-American immigrants, decides to make Texas an independent state (with institutionalized slavery). The leaders of this movement include William Barret Travis (Patrick Wilson), something of a martinet who desires to take command of the Alamo. In reality, he had abandoned his wife and children in New Orleans and had let one of his slaves take the blame for a killing.

Davy Crockett arrives with his men with much bravado built over years of being an "Indian fighter." Another rebel leader is another legend in his own lifetime, Jim Bowie (Jason Patric), who had a long history of adventure, violence, and slave smuggling. During February 1836, General Antonio López de Santa Ana (Emilio Echevarría, from *Amores Perros*) arrives to put down the rebellion.

The siege of the Alamo ends in March 1836 and all the defenders are killed in the battle. Davy Crockett, contrary to popular belief, does not die in battle but is taken prisoner and executed by a firing squad. The film goes on to document the defeat of Santa Ana in the Battle of San Jacinto at the hands of Sam Houston. Santa Ana is wounded and taken prisoner, and is compelled to sign a document recognizing the independence of Texas (one that the Mexican congress would subsequently dismiss as unconstitutional). Texas' 1836 constitution formalized the institution of slavery as the law of the land.

The film went to great lengths to make everything authentic, the costumes, locations, music, and other details. However, the truths behind this historical event have been obscured by mythology and Hollywood films. As a consequence, this film only barely touches the demystification of the Alamo.

The film cost an estimated $145 million and grossed only $25,819,961 worldwide. This film went on to become one of the biggest "bombs" in film history. What is perplexing is that in a decade filled with xenophobia, English Only laws, racial profiling, and the demonization of Otherness, moviegoers simply turned away from an event of distorted history.

Before Night Falls (2000, Fine Line Features)

This film was directed by Julian Schnabel and the screenplay was written by Schnabel, Cunningham O'Keefe, and Lázaro Gómez Carriles. The script was based on the autobiography of Reinaldo Arenas entitled *Before Night Falls.* The film was distributed by Fine Line Features.

The film documents the life of Reinaldo Arenas, who was born in Oriente Province, Cuba, in 1943. He was raised by a single mother and his grandparents. It is after Arenas moves to Havana to continue his studies that he starts exploring his sexuality and becomes openly gay. He manages to find his voice through his published writings and his lifestyle.

In the early 1970s, Arenas was arrested for assaulting minors (of which he argued he was innocent) and publishing outside the country without consent. After being arrested several times, he leaves Cuba in 1980. He moves to Miami and then to New York City, where he lives with his lover Lázaro Gómez Carilles. There, he finds he has AIDS and commits suicide.

Spanish actor Javier Bardem was cast as Arenas and in actuality had a striking physical resemblance to the late writer. Bardem was nominated for an Academy Award for Best Actor and received much critical acclaim. Johnny Depp and Diego Luna made cameo appearances. Others in the cast included Oliver Martinez, Santiago Magill, and Andrea Di Stefano. The *New York Times* wrote, "This haunting film portrays that homosexual dissident writer as a desperate unfulfilled searcher for a lost heaven on earth that he experiences only briefly as a very young man."[19]

A Better Life (2011, Summit Entertainment)

The film *A Better Life,* which chronicled the hard and difficult life of an undocumented Mexican laborer, was an unexpected critical and commercial success.

The film was based on a screenplay called *The Gardener* by Eric Eason, which was based on a story by Roger L. Simon. It was directed by Chris Weitz, the son of Mexican-American actress Susan Kohner. She was the daughter of Lupita Tovar (Kohner), one of the first Mexican film stars in Hollywood in the 1920s. The evocative cinematography was done by Javier Aguirresarobe, the award-winning Spanish Basque cinematographer. It was released by Lime Orchard Productions and distributed by Summit Entertainment.

The film was shot on location in East Los Angeles and caught the cultural nuances of the Mexican-American community. Director Weitz enlisted the help of Father Gregory Boyle, a well-known advocate for gang youth. Boyle founded Homeboy Industries to provide jobs for former gang members, and through their assistance Weitz was able to identify evocative locales in the barrio for the film. Weitz in turn provided acting employment for many of the former gang youth in the film, which added much to the authenticity (in language and culture) of the film itself.

The film told the story of Carlos Galindo (Demián Bichir), an undocumented Mexican gardener, and his increasingly difficult relationship with his U.S.–born son Luis (José Julián). Carlos wants to start his own landscaping business and have a better life to share with his son. Carlos borrows money from his sister Anna (Dolores Heredia). He then hires a hard-pressed laborer, Santiago (Carlos Linares), on the street. Unfortunately, one day when Carlos is trimming a palm tree, Santiago takes off with his truck and equipment.

In the meantime, Carlos' son Luis (who is in high school and dating a gang-affiliated girl) is increasingly pressured by his gang-affiliated friends to join their gang. Luis helps his father finally track down Santiago. However, their mutual effort is undermined by Luis' growing resentment of his own culture and language as a first-generation U.S.–born adolescent. Luis runs away from his father.

However, in the morning, Luis realizes that he has nobody and that he must help his father track down the stolen truck. They finally are able to retrieve it, but the police intervene and Carlos is arrested by the U.S. Immigration and Customs Enforcement (ICE) and deported. Before they are separated, he and his son are able to meet in prison. Carlos is over-whelmed by the parting and emotionally tells his son about all his hopes and dreams for them.

The film ends on an upbeat note with Luis playing at a soccer game. In the audience is his aunt and two children. Carlos is in the desert once again with a *coyote* (smuggler) and a group of undocumented workers beginning their long trek back to the United States.

The film earned glowing reviews, most of which praised Demián Bichir's outstanding performance. Manohla Dargis of the *New York Times* said of the film, "Set largely in East Los Angeles, an area that doesn't often pop up in movies except as a scary, nominally exotic backdrop (unless Cheech and Chong are going up in smoke), *A Better Life* involves a struggle to hold onto a home of one's own.... Mr. Bichir, a Mexican actor with a long list of credits in his country, and Mr. Julian (who was 16 during the shoot), are both sympathetic, and they hold your attention despite some awkwardly directed patches."[20] Demián Bichir won an Academy Award nomination for Best Actor for his heartbreaking performance as the dis-traught father.

Che (2008, IFC Films)

Che was the second film during the 2000s to depict part of the life of Argentinean-born Ernesto "Che" Guevara. A doctor by profession, Guevara witnessed the U.S.–led intervention in Guatemala in 1954 and subsequently became one of the key leaders of the Cuban Revolution. Another film, *The Motorcycle Diaries,* depicted the travels of the young medical student through South America. The film *Che* dramatized the period when he joins the Cuban revolutionaries in Mexico City in 1956, the guerrilla war that toppled the Cuban dictator Fulgencio Batista in 1959, and his guerrilla campaign in Bolivia during 1966 and 1967.

The film was directed by Steven Soderbergh and scripted by Benjamin A. van der Veen and Peter Buchman. It was produced by Benicio Del Toro and Laura Bickford. It was released by Telecinco Cinema and Wild Bunch and distributed by IFC Films (USA) and Optimum Releasing (UK).

The film is a two-part biography about Ernesto "Che" Guevara that was initially screened as one film at the Cannes Film Festival in 2008. Thereafter, the film was divided into two parts: *Che, Part 1: The Argentine* and *Che, Part 2: Guerrilla.* Part 1 begins with Che's interactions with Cuban revolutionaries Fidel and Raúl Castro and others in Mexico City. Many of them were political prisoners recently released by Cuban dictator Fulgencio Batista. During 1957, they sail to Cuba and begin a guerrilla war against the dictator, cul-minating with the battle of Santa Clara in October 1958. The revolutionaries take power. Guevara enters Havana and comments, "We won the war, the revolution starts now."

Part 2 begins with Guevara arriving in Bolivia incognito in 1966 to head a guerrilla *foco* (in Marxist revolutionary ideology a small, fast-moving group of fighters providing a focus for popular discontent with a sitting regime and thereby leading a general uprising) in the Andean mountains. Although the groundwork for the movement has been meticu-lously organized, there soon is ideological division within the leftist movement. Mario Monje, the leader of the Bolivian Communist Party, decides not to support the guerrilla movement and works to isolate it. The Bolivian army detects the group before they are completely prepared to do battle. One contact, Tamara "Tania" Bunke, and French intellectual Régis Debray are compelled to stay with the guerrillas. Subsequently, Tania and one group of guerrillas are ambushed by the army and Debray is captured while trying to leave the camp. Supported by U.S. military advisors and the C.I.A., the Bolivian army pursues Guevara's guerrillas. Guevara is wounded, taken prisoner, and then executed on October 9, 1967.

The film was a long-term mission for actor Benicio Del Toro, who had wanted to make a film about Guevara for many years. Del Toro undertook meticulous research about the man he would portray. He spent seven years obsessively researching Guevara's life. Del Toro met numerous people at different stages of Guevara's life, including his younger brother, Guevara's widow, childhood friends, and comrades-in-arms. Although there were many drafts of the screenplay, the two most important historical sources about Guevara were two of his books: *Reminiscences of the Cuban Revolutionary War* and *Bolivian Diary*.

Initially, the film was going to be shot in English, but it ended up in Spanish. Director Steven Soderbergh commented, "I'm hoping the days of that sort of specific brand of cultural imperialism have ended." The first film was going to be shot initially in Cuba, but they were prohibited by the U.S. embargo against Cuba. The climactic Battle of Santa Clara scene was shot in Campeche, Mexico.

The two film parts were shot beginning in July 2007 with *Guerrilla* first, in Spain for thirty-nine days, and *The Argentine,* shot in Puerto Rico and Mexico over thirty-nine days. Missing from Guevara's life is the period he spent in the Congo during 1966 leading another guerrilla movement, against the South African forces.

The large cast was headlined by Benicio Del Toro as Che, Demián Bichir as Fidel Castro, Catalina Sandino Moreno as Aleida March, Lou Diamond Phillips as Mario Monje, Matt Damon as Fr. Schwartz, Rodrigo Santoro as Raúl Castro, and Franka Potente as Tania.

The film did poorly in the United States and had a limited engagement in a few cities, but in the rest of the world had a gross in excess of $30 million. The film was released on DVD in January 2009.

Predictably, U.S. film critics gave the film mixed reviews, while in the rest of the world they were glowing. The *New York Times* commented, "Benicio Del Toro's performance is technically flawless.... But the film's formal sophistication is ultimately an evasion of the moral reckoning that Ernesto "Che" Guevara, more than 40 years and several million T-shirts after his death, surely deserves. Mr. Soderbergh once again offers a master class in film-making. As history, though, *Che* is finally not an epic but romance. It takes great care to be true to the factual record, but it is, nonetheless, a fairy tale."[21]

Benicio Del Toro won the French Prix d'Interpretation Masculine (Best Actor); the Spanish Goya Award (2009) for Best Spanish Lead Actor; and Cuba's Tomás Gutiérrez Alea (named after the prolific Cuban filmmaker) prize for his role. In the United States, actor Sean Penn expressed his dismay that Benicio Del Toro had not been nominated for an Academy Award or a Screen Actors Guild Award.

Frida (2002, Miramax Films)

Mexican painter Frida Kahlo (1907–1954) had been the object of a growing cult and fame for decades. A U.S. film project had been decades in the making by various directors and studios. The fact that a Hollywood film was finally made and proved to be both critically and commercially successful was a tribute to the creative force behind it, Mexican actress Salma Hayek.

The film was directed by Julie Taymor and scripted by Anna Thomas, Gregory Nava, Diane Lake, and Clancy Sigal, based on the book *Frida: A Biography of Frida Kahlo* by Hayden Herrera. It was distributed by Miramax Films.

The making of the film had a long and tumultuous path going back to the 1980s. Initially, Nancy Hardin, a former book agent and literary agent, optioned Hayden Herrera's biography on Frida Kahlo, but studios were not interested. During this time, Madonna announced she would play the role, much to the disappointment of Latinos. During 1991, Chicano playwright and director Luis Valdez began a film about Kahlo that had Laura San Giacomo in the title role. A wave of protest occurred due to the casting. Latinos are in effect not permitted to audition for non–Latino roles, and when there is a Latino role, it is often taken by a Euro-American performer.

In 1993, Luis Valdez had retitled the proposed film as *The Two Fridas* with both Laura San Giacomo and Mexican actress Ofelia Medina (who had played the role previously in a well-received Mexican film). Raúl Juliá was scheduled to play Diego Rivera, but his death further put the production on hold. All this time, a young Salma Hayek had been trying to convince Valdez to cast her, and kept pushing for the role despite all the filming mishaps. Hayek recollected later, "At that age I did not like her work.... But something intrigued me, and the more I learned, the more I started to appreciate her work.... Some people see only pain, but I also see irony and humor. I think what draws me to her is what Diego saw in her. She was a fighter. Many things could have diminished her spirit, like the accident or Diego's infidelities. But she wasn't crushed by anything."[22]

Hayek sought out Dolores Olmedo Patino, one of Diego Rivera's lovers and administrator of the rights of Rivera's artworks. Hayek secured the use of the art for the film and began to seek the cast, including Alfred Molina, who would play Diego Rivera. During August 2000, the casting of Jennifer Lopez was announced for the Valdez project. However, Hayek and Miramax had begun production during the spring of 2001. The film was shot entirely in Mexico, using the Rivera-Kahlo San Angel studio house and other historic sites. Interior scenes were shot in Mexico's legendary Churubusco Studios in Mexico City.

The film depicts the trolley car accident that Frida (Salma Hayek) underwent at eighteen years of age. In order to help her rehabilitate herself, her father provides painting materials. She begins to paint and discovers a powerful creative force within herself.

She becomes involved with Mexico's great muralist Diego Rivera (Alfred Molina), whom she eventually marries. It is a tumultuous relationship full of infidelities on his part, quarrels, jealousies, and passionate highs and lows. In New York City, he defies Nelson Rockefeller's censorship of one of his murals, which is later destroyed. While there, Frida suffers a miscarriage. They return to Mexico, but he has an affair with her sister and leaves. She sinks into depression and alcoholism.

Diego and Frida reunite when Russian revolutionary and exile Leon Trotsky (Geoffrey Rush) seeks political asylum in Mexico. However, her affair with the revolutionary breaks up the marriage once again. Frida goes to Paris, where she discovers an exciting bohemian lifestyle. Upon her return to Mexico, Trotsky is assassinated, and both Rivera and she are temporarily arrested. Rivera gets her released and they undergo reconciliation. They remarry. She loses a leg to gangrene. Before her death, she is able to have an art exhibit in Mexico City, a historic achievement.

The film *Frida* premiered on August 29, 2002, at the Venice International Film Festival and premiered in Mexico City at the Palacio de Bellas Artes on November 8, 2002. The film was an immediate critical and commercial hit. The film received six Academy Award nominations, including Best Actress (the first for a Mexican actress in a leading role; Katy Jurado had previously been nominated for Best Supporting Actress for *Broken Lance* in 1954), Best Art Direction–Set Decoration, Best Costume Design, Best Music Score (Elliot Goldenthal), Best Original Song ("Burn It Blue" by Julie Taymor and Elliot Goldenthal), and Best Makeup (John E. Jackson, Beatriz De Alba). It won Oscars for Best Makeup and Best Original Music Score. In addition, Salma Hayek was nominated for Best Actress by the Golden Globes, the Screen Actors Guild, and the BAFTA Awards.

The film remains Salma Hayek's crowning achievement, as an actress, filmmaker, and creative force.

Girlfight (2000, Screen Gems)

Girlfight was the first film to feature a Latina's entry into the fight game, historically a male preserve until recent years. Both the novelty and the presence of newcomer Michelle Rodriguez made the film a contender for good reviews, good box-office, and a good story.

The film marked the directorial debut of Karyn Kusama (who also wrote the screenplay). The film depicts the life of Diane Guzman (Michelle Rodriguez), an angry and troubled bully of a girl in Brooklyn, New York City. She lives in a housing project with her abusive father, Sandro (Paul Calderon), and her younger brother, Tiny (Ray Santiago). The relationship between Diane and her father is one of turbulence and pain.

Diane channels her anger into boxing, where she is grudgingly accepted by the macho culture. At this point she meets an aspiring featherweight, Adrian (Santiago Douglas), with whom she slowly finds tenderness and love in her life. Diane's big opportunity comes when the state determines that amateur tournaments must include both males and females. In reality, mixed-gender fights are almost never held and do not have the endorsement of either female or male boxing associations. At the end, Diane faces Adrian in a boxing match (here the film takes a melodramatic downturn, unfortunately).

However, the film captures the novelty of Latinas as boxers in a male preserve, the feel and stench of sweat of boxing gyms, and the hopes and dreams of the most marginalized.

The film received wide critical praise and became commercially successful. The *New York Times* wrote, "The plot takes some unexpected—if occasionally contrived—turns.... But the film belongs to Ms. Rodriguez. With her slightly crooked nose and her glum, sensual mouth, she looks a little like Marlon Brando in his smoldering prime, and she has some of his slow, intense physicality. She doesn't so much transcend gender as redefine it."[23] The film won the Director's Award and the Grand Jury Prize, tied with Kenneth Lonergan's *You Can Count Me Out,* at the Sundance Film Festival in 2000.

Both *Girlfight* and *Price of Glory* offer perceptive insights into the Latino experience in boxing.

Innocent Voices (2004, 20th Century–Fox)

The film *Innocent Voices* focused on the Salvadoran civil war of the 1970s and 1980s. Hollywood film studios had previously tackled the issue in two films. Oliver Stone's *Salvador* (1986) focused on a U.S. journalist (played by James Woods) who covers the civil war as an outsider witness. In turn, Roger Spottiswoode's *Under Fire* (1988) documented the multiple viewpoints of a trio of U.S. journalists (Nick Nolte, Joanna Cassidy, and Gene Hackman) as they covered the Nicaraguan revolution against the Somoza dynasty. What was long overdue was a film from the actual participants caught up in these important Central American wars.

Innocent Voices was directed by Luis Mandoki and scripted by Mandoki and Oscar Orlando Torres. Much of the script was based on Torres' own childhood during the civil war. It was produced by Lawrence Bender and distributed by 20th Century–Fox.

The film is set in El Salvador and follows the story of a narrator, a boy named Chava (Carlos Padilla). He is eleven years of age and the eldest son of Kella (Leonor Varela). His Mama Toya or grandmother (Ofelia Medina) lives nearby. His father left at the beginning of the civil war and the town is a battleground for the army and the guerrillas. His mother makes a living by sewing and the boy helps her sell her crafts at a shop. He also helps a bus driver announce the various stops along the way. His mother is always afraid for him, as he is nearing the age when he could be conscripted by the army.

One day, his uncle Beto (a guerrilla) comes to visit them. He wants to take Chava in order to save him from conscription, but Kella does not allow him to leave. Over time Chava is radicalized by the brutality of the army and the suffering of the innocent.

The film garnered excellent reviews, and good word of mouth resulted in its commercial success. However, one criticism of the film was that the protagonists did not speak in the Salvadoran accent of *voseo* or *Caliche*. The film has become for many the definitive film made thus far about the Salvadoran civil war.

Maria Full of Grace (2004, HBO/Journeyman Films)

Maria Full of Grace was a small independent film which depicted the odyssey of a young and impoverished Colombian woman who becomes a "drug mule," smuggling illicit drugs inside her stomach, in order to carry them into the United States. It humanized the gullible and desperate who become involved in drug smuggling. The film introduced a new actress, Catalina Sandino Moreno. Incredibly, the young actress was nominated for the Best Actress Academy Award (the first Colombian actress to be so honored).

The film was directed and scripted by Joshua Marston. It was produced by Paul S. Mezy and distributed by Fine Line Features. Although the film is mostly set in Colombia, it was actually shot in Ecuador, and eventually in New York City. The title of the film makes reference to the "Hail Mary" prayer which begins, "Hail Mary, full of grace. The Lord is with thee." The film poster (with actress Catalina Sandino Moreno kneeling and looking up to receive a piece of white material) makes an allusion to the Catholic ritual of Holy Communion. But it also represents what Maria smuggles, inside her stomach, into the United States: an illegal drug.

The film documents the story of a seventeen-year-old Colombian named Maria Alvarez (Catalina Sandino Moreno) who works on a rural flower plantation. Her income supports her mother, as well as an unemployed older sister who is a single mother. Maria has frequent conflicts with her, which reinforces her desire to leave this type of life.

She is involved with a young man and becomes pregnant, but he proves to be irresponsible and uncaring. She quits her job, much to the disapproval of her mother, and leaves for Bogotá. Through a male acquaintance, she is offered employment as a "drug mule," agreeing to ingest drugs in plastic bags and smuggle them into the United States in return for payment. (Oftentimes, however, the bags burst and the smuggler dies instantly.) Although anxious about the entire enterprise, she takes the job and swallows sixty-two wrapped pellets of heroin. She is flown to New York City. Unfortunately, her perpetually nagging and stressed-out friend Blanca accompanies her as another drug mule.

The tantrums of her friend, the possibility of arrest by U.S. customs agents, and the dangerous nature of the job results in unforeseen consequences in New York City. At the end, Maria decides to stay in the United States, facing a dire and daunting future.

The film received widespread critical acclaim and much of it went to Catalina Sandino Moreno. She became the first Colombian-origin actress to receive an Academy Award nomination for Best Actress. The *New York Times* commented, "In a performance that feels lived in rather than acted, Ms. Moreno's Maria is an attractive, smart, spirited young woman who faces challenges fending for herself with a fierce determination and an ingenuity that compromises but never undermines her essential decency and morality."[24]

The Motorcycle Diaries (2004, Focus Features)

The Motorcycle Diaries was a co-production that depicted the travels of a young medical student, Ernesto "Che" Guevara, through South America. It was based on Guevara's book and provided a glimpse into a young man bewildered by his idealism and the widespread poverty and injustice in Latin America.

Ernesto "Che" Guevara had been the subject of a 1969 Hollywood film entitled *Che* (20th Century–Fox) in which he was played by Omar Sharif and Fidel Castro was played by Jack Palance. It was unremarkable, unsuccessful, and partisan. Soon after its release, it sank into cinematic memory and history. Thirty-six years later proved to be a more opportune time to tell young Che's story. Guevara was the subject of two films during the 2000s. The second film, *Che* (2008), featured Benicio Del Toro as the adult revolutionary.

The film *The Motorcycle Diaries* was directed by Walter Salles and scripted by Jose Rivera (based on the book *The Motorcycle Diaries* by Ernesto "Che" Guevara). It was produced by Edgard Tenenbaum, Michael Nozik, and Karen Tenkhoff and released by Film Four and BD Cine. It was distributed by Focus Features.

The film is set in 1952, when Ernesto "Che" Guevara (Gael García Bernal) is about to complete his medical degree. He and his older friend Alberto Granado (Rodrigo De la Serna, in real life related to the Guevara family), a biochemist, decide to travel across South America.

They hope to cross the continent (some 5,000 miles) in four and a half months, have fun, find adventure, and work in a leper colony. They travel on Alberto's old Norton 500 motorcycle, christened as *La Poderosa*.

They have adventures and fun, but the trip transforms them, especially Guevara. They work in the leper colony, witnessing the mass poverty of the indigenous peoples, the exploitation of workers, and the despair of millions. The film ends with footage of the real Dr. Alberto Granado, now 82 years old, photographs of the real journey, and of Guevara's CIA-sponsored execution in Bolivia in 1967. Granado left for Cuba after the revolution, founded a medical clinic, and died there in 2010.

The film was shot in Peru, Argentina, Chile, and Venezuela, locations which contributed much to the evocative journey. The film was released to excellent reviews and caught the imagination of millions around the world. The *New York Times* wrote, "In it he [Guevara] evokes a pan–Latin American identity that transcends the arbitrary boundaries of nation and race. *The Motorcycle Diaries*, combining the talents of a Brazilian director and leading actors from Mexico (Mr. Bernal) and Argentina (Mr. de la Serna), pays heartfelt tribute to this idea. In an age of mass tourism, it also unabashedly revives the venerable, romantic notion that travel can enlarge the soul, and even change the world."[25]

Nacho Libre (2006, Paramount)

Masks have always been one of the central motifs in Mexican art and history, from pre–Columbian times to the present. During the latter part of the golden age of Mexican cinema in the 1950s, dozens of films about a masked avenger for social justice were made. The most famous of these were those featuring a real-life wrestler and icon named El Santo. His films and those of others, like Blue Demon, provided endless fascination and entertainment for millions of working-class Mexicans and other marginalized people. The film *Nacho Libre* continued the Mexican fascination with wrestlers that tackled poverty and injustice.

The film was directed by Jared Hess and scripted by Hess and Mike White. It was produced by Jack Black, Mike White, Ricardo del Rio, and David Klawans and distributed by Nickelodeon Movies and Paramount Pictures.

The film focuses on the ambitions of Ignacio (Jack Black), the son of a Lutheran missionary by way of Scandinavia and a wayward Mexican deacon. Orphaned at a young age, Ignacio becomes a cook at a monastery. Ignacio is motivated to become a *luchador* (a wrestler) and help the orphanage. The arrival of Sister Encarnación (Ana de la Reguera) and her encouragement does much to propel him in his endeavor.

As a masked wrestler he struggles, winning some and losing some. Eventually, he becomes champion. With his earnings he buys a bus for the orphanage that they can use for field trips.

The film built on the Mexican pre–Columbian fascination with masks and the duality of life. It also connected to the long history of masked heroes, such as El Santo and Blue Demon, who had long and successful careers both in the wrestling ring and in the Mexican proletarian films of the 1950s and 1960s.

Upon its release, *Nacho Libre* received mixed reviews by critics, but it endeared itself to filmgoers. The film became a modest hit and something of a cult film.

Piñero (2001, Miramax Films)

Piñero was one of three films in the decade to dramatize the real-life story of three prominent Latino artists. This particular film depicted the life of poet and playwright Miguel Piñero (the others depicted Mexican painter Frida Kahlo in *Frida*; and the Cuban gay poet Reinaldo Arenas in *Before Night Falls*).

The film was directed and scripted by Cuban filmmaker Leon Ichaso. It was produced by John Leguizamo, John Penotti, and Tim Williams. It was distributed by Miramax Films. Benjamin Bratt played Piñero and the cast included Rita Moreno as his mother, Talisa Soto as Sugar, and Giancarlo Esposito as Miguel Algarin.

The film depicts the life of Puerto Rican poet and playwright Miguel Piñero (1946–1988). Some proposed that his hard and gritty urban poetry was a precursor to contemporary rap and hip-hop lyrics. He was born poor and marginalized, and became involved in petty thefts and later drug dealing. He served a prison term at Sing Sing. The experience turned his life around and it became the subject of his Tony-nominated play *Short Eyes*. In the 1970s, he co-founded the Nuyorican Poets Café.

In 1977, his play *Short Eyes* was made into a film by director Robert M. Young. Piñero became famous and was deluged with film roles, television writing assignments, and the temptations of fame and fortune. However, his fast and reckless lifestyle caught up with him. He died of cirrhosis in 1988.

In real life Piñero was a diminutive man, very different from the six-feet-plus actor Benjamin Bratt, who plays him on the screen. Bratt, who is of Peruvian-German heritage, was not the first choice for the film. Bratt had given an excellent performance as a Chicano gang member in *Blood In, Blood Out* in 1993, but thereafter had starred in several television series, most notably in *Law & Order*. However, his performance as Miguel Piñero was a revelation. He was nominated for an Academy Award as Best Actor and earned widespread critical acclaim. The *New York Times* wrote, "What's so impressive about Mr. Bratt's evocation of the Puerto Rican playwright who crashed into the theatrical scene in the early 1970s ... is that he doesn't overplay his hand. Even in the most unstrung moments, Mr. Bratt's Piñero retains a layer of sinuous craftiness."[26]

Price of Glory (2000, New Line Cinema)

Boxing has always been a way into glory and fame for the most marginalized in society. Mexicans have a long history in the United States of being marginalized and seeking a way out of poverty and obscurity. *Price of Glory* was an excellent entry into the boxing genre. Unfortunately, the studio half-heartedly promoted the film and it quickly sank into obscurity and red ink.

The film was the directorial debut of Carlos Ávila and it was scripted by Phil Berger, a former *New York Times* writer who covered boxing. The film was released by Fine Line Cinema. The film focuses on Arturo Ortega (Jimmy Smits), a Mexican American, an embittered man who lives with the burning memory of having been a champion boxer until he was overmatched by his corrupt manager. He lives in a small border town in Arizona. Now, married and with three small sons, he dreams of training them to be champions. His obsession to have his sons relive his days of glory takes a toll on his marriage and his wife (Maria del Mar).

As adults, the sons, Jimmy (Clifton Collins, Jr.), Sonny (Jon Seda, a real and former Golden Gloves boxer in his youth), and Johnny (Ernesto Hernández), strive hard to win the respect and love of their demanding father. They are trained by Hector (Sal Lopez) and Oscar (Carlos Palomino, a real former welterweight champion, 1976–1979). Inevitably, corrupt characters enter the lives of the young boxers and destroy their dreams.

Price of Glory is a special film about the Mexican-American experience in the sport of boxing. It captures the pressures and expectations of second-generation boxers, the excitement of the amateur tournaments, the sacrifices and dreams of young boxers, the transition into professional boxing, and the vast array of temptations and corrupt money like no other boxing film ever has, with the exception of *The Ring* (1952).

The film features perhaps Jimmy Smits' best performance. The film has more boxing heart and reality than the all the *Rocky* movies combined.

Real Women Have Curves (2002, HBO)

Real Women Have Curves was another film which explored new frontiers within the Latino experience in the United States. It depicted the trials and tribulations of a Mexican-American adolescent struggling to fit into the white image of beauty and youth.

The film was directed by Patricia Cardoso and the screenplay was written by Josefina López (based on her play of the same name) and George LaVoo. It was produced by George LaVoo and distributed by HBO Films.

The film told the story of Ana García (America Ferrera), a Mexican-American student at Beverly Hills High School. She is a successful student, but must work in her sister's sweat-shop dress factory. She works, along with her mother, Carmen (Lupe Ontiveros), in order to survive economically. Ana has dreams of attending the Ivy League Columbia University in New York City. She is encouraged in her ambitions by a sympathetic teacher, Mr. Guzman (George Lopez). However, her mother's view of what's appropriate for a traditional young Mexican-American woman differs from her own. Nevertheless, Ana is determined to reshape both her self-image and her goals.

The play had been popular among Mexican-Americans for several years before the film was made. However, the fact that it focused on two poor Mexican-American women was a challenge to some in Hollywood to make into a film.

Nonetheless, the film defied expectations and struck a chord with ethnic audiences. The film debuted at the Sundance Film Festival and won the Audience Award. In addition, it won Special Jury Prizes for America Ferrera and Lupe Ontiveros. The screenplay earned the Humanities Prize and the film went on to win the National Board of Review Award for Special Recognition for Excellence in Filmmaking. Both Ferrera and Ontiveros won widespread critical acclaim. The *New York Times* noted, "*Curves* was produced for television by HBO but deserves to be seen by appreciative audiences in theaters. A cross-section of movie-goers who transcend Latino demographics may feel that understandable versions of themselves have made it to the screen. We're lucky this film didn't come out of a studio, where

Ana would have been played by Jennifer Lopez. Instead, *Curves* has a different kind of reward, the beauty of talent bursting to prove itself."[27]

Spy Kids (2001, Dimension Films)

Spy Kids was a unique film: it was both Latino-themed and a family film. Director Robert Rodriguez went against long-established Hollywood conventions and fashioned a film which promoted Latino family values, expanded the spy genre, and was hugely successful. It spawned several sequels: *Spy Kids 2, Spy Kids 3,* and *Spy Kids 4.*

The film was directed and scripted by Robert Rodriguez, and co-produced with Harvey Weinstein, Elizabeth Avellan, and Bob Weinstein. It was released by Troublemaker Studios.

In the film, ten-years-retired spies Gregory Cortez (Antonio Banderas) and his wife Ingrid (Carla Gugino) are called back for an important assignment. However, they are both captured. Their children, Carmen (Alex Vega) and Juni (Daryl Sabara), discover the true profession of their parents and attempt to rescue them. The children enlist the services of their estranged uncle Machete (Danny Trejo), who is a gadget-inventor genius. Juni also brings in Fegan Foop (Alan Cumming) and they all manage to defeat the plans of Alexander Minion (Tony Shalhoub) to develop an army of androids disguised as children.

As simple as the narrative is, however, director Robert Rodriguez managed to infuse the whole film with a child's sense of wonder and adventure. While critics were mixed, the films were an unexpected commercial hit. McDonald's released Spy Kids toys with its Happy Meals, furthering the appeal of the film. The success of the film spawned three sequels, all of them directed and scripted by Rodriguez: *Spy Kids 2: The Island of Lost Dreams* (2002); *Spy Kids 3-D: Game Over* (2003); and *Spy Kids 4: All the Time in the World* (2011).

The *Spy Kids* films were influenced by the James Bond films, but Rodriguez infused them with both humor and family well-being. The films became a Latino film franchise which has grossed in excess of $450 million. One of the great pleasures of *Spy Kids* films was the casting of several generations of Latino film stars: Ricardo Montalbán from the 1940s, Cheech Marin from the 1970s, Salma Hayek from the 1990s, and Jessica Alba from the 2000s.

Traffic (2000, USA Films)

After decades of U.S. films depicting the scourge of the drug trade and drug cartels, the film *Traffic* brought something new and refreshing. The film depicted the impact of the drug trade upon several individuals in the United States and Mexico. More importantly, it dramatized the high demand of illicit drugs in the U.S. as the driving force of supply. The film told the story of drug traffic from four perspectives: a user, an enforcer, a politician, and a trafficker.

Traffic was directed by Steven Soderbergh and scripted by Stephen Gaghan. The film was adapted from the British Channel 4 television series of the same name. Soderbergh operated the camera and gave each of the stories a different look. The film was distributed by USA Films.

The first story takes place in Mexico, where two police officers (Benicio Del Toro, Jacob Vargas) are arrested. However, the arrest is stopped by men loyal to General Salazar (Tomas Milan). The two police officers are let go, but under the condition that they apprehend Francisco Salazar (Clifton Collins, Jr.), a hit man for the Tijuana cartel.

The second story focuses on Robert Wakefield (Michael Douglas), an Ohio judge who has been appointed by the president of the United States to become the drug czar. He and his wife (Amy Irving) are unaware that their daughter and her boyfriend are cocaine users. Both are subsequently arrested for trying to buy illicit drugs.

The third story is set in San Diego, California, and involves the undercover investigation of the Drug Enforcement Agency (DEA) by two agents (Luis Guzmán, Don Cheadle) to arrest Eduardo Ruiz (Miguel Ferrer), an important dealer. The agents convince Ruiz to deliver his boss, Carlos Ayala (Steven Bauer), the biggest distributor for the Obregon brothers in the United States. Ayala's wife hires hit men to get the agents.

The fourth and last story is set back in Tijuana, where Flores (Clifton Collins, Jr.), a hit man for the Tijuana cartel, is captured and tortured. He is compelled to give Salazar the names of many of his criminal associates. Salazar himself is from the Juárez cartel, which is at war with the Tijuana cartel.

Most of the Mexican scenes were shot in the border town of Nuevo Laredo, State of Tamaulipas, Mexico, opposite the city of Laredo, Texas, due to the real-life cartel violence in Tijuana, Baja California. Actor Benicio Del Toro (a native of Puerto Rico) worked hard to enunciate the Mexican Spanish inflections, fearing that he would be dubbed or that the Mexican scenes would be shot in English (thankfully they were kept in Spanish). Salma Hayek made a cameo appearance as the mistress of a drug lord. Soderbergh's camera work contributed much to giving the feeling that the film footage was "caught" and not staged. He cited the influence of *The Battle of Algiers* and *Z*, as well as the work of Jean-Luc Godard and Richard Lester.

The film opened to critical acclaim and huge commercial success. The film won Academy Awards for Best Supporting Actor (Benicio Del Toro), Best Director, Best Film Editing, and Best Adapted Screenplay. It was also nominated for Best Picture, but lost to *Gladiator*. Del Toro won the Best Actor Award from the Screen Actors Guild and numerous other awards. The *New York Times* noted, "The most indelible performances belong to Benicio Del Toro as a burly, eagle-eyed Mexican state policeman of pluck and resourcefulness who has the street smarts to wriggle out of almost any squeeze.... *Traffic* is a tragic cinematic mural of a war being fought and lost. That failure, the movie suggests, has a lot to do with greed and economic inequity (third world cartels have endless financial resources to fight back). But the ultimate culprit, the movie implies, is human nature."[28]

Perhaps the most important contribution that the film made was that it informed the audience that the drug trade is interdependent, involving demand (in the First World) and supply (from the Third World).

Latino Film Stars and Filmmakers

Jessica Alba

Jessica Alba became one of the most prominent Latina actresses of the 2000s through a number of diverse films and genres. Her good looks garner her acclaim as a sex symbol.

Jessica Marie Alba was born on April 28, 1983, in Pomona, California. Her mother, Catherine (née Jensen), was of French Canadian and Danish ancestry and her father, Mark

Alba, is Mexican American. Jessica Alba faced a number of physical adversities during her childhood: collapsed lungs, pneumonia, a ruptured appendix, and a tonsillar cyst.

She began acting the age of five, making her film debut in the 1994 film *Camp Nowhere*. Thereafter, she appeared in television commercials and several independent films. During 1994, she gained notice in a recurring role in the Nickelodeon series *The Secret World of Alex Mack,* and then costarred for two seasons in the series *Flipper*. In the meantime, she polished her acting chops at the Atlantic Theater Company, under the guidance of William H. Macy and his wife Felicity Huffman.

During 2001 and 2002, she played the title role on the Fox sci-fi television series *Dark Angel,* which won her much critical acclaim and praise. Film stardom came with her role as the exotic dancer in *Sin City* (2005). She married actor Cash Warren on May 8, 2008, and the couple had a child, Honor Maire Warren, on June 7, 2008.

Her films include *Fantastic Four* (2005); *Good Luck Chuck* (2007); *Valentine's Day* (2008); *Little Fockers* (2010); and two directed by Robert Rodriguez, *Machete* (2010) and *Spy Kids 4: All the Time in the World* (2011).

CARLOS ÁVILA

Mexican American director Carlos Ávila grew up in the Los Angeles barrio of Echo Park and graduated from the UCLA Film School. Ávila first caught the attention of the film industry with a short film entitled *Distant Water*, a coming-of-age drama set in Los Angeles. It won the Inaugural Film Festival of International Cinema Students in Tokyo Award and the film went on to screened at the Sundance Film Festival.

Since then, Ávila has directed one feature film, several film shorts, and a television series documentary (*Independent Lens* in 2003). He has branched out as a director, writer, and producer.

He made his directorial film debut with *Price of Glory* (2000), an evocative story of a former championship boxer (Jimmy Smits) who tries to make up for his lost glory through the boxing of his three sons. Sadly, the film was virtually ignored by both critics and the public and only half-heartedly supported by its studio. Former welterweight champion Carlos Palomino was cast as a trainer. The film has more boxing heart and genuineness than the overrated *Rocky* and its sequels.

JAVIER BARDEM

Spanish-born Javier Bardem became the most critically acclaimed Latino actor of the decade when he scored with both critics and audiences in a series of high-profile films.

He was born in Las Palmas de Gran Canaria, in the Canary Islands, Spain, on March 1, 1969. His ancestors were pioneers in Spanish cinema. He made his film debut in *El Pícaro* at the age of six and thereafter appeared on Spanish television.

His film breakthrough came with his role of the pimp in the controversial film *Las Edades de Lulú* in 1990. In 1992, he hit a career high with the dark comedy *Jamón, Jamón* in which he played a macho gigolo courting Penélope Cruz. The film was an international success critically and commercially, earning accolades for both Bardem and Cruz. Bardem continued with a series of successful Spanish films: *The Bilingual Lover* (1993); *Huídos* (1993); *Golden Balls* (1993); the short film *Pronòstic Reservat* (1993); *The Detective and Death* (1994); *Boca a Boca* (1995); *Éxtasis* (1996); *Not Love, Just Frenzy* (1996), in which he was reunited with Penélope Cruz; *Love Can Seriously Damage Your Health* (1996), again with Penélope Cruz); *Airbag* (1997); Pedro Almodóvar's *Live Fresh* (1997), with Penélope Cruz; and *Between Your Legs* (1999).

Bardem's success did not go unnoticed in other national cinemas, especially in the English-language film industry. However, his inability to speak English at this time hampered his transition. In 2000, Bardem made his English-language film debut playing the lead role of gay Cuban poet and novelist Reinaldo Arenas in Julian Schnabel's *Before Night Falls*. He became the first Spanish actor to be nominated for an Academy Award for Best Actor. It garnered Bardem worldwide acclaim and demand for his services.

Bardem did a cameo in *Don't Tempt Me* (2000) with Penélope Cruz; played the lead in John Malkovich's *The Dancer Upstairs* (2002); appeared in *Mondays in the Sun* (2002) and *Variaciones* (2002), which won Bardem a Goya for Best Actor; and won the Best Actor Venice Film Festival Award for his role in *Mar Adentro* in 2004. After these successes, Hollywood beckoned again and Bardem heeded the call. Bardem played the sociopathic hit man in the Coen brothers' *No Country for Old Men* (2007). Bardem became the first Spanish actor to win an Academy Award for Best Supporting Actor (although he actually played the lead role), as well as a Golden Globe Award and Screen Actors Guild (SAG) Award for Best Supporting Actor. Bardem played the lead role in the film adaptation of Gabriel García Márquez' novel *Love in the Time of Cholera* (2007), but the film met with limited success. More recently, he appeared in Woody Allen's *Vicky Cristina Barcelona* (2008) and Alejandro González Iñárritu's *Biutiful* (2010), for which he won the Best Actor Award at the Cannes Film Festival, as well as a Best Actor Academy Award nomination.

During July 2010, Bardem married his frequent film costar Penélope Cruz. Bardem states that he is a "worker" and not an actor. It is said he does not know how to drive and that he considers himself an atheist.

ADRIANA BARRAZA

Adriana Barraza was the third Mexico-born actress to be nominated for an Academy Award (the others are Katy Jurado and Salma Hayek). However, she had worked for decades in relative anonymity in Mexico before she gained widespread notice.

She was born on March 5, 1956, in Toluca, Estado de Mexico, Mexico. She has lived in the Mexican state of Chihuahua since 1974 with her Argentine husband. Her husband taught philosophy at the University of Chihuahua. She studied acting at a fine arts school.

In 1985, she moved to Mexico City to work in theater as a director. She has worked extensively in Mexican television. She was prominent in several Mexican *telenovelas*: *Bajo un Mismo Rostro*, *La Paloma*, *Imperio de Cristal*, and *Alguna Vez Tendremos Alas*.

She first came to film prominence with the role of the distraught mother in *Amores Perros* (2000). In 2006, she was cast as the nanny in the film *Babel*. Both the film and she won numerous international awards. She was nominated for an Academy Award for Best Actress.

She currently is an acting coach for Telemundo and has made several more U.S. films. In 2011, she had roles in *From Prada to Nada* and *Thor*.

DEMIÁN BICHIR

Mexican actor Demián Bichir's breakthrough role came playing an overworked, undocumented Mexican laborer in the film *A Better Life* in 2011. However, he had toiled at his craft with growing recognition in Mexican films and *telenovelas* for many years.

Demián Bichir Nájera was born in Mexico City on August 1, 1963, to actors Alejandro Bichir and Maricruz Nájera. Demián began acting at age fourteen in the Mexican *telenovela Rina* with Ofelia Medina in 1977. His second role in a *telenovela* came in 1982 as an adult character in *Vivir Enamorada*. Since then he has starred in several more Mexican *telenovelas*: *Cuando los Hijos Se Van* (1983); *Guadalupe* (1984); *Los Años Felices* (1984); *El Rincón de los Prodigios* (1988); *Lazos de Amor* (1996); *Demasiado Corazón* (1998); *Nada Personal* (1999); and *La Otra Mitad del Sol* (2005).

He made his film debut in the U.S. production *Choices of the Heart* (1983) and his first Mexican film debut in *Astacia* in 1986. As his career progressed he played in every type of genre film: *Rojo Amanecer* (1989), about the 1968 Tlatelolco student massacre; *Miroslava* (1993), about the tragic Czech-Mexican film star Miroslava Stern; the remake *Salón México* (1996); the cult favorite *Santitos* (1999); and critical and commercial hit *Sexo, Pudor y Lágrimas* (1999), which catapulted him to film stardom. Since then he has played Emiliano Zapata in the Mexican miniseries *Zapata: Amor en Rebeldía* in 2004 and leads in several Mexican films, *Bendito Infierno* (2001) with Penélope Cruz and compatriot Gael García Bernal; *Noche de Lima* (2004); *Hipnos* (2004); and *Fuera del Cielo* (2007).

He began a parallel film career in U.S. films at the same time. His credits include *The Penitent* (1988); Disney's animated film *Aladdin* (1992); *Perdita Durango* (1997); *In the Time of the Butterflies* (2001); *Heartbreak Hospital* (2002); *Che* (2008) with Benicio Del Toro, in which he played Fidel Castro; *American Visa* (2007); and *The Runway* (2010).

His breakout role in U.S. films came with *A Better Life* in 2011. He received glowing reviews and many awards, including the ALMA Award as Favorite Movie Actor; the Independent Spirit Award for Best Male Lead; and the Screen Actors Guild Award for Outstanding Performance by a Male Actor in a Leading Role. However, his crowning recognition came with an Academy Award nomination for Best Actor of the Year (the first Mexican actor to be so nominated since Anthony Quinn for *Zorba the Greek* in 1964).

One recent role was that of a ruthless Baja drug cartel leader in Oliver Stone's *Savages* (2012) with Salma Hayek and Benicio Del Toro.

Acting continues to be a family tradition. He has two brothers, Odiseo and Bruno Bichir, who are up-and-coming actors in Mexico. On the personal side, Bichir has been married to singer Lisset Gutiérrez.

PENÉLOPE CRUZ

Penélope Cruz is Spain's most successful female film star since Sarita Montiel. She has garnered international critical acclaim for her acting talent, as well as her physical allure.

She was born Penélope Cruz Sanchez on April 28, 1974, in Alcobendas, Madrid, Spain. Her mother was a hairdresser and personal manager and her father an auto mechanic. Penélope was initially attracted to classical dancing. She had three years of ballet training and then four years of acting at Cristina Rota's New York school. By her early teens she became fascinated by acting.

In 1989, at the age of fifteen, Cruz debuted in the video clip of the song "La Fuerza del Destino" of the musical trio *Mecano*. From 1990 to 1997, she hosted a Spanish television show, *La Quinta Marcha*. In 1992, she made her film debut by playing the title role in the comedy-drama *Jamón, Jamón*. She played a young woman who expects to have a child with a man her mother does not like. Overnight, Penélope Cruz became a film sensation, praised both for her acting talent and her sensual allure. The same year, she scored another big hit in the Academy Award–winning film *Belle Époque*, in which she played a virginal young lady.

Between 1993 and 1996, she starred in ten Spanish and Italian films. They included: *For Love, Only for Love* (1993); *The Great Labyrinth* (1993); *The Rebel* (1993); *Alegre ma non Troppo* (1994); *Todo es Mentira* (1994); *Entre Rojas* (1995); and *El Efecto Mariposa* (1995), among others.

Penélope Cruz's international acclaim as an actress and sex symbol brought Hollywood studios to her door. In 1998, she made her U.S. film debut in *The Hi-Lo Country*. However, the film met with both critical and commercial failure, although she won praise for her performance. She followed this film with *Don Juan* (1998) and *The Girl of Your Dreams* (1998), for which she was given a Goya Award and Spanish Actors Union Award. In 1999, she was reunited with director Pedro Almodóvar (who had previously directed her in *Live Flesh* in 1998) for the film *All About My Mother,* in which she played a nun who is pregnant and has AIDS. She then played the lead in the U.S. film *Woman on Top* (2000), portraying a famous chef who suffers from motion sickness. She costarred with Matt Damon in *All the Pretty Horses* (2000), but the film met with limited success. In 2001, she costarred with Tom Cruise in *Vanilla Sky*, which was very successful, and appeared in *Blow* with Johnny Depp, which was less successful. As always, she earned praise for her acting.

During the 2000s, her films have included: *Captain Corelli's Mandolin* (2001), set in World War II Italy; *Sahara* (2005), a flop; *Chromophobia* (2005); *Bandidas* (2006), a western with Salma Hayek; and Pedro Almodóvar's *Volver* (2006), a major critical and commercial success, for which she won the Goya Award and the European Film Award for her sensitive performance. Throughout the decade she was flooded with films: *Manolete* (2007); *Elegy* (2008); and Woody Allen's comedy *Vicky Cristina Barcelona* (2008). For the last-named film, she became the first Spanish actress to win a Best Supporting Actress Academy Award. She next starred in the animated film *G-Force* (2009), which was hugely successful; *Nine* (2009), a film musical with Sophia Loren and Daniel Day-Lewis; and *Pirates of the Caribbean 4* (2011), which reunited her again with Johnny Depp.

Penélope Cruz continues to be a glamorous icon, movie star, award-winning actress, philanthropist, cosmetics spokeswoman, and more recently mother. She married her frequent film costar Javier Bardem on July 2010. They had a boy the next year.

ROSARIO DAWSON

Rosario Dawson was one of a handful of U.S.–born Latina actresses who came to prominence during the early years of the new millennium.

Rosario Isabel Dawson was born on May 9, 1979, in New York City. Her mother, Isabel

Celeste, was an accomplished singer and writer of Puerto Rican, Taíno (Caribbean Native American), and Afro-Cuban ancestry. Her biological father was Patrick Harris, but Rosario carries the surname of Greg Dawson, her stepfather. Rosario grew up in poverty in the Lower East Side of Manhattan.

She made her film debut in the controversial film *Kids* in 1995. Since then she has starred in a variety of films, everything from independent films to big-budget blockbusters. She has also appeared in numerous music videos with such luminaries as Prince and the Chemical Brothers. Her key films include Spike Lee's drug drama *25th Hour* (2002) with Edward Norton; the film version of the stage musical *Rent* (2005); Oliver Stone's uneven *Alexander* (2004), about Alexander the Great; *Clerks II* (2006); the drama *Seven Pounds* (2008); and the action thriller *Unstoppable* (2010).

She has appeared on stage and is involved in numerous charitable causes.

AMERICA FERRERA

America Ferrera was one of the new young Latina actresses who emerged in the early 2000s. Her coming-of-age roles in film and television mirrored the socioeconomic experiences of many young Latinas.

She was born America Georgina Ferrera on April 18, 1984, in Los Angeles, California. She was the youngest of six children of Honduran parents who immigrated to the United States from civil war–torn Central America in the mid–1970s.

From the age of seven she was attracted to acting and performed in many school productions. She made her television film debut in *Gotta Kick It Up!* (2002, Disney Channel). That same year she played the Latina teen girl who wants to pursue her dream of going to college in the independent film *Real Women Have Curves*. Both the film and its stars, America Ferrera and Lupe Ontiveros (who played her mom), won critical praise. This became America's signature role and one for which she will long be remembered.

She followed her breakout role with several roles in top-rated television series like *Touched by an Angel*. In 2006, she was cast to play the lead role in the U.S. television version of the Colombian series *Ugly Betty*. Ferrera played an adolescent whose peers find her not only unattractive but culturally different as a Latina. The series, which was produced by Salma Hayek, ran until April 2010. Ferrera won the 2007 Golden Globe Award for Best Performance by an Actress in a Television Series, as well as the Screen Actors Guild Award for Best Female Actress in a Comedy Series.

Her films include *The Sisterhood of the Traveling Pants* (2004); *Under the Same Moon* (2007); *Our Family Wedding* (2010); and *How to Train Your Dragon 2* (2014).

GAEL GARCÍA BERNAL

One of the brightest Mexico-born film stars who won wide acclaim for his acting was Gael García Bernal. He had the good fortune to star in several films that were not only critically acclaimed, but also wide commercial hits.

He was born on November 30, 1978, in Guadalajara, Mexico, to Patricia Bernal (an actress and former model) and Jose Ángel García (an actor and director). Gael began acting in Mexican *telenovelas* at the age of one, and as a youth he studied for the International Baccalaureate.

At the age of nineteen he left for London, England, to study acting at the Central School of Speech and Drama. In 2000, Mexican director Alejandro González Iñárritu cast him for one of the leads in his film *Amores Perros,* about two feuding brothers in a poor barrio in Mexico City. The film was an international success and placed Bernal front and center as Mexico's most important male film star. Two equally successful films followed: *Y Tu Mamá También* (2001) and *El Crimen del Padre Amaro* (2002). He capped those years with the lead in the Federico García Lorca play *Bodas de Sangre* in 2005 in London.

He then entered the U.S. film market playing Argentine revolutionary Ernesto "Che" Guevara in the cable film *Fidel* (2002). He returned to play a young Guevara in Walter Salles' evocative coming-of-age biopic *The Motorcycle Diaries* (based on Guevara's own writings). During this period, he and fellow actor Diego Luna founded their own production company, Canana Productions. In 2010, García codirected (with Marc Siver) four short films for Amnesty International about the plight of Central American immigrants. García is very involved with social causes, including the plight of indigenous peoples.

His films include *Bad Education* (2003); *Babel* (2005); *Rudo y Cursi* (2008); *Even the Rain* (2010); and *A Little Bit of Heaven* (2011).

ALEJANDRO GONZÁLEZ IÑÁRRITU

One of the most acclaimed Mexico-born directors to cross over into U.S. films is Alejandro González Iñárritu. He has had several critically and commercially successful films.

He was born on August 15, 1963, in Mexico City, Mexico, to Luz Maria Iñárritu and Hector González Gama. He grew up in the wealthy neighborhood of Las Águilas in southern Mexico City. His father, a wealthy banker, went bankrupt and became a fruit and vegetable seller.

Alejandro began his show business career as a DJ in 1984 on WFM radio. He then composed music for Mexican films and studied filmmaking in Maine and Los Angeles under the direction of Polish director Ludwik Margules and Judith Weston. He utilized this experience to become the head of production at the Mexican television network Televisa and subsequently a television director. In 1991, he set up his own company, Zeta Films.

In 1995, he directed his half-feature film entitled *Detrás del Dinero* for Televisa. In 2000, he directed his breakthrough film, *Amores Perros.* Among the many recognitions the film garnered was the Academy Award nomination for Best Foreign Film. Hollywood beckoned and he made his directorial U.S. film debut with *21 Grams* (2003) with Benicio Del Toro and Naomi Watts, both of whom were nominated for Academy Awards for their performances.

In 2006, he directed *Babel,* a film about four stories in four different time frames and four countries: Japan, the United States, Morocco, and Mexico. It earned him the Best Director Prize (Prix de Mise-en-Scène) at the Cannes Film Festival that year and the film earned many international awards. However, all this was marred by his feud with screenwriter Guillermo Arriaga and a dispute over writing credit. *Babel* went on to be nominated for seven Academy Awards, including Best Picture and Best Director (he was the first Mexican film director to be so honored).

After this great success he produced the film *Rudo y Cursi* (2008), with Gael García Bernal and Diego Luna, about two feuding soccer star brothers. He directed a soccer-themed commercial for Nike for the 2010 FIFA World Cup. More recently he directed *Biutiful* (2010) with Javier Bardem.

The director lives in Los Angeles with his wife Maria Eladia Hagerman de González. They have two children.

LUIS GUZMÁN

Over the decade character actor Luis Guzmán became almost as well known as the big film stars that he supported in many diverse roles.

He was born Pedro Lambroy on August 28, 1956, in Cayey, Puerto Rico. He was raised in Greenwich Village and the Lower East Side in New York City. His father was a television repairman and his mother a hospital worker. Luis graduated from American University and began a career as a social worker, and acting became a side vocation. Nevertheless he became very busy in theater and later in independent films, which led to Hollywood films.

He was initially typecast as a thug, a criminal, and other assorted lowlifes, but gradually he earned critical acclaim and was cast in both comedies and dramas. He made his film debut in the film version of Miguel Piñero's *Short Eyes* in 1977. His films include *Crocodile Dundee 2* (1988); *Q & A* (1990); *Carlito's Way* (1993); *The Limey* (1999); *Traffic* (2000); *The Count of Monte Cristo* (2002); *Fast Food Nation* (2006); and *Arthur* (2011). He has appeared extensively on episodic television and costarred in a Latino-themed series with John Leguizamo entitled *House of Buggin'* in 1995. However, the series was cancelled before the end of the first season.

He is married to Yoruba Guzmán and has five children. They live in Barnet, Vermont.

JAY HERNANDEZ

One of the youngest and most promising Latino leading men during the decade was Jay Hernandez.

He was born Javier Manuel Hernandez, Jr., on February 20, 1978, in Montebello, California, to Javier Hernandez, Sr., a mechanic, and Isis Maldonado, a secretary and accountant. His parents were third-generation Mexican Americans. He attended Don Bosco Technical Institute and later Schurr High School in Montebello.

One day, while riding an elevator in a high-rise, he was approached by talent manager Howard Tyner, who told him that he had the makings of a Hollywood film star. He enrolled Hernandez in acting classes and sent him around to casting agents. He made his film debut in *Living the Life* in 2000 and made a big impression in *Crazy/Beautiful* in 2001 opposite Kirsten Dunst. He played the lead in the very successful horror film *Hostel* (2005) and costarred in *World Trade Center* (2005). Other films include *Ladder 49* (2004); *Grindhouse* (2006); *Hostel II* (2007); *Lakeview Terrace* (2008); and *Takers* (2010).

He has appeared in episodic television.

LAURA HARRING

One of the talented Mexican actresses to cross over into U.S. films during the 2000s was Laura Harring.

She was born Laura Elena Harring Martinez on March 3, 1964, in Los Mochis, Sinaloa, Mexico. Her mother, Maria Elena Cairo, was a realtor and psychotherapist, and her father, Raymond Herring (of Austrian-German ancestry), an organic farmer. They divorced in 1971. Laura spent ten years in her native Mexico before her family moved to San Antonio, Texas.

In Texas, she was hit by a stray bullet in the head from a drive-by shooting and miraculously recovered and went on to study in Switzerland at AEGON College. Upon her return to the United States, she moved to El Paso, Texas, where she competed in numerous beauty pageants, winning Miss El Paso, Miss USA (the first Latina to do so), and Miss Texas USA, and made the top ten of the 1985 Miss Universe pageant. She became a social worker in India and married Count Carl-Eduard von Bismarck-Schonhausen, the great-grandson of the famous statesman Otto von Bismarck. Thereafter, Harring studied at the London Academy of Performing Arts.

She made her television debut in the film *The Alamo: Thirteen Days of Glory* in 1987 as General Santa Ana's bride, and thereafter appeared in numerous episodic television shows. She was a star of two popular television shows: the soap opera *General Hospital* (1990–1991) and *Sunset Beach* (1997).

Her most important film roles have been in three David Lynch films: *Mulholland Drive* (2001); *Rabbits* (2002); and *Inland Empire* (2006). Her films include *The Punisher* (2004) with John Travolta; *Mi casa es su casa* (2006); and *Love in the Time of Cholera* (2007). She also appeared on the TV show *Gossip Girl* in 2010.

MARIO LÓPEZ

One of the most popular Mexican-American performers during the decade was Mario López, who became popular on television.

He was born Mario Michael López, Jr., on October 10, 1973, in San Diego, California. He made his television debut in the series *a.k.a. Pablo* in 1973 and appeared on many other episodic television shows. He became famous, especially among teenage girls, when he was cast in the role of A.C. Slater in the comedy series *Saved by the Bell,* which ran from 1989 to 1993. He later reprised his role in the short-lived *Saved by the Bell: The College Years.*

In 1997, he played Olympic diver Greg Louganis in the television film *Breaking the Surface: The Greg Louganis Story,* which garnered him excellent reviews for his performance. Thereafter he was a regular for two years on the USA network show *Pacific Blue.* He played a doctor on the daytime soap opera *The Bold and the Beautiful* during 2006 and guest-starred in other television shows.

Since 1992, he has hosted an assortment of television programs: *Name Your Adventure* (1992); *Masters of the Maze* (1995); and *The Other Half* (2001), among others. Since 2006, he has been the celebrity guest host for the syndicated entertainment show *Extra.*

He has been married to Ali Landry since 2004 and they have one child.

DIEGO LUNA

One of the brightest Mexico-born actors during the decade was Diego Luna. He was part of a group of Mexican actors and filmmakers who blossomed and crossed over into the Hollywood film industry.

He was born Diego Luna Alexander on December 29, 1979, in Mexico City, Mexico. He was the son of Alejandro Luna, a Mexican film set designer, and Fiona Alexander, an English costume designer. His mother died when Diego was two years old. As a child, he was brought to theater and film sets and gained an affinity for theater and film.

Beginning at an early age, Diego performed on Mexican television, and in film and theater. He made his television film debut in *El Último Fin de Año* in 1991. He scored a big success with his role in the *telenovela El Abuelo y Yo* in 1992, which also costarred Gael García Bernal; and followed up with another popular *telenovela, El Premio Mejor*, in 1995.

In 2001, he costarred with Gael García Bernal in the critical and commercial hit *Y Tu Mamá También*. He made his U.S. film debut in *Frida* (2002) as Frida Kahlo's boyfriend. His films include *Open Range* (2003) with Kevin Costner; *Nicotine* (2003); *Dirty Dancing: Havana Nights* (2004); *Fade to Black* (2006); *Rudi y Cursi* (2008); *Milk* (2008); *Casa de Mi Padre* (2011); *Contraband* (2012); and *Elysium* (2013). He made his directorial debut with *JC Chavez* in 2007, about the career downside of boxing legend Julio Cesar Chavez.

Luna and Gael García Bernal co-founded Cinema Productions. Luna married Mexican actress Camila Sodio on February 5, 2008. They have a son and a daughter.

He most recently directed *Cesar Chavez* (2014), a biopic about the Chicano civil rights leader.

LUIS MANDOKI

Luis Mandoki was one of several Mexico-born directors who came to Hollywood during the decade and enriched the Hollywood film landscape.

He was born in Mexico City, Mexico, in 1954. He studied at the Fine Arts (Bellas Artes) school in Mexico City, the San Francisco Art Institute, the London College of Printing, and the London International Film School. While studying at the last-named college, he directed his first short film, entitled *Silent Film,* which went on to win an award at the International Amateur Film Festival, part of the Cannes Film Festival, in 1976.

Upon his return to Mexico, he directed documentaries and short films for the Instituto Nacional Indigenista, Conacine (National Commission of Film), and the Centro de Producción de Cortometrajse (Center for the Production for Short Films). He won the Mexican Ariel award for his short film *El Secreto* in 1980. In 1984, Mandoki directed his breakthrough film, *Motel.* The film was a critical and commercial success and was exhibited around the world in film festivals.

In 1987, he directed *Gaby: A True Story*, which focused on Gaby Brimer, a physically challenged Mexican writer. The film earned Norma Aleandro an Academy Award nomination for Best Supporting Actress. In 2004, Mandoki directed *Innocent Voices/Voces Inocentes,* perhaps the best film yet made on the Salvadoran civil war of the 1970s and 1980s. The film earned the Mexican Ariel for Best Film and it was nominated for an Academy Award as Best Foreign Film. The film was both a commercial and critical success.

His films include *White Palace* (1990); *Born Yesterday* (1993); *Message in a Bottle* (1999); *Angel Eyes* (2001); *The Edge* (2003); *Amapola* (2005); and *The Translator* (2009). In 2007, he directed the documentary *Fraude,* about the 2006 Mexican presidential election and the documented evidence of massive fraud.

Mandoki lives in Mexico City with his wife Olivia and three children.

MICHAEL PEÑA

One of the few Mexican-American actors to come to prominence during the decade was Michael Peña.

He was born Michael Anthony Peña on January 13, 1976, in Chicago, Illinois. His mother was an assistant to a social worker and his father was employed in a button factory. Michael attended Hubbard High School in Chicago. He made his film debut in *My Fellow Americans* in 1996 opposite Jack Lemmon and James Garner. He made his first big impression in the role of the Mexican-American perceived as a gang member in the Academy Award–winning film *Crash* in 2003. In 2005, he played Sal Castro, the high school teacher in *Walkout* (HBO), the true story of the high school walkouts in East Los Angeles. In 2006, he played second leading roles in three important and successful films: *Babel, World Trade Center,* and *Shooter.*

His films include *Gone in 60 Seconds* (2000); *Buffalo Soldiers* (2001); *Observe and Report* (2009); *Battle: Los Angeles* (2011); and *Tower Heist* (2011). He was selected to play labor leader Cesar Chavez by actor/director Diego Luna in the film *Cesar Chavez* (2014).

He is married to Brie Shaffer and they have one child.

EFREN RAMIREZ

Efren Ramirez became a cult figure when he played the outcast Latino character in *Napoleon Dynamite.*

He was born Efraín Antonio Ramirez on October 2, 1973, in Los Angeles, California. He is of Mexican and Salvadoran ancestry.

He made his film debut in *Tammy and the T-Rex* in 1994. His breakthrough film was *Napoleon Dynamite* in 2004, in which he played the character of Pedro Sanchez. Both the film and Ramirez received acclaim. Since then, his films include *Employee of the Month* (2006); *Crossing the Heart* (2007); *American Summer* (2008); *Crank: High Voltage* (2009); and *When in Rome* (2010).

He has appeared extensively on television since 1994. He was married to Iyari Linmon, but the marriage was later annulled. He is a traveling DJ and also a musician.

MICHELLE RODRIGUEZ

One of the most popular young Latina performers during the decade was Michelle Rodriguez, who specialized in action dramas.

She was born Mayte Michele Rodriguez on July 12, 1978, in San Antonio, Texas. She is the daughter of Rafael Rodriguez, a Puerto Rican serviceman, and Carmen Milady Pared of the Dominican Republic. Michelle had ten siblings or half-siblings. She moved to the Dominican Republic with her mother when she was eight and then lived in Puerto Rico at the age of eleven. She attended high school in New Jersey, dropping out of school after being kicked out of five schools. Nevertheless, she earned her GED degree and then went on to attend business school. However, the acting bug propelled her in a different direction.

In 2000, she beat out 350 actresses for the role of the troubled adolescent who becomes a boxer in the film *Girlfight*. The independent film won numerous awards, as well as critical acclaim for Rodriguez. Since that role, she has been often typecast as an assertive and tough girl in several action films.

She continues to be popular among filmgoers. He films include *The Fast and the Furious* (2000); *Resident Evil* (2002); *S.W.A.T.* (2003); *Fast and Furious 2* (2009); *Avatar* (2009); *Machete* (2010); *Battle Los Angeles* (2011); *Army of Two* (2011); and *Fast & Furious 6* (2013).

She has appeared extensively on television since 2005. During the periods 2005–06 and 2009–10, she was a regular on the series *Lost*.

WALTER SALLES

One of several Latin American directors who infused the Hollywood film industry with new vitality and vision was during the decade was Walter Salles.

He was born Walther Moreira Salles, Jr., on April 12, 1956, in Río de Janeiro, Brazil. He is the son of Walther Moreira Salles and Elizinha Goncalves. His father was an ambassador and banker. His brother, João Moreira Salles, is a prominent Brazilian filmmaker. Walter studied film at the University of Southern California School of Cinematic Arts.

He made his directorial film debut in 1995 with *Terra Estrangeira (Foreign Land)*. In 1998, his film *Central do Brasil (Central Station)* garnered him worldwide acclaim. The film was nominated for Academy Awards for Best Foreign Film and Best Actress (Fernanda Montenegro). In 2001, he had another huge success with *April Despedacado (Behind the Sun)*. The film was nominated for Best Foreign Film at the Golden Globes.

In 2004, he directed *Diarios de Motocicleta* (The Motorcycle Diaries), based on the book by Ernesto "Che" Guevara about his travels through South America before he became a revolutionary. The film was huge international success. In 2005, Salles made his U.S. directorial debut with *Dark Water* and produced the Argentine film *Hermanos*.

During 2006, he directed his first French film, *Paris Je t'aime (Paris, I Love You)*, a collection of eighteen segments with the participation of twenty-one directors that was set in different parts of Paris. In 2007, he followed it up with another French film, *To Each His Own Cinema (Chacon Son Cinema)*. His third French film, *Linha de Passe,* in 2008 focused on the plight of a poor family and their dreams. The film was nominated for the Golden Palm. Salles also directed a film version of Jack Kerouac's *On the Road* (2012).

CATALINA SANDINO MORENO

Catalina Sandino Moreno became the first Colombian-born actress to find Hollywood film industry success and be nominated for an Academy Award for Best Actress.

She was born Catalina Sandino Moreno on April 19, 1981, in Bogotá, Colombia. Her father was a cattle breeder and her mother a pathologist. She studied at the Pontificia Universidad Javieriana in Bogotá. In 2004, she moved to New York City after winning the attention of several filmmakers while attending the Ruben Di Pietro acting school in Bogotá.

During 2004, she won the coveted role of the young Colombian girl attracted to smuggling drugs into New York City in the film *Maria Full of Grace*. She had auditioned for the role and beat out some nine hundred other actresses for the role. She became the first Columbian actress to be nominated for an Academy Award for Best Actress. The film was an international critical and commercial success and put the young actress in the forefront.

Her subsequent films include *Fast Food Nation* (2006); *Paris Je t'aime* (2006); *Che Part One* (2008); *Che Part Two* (2008); *Twilight Saga: Eclipse* (2010); and *For Greater Glory* (2011).

She married David Elwell in 2006.

José Luis Valenzuela

José Luis Valenzuela directed theater for many years before making his directorial debut in film.

Valenzuela made his directorial film debut with a film short entitled *How Else Am I Supposed to Know I Am Still Alive* in 1991. In 2000, he made his feature film debut with *Luminarias,* based on the play of the same name and scripted by his wife Evelina Fernández. Since then he has directed the film short *Til Parole Do Us Part* in 2005 and a second feature film, *Moe,* in 2008.

He continues to work in theater.

Alexa Vega

One of the few Latina child performers who grew up to be successful was Alexa Vega.

She was born Alexa Ellesse Vega on August 27, 1988, in Miami, Florida. Her mother was Gina Rue, a Euro-American, and her father was Colombian.

She made her television debut in the series *Evening Shade* with Burt Reynolds during the 1993–94 season, and thereafter appeared in many episodic television shows. She made her film debut in *Little Giants* in 1994. However, it was her appearance as Carmen Diaz, the precocious daughter of Antonio Banderas in Robert Rodriguez's *Spy Kids* (2001), which brought her to prominence. She subsequently repeated her role in *Spy Kids 2: Island of Lost Dreams* (2002); *Spy Kids 3-D: Game Over* (2003); and *Spy Kids 4: All the Time in the World* (2012).

In 2006, she played Paula Chrisostomo, the high school student activist in *Walkout* (2006), about the East Los Angeles walkouts. Her films include *Innocent* (2008); *From Prada to Nada* (2011); and *Summer Song* (2011).

Chris Weitz

In recent years, many creative talents of mixed heritage have emerged in the film industry. One of the most successful in recent years has been Chris Weitz.

Christopher John "Chris" Weitz was born on November 30, 1969, in New York City. His mother is actress Susan Kohner and his father was novelist and fashion designer John Weitz. His grandmother is Mexican actress Lupita Tovar, one of the pioneer Mexican Hollywood film stars of the 1920s. His grandfather was film producer/agent Paul Kohner. He has a brother, Paul Weitz, who is also a screenwriter, producer, and director.

He studied at St. Paul's School in London and graduated from Trinity College in Cambridge with an English degree.

He began in the film industry as a co-writer (with Todd Alcott) of the animated film *Antz* in 1998. He subsequently scripted a revival of *Fantasy Island* during 1998 and 1999 and the films *Nutty Professor II: The Klumps* and *About a Boy* (2002), which he codirected with his brother, Paul Weitz. On his own he has directed the following films: *The Golden Compass* (2007); *The Twilight Saga: New Moon* (2009), which became a huge commercial success; and *A Better Life* (2011), which signaled a return to smaller and more personal films.

Chris Weitz has also been an actor. He did a cameo in *American Pie* (1999); played the lead role in *Chuck and Buck* (2000); appeared in and executive-produced *See This Movie* (2004); appeared in *Mr. & Mrs. Smith* (2005); and did a voice-over in the animated feature *Bickford Shmeckler's Coral Ideals* (2006). He is married to Mercedes Martinez (a Mexican-Cuban) and they have one son.

POSTSCRIPT

Beyond the 2000s
Looking Back and Looking Forward

As one looks back into more than one hundred and six years of the Latino presence in U.S. cinema, it is filled with both good and bad, triumphs and setbacks, especially in the recent decades. Latinos have since their first filmic image in 1894 been portrayed in a distorted and stereotypical manner more often than not. Fundamental to understanding these images are the historical concepts and events that preceded the advent of film images. Such historical concepts and events such as the Monroe Doctrine, Manifest Destiny, and the Mexican-American War, among others, left an array of permanent distorted images and attitudes about what Latinos are or are not. Later, popular literature, dime novels, and Buffalo Bill's Wild West Show perpetuated these stereotypes, from which they were transported into the infant film art form.

Thereafter (as before), the social disorientation caused by crises such as war and economic dislocations, especially depressions and economic downturns, resulted in xenophobia and a scapegoating of Latinos. They directly worsened Latino filmic images, as well as the curtailment of opportunities. During the first stage of the evolution of Latino images, 1894 to 1922, Latino characters were portrayed for the most part by non–Latino performers, with some minor exceptions. Again, several political and economic downturns affected the filmic images for the worse: the Mexican Revolution, World War I, and the Red Scare. During the 1920s, the first group of Latino film stars (Ramon Novarro, Dolores del Río, Lupe Vélez, Gilbert Roland, and Lupita Tovar, among others) emerged. Although they did not always portray Latino characters, they were afforded the opportunity to play a diversity of roles which remains unprecedented. The roles in which they did portray Latino characters were in general a vast improvement to those of non–Latino performers. Of course, there were exceptions to this pattern.

During the 1930s and 1940s, under the studio system a new group of major Latino stars (Rita Hayworth, Anthony Quinn, Cesar Romero, Maria Montez, Ricardo Montalbán, etc.) and character actors continued to flourish. The advent of the depression ushered in a mass repatriation of Mexicans and Mexican-Americans that directly contributed to a return of the Mexican *bandido* and "desperado" and his frenzied and sleazy *cantinera* counterpart. The 1930s also brought the first opportunities for Latinos to direct, produce, and script U.S. films, especially in the more than one hundred Spanish-language films that were produced in Hollywood during the period 1930–1939. The end of the 1940s brought pivotal changes in the Hollywood film industry, in particular the decline of the studio system and the McCarthy era of blacklisting. Between 1949 and 1954, a "premature Chicano cinema" developed with films such as *Salt of the Earth* (1954) that began to address the social plight of Mexican-Americans. However, the political climate of the Cold War, the Korean War, and the McCarthy witch-hunt removed a whole generation of progressive filmmakers and cowed the next generation of Hollywood filmmakers.

The 1950s and 1960s saw the complete demise of the old Hollywood studio system and the rise of talent agencies and independent filmmakers, as well as freelancing film stars. The period was characterized by the marked of absence of new Latino film stars and the short-term use or misuse of imported Mexican and Latin American talent. The decline of the western genre, which has historically used more Latino characters, further diminished the Latino presence. The rise of the "spaghetti western" in Italy and elsewhere brought back some of the most reprehensible stereotypes, specifically those of Mexicans. The specter of revolution in Latin America and a rabid anticommunism, as well as such pivotal events as the Civil Rights movement and the advent of domestic Latino movements (Chicano and Puerto Rican, among others) further blurred and narrowed the Hollywood view of Latinos and other people of color. Nonetheless, Latinos developed organizations like Nosotros and others to advocate for better opportunities and for the eradication of negative images.

The 1970s brought a renaissance of the Hollywood film industry, as well as the emergence of several domestic Latino cinemas, especially Chicano cinema. This cinema saw films directed, written, produced, and acted by Chicano talent, and which addressed the pressing social issues confronting the community. The 1980s saw the flourishing of Chicano cinema, as well as the emergence of Puerto Rican and Cuban-American cinemas. In addition, for the first time since the 1940s, several new Latino film stars (Edward James Olmos, Salma Hayek, Jennifer Lopez, Raúl Juliá, and Jimmy Smits) rose in Hollywood. A group of Chicano, Puerto Rican, and Cuban filmmakers also emerged. During this period, a recession, revolution in Central America, and the dramatic growth in the population of undocumented Mexican and Central American laborers in the U.S. contributed to an anxiety of the Euro-American psyche and fanned the flames of xenophobia.

The 1990s witnessed the end of the Cold War and the beginning of the post-nation-states and globalization. These events, coupled with changing Latino demographics, created a cultural disorientation and the passage of a series of exclusionary policies directed at Latinos. Predictably, film and television portrayed Latinos as the "Other." The majority of Latino roles became incidental or subsidiary, as the Hollywood film industry undertook an overdose of self-denial in the very midst of the Latino critical mass.

As we enter the second decade of the new century and the millennium, the demographics are irreversible. Latinos have already become the largest U.S. minority and are likely to continue to make up a substantial portion of the nation's population. The Latino presence has already affected U.S. popular music and literature; language and cuisine, schools and universities, and politics and government. Only film and television continue to espouse a *de facto* cultural apartheid. Despite all this, Latinos have historically made significant contributions to the Hollywood film industry and will continue to do so.

The technological revolution of videos, DVDs, digital cameras, computers, smartphones, downloads, and other technologies provides an informal education for future Latino actors and filmmakers. These technologies offer the opportunity for diverse voices, which have previously been denied access or have been silenced.

This writer is optimistic about the future. In the future, there will be Latino stories of everyday life: of struggle and hope, of history and culture, and of dreams and love. The settings will be diverse: reservations and barrios, *favelas* and agricultural fields, as well as suburbs and in professional workplaces. Latinos will be protagonists, not merely incidental beings in their nations or in the world, but proactive in their lives and destinies. They will come in different anatomies, colors and hues: brown and black, *mestizo* and mulatto, lighter skin and every color in between. They will speak Native American languages and dialects, Spanish and Spanglish, Portuguese and French, and even English.

And they will speak with the voice of film.

Chapter Notes

Introduction

1. Ángel R. Oquendo, "Re-Imagining the Latino/a Race," in Richard Delgado and Jean Stefancic, eds., *The Latino/a Condition: A Critical Reader* (New York: New York University Press, 1998), p. 63.

2. Suzanne Oboler, "Hispanic? That's What They Call Us," in Delgado and Stefancic, eds., p. 4.

3. Juan Flores, "The Latino Imaginary: Dimensions of Community and Identity," in Francis R. Aparicio and Susana Chávez-Silverman, eds., *Tropicalization: Transcultural Representations of Latinidad* (Hanover, NH: University Press of New England, 1997), p. 186.

4. Frances R. Aparicio, "On Subversive Signifiers: Tropicalizing Language in the United States," in Aparicio and Chávez-Silverman, eds., *Tropicalizations: Transcultural Representations of Latinidad* (Hanover, NH: University Press of New England, 1997), p. 196.

5. Beatriz Urraca, "A Textbook of Americanism: Richard Harding Davis' Soldiers of Fortune," in Aparicio and Susana Chávez-Silverman, eds., p. 22.

Chapter I

1. Thomas Jefferson, *Notes on the State of Virginia, Query XIV*, reprinted in Thomas Jefferson, *Thomas Jefferson: Writings: Autobiography / Notes on the State of Virginia / Public and Private Papers / Addresses / Letters*, edited by Merrill D. Peterson (New York: Library of America, 1984), pp. 264, 265.

2. *Congressional Record, 30th Congress, 1st session*, 48 (1846), excerpted in David Weber, *Foreigners in Their Native Land: Historical Roots of the Mexican-Americans* (Albuquerque: University of New Mexico Press, 2003, p. 135.

3. Weber, *Foreigners in Their Native Land,* pp. 59–60.

4. LeRoy R. Hafen and Ann W. Hafen, eds., *Rufus S. Sage: His Letters and Papers, 1836–1847* (Glendale, CA: A.H. Clark, 1956), excerpted in Weber, *Foreigners in Their Native Land,* pp. 72, 74.

5. Walter P. Webb, *The Texas Rangers: A Century of Frontier Defense*, 2d ed. (Austin: University of Texas Press, 1965), excerpted in Weber, *Foreigners in Their Native Land*, p. 77.

6. Paul Johnson, *A History of the American People* (New York: Harper-Collins, 1999), p. 621. See also Karl Berman, *Under the Big Stick: Nicaragua and the United States Since 1848* (Boston: Compita, 1986).

7. Dwight Conquerwood, "Rethinking Ethnography: Towards a Critical Cultural Politics," *Communication Monographs* 58 (1991): 179.

8. Gloria Anzaldúa, "Borderlands," in Richard Delgado and Stefanie Delgado, eds., *The Latino/a Condition: A Critical Reader* (New York: New York University Press, 1998), p. 628.

9. Rodolfo Acuña, *Occupied America: A History of Chicanos* (New York: Harper & Row, 1988).

10. Juan González, *Harvest of Empire: A Story of Latinos in America* (New York: Viking, 2000), p. 96.

11. González, *Harvest of Empire*, p. 255.

12. González, *Harvest of Empire*, p. 63.

13. Marcelo Suárez-Orozco, "State Terrors: Immigrants and Refugees in the Post-National Space," in Yali Zou and Enrique Trueba, eds., *Ethnic Identity and Power: Cultural Contexts of Political Action in Schools and Society*, 283–319 (Albany: State University of New York Press, 1998).

14. Bob Herbert, "The Company They Keep," *New York Times*, February 17, 1996.

15. Suárez-Orozco, "State Terrors," in Zou and Trueba, eds., p. 299.

16. *Los Angeles Times*, June 15, 1996.

Chapter II

1. Arthur Pettit, *Images of the Mexican in Fiction and Film* (College Station: Texas A&M, 1980); Joy S. Kasson, *Buffalo Bill's Wild West: Celebrity, Memory and Popular History* (New York: Hill & Wang, 2000).

2. Pettit, *Images of the Mexican in Fiction and Film*, pp. ix–xx.

3. Pettit, *Images of the Mexican in Fiction and Film*, p. xx.

4. Pettit, *Images of the Mexican in Fiction and Film*, p. xx.

5. Pettit, *Images of the Mexican in Fiction and Film*, p. 40.

6. Pettit, *Images of the Mexican in Fiction and Film*, p. 62.

7. Christine List, *Chicano Images: Refiguring Ethnicity in Mainstream Film* (New York: Garland, 1993), pp. 132–133.

8. Margarita De Orellano, "The Circular Look: The Incursion of North American Fictional Cinema 1911–1917 into the Mexican Revolution," in John King, Ana M. López and Manuel Alvarado, eds., *Mediating Two Worlds: Cinematic Encounters in the Americas* (London: British Film Institute, 1993), p. 13.

Chapter III

1. President John F. Kennedy's Inaugural Address, January 20, 1961.

2. Rodolfo Acuña, *Occupied America: A History of Chicanos* (New York: Harper & Row, 1998), p. 436.

3. Christopher Frayling, *Sergio Leone: Something to Do with Death*

(London: Faber and Faber, 2000), p. 311.

4. Chon A. Noriega, *Shot in America: Television, the State, and the Rise of Chicano Cinema* (Minneapolis: University of Minnesota Press, 2000), p. 3.

5. Rosa Linda Fregoso, *The Bronze Screen: Chicana and Chicano Film* (Minneapolis: University of Minnesota Press), p. xix.

6. Rodney Farnsworth, "John Wayne's Epic of Contradictions," *Film Quarterly* 52, no. 2 (Winter 1998–99).

7. *Hollywood Reporter*, September 5, 1969.

8. *Newsweek*, December 9, 1968.

9. See Jon Lee Anderson, *Che Guevara: A Revolutionary Life* (New York: Grove Press, 1997); Paco Ignacio Taibo II, *Guevara: Also Known As Che* (New York: St. Martin's Press, 1997); Jorge Castañeda, *Compañero: The Life and Death of Che Guevara* (New York: Vintage, 1998).

10. William Tusher, "Sy Barlett Calls Mexico Banning of 'Che' Unfair," *Hollywood Reporter,* September 5, 1967.

11. *Newsweek*, December 17, 1968.

12. *Variety*, May 29, 1969.

13. *Time*, June 13, 1969.

14. Frayling, *Sergio Leone*, p. 312.

15. *Los Angeles Herald-Examiner*, "For a Few Dollars More," June 12, 1967.

16. Christopher Frayling, *Spaghetti Westerns: Cowboys and Europeans from Karl May to Sergio Leone* (London: I.B. Tauris, 1991), p. 256.

17. "For a Few Dollars More," *New York Daily News,* July 4, 1967.

18. "For a Few Dollars More," *New York Times,* July 4, 1967.

19. *New York Times*, December 25, 1968.

20. *Time*, February 9, 1968.

21. James Robert Parish and Michael R. Pitts, *The Great Western Pictures* (Metuchen, NJ: Scarecrow Press, 1976), p. 288.

22. Parish and Pitt, *The Great Western Pictures*, p. 291.

23. Parish and Pitt, *The Great Western Pictures*, p. 292.

24. Parish and Pitt, *The Great Western Pictures*, p. 292.

25. "One-Eyed Jacks," *New York Times,* March 31, 1961.

26. *Take One* interview, 1969.

27. *The Motion Picture Herald*, March 27, 1968.

28. *Los Angeles Times*, July 31, 1968.

29. Sonia Nieto, "Fact and Fiction: Stories of Puerto Ricans in the U.S. Schools," in *Harvard Educational Review, Symposium: Colonialism, and Working-Class Resistance: Puerto Rican Education in the United States* 69, no. 2 (Summer 1998).

30. Arthur G. Pettit, *Images of the Mexican American in Fiction and Film* (College Station: Texas A&M University Press, 1980), pp. 233–234.

31. Publicity Department, Press Release, Buena Vista Co., 1971.

32. *Entertainment Today*, August 11–17, 1995.

33. *Entertainment Today,* August 11–17, 1995.

34. *Los Angeles Times*, August 6, 1995.

35. *Los Angeles Times,* August 6, 1995.

36. *Entertainment Today*, August 11–17, 1995.

37. *Los Angeles Times,* August 6, 1995.

38. *Entertainment Today,* August 11–17, 1995.

39. *Siempre*, June 3, 1965.

40. *Los Angeles Mirror*, July 20, 1961.

41. *Los Angeles Mirror,* July 20, 1961.

42. *Los Angeles Times TV Times*, July 26–August 1, 1970.

43. *Los Angeles Herald-Examiner TV Weekly*, October 29–November 4, 1967.

44. *Los Angeles Times TV Times,* July 26–August 1, 1970.

45. *TV Guide,* November 2, 1968.

46. *Cineavance,* Mexico City, 1962.

47. *Cineavance,* Mexico City, 1962.

48. *Cineavance,* Mexico City, 1966.

49. *Variety*, November 30, 1966.

50. *Cineavance,* Mexico City, 1966.

51. *Cineavance,* Mexico City, 1966.

52. *The Wild Bunch* press release, Warner Bros., 1969.

53. *The Wild Bunch* press release, Warner Bros., 1969.

54. *Hollywood Drama-Logue,* March 19, 1981.

55. *Hollywood Drama-Logue,* March 19, 1981.

56. *New York Times*, September 8, 1965.

57. *Playboy*, January 1970.

58. John Wallace, *Screen World 1968* 19 (New York: Crown, 1968); *Screen World 1969* 20 (New York: Crown, 1969); *Screen World 1970* 21 (New York: Crown, 1970); *Screen World 1972* 23 (New York: Crown, 1972).

59. *Newsweek*, December 10, 1967.

60. *Los Angeles Times*, April 15, 1969.

61. *Los Angeles Times*, November 11, 1969.

62. *Look Magazine*, April 15, 1969.

63. *Time*, November 28, 1969.

64. *New York Daily News*, April 12, 1930.

65. *New York Times*, April 12, 1970.

66. *Time*, April 4, 1969.

67. *Time*, April 4, 1969.

68. *Time*, August 14, 1972.

69. *Los Angeles Herald-Examiner*, April 20, 1972.

70. *Hollywood Reporter*, August 3, 1972.

71. *Los Angeles Times*, March 28, 1974.

72. *Time*, March 25, 1974.

73. Glenn Collins, "Raquel Welch: 'I Like a Woman with Backbone,'" *New York Times*, May 20, 1982.

74. *Playboy*, January 1970.

75. *Dick Cavett Show*, June 25, 1970.

Chapter IV

1. Rodolfo Acuña, *Occupied America: A History of Chicanos* (New York: Harper & Row, 1988), p. 372.

2. Robyn Karney, ed., *The Movie Stars Story* (New York: Crescent Books, 1984), p. 253.

3. Rosa Linda Fregoso, *The Bronze Screen: Chicana and Chicano Film Culture* (Minneapolis: University of Minnesota Press, 1993), p. 15.

4. Fregoso, *The Bronze Screen*, pp. 93–121.

5. James Diego Vigil, *Barrio Gangs: Street Life and Identity in Southern California* (Austin: University of Texas Press, 1988), p. 49.

6. *New York Times*, March 23, 1979.

7. *Los Angeles Herald-Examiner*, March 23, 1979.

8. *Los Angeles Times*, March 17, 1979.

9. Tony Thomas, *The Films of Marlon Brando* (Secaucus, NJ: Citadel Press, 1973).

10. *Los Angeles Herald-Examiner*, December 18, 1970.

11. "Only Once in a Lifetime," *The Hollywood Reporter*, date unknown.

12. Christine List, *Chicano Images: Refiguring Ethnicity in Mainstream Film* (New York: Garland, 1996), p. 128.

13. *Los Angeles Times*, June 3, 1979.

14. *Variety*, June 14, 1979.

15. Fregoso, The Bronze Screen, p. 86.

16. Franco Solinas, *State of Seige* (New York: Ballantine, 1973).

17. Solinas, State of Seige.

18. *Los Angeles Herald-Examiner*, May 19, 1973. New York Times, April 29, 1979.

19. *New York Times*, April 29, 1979.

20. *Los Angeles Times*, November 20, 1977.

21. *On Location*, September/October 1979.

22. *On Location*, September/October 1979.

23. *On Location*, September/October 1979.

24. *On Location*, September/October 1979.

25. *Millimeter*, March 1976.

26. *Playboy*, July 1977.

27. *Los Angeles Times*, May 28, 1976.

28. *Playboy*, March 1982.

29. *Playboy*, March 1982.

30. *Los Angeles Herald-Examiner*, October 30, 1983.

31. "Bobbie Joe and the Outlaw," *Los Angeles Times*, July 7, 1976.

32. *Los Angeles Times*, March 4, 1990.

33. *Los Angeles Times*, March 4, 1990.

34. *Los Angeles Times TV Guide*, October 30–November 5, 1994.

35. *El Mandato*, November 1992.

36. *New York Times*, March 23, 1979.

37. *Variety*, March 23, 1979.

38. *Los Angeles Times*, March 23, 1979.

39. *Hollywood Drama-Logue*, May 4, 1979.

40. *Hollywood Drama-Logue*, May 4, 1979.

41. Author interview with Danny De La Paz, August 2, 1996.

42. Author interview with Danny De La Paz, August 2, 1996.

43. Author interview with Danny De La Paz, August 2, 1996.

44. *Hollywood Drama-Logue*, May 4, 1979.

45. *Hollywood Drama-Logue*, May 4, 1979.

46. *Village Voice*, March 16, 1992.

47. *El Mandato*, November 1992.

48. Author interview with Danny De La Paz, August 2, 1996.

49. *El Mandato,* November 1992.

50. Author interview with Danny De La Paz, August 2, 1996.

51. *Variety*, September 17, 1971.

52. *Los Angeles Times*, July 19, 1972.

53. Gregg Barrios, "A Cinema of Failure, a Cinema of Hunger: The Films of Efraín Gutiérrez," in Gary Keller, ed., *Chicano Cinema: Research, Reviews and Resources* (Binghamton, NY: Bilingual Review Press, 1985), p. 179.

54. *Lubbock Avalanche-Journal,* August 19, 1979.

55. *Hispanic,* November 1996.

56. Author interview with Efraín Gutiérrez, April 21, 1999.

57. Author interview with Efraín Gutiérrez, April 21, 1999.

58. *Lubbock Avalanche-Journal*, August 19, 1979.

59. *Laredo News*, July 29, 1979.

60. Author interview with Efraín Gutiérrez, April 21, 1999.

61. *Laredo News*, July 29, 1979.

62. *Laredo News,* July 29, 1979.

63. *San Antonio Express-News*, June 11, 1979.

64. Author interview with Efraín Gutiérrez, April 21, 1999.

65. *Los Angeles Herald-Examiner*, November 23, 1972.

66. *Los Angeles Times*, June 15, 1972.

67. *Drama-Logue*, August 17–23, 1989.

68. *Drama-Logue*, August 17–23, 1989.

69. *Playboy*, September 1982.

70. *Playboy*, September 1982.

71. *Playboy*, September 1982.

72. *L.A. Weekly,* August 28–September 3, 1987.

73. *L.A. Weekly,* August 28–September 3, 1987.

74. *Los Angeles Times,* September 6, 1987.

75. *New York Times*, August 16, 1989.

76. *Los Angeles Times,* June 13, 1996.

77. *Premiere*, June 1996.

78. *Los Angeles Times,* June 5, 1994.

79. *Los Angeles Times*, September 24, 1978.

80. *Los Angeles Times*, June 5, 1994.

81. *Los Angeles Times*, June 5, 1994.

82. *Los Angeles Times*, September 24, 1978.

83. *TV Guide*, November 11, 1989.

84. *TV Guide,* November 11, 1989.

85. *Los Angeles Times*, June 5, 1994.

86. *Los Angeles Times,* June 5, 1994.

87. *TV Guide*, November 11, 1989.

88. *TV Guide*, November 11, 1989.

89. *TV Guide*, November 11, 1989.

90. *Los Angeles Herald-Examiner,* December 13, 1978.

91. *Los Angeles Herald-Examiner,* December 13, 1978.

92. *Los Angeles Herald-Examiner,* December 13, 1978.

93. *Los Angeles Herald-Examiner,* December 13, 1978.

94. *Los Angeles Herald-Examiner,* May 31, 1985.

95. *Los Angeles Times*, August 3, 1977.

96. *Los Angeles Herald-Examiner,* May 31, 1985.

97. *Los Angeles Herald-Examiner,* May 31, 1985.

98. *Los Angeles Herald-Examiner,* May 31, 1985.

99. *Los Angeles Times,* December 10, 1970.

100. *Los Angeles Times,* December 10, 1978.

101. *Variety*, August 12, 1970.

102. *Los Angeles Times*, May 14, 1989.

103. *Los Angeles Times*, May 14, 1989.

104. *Los Angeles Times*, May 14, 1989.

105. *Los Angeles Times*, May 14, 1989.

106. *Drama-Lounge*, July 28–August 3, 1988.

107. *Los Angeles Times*, February 3, 1994.

108. *Los Angeles Times*, February 3, 1996.

109. *Los Angeles Times*, February 3, 1996.

110. *New York Times*, November 22, 1996.

111. *New York Times*, November 22, 1996.

112. *New York Times*, November 22, 1996.

113. *Elle*, July 1987.

114. *Los Angeles Times*, November 22, 1996.

115. *New York Times*, November 22, 1996.

116. Author interview with Jesús Salvador Treviño, October 12, 1996.

117. Author interview with Jesús Salvador Treviño, October 12, 1996.

118. Author interview with Jesús Salvador Treviño, October 12, 1996.

119. Barbara Zheutlin, *Creative Differences: Profiles of Hollywood Dissidents* (Boston: South End Press, 1978).

120. *Variety*, June 14, 1979.

121. Zheutlin, *Creative Differences*.

122. Author interview with Jesús Salvador Treviño, October 12, 1996.

123. Author interview with Jesús Salvador Treviño, October 12, 1996.

124. Author interview with Jesús Salvador Treviño, October 12, 1996.

125. Zheutlin, *Creative Differences*.

126. Zheutlin, *Creative Differences*.

127. *Los Angeles Times*, August 24, 1980.

128. Author interview with Jesús Salvador Treviño, October 12, 1996.

129. Author interview with Jesús Salvador Treviño, October 12, 1996.

130. Author interview with Jesús Salvador Treviño, October 12, 1996.

131. Author interview with Jesús Salvador Treviño, October 12, 1996.

132. Enrique Berumen, "Knocking on Resurrection Blvd: A Conversation with Director Jesús Treviño," *Boca* 2, no. 4 (October 2000): 13.

133. Berumen, "Knocking on Resurrection Blvd."

134. Berumen, "Knocking on Resurrection Blvd."

135. *South Bay*, November 1981.

136. *South Bay*, November 1981.

137. *Playboy*, July 1974.

138. *Playboy*, July 1974.

139. *Variety*, August 7, 1974.

140. *Los Angeles Times*, June 8, 1974.

141. *Los Angeles Herald-Examiner*, June 8, 1974.

142. *Newsweek*, August 8, 1974.

143. *Films and Filming*, February 1975.

144. *The Hollywood Reporter*, August 8, 1974.

145. *Los Angeles Times*, August 10, 1974.

146. Author interview with Richard Yniguez, September 11, 1996.

147. *Los Angeles Herald-Examiner*, January 14, 1978.

148. *Los Angeles Herald Examiner*, January 14, 1978.

149. Author interview with Richard Yniguez, September 11, 1996.

150. *Los Angeles Times*, January 13, 1978.

151. *Variety*, March 23, 1979.

152. Author interview with Richard Yniguez, September 11, 1996.

153. *Los Angeles Times*, June 3, 1979.

154. *Variety*, June 4, 1979.

155. Author interview with Richard Yniguez, September 11, 1996.

156. Author interview with Richard Yniguez, September 11, 1996.

157. *Vista Magazine*, March 12, 1989.

158. *Vista Magazine*, March 12, 1989.

Chapter V

1. Rodolfo Acuña, *Occupied America: A History of Chicanos* (New York: Harper & Row, 1988), p. 440.

2. Acuña, *Occupied America*, p. 449.

3. Joel W. Finler, *The Hollywood Story* (New York: Crown, 1988), p. 35.

4. Chon A. Noriega, "Imagined Borders: Locating Chicano Cinema in America/América," in Chon A. Noriega and Ana M. López, eds., *The Ethnic Eye* (Minneapolis: University of Minnesota Press, 1996), p. 4.

5. Silvia Morales, "Chicano-Produced Celluloid Mujeres," in Gary D. Keller, ed., *Chicano Cinema: Research, Reviews, and Resources* (Binghamton, NY: Bilingual Press, 1985), p. 93.

6. Rosa Linda Fregoso, "Chicano/a Film Practices: Confronting the 'Many-Headed Demon of Oppression,'" in Chon A. Noriega, ed., *Chicanos and Film: Representation and Resistance* (Minneapolis: University of Minnesota Press, 1992), p. 169.

7. Lillian Jimenez, "Moving toward the Center: Puerto Rican Cinema in New York," in Chon A. Noriega and Ana M. López, eds., *The Ethnic Eye: Latino Media Arts* (Minneapolis: University of Minnesota Press, 1996), p. 35.

8. Chon A. Noriega, "What Is Chicano Cinema," *Tonantzin* no. 7 (January–February 1990), p. 18.

9. Michael Ybarra and Diane Haithman, "Taking a Look at TV's Racial Picture," *Los Angeles Times*, August 23, 1989.

10. Ybarra and Haithman, "Taking a Look at TV's Racial Picture."

11. Ybarra and Haithman, "Taking a Look at TV's Racial Picture."

12. *Village Voice*, November 18, 1983.

13. *Los Angeles Times*, September 30, 1982.

14. Rosa Linda Fregoso, *The Bronze Screen: Chicana and Chicano Film Culture* (Minneapolis: University of Minnesota Press, 1993), pp. 74–75.

15. *Los Angeles Times*, July 19, 1987.

16. *Los Angeles Times*, July 19, 1987.

17. *New York Times*, July 24, 1987.

18. *New York Times*, July 24, 1987.

19. *Variety*, May 20, 1987.

20. List, *Chicano Images*, p. 31.

21. Christine List, "Self-Directed Stereotyping in the Films of Cheech Marin," In Chon A. Noriega, *Chicanos and Film: Representation and Resistance.*

22. *Americas 2001*, Vol. 1, No. 1, June–July 1987.

23. *L.A. Weekly*, March 10–15, 1989.

24. *Los Angeles Times*, March 18, 1989.

25. List, *The Bronze Screen*, p. 95.

26. *New York Times*, August 23, 1995.

27. *Latino* press kit.

28. *Variety*, may 22, 1985.

29. *Los Angeles Herald-Examiner*, November 13, 1985.

30. *Los Angeles Times*, November 13, 1985.

31. *La Gente*, November 1985.

32. *El Norte* press kit.

33. *Mother Jones,* February/March 1984.

34. *New York Times*, January 11, 1984.

35. *Los Angeles Times*, March 8, 1984.

36. List, *Chicano Images*, pp. 111–112.

37. *L.A. Weekly,* September 13–19, 1985.

38. *Los Angeles Times,* August 24, 1980.

39. Rosa Linda Fregoso, in Gary D. Keller, ed., *Chicano Cinema: Research, Reviews, and Resources* (Binghamton, NY: Bilingual Review Press), p. 148.

40. *Stand and Deliver,* production information packet.

41. *Stand and Deliver,* production information packet, 1988.

42. *Stand and Deliver,* production information packet, 1988.

43. *Los Angeles Times,* March 10, 1988.

44. Mario Barrera, "Story Structure in Latino Feature Films," in Chon A. Noriega, ed., *Chicanos and Film: Representation and Resistance* (Minneapolis: University of Minnesota Press, 1992), p. 236.

45. *Los Angeles Times,* March 3, 1981.

46. *Los Angeles Times,* October 4, 1983.

47. Author interview with María Conchita Alonso, November 3, 1998.

48. *Chicago Tribune,* August 7, 1986.

49. *Chicago Tribune,* August 7, 1986.

50. Author interview with María Conchita Alonso, November 3, 1998.

51. *Boston Globe,* August 7, 1996.

52. *Chicago Tribune,* October 4, 1996.

53. Author interview with María Conchita Alonso, November 3, 1998.

54. *People,* January 15, 1990.

55. *People,* January 15, 1990.

56. *Lone Wolf McQuade* pressbook.

57. *Hollywood Drama-Logue,* June 8, 1989.

58. *Hollywood Drama-Logue,* June 8, 1989.

59. *Hollywood Drama-Logue,* June 8, 1989.

60. *The Hollywood Reporter,* April 18, 1991.

61. *Current Biography,* 1986.

62. *New York Times,* March 19, 1985.

63. *New York Times,* March 19, 1985.

64. *Chicago Tribune,* September 26, 1985.

65. *Chicago Tribune,* September 26, 1985.

66. *Los Angeles Times,* June 7, 1984.

67. *Los Angeles Times,* June 7, 1984.

68. *Los Angeles Times,* June 7, 1984.

69. *Los Angeles Times,* June 8, 1984.

70. *Newsweek,* September 8, 1985.

71. *Los Angeles Times,* June 8, 1984.

72. Los Angeles Times, June 8, 1984.

73. *Village Voice,* April 5, 1988.

74. *Playboy,* July 1989.

75. *Hollywood Drama-Logue,* June 1–7, 1989.

76. *Hollywood Drama-Logue,* June 1–7, 1989.

77. *Hollywood Drama-Logue,* June 1–7, 1989.

78. *The Hollywood Reporter,* April 18, 1991.

79. *Variety,* April 9, 1991.

80. Jennifer Foote, "Hispanic Hollywood," *Newsweek,* August 17, 1987, pp. 66–67.

81. Foote, "Hispanic Hollywood."

82. *Universal News,* December 10, 1981.

83. *Universal News,* December 10, 1981.

84. *Universal News,* December 10, 1981.

85. *Los Angeles Times Magazine,* January 1982.

86. *Los Angeles Times Magazine,* January 1982.

87. *Los Angeles Times,* May 3, 1985.

88. *La Opinión,* May 30, 1995.

89. *New York Times,* April 15, 1995.

90. *La Bamba* pressbook.

91. *La Bamba* pressbook.

92. *La Bamba* pressbook.

93. *Los Angeles Times,* March 28, 1990.

94. *Los Angeles Times,* March 28, 1990.

95. *American Premiere,* August 1990.

96. *American Premiere,* August 1990.

97. *American Premiere,* August 1990.

98. *American Premiere,* August 1990.

99. *New York Times,* November 22, 1996.

100. *Los Angeles Times,* November 22, 1996.

101. *Los Angeles Times,* June 19, 1989.

102. *Drama-Logue,* October 26–November 1, 1989.

103. *Drama-Logue,* October 26–November 1, 1989.

104. *TV Guide,* September 29, 1990.

105. *People Magazine,* May 5, 1986.

106. *Los Angeles Times,* April 15, 1995.

107. *Tolucan/Canyon Crier,* August 17, 1988.

108. *Tolucan/Canyon Crier,* August 17, 1988.

109. *Daily News,* June 29, 1988.

110. *Drama-Logue,* June 29, 1988.

111. Author interview with Silvana Gallardo, April 5, 1991.

112. Author interview with Silvana Gallardo, April 5, 1991.

113. *Drama-Logue,* November 28–December 4, 1985.

114. *Tolucan/Canyon Crier,* August 17, 1985.

115. *Tolucan/Canyon Crier,* August 17, 1985.

116. Author interview with Silvana Gallardo, April 5, 1991.

117. Author interview with Silvana Gallardo, April 5, 1991.

118. Author interview with Silvana Gallardo, April 5, 1991.

119. *Los Angeles Herald-Examiner,* June 5, 1987.

120. *Los Angeles Herald-Examiner,* June 5, 1987.

121. *Los Angeles Herald-Examiner,* June 5, 1987.

122. *Vanity Fair,* November 1986.

123. *New York Times,* August 23, 1985.

124. *Los Angeles Times,* November 22, 1996.

125. *People,* May 2, 1977.

126. *People,* May 2, 1977.

127. *Harper's Bazaar,* March 1983.

128. *Harper's Bazaar,* March 1983.

129. *Cue,* November 28, 1970.

130. *Los Angeles Times,* July 20, 1982.

131. *Los Angeles Times,* July 20, 1982.

132. *Los Angeles Times,* July 20, 1982.

133. *Los Angeles Times,* September 7, 1989.

134. *Los Angeles Times,* September 7, 1989.

135. *Los Angeles Times,* September 7, 1989.

136. *Variety*, June 7, 1989.

137. *Los Angeles Herald-Examiner,* September 8, 1989.

138. *Chicago Sun-Times,*

139. *Los Angeles Times,* September 7, 1989.

140. *Los Angeles Times,* October 25, 1994.

141. *Los Angeles Times TV Guide,* September 11–17, 1994

142. *Boston Globe,* September 20, 1995.

143. *Los Angeles Times,* October 25, 1994.

144. Author interview with Alma Martínez, September 12, 1996.

145. *Variety,* November 26, 1988.

146. *Variety,* January 16, 1991.

147. *Los Angeles Times,* January 11, 1991.

148. Author interview with Alma Martínez, September 12, 1996.

149. Author interview with Alma Martínez, September 12, 1996.

150. Author interview with Alma Martínez, September 12, 1996.

151. *La Bamba* pressbook

152. *Variety,* May 20, 1987.

153. *La Bamba* pressbook.

154. Jennifer Foote, "Hispanic Hollywood," *Newsweek,* August 17, 1987, pp. 66–67.

155. *LA Weekly,* September 9–15, 1994.

156. *New York Times,* May 14, 1999.

157. *Drama-Logue,* February 8–14, 1996.

158. *El Norte* press kit.

159. *Mother Jones,* February/March, 1984.

160. *New York Times,* January 11, 1984.

161. *Los Angeles Times,* March 8, 1984.

162. *Los Angeles Times,* June 4, 1995.

163. *Los Angeles Times,* May 3, 1995.

164. *Los Angeles Times,* August 28, 1998.

165. *Los Angeles Herald-Examiner,* March 8, 1988.

166. *Los Angeles Times,* March 19, 1989.

167. *Los Angeles Times,* March 19, 1989.

168. *Los Angeles Times,* March 19, 1989.

169. *Los Angeles Times,* March 19, 1989.

170. *Los Angeles Times,* March 19, 1989.

171. Guy Garcia, "Frente a Frente con Edward James Olmos," *Mas,* March/April, 1991, pp. 58–64.

172. Garcia, "Frente a Frente con Edward James Olmos."

173. *Premiere,* April 1992.

174. *The Hollywood Reporter,* March 16, 1992.

175. *Village Voice,* March 13–19, 1992.

176. *Variety,* March 16, 1992.

177. *Los Angeles Times,* June 4, 1995.

178. *Los Angeles Times,* May 3, 1995.

179. *LA Weekly,* March 11, 1988.

180. *Drama-Logue,* October 1, 1987.

181. *New York Times,* May 22, 1998.

182. *New York Times,* September 25, 1996.

183. *Variety,* May 20, 1987.

184. *Los Angeles Times,* June 21, 1996.

185. Jennifer Foote, "Hispanic Hollywood," *Newsweek,* August 17, 1996, pp. 66–67.

186. Foote, "Hispanic Hollywood."

187. Foote, "Hispanic Hollywood."

188. *La Opinión,* June 6, 1996.

189. *Los Angeles Times,* March 14, 1997.

190. Associated Press, June 18, 1988.

191. Author interview with Tony Plana, January 6, 1996.

192. *Los Angeles Times,* July 6, 1987.

193. Author interview with Tony Plana, July 6, 1996.

194. *Drama-Logue,* January 8–14, 1987.

195. *Drama-Logue,* January 8–14, 1987.

196. *Variety,* May 22, 1985.

197. *Drama-Logue,* January 8–14, 1987.

198. *Drama-Logue,* January 8–14, 1987.

199. Author interview with Tony Plana, January 6, 1996.

200. Author interview with Tony Plana, January 6, 1996.

201. Author interview with Tony Plana, January 6, 1996.

202. Author interview with Tony Plana, January 6, 1996.

203. *The Hollywood Reporter,* June 5, 1996.

204. *La Opinión,* May 4, 1995.

205. *Los Angeles Times,* August 7, 1992.

206. *Born in East L.A.* pressbook.

207. *Drama-Logue,* August 14–20, 1986.

208. *Drama-Logue,* August 14–20, 1986.

209. *TV Guide,* February 3, 1990.

210. *Los Angeles Times,* May 12, 1994.

211. *Los Angeles Times,* May 12, 1994.

212. *Los Angeles Times,* May 13, 1995.

213. *TV Guide,* February 3, 1990.

214. *L.A. Weekly,* March 10–16, 1989.

215. *Los Angeles Times,* September 18, 1998.

216. *Boston Globe,* July 15, 1990.

217. *American Premiere,* August 1980.

218. *American Premiere,* August 1980.

219. *American Premiere,* August 1990.

220. *American Premiere,* August 1990.

221. *Los Angeles Daily News,* March 15, 1991.

222. *American Premiere,* August 1990.

223. *After Dark,* March 1981.

224. *Us,* June 25, 1990.

225. *Us,* June 25, 1990.

226. *Us,* June 25, 1990.

227. *Us,* June 25, 1990.

228. *Box-Office,* May 1981.

229. *Playboy,* May 1981.

230. *US,* June 25, 1990.

231. *Newsweek,* June 11, 1990.

232. *Us,* June 25, 1990.

233. Author interview with Luis Valdez, April 2, 1999.

234. uthor interview with Luis Valdez, April 2, 1999.

235. Author interview with Luis Valdez, April 2, 1999.

236. Author interview with Luis Valdez, April 2, 1999.

237. Author interview with Luis Valdez, April 2, 1999.

238. *New York Times,* February 27, 1981.

239. Author interview with Luis Valdez, April 2, 1999.

240. *Los Angeles Times,* July 29, 1990.

241. *Los Angeles Times,* July 29, 1990.

242. *Los Angeles Times*, July 29, 1990.

243. *Los Angeles Times*, July 29, 1990.

244. *Los Angeles Times*, July 29, 1990.

245. Author interview with Luis Valdez, April 2, 1999.

246. *Los Angeles Times*, July 29, 1990.

247. July 29, 1990.

248. *Los Angeles Times*, July 29, 1990.

249. *Los Angeles Times*, July 29, 1990.

250. Author interview with Luis Valdez, April 2, 1999.

251. Author interview with Luis Valdez, April 2, 1999.

Chapter VI

1. *Los Angeles Times,* April 1, 1991.

2. *Los Angeles Times*, April 1, 1991.

3. *Boston Globe*, March 3, 1999.

4. *Los Angeles Times,* March 11, 1981.

5. *Los Angeles Times*, January 25, 1991.

6. *Time*, May 14, 1990.

7. *La Opinión*, January 11, 1990.

8. *Los Angeles Times*, December 7, 1990.

9. *Los Angles Times*, September 3, 1990.

10. *Los Angeles Times*, December 12, 1990.

11. *Los Angeles Times*, May 14, 1990.

12. *Los Angles Times*, August 29, 1990.

13. *The Hollywood Reporter*, April 18, 1991.

14. *TV Guide*, June 29, 1991.

15. *TV Guide*, June 29, 1991.

16. *Los Angeles Times*, "Television Guide," August 18–24, 1991.

17. *Los Angles Times*, September 11, 1991.

18. *TV Guide*, August 31, 1991.

19. *Los Angeles Times*, April 14, 1995.

20. *Los Angeles Times*, May 12, 1995.

21. Henry Giroux, "Race, Pedagogy, and Whiteness in Dangerous Minds," *Cineaste* 22, no. 4 (1997), p. 49.

22. *Los Angeles Times*, July 30, 1997.

23. *Los Angeles Times*, March 14, 1997.

24. *Los Angeles Times*, April 4, 1994.

25. *Los Angeles Times*, August 3, 1994.

26. *Hollywood Drama-Logue*, May 9–15, 1996.

27. *Los Angeles Times*, November 22, 1996.

28. *Los Angeles Times*, September 29, 1996.

29. *Los Angeles Times*, September 24, 1999.

30. *L.A. Weekly*, November 5–11, 1999.

31. *Los Angeles Times*, September 8, 1994.

32. Screen Actors Guild, 1998.

33. *Los Angeles Times*, July 7, 1999.

34. *Los Angeles Times*, July 20, 1999.

35. *Los Angeles Times*, September 11, 1999.

36. Elizabeth Jensen and Kevin Baxter, "Univision: TV Success Story That Will Last?" *Los Angeles Times,* July 13, 1999. Spanish-language television in the United States is dominated by three networks: the Los Angeles–based Univision, the Mexico City–based Telemundo, and Grupo Televisa. By far the most successful is Univision. According to Nielsen Media Research, the network maintains 92 percent of the audience that watches Spanish-language television. This translates into 8.3 million households and some 28.3 million viewers ages two and older. For 1998, Univision reported revenue of $577.1 million. This was up 25.6 percent from the previous year, when their profit was $104.4 million on operating revenue of $459.7 million.

37. Cindy Rodriguez, "How Can Latino Viewers Get Their Screens to Fade to Brown?" *Boston Globe*, September 26, 1999.

38. *Village Voice*, March 13, 1992.

39. *Variety*, March 16, 1992.

40. *The* Hollywood Reporter, March 9, 1997.

41. Christine List, *Chicano Images Refiguring Ethnicity in Mainstream Film* (New York: Garland, 1996), p. 132.

42. *New York Times*, April 30, 1992.

43. *Los Angeles Times*, April 30, 1992.

44. *Variety*, May 23, 1994.

45. *New York Times*, October 14, 1994.

46. *Drama-Logue*, November 10, 1994.

47. *Los Angeles Times*, October 14, 1994.

48. *Variety*, September 14, 1993.

49. *New York Times*, February 26, 1993.

50. *New York Times*, July 17, 1998.

51. *Boston Globe*, July 17, 1998.

52. *Men with Guns* press kit.

53. *The Hollywood Reporter*, September 15, 1997.

54. *New York Times*, March 6, 1998.

55. Joan W. Moore, *Going Down to the Barrio: Homeboys and Homegirls in Change* (Philadelphia: Temple University Press, 1991), p. 48.

56. *Variety*, July 7, 1993.

57. *New York Times*, July 15, 1994.

58. *Los Angeles Times*, July 22, 1994.

59. *Los Angeles Times*, May 3, 1995.

60. *La Opinión*, February 13, 1996.

61. *New York Times*, February 14, 1996.

62. *Los Angeles Times*, October 18, 1996.

63. *Los Angeles Times*, March 16, 1997.

64. *People*, December 8, 1996.

65. *New York Times*, March 21, 1997.

66. *Boston Globe*, March 21, 1997.

67. *Los Angeles Times*, July 23, 1997.

68. *Star Maps* press kit.

69. Author interview with Miguel Arteta, June 20, 1998.

70. *Los Angeles Times*, July 20, 1997.

71. Author interview with Miguel Arteta, June 20, 1997.

72. *Los Angeles Times*, July 23, 1997.

73. *Star Maps* press kit.

74. Author interview with Miguel Arteta, June 28, 1998.

75. *Los Angeles Times*, August 21, 1995.

76. *Variety*, May 2, 1995.

77. *Los Angeles Times*, May 10, 1996.

78. *New York Times*, August 21, 1995.

79. *New York Times*, October 22, 1999.

80. *Los Angeles Times*, December 24, 1999.

81. *Los Angeles Times*, December 25, 1992.

82. *Los Angeles Times*, December 25, 1992.

83. *Los Angeles Times*, December 25, 1992.

84. *Los Angeles Times*, April 30, 1993.

85. *New York Times*, April 30, 1993.

86. *Los Angeles Times*, October 15, 1995.

87. *Los Angeles Times*, October 15, 1995.

88. Author interview with Lumi Cavazos, July 30, 1996.

89. *Los Angeles Times*, October 17, 1994.

90. Author interview with Lumi Cavazos, October 17, 1996.

91. *Time*, April 3, 1983.

92. Author interview with Lumi Cavazos, October 17, 1996.

93. Author interview with Lumi Cavazos, July 30, 1996.

94. *Los Angeles Times*, October 17, 1994.

95. *La Opinión*, September 4, 1994.

96. *Los Angeles Times*, August 29, 1996.

97. *Los Angeles Times*, August 29, 1996.

98. *China Moon* press kit.

99. *Newsweek*, January 15, 1996.

100. *Newsweek*, January 15, 1996.

101. *Boston Globe*, September 5, 1995.

102. *Los Angeles Times*, August 22, 1997.

103. *Los Angeles Times TV Times*, February 9–15, 1992.

104. *Venice*, November 1996.

105. *Los Angeles Times TV Times*, February 9–15, 1992.

106. *Venice,* November 1996.

107. Lorenzo Munoz, "The Warrior Within," *Los Angeles Times*, September 5, 1999.

108. *Los Angeles Times*, July 23, 1997.

109. Author interview with Rubén González, December 27, 1997.

110. Author interview with Rubén González, December 27, 1997.

111. Author interview with Rubén González, December 27, 1997.

112. *Los Angeles Times*, October 17, 1992.

113. *Los Angeles Times,* October 17, 1992.

114. *Premiere*, March 1996.

115. *Boston Globe*, March 14, 1997.

116. *Los Angeles Times*, June 19, 1996.

117. *Los Angeles Times*, February 26, 1997.

118. *Boston Herald*, February 14, 1997.

119. *Boston Herald*, February 14, 1997.

120. *Los Angeles Times*, August 28, 1998.

121. *Los Angeles Times*, July 13, 1999.

122. *Los Angeles Times*, July 13, 1999.

123. *Los Angeles Times*, June 30, 1999.

124. *New York Times*, July 16, 1999.

125. *Los Angeles Times*, July 17, 1999.

126. *Boston Globe*, November 12, 1999.

127. *Los Angeles Times*, July 27, 1997.

128. *Los Angeles Times*, July 27, 1997.

129. *Los Angeles Times,* July 27, 1997.

130. *Vibe*, June/July 1997.

131. *La Opinión*, August 4, 1994.

132. *Los Angeles Times*, February 21, 1997.

133. *Buzz*, April 1997.

134. *Buzz,* April 1997.

135. *Los Angeles Times*, March 21, 1997.

136. *New York Times*, March 31, 1997.

137. *Boston Globe*, March 21, 1997.

138. *Time,* March 24, 1997.

139. *New York Times*, June 26, 1999.

140. *Vibe,* June/July 1997.

141. *Los Angeles Times*, March 30, 1999.

142. *Los Angeles Times*, May 30, 1999.

143. Author interview with Sal Lopez, August 27, 1996.

144. Author interview with Sal Lopez, August 27, 1996.

145. Author interview with Sal Lopez, August 27, 1996.

146. *Men with Guns* press kit.

147. *Men with Guns* press kit.

148. Author interview with Annette Murphy, September 10, 1997.

149. Author interview with Lupe Ontiveros, August 7, 1996.

150. Author interview with Lupe Ontiveros, August 7, 1996.

151. Author interview with Lupe Ontiveros, August 7, 1996.

152. Author interview with Lupe Ontiveros, August 7, 1996.

153. Author interview with Lupe Ontiveros, August 7, 1996.

154. *Parade,* September 19, 1993.

155. *Long Beach Press-Telegram*, April 6, 1992.

156. *Long Beach Press-Telegram*, April 6, 1992.

157. *Newsweek*, May 4, 1992.

158. *Newsweek*, May 4, 1992.

159. *Los Angeles Times*, November 15, 1993.

160. *Time*, November 18, 1993.

161. *Los Angeles Times,* September 29, 1994.

162. *Parade*, September 19, 1993.

163. *Los Angeles Times*, September 27, 1996.

164. *New York Times*, April 25, 1997.

165. *Boston Globe*, February 19, 1999.

166. *Boston Globe*, April 23, 1999.

167. *Miami Herald*, June 8, 1996.

168. *Time*, March 8, 1993.

169. *Los Angeles Times,* February 26, 1993.

170. *New York Times*, February 26, 1993.

171. *Time,* March 8, 1993.

172. *Los Angeles Times*, November 27, 1984.

173. *Los Angeles Times*, November 27, 1994.

174. *Los Angeles Times*, November 27, 1994.

175. *Daily Variety*, May 25, 1995.

176. *Profile,* November 1995.

177. Author interview with Julieta Rosen, September 21, 1998.

178. Author interview with Julieta Rosen, September 21, 1998.

179. Ephraim Katz, *The Film Encyclopedia* (New York: HarperCollins, 1994).

180. *Los Angeles Times*, September 5, 1997.

181. *Los Angeles Times*, September 11, 1998.

182. *Drama-Logue*, October 20–26, 1994.

183. *Variety*, May 20, 1994.

184. *Playboy*, October 1996.

185. *Los Angeles Times TV Times*, November 6–12, 1994.

186. *Los Angeles Times TV Times*, November 6–12, 1994.

187. *Playboy*, October 1996.

188. *Playboy*, October 1996.

189. *Playboy*, October 1996.

190. *Latin Style,* December/January 1998.

191. *People,* May 31, 1999.

192. *Drama-Logue,* November 20–26, 1986.

193. *Drama-Logue,* October 20–26, 1994.

194. *Drama-Logue,* October 20–26, 1994.

195. *Drama-Logue,* October 20–26, 1994.

196. *New York Times,* November 14, 1994.

197. *Variety,* May 20, 1994.

198. *TV Guide,* November 2, 1996.

199. *Los Angeles Times,* May 20, 1996.

Chapter VII

1. On June 26, 2012, the United States Supreme Court struck down three measures of SB 1070, but kept one section "which directs police to check the immigration status of people they suspect are in this country illegally when they make lawful stops for other reasons." David G. Savage, "Supreme Court Rejects Most of Immigration Law." *Los Angeles Times,* June 26, 2012.

2. "A Lesson for Arizona," *Los Angeles Times,* June 10, 2011. Ethnic studies were established in the 1960s as an effort to educate students about the diverse cultural history of the United States. The Arizona law targeted Chicano studies specifically and no other ethnic studies programs such as Native American studies or African-American studies.

3. Diane Ravitch, *Reign of Terror: The Hoax of the Privatization Movement and the Dangers to America's Public Schools* (New York: Alfred A. Knopf, 2013), 4.

4. *Los Angeles Times,* April 16, 2010.

5. "Controversy Surrounds 'Colombiana' Film for Stereotyping," News Taco, August 16, 2011.

6. *Los Angeles Times,* March 16, 2012.

7. *Los Angeles Times,* May 31, 2002.

8. Chris Johnson, "Book-to-Film Heroine," *Los Angeles Times,* March 11, 2013.

9. Chris Johnson, "Book-to-Film Heroine," *Los Angeles Times,* March 11, 2013.

10. "Box-Office Mojo Franchises," boxofficemojo.com, accessed March 18, 2013.

11. Tracy Wilkerson, "Diego Luna's Cesar Chavez Movie Marches on in Mexico," *Los Angeles Times,* July 1, 2012.

12. *Los Angeles Times,* March 27, 2014.

13. *New York Times,* March 27, 2014.

14. Reed Johnson, "Mexican Stars Chasing the Hollywood Dream," *Los Angeles Times,* July 10, 2011.

15. Christine Hoag, "Actores Protestan por Falta de Apoyo," *La Opinión,* July 14, 2011.

16. John Horn, Nicole Sperling, and Doug Smith, "Unmasking the Academy," *Los Angeles Times,* February 19, 2012.

17. Ben Fritz, "The Revolution Will Be Downloaded," *Los Angeles Times,* September 25, 2012.

18. Ben Fritz, "The World Is Watching (They Hope)," *Los Angeles Times,* April 28, 2012.

19. *New York Times,* October 6, 2000.

20. *New York Times,* June 23, 2011.

21. *New York Times,* December 12, 2008.

22. Stephen Farber, "Salma and Frida," *The BookLA.com,* http://the bookla.com/s_2000_hayek.html.

23. *New York Times,* September 29, 2000.

24. *New York Times,* July 16, 2004.

25. *New York Times,* September 24, 2004.

26. *New York Times,* December 12, 2001.

27. *New York Times,* March 22, 2002.

28. *New York Times,* December 27, 2000.

Bibliography

Acuña, Rodolfo F. *Anything But Mexican: Chicanos in Contemporary Los Angeles.* New York: Verso, 1998.

_____. *Occupied America: A History of Chicanos.* New York: HarperCollins, 1998.

Anderson, John Lee. *Che Guevara: A Revolutionary Life.* New York: Grove Press, 1997.

Aparicio, Francis R., and Susana Chavez-Silverman, eds. *Tropicalization: Transcultural Representations of Latinidad.* Hanover, NH: University Press of New England, 1997.

Balderrama, Francisco E., and Raymond Rodriguez. *Decade of Betrayal.* Albuquerque: University of New Mexico Press, 1996.

Basinger, Jeanine. *Silent Stars.* New York: Alfred A. Knopf, 1999.

Bergan, Ronald. *The United Artists Story.* New York: Crown, 1988.

Berman, Karl. *Under the Big Stick: Nicaragua and the United States Since 1848.* Boston: Compita, 1986.

Berumen, Frank Javier Garcia. *Brown Celluloid: Latino/a Film Icons and Images in the Hollywood Film Industry, Volume 1 (1894–1959).* New York: Vantage Press, 2003.

_____. *The Chicano/Hispanic Image in American Film.* New York: Vantage Press, 1996.

_____. *Ramon Novarro: The Life and Films of the First Latino Hollywood Superstar.* New York: Vantage Press, 2001.

Blum, Daniel C. *The New Pictorial History of the Talkies.* New York: G.P. Putnam's Sons, 1968.

_____. *A Pictorial History of the Silent Screen.* New York: G.P. Putnam's Sons, 1953.

Blum, Daniel C. *Screen World 1949–1967.* New York: Crown, 1967.

"Bobbie Joe and the Outlaw." *Los Angeles Times,* July 7, 1976.

Branch, Taylor. *Parting the Waters: America in the King Years, 1954–1963.* New York: Simon & Schuster, 1998.

Castañeda, Jorge. *Compañero: The Life and Death of Che Guevara.* New York: Vintage, 1998.

"Controversy Surrounds 'Colombiana' Film for Stereotyping." News Taco, August 16, 2011.

Del Castillo, Griswold, and Arnulfo De León. *North to Aztlán: A History of Mexican Americans in the United States.* New York: Twayne, 1996.

Delgado, Richard, and Jean Stefancic, eds. *The Latino/a Condition: A Critical Reader.* New York: New York University Press, 1998.

Eames, John Douglas. *The MGM Story.* New York: Crown, 1982.

_____. *The Paramount Story.* New York: Crown, 1985.

Fairbanks, Douglas, Jr. *The Fairbanks Album.* Boston: New York Graphic Society, 1975.

Farber, Stephen. *Salma and Frida.* The BookLA. com. http//the bookla.com/s_2000_hayek.html.

Farnsworth, Rodney. "John Wayne's Epic of Contradiction." *Film Quarterly* 52, no. 2 (Winter 1998–99).

Finler, Joel W. *The Hollywood Story.* New York: Crown, 1998.

_____. *The Movie Directors Story.* New York: Crescent Books, 1985.

Foote, Jennifer. "Hispanic Hollywood." *Newsweek,* August 17, 1987.

"For a Few Dollars More." *Los Angeles Herald-Examiner,* June 12, 1967.

"For a Few Dollars More," *New York Daily News,* July 4, 1967.

"For a Few Dollars More." *New York Times,* July 4, 1967.

Franklin, Joe. *Classics of the Silent Screen.* New York: Cadillac, 1959.

Frayling, Christopher. *Sergio Leone: Something to Do with Death.* London: Faber and Faber, 2000.

_____. *Spaghetti Westerns: Cowboys and Europeans from Karl May to Sergio Leone.* London: I. B. Tauris, 1998.

Fregoso, Rosa Linda. *The Bronze Screen: Chicana and Chicano Film Culture.* Minneapolis: University of Minnesota Press, 1993.

Fritz, Ben. "The Revolution Will Be Downloaded." *Los Angeles Times,* September 25, 2012.

_____. "The World Is Watching (They Hope)." *Los Angeles Times,* April 28, 2012.

García, Mario T. *Memories of Chicano History: The*

Life and Times of Bert Corona. Berkeley: University of California Press, 1994.

_____. *Mexican Americans: Leadership, Ideology and Identity, 1930–1960*. New Haven: Yale University Press, 1989.

Giroux, Henry. "Race, Pedagogy, and Whiteness in *Dangerous Minds*." *Cineaste* 22, no. 4 (1997).

Gómez-Quiñonez, Juan. *Chicano Politics: Reality and Promise, 1940–1990*. Albuquerque: University of New Mexico Press, 1990.

_____. *Roots of Chicano Politics, 1600–1940*. Albuquerque: University of New Mexico Press.

Gonzalez, Gilbert G. *Chicano Education in the Era of Segregation*. Philadelphia: The Balch Institute Press, 1990.

González, Juan. *Harvest of Empire : A History of Latinos in America*. New York: Viking, 2000.

Gutiérrez, José Ángel. *The Making of a Chicano Militant: Lessons from Cristal*. Madison: University of Wisconsin Press, 1998.

Heinink, Juan B., and Robert G. Dickson. *Cita en Hollywood: Antología de las Películas Norteamericanas Habladas en Español*. Bilbao, Spain: Ediciones Mensajero, 1990.

Hirschhorn, Clive. *The Universal Story*. London: Octopus Books, 1985.

_____. *The Warner Brothers Story*. New York: Crown, 1979.

Hoag, Christine. "Actores Protestan por Falta de Apoyo." *La Opinión*, July 14, 2011.

Horn, John, Nicole Sperling, and Doug Smith. "Unmasking the Academy." *Los Angeles Times*, February 19, 2012.

Jefferson, Thomas. *Notes on the State of Virginia*, *Query XIV*. In *Thomas Jefferson: Writings: Autobiography / Notes on the State of Virginia / Public and Private Papers / Addresses / Letters*. Merrill D. Peterson, ed. New York: Library of America, 1984.

Jensen, Elizabeth, and Kevin Baxter. "Univision: TV Success Story That Will Last?" *Los Angeles Times*, July 13, 1999.

Jewell, Richard B., and Vernon Harbin. *The RKO Story*. London: Arlington House, 1982.

Johnson, Chris. "Book-to-Film Heroine." *Los Angeles Times*, March 11, 2013.

Johnson, Paul. *A History of the American People*. New York: HarperCollins, 1999.

Johnson, Reed. "Mexican Stars Chasing the Hollywood Dream." *Los Angeles Times*, July 10, 2011.

Karney, Robyn, ed. *The Movie Stars Story*. New York: Crescent Books, 1984.

Kasson, Joy S. *Buffalo Bill's Wild West: Celebrity, Memory, and Popular History*. New York: Hill & Wang, 2000.

Katz, Ephraim. *The Film Encyclopedia*. New York: HarperPerennial, 1998.

Keller, Gary D. *A Biographical Handbook of Hispanics and United States Film*. Tempe: Bilingual Press/Editorial Bilingue, 1997.

Keller, Gary D., ed. *Chicano Cinema: Research, Reviews, and Resources*. Binghamton, NY: Bilingual Press, 1985.

King, John, Ana M. López, and Manuel Alvarado, eds. *Mediating Two Worlds: Cinematic Encounters in the Americas*. London: British Film Institute, 1993.

Lamparski, Richard. *Whatever Became Of ... ? Volume 8*. New York: Crown, 1982.

"A Lesson for Arizona." *Los Angeles Times*, June 10, 2011.

List, Christine. *Chicano Images: Refiguring Ethnicity in Mainstream Film*. New York: Garland, 1996.

Maciel, David R. *El Bandolero, el Pocho, y la Raza: Imágenes Cinematográficas del Chicano*. Albuquerque: University of New Mexico Press, 1994.

Maltin, Leonard. *The Disney Films*. New York: Crown, 1984.

Martinez, Joel L., and Richard H. Mendoza, eds. *Chicano Psychology*. New York: Academic Press, 1984.

McGilligan, Patrick, and Paul Buhle. *Tender Comrades: A Backstory of the Hollywood Blacklist*. New York: St. Martin's Press, 1997.

McWilliams, Carey. *North from Mexico: The Spanish-Speaking Peoples of the United States*. New York: Greenwood Press, 1968.

Mirande, Alfredo, and Evangelina Enríquez. *La Chicana: The Mexican-American Women*. Chicago: University of Chicago Press, 1979.

Monaco, James, and the editors of Baseline. *The Encyclopedia of Film*. New York: Perigee Books, 1991.

Moore, Joan W. *Going Down to the Barrio: Homeboys and Homegirls in Change*. Philadelphia: Temple University Press, 1991.

_____. *Homeboys, Gangs, and Prison in the Barrios of Los Angeles*. Philadelphia: Temple University Press, 1978.

Mora, Carl J. *Mexican Cinema: Reflections of a Society, 1896–1980*. Berkeley: University of California Press, 1982.

Munoz, Lorenzo. "The Warrior Within." *Los Angeles Times*, September 5, 1999.

Nash, Jay Robert, and Stanley Ralph Ross. *The Motion Picture Guide, 1927–1983*. Chicago: Cinebooks, 1985.

Nevares, Beatriz Reyes. *The Mexican Cinema: Interviews with Thirteen Directors*. Albuquerque: University of New Mexico Press, 1979.

Nieto, Sonia. "Fact and Fiction: Stories of Puerto Ricans in the U.S. Schools." In *Harvard Educational*

Review, Symposium: Colonialism, and Working-Class Resistance: Puerto Rican Education in the United States 69, no. 2 (Summer 1998).

Noriega, Chon A. *Shot in America: Television, the State, and the Rise of Chicano Cinema*. Minneapolis: University of Minnesota, 2000.

Noriega, Chon A., ed. *Chicanos and Film: Representation and Resistance*. Minneapolis: University of Minnesota Press, 1992.

Noriega, Chon A., and Ana M. López, eds. *The Ethnic Eye: Latino Media Arts*. Minneapolis: University of Minnesota Press, 1996.

"One-Eyed Jacks." *New York Times,* March 31, 1961.

Paranaguá, Paulo Antonio, ed. *Mexican Cinema*. London: British Film Institute, 1995.

Parish, James Robert, and William T. Leonard. *Hollywood Players: The Thirties*. Carlsbad, NJ: Rainbow Books, 1976.

Parish, James Robert, and Michael R. Pitts. *The Great Western Pictures*. Metuchen, NJ: Scarecrow Press, 1976.

Pettit, Arthur. *Images of the Mexican-American in Fiction and Film*. College Station: Texas A&M, 1980.

Quinlan, David. *Quinlan's Illustrated Registry of Film Stars*. New York: Henry Holt , 1991.

Riera, Emilio García. *Emilio Fernández: 1904–1986*. Guadalajara, Mexico: University of Guadalajara, 1987.

_____. *Historia Documental del Cine Mexicano, 1946–1965*. Guadalajara, Mexico: University of Guadalajara, 1992.

_____. *México Visto por el Cine Extranjero, Volúmenes 1–5*. Guadalajara, Mexico: University of Guadalajara, 1987.

Ringgold, Gene, and DeWitt Bodee. *The Films of Cecil B. DeMille*. New York: Citadel Press, 1969.

Rodriguez, Cindy. "How Can Latino Viewers Get Their Screens to Fade to Brown?" *Boston Globe*, September 26, 1999.

Rosebaum, Robert J. *Mexican Resistance in the Southwest*. Dallas: Southern Methodist University Press, 1987.

San Miguel, Guadalupe, Jr., and Richard R. Valencia. "From the Treaty of Guadalupe Hidalgo to Hopewood: The Educational Plight and Struggle of Mexican Americans in the Southwest." *Harvard Educational Review* 68 (Fall 1998): 353–412.

Savage, David G. "Supreme Court Rejects Most of Immigration Law." *Los Angeles Times,* June 26, 2012.

Sennett, Ted. *Warner Brothers Presents*. New York: Castle Books, 1971.

Shipman, David. *The Great Movie Stars: The Golden Years*. New York: Little, Brown, 1995.

_____. *The Great Movie Stars: The International Years*. New York: Little, Brown, 1995.

Solinas, Franco. *State of Siege*. New York: Ballantine, 1973.

Stavans, Ilan. *The Hispanic Condition: Reflections & Identity in America*. New York: HarperPerennial, 1995.

Suárez-Orozco, Carola, and Marcelo Suárez-Orozco. *Transformations: Immigration, Family Life and Achievement Motivation among Latino Adolescents*. Stanford: Stanford University Press, 1995.

Suárez-Orozco, Marcelo, ed. *Crossings: Mexican Immigration in Interdisciplinary Perspectives*. Cambridge: Harvard University, 1998.

Taibo, Paco Ignacio, I. *"Indio" Fernández: El Cine por Mis Pistolas (Genio y Figura)*. Mexico City: Editorial Joaquín Mortiz, S.A., 1986.

Taibo, Paco Ignacio, II. *Guevara: Also Known As Che*. New York: St. Martin's Press, 1997.

Thomas, Tony. *The Films of Marlon Brando*. Secaucus, NJ: Citadel Press, 1973.

Thomas, Tony, and Aubrey Solomon. *The Films of 20th Century–Fox: A Pictorial History* Secaucus, NJ: Citadel Press, 1985.

Trelles Plazaola, Luis. *Imágenes Cambiantes: Descubrimiento, Conquista, y Colonización de América Hispana Vista por el Cine de Ficción y Largometraje*. San Juan: Editorial de la Universidad de Puerto Rico, 1996.

Tusher, William. "Sy Barlett Calls Mexico Banning of 'Che' Unfair." *Hollywood Reporter,* September 5, 1967.

Valdez, Luis. *Zoot Suit and Other Plays*. Houston: Arte Público Press, 1992.

Vásquez, Blanca, ed. "Focus en Foco: Latinos and the Media." *Centro* 3, no. 1 (1998).

Vermilye, Jerry. *The Films of the Twenties*. Secaucus, NJ: Citadel Press, 1985.

Vigil, James Diego. *Barrio Gangs: Street Life and Identity in Southern California*. Austin: University of Texas Press, 1998.

_____. *From Indians to Chicanos: The Dynamics of Mexican-American Culture*. Prospect Heights, IL: Waveland Press, 1996.

Villarreal, Robert E., Norma G. Hernandez, and Howard D. Neighbor, eds. *Latino Empowerment: Progress, Problems, and Prospects*. New York: Praeger, 1988.

Weaver, John T. *Forty Years of Screen Credits 1929–1969*, vols. 1 and 2. Metuchen, NJ: Scarecrow Press, 1970.

Webb, Walter Prescott. *Texas Rangers: A Century of Frontier Defense*, 2d ed. Austin: University of Texas Press, 1965.

Weber, David. *Foreigners in Their Native Land: Historical Roots of the Mexican Americans*. Albuquerque: University of New Mexico Press, 2003.

Willis, John. *Screen World, 1949–1997.* New York: Crown, 1997.

Wlaschin, Ken. *The Illustrated History of the World's Great Movie Stars and Their Films: From 1900 to the Present Day.* New York: Harmony Books, 1983.

Woll, Allen L. *The Latin Image in American Film.* Los Angeles: UCLA Latin American Center Publications, 1980.

Ybarra, Michael, and Diane Haithman. "Taking a Look at TV's Racial Picture." *Los Angeles Times,* August 23, 1989.

Zheutlin, Barbara. *Creative Differences: Profiles of Hollywood Dissidents.* Boston: South End Press, 1978.

Zou, Yali, and Enrique Trueba, eds. *Ethnic Identity and Power: Cultural Contexts of Political Action in School and Society.* New York: State University of New York Press, 1998.

Interviews

Alonso, María Conchita. November 3, 1998.

Arteta, Miguel. June 20, 1998.

Cavazos, Lumi. July 30, 1996.

De La Paz, Danny. August 2, 1996.

Figueroa, Efrain. September 2, 1997.

Gallardo, Silvana. April 5, 1991.

González, Rubén. December 27, 1996.

Gutiérrez, Efraín. April 21, 1999.

Kohner, Lupita Tovar. January 13 and September 22, 1998.

Lopez, Sal. August 27, 1996.

Martínez, Alma. September 12, 1996.

Montalbán, Ricardo. August 21, 1997.

Morones, Bob. January 14, 1997.

Murphy, Annette. September 10, 1997.

Olmos, Edward James. December 1996.

Ontiveros, Lupe. August 7, 1996.

Pellicer, Pilar. November 25, 1993.

Plana, Tony. January 6, 1996.

Revueltas, Rosaura. February 14, 1992.

Rosen, Julieta. September 21, 1998.

Treviño, Jesús Salvador. October 12, 1996.

Valdez, Luis. April 2, 1999.

Yniguez, Richard. September 11, 1996.

Newspapers

Boston Globe
El Mandato
La Opinión
L.A. Weekly
Laredo News
Los Angeles Free Press
Los Angeles Herald-Examiner
Los Angeles Times
Long Beach Press-Telegram
Lubbock Avalanche-Journal
Miami Herald
New York Daily News
New York Times
San Antonio Express-News
Tolucan Canyon Crier
UCLA La Gente
The Village Voice
Washington Press

Index